2004 CASE SUPPLEMENT AND STATUTORY APPENDIX

CASES AND MATERIALS

COPYRIGHT

SIXTH EDITION

D1319415

by

ROBERT A. GORMAN
Professor of Law
Arizona State University College of Law
Kenneth W. Gemmill Professor of Law Emeritus
University of Pennsylvania

JANE C. GINSBURG
Morton L. Janklow Professor of
Literary and Artistic Property Law
Columbia University School of Law

FOUNDATION PRESS

NEW YORK, NEW YORK

2004

© 2002, 2003 FOUNDATION PRESS
© 2004 By FOUNDATION PRESS
       395 Hudson Street
       New York, NY 10014
       Phone Toll Free 1–877–888–1330
       Fax (212) 367–6799
       fdpress.com

Printed in the United States of America

ISBN 1–58778–800–4

 TEXT IS PRINTED ON 10% POST CONSUMER RECYCLED PAPER

TABLE OF CONTENTS

*

TABLE OF CASES

Principal cases are in bold type. Non-principal cases are in roman type. References are to Pages.

*

2004 CASE SUPPLEMENT AND STATUTORY APPENDIX

CASES AND MATERIALS

COPYRIGHT

*

CHAPTER 1

THE CONCEPT OF COPYRIGHT

C. OVERVIEW OF COPYRIGHT LAW

4. SCOPE OF EXCLUSIVE RIGHTS UNDER COPYRIGHT

b. COPYRIGHT LITIGATION

Page 44: Add the following to the first paragraph of the textual Note:

The Supreme Court of Indiana has held that in a contract action brought by a publisher against an author, in which the author files a counterclaim against the publisher for copyright infringement, a state court may hear and decide the copyright counterclaim. The court examined 28 U.S.C. § 1338(a), which gives exclusive jurisdiction to federal courts over copyright actions, and concluded that the case—the claim and counterclaim together—was not a "civil action arising under any Act of Congress relating to ... copyrights." (Presumably, had the author sued first for copyright infringement, the federal court would have had exclusive jurisdiction and could also have ruled upon the publisher's contract counterclaim. Are the policies that provide for such exclusive jurisdiction overridden when the publisher gets to the state court first?) See Green v. Hendrickson Pubs., Inc., 770 N.E.2d 784, 63 U.S.P.D.Q.2d 1852 (Ind. 2002).

E. DISTINCTIONS: TRADEMARKS

Page 70: Before Questions add the following:

Dastar Corp. v. Twentieth Century Fox Film Corp. 539 U.S. 23 (2003). In 1949, Twentieth Century Fox produced a multi-part television series, "Crusade in Europe," based on then-General Eisenhower's campaign memoirs. In 1977, after Fox failed to renew the copyright registration, the work went into the public domain. In 1995, Dastar released a set of videos, "Campaigns in Europe," substantially copied from "Crusade." Dastar listed itself as the producer of "Campaigns," without reference to "Crusade" or Fox. Fox sued, claiming that Dastar's release of the videos under its own name constituted "reverse passing off" in violation of the Lanham Federal Trademarks Act, section 43(a). Fox contended that substituting Dastar's name for Fox's constituted a "false designation of origin," because Fox, the original producer, was the originator of the "Crusade" television series that "Campaigns" "bodily appropriated." The District Court agreed, and awarded Fox double Dastar's profits. The Ninth Circuit

1

affirmed in an unpublished opinion. The Supreme Court reversed, 8–0 (Justice Breyer recused).

Justice Scalia's opinion holds that "origin" as used in the Lanham Act does not mean original creator of a work from which copies are made, but rather the source of the particular copies (goods) that are being distributed.

The dictionary definition of "origin" is "[t]he fact or process of coming into being from a source," and "[t]hat from which anything primarily proceeds; source." Webster's New International Dictionary 1720–1721 (2d ed. 1949). And the dictionary definition of "goods" (as relevant here) is "[w]ares; merchandise." *Id.*, at 1079. We think the most natural understanding of the "origin" of "goods"—the source of wares—is the producer of the tangible product sold in the marketplace, in this case the physical Campaigns videotape sold by Dastar. The concept might be stretched ... to include not only the actual producer, but also the trademark owner who commissioned or assumed responsibility for ("stood behind") production of the physical product. But as used in the Lanham Act, the phrase "origin of goods" is in our view incapable of connoting the person or entity that originated the ideas or communications that "goods" embody or contain. Such an extension would not only stretch the text, but it would be out of accord with the history and purpose of the Lanham Act and inconsistent with precedent.

... The consumer who buys a branded product does not automatically assume that the brand-name company is the same entity that came up with the idea for the product, or designed the product—and typically does not care whether it is. The words of the Lanham Act should not be stretched to cover matters that are typically of no consequence to purchasers.

It could be argued, perhaps, that the reality of purchaser concern is different for what might be called a communicative product—one that is valued not primarily for its physical qualities, such as a hammer, but for the intellectual content that it conveys, such as a book or, as here, a video. The purchaser of a novel is interested not merely, if at all, in the identity of the producer of the physical tome (the publisher), but also, and indeed primarily, in the identity of the creator of the story it conveys (the author). And the author, of course, has at least as much interest in avoiding passing-off (or reverse passing-off) of his creation as does the publisher. For such a communicative product (the argument goes) "origin of goods" in § 43(a) must be deemed to include not merely the producer of the physical item (the publishing house Farrar, Straus and Giroux, or the video producer Dastar) but also the creator of the content that the physical item conveys (the author Tom Wolfe, or—assertedly—respondents).

The problem with this argument according special treatment to communicative products is that it causes the Lanham Act to conflict with the law of copyright, which addresses that subject specifically. The right to copy, and to copy without attribution, once a copyright has expired, like "the right to make [an article whose patent has expired]—including the right to make it in precisely the shape it carried when patented—passes to the public." *Sears, Roebuck & Co.* v. *Stiffel Co.*, 376 U.S. 225, 230 (1964); see also *Kellogg Co.* v. *National Biscuit Co.*, 305 U.S. 111, 121–122 (1938). "In general, unless an intellectual property right such as a patent or copyright protects an item, it will be subject to copying." *TrafFix Devices, Inc.* v. *Marketing Displays, Inc.*, 532 U.S. 23, 29 (2001). The rights of a patentee or copyright holder are part of a "carefully crafted bargain," *Bonito Boats, Inc.* v. *Thunder Craft Boats, Inc.*, 489 U.S. 141, 150–151 (1989), under which, once the patent or copyright monopoly has expired, the public may use the invention or work at will and without attribution. Thus, in construing the Lanham Act, we have been "careful to caution against misuse or over-extension" of trademark and related protections into areas traditionally occupied by patent or copyright. *TrafFix*, 532 U.S., at 29. "The Lanham Act," we have said, "does not exist to reward manufacturers for their innovation in creating a particular device; that is the purpose of the patent law and its period of exclusivity." *Id.*, at 34. Federal trademark law "has no necessary relation to invention or discovery," *Trade–Mark Cases,* 100 U.S. 82, 94 (1879), but rather, by preventing competitors from copying "a source-identifying mark," "reduce[s] the customer's costs of shopping and making purchasing decisions," and "helps assure a producer that it (and not an imitating competitor) will reap the financial, reputation-related rewards associated with a desirable product," *Qualitex Co.* v. *Jacobson Products Co.*, 514 U.S. 159, 163–164 (1995) (internal quotation marks and citation omitted). Assuming for the sake of argument that Dastar's representation of itself as the "Producer" of its videos amounted to a representation that it originated the creative work conveyed by the videos, allowing a cause of action under § 43(a) for that representation would create a species of mutant copyright law that limits the public's "federal right to 'copy and to use,' " expired copyrights, *Bonito Boats*, *supra*, at 165.

. . . In sum, reading the phrase "origin of goods" in the Lanham Act in accordance with the Act's common-law foundations (which were *not* designed to protect originality or creativity), and in light of the copyright and patent laws (which *were*), we conclude that the phrase refers to the producer of the tangible goods that are offered for sale, and not to the author of any idea, concept, or communication embodied in those goods. Cf. 17 U.S.C. § 202 (distinguishing between a copyrighted work and "any material object in which the work is embodied"). To hold otherwise would be akin to finding that § 43(a) created a species of perpetual patent and copyright, which Congress may not do. See *Eldred* v. *Ashcroft*, 537 U.S. 186, 208 (2003).

Page 70: Add new Question 3:

3. Is *Frederick Warne* still good law after *Dastar*? Would it matter if the Peter Rabbit images were still under copyright?

CHAPTER 2

COPYRIGHTABLE SUBJECT MATTER

A. IN GENERAL

Page 79: Add to note citing *Tin Pan Apple*. For an example from the realm of visual creations, see Mattel, Inc. v. Goldberger Doll Mfg. Co., 365 F.3d 133 (2d Cir. 2004), in which the court of appeals overturned a summary judgment favoring the defendant's Radio City Rockette doll which had allegedly been copied from Barbie; although Barbie's upturned nose, bow lips and widely spaced eyes were standard features for dolls, they can be combined in a minimally creative way so that the "particularized expression" (rather than mere idea) is copyrightable.

C. FACTS AND COMPILATIONS

2. COMPILATIONS

Page 155: Add following Question 4:

4. Dorothy Parker was a well-known American author, who wrote principally in the 1920s and 1930s. Many of her poems were published in such magazines as Vanity Fair and the New Yorker, and she gathered many of her poems and published them as compilations. Recently, a Parker scholar scoured her letters, manuscripts and other unpublished materials, and (with the consent of the present copyright owner) published a collection of 122 items purporting to be "all of the unpublished poems of Dorothy Parker." The defendant has published a book containing 121 of those items, and has been sued by the Parker scholar for copyright infringement. The defendant claims that collecting "all" of the Parker poems, although perhaps the product of arduous scholarly searching, lacks copyrightable originality. The Parker scholar, on the other hand, contends that identifying a work as a "poem"—in the absence of a clear such designation by Parker herself—requires subjective literary judgment. What should be the outcome of the litigation? See Silverstein v. Penguin Putnam, Inc., 368 F.3d 77 (2d Cir. 2004).

Assessment Technologies of WI, LLC V. WIREdata, Inc.

350 F.3d 640 (7th Cir. 2003).

■ POSNER, CIRCUIT JUDGE. This case is about the attempt of a copyright owner to use copyright law to block access to data that not only are neither copyrightable nor copyrighted, but were not created or obtained by the copyright owner. The owner is trying to secrete the data in its copyrighted program—a program the existence of which reduced the likelihood that the data would be retained in a form in which they would have been readily accessible. It would be appalling if such an attempt could succeed.

Assessment Technologies (AT, we'll call it) brought suit for copyright infringement and theft of trade secrets against WIREdata, and the district court after an evidentiary hearing issued a permanent injunction on the basis of AT's copyright claim alone.

The copyright case seeks to block WIREdata from obtaining noncopyrighted data. AT claims that the data can't be extracted without infringement of its copyright. The copyright is of a compilation, and the general issue that the appeal presents is the right of the owner of such a copyright to prevent his customers (that is, the copyright licensees) from disclosing the compiled data even if the data are in the public domain.

WIREdata, owned by Multiple Listing Services, Inc., wants to obtain, for use by real estate brokers, data regarding specific properties—address, owner's name, the age of the property, its assessed valuation, the number and type of rooms, and so forth—from the southeastern Wisconsin municipalities in which the properties are located. The municipalities collect such data in order to assess the value of the properties for property-tax purposes. Ordinarily they're happy to provide the data to anyone who will pay the modest cost of copying the data onto a disk. Indeed, Wisconsin's "open records" law, Wis. Stat. § § 19.31–.39; *State ex rel. Milwaukee Police Ass'n v. Jones*, 2000 WI App 146, 615 N.W.2d 190, 194–96, 237 Wis. 2d 840 (Wis. App. 2000), which is applicable to data in digital form, see *id.* at 195–96; Wis. Stat. § 19.32(2), requires them to furnish such data to any person who will pay the copying cost. However, three municipalities refused WIREdata's request. They (or the contractors who do the actual tax assessment for them) are licensees of AT. The open-records law contains an exception for copyrighted materials, *id.*, and these municipalities are afraid that furnishing WIREdata the requested data would violate the copyright. WIREdata has sued them in the state courts of Wisconsin in an attempt to force them to divulge the data, and those suits are pending. Alarmed by WIREdata's suits, AT brought the present suit to stop WIREdata from making such demands of the municipalities and seeking to enforce them by litigation.

The data that WIREdata wants are collected not by AT but by tax assessors hired by the municipalities. The assessors visit the property and by talking to the owner and poking around the property itself obtain the information that we mentioned in the preceding paragraph—the age of the property, the number of rooms, and so forth. AT has developed and copyrighted a computer program, called "Market Drive," for compiling these data. The assessor types into a computer the data that he has obtained from his visit to the property or from other sources of information and then the Market Drive program, in conjunction with a Microsoft database program (Microsoft Access), automatically allocates the data to 456 fields (that is, categories of information) grouped into 34 master categories known as tables. Several types of data relating to a property, each allocated to a different field, are grouped together in a table called "Income Valuations," others in a table called "Residential Buildings," and so on. The data collected by the various assessors and inputted in the manner just described are stored in an electronic file, the database. The municipality's tax officials can use various queries in Market Drive or Market Access to view the data in the file. . . .

. . . AT has a valid copyright; and if WIREdata said to itself, "Market Drive is a nifty way of sorting real estate data and we want the municipalities to give us their data in the form in which it is organized in the database, that is, sorted into AT's 456 fields grouped into its 34 tables," and the municipalities obliged, they would be infringing AT's copyright because they are not licensed to make copies of Market Drive for distribution to others; and WIREdata would be a contributory infringer. . . . But WIREdata doesn't want the Market Drive compilation. It isn't in the business of making tax assessments, which is the business for which Market Drive is designed. It only wants the raw data, the data the assessors inputted into Market Drive. Once it gets those data it will sort them in accordance with its own needs, which have to do with providing the information about properties that is useful to real estate brokers as opposed to taxing authorities. . . .

. . . A work that merely copies uncopyrighted material is wholly unoriginal and the making of such a work is therefore not an infringement of copyright. The municipalities would not be infringing Market Drive by extracting the raw data from the databases . . . and handing those data over to WIREdata; and since there would thus be no direct infringement, neither would there be contributory infringement by WIREdata. It would be like a Westlaw licensee's copying the text of a federal judicial opinion that he found in the Westlaw opinion database and giving it to someone else. Westlaw's compilation of federal judicial opinions is copyrighted and copyrightable because it involves discretionary judgments regarding selection and arrangement. But the opinions themselves are in the public domain (federal law forbids assertion of copyright in federal documents, 17 U.S.C. § 105), and so Westlaw cannot prevent its licensees from copying the opinions themselves as distinct from the aspects of the database that are copyrighted. See *Matthew Bender & Co. v. West Publishing Co.*, 158 F.3d 693 (2d Cir. 1998); *Matthew Bender & Co. v. West Publishing Co.*, 158 F.3d 674 (2d Cir. 1998).

* * *

AT argues that WIREdata doesn't need to obtain the data in digital form because they exist in analog form, namely in the handwritten notes of the assessors, notes that all agree are not covered by the Market Drive copyright. But we were told at argument without contradiction that some assessors no longer make handwritten notes to copy into a computer at a later time. Instead they take their laptop to the site and type the information in directly. So WIREdata could not possibly obtain all the data it wants (all of which data are in the public domain, we emphasize) from the handwritten notes. But what is more fundamental is that since AT has no ownership or other legal interest in the data collected by the assessor, it has no legal ground for making the acquisition of that data more costly for WIREdata. AT is trying to use its copyright to sequester uncopyrightable data, presumably in the hope of extracting a license fee from WIREdata.

We are mindful of pressures, reflected in bills that have been pending in Congress for years, Jonathan Band & Makoto Kono, "The Database Protection Debate in the 106th Congress," 62 *Ohio St. L.J.* 869 (2001), to provide legal protection to the creators of databases, as Europe has already done. Jane C. Ginsburg, "Copyright, Common Law, and Sui Generis Protection of Databases in the United States and Abroad," 66 *U. Cin. L. Rev.* 151 (1997).... The creation of massive electronic databases can be extremely costly, yet if the database is readily searchable and the data themselves are not copyrightable (and we know from *Feist* that mere data are indeed not copyrightable) the creator may find it difficult or even impossible to recoup the expense of creating the database. Legal protection of databases as such (as distinct from programs for arranging the data, like Market Drive) cannot take the form of copyright, as the Supreme Court made clear in *Feist* when it held that the copyright clause of the Constitution does not authorize Congress to create copyright in mere data. But that is neither here nor there; what needs to be emphasized in this case is that the concerns (whether or not valid, as questioned in Ginsburg, *supra*, and also J.H. Reichman & Pamela Samuelson, "Intellectual Property Rights in Data?" 50 *Vand. L. Rev.* 51 (1997), and Stephen M. Maurer & Suzanne Scotchmer, "Database Protection: Is It Broken and Should We Fix It?" 284 *Sci.* 1129 (1999)) that actuate the legislative proposals for database protection have no relevance because AT is not the collector of the data that go into the database. All the data are collected and inputted by the assessors; it is they, not AT, that do the footwork, the heavy lifting....

QUESTION

Judge Posner's opinion refers to legislative proposals to protect databases; one of these is set out at pp. 157–60 of the Casebook. Had this bill been enacted and in force at the time WIREData sought to obtain the information from the state agencies, would it have prohibited WIREData's acquisition of the data? Why or why not? Is this result consistent with the bill's goals?

Page 165: Insert the following after the *Mason* case:

[In Sparaco v. Lawler, Matusky, Skelly, Engineers LLP, 303 F.3d 460 (2d Cir.2002), Judge Leval offered a somewhat different—and perhaps narrower—approach to the copyrightability of maps. He characterized the older decisions sustaining map copyright as having been based on "sweat of the brow." He held that a site map that depicted only existing physical characteristics simply showed "facts" and was thus not copyrightable. However, a map showing the details of proposed improvements to the site is copyrightable.]

D.   DERIVATIVE WORKS

Page 177:   Add the following after the first full paragraph on the page:

(After the struggle to characterize the vodka-bottle photographs as not derivative works, and thus more readily copyrightable, the court of appeals at a later stage of the proceedings ultimately held that the defendant's photographs did not infringe, by application of doctrines of "merger" and "scenes a faire" to be studied in greater detail in Chapter 6, *infra*. The court concluded that the plaintiff's photograph was a standard depiction of a liquor product, that there were few different ways to portray the vodka bottle, that the plaintiff's copyright was therefore "thin," and that it could be infringed only by a "virtually identical" copy. Here, the defendant's photographs were different in lighting, angles, shadows and highlighting, reflections and background, and were thus non-infringing. Ets–Hokin v. Skyy Spirits, Inc., 323 F.3d 763 (9th Cir.2003).)

Ets-Hokin
Photograph

Defendant's
Photograph

F. PICTORIAL, GRAPHIC AND SCULPTURAL WORKS

Page 203: Add the following after the textual Note:

See Celebration Intern., Inc. v. Chosun Intern., Inc., 234 F.Supp.2d 905 (S.D.Ind.2002), in which the court held that the body of a tiger costume was not separable from its useful function as clothing, but that the head was separable and thus copyrightable. The court ultimately, however, ruled against the plaintiff costume designer. The protection accorded to the costume head was limited because it was designed to appear like a "real" tiger. Although even under that stringent test, the court found that there was "substantial similarity," it nonetheless concluded that the defendant's tiger head was an independent creation and was not copied from the plaintiff's.

Pages 203–18: Substitute the following (while consulting the photographs at pp. 204, 210, 212, 218):

PIVOT POINT INTERNATIONAL, INC. v. CHARLENE PRODS., INC.

___ F.3d ___, 2004 WL 1416584 (7th Cir.2004).

■ RIPPLE, CIRCUIT J.

Pivot Point International, Inc. ("Pivot Point"), brought this cause of action against Charlene Products, Inc., and its president Peter Yau (collectively "Charlene"), for copyright infringement pursuant to 17 U.S.C. § 501(b). The district court granted summary judgment for the defendants on the ground that the copied subject matter, a mannequin head, was not copyrightable under the Copyright Act of 1976 ("1976 Act"), 17 U.S.C. § 101 et seq. For the reasons set forth in the following opinion, we reverse the judgment of the district court and remand the case for proceedings consistent with this opinion.

I

BACKGROUND

A. Facts

Pivot Point develops and markets educational techniques and tools for the hair design industry. It was founded in 1965 by Leo Passage, an internationally renowned hair designer. One aspect of Pivot Point's business is the design and development of mannequin heads, "slip-ons" (facial forms that slip over a mannequin head) and component hair pieces.

In the mid–1980s, Passage desired to develop a mannequin that would imitate the "hungry look" of high-fashion, runway models. Passage believed that such a mannequin could be marketed as a premium item to cutting-edge hair-stylists and to stylists involved in hair design competi-

Mara

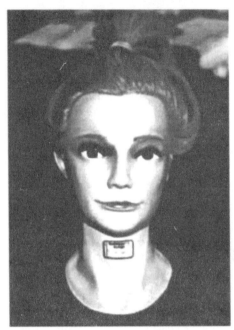

Liza

tions. Passage then worked with a German artist named Horst Heerlein to create an original sculpture of a female human head. Although Passage discussed his vision with Heerlein, Passage did not give Heerlein any specific dimensional requirements. From Passage's description, Heerlein created a sculpture in plaster entitled "Mara."

Wax molds of Mara were made and sent to Pivot Point's manufacturer in Hong Kong. The manufacturer created exact reproductions of Mara in polyvinyl chloride ("PVC"). The manufacturer filled the PVC form with a liquid that expands and hardens into foam. The process of creating the Mara sculpture and of developing the mannequin based on the sculpture took approximately eighteen months. In February of 1988, when Pivot Point first inspected the PVC forms of Mara, it discovered that the mannequin's hairline had been etched too high on the forehead. The manufacturer corrected the mistake by adding a second, lower hairline. Although the first, higher hairline was visible upon inspection, it was covered with implanted hair. The early PVC reproductions of Mara, and Pivot Point's first shipment of the mannequins in May of 1988, possessed the double hairlines.

About the same time that it received its first shipment of mannequins, Pivot Point obtained a copyright registration for the design of Mara, specifically the bareheaded female human head with no makeup or hair. Heerlein assigned all of his rights in the Mara sculpture to Pivot Point. Pivot Point displayed the copyright notice in the name of Pivot Point on each mannequin.

Pivot Point enjoyed great success with its new mannequin. To respond to customer demand, Pivot Point began marketing the Mara mannequin with different types and lengths of hair, different skin tones and variations in makeup; however, no alterations were made to the facial features of the mannequin. For customer ease in identification, Pivot Point changed the name of the mannequin based on its hair and skin color; for instance, a Mara mannequin implanted with yak hair was called "Sonja," and the Mara mannequin implanted with blonde hair was called "Karin."

At a trade show in 1989, Charlene, a wholesaler of beauty products founded by Mr. Yau,[2] displayed its own "Liza" mannequin, which was very close in appearance to Pivot Point's Mara. In addition to the strikingly similar facial features, Liza also exhibited a double hairline that the early Mara mannequins possessed. On September 24, 1989, Pivot Point noticed Charlene for copyright infringement. When Charlene refused to stop importing and selling the Liza mannequin, Pivot Point filed this action.

B. District Court Proceedings

Pivot Point filed a multi-count complaint in district court against Charlene. It alleged violations of federal copyright law as well as state-law claims; Charlene both answered the complaint and counterclaimed. After extensive discovery, Pivot Point filed a comprehensive motion for summary judgment on its complaint and Charlene's counterclaims. Charlene filed several cross-motions for summary judgment as well. The district court tentatively ruled on these motions in July 2001 and issued a final ruling in October 2001.

1. Merits

In its opinion, the district court stated that "[t]he principal dispute is whether a human mannequin head is copyrightable subject matter. If it is, then there must be a trial on the question whether Liza is a knock off of Mara." R.401 at 1. The district court explained that, although sculptural works are copyrightable under 17 U.S.C. § 102(a)(5), sculptures that may be copyrighted are limited by the language of 17 U.S.C. § 101, which provides in relevant part:

> Such works shall include works of artistic craftsmanship insofar as their form but not their mechanical or utilitarian aspects are concerned; the design of a useful article, as defined in this section, shall be considered a pictorial, graphic or sculptural work only if, and only to the extent that, such design incorporates pictorial, graphic, or sculptural features that can be identified separately from, and are capable of existing independently of, the utilitarian aspects of the article.

According to the district court, there was no question that Mara was a sculpture. However, in the district court's view, the sculpture served

---

2. Mr. Yau was not unfamiliar with Pivot Point. Shortly before founding Charlene Products in 1985, Mr. Yau had worked for Pivot Point.

utilitarian ends. "Students in beauty schools practice styling hair on Mara's head and may practice other skills by applying makeup to Mara's eyes, lips, and cheeks. The parties dispute which functions are primary." R.401 at 2.

The district court then explored whether the artistic and utilitarian aspects of Mara were "separable" for purposes of the piece's copyrightability: "The statutory separability requirement confines copyright protection to those aspects of the design that exist apart from its utilitarian value, and that could be removed without reducing the usefulness of the item." *Id.* at 3. The district court observed that drawing this line is particularly troublesome.

The statute, continued the district court, is generally recognized to suggest two types of separability: physical separability and conceptual separability. The district court explained that physical separability occurs when the ornamental nature of the object can be physically removed from the object and that

> [c]onceptual separability differs from physical separability by asking not whether the features to be copyrighted could be sliced off for separate display, but whether one can conceive of this process. Relying on a comment in the House Report on the 1976 amendments, the second circuit in *Kieselstein-Cord* [*v. Accessories by Pearl, Inc.,* 632 F.2d 989 (2d Cir.1980),] purported to adopt conceptual separability as the exclusive test (632 F.2d at 992, contrasting that approach with *Esquire* [*v. Ringer,* 591 F.2d 796 (D.C.Cir.1978)], which opted for physical separability, 591 F.2d at 803–04). Why a court should repair to the legislative history is unclear; the second circuit did not identify any ambiguity in § 101 that needed to be resolved, and a statement in the House Report that what appears on the face of the statutory text to be two requirements (physical and conceptual separability) should be administered as just one is not a proposition that in today's legal climate can be indulged. The Supreme Court does not permit the use of legislative history to alter, as opposed to elucidate, a statutory text.

Id. at 4.

Despite this lack of statutory moorings, the district court nevertheless reviewed the differing formulations for conceptual separability and determined that the definition proposed by Professor Paul Goldstein was the best one: "a pictorial, graphic or sculptural feature incorporated in the design of a useful article is conceptually separable if it can stand on its own as work of art traditionally conceived, and if the useful article in which it is embodied would be equally useful without it." R.401 at 5 (quoting 1 Paul Goldstein, *Copyright: Principles, Law & Practice* § 2.5.3, at 109 (1989)). The district court believed that the strength of this definition "comes from the fact that it differs little, if at all, from the test of physical separability embraced by the D.C. Circuit in *Esquire* and by the majority in *Carol Barnhart* [*Inc., v. Economy Cover Corp.,* 773 F.2d 411, 418 (2d Cir.1985)]." *Id.* Applying this test led the district court to conclude that

13

Mara cannot be copyrighted because, even though one can conceive of Mara as a sculpture displayed as art, it would not be *equally* useful if the features that Pivot Point want to copyright were removed. So long as *a* utilitarian function is makeup tutoring and practice and the fact that Pivot Points sells Mara without eye or lip coloring shows that this is *a* function even if not, in Pivot Point's view, the "primary" one—the utilitarian value would be diminished by removing the aesthetic features that Pivot Point wants to protect by copyright.

Id.

As a final matter, the district court distinguished two cases, *Hart v. Dan Chase Taxidermy Supply Co.,* 86 F.3d 320 (2d Cir.1996), and *Superior Form Builders, Inc. v. Dan Chase Taxidermy Supply Co., Inc.,* 74 F.3d 488 (4th Cir.1996), which upheld the copyrightability of animal and fish mannequins. The district court found the *Hart* case unpersuasive, but concluded that "one cannot say of Mara what the fourth circuit said of animal mannequins: Mara is valued not for 'its own appearance' but for what it enables students to do and learn. Mara is a 'useful article' as § 101 and *Superior Form Builders* deploy that term." *Id.* at 6.

* * *

II

ANALYSIS

* * *

B.   Copyrightability

The central issue in this case is whether the Mara mannequin is subject to copyright protection. This issue presents, at bottom, a question of statutory interpretation. We therefore begin our analysis with the language of the statute. Two provisions contained in 17 U.S.C. § 101 are at the center of our inquiry. The first of these is the description of pictorial, graphic and sculptural works:

> "Pictorial, graphic, and sculptural works" include two-dimensional and three-dimensional works of fine, graphic, and applied art, photographs, prints and art reproductions, maps, globes, charts, diagrams, models, and technical drawings, including architectural plans. Such works shall include works of artistic craftsmanship insofar as their form but not their mechanical or utilitarian aspects are concerned; the design of a *useful article,* as defined in this section, shall be considered a pictorial, graphic, or sculptural work *only if, and only to the extent that, such design incorporates pictorial, graphic, or sculptural features that can be identified separately from, and are capable of existing independently of, the utilitarian aspects of the article.*

The definition section further provides that "[a] 'useful article' is an article having an intrinsic utilitarian function that is not merely to portray the appearance of the article or to convey information. An article that is normally a part of a useful article is considered a 'useful article.'" 17

U.S.C. § 101. As is clear from the definition of pictorial, graphic and sculptural work, only "useful article[s]," as the term is further defined, are subject to the limitation contained in the emphasized language above. If an article is not "useful" as the term is defined in § 101, then it is a pictorial, graphic and sculptural work entitled to copyright protection (assuming the other requirements of the statute are met).

1. Usefulness

[Pivot Point argued that the Mara mannequin is not a "useful article" because "its inherent nature is to portray the appearance of runway models. Its value resides in how well it portrays the appearance of runway models," just as the value of a bust of Cleopatra would lie in how well it approximates her likely appearance. Pivot Point relied upon the decisions of the Fourth Circuit in *Superior Form Builders* and the Second Circuit in *Hart*. Charlene, however, contended that the Mara mannequin had an additional function, and a useful one: it is marketed and used for practicing the art of makeup application. Therefore, it is a useful article subject to the limiting language of section 101.]

. . . [W]e shall assume that the district court correctly ruled that Mara is a useful article and proceed to examine whether, despite that usefulness, it is amenable to copyright protection.

2. Separability

We return to the statutory language. A useful article falls within the definition of pictorial, graphic or sculptural works *only if, and only to the extent that, such design incorporates pictorial, graphic, or sculptural features that can be identified separately from, and are capable of existing independently of, the utilitarian aspects of the article.*" 17 U.S.C. § 101.[6] It is common ground between the parties and, indeed, among the courts that

---

6. Prior to the addition of this language in the 1976 Act, Congress had not explicitly authorized the Copyright Office to register "useful articles." Indeed, when Congress first extended copyright protection to three-dimensional works of art in 1870, copyright protection was limited to objects of fine art; objects of applied art still were not protected. *See* Paul Goldstein, 1 *Copyright* § 2.5.3 at 2:58 (2d ed.2004). This changed with the adoption of the Copyright Act of 1909 ("1909 Act"); Professor Goldstein explains:

The 1909 Act, which continued protection for three-dimensional works of art, dropped the requirement that they constitute fine art and thus opened the door to protection of useful works of art. In 1948, the Copyright Office broadened the scope of protection for three-dimensional works of art to cover "works of artistic craftsmanship insofar as their form but

not their utilitarian aspects are concerned." The United States Supreme Court upheld this interpretation in *Mazer v. Stein,* [347 U.S. 201, 213 (1954),] holding that the fact that statuettes in issue were intended for use in articles of manufacture—electric lamp bases—did not bar them from copyright. Five years later, in 1959, the Copyright Office promulgated a rule that if "the sole intrinsic function of an article is its utility, the fact that the work is unique and attractively shaped will not qualify it as a work of art." The regulation did, however, permit registration of features of a utilitarian article that "can be identified separately and are capable of existing independently as a work of art."

Id. (quoting 37 C.F.R. § 207.8(a) (1949) and 37 C.F.R. § 202 .10(c) (1959); footnotes omitted).

have examined the issue, that this language, added by the 1976 Act, was intended to distinguish creative works that enjoy protection from elements of industrial design that do not. *See* H.R.Rep. No. 94–1476, at 55 (1976), *reprinted in* 1976 U.S.C.C.A.N. 5659, 5668 (stating that the purpose behind this language was "to draw as clear a line as possible between copyrightable works of applied art and uncopyrighted works of industrial design"). Although the Congressional goal was evident, application of this language has presented the courts with significant difficulty. Indeed, one scholar has noted: "Of the many fine lines that run through the Copyright Act, none is more troublesome than the line between protectible pictorial, graphic and sculptural works and unprotectible utilitarian elements of industrial design." Paul Goldstein, 1 *Copyright* § 2.5.3, at 2:56 (2d ed.2004).

The difficulty in the application of this language would not have come, in all likelihood, as a surprise to the Congressional drafters. The language employed by Congress is not the language of a bright-line rule of universal application. Indeed, the circuits that have addressed the interpretative problem now before us uniformly have recognized that the wording of the statute does not supply categorical direction, but rather requires the Copyright Office and the courts "to continue their efforts to distinguish applied art and industrial design." Robert C. Denicola, *Applied Art & Industrial Design: A Suggested Approach to Copyright in Useful Articles,* 67 Minn. L.Rev. 707, 730 (1983). In short, no doubt well-aware of the myriad of factual scenarios to which its policy guidance would have to be applied, Congress wisely chose to provide only general policy guidance to be implemented on a case-by-case basis through the Copyright Office and the courts.

Even though the words of the statute do not yield a definitive answer, we believe that the statutory language nevertheless provides significant guidance in our task. We therefore shall examine in more detail what that language has to tell us, and we return to the necessary starting point of our task, § 101.

The statutory language provides that "the design of a useful article . . . shall be considered a pictorial, graphic, or sculptural work only if, and only to the extent that, such design incorporates pictorial, graphic, or sculptural features *that can be identified separately from and are capable of existing independently of, the utilitarian* aspects of the article." Although the italicized clause contains two operative phrases—"*can be identified separately from* "and "*are capable of existing independently of* "—we believe, as have the other courts that have grappled with this issue, that Congress, in amending the statute, intended these two phrases to state a single, integrated standard to determine when there is sufficient separateness between the utilitarian and artistic aspects of a work to justify copyright protection.

Certainly, one approach to determine whether material can be "identified separately," and the most obvious, is to rely on the capacity of the artistic material to be severed physically from the industrial design. *See Mazer v. Stein,* 347 U.S. 201, 74 S.Ct. 460, 98 L.Ed. 630 (1954) (holding that a statuette incorporated into the base of a lamp is copyrightable).

When a three-dimensional article is the focus of the inquiry, reliance on physical separability can no doubt be a helpful tool in ascertaining whether the artistic material in question can be separated from the industrial design. As Professor Denicola points out, however, such an approach really is not of much use when the item in question is two-dimensional. *See* Denicola, *supra,* at 744. Indeed, because this provision, by its very words, was intended to apply to two-dimensional material, it is clear that a physical separability test cannot be the exclusive test for determining copyrightability.

It seems to be common ground between the parties and, indeed, among the courts and commentators, that the protection of the copyright statute also can be secured when a conceptual separability exists between the material sought to be copyrighted and the utilitarian design in which that material is incorporated.[8] The difficulty lies not in the acceptance of that

---

8. Although the district court was skeptical that the statutory language encompassed both physical and conceptual separability, circuits have been almost unanimous in interpreting the language of § 101 to include both types of separability. *See Superior Form Builders, Inc. v.Dan Chase Taxidermy Supply Co., Inc.,* 74 F.3d 488, 494 (4th Cir. 1996) (asking whether functional aspects of animal mannequins are "conceptually separable from the works' sculptural features"); *Brandir Int'l, Inc. v. Cascade Pac. Lumber Co.,* 834 F.2d 1142, 1144 (2d Cir.1987) (stating that " '[c]onceptual separability' is alive and well"); *Carol Barnhart Inc. v. Econ. Cover Corp.,* 773 F.2d 411, 418 (2d Cir.1985) (judging copyrightability of mannequin torsos based on whether "forms possess aesthetic or artistic features that are physically or conceptually separable from the forms' use as utilitarian objects to display clothes"); *Norris Indus., Inc. v. Int'l Tel. & Tel. Corp.,* 696 F.2d 918, 923 (11th Cir.1983) ("Both case law and legislative history indicate that separability encompasses works of art that are either physically severable from the utilitarian article or conceptually severable."); *Kieselstein-Cord v. Accessories by Pearl, Inc.,* 632 F.2d 989, 993 (2d Cir.1980) (applying test of conceptual separability).

Only one appellate court has rejected the idea of conceptual separability. *See Esquire, Inc. v. Ringer,* 591 F.2d 796 (D.C.Cir.1978). In that case, arising under the 1909 Act, the Copyright Office had refused to register a design for outdoor lighting fixtures. The district court, however, believed the fixtures were copyrightable and issued a writ of mandamus that the copyright issue. However, the

D.C. Circuit reversed. The precise question before the court was whether the regulation implementing the 1909 Act mandated that the Copyright Office register a copyright for the lighting fixtures. The regulation at issue provided:

> "(c) If the sole intrinsic function of an article is its utility, the fact that the article is unique and attractively shaped will not qualify it as a work of art. However, if the shape of a utilitarian article incorporates features, such as artistic sculpture, carving, or pictorial representation, which can be identified separately and are capable of existing independently as a work of art, such features will be eligible for registration."

Id. at 800 (quoting 37 C.F.R. § 202.10(b) (1976)). The Copyright Office took the position that the regulation barred "copyright registration for the overall shape or configuration of a utilitarian article, no matter how aesthetically pleasing that shape or configuration may be." *Id.* In determining whether to accept or reject the proffered interpretation, the court noted that "[c]onsiderable weight is to be given to an agency's interpretation of its regulations," especially when "an administrative interpretation relates to a matter within the field of administrative expertise." *Id.* at 801. The court concluded that the Copyright Office had adopted a "reasonable and well-supported interpretation of § 202.10(c)." *Id.* at 800. In the court's view, the interpretation was grounded in "the principle that industrial designs are not eligible for copyright." *Id.* The court also believed that the interpretation found support in the legislative history of the newly enacted 1976

proposition, which the statutory language clearly contemplates, but in its application. As noted by Pivot Point, the following tests have been suggested for determining when the artistic and utilitarian aspects of useful articles are conceptually separable: 1) the artistic features are "primary" and the utilitarian features "subsidiary," *Kieselstein-Cord,* 632 F.2d at 993; 2) the useful article "would still be marketable to some significant segment of the community simply because of its aesthetic qualities," Melville B. Nimmer & David Nimmer, 1 *Nimmer on Copyright* § 2.08[B][3], at 2–101 (2004); 3) the article "stimulate[s] in the mind of the beholder a concept that is separate from the concept evoked by its utilitarian function," *Carol Barnhart,* 773 F.2d at 422 (Newman, J., dissenting); 4) the artistic design was not significantly influenced by functional considerations, *see Brandir Int'l,* 834 F.2d at 1145 (adopting the test forwarded in Denicola, *supra,* at 741); 5) the artistic features "can stand alone as a work of art traditionally conceived, and ... the useful article in which it is embodied would be equally useful without it," Goldstein, 1 *Copyright* § 2.5.3, at 2:67; and 6) the artistic features are not utilitarian, *see* William F. Patry, 1 *Copyright Law & Practice* 285 (1994). . . .

In articulating a meaningful approach to conceptual separability, we note that we are not the first court of appeals to deal with this problem. The work of our colleagues in the other circuits provides significant insights into our understanding of Congressional intent. Indeed, even when those judges have disagreed on the appropriate application of the Congressional mandate to the case before them, their insight yield a bountiful harvest for those of us who now walk the same interpretative path.

Among the circuits, the Court of Appeals for the Second Circuit has had occasion to wrestle most comprehensively with the notion of "conceptual separability." Its case law represents, we believe, an intellectual journey that has explored the key aspects of the problem. We therefore turn to a study of the key stages of doctrinal development in its case law.

Act. The court acknowledged, however, that the legislative history was not "free from ambiguity"; it explained:

Esquire could arguably draw some support from the statement that a protectable element of a utilitarian article must be separable "physically *or conceptually* "from the utilitarian aspects of the design. But any possible ambiguity raised by this isolated reference disappears when the excerpt is considered in its entirety. The underscored passages indicate unequivocally that the overall design or configuration of a utilitarian object, even if it is determined by aesthetic as well as functional considerations, is not eligible for copyright. Thus the legislative history, taken as congressional understanding of existing law, reinforces the Register's position.

Id. at 803–04.

As is evident from the passages set forth above, the issue addressed by the D.C. Circuit in *Esquire* arose in a much different procedural and legal environment than the issue in the present case. The court's focus in *Esquire* was a regulation adopted pursuant to the former law and its obligation to defer to the agency's interpretation of the law embodied in that regulation. Furthermore, the court acknowledged that the 1976 Act was "not applicable to the case before" it. *Id.* at 803. Given these differences, we do not believe that the D.C. Circuit would conclude that its decision in *Esquire* disposed of the issue of conceptual separability presently before this court.

a.

The Second Circuit first grappled with the issue of conceptual separability in *Kieselstein-Cord v. Accessories by Pearl, Inc.,* 632 F.2d 989 (2d Cir.1980). In that case, Kieselstein–Cord, a jewelry designer, had created a line of decorative and jeweled belt buckles inspired by works of art; he obtained copyright registrations for his designs. When the line was successful, Accessories by Pearl, Inc., ("Pearl") copied the designs and marketed its own, less-expensive versions of the belt buckles. Kieselstein–Cord then sued Pearl for copyright infringement; however, Pearl claimed that the belt buckles were not copyrightable because they were " 'useful articles' with no 'pictorial, graphic, or sculptural features that can be identified separately from, and are capable of existing independently of, the utilitarian aspects' of the buckles." *Id.* at 991–92. The Second Circuit disagreed. Although it did not articulate a specific test for evaluating conceptual separability, it focused on the "primary" and "subsidiary" elements of the article and concluded:

> We see in appellant's belt buckles conceptually separable sculptural elements, as apparently have the buckles' wearers who have used them as ornamentation for parts of the body other than the waist. The primary ornamental aspect of the Vaquero and Winchester buckles is conceptually separable from their subsidiary utilitarian function. This conclusion is not at variance with the expressed congressional intent to distinguish copyrightable applied art and uncopyrightable industrial design. Pieces of applied art, these buckles may be considered jewelry, the form of which is subject to copyright protection.

Id. at 993 (internal citations omitted).

b.

The Second Circuit revisited the issue of conceptual separability in *Carol Barnhart Inc. v. Economy Cover Corp.,* 773 F.2d 411 (2d Cir.1985). In that case, Carol Barnhart, a provider of retail display items, developed four mannequins consisting of human torsos for the display of shirts and jackets. It obtained copyright registrations for each of the forms. When a competitor, Economy Cover, copied the designs, Carol Barnhart claimed infringement of that copyright. The Second Circuit held that the designs were not copyrightable. It explained:

> [W]hile copyright protection has increasingly been extended to cover articles having a utilitarian dimension, Congress has explicitly refused copyright protection for works of applied art or industrial design which have aesthetic or artistic features that cannot be identified separately from the useful article. Such works are not copyrightable regardless of the fact that they may be "aesthetically satisfying and valuable."
>
> Applying these principles, we are persuaded that since the aesthetic and artistic features of the Barnhart forms are inseparable from the forms' use as utilitarian articles the forms are not copyrightable.... [Barnhart] stresses that the forms have been responded to as sculptur-

al forms, and have been used for purposes other than modeling clothes, e.g., as decorating props and signs without any clothing or accessories. While this may indicate that the forms are "aesthetically satisfying and valuable," it is insufficient to show that the forms possess aesthetic or artistic features that are physically or conceptually separable from the forms' use as utilitarian objects to display clothes. On the contrary, to the extent the forms possess aesthetically pleasing features, even when these features are considered in the aggregate, they cannot be conceptualized as existing independently of their utilitarian function.

Id. at 418 (internal citations omitted). The court also rejected the argument that *Kieselstein-Cord* was controlling. The majority explained that what distinguished the Kieselstein–Cord buckles from the Barnhart forms was "that the ornamented surfaces of the buckles were not in any respect required by their functions; the artistic and aesthetic features would thus be conceived as having been added to, or superimposed upon, an otherwise utilitarian article." *Id.* at 419.

Perhaps the most theoretical and comprehensive discussion of "conceptual separability," as opposed to physical separability, can be found in the dissenting opinion of Judge Newman in *Carol Barnhart,* 773 F.2d at 419. After reviewing the possible ways to determine conceptual separability, Judge Newman set forth his choice and rationale:

How, then, is "conceptual separateness" to be determined? In my view, the answer derives from the word "conceptual." For the design features to be "conceptually separate" from the utilitarian aspects of the useful article that embodies the design, the article must stimulate in the mind of the beholder a concept that is separate from the concept evoked by its utilitarian function. The test turns on what may reasonably be understood to be occurring in the mind of the beholder or, as some might say, in the "mind's eye" of the beholder....

. . .

The "separateness" of the utilitarian and non-utilitarian concepts engendered by an article's design is itself a perplexing concept. I think the requisite "separateness" exists whenever the design creates in the mind of the ordinary observer two different concepts that are not inevitably entertained simultaneously. Again, the example of the artistically designed chair displayed in a museum may be helpful. The ordinary observer can be expected to apprehend the design of a chair whenever the object is viewed. He may, in addition, entertain the concept of a work of art, but, if this second concept is engendered in the observer's mind simultaneously with the concept of the article's utilitarian function, the requisite "separateness" does not exist. The test is not whether the observer fails to recognize the object as a chair but only whether the concept of the utilitarian function can be displaced in the mind by some other concept. That does not occur, at least for the ordinary observer, when viewing even the most artistically designed chair. It may occur, however, when viewing some other object if the utilitarian function of the object is not perceived at all; it may also occur, even when the utilitarian function is perceived by observation, perhaps aided by explanation, if the concept of the utilitarian function can be displaced in the observer's mind while he entertains the separate concept of some non-utilitarian function. The separate concept will normally be that of a work of art.

Id. At 422–23

c.

The Second Circuit soon addressed conceptual separability again in *Brandir International, Inc. v. Cascade Pacific Lumber Co.*, 834 F.2d 1142 (2d Cir.1987). That case involved the work of an artist, David Levine; specifically, Levine had created a sculpture of thick, interwoven wire. A cyclist friend of Levine's realized that the sculpture could, with modification, function as a bicycle rack and thereafter put Levine in touch with Brandir International, Inc. ("Brandir"). The artist and the Brandir engineers then worked to modify the sculpture to produce a workable and marketable bicycle rack. Their work culminated in the "Ribbon Rack," which Brandir began marketing in 1979. Shortly thereafter, Cascade Pacific Lumber Co. ("Cascade") began selling a similar product, and, in response, Brandir applied for copyright protection and began placing copyright notices on its racks. The Copyright Office, however, rejected the registration on the ground that the rack did not contain any element that was "capable of independent existence as a copyrightable pictorial, graphic or sculptural work apart from the shape of the useful article." *Id*. at 1146.

The court first considered the possible tests for conceptual separability in light of its past decisions and, notably, attempted to reconcile its earlier attempts:

Perhaps the differences between the majority and the dissent in *Carol Barnhart* might have been resolved had they had before them the Denicola article on *Applied Art and Industrial Design: A Suggested Approach to Copyright in Useful Articles*, [67 Minn. L.Rev. 707 (1983)].... Denicola argues that "the statutory directive requires a distinction between works of industrial design and works whose origins lie outside the design process, despite the utilitarian environment in which they appear." He views the statutory limitation of copyrightability as "an attempt to identify elements whose form and appearance reflect the unconstrained perspective of the artist," such features not being the product of industrial design. *Id*. at 742. "Copyrightability, therefore, should turn on the relationship between the proffered work and the process of industrial design." *Id*. at 741. He suggests that "the dominant characteristic of industrial design is the influence of non-aesthetic, utilitarian concerns" and hence concludes that copyrightability "ultimately should depend on the extent to which the work reflects artistic expression uninhibited by functional considerations." *Id*. To state the Denicola test in the language of conceptual separability, if design elements reflect a merger of aesthetic and functional considerations, the artistic aspects of a work cannot be said to be conceptually separable from the utilitarian elements. Conversely, where design elements can be identified as reflecting the designer's artistic judgment exercised independently of functional influences, conceptual separability exists.

We believe that Professor Denicola's approach provides the best test for conceptual separability and, accordingly, adopt it here for several reasons. First, the approach is consistent with the holdings of our previous cases. In *Kieselstein-Cord,* for example, the artistic aspects of the belt buckles reflected purely aesthetic choices, independent of the buckles' function, while in *Carol Barnhart* the distinctive features of the torsos—the accurate anatomical design and the sculpted shirts and collars—showed clearly the influence of functional concerns.... Second, the test's emphasis on the influence of utilitarian concerns in the design process may help ... "alleviate the de facto discrimination against nonrepresentational art that has regrettably accompanied much of the current analysis." *Id.* at 745.

Id. at 1145 (footnotes omitted).

Applying Professor Denicola's test to the Ribbon Rack, the court found that the rack was not copyrightable. The court stated that, "[h]ad Brandir merely adopted one of the existing sculptures as a bicycle rack, neither the application to a utilitarian end nor commercialization of that use would have caused the object to forfeit its copyrighted status." *Id.* at 1147. However, when the Ribbon Rack was compared to earlier sculptures, continued the court, it was "in its final form essentially a product of industrial design." *Id.*

In creating the RIBBON Rack, the designer ... clearly adapted the original aesthetic elements to accommodate and further a utilitarian purpose. These altered design features of the RIBBON Rack, including the spacesaving, open design achieved by widening the upper loops ... , the straightened vertical elements that allow in-and above-ground installation of the rack, the ability to fit all types of bicycles and mopeds, and the heavy-gauged tubular construction of rustproof galvanized steel, are all features that combine to make for a safe, secure, and maintenance-free system of parking bicycles and mopeds.

. . .

... While the RIBBON Rack may be worthy of admiration for its aesthetic qualities alone, it remains nonetheless the product of industrial design. Form and function are inextricably intertwined in the rack, its ultimate design being as much the result of utilitarian pressures as aesthetic choices.... Thus there remains no artistic element of the RIBBON Rack that can be identified as separate and "capable of existing independently, of, the utilitarian aspects of the article."

Id. at 1146–47.

d.

We believe that the experience of the Second Circuit is also reflected in the more recent encounter of the Fourth Circuit with the same problem. In *Superior Form Builders, Inc. v. Dan Chase Taxidermy Supply Co., Inc.,* 74 F.3d 488 (4th Cir.1996), the court considered whether animal mannequins qualified for copyright protection. The Fourth Circuit first considered whether the mannequins were useful articles as defined by § 101 and concluded that they were not:

> A mannequin provides the creative form and expression of the ultimate animal display.... Even though covered with a skin, the mannequin is not invisible but conspicuous in the final display. The angle of the animal's head, the juxtaposition of its body parts, and the shape of the body parts in the final display is little more than the portrayal of the underlying mannequin.... None of these expressive aspects of a mannequin is lost by covering the mannequin with a skin. Thus, any utilitarian aspect of the mannequin exists "merely to portray the appearance" of the animal. *See* 17 U.S.C. § 101.

> ... It is the portrayal of the animal's body expression given by the mannequin that is thus protectable under the Copyright Act. We therefore agree with the district court in this case because "the usefulness of the forms is their portrayal of the appearance of animals." The mannequin forms "by definition are not useful articles."

> *Id.* at 494 (quoting *Superior Form Builders v. Dan Chase Taxidermy Supply Co., Inc.,* 851 F.Supp. 222, 223 (E.D.Va.1994)).

The court, however, also considered whether, if useful, the utilitarian and aesthetic aspects of the mannequin were separable:

> To the extent that an argument can be made that the mannequins in this case perform a utilitarian function—other than portraying themselves—by supporting the mounted skins, we believe the function to be conceptually separable from the works' sculptural features. *See Brandir Int'l, Inc. v. Cascade Pac. Lumber Co.,* 834 F.2d 1142, 1145 (2d Cir.1987) ("Where design elements can be identified as reflecting the designer's artistic judgment exercised independently of functional influences, conceptual separability exists."); *Kieselstein-Cord v. Accessories by Pearl, Inc.,* 632 F.2d 989, 993 (2d Cir.1980) (finding sculptural element of belt buckle conceptually separable from utilitarian function).

Id. Thus, without specifically adopting one of the tests of conceptual separability, the Fourth Circuit determined that artistic work put into the design of the animal frame was copyrightable; the fact that a skin was placed on the model and that the model, therefore, was useful in the display of the skin did not negate the artistic elements of the design.[11]

* * *

---

11. Notably, in *Hart v. Dan Chase Taxidermy Supply Co.,* 86 F.3d 320 (2d Cir.1996), the Second Circuit shortly thereafter addressed the question whether a fish manne-

C. Application

.... The Second Circuit cases exhibit a progressive attempt to forge a workable judicial approach capable of giving meaning to the basic Congressional policy decision to distinguish applied art from uncopyrightable industrial art or design. In *Kieselstein-Cord,* the Second Circuit attempted to distinguish artistic expression from industrial design by focusing on the present use of the item, i.e., the "primary ornamental aspect" versus the "subsidiary utilitarian function" of the object at issue. 632 F.2d at 993. In *Carol Barnhart,* the Second Circuit moved closer to a process-oriented approach:

> What distinguishes those [Kieselstein–Cord] buckles from the Barnhart forms is that the ornamented surfaces of the buckles were not in any respect required by their utilitarian functions; the artistic and aesthetic features could thus be conceived of as having been added to, or superimposed upon, an otherwise utilitarian article. The unique artistic design was wholly unnecessary to performance of the utilitarian function. In the case of the Barnhart forms, on the other hand, the features claimed to be aesthetic or artistic, e.g., the life-size configura-

quin was copyrightable. Although the court did not address specifically the issue before us today, its analysis is nevertheless helpful. Referring to its decision in *Carol Barnhart,* the Second Circuit posed the question rather simplistically: "Is taxidermy different [for purposes of copyright protection]?" *Id.* at 321. The Second Circuit resolved that it is:

> We do not agree that *Barnhart* mandates a finding that fish mannequins are "useful articles" undeserving of copyright protection.... [W]e do not believe that the *Barnhart* torsos can be analogized to the fish in this case. In *Barnhart,* the headless, armless, backless styrene torsos were little more than glorified coat-racks used to display clothing in stores. The torsos were designed to present the clothing, not their own forms. In taxidermy, by contrast, people look for more than a fish skin; they wish to see a complete "fish." The superficial characteristics of the fish, such as its color and texture, are admittedly conveyed by the skin, but the shape, volume, and movement of the animal are depicted by the underlying mannequin. Whether the fish is shown as resting, jumping, wiggling its tail, or preparing to munch on some plankton, is dictated by the mannequin and by its particular form, not by the skin.

> In short, the fish mannequin is designed to be looked at. That the fish mannequin is meant to be viewed clothed by a fish skin, rather than naked and on its own, makes no difference. The function of the fish form is to portray its own appearance, and that fact is enough to bring it within the scope of the Copyright Act. 17 U.S.C. § 101; *accord Superior Form Builders v. Dan Chase Taxidermy Supply Co.,* 74 F.3d 488 (4th Cir. 1996) (distinguishing *Barnhart* and holding that mammal taxidermy mannequins are "sculptural works" rather than "useful articles" because their utilitarian aspects serve "merely to portray the appearance" of the animal)....

> We conclude that fish mannequins even if considered "useful articles," are useful insofar as they "portray the[ir] appearance." 17 U.S.C. § 101. That makes them copyrightable.

Id. at 323 (internal citation omitted). Thus, the Second Circuit distinguished fish mannequins from human mannequins; however, it did so on the basis that the fish mannequins were not "useful articles" as that term is defined in § 101, not on the basis that, although useful, the artistic aspects were physically or conceptually separable from the useful aspects of the article.

tion of the breasts and the width of the shoulders, are inextricably intertwined with the utilitarian feature, the display of clothes. Whereas a model of a human torso, in order to serve its utilitarian function, must have some configuration of the chest and some width of shoulders, a belt buckle can serve its function satisfactorily without any ornamentation of the type that renders the Kieselstein–Cord buckles distinctive.

773 F.2d at 419. Thus, it was the fact that the creator of the torsos was driven by utilitarian concerns, such as how display clothes would fit on the end product, that deprived the human torsos of copyright protection.

This process-oriented approach for conceptual separability—focusing on the process of creating the object to determine whether it is entitled to copyright protection—is more fully articulated in *Brandir* and indeed reconciles the earlier case law pertaining to conceptual separability.

[T]he approach is consistent with the holdings of our previous cases. In *Kieselstein-Cord,* for example, the artistic aspects of the belt buckles reflected purely aesthetic choices, independent of the buckles' function, while in *Carol Barnhart* the distinctive features of the torsos—the accurate anatomical design and the sculpted shirts and collars—showed clearly the influence of functional concerns. Though the torsos bore artistic features, it was evident the designer incorporated those features to further the usefulness of the torsos as mannequins.

Brandir, 834 F.2d at 1145.

Furthermore, *Brandir* is not inconsistent with the more theoretical rendition of Judge Newman in his *Carol Barnhart* dissent—that "the requisite 'separateness' exists whenever the design creates in the mind of an ordinary observer two different concepts that are not inevitably entertained simultaneously." 773 F.2d at 422. When a product has reached its final form as a result of predominantly functional or utilitarian considerations, it necessarily will be more difficult for the observer to entertain simultaneously two different concepts—the artistic object and the utilitarian object. In such circumstances, *Brandir* has the added benefit of providing a more workable judicial methodology by articulating the driving principle behind conceptual separability—the influence of industrial design. When the ultimate form of the object in question is "as much the result of utilitarian pressures as aesthetic choices," "[f]orm and function are inextricably intertwined," and the artistic aspects of the object cannot be separated from its utilitarian aspects for purposes of copyright protection. *Brandir,* 834 F.2d at 1147.

Conceptual separability exists, therefore, when the artistic aspects of an article can be "conceptualized as existing independently of their utilitarian function." *Carol Barnhart,* 773 F.2d at 418. This independence is necessarily informed by "whether the design elements can be identified as reflecting the designer's artistic judgment exercised independently of functional influences." *Brandir,* 834 F.3d at 1145. If the elements do reflect the independent, artistic judgment of the designer, conceptual separability exists. Conversely, when the design of a useful article is "as much the result of utilitarian pressures as aesthetic choices," *id.* at 1147, the useful and aesthetic elements are not conceptually separable.

Applying this test to the Mara mannequin, we must conclude that the Mara face is subject to copyright protection. It certainly is not difficult to conceptualize a human face, independent of all of Mara's specific facial features, i.e., the shape of the eye, the upturned nose, the angular cheek and jaw structure, that would serve the utilitarian functions of a hair stand and, if proven, of a makeup model. Indeed, one is not only able to conceive of a different face than that portrayed on the Mara mannequin, but one easily can conceive of another visage that portrays the "hungry look" on a high-fashion runway model. Just as Mattel is entitled to protection for "its own particularized expression" of an "upturned nose[ ], bow lips, and widely spaced eyes," *Mattel [Inc. v. Goldberger Doll Mfg. Co.],* 365 F.3d 133, 136 [(2d Cir. 2004)], so too is Heerlein (and, therefore, Pivot Point as assignee of the copyright registration) entitled to have his expression of the "hungry look" protected from copying.

Mara can be conceptualized as existing independent from its use in hair display or make-up training because it is the product of Heerlein's artistic judgment. When Passage approached Heerlein about creating the Mara sculpture, Passage did not provide Heerlein with specific dimensions or measurements; indeed, there is no evidence that Heerlein's artistic judgment was constrained by functional considerations. Passage did not require, for instance, that the sculpture's eyes be a certain width to accommodate standard-sized eyelashes, that the brow be arched at a certain angle to facilitate easy make-up application or that the sculpture as a whole not exceed certain dimensional limits so as to fit within Pivot Point's existing packaging system. Such considerations, had they been present, would weigh against a determination that Mara was purely the product of an artistic effort. By contrast, after Passage met with Heerlein to discuss Passage's idea for a "hungry-look" model, Heerlein had carte blanche to implement that vision as he saw fit. Consequently, this is not a situation, such as was presented to the Second Circuit in *Carol Barnhart,* in which certain features ("accurate anatomical design and the sculpted shirts and collars") were included in the design for purely functional reasons. *Brandir,* 834 F.2d at 1145. Furthermore, unlike "the headless, armless, backless styrene torsos" which "were little more than glorified coat-racks used to display clothing in stores," *Hart,* 86 F.3d at 323, the creative aspects of the Mara sculpture were meant to be seen and admired. Thus, because Mara was the product of a creative process unfettered by functional concerns, its sculptural features "can be identified separately from, and are capable of existing independently of," its utilitarian aspects. It therefore meets the requirements for conceptual separability and is subject to copyright protection.

Conclusion

The Mara mannequin is subject to copyright protection. We therefore must reverse the summary judgment in favor of Charlene Products and Mr.

Yau; the case is remanded for a trial on Pivot Point's infringement claim....

■ KANNE, CIRCUIT JUDGE, dissenting.

Writing for the majority, Judge Ripple has applied his usual thorough and scholarly approach to this difficult intellectual property problem; however, I cannot join the majority opinion because I am not persuaded that the "Mara" mannequin is copyrightable. All functional items have aesthetic qualities. If copyright provided protection for functional items simply because of their aesthetic qualities, Congress's policy choice that gives less protection in patent than copyright would be undermined. *See American Dental Ass'n v. Delta Dental Plans Ass'n,* 126 F.3d 977, 980 (7th Cir.1997).

The majority rightly assumes that Mara is a "useful article" as defined in 17 U.S.C. § 101. Opinion at 13. To receive copyright protection as a "sculptural work," then, Mara must come within the narrow restrictions placed on "useful articles" in the definition of pictorial, graphic, and sculptural works:

> [T]he design of a useful article ... shall be considered a ... sculptural work only if, and only to the extent that, such design incorporates ... sculptural features that can be identified separately from, *and* are capable of existing independently of, the utilitarian aspects of the article.

17 U.S.C. § 101 (emphasis added). As the district court noted, the statute requires, on its face, that sculptural features must be separately identified from the utilitarian aspects of the article ("conceptual separability") and they must exist independently from the utilitarian aspects of the article ("physical separability") in order to receive copyright protection. As to whether both conceptual and physical separability are required for copyrightability, most courts and commentators have concluded that only one or the other test is appropriate. But that issue is not presented here because Mara is not copyrightable regardless of whether both or either is applied.

Taking physical separability first, the district court used examples from case law to illustrate that the sculptural features in many useful items can be physically removed from the object and sold separately without affecting the functionality of the useful article. *See, e.g., Mazer v. Stein,* 347 U.S. 201, 74 S.Ct. 460, 98 L.Ed. 630 (1954) (holding that a sculpture of a dancer carved into the base of a lamp may be copyrighted); *Kieselstein-Cord v. Accessories by Pearl, Inc.,* 632 F.2d 989 (2d Cir.1980) (holding that decorative belt buckles could be copyrighted as separate objects sold not to hold up one's pants).

Mara, on the other hand, has only functional attributes. Thus, any physical separation of a portion of her would not be independent of her utilitarian aspects. She is sold to beauty schools as a teaching device; students style her hair and apply makeup as realistic training for such pursuits on live subjects. A mannequin head without a neck, or with different eyes and musculature, would not serve the utilitarian purpose of applying makeup or teaching the art of matching hair styles to facial features. As the district court explained: "Beauty students style hair to flatter the face, not to be worn on featureless ovoids. The use of a mannequin head in training students of beauty schools *lies in its aesthetic qualities.*" There is nothing in Mara that we could physically remove that would not be part of Mara's utility as a teaching aid. Like mannequins of human torsos, *Carol Barnhart Inc. v. Economy Cover Corp.,* 773 F.2d 411, 418–19 (2d Cir.1985), mannequins of human faces are not physically separable from their functional purpose and are therefore not copyrightable.

Next, the district court considered various restatements of the meaning of "conceptual separability" (whether features can be identified or conceived of separately from the utilitarian aspects) and applied the most appropriate one to Mara. Professor Goldstein, in his treatise, *Copyright: Principles, Law & Practice,* presents a reasonable explanation of the statutory text: "a . . . sculptural feature incorporated in the design of a useful article is conceptually separable if it can stand on its own as a work of art traditionally conceived, and if the useful article in which it is embodied would be equally useful without it." Mara has no conceptually separable features to which copyright protection could be granted. Her features are incapable of being identified separately from the utilitarian use of those features. Without features, the mannequin's head and neck would be little more than an egg on a stick, useless for its intended purpose. Mara possesses neither physical nor conceptual separability.

The majority, concluding that Congress intended "to state a single, integrated standard," deduced that the standard must be "conceptual separability." This may be correct, as it is very difficult to divine the distinction between physical and conceptual separability if those standards are properly stated. In my view, however, the majority's explanation of conceptual separability lacks a basis in the statute. As the majority sees it, conceptual separability "exists . . . when the artistic aspects of an article can be conceptualized as existing independently of their utilitarian function." Opinion at 36. The majority further explains that the way to determine if this is the case is to look to the process of design: if independent "artistic" choices were made in the sculpture's creation, and such choices were not later sullied by the influence of industrial design, then some of the useful article is a conceptually separable sculpture and therefore copyrightable, Opinion at 36–37.

Problematically, the majority's test for conceptual separability seems to bear little resemblance to the statute. The statute asks two questions: Does the useful article incorporate "sculptural features that can be identified separately from the utilitarian aspects" of the article? And are these features "capable of existing independently" from the utilitarian aspects? The copyright statute is concerned with protecting only non-utilitarian features of the useful article. To be copyrightable, the statute requires that the useful article's functionality remain intact once the copyrightable material is separated. In other words, Pivot Point needs to show that Mara's face is not a utilitarian "aspect" of the product "Mara," but rather a separate non-utilitarian "feature." The majority, by looking only to whether the features could also "be conceptualized as existing independently of *their utilitarian function*" and ignoring the more important question of whether the features themselves are utilitarian *aspects* of the useful article, mistakenly presupposes that utilitarian aspects of a useful article can be copyrighted. If we took away Mara's facial features, her functionality would be greatly diminished or eliminated, thus proving that her features cannot be copyrighted.

Moreover, the "process-oriented approach," advocated by the majority drifts even further away from the statute. Opinion at 35. The statute looks to the useful article as it exists, not to how it was created. I believe it simply is irrelevant to inquire into the origins of Mara's eyes, cheekbones, and neck. If such features have been fully incorporated as functional aspects of the mannequin, then copyright does not provide protection. Even if we were to look at the "process" that led to the creation of Mara, it is undeniable that, from the beginning, Pivot Point intended Mara to serve a functional purpose and commissioned her creation to fulfill that purpose (not to create a work of art for aesthetic beauty).

The majority, as evidenced by its emphasis on the fact that Charlene Products apparently copied Mara with its doll, "Liza," seems unduly concerned in this context with Charlene's questionable business practices. This is immaterial to the determination of whether the Mara doll is protected by copyright law. Importantly, other possible legal protections for Pivot Point's intellectual property—design patent, trademark, trade dress, and state unfair competition law—are available to address the majority's concerns. Copyright does not protect functional products. Charlene is free, under its own brand name, to copy and sell copies of useful articles that do not have patent protection. *See, e.g., TrafFix Devices, Inc. v. Marketing Displays, Inc.*, 532 U.S. 23, 121 S.Ct. 1255, 149 L.Ed.2d 164 (2001); *Bonito Boats, Inc. v. Thunder Craft Boats, Inc.*, 489 U.S. 141, 109 S.Ct. 971, 103 L.Ed.2d 118 (1989); *Sears, Roebuck & Co. v. Stiffel Co.*, 376 U.S. 225, 84 S.Ct. 784, 11 L.Ed.2d 661 (1964). I fear that the majority's opinion grants copyright protection to functional aspects of a useful article. I would, therefore, affirm the district court's grant of summary judgment in favor of Charlene Products and Mr. Yau.

[See Collezione Europa U.S.A., Inc. v. Hillsdale House, Ltd., 243 F.Supp.2d 444 (M.D.N.C.2003). There, sculpted leaf forms were incorporated as part of the metal back supports on furniture manufactured by Hillsdale, the defendant in this declaratory judgment action. The declaratory plaintiff copied those forms. (Photographs are set forth in the F.Supp.2d court report.) The court, relying heavily on the district court decision in *Pivot Point*, held that the proper "separability" test is not whether the sculpted forms can be broken off and exist as a work of art, but rather whether one can "conceive" of that process. Thus, "conceptual" separability. Applying that test, the court held that the leaf forms—like the lamp-base statue in *Mazer*—were separable from the chair and were copyrightable.]

H. CHARACTERS

Page 242: The Second Circuit has affirmed the district court's decision in a later stage of the case: *Archie Comic Pubs, Inc. v. DeCarlo*, 258 F.Supp.2d 315 (S.D.N.Y. 2003), *aff'd*, 88 Fed. Appx. 468 (2d Cir. 2004).

Page 244: add the following after *Detective Comics*:

Gaiman v. McFarlane

360 F.3d 644 (7th Cir. 2004).

■ POSNER, CIRCUIT JUDGE

. . . Gaiman and McFarlane are both celebrated figures in the world of comic books, but they play different though overlapping roles. Gaiman just writes scripts; McFarlane writes scripts too, but he also illustrates and publishes the comic books. In 1992, shortly after forming his own publishing house, McFarlane began publishing a series of comic books entitled *Spawn*, which at first he wrote and illustrated himself. "Spawn," more precisely "Hellspawn," are officers in an army of the damned commanded by a devil named Malebolgia, who hopes one day to launch his army against Heaven. The leading character in the series is a man named Al Simmons, who is dead but has returned to the world of the living as a Hellspawn.

Al's story is an affecting one. Born in a quiet neighborhood outside of Pittsburgh, he was recruited by the CIA and eventually became a member of an elite military unit that guards the President. He saved the President from an assassin's bullet and was rewarded with a promotion to lieutenant colonel. He was placed under the command of Jason Wynn, who became his mentor and inducted him into the sinister inner recesses of the intelligence community. When Al began to question Wynn's motives, Wynn sent two agents, significantly named Chapel and Priest, to kill Al with laser weapons, and they did, burning him beyond recognition. Al was buried with great fanfare in Arlington National Cemetery.

Now Al had always had an Achilles' heel, namely that he loved his wife beyond bearing and so, dying, he vowed that he would do anything to see her again. Malebolgia took him at his word ("would do anything") and returned Al to Earth. But a deal with the devil is always a Faustian pact. Al discovered that he was now one of Malebolgia's handpicked Hellspawn and had been remade (a full makeover, as we'll see) and infused with Hell-born energy.

Returned to Earth in his new persona, Al discovers that his wife has remarried his best friend, who was able to give her the child he never could. He absorbs the blow but thirsts for revenge against Jason Wynn. He bides his time, living with homeless people and pondering the unhappy fact that once he exhausts his Hell-born energy he will be returned to Malebolgia's domain and become a slave in an army of the damned with no hope of redemption. He must try somehow to break his pact with the devil.

The early issues in the series were criticized for bad writing, so McFarlane decided to invite four top writers each to write the script for one issue of *Spawn*. One of those invited was Gaiman. He accepted the invitation and wrote the script for *Spawn* issue No. 9. Their contract, made in 1992, was oral. There was no mention of copyright, nor, for that matter, of how Gaiman would be compensated for his work, beyond McFarlane's assuring Gaiman that he would treat him "better than the big guys" did. The reference was to the two leading comic book publishers, Marvel Comics (not to be confused with Gaiman's company, Marvels and Miracles) and DC Comics, for which Gaiman and other writers write on a "work made for hire" basis. 17 U.S.C. § 101. This means that the publishers own the copyrights on their work. § 201(b).

It might seem that when McFarlane told Gaiman that he would treat Gaiman "better than the big guys" did, he just meant he'd compensate him more generously for work made for hire. But McFarlane rightly does not argue this. Gaiman's work for him was not work made for hire....

In his script for *Spawn* No. 9, Gaiman introduced three new characters—Medieval Spawn (as he was later called by McFarlane—Gaiman had not named it and in the issue he is just referred to as a Spawn, with no further identifier), Angela (no last name), and Count Nicholas Cogliostro. Gaiman described, named, and wrote the dialogue for them, but McFarlane drew them....

Spawn No. 9 was a huge success, selling more than a million copies. McFarlane paid Gaiman $100,000 for his work on it. Gaiman testified that this was about what he would have expected to receive from DC Comics had he written the script of *Spawn* No. 9 for that company as a work made for hire....

[McFarlane disputes Gaiman's claim for an accounting for profits from the Spawn characters on two grounds, first that Gaiman is not a coauthor of the work and therefore is not entitled to an accounting—see *infra* Chapter 3 of this Supplement for this aspect of the decision; second that the characters are not copyrightable]

McFarlane's second argument against the copyrightability of Medieval Spawn and Cogliostro appeals to the confusingly named doctrine of "scenes a faire" (literally "scenes for action," a theatrical term meaning the climactic scene in a play or opera, which is not the legal meaning). Related to the fundamental idea-expression dichotomy ..., the doctrine teaches that "a copyright owner can't prove infringement by pointing to features of his work that are found in the defendant's work as well but that are so rudimentary, commonplace, standard, or unavoidable that they do not serve to distinguish one work within a class of works from another."

31

Bucklew v. Hawkins, Ash, Baptie & Co., 329 F.3d 923, 929 (7th Cir. 2003) [additional citations omitted]. If standard features could be used to prove infringement, not only would there be great confusion because it would be hard to know whether the alleged infringer had copied the feature from a copyrighted work or from the public domain, but the net of liability would be cast too wide; authors would find it impossible to write without obtaining a myriad of copyright permissions.

A stock character is a stock example of the operation of the doctrine, and a drunken old bum is a stock character. If a drunken old bum were a copyrightable character, so would be a drunken suburban housewife, a gesticulating Frenchman, a fire-breathing dragon, a talking cat, a Prussian officer who wears a monocle and clicks his heels, a masked magician, and, in Learned Hand's memorable paraphrase of *Twelfth Night*, "a riotous knight who kept wassail to the discomfort of the household, or a vain and foppish steward who became amorous of his mistress." It would be difficult to write successful works of fiction without negotiating for dozens or hundreds of copyright licenses, even though such stereotyped characters are the products not of the creative imagination but of simple observation of the human comedy.

McFarlane argues that even as dolled up by the penciler, the inker, and the colorist, Cogliostro is too commonplace to be copyrightable. Gaiman could not copyright a character described merely as an unexpectedly knowledgeable old wino, that is true; but that is not his claim. He claims to be the joint owner of the copyright on a character that has a specific name and a specific appearance. Cogliostro's age, obviously phony title ("Count"), what he knows and says, his name, and his faintly Mosaic facial features combine to create a distinctive character. No more is required for a character copyright. ... As long as the character is distinctive, other authors can use the stock character out of which it may have been built without fear (well, without too much fear) of being accused as infringers.

We are mindful that the Ninth Circuit denied copyrightability to Dashiell Hammett's famously distinctive detective character Sam Spade in *Warner Bros. Pictures, Inc. v. Columbia Broadcasting System, Inc.*, 216 F.2d 945 (9th Cir. 1954). That decision is wrong, though perhaps understandable on the "legal realist" ground that Hammett was not claiming copyright in Sam Spade—on the contrary, he wanted to reuse his own character but to be able to do so he had to overcome Warner Brothers' claim to own the copyright. The Ninth Circuit has killed the decision, see *Olson v. National Broadcasting Co.*, 855 F.2d 1446, 1452 and n. 7 (9th Cir. 1988); *Walt Disney Productions v. Air Pirates*, *supra*, 581 F.2d at 755 and n. 11, though without the usual obsequies, but even if the decision were correct and were binding authority in this circuit, it would not rule this case. The reason is the difference between literary and graphic expression. The description of a character in prose leaves much to the imagination, even when the description is detailed—as in Dashiel Hammett's description of Sam Spade's physical appearance in the first paragraph of *The Maltese Falcon*: "Samuel Spade's jaw was long and bony, his chin a jutting v under the more flexible v of his mouth. His nostrils curved back to make another, smaller, v. His yellow-grey eyes were horizontal. The v *motif* was picked up again by thickish brows rising outward from twin creases above a hooked nose, and his pale brown hair grew down—from high flat temples—in a point on his forehead. He looked rather pleasantly like a blond Satan." Even after all this, one hardly knows what Sam Spade looked like. But everyone knows what Humphrey Bogart looked like. A reader of unillustrated fiction completes the work in his mind; the reader of a comic book or the viewer of a movie is passive. That is why kids lose a lot when they don't read fiction, even when the movies and television that they watch are aesthetically superior.

Although Gaiman's verbal description of Cogliostro may well have been of a stock character, once he was drawn and named and given speech he became sufficiently distinctive to be copyrightable. . . .

I. Sound Recordings

House Report

H.R. Rep. No. 94–1476, 94th Cong., 2d Sess. 55–56 (1976).

. . . .

Enactment of Public Law 92–140 in 1971 marked the first recognition in American copyright law of sound recordings as copyrightable works. As defined in section 101, copyrightable "sound recordings" are original works of authorship comprising an aggregate of musical, spoken, or other sounds that have been fixed in tangible form. The copyrightable work comprises the aggregation of sounds and not the tangible medium of fixation. Thus, "sound recordings" as copyrightable subject matter are distinguished from "phonorecords," the latter being physical objects in which sounds are fixed. They are also distinguished from any copyrighted literary, dramatic, or musical works that may be reproduced on a "phonorecord."

As a class of subject matter, sound recordings are clearly within the scope of the "writings of an author" capable of protection under the Constitution, and the extension of limited statutory protection to them was too long delayed. Aside from cases in which sounds are fixed by some purely mechanical means without originality of any kind, the copyright protection that would prevent the reproduction and distribution of unauthorized phonorecords of sound recordings is clearly justified.

The copyrightable elements in a sound recording will usually, though not always, involve "authorship" both on the part of the performers whose performance is captured and on the part of the record producer responsible for setting up the recording session, capturing and electronically processing the sounds, and compiling and editing them to make the final sound recording. There may, however, be cases where the record producer's contribution is so minimal that the performance is the only copyrightable element in the work, and there may be cases (for example, recordings of bird calls, sounds of racing cars, et cetera) where only the record producer's contribution is copyrightable.

On the Distinction Between a Sound Recording and the Musical Composition or Other Work Fixed on the Recording

Sound recordings typically incorporate copyrighted works, most often musical compositions. Indeed, a sound recording may serve as the medium of first fixation of a musical composition—imagine a recording of a performance of a spontaneous jazz composition: once the work is recorded, it meets the fixation threshold for federal copyright protection. The musical composition now comes within federal copyright regardless of whether or not the composition is subsequently reduced to sheet music form. Whether recorded in an audible format or in notation, the musical composition exists as a copyrighted work apart from its medium of fixation. The sound recording evidences the composition, but in copyright terms it is also a work in its own right, assuming the performance or process of recording it demonstrate sufficient originality. Hence, copyright will protect a sound recording of Mozart's 41st Symphony, not on account of the musical composition (which is in the public domain), but because of the authorship manifested in the playing of the orchestra and the engineering of the recording. By the same token, a copyrighted sound recording of a public domain musical composition will not restore the recorded work to copyright protection: any one else is free to make her own performance and/or recording of Mozart's 41st.

Students, and even courts, sometimes conflate the categories of a sound recording and the work it records. Where, for example, a musical composition is confused with a sound recording, failure to recognize the distinct character of the works has consequences for their ownership and scope of protection (as we will see in Chapter 6, the scope of copyright in a sound recording is narrower than for other § 102 categories of works). As you study the majority and dissenting opinions in the following decision, consider which characterization of the work at issue you find more persuasive.

Newton v. Diamond

349 F.3d 591 (9th Cir. 2003).

■ SCHROEDER, CHIEF JUDGE:

* * *

Background and Procedural History

The plaintiff and appellant in this case, James W. Newton, is an accomplished avant-garde jazz flutist and composer. In 1978, he composed the song "Choir," a piece for flute and voice intended to incorporate elements of African–American gospel music, Japanese ceremonial court music, traditional African music, and classical music, among others. According to Newton, the song was inspired by his earliest memory of music, watching four women singing in a church in rural Arkansas. In 1981, Newton performed and recorded "Choir" and licensed all rights in the sound recording to ECM Records for $5000. The license covered only the sound recording, and it is undisputed that Newton retained all rights to the composition of "Choir." Sound recordings and their underlying compositions are separate works with their own distinct copyrights. 17 U.S.C. § 102(a)(2), (7).

The defendants and appellees include the members of the rap and hip-hop group Beastie Boys, and their business associates. In 1992, Beastie Boys obtained a license from ECM Records to use portions of the sound recording of "Choir" in various renditions of their song "Pass the Mic" in exchange for a one-time fee of $1000. Beastie Boys did not obtain a license from Newton to use the underlying composition.

The portion of the composition at issue consists of three notes, C—D flat—C, sung over a background C note played on the flute. When played on the sound recording licensed by Beastie Boys, the segment lasts for approximately six seconds. The score to "Choir" also indicates that the entire song should be played in a "largo/senza-misura" tempo, meaning "slowly/without-measure." Apart from an instruction that the performer sing into the flute and finger simultaneously, the score is not further orchestrated.

The dispute between Newton and Beastie Boys centers around the copyright implications of the practice of sampling, a practice now common to many types of popular music. . . .

. . . Pursuant to their license from ECM Records, Beastie Boys digitally sampled the opening six seconds of Newton's sound recording of "Choir." Beastie Boys repeated or "looped" this six-second sample as a background element throughout "Pass the Mic," so that it appears over forty times in various renditions of the song. In addition to the version of "Pass the Mic" released on their 1992 album, "Check Your Head," Beastie Boys included the "Choir" sample in two remixes, "Dub the Mic" and "Pass the Mic (Pt. 2, Skills to Pay the Bills)." . . .

. . . This case involves not only use of a composition, . . . but also use of a sound recording of a performance of that composition. Because the defendants licensed the sound recording, our inquiry is confined to whether the unauthorized use of the composition itself was substantial enough to sustain an infringement claim. Therefore, we may consider only Beastie Boys' appropriation of the song's compositional elements and must remove from consideration all the elements unique to Newton's performance. Stated another way, we must "filter out" the licensed elements of the sound recording to get down to the unlicensed elements of the composition, as the composition is the sole basis for Newton's infringement claim.

In filtering out the unique performance elements from consideration, and separating them from those found in the composition, we find substantial assistance in the testimony of Newton's own experts. His experts reveal the extent to which the sound recording of "Choir" is the product of Newton's highly developed performance techniques, rather than the result of a generic rendition of the composition. As a general matter, according to

Newton's expert Dr. Christopher Dobrian, "the contribution of the performer is often so great that s/he in fact provides as much musical content as the composer." This is particularly true with works like "Choir," given the nature of jazz performance and the minimal scoring of the composition. Indeed, as Newton's expert Dr. Oliver Wilson explained:

> The copyrighted score of "Choir", as is the custom in scores written in the jazz tradition, does not contain indications for all of the musical subtleties that it is assumed the performer-composer of the work will make in the work's performance. The function of the score is more mnemonic in intention than prescriptive.

And it is clear that Newton goes beyond the score in his performance....

... Whatever copyright interest Newton obtained in this "dense cluster of pitches and ambient sounds," he licensed that interest to ECM Records over twenty years ago, and ECM Records in turn licensed that interest to Beastie Boys. Thus, regardless of whether the average audience might recognize "the Newton technique" at work in the sampled sound recording, those performance elements are beyond consideration in Newton's claim for infringement of his copyright in the underlying composition. Having licensed away his interest in the recording of his performance, Newton's only claim is for a violation of his rights in the three-note sequence transcribed in the composition.

Once we have isolated the basis of Newton's infringement action—the "Choir" composition, devoid of the unique performance elements found only in the sound recording—we turn to the nub of our inquiry: whether Beastie Boys' unauthorized use of the composition, as opposed to their authorized use of the sound recording, was substantial enough to sustain an infringement action. [The court held that the taking from the composition was *de minimis*, and therefore not actionable.]

■ GRABER, CIRCUIT JUDGE, dissenting:

I respectfully dissent....

... The majority is correct that James Newton's considerable skill adds many recognizable features to the performance sampled by Beastie Boys. Even after those features are "filtered out," however, the composition, standing alone, is distinctive enough for a jury reasonably to conclude that an average audience would recognize the appropriation of the sampled segment and that Beastie Boys' use was therefore not de minimis.

Newton has presented evidence that the compositional elements of "Choir" are so compositionally distinct that a reasonable listener would recognize the sampled segment even if it were performed by the featured flautist of a middle school orchestra. It is useful to begin by observing that the majority's repeated references to the sampled segment of "Choir" as a "3–note sequence" are overly simplified. The sampled segment is actually a three-note sequence sung above a fingered held C note, for a total of four separate tones. Even passages with relatively few notes may be qualitatively significant. The opening melody of Beethoven's Fifth Symphony is relatively simple and features only four notes, but it certainly is compositionally distinctive and recognizable.

The majority is simply mistaken in its assertion, that Newton's experts did not present evidence of the qualitative value of the compositional elements of the sampled material sufficient to survive summary judgment. The majority is similarly mistaken when it says that Newton's experts failed to distinguish between the sound recording and the composition. To the contrary, Newton presented considerable expert evidence that the composition *alone* is distinctive and recognizable.

First, Newton offered a letter from Professor Olly Wilson of the University of California at Berkeley. Professor Wilson acknowledges that much of the distinctiveness of the sampled material is due to Newton's performance and that the copyrighted score does not fully convey the quality of the piece as performed. Nevertheless, Professor Wilson concludes that the score

> clearly indicates that the performer will simultaneously sing and finger specific pitches, gives a sense of the rhythm of the piece, and also provides the general structure of this section of the piece. Hence, in my opinion, the digital sample of the performance ... is clearly a realization of the musical score filed with the copyright office.

Second, Newton presented a letter from Professor Christopher Dobrian of the University of California, Irvine. The majority deals with Professor Dobrian's evidence by stating: "Dr. Dobrian described the three-note sequence at issue as 'a simple, "neighboring tone" figure.' " As the passage quoted below demonstrates, the majority fundamentally misreads Professor Dobrian's statement by taking it out of context; in the process the majority reverses his intended meaning. Professor Dobrian actually concludes:

> Applying traditional analysis to this brief excerpt from Newton's "Choir"—i.e., focusing solely on the notated pitches—a theorist could conclude (erroneously, in my opinion) that the excerpt contains an insignificant amount of information because it contains a simple "neighboring-tone" figure: C to D-flat and back to C.... If, on the other hand, one considers the special playing technique *described in the score* (holding one fingered note constant while singing the other pitches) and the resultant complex, expressive effect that results, it is clear that the "unique expression" of this excerpt is not solely in the pitch choices, but is actually in those particular pitches performed in that particular way on that instrument. These components in this particular combination are not found anywhere else in the notated music literature, and they are *unique and distinctive* in their sonic/musical result.

(Emphasis added.)

It is important to note that Professor Dobrian is *not* talking about Newton's performance of the sampled portion. Rather, he is speaking of the distinctiveness *of the underlying composition*. The "playing technique" is not a matter of personal performance, but is a built-in feature of the score itself. In essence, Dobrian is stating that *any* flautist's performance of the sampled segment would be distinctive and recognizable, because the score itself is distinctive and recognizable.

The majority, then, misreads the record when it states that Newton failed to offer evidence that the sampled material is qualitatively significant. In fact, Newton presented evidence, as described above, to show that an average and reasonable listener would recognize Beastie Boys' appropriation of the *composition* of the sampled material. . . .

QUESTION

Suppose a composer has fixed her composition in sheet music. She then performs the composition, adding new variations to the previously fixed theme. The performance is recorded. Are the variations a "musical composition," or a "recorded performance" distinct from and exclusive of the composition?

J.   GOVERNMENT WORKS AND OTHER PUBLIC POLICY ISSUES

Page 252:   Substitute the following for the paragraph discussing the panel decision in the *Veeck* case:

Veeck v. Southern Bldg. Code Cong. Internat'l, Inc.

293 F.3d 791 (5th Cir. en banc 2002).

■ Before KING, CHIEF JUDGE, JOLLY, HIGGINBOTHAM, DAVIS, JONES, SMITH, WIENER, BARKSDALE, EMILIO M. GARZA, DEMOSS, BENAVIDES, STEWART, PARKER, DENNIS and CLEMENT, CIRCUIT JUDGES.

■ EDITH H. JONES, CIRCUIT JUDGE:

The issue in this *en banc* case is the extent to which a private organization may assert copyright protection for its model codes, after the models have been adopted by a legislative body and become "the law". Specifically, may a code-writing organization prevent a website operator from posting the text of a model code where the code is identified simply as the building code of a city that enacted the model code as law? Our short answer is that as *law*, the model codes enter the public domain and are not subject to the copyright holder's exclusive prerogatives. As model codes, however, the organization's works retain their protected status.

BACKGROUND

Peter Veeck individually operates "RegionalWeb" (<http://regional-web.texoma.net>), a non-commercial website that provides information about north Texas. Sometime in 1997, Veeck decided to post on Regional-Web the local building codes of Anna and Savoy, two small towns in north Texas that had adopted the 1994 edition of the Standard Building Code written by appellee, Southern Building Code Congress International, Inc. ("SBCCI"). Veeck made a few attempts to inspect several towns' copies of the Building Code, but he was not able to locate them easily. Eventually, Veeck purchased the 1994 model building codes directly from SBCCI; he paid $72.00 and received a copy of the codes on disk. Although the software licensing agreement and copyright notice indicated that the codes could not be copied and distributed, Veeck cut and pasted their text onto his RegionalWeb. Veeck's website did not specify that the codes were written by SBCCI. Instead, he identified them, correctly, as the building codes of Anna and Savoy, Texas.

The author of the codes, SBCCI, is a non-profit organization consisting of approximately 14,500 members from government bodies, the construction industry, business and trade associations, students, and colleges and universities. Since 1940, SBCCI's primary mission has been to develop, promote, and promulgate model building codes, such as the Standard Plumbing Code, the Standard Gas Code, the Standard Fire Prevention Code, and the Standard Mechanical Code. SBCCI encourages local government entities to enact its codes into law by reference, without cost to the governmental entity. No licensing agreements are executed in connection with legislative adoption, nor does SBCCI keep track of the entities that have adopted its codes. Although SBCCI is a non-profit organization, its annual budget, exceeding $9 million, derives in part from sales of its model codes and is used to fund continuing activities. There are no restrictions or requirements on membership in SBCCI, but non-members are charged considerably more for copies of its codes than are members.

While SBCCI continues to assert its copyright prerogatives—exclusively to publish the codes and license their reproduction and distribution—even as to codes that have been adopted by local entities, the organization insists that it grants liberal permission for copying. To support this contention, SBCCI offered in evidence several dozen letters of permission written to entities as diverse as book publishers, seminar providers, and municipal inspection agencies. Notably, each permit letter carefully circumscribed the amount of copying allowed.

SBCCI's generosity did not extend to Veeck's public-service posting of the Anna and Savoy building codes on his website. The organization demanded that he cease and desist from infringing its copyrights. Veeck filed a declaratory judgment action seeking a ruling that he did not violate the Copyright Act. SBCCI counterclaimed for copyright infringement, unfair competition and breach of contract. Both parties moved for summary judgment on the copyright infringement issue.

Finding no genuinely disputed material facts, the district court granted summary judgment in favor of SBCCI, including a permanent injunction and monetary damages. On appeal, a divided panel of this court upheld SBCCI's copyrights in the municipal building codes posted by Veeck, and it rejected his defenses to infringement based on due process, merger, fair use, copyright misuse and waiver.

We elected to rehear this case *en banc* because of the novelty and importance of the issues it presents.

DISCUSSION

As the organizational author of original works, SBCCI indisputably holds a copyright in its model building codes. See 17 U.S.C. § 102(a). Copyright law permits an author exclusively to make or condone derivative works and to regulate the copying and distribution of both the original and derivative works. 17 U.S.C. § 106. The question before us is whether Peter Veeck infringed SBCCI's copyright on its model codes when he posted them only as what they became—building codes of Anna and Savoy, Texas—on his regional website. Put otherwise, does SBCCI retain the right wholly to exclude others from copying the model codes after and only to the extent to which they are adopted as "the law" of various jurisdictions?

The answer to this narrow issue seems compelled by three sources: the Supreme Court's holding that "the law" is not copyrightable; alternatively, the Copyright Act's exclusion from its scope of "ideas" or "facts"; and the balance of caselaw.

I. *The Supreme Court's View*

Excluding "the law" from the purview of the copyright statutes dates back to this nation's earliest period. In 1834, the Supreme Court interpreted the first federal copyright laws and unanimously held that "no reporter has or can have any copyright in the written opinions delivered by this Court ... " *Wheaton v. Peters*, 33 U.S. (8 Pet.) 591, 668, 8 L.Ed. 1055 (1834). The case arose when one of the Court's official reporters was asserting copyright protection for his annotated compilations of Supreme Court opinions. The Court distinguished between the reporter's individual work and the Justices' opinions. The Court's rejection of copyright for judicial opinions paralleled the principle—recognized by attorneys for both parties—that "[s]tatutes were never copyrighted." Based on the acknowledged and incontestable analogy with legislative acts, *Wheaton* held unanimously that "the law" in the form of judicial opinions may not be copyrighted.

The same broad understanding of what constitutes "the law" for copyright purposes underlies the Court's later decision in *Banks v. Manchester*, 128 U.S. 244, 9 S.Ct. 36, 32 L.Ed. 425 (1888). The Court there denied a copyright to a court reporter in his printing of the opinions of the Ohio Supreme Court. The Court first noted that whatever work the judges perform in their official capacity cannot be regarded as authorship under the copyright law. As a question of "public policy," the Court stated that,

> there has always been a judicial *consensus*, from the time of the decision in the case of *Wheaton v. Peters*, 8 Pet. 591, 8 L.Ed. 1055, that no copyright could, under the statutes passed by Congress, be secured in the products of the labor done by judicial officers in the discharge of their judicial duties. *The whole work done by the judges constitutes the authentic exposition and interpretation of the law, which, binding every citizen, is free for publication to all, whether it is a declaration of unwritten law, or an interpretation of a constitution or statute.*

Banks, 128 U.S. at 253, 9 S.Ct. at 40. (emphasis added). At this point, *Banks* relied upon a decision of the Massachusetts Supreme Judicial Court, which stated,

> [I]t needs no argument to show that justice requires that all should have free access to the opinions, and that it is against sound public policy to prevent this, or to suppress and keep from the earliest knowledge of the public the statutes, or the decisions and opinions of the Justices.

Nash v. Lathrop, 142 Mass. 29, 6 N.E. 559 (1886). The court in *Nash* further observed that a legislature likewise could not deny public access to statutes. *Banks* represents a continuous understanding that "the law," whether articulated in judicial opinions or legislative acts or ordinances, is in the public domain and thus not amenable to copyright. Modern decisions have followed suit. Significantly, the 1976 Copyright Act specifically denies protection to federal statutes and regulations. 17 U.S.C. § 105. Given the state law foundation of *Banks* and its progeny, there is no reason to believe that state or local laws are copyrightable. * * * *

As governing law, pursuant to *Banks*, the building codes of Anna and Savoy, Texas cannot be copyrighted. SBCCI and its numerous amici must limit or circumvent the *Banks* line of cases in order to prevail. Initially, SBCCI divides *Banks* into two holdings and concludes that either holding must be squared with the policies and purposes of copyright law. This not insubstantial mode of analysis must be carefully reviewed.

The first holding of *Banks* is said to deny copyright to judicial opinions because judges, whose salaries are paid by the government, cannot claim to be "authors" of their official works. SBCCI contends that this discussion shows only that judges have no need of the Copyright Act's economic incentives in order to author judicial opinions. *Banks*, it is implied, articulates a utilitarian rationale for denying copyright protection to judicial opinions. SBCCI contrasts government employees with the private "authors" of model codes who allegedly depend on copyright incentives in order to perform their public service. SBCCI concludes that this "prong" of *Banks* does not apply to private code-writing organizations whose work has been adopted or incorporated into statutes, ordinances, or government regulations. Two courts, in addition to the panel that originally heard this case, have identified the consideration of authorship incentives as a "holding" of *Banks*. See Practice Management Info. Corp. v. American Medical Ass'n, 121 F.3d 516, 518 (9th Cir.1997), *opinion amended by* 133 F.3d 1140 (9th Cir.1998); County of Suffolk v. First American Real Estate Solutions, 261 F.3d 179, 194 (2d Cir.2001).

The second "holding" of *Banks*, which requires "the law" or its exposition to be "free for publication to all," is recharacterized by SBCCI as a "due process" argument. That argument devolves into a factual question concerning public "access" to the law. Because SBCCI contends that there is no dispute about the adequacy of public "access" to its model codes, after their enactment as the building codes of Anna and Savoy, *Banks* is inapplicable.

The "dual holding" analysis seems to foist on *Banks* a rationale that the Supreme Court never explicitly articulated. *Banks*, however, does not bifurcate its holding based on the particular authors' need of the Copyright Act's incentives or a factual calculus concerning the "adequacy" of public access to the law. * * * *

There is simply no independent holding in *Banks* that judges are not "authors" under the copyright law because, as public officials, they do not need the "incentives" that copyright law affords in order to write opinions. Instead, *Banks* refers to the source of the judges' salary in order to explain that it is the public at large, not the judges, who have the "pecuniary interest or proprietorship" in "the fruits of their judicial labors." The whole of those judicial labors, as *Banks* immediately defines them, "constitutes the authentic exposition and interpretation of the law," which is "free for publication to all . . ." *Id.*

Moreover, when viewed in light of *Wheaton*, the last case relied on by *Banks*'s analysis, the argument for bifurcation is seriously weakened. *Wheaton*'s holding, as has been shown, derives from an analogy between judicial opinions and legislative acts as together constituting "the law," which is not subject to copyright.

The origin of the bifurcated holding interpretation of *Banks* seems to lie in the First Circuit's thoughtful opinion in *Building Officials and Code Adm. v.Code Technology, Inc.*, 628 F.2d 730 (1st Cir.1980), but the First Circuit does not endorse bifurcation. In this opinion, which will be discussed further *infra*, the First Circuit considered the argument of BOCA, the model code writer, urging copyright protection for a model building code similar in origin and purpose to the one before us. BOCA's argument, the court said, "implies that the rule of *Wheaton v. Peters* was based on the public's property interest in work produced by legislators and judges, who are, of course, government employees." *BOCA*, 628 F.2d at 734.

While acknowledging that this interpretation is "not without foundation," the First Circuit cautioned: "But BOCA's argument overlooks another aspect of the ownership theory discussed in these cases." *Id.* BOCA then identifies the real premises of Banks and related cases: the "metaphorical concept of citizen authorship" of the law, together with "the very important and practical policy that citizens must have free access to the laws which govern them." *Id.* BOCA cited the authorship rationale for *Banks* only to find it unsatisfactory. In our view, *BOCA* was correct.

Only by bifurcating *Banks* can SBCCI achieve its purpose of claiming authorship of "the law" and proprietary rights in its codes that have been enacted into law. However, the acceptance of SBCCI's and the dissent's theory, that non-governmental employees who draft model statutes or regulations may be entitled to copyright protection, raises troubling issues. The complexities of modern life and the breadth of problems addressed by government entities necessitate continuous participation by private experts and interest groups in all aspects of statutory and regulatory lawmaking. According to SBCCI, a utilitarian test should be invoked to determine which organizations "need" the incentives provided by the Copyright Act in order to perform the public service of drafting specialized statutes, ordinances or regulations. Alternatively, perhaps SBCCI and the dissent intend that whenever any private "author" finds his or her proposal adopted verbatim in law, copyright protection may be claimed. As an example, three law professors have taken credit for drafting a recent federal statute on supplemental federal court jurisdiction. See 28 U.S.C. § 1367; Christopher M. Fairman, *Abdication to Academia: The Case of the Supplemental Jurisdiction Statute*, 28 U.S.C. § 1367, 19 SETON HALL LEGIS. J. 157 (1994). Under SBCCI's reasoning, it is likely that these professors, had they so desired, could have asserted a copyright in their "model supplemental jurisdictional provision." SBCCI offers no outer limit on claims of copyright prerogatives by nongovernmental persons who contribute to writing "the law."

Not only is the question of authorship of "the law" exceedingly complicated by SBCCI's and the dissent's position, but in the end, the "authorship" question ignores the democratic process. Lawmaking bodies in this country enact rules and regulations only with the consent of the governed. The very process of lawmaking demands and incorporates contributions by "the people," in an infinite variety of individual and organizational capacities. Even when a governmental body consciously decides to enact proposed model building codes, it does so based on various legislative considerations, the sum of which produce its version of "the law." In performing their function, the lawmakers represent the public will, and the public are the final "authors" of the law.

The *BOCA* decision put it thus:

> The citizens are the authors of the law, and therefore its owners, regardless of who actually drafts the provisions, because the law derives its authority from the consent of the public, expressed through the democratic process. 628 F.2d at 734.[11] This "metaphorical concept of citizen authorship" together with the need for citizens to have free access to the laws are the ultimate holding of *Banks*.

Id.

BOCA described free access as a policy "based on the concept of due process," the people's right to know what the law requires so that they may obey it and avoid its sanctions. SBCCI and the dissent contend that this "due process" reasoning involves nothing more than the factual issue of "sufficient" public access to the building codes of Anna and Savoy. Since a copy of the codes is available for inspection and individual copying in a public office, SBCCI contends that the obligations of due process are fulfilled.

---

11. Technically, citizen "ownership" of the law might suggest that local governmental entities, as public representatives, could prevent copying of the law. As Goldstein notes, the decisions holding that statutes are in the public domain prevent any such misunderstanding. 1 GOLDSTEIN, COPYRIGHT, § 2.48 at n. 42.

We disagree that the question of public access can be limited to the minimum availability that SBCCI would permit. *Banks* does not use the term "due process." There is also no suggestion that the *Banks* concept of free access to the law is a factual determination or is limited to due process, as the term is understood today. Instead, public ownership of the law means precisely that "the law" is in the "public domain" for whatever use the citizens choose to make of it. Citizens may reproduce copies of the law for many purposes, not only to guide their actions but to influence future legislation, educate their neighborhood association, or simply to amuse. If a citizen wanted to place an advertisement in a newspaper quoting the Anna, Texas building code in order to indicate his dissatisfaction with its complexities, it would seem that he could do so. In our view, to say, as *Banks* does, that the law is "free for publication to all" is to expand, not factually limit, the extent of its availability.

Moreover, as the *BOCA* decision observed, it is difficult to reconcile the public's right to know the law with the statutory right of a copyright holder to exclude his work from any publication or dissemination. SBCCI responds that due process must be balanced against its proprietary rights and that the fair use doctrine as well as its honorable intentions will prevent abuse. Free availability of the law, by this logic, has degenerated into availability as long as SBCCI chooses not to file suit.[12]

For these reasons, we reject SBCCI's deconstruction of *Banks* into merely utilitarian and factual issues. Instead, we read *Banks*, *Wheaton*, and related cases consistently to enunciate the principle that "the law," whether it has its source in judicial opinions or statutes, ordinances or regulations, is not subject to federal copyright law.

To sum up this section, we hold that when Veeck copied *only* "the law" of Anna and Savoy, Texas, which he obtained from SBCCI's publication, and when he reprinted only "the law" of those municipalities, he did not infringe SBCCI's copyrights in its model building codes. The basic proposition was stated by Justice Harlan, writing for the Sixth Circuit: "any person desiring to publish the statutes of a state may use any copy of such statutes to be found in any printed book . . ." Howell v. Miller, 91 F. 129, 137 (6th Cir.1898).[14] See Jerry E. Smith, Government Documents: Their Copyright and Ownership, 22 Copyright Symposium 147, 174 (ASCAP 1977), reprinted in 5 TEX. TECH L. REV. 71, 92 (1973).

---

12. SBCCI does not permit governmental entities to publish its model codes when they are enacted. Instead, it permits their adoption by reference and furnishes a copy of the adopted code to the entity. SBCCI also generously allows that if a governmental entity were to publish the building code on an Internet site to meet its due process obligation, that would be a fair use. But when the North Carolina Building Officials were permitted to publish a model code on their non-public access website, SBCCI expressly reserved its rights.

14. Our decision might well be the opposite, if Veeck had copied the model codes as model codes, or if he had indiscriminately mingled those portions of "the law" of Anna and Savoy adopted by their town councils with other parts of the model codes not so adopted.

II. *The Copyright Act*

A. *The Merger Doctrine*

As we earlier stated, SBCCI is the "author" of model building codes that, qua model building codes, are facially copyright-protected. This is true even if *Banks* places the building codes of Anna and Savoy, and other governmental entities that adopted part or all of SBCCI's model codes, in the public domain. But if the holding of *Banks* fails, Veeck alternatively asserts a defense under the Copyright Act to the protection of the model codes after they have been enacted into positive law. Once adopted, he asserts, the model codes become "facts" that are not protected under the Copyright Act. Further, because there is only one way to express the meaning of the building codes, the "idea" embodied in the law merges with SBCCI's expression, and at that point, renders copyright protection un-available.

It is not the sole purpose of copyright law to secure a fair return for an author's creative labor. * * * * The statute excludes from copyright protection ideas, procedures, processes, systems, methods of operation, or information in the public domain. * * * * If an idea is susceptible to only one form of expression, the merger doctrine applies and § 102(b) excludes the expression from the Copyright Act. * * * *

Veeck copied the building code of the towns of Anna and Savoy, Texas, based on their adoption of a version of the SBCCI model code. The codes are "facts" under copyright law. They are the unique, unalterable expression of the "idea" that constitutes local law. Courts routinely emphasize the significance of the precise wording of laws presented for interpretation. * * * * Judge Little, dissenting from the panel opinion in this case, observed that

> ... the merger doctrine is especially appropriate because other methods of expressing the idea are foreclosed. [citation omitted] An individual wishing to publish the text of a law cannot develop his own, unique version and still publish an authoritative copy.

Veeck v. Southern Bldg. Code Cong. Int'l, 241 F.3d 398, 416 (5th Cir. 2001)(Little, J., dissenting). It should be obvious that for copyright purposes, laws are "facts": the U.S. Constitution is a fact; the Federal Tax Code and its regulations are facts; the Texas Uniform Commercial Code is a fact. Surely, in principle, the building codes of rural Texas hamlets are no less "facts" than the products of more august legislative or regulatory bodies. While the Supreme Court has not stated directly that laws are "facts," it has broadly observed that, as with census data, "the same is true of all facts—scientific, historical, biographical and news of the day. 'They may not be copyrighted and are part of the public domain available to every person.' " *Feist*, 499 U.S. at 348, 111 S.Ct. at 1289.

Emphasizing not the language of § 102(b), but the "policy" of the merger doctrine, SBCCI contends that merger poses no bar to copyright protection here. * * * Veeck's merger argument ignores the goal of foster-ing competition in creativity. SBCCI thus asserts that "merger would only apply in this case if a subsequent author seeking to create a building code for Anna or Savoy would have to use the same expression to convey the idea." SBCCI supplemental en banc brief at 7. This argument effectively converts the merger doctrine from a limit on copyrightability into a mere defense against infringement based on the identity of the author. In our view § 102(b) does foster the creativity that SBCCI applauds, but it does so by permitting the free flow of information in facts and ideas from their emergence, rather than as a defense to infringement claims. *See Kern River* at 1460; Mason v. Montgomery Data, Inc., 967 F.2d 135, 138 n. 5 (5th Cir.1992) ("Mason argues that application of the merger doctrine does not render a work *uncopyrightable*, but rather prevents a finding of *infringement* of an otherwise copyrightable work. But this court has applied the merger doctrine to the question of copyrightability.").

SBCCI and the dissent next urge the inapplicability of the merger doctrine because there are many possible ways to express model codes: both the multiplicity of building standards and the variety of ways to express those standards compel the conclusion that the ideas have not merged with their expression. Cf. *Mason*, 967 F.2d at 139 (rejecting merger because the idea embodied in the author's maps can be expressed in a variety of ways). What SBCCI and the dissent ignore, however, is the graphic merger of its model building codes with "the law" as enacted by Anna and Savoy, Texas. Veeck copied from SBCCI's model codes, 1994 edition, because those codes were transformed into the "fact" and "idea" of the towns' building codes. Veeck could not express the enacted law in any other way. * * * *

We emphasize that in continuing to write and publish model building codes, SBCCI is creating copyrightable works of authorship. When those codes are enacted into law, however, they become to that extent "the law" of the governmental entities and may be reproduced or distributed as "the law" of those jurisdictions. * * * *

III.   *The Caselaw; Model Codes Versus Standards*

Until recently in our history, it was understood that *Wheaton, Banks* and nearly every other pertinent case held that copyright protection may not be asserted for the text of "the law". * * * * [W]e have no hesitation in confirming *BOCA*'s predisposition against the copyrightability of model codes to the extent they have been adopted as law. But the limits of this holding must be explained. Several national standards-writing organizations joined SBCCI as *amici* out of fear that their copyrights may be vitiated simply by the common practice of governmental entities' incorporating their standards in laws and regulations. This case does not involve references to extrinsic standards. Instead, it concerns the wholesale adoption of a model code promoted by its author, SBCCI, precisely for use as legislation. Caselaw that derives from official incorporation of extrinsic standards is distinguishable in reasoning and result. *See* CCC Info. Services v. Maclean Hunter Market Reports, Inc., 44 F.3d 61 (2d Cir.1994); and Practice Management Info. Corp. v. American Medical Ass'n, 121 F.3d 516 (9th Cir.1997), *opinion amended by* 133 F.3d 1140 (9th Cir.1998).

In *CCC Information Services*, a New York statute required insurance companies to use the "Red Book," a privately prepared and copyrighted list of projected automobile values, as one of several standards in calculating the payments upon the total loss of a vehicle. CCC Information Services systematically loaded portions of the Red Book onto its computer network and distributed the information to its customers. One of CCC's theories was that the Red Book had entered the public domain. The Second Circuit addressed the public domain issue briefly, stating that "we are not prepared to hold that a state's reference to a copyrighted work as a legal standard for valuation results in loss of the copyright." *CCC Info. Services*, 44 F.3d at 74. *CCC* notes the infringer's reliance on the *BOCA* decision, but it does not opine on that case, confining itself to the precise facts before the court.

Practice Management involved the American Medical Association's copyrighted coding system for reporting physicians' services and medical procedures. The Federal Health Care Financing Administration (HCFA) contacted and then agreed with AMA to use the AMA's coding system for identifying physicians' services on Medicare and Medicaid reimbursement forms. AMA granted a "non-exclusive, royalty-free and irrevocable" license to HCFA, without restrictions on the government's ability to reproduce or distribute AMA's codes. There was no evidence that AMA had restricted the code's availability to anyone. The Ninth Circuit held that the HCFA's decision to adopt regulations requiring physicians to use a version of the AMA code on Medicaid claim forms did not place the code in the public domain under *Banks*. *Practice Management*, 121 F.3d at 519 ("[T]he AMA's right under the Copyright Act to limit or forgo publication of the [coding system] poses no realistic threat to public access.").

Both the Second and Ninth Circuits feared that reaching the opposite conclusion in those cases would have "expose[d] copyrights on a wide range of privately authored model codes, standards, and reference works to invalidation." *Practice Management*, 121 F.3d at 519. The Ninth Circuit suggested that federal court rules regarding citations could invalidate the copyrightability of the Blue Book. *Id.* at 519 n. 5. The Second Circuit feared that a ruling in favor of CCC Information Systems would call into question the copyrightability of school books once they were assigned as part of a mandatory school curriculum. *CCC Info Services*, 44 F.3d at 74.

These decisions, and the hypothetical situations they discuss, are all distinguishable from *Veeck*. If a statute refers to the Red Book or to specific school books, the law requires citizens to consult or use a copyrighted work in the process of fulfilling their obligations. The copyrighted works do not "become law" merely because a statute refers to them. See 1 GOLDSTEIN COPYRIGHT, § 2.49 at n. 45.2 (noting that *CCC* and *Practice Management* "involved compilations of data that had received governmental approval, not content that had been enacted into positive law"). Equally important, the referenced works or standards in *CCC* and *Practice Management* were created by private groups for reasons other than incorporation into law. To the extent incentives are relevant to the existence of copyright protection, the authors in these cases deserve incentives. And neither CCC nor AMA solicited incorporation of their standards by legislators or regulators. In the case of a model code, on the other hand, the text of the model serves no other purpose than to become law. SBCCI operates with the sole motive and purpose of creating codes that will become obligatory in law.

* * * * [T]he result in this case would have been different if Veeck had published not the building codes of Anna and Savoy, Texas, but the SBCCI model codes, as model codes.

IV. *Policy Arguments*

Many of SBCCI's and the dissent's arguments center on the plea that without full copyright protection for model codes, despite their enactment as the law in hundreds or thousands of jurisdictions, SBCCI will lack the revenue to continue its public service of code drafting. Thus SBCCI needs copyright's economic incentives.

Several responses exist to this contention. First, SBCCI, like other code-writing organizations, has survived and grown over 60 years, yet no court has previously awarded copyright protection for the copying of an enacted building code under circumstances like these. Second, the success of voluntary code-writing groups is attributable to the technological complexity of modern life, which impels government entities to standardize their regulations. The entities would have to promulgate standards even if SBCCI did not exist, but the most fruitful approach for the public entities and the potentially regulated industries lies in mutual cooperation. The self-interest of the builders, engineers, designers and other relevant tradesmen should also not be overlooked in the calculus promoting uniform codes. As one commentator explained,

> ... it is difficult to imagine an area of creative endeavor in which the copyright incentive is needed less. Trade organizations have powerful reasons stemming from industry standardization, quality control, and self-regulation to produce these model codes; it is unlikely that, without copyright, they will cease producing them.

1 Goldstein § 2.5.2, at 2:51.

Third, to enhance the market value of its model codes, SBCCI could easily publish them as do the compilers of statutes and judicial opinions, with "value-added" in the form of commentary, questions and answers, lists of adopting jurisdictions and other information valuable to a reader. The organization could also charge fees for the massive amount of interpretive information about the codes that it doles out. In short, we are unpersuaded that the removal of copyright protection from model codes only when and to the extent they are enacted into law disserves "the Progress of Science and useful Arts." U.S. Const. art. I. § 8, cl. 8.

CONCLUSION

For the reasons discussed above, we REVERSE the district court's judgment against Peter Veeck, and REMAND with instructions to dismiss SBCCI's claims.

■ Patrick E. Higginbotham, Circuit Judge, joined by King, Chief Judge, and W. Eugene Davis and Carl E. Stewart, Circuit Judges, dissenting:

In this difficult case I am persuaded to join the view that would affirm the judgment of the district court. It is undisputed that Veeck copied the copyrighted product of SBCCI. That parts of the copied material contain the same expressions as the adopted codes of two Texas cities is no defense unless the use by the cities of the protected expression somehow invalidated SBCCI's copyright. * * * *

Nothing suggests that private entities will control access to "the law." A contrary vision persists while ignoring the assured access of persons interested in the language of the ordinance. We are not told what impediment a person interested in the ordinance will face that will not be avoided by the doctrines of fair use and implied license or the constitutionally footed right of persons to access the law. Nor does developed case law tell us.

Banks holds that judges, as public employees, cannot have a financial interest in the fruits of their judicial labors. It is a case about authorship, about the acquiring of copyrights by public officials, not a case invalidating the copyrights held by private actors when their work is licensed by lawmakers.

As for the merger doctrine, I am not persuaded that it brings anything more to the table. That doctrine reflects the narrow circumstance where an idea can be expressed only one way and hence protection of its expression gives way. A complex code, even a simple one, can be expressed in a variety of ways. That reality is not ended by choosing one manner of expression to enact and then pronouncing that this normative rule—"the law"—can only be expressed in one way. Of course, you have adopted the protected expression; the reasoning is wholly tautological. It is a restatement of the conclusion that adopting the codes invalidated the copyright, not an independent reason why that is so.

There is a strong argument for that conclusion and it can be simply stated without calling on the illusion of the merger doctrine: the thinness of the protection enjoyed by this specie of copyright is overcome by the stronger public policy of unfettered access to enacted law, a victory expressed in the conclusion that enacting the code into law put the expression in the public domain. Whether that is so is our question and the merger doctrine does not answer it. * * * *

Significantly the absence of easily-found answers to the large, broadly-stated policy choices calls for caution. As I earlier observed, these small cities were empowered by the work of SBCCI; they gained the benefit of uniformity in regulation with other cities in their codes as well as proven quality—with the ability to charge a small fee for copies. Any person wishing a copy of the code can obtain it. They can reproduce it for critical commentary or to express their displeasure with its content, even make copies to circulate in a campaign urging that it be rescinded.

49

* * * * When Veeck did his work, the code was already available on the internet, albeit subject to the terms of its license. Veeck's effort was to put the code on the internet free of license. To accept Veeck's contention would invalidate the copyright on every model code except those in inventory that had never been adopted by any governmental body. * * * *

In sum, the suggestion that SBCCI's position asks this Court to extend the reach of the copyright law is exactly backwards. The copyrights at issue here were concededly valid before the cities adopted them as codes. The proper question is whether we should invalidate an otherwise valid copyright as well as the solemn contract between the governmental body and SBCCI. * * * * I conclude that Veeck violated the explicit terms of the license he agreed to when he copied model codes for the internet and posted them. I decide no more.

■ WIENER, CIRCUIT JUDGE, joined by KING, CHIEF JUDGE, and PATRICK E. HIGGINBOTHAM, W. EUGENE DAVIS, CARL E. STEWART, and DENNIS, CIRCUIT JUDGES, dissenting:

Technical codes and standards have become necessary, pervasive, and indispensable ingredients of Twenty–First Century life in this country; regrettably, today's majority opinion has a real potential of drastically changing the societal landscape through that opinion's predictably deleterious effects on these codes and standards, their authors, and the public and private entities that daily use and depend on them. Despite efforts to clothe its ruling in classic copyright lingo—"public domain," "fact/expression," "merger"—in holding for Veeck under the discrete facts of this case, the majority had to (and did) adopt a *per se* rule that a single municipality's enactment of a copyrighted model code into law by reference strips the work of all copyright protection, *ipso facto*. Firmly believing that for this court to be the first federal appellate court to go that far is imprudent, I respectfully dissent.

* * * *

II. ANALYSIS

* * * *

B. *Merits*

1. *Overview*

* * * * My analysis is necessarily delimited by the particular, undisputed facts of the case: Veeck is a non-commercial, non-educational, non-contractor, non-official, non-resident of either Anna or Savoy, who purchased a copyrighted work, replete with warnings about infringement, and published that work virtually in its entirety on the internet. Veeck published on his website the entire substantive portion of the model building code that he purchased from SBCCI, redacting only the identity of the code's author (SBCCI) and the statement that the code was copyright protected, and inserting that they were the codes of Anna and Savoy. Veeck's only professed justification for infringing SBCCI's copyrights was that two or more small municipalities in northern Texas—of which Veeck was neither a resident nor otherwise related to in any capacity, official or unofficial—had, at the invitation of the code's author, enacted the codes into law by reference. Because he cannot, Veeck does not contend that Anna or Savoy denied him access to their codes or that he (or anyone else) was unable to view the law to which the citizens of Anna and Savoy are subject. Had Anna, Savoy, or SBCCI blocked the code's availability, I would be among the first to recognize Veeck's (and anyone else's) right of access to "THE law." That, however, is simply not the case before us; this is not a free access case and cannot be so classified. * * * *

2. *Due Process/Public Domain*

a. *Absence of Controlling Legal Authority*

In the absence of an expressed pronouncement from either the Supreme Court or Congress, our creation of an automatic rule rendering the copyright of a model code nugatory *per se* when and if it is enacted into law is unwise, imprudent, and far in excess of our authority. *Before* such a work is enacted into law, the Copyright Act unquestionably affords copyright protection to its author; and Congress has given no indication that, on enactment, this protected status evanesces *ipso facto* as to the whole universe of potential copiers. As I discuss in greater detail below, recent congressional enactments and accompanying federal agency policies strongly predict that, were Congress to address the issue here presented, it would preserve the protection of SBCCI's copyright, at least under circumstances like those we consider today.

As for the Supreme Court, its most analogous opinion, *Banks v. Manchester*, falls markedly short of answering the question. The Court grounded its century-and-one-quarter old *Banks* holding—that judicial opinions cannot be copyrighted—in the logic that, as the product of judges who are paid from public coffers and elected or appointed for the sole purpose of interpreting and applying the law, judicial opinions can never be copyrighted. Thus *Banks* turns not on the nature of the *work* but on the nature of the *author*. By its own terms, the *Banks* holding is obviously limited to the work of taxpayer-paid public officials who produce or interpret the law. The majority's stretching of *Banks* to the facts of the instant case constitutes a clear overreaching that finds no definitive support from any controlling authority.

* * * * If Congress or the Supreme Court wishes to strip totally the copyright protection otherwise enjoyed by model codes as an automatic result of being enacted into law, and to justify such emasculation by invoking the doctrines of free speech, due process, merger, or the like, that would be their prerogative. Prudence demands, however, that so large a step beyond all established legal boundaries should not have been taken first by an intermediate appellate court. Indeed, recent appellate case law, congressional pronouncements, and federal agency actions, predict the diametrically opposite result: a discernable trend towards greater governmental adoption of privately created codes with concomitant retention of copyright protection, tempered, of course, by express or implied consent or waiver—or even fair use—for those officials, residents, contractors, subcon-

tractors, and design professionals who have a need to view and copy portions of codes to comply with their provisions.

b.   *Policy Analysis for Copyright Protection*

What *Banks* and other opinions undeniably teach about assessing the copyright protection of works like the codes here at issue is that "[t]he question is one of public policy...." Accordingly, these decisions do not stand for the abstract and generic proposition that all law *qua* law, regardless of its form, authorship, or content, is automatically unprotected fair game as to all copiers, without distinction. Hence, courts are given the weighty task of balancing, on the one hand, the policy concerns that favor the constitutionally mandated retention of copyright protection for privately authored works and, on the other hand, the policy concerns that would permit stripping the author of a privately created work of copyright protection once that work is enacted into law. I do not dismiss lightly the policy considerations supporting this latter concern. Yet, when properly limited to the narrow set of facts before us, the scale of countervailing policy considerations is tipped—slightly yet undeniably—in favor of enforcing SBCCI's copyright, vis-à-vis Veeck and any others (but only they) who are identically situated.

I begin with an assessment of the policy consideration supporting Veeck's position—namely, the due process and public domain concerns. As an initial matter, the type of due process asserted by Veeck is murky at best. He was not denied access to the codes by either the towns or SBCCI (indeed, he has never alleged that he even tried to attain access directly from either town, or his home forum for that matter), and he was never charged with or prosecuted for a code violation; therefore, his claim cannot be based on procedural due process. And, inasmuch as copyright is a federal law, no state action could deprive him of a fundamental right that would trigger a substantive due process claim. Neither has Veeck pointed to any state actor who has purportedly denied him due process. Yet despite his unimpeded access to the law and the absence of state action, Veeck argues amorphously that his due process rights somehow allow him freely to copy and publish otherwise copyright-protected codes once they are enacted into law by reference.

I reiterate for emphasis that this would be an entirely different case if Veeck's (or anyone's) access to the law had been denied or obstructed; instead, we deal here only with Veeck's bald pronouncement—now legitimated by the majority opinion—that, once a code is enacted into law, due process does not merely afford him access, but also gives him unfettered copying and dissemination rights. The majority's acceptance of Veeck's position is truly a novel extension of any prior judicial recognition of a due process right. True enough, Veeck can copy and publish judicial opinions and statutes on his website with impunity. He can do so, however, not because of his due process rights, but rather because—as judicial opinions and legislatively drafted statutes have never enjoyed copyright protection, could never enjoy such protection, and are in the public domain from the moment of their inception—such works are entitled to no copyright protection or restrictions.

Logically then, the only possible support for Veeck's due process position is his wholly unsupported assertion that, by virtue of their adoption into law by reference, the codes have entered the *public domain* and are therefore denuded of all copyright protection whatsoever, regardless of their content or the identity of the author or other interested parties. * * * *

Admittedly, the majority's argument finds rhetorical support from the First Circuit's dicta in *Building Officials & Code Admin. v. Code Technology, Inc. (BOCA)*, in which that court stated "[t]he citizens are the authors of the law, and therefore its owners, regardless of who actually drafts the provisions because the law derives its authority from the consent of the public, expressed through the democratic process." Undoubtedly, this metaphorical concept of citizen authorship cum ownership has great symbolic, "feel-good" appeal. The majority's uncritical application of that proposition to the instant case, however, naively treats all manifestations of "THE law" in our increasingly complex society monolithically and without differentiation. The Supreme Court took no such position in *Banks*; in fact, *Banks* addresses only judicial opinions and other pronouncements of the law created *ab initio* by publicly paid officials. * * * *

* * * Congress itself has provided the strongest support for the proposition that these privately created codes should be treated differently than other laws. Recognizing that the production of a comprehensive technical code requires a great deal of research, labor, time, and expertise, Congress in the National Technology and Transfer Act of 1995 (the "NTTA") expressly directs that "Federal agencies and departments shall use technical standards that are developed or adopted by voluntary consensus standards bodies...." The OMB, in its Circular A 119, which was designed to provide guidance to federal agencies in the wake of the NTTA, requires that "[i]f a voluntary standard is used and published in an agency document, your *agency must observe and protect the rights of the copyright holder and any other similar obligations*." These pronouncements by Congress and the OMB strongly evince a recognition that the privately created regulatory codes and standards differ greatly from either judicial opinions or a statutes. Technical codes are indispensable resources in today's increasingly complex, high-tech society, and they deserve authorship protections not afforded to other types of "THE law."

* * * * [R]ecent appellate case law supports the recognition of the clear differences between, on the one hand, privately developed standards that are adopted into law by reference and, on the other hand, law created by legislators and judges.[23] * * * * The policy considerations that dictate

---

23. See County of Suffolk v. First American Real Estate Solutions, 261 F.3d 179 (2d Cir.2001) (developing a two-pronged economic incentive/public need test to determine whether tax maps developed by the County of Suffolk were in the public domain from inception and therefore stripped of copyright protection; citing *Practice Manage-*

unlimited and unrestricted publishing of judicial opinions and statutes simply do not appertain here.

The policy concerns supporting the retention of at least some copyright protection for SBCCI are more persuasive and probative. First and most importantly, unlike judges and legislators who are paid from public funds to issue opinions and draft laws, SBCCI is a private sector, not-for-profit organization which relies for its existence and continuing services, in significant part, on revenues from the sale of its model codes. * * * *

The importance of affording organizations like SBCCI protection from attenuated third parties like Veeck—even when motives are pure and unfair financial competition is not the goal—is best underscored by verbalizing the natural consequence of reducing the revenues, and thus the creative incentives, for organizations like SBCCI. Without private code-creating entities, our smaller towns—and even some of our larger cities, states, and agencies of the federal government—would be forced to author their own regulatory codes. Such a task would inefficiently expend the time and resources of the legislative and executive bodies of these governmental entities, not to mention the question of available expertise. To create codes of appropriate detail, accuracy, and information, governmental bodies would have to enlist the aid of technical experts, undoubtedly at considerable cost. Finally, causing municipalities, states, and the federal agencies to engage in this activity could lead to innumerable variations of any given code, thereby undermining uniformity and, with it, safety and efficiency. For small towns like Anna and Savoy, such a result could be even more detrimental, as their limited resources well might be insufficient to absorb the costs of creating their own codes. Ultimately, taxpayers would end up paying for a service that is currently provided efficiently, expertly, and at no expense to them. * * * *

Finally, denying the Veecks of the world unrestricted republication and dissemination rights does not obstruct reasonable and necessary usage of and compliance with the adopted codes. I remain confident that the copyright doctrines of fair use and implied license or waiver are more than adequate to preserve the ability of residents and construction industry participants to copy any portions of the code that they want or need to view. The fair use doctrine would also protect the use of the code, or portions of the code, as a teaching tool and would allow experts, lawyers, and judges freely to cite the code in their briefs or opinions without infringing SBCCI's copyright. These existing internal safeguards in copy-

---

ment and the panel opinion in *Veeck*, deciding that, as a matter of law, the county's tax maps were not in the public domain); *Practice Management*, 121 F.3d 516, *cert. denied*, 522 U.S. 933, 118 S.Ct. 339, 139 L.Ed.2d 263, *opinion amended by* 133 F.3d 1140 (finding that the American Medical Association did not lose the right to enforce its copyright when use of its promulgated coding system was required by government regulations);

CCC, 44 F.3d 61, *cert. denied*, 516 U.S. 817, 116 S.Ct. 72, 133 L.Ed.2d 32 (upholding copyright of privately prepared listing of automobile values that states required insurance companies to use); see also 1Melville B. Nimmer & David Nimmer, Nimmer on Copyright § 5.06[C], at 5–91 (2000) ("It is questionable whether [the due process clause] justifies the denial of copyright to a private person or group who produces such a model code.").

right law show up the majority's dire predictions for the unrealistic hyperbole that they are.

* * * *

3. *The Idea/Expression Dichotomy and Merger*

Veeck insists (and now a majority of the active judges of this court agree) that the model codes lose their copyright protection by virtue of the idea/expression (or fact/expression) dichotomy in copyright law. Veeck's basic contention is that when a model code is enacted into law by being adopted by reference, it automatically metamorphoses from "expression" to emerge as an "idea"—and that as an idea, it cannot be protected. Relatedly, he contends that the doctrine of "merger" applies to nullify protection for expressions of an idea any time that there are only one or a very limited number of ways to express a given idea. The cornerstone of both arguments is the definition of "idea" in the context of a model code that has been enacted by reference.

a. Defining "Idea"

Veeck's argument fails because it misapprehends and misapplies the "idea" concept in copyright law. "Idea" in copyright law is a term of art which does not track its everyday, dictionary meaning. What constitutes an "idea" in the lexicon of copyright law cannot be determined by empirically analyzing a given fact situation until the nascent dividing line between the "idea" and its "expression" finally crystallizes; indeed, just the reverse is true. Case law reveals that identification of the "idea" in a work is not the starting point but the *result* of a judicial exercise that in turn is highly dependent on the precise factual situation being tested. Therefore, designation of the enacted code as an idea *vel non* is a legal *conclusion* to be reached by a court, not an initial factual finding to be gleaned intuitively. That determination of idea is *not antecedent* to a policy determination regarding the "copyrightability" of the code; to the contrary, it is the logical *end-product* reached after competing concerns are weighed judicially.

* * * *

Our task in this case should have been to decide whether the "idea" embodied in the code is defined, at one extreme of the continuum, as the entire code itself in its tangible form, or if instead the "idea" is defined at a more removed and abstract level further along that continuum.

My foregoing analysis has already demonstrated that the policy considerations weigh in favor of granting SBCCI protection against Veeck and other copiers and republishers identically situated. Having laboriously arrived at this conclusion, and accepting that a building code can be expressed in myriad ways, I am convinced that the code in its tangible entirety is not the unprotected "idea" in this situation.[34] None question that this is true for codes that have not been enacted globally into law by reference, and nothing of which I am aware can magically change the

---

34. In doing so, I acknowledge that specific portions and discrete facts within the code could be considered facts or ideas, and therefore unprotectable.

expression that is the copyrighted code into a copyright *idea* by the simple act of adoption as a body of law. * * * *

b. Merger

* * * * The merger doctrine ... is a limited exception in copyright law, intended to shelter only those rare cases in which the "idea" is susceptible of more than one expression, but the number of possible *expressions* is so finite and small as to have effectively "merged" with the *idea.* * * * *

Again, Veeck can find no immunity in the merger doctrine because there exists a plethora of ways to *express* a building code, thereby making the merger doctrine inapplicable. Although some among the many highly specific, technical, and detailed provisions within a building code might be susceptible of being expressed in only one or a handful of ways—and thus conceivably be subject to merger—a total, unitary building code, *in globo,* may be written, organized, and presented in any one of innumerable forms. All concede that many code-drafting organizations like SBCCI exist and that they are constantly creating competing versions of topical codes; yet each is expressed differently—and each is copyrighted. As there exist considerably more than a tiny, finite number of ways to express a building code, the merger doctrine is inapplicable and thus unavailable to insulate Veeck's infringement from copyright protection.

* * * *

QUESTIONS

1. Apart from the special case of pictorial, graphic and sculptural works, the author's intentions in creating the work are generally irrelevant to its copyrightability. But isn't the majority here holding that creation of text, in the hope that it will be adopted as law, deprives an original work of authorship of copyright should the text in fact become law? Does this make sense? Is there a better way to resolve the potential conflict between copyright and due process concerns?

2. The majority quotes approvingly Professor Paul Goldstein's suggestion that copyright for model codes may be inappropriate because copyright does not supply an incentive to create these texts. Should courts be inquiring into whether or not copyright serves as an incentive to create a particular work? To create a class of works?

CHAPTER 3

OWNERSHIP

A. INITIAL OWNERSHIP

2. WORKS MADE FOR HIRE

Page 274: Add to Question 5:

In a recent copyright ownership dispute concerning some of the true cultural treasures of the mid-twentieth century—the choreographic works of Martha Graham—the legatee named in Ms. Graham's will was held to own copyright in only one of the 70 dances that were being contested. Of those 70, 34 were found to have been created as works made for hire and thus owned by the Martha Graham Center of Contemporary Dance, Inc.; Ms. Graham began her employment in 1956, and so the work-for-hire decisions under the 1909 Act governed. Of the remaining 36 dances of Ms. Graham, 10 were published but were not renewed in their twenty-eighth year and thus fell into the public domain. Of 21 dances held to have been unpublished, and initially owned by Ms. Graham, the court concluded that the common law copyrights were conveyed by her to the Center through oral communications and course of conduct. (How would that result differ had the 1976 Act applied?) Martha Graham's legatee was declared by the court to be the owner of only one of those latter dances, because it was later published and—as will be seen in Chapter 4—thus fell within the renewal provisions of the 1909 Act, which (with a deceased author and no surviving family) could be invoked by the person named in the author's will. Martha Graham School & Dance Foundation, Inc. v. Martha Graham Center of Contemporary Dance, Inc., 224 F.Supp.2d 567 (S.D.N.Y.2002).

Page 295: Insert after *Aalmuhammed v. Lee:*

Gaiman v. McFarlane, 360 F.3d 644 99 (7th Cir. 2004). [For the facts of this case, see *supra*, this Supplement Chapter 2.] Judge Posner expressed general doubt about the persuasiveness of the requirement that co-authorship requires each contribution to be copyrightable. In the context of comic books, he went further, to reject the requirement altogether:

> McFarlane makes two arguments for why Gaiman does not have copyright in Medieval Spawn (the name that McFarlane settled on for Olden Days Spawn) or Cogliostro. The first is that all that Gaiman contributed was the idea for the characters, and ideas are not copyrightable, only expression is and the expression was due to McFarlane's drawing of the characters. It is true that people who contribute merely nonexpressive elements to a work are not copyright owners. As

we said in *Seshadri v. Kasraian, supra*, 130 F.3d at 803, "the assistance that a research assistant or secretary or draftsman or helpfully commenting colleague provides in the preparation of a scholarly paper does not entitle the helper to claim the status of a joint author." There has to be *some* original expression contributed by anyone who claims to be a co-author, and the rule (we'll consider an exception momentarily) is that his contribution must be independently copyrightable. E.g., *Erickson v. Trinity Theatre, Inc., supra*, 13 F.3d at 1071; *Aalmuhammed v. Lee, supra*, 202 F.3d at 1231; 1 William F. Patry, *Copyright Law and Practice* 362–65 (1994). Had someone merely remarked to McFarlane one day, "you need a medieval Spawn" or "you need an old guy to move the story forward," and McFarlane had carried it from there, and if later a copyeditor had made some helpful editorial changes, neither the suggester nor the editor would be a joint owner. Cf. *Erickson v. Trinity Theatre, Inc., supra*, 13 F.3d at 1064, 1071–72. Otherwise almost every expressive work would be a jointly authored work, and copyright would explode.

But where two or more people set out to create a character jointly in such mixed media as comic books and motion pictures and succeed in creating a copyrightable character, it would be paradoxical if though the result of their joint labors had more than enough originality and creativity to be copyrightable, no one could claim copyright. That would be peeling the onion until it disappeared. The decisions that say, rightly in the generality of cases, that each contributor to a joint work must make a contribution that if it stood alone would be copyrightable weren't thinking of the case in which it *couldn't* stand alone because of the nature of the particular creative process that had produced it.

Here is a typical case from academe. One professor has brilliant ideas but can't write; another is an excellent writer, but his ideas are commonplace. So they collaborate on an academic article, one contributing the ideas, which are not copyrightable, and the other the prose envelope, and unlike the situation in the superficially similar case of *Balkin v. Wilson*, 863 F.Supp. 523 (W.D. Mich. 1994), they sign as coauthors. Their intent to be the joint owners of the copyright in the article would be plain, and that should be enough to constitute them joint authors within the meaning of 17 U.S.C. § 201(a). This is the valid core of the Nimmers' heretical suggestion that "if authors *A* and *B* work in collaboration, but *A*'s contribution is limited to plot ideas that standing alone would not be copyrightable, and *B* weaves the ideas into a completed literary expression, it would seem that *A* and *B* are joint authors of the resulting work." 1 Nimmer & Nimmer, *supra*, § 6.07, p. 6–23; see also 1 Patry, *supra*, at 365–66.

The contents of a comic book are typically the joint work of four artists—the writer, the penciler who creates the art work (McFarlane), the inker (also McFarlane, in the case of *Spawn* No. 9, but it would often be a different person from the penciler) who makes a black and white plate of the art work, and the colorist who colors it. The finished product is copyrightable, yet one can imagine cases in which none of the separate contributions of the four collaborating artists would be. The writer might have contributed merely a stock character (not copyrightable, as we're about to see) that achieved the distinctiveness required for copyrightability only by the combined contributions of the penciler, the inker, and the colorist, with each contributing too little to have by his contribution alone carried the stock character over the line into copyright land. . . .

B. Transfer of Copyright Ownership

1. Divisibility and Formal Requirements

Page 299: Add the following to the end of the textual Note:

Despite the clear intent of Congress in 1976 to eliminate the doctrine of "indivisibility" that had prevailed under the 1909 Act, and to accord greater status and rights to the holder of particular exclusive rights, old doctrine sometimes carries forward, as shown by cases such as **Gardner v. Nike, Inc.**, 279 F.3d 774 (9th Cir.2002). Under the 1909 Act, courts had held that a person taking a transfer of a part of the copyright from the "proprietor" or copyright owner had no power to re-transfer that right to a third party without securing the consent of the copyright owner. In the *Gardner* case, arising under the 1976 Act, the court of appeals—relying upon the 1909 Act jurisprudence in spite of the abandonment in the 1976 Act of the doctrine of indivisibility—held that the transferee of an exclusive copyright license may not further transfer those rights without the consent of the transferor. The case involved a cartoon character created by Nike and exclusively licensed to Sony for "perpetual" and "worldwide" use in the marketing of recordings and clothing; Sony purported to convey those rights in turn to Gardner, but the Court of Appeals for the Ninth Circuit held that the transfer to Gardner was invalid.

The court relied on the text of the statute and upon copyright policy. It viewed Section 201(d)(2) as giving the exclusive licensee no more than the "protection and remedies" accorded a copyright owner, and interpreted this phrase not to embrace the power freely to sublicense to a third party. The court reasoned: "This explicit language limits the rights afforded to an owner of exclusive rights. Based on basic principles of statutory construction, the specific language of § 201(d)(2) is given precedence over the more general language of § 101 and § 201(d)(1). Further, . . . Congress was aware that prior to the 1976 Act, licensees could not sublicense their right in an exclusive license [without the express consent of the licensor]. With that knowledge in hand, however, Congress chose to limit exclusive licensees' 'benefits' under the 1976 Act to 'protection and remedies.' " As to policy, the court viewed the 1976 Act as impliedly carrying forward the earlier concern to have the copyright owner "monitor" the economic and creative viability of the sub-licensee.

Do you agree with the court's reasoning?

Page 303:   Add the following after the *Effects Associates* case:

[See Nelson–Salabes, Inc. v. Morningside Development, 284 F.3d 505 (4th Cir.2002), for a suggested group of factors to assess in determining whether an implied license has been granted.]

Page 304:   Add new Questions 6 and 7:

6.   Norton Novelist authorizes Priscilla Playwright to create a stage play based on his novel. The parties expect that Norton will himself direct his wife's troupe, Theresa's Theatricals, in the world premiere performance of Priscilla's play. Before the play opens, Norton and Priscilla have a falling-out, but Norton opens on Broadway anyway. Priscilla claims that, the parties never having executed a written agreement giving Norton the exclusive right of first public performance, Norton has infringed her copyright in the play. Norton responds that, as the copyright owner of the underlying work on which the play was based, he owns the exclusive right to authorize the making of derivative works, and therefore is entitled to exploit the play as well. How should the court rule? Would it make any difference if Norton claims that his original authorization to Priscilla did not extend to allowing her to claim a copyright in her adaptation? Would sec. 204(a) require such a limitation to be in writing? (Would sec. 204(a) have required a writing had Norton claimed that his original agreement with Patty required her to assign her copyright to him?) See, e.g., Liu v. Price Waterhouse, 302 F.3d 749 (7th Cir.2002).

7.   Frank Foto began to work as a full-time photographer for Brown University in 1980. He took photos of Brown's students, faculty, facilities and environs for the purpose of creating a positive image of the University, and his work was reproduced in various Brown publications. In 1985, Brown published a Policy on Copyright, which had the following provision: "*Ownership:* It is the University's position that, as a general premise, ownership of copyrightable property which results from performance of one's University duties and activities will belong to the author or origina-tor. This applies to books, art works, software, etc." Foto has recently retired from his post at Brown, and he consults you on the question whether he, or the University, is the owner of the photographs he took during his years on the staff. What advice do you give? See *Foraste v. Brown Univ.*, 290 F.Supp.2d 234 (D.R.I. 2003).

Page 306:   Add the following to the textual Note:

In its decision in **In re World Auxiliary Power Co.**, 303 F.3d 1120 (9th Cir.2002), the Court of Appeals for the Ninth Circuit endorsed the outcome in *National Peregrine* while limiting it to the situation of a registered copyright: the only way for a creditor to perfect its security interest in a *registered* copyright is by recording in the Copyright Office. When, however, the creditor holds a security interest in unregistered copyrights—for example, copyrights yet to be acquired by the debtor in the future—the creditor perfects its interest, and thus later prevails against the debtor's trustee in bankruptcy, by filing under the Uniform Commercial Code in the appropriate state office. The court held that the so-called "step back" provisions of the UCC do not apply with respect to unregistered copyrights. Moreover, there is no "conflict preemption" of the filing provisions of the UCC, as there is no competing federal filing system for unregistered copyrights. (The court of appeals thus rejected two district court decisions within the Ninth Circuit which had applied *Peregrine* to security interests in unregistered copyrights.)

Page 322:   Add the following at the end of the *Rosetta Books* case:

[The Court of Appeals for the Second Circuit held, 283 F.3d 490 (2d Cir.2002), that it was not an abuse of discretion for the trial court to decline to enjoin publication of e-books, in light of the hardship that would result to the defendant and the failure of the plaintiff to prove a likelihood of success on the merits.]

Page 323:   Add new Question 4:

4.   Frances Fascinating granted Max Mogul motion picture rights in her autobiographical play, "My Wonderful Life." She subsequently wrote an autobiographical novel, "My Excellent Existence," and has sold movie rights to that. Max objects that his agreement with Frances covering "derivative works based on the play" gives him the rights to Frances' subsequent autobiographical works. How should the court rule? See Houlihan v. McCourt, 2002 WL 1759822 (N.D.Ill.2002).

Page 335: Add to end of Question 2:

Compare *Faulkner v. National Geog. Soc'y*, 294 F.Supp.2d 523 (S.D.N.Y. 2003).

CHAPTER 4

DURATION AND RENEWAL, AND TERMINATION OF TRANSFERS

Pages 343–37: Substitute the following for the textual Note:

Eldred v. Ashcroft

537 U.S. 186, 123 S.Ct. 769 (2003).

■ JUSTICE GINSBURG delivered the opinion of the Court.

This case concerns the authority the Constitution assigns to Congress to prescribe the duration of copyrights. The Copyright and Patent Clause of the Constitution, Art. I, § 8, cl. 8, provides as to copyrights: "Congress shall have Power ... [t]o promote the Progress of Science ... by securing [to Authors] for limited Times ... the exclusive Right to their ... Writings." In 1998, in the measure here under inspection, Congress enlarged the duration of copyrights by 20 years. Copyright Term Extension Act (CTEA), Pub.L. 105–298, § 102(b) and (d), 112 Stat. 2827–2828 (amending 17 U.S.C. §§ 302, 304). As in the case of prior extensions, principally in 1831, 1909, and 1976, Congress provided for application of the enlarged terms to existing and future copyrights alike.

Petitioners are individuals and businesses whose products or services build on copyrighted works that have gone into the public domain. They seek a determination that the CTEA fails constitutional review under both the Copyright Clause's "limited Times" prescription and the First Amendment's free speech guarantee. Under the 1976 Copyright Act, copyright protection generally lasted from the work's creation until 50 years after the author's death. Pub.L. 94–553, § 302(a), 90 Stat. 2572 (1976 Act). Under the CTEA, most copyrights now run from creation until 70 years after the author's death. 17 U.S.C. § 302(a). Petitioners do not challenge the "life-plus-70–years" time span itself. "Whether 50 years is enough, or 70 years too much," they acknowledge, "is not a judgment meet for this Court." Brief for Petitioners 14.[1] Congress went awry, petitioners maintain, not with respect to newly created works, but in enlarging the term for published works with existing copyrights. The "limited Tim[e]" in effect when a copyright is secured, petitioners urge, becomes the constitutional boundary, a clear line beyond the power of Congress to extend. See *ibid*. As to the

---

1. JUSTICE BREYER's dissent is not similarly restrained. He makes no effort meaningfully to distinguish existing copyrights from future grants. See, *e.g., post*, at 801, 807–810, 812–813. Under his reasoning, the CTEA's 20–year extension is globally unconstitutional.

First Amendment, petitioners contend that the CTEA is a content-neutral regulation of speech that fails inspection under the heightened judicial scrutiny appropriate for such regulations.

In accord with the District Court and the Court of Appeals, we reject petitioners' challenges to the CTEA. In that 1998 legislation, as in all previous copyright term extensions, Congress placed existing and future copyrights in parity. In prescribing that alignment, we hold, Congress acted within its authority and did not transgress constitutional limitations.

I

A

We evaluate petitioners' challenge to the constitutionality of the CTEA against the backdrop of Congress' previous exercises of its authority under the Copyright Clause. The Nation's first copyright statute, enacted in 1790, provided a federal copyright term of 14 years from the date of publication, renewable for an additional 14 years if the author survived the first term. Act of May 31, 1790, ch. 15, § 1, 1 Stat. 124 (1790 Act). The 1790 Act's renewable 14–year term applied to existing works (*i.e.*, works already published and works created but not yet published) and future works alike. *Ibid.* Congress expanded the federal copyright term to 42 years in 1831 (28 years from publication, renewable for an additional 14 years), and to 56 years in 1909 (28 years from publication, renewable for an additional 28 years). Act of Feb. 3, 1831, ch. 16, §§ 1, 16, 4 Stat. 436, 439 (1831 Act); Act of Mar. 4, 1909, ch. 320, §§ 23–24, 35 Stat. 1080–1081 (1909 Act). Both times, Congress applied the new copyright term to existing and future works, 1831 Act §§ 1, 16; 1909 Act §§ 23–24; to qualify for the 1831 extension, an existing work had to be in its initial copyright term at the time the Act became effective, 1831 Act §§ 1, 16.

In 1976, Congress altered the method for computing federal copyright terms. 1976 Act §§ 302–304. For works created by identified natural persons, the 1976 Act provided that federal copyright protection would run from the work's creation, not—as in the 1790, 1831, and 1909 Acts—its publication; protection would last until 50 years after the author's death. § 302(a). In these respects, the 1976 Act aligned United States copyright terms with the then-dominant international standard adopted under the Berne Convention for the Protection of Literary and Artistic Works. See H.R.Rep. No. 94–1476, p. 135 (1976), U.S.Code Cong. & Admin.News 1976, p.5659. For anonymous works, pseudonymous works, and works made for hire, the 1976 Act provided a term of 75 years from publication or 100 years from creation, whichever expired first. § 302(c).

These new copyright terms, the 1976 Act instructed, governed all works not published by its effective date of January 1, 1978, regardless of when the works were created. §§ 302–303. For published works with existing copyrights as of that date, the 1976 Act granted a copyright term of 75 years from the date of publication, § 304(a) and (b), a 19–year increase over the 56–year term applicable under the 1909 Act.

The measure at issue here, the CTEA, installed the fourth major duration extension of federal copyrights.[2] Retaining the general structure of the 1976 Act, the CTEA enlarges the terms of all existing and future copyrights by 20 years. For works created by identified natural persons, the term now lasts from creation until 70 years after the author's death. 17 U.S.C. § 302(a). This standard harmonizes the baseline United States copyright term with the term adopted by the European Union in 1993. See Council Directive 93/98/EEC of 29 October 1993 Harmonizing the Term of Protection of Copyright and Certain Related Rights, 1993 Official J. Eur. Cmty. 290 (EU Council Directive 93/98). For anonymous works, pseudonymous works, and works made for hire, the term is 95 years from publication or 120 years from creation, whichever expires first. 17 U.S.C. § 302(c).

Paralleling the 1976 Act, the CTEA applies these new terms to all works not published by January 1, 1978. §§ 302(a), 303(a). For works published before 1978 with existing copyrights as of the CTEA's effective date, the CTEA extends the term to 95 years from publication. § 304(a) and (b). Thus, in common with the 1831, 1909, and 1976 Acts, the CTEA's new terms apply to both future and existing copyrights.[3]

B

Petitioners' suit challenges the CTEA's constitutionality under both the Copyright Clause and the First Amendment. [The District Court entered judgment on the pleadings in favor of the Attorney General, and the Court of Appeals affirmed, one judge dissenting in part.]

We granted certiorari to address two questions: whether the CTEA's extension of existing copyrights exceeds Congress' power under the Copyright Clause; and whether the CTEA's extension of existing and future copyrights violates the First Amendment. 534 U.S. 1126 and 1160, 122 S.Ct. 1062 and 1170, 151 L.Ed.2d 966 and 152 L.Ed.2d 115 (2002). We now answer those two questions in the negative and affirm.

2. Asserting that the last several decades have seen a proliferation of copyright legislation in departure from Congress' traditional pace of legislative amendment in this area, petitioners cite nine statutes passed between 1962 and 1974, each of which incrementally extended existing copyrights for brief periods. See Pub.L. 87–668, 76 Stat. 555; Pub.L. 89–142, 79 Stat. 581; Pub.L. 90–141, 81 Stat. 464; Pub.L. 90–416, 82 Stat. 397; Pub.L. 91–147, 83 Stat. 360; Pub.L. 91–555, 84 Stat. 1441; Pub.L. 92–170, 85 Stat. 490; Pub.L. 92–566, 86 Stat. 1181; Pub.L. 93–573, Title I, 88 Stat. 1873. As respondent (Attorney General Ashcroft) points out, however, these statutes were all temporary placeholders subsumed into the systemic changes effected by the 1976 Act. Brief for Respondent 9.

3. Petitioners argue that the 1790 Act must be distinguished from the later Acts on the ground that it covered existing works but did not extend existing copyrights. Reply Brief 3–7. The parties disagree on the question whether the 1790 Act's copyright term should be regarded in part as compensation for the loss of any then existing state- or common-law copyright protections. See Brief for Petitioners 28–30; Brief for Respondent 17, n. 9; Reply Brief 3–7. Without resolving that dispute, we underscore that the First Congress clearly did confer copyright protection on works that had already been created.

II

A

We address first the determination of the courts below that Congress has authority under the Copyright Clause to extend the terms of existing copyrights. Text, history, and precedent, we conclude, confirm that the Copyright Clause empowers Congress to prescribe "limited Times" for copyright protection and to secure the same level and duration of protection for all copyright holders, present and future.

The CTEA's baseline term of life plus 70 years, petitioners concede, qualifies as a "limited Tim[e]" as applied to future copyrights.[4] Petitioners contend, however, that existing copyrights extended to endure for that same term are not "limited." Petitioners' argument essentially reads into the text of the Copyright Clause the command that a time prescription, once set, becomes forever "fixed" or "inalterable." The word "limited," however, does not convey a meaning so constricted. At the time of the Framing, that word meant what it means today: "confine[d] within certain bounds," "restrain[ed]," or "circumscribe[d]." S. Johnson, A Dictionary of the English Language (7th ed. 1785); see T. Sheridan, A Complete Dictionary of the English Language (6th ed. 1796) ("confine[d] within certain bounds"); Webster's Third New International Dictionary 1312 (1976) ("confined within limits"; "restricted in extent, number, or duration"). Thus understood, a time span appropriately "limited" as applied to future copyrights does not automatically cease to be "limited" when applied to existing copyrights. And as we observe, there is no cause to suspect that a purpose to evade the "limited Times" prescription prompted Congress to adopt the CTEA.

To comprehend the scope of Congress' power under the Copyright Clause, "a page of history is worth a volume of logic." New York Trust Co. v. Eisner, 256 U.S. 345, 349, 41 S.Ct. 506, 65 L.Ed. 963 (1921) (Holmes, J.). History reveals an unbroken congressional practice of granting to authors of works with existing copyrights the benefit of term extensions so that all under copyright protection will be governed evenhandedly under the same regime. As earlier recounted, the First Congress accorded the protections of the Nation's first federal copyright statute to existing and future works alike. 1790 Act § 1.[5] Since then, Congress has regularly applied duration extensions to both existing and future copyrights. 1831 Act §§ 1, 16; 1909 Act §§ 23–24; 1976 Act §§ 302–303; 17 U.S.C. §§ 302–304.[6]

---

4. We note again that Justice BREYER makes no such concession. He does not train his fire, as petitioners do, on Congress' choice to place existing and future copyrights in parity. Moving beyond the bounds of the parties' presentations, and with abundant policy arguments but precious little support from precedent, he would condemn Congress' entire product as irrational.

5. This approach comported with English practice at the time. The Statute of Anne, 1710, 8 Ann. c. 19, provided copyright protection to books not yet composed or published, books already composed but not yet published, and books already composed and published. * * *

6. Moreover, the precise duration of a federal copyright has never been fixed at the time of the initial grant. The 1790 Act pro-

Because the Clause empowering Congress to confer copyrights also authorizes patents, congressional practice with respect to patents informs our inquiry. We count it significant that early Congresses extended the duration of numerous individual patents as well as copyrights. See, *e.g.*, Act of Jan. 7, 1808, ch. 6, 6 Stat. 70 (patent); Act of Mar. 3, 1809, ch. 35, 6 Stat. 80 (patent); Act of Feb. 7, 1815, ch. 36, 6 Stat. 147 (patent); Act of May 24, 1828, ch. 145, 6 Stat. 389 (copyright); Act of Feb. 11, 1830, ch. 13, 6 Stat. 403 (copyright); see generally Ochoa, Patent and Copyright Term Extension and the Constitution: A Historical Perspective, 49 J. Copyright Society 19 (2001). The courts saw no "limited Times" impediment to such extensions; renewed or extended terms were upheld in the early days, for example, by Chief Justice Marshall and Justice Story sitting as circuit justices. See Evans v. Jordan, 8 F. Cas. 872, 874 (No. 4,564) (CC Va. 1813) (Marshall, J.) ("Th[e] construction of the constitution which admits the renewal of a patent is not controverted. A renewed patent ... confers the same rights, with an original."), aff'd, 9 Cranch 199, 3 L.Ed. 704 (1815); Blanchard v. Sprague, 3 F. Cas. 648, 650 (No. 1,518) (CC Mass. 1839) (Story, J.) ("I never have entertained any doubt of the constitutional authority of congress" to enact a 14–year patent extension that "operates retrospectively"); see also Evans v. Robinson, 8 F. Cas. 886, 888 (No. 4,571) (CC Md. 1813) (Congresses "have the exclusive right ... to limit the times for which a patent right shall be granted, and are not restrained from renewing a patent or prolonging" it.).[7]

Further, although prior to the instant case this Court did not have occasion to decide whether extending the duration of existing copyrights complies with the "limited Times" prescription, the Court has found no constitutional barrier to the legislative expansion of existing patents.[8]

---

vided a federal copyright term of 14 years from the work's publication, renewable for an additional 14 years *if* the author survived and applied for an additional term. § 1. Congress retained that approach in subsequent statutes. See Stewart v. Abend, 495 U.S. 207, 217, 110 S.Ct. 1750, 109 L.Ed.2d 184 (1990) ("Since the earliest copyright statute in this country, the copyright term of ownership has been split between an original term and a renewal term."). Similarly, under the method for measuring copyright terms established by the 1976 Act and retained by the CTEA, the baseline copyright term is measured in part by the life of the author, rendering its duration indeterminate at the time of the grant. See 1976 Act § 302(a); 17 U.S.C. § 302(a).

7. Justice STEVENS would sweep away these decisions, asserting that Graham v. John Deere Co. of Kansas City, 383 U.S. 1, 86 S.Ct. 684, 15 L.Ed.2d 545 (1966), "flatly contradicts" them. Post, at 798. Nothing but wishful thinking underpins that assertion.

The controversy in *Graham* involved no patent extension. *Graham* addressed an invention's very eligibility for patent protection, and spent no words on Congress' power to enlarge a patent's duration.

8. Justice STEVENS recites words from Sears, Roebuck & Co. v. Stiffel Co., 376 U.S. 225, 84 S.Ct. 784, 11 L.Ed.2d 661 (1964), supporting the uncontroversial proposition that a State may not "extend the life of a patent beyond its expiration date," id., at 231, 84 S.Ct. 784, then boldly asserts that for the same reasons Congress may not do so either. See post, at 790, 792. But *Sears* placed no reins on Congress' authority to extend a patent's life. The full sentence in *Sears*, from which Justice STEVENS extracts words, reads: "Obviously a State could not, consistently with the Supremacy Clause of the Constitution, extend the life of a patent beyond its expiration date or give a patent on an article which lacked the level of invention required for federal patents." 376 U.S., at

McClurg v. Kingsland, 1 How. 202, 11 L.Ed. 102 (1843), is the pathsetting precedent. The patentee in that case was unprotected under the law in force when the patent issued because he had allowed his employer briefly to practice the invention before he obtained the patent. Only upon enactment, two years later, of an exemption for such allowances did the patent become valid, retroactive to the time it issued. *McClurg* upheld retroactive application of the new law. The Court explained that the legal regime governing a particular patent "depend[s] on the law as it stood at the emanation of the patent, together with such changes as have been since made; for though they may be retrospective in their operation, that is not a sound objection to their validity." *Id.*, at 206. Neither is it a sound objection to the validity of a copyright term extension, enacted pursuant to the same constitutional grant of authority, that the enlarged term covers existing copyrights.

Congress' consistent historical practice of applying newly enacted copyright terms to future and existing copyrights reflects a judgment stated concisely by Representative Huntington at the time of the 1831 Act: "[J]ustice, policy, and equity alike forb[id]" that an "author who had sold his [work] a week ago, be placed in a worse situation than the author who should sell his work the day after the passing of [the] act." 7 Cong. Deb. 424 (1831); accord Symposium, *The Constitutionality of Copyright Term Extension*, 18 Cardozo Arts & Ent. L.J. 651, 694 (2000) (Prof.Miller) ("[S]ince 1790, it has indeed been Congress's policy that the author of yesterday's work should not get a lesser reward than the author of tomorrow's work just because Congress passed a statute lengthening the term today."). The CTEA follows this historical practice by keeping the duration provisions of the 1976 Act largely in place and simply adding 20 years to each of them. Guided by text, history, and precedent, we cannot agree with petitioners' submission that extending the duration of existing copyrights is categorically beyond Congress' authority under the Copyright Clause.

Satisfied that the CTEA complies with the "limited Times" prescription, we turn now to whether it is a rational exercise of the legislative authority conferred by the Copyright Clause. On that point, we defer substantially to Congress. *Sony*, 464 U.S., at 429, 104 S.Ct. 774 ("[I]t is

231, 84 S.Ct. 784. The point insistently made in *Sears* is no more and no less than this: *States* may not enact measures inconsistent with the federal patent laws. *Ibid.* ("[A] State cannot encroach upon the federal patent laws directly . . . [and] cannot . . . give protection of a kind that clashes with the objectives of the federal patent laws."). A decision thus rooted in the Supremacy Clause cannot be turned around to shrink congressional choices.

Also unavailing is Justice STEVENS' appeal to language found in a private letter written by James Madison.; see also dissenting opinion of BREYER, J. Respondent points to a better "demonstrat[ion]," (STEVENS, J., dissenting), of Madison's and other Framers' understanding of the scope of Congress' power to extend patents: "[T]hen-President Thomas Jefferson—the first administrator of the patent system, and perhaps the Founder with the narrowest view of the copyright and patent powers—signed the 1808 and 1809 patent term extensions into law; . . . James Madison, who drafted the Constitution's 'limited Times' language, issued the extended patents under those laws as Secretary of State; and . . . Madison as President signed another patent term extension in 1815." Brief for Respondent 15.

Congress that has been assigned the task of defining the scope of the limited monopoly that should be granted to authors . . . in order to give the public appropriate access to their work product.").[10]

The CTEA reflects judgments of a kind Congress typically makes, judgments we cannot dismiss as outside the Legislature's domain. As respondent describes, see Brief for Respondent 37–38, a key factor in the CTEA's passage was a 1993 European Union (EU) directive instructing EU members to establish a copyright term of life plus 70 years. EU Council Directive 93/98, p. 4; see 144 Cong. Rec. S12377–S12378 (daily ed. Oct. 12, 1998) (statement of Sen. Hatch). Consistent with the Berne Convention, the EU directed its members to deny this longer term to the works of any non-EU country whose laws did not secure the same extended term. See Berne Conv. Art. 7(8); P. Goldstein, International Copyright § 5.3, p. 239 (2001). By extending the baseline United States copyright term to life plus 70 years, Congress sought to ensure that American authors would receive the same copyright protection in Europe as their European counterparts.[11] The CTEA may also provide greater incentive for American and other authors to create and disseminate their work in the United States. See Perlmutter, Participation in the International Copyright System as a Means to Promote the Progress of Science and Useful Arts, 36 Loyola (LA) L.Rev. 323, 330 (2002) ("[M]atching th[e] level of [copyright] protection in the United States [to that in the EU] can ensure stronger protection for U.S. works abroad and avoid competitive disadvantages vis-a-vis foreign rightholders."); see also *id.*, at 332 (the United States could not "play a leadership role" in the give-and-take evolution of the international copyright system, indeed it would "lose all flexibility," "if the only way to

---

10. Justice BREYER would adopt a heightened, three-part test for the constitutionality of copyright enactments. He would invalidate the CTEA as irrational in part because, in his view, harmonizing the United States and European Union baseline copyright terms "apparent[ly]" fails to achieve "significant" uniformity. The novelty of the "rational basis" approach he presents is plain. Cf. Board of Trustees of Univ. of Ala. v. Garrett, 531 U.S. 356, 383, 121 S.Ct. 955, 148 L.Ed.2d 866 (2001) (BREYER, J., dissenting) ("Rational-basis review—with its presumptions favoring constitutionality—is 'a paradigm of judicial restraint.' ") (quoting FCC v. Beach Communications, Inc., 508 U.S. 307, 314, 113 S.Ct. 2096, 124 L.Ed.2d 211 (1993)). Rather than subjecting Congress' legislative choices in the copyright area to heightened judicial scrutiny, we have stressed that "it is not our role to alter the delicate balance Congress has labored to achieve." Stewart v. Abend, 495 U.S., at 230, 110 S.Ct. 1750; see Sony Corp. of America v. Universal City Studios, Inc., 464 U.S. 417, 429, 104 S.Ct. 774, 78 L.Ed.2d 574 (1984). Congress' exercise of its Copyright Clause authority must be rational, but Justice BREYER's stringent version of rationality is unknown to our literary property jurisprudence.

11. Responding to an inquiry whether copyrights could be extended "forever," Register of Copyrights Marybeth Peters emphasized the dominant reason for the CTEA: "There certainly are proponents of perpetual copyright: We heard that in our proceeding on term extension. The Songwriters Guild suggested a perpetual term. However, our Constitution says limited times, but there really isn't a very good indication on what limited times is. The reason why you're going to life-plus–70 today is because Europe has gone that way. . . ." Copyright Term, Film Labeling, and Film Preservation Legislation: Hearings on H.R. 989 et al. before the Subcommittee on Courts and Intellectual Property of the House Committee on the Judiciary, 104th Cong., 1st Sess., 230 (1995) (hereinafter House Hearings).

promote the progress of science were to provide incentives to create new works'').

In addition to international concerns, Congress passed the CTEA in light of demographic, economic, and technological changes, Brief for Respondent 25–26, 33, and nn. 23 and 24,[14] and rationally credited projections that longer terms would encourage copyright holders to invest in the restoration and public distribution of their works, id., at 34–37; see H.R.Rep. No. 105–452, p. 4 (1998) (term extension "provide[s] copyright owners generally with the incentive to restore older works and further disseminate them to the public'').[15]

In sum, we find that the CTEA is a rational enactment; we are not at liberty to second-guess congressional determinations and policy judgments of this order, however debatable or arguably unwise they may be. Accord-

14. Members of Congress expressed the view that, as a result of increases in human longevity and in parents' average age when their children are born, the pre-CTEA term did not adequately secure "the right to profit from licensing one's work during one's lifetime and to take pride and comfort in knowing that one's children—and perhaps their children—might also benefit from one's posthumous popularity." 141 Cong. Rec. 6553 (1995) (statement of Sen. Feinstein); see 144 Cong. Rec. S12377 (daily ed. Oct. 12, 1998) (statement of Sen. Hatch) ("Among the main developments [compelling reconsideration of the 1976 Act's term] is the effect of demographic trends, such as increasing longevity and the trend toward rearing children later in life, on the effectiveness of the life-plus-fifty term to provide adequate protection for American creators and their heirs."). Also cited was "the failure of the U.S. copyright term to keep pace with the substantially increased commercial life of copyrighted works resulting from the rapid growth in communications media." Ibid. (statement of Sen. Hatch); cf. Sony, 464 U.S., at 430–431, 104 S.Ct. 774 ("From its beginning, the law of copyright has developed in response to significant changes in technology.... [A]s new developments have occurred in this country, it has been the Congress that has fashioned the new rules that new technology made necessary.").

15. Justice BREYER urges that the economic incentives accompanying copyright term extension are too insignificant to "mov[e]" any author with a "rational economic perspective." Calibrating rational economic incentives, however, like "fashion[ing]

... new rules [in light of] new technology," Sony, 464 U.S., at 431, 104 S.Ct. 774, is a task primarily for Congress, not the courts. Congress heard testimony from a number of prominent artists; each expressed the belief that the copyright system's assurance of fair compensation for themselves and their heirs was an incentive to create. See, e.g., House Hearings 233–239 (statement of Quincy Jones); Copyright Term Extension Act of 1995: Hearings before the Senate Committee on the Judiciary, 104th Cong., 1st Sess., 55–56 (1995) (statement of Bob Dylan); id., at 56–57 (statement of Don Henley); id., at 57 (statement of Carlos Santana). We would not take Congress to task for crediting this evidence which, as Justice BREYER acknowledges, reflects general "propositions about the value of incentives" that are "undeniably true."

Congress also heard testimony from Register of Copyrights Marybeth Peters and others regarding the economic incentives created by the CTEA. According to the Register, extending the copyright for existing works "could ... provide additional income that would finance the production and distribution of new works." House Hearings 158. "Authors would not be able to continue to create," the Register explained, "unless they earned income on their finished works. The public benefits not only from an author's original work but also from his or her further creations. Although this truism may be illustrated in many ways, one of the best examples is Noah Webster[,] who supported his entire family from the earnings on his speller and grammar during the twenty years he took to complete his dictionary." Id., at 165.

ingly, we cannot conclude that the CTEA—which continues the unbroken congressional practice of treating future and existing copyrights in parity for term extension purposes—is an impermissible exercise of Congress' power under the Copyright Clause.

B

Petitioners' Copyright Clause arguments rely on several novel readings of the Clause. We next address these arguments and explain why we find them unpersuasive.

1

Petitioners contend that even if the CTEA's 20–year term extension is literally a "limited Tim[e]," permitting Congress to extend existing copyrights allows it to evade the "limited Times" constraint by creating effectively perpetual copyrights through repeated extensions. We disagree.

As the Court of Appeals observed, a regime of perpetual copyrights "clearly is not the situation before us." 239 F.3d, at 379. Nothing before this Court warrants construction of the CTEA's 20–year term extension as a congressional attempt to evade or override the "limited Times" constraint.[16] Critically, we again emphasize, petitioners fail to show how the

---

16. Justice BREYER agrees that "Congress did not intend to act unconstitutionally" when it enacted the CTEA, yet in his very next breath, he seems to make just that accusation. What else is one to glean from his selection of scattered statements from individual members of Congress? He does not identify any statement in the statutory text that installs a perpetual copyright, for there is none. But even if the statutory text were sufficiently ambiguous to warrant recourse to legislative history, Justice BREYER's selections are not the sort to which this Court accords high value: "In surveying legislative history we have repeatedly stated that the authoritative source for finding the Legislature's intent lies in the Committee Reports on the bill, which 'represen[t] the considered and collective understanding of those [members of Congress] involved in drafting and studying proposed legislation.'" Garcia v. United States, 469 U.S. 70, 76, 105 S.Ct. 479, 83 L.Ed.2d 472 (1984) (quoting Zuber v. Allen, 396 U.S. 168, 186, 90 S.Ct. 314, 24 L.Ed.2d 345 (1969)). The House and Senate Reports accompanying the CTEA reflect no purpose to make copyright a forever thing. Notably, the Senate Report expressly acknowledged that the Constitution "clearly precludes Congress from granting unlimited protection for copyrighted works," S.Rep. No. 104–315, p. 11 (1996), and disclaimed any intent to contravene that prohibition, *ibid.* Members of Congress instrumental in the CTEA's passage spoke to similar effect. See, *e.g.*, 144 Cong. Rec. H1458 (daily ed. Mar. 25, 1998) (statement of Rep. Coble) (observing that "copyright protection should be for a limited time only" and that "[p]erpetual protection does not benefit society").

Justice BREYER nevertheless insists that the "economic effect" of the CTEA is to make the copyright term "virtually perpetual." Relying on formulas and assumptions provided in an *amicus* brief supporting petitioners, he stresses that the CTEA creates a copyright term worth 99.8% of the value of a perpetual copyright. If Justice BREYER's calculations were a basis for holding the CTEA unconstitutional, then the 1976 Act would surely fall as well, for—under the same assumptions he indulges—that Act secures 99.4% of the value of a perpetual term. See Brief for George A. Akerloff et al. as *Amici Curiae* 6, n. 6 (describing the relevant formula). Indeed, on that analysis even the "limited" character of the 1909 (97.7%) and 1831 (94.1%) Acts might be suspect. Justice BREYER several times places the Founding Fathers on his side. It is doubtful, however, that those architects of our Nation, in framing the "limited Times" prescription, thought in terms of the calculator rather than the calendar.

CTEA crosses a constitutionally significant threshold with respect to "limited Times" that the 1831, 1909, and 1976 Acts did not. * * * Those earlier Acts did not create perpetual copyrights, and neither does the CTEA.[17]

2

Petitioners dominantly advance a series of arguments all premised on the proposition that Congress may not extend an existing copyright absent new consideration from the author. They pursue this main theme under three headings. Petitioners contend that the CTEA's extension of existing copyrights (1) overlooks the requirement of "originality," (2) fails to "promote the Progress of Science," and (3) ignores copyright's *quid pro quo.*

Petitioners' "originality" argument draws on Feist Publications, Inc. v. Rural Telephone Service Co., 499 U.S. 340, 111 S.Ct. 1282, 113 L.Ed.2d 358 (1991). In *Feist*, we observed that "[t]he *sine qua non* of copyright is originality," *id.*, at 345, 111 S.Ct. 1282, and held that copyright protection is unavailable to "a narrow category of works in which the creative spark is utterly lacking or so trivial as to be virtually nonexistent," *id.*, at 359, 111 S.Ct. 1282. Relying on *Feist*, petitioners urge that even if a work is sufficiently "original" to qualify for copyright protection in the first instance, any extension of the copyright's duration is impermissible because, once published, a work is no longer original.

Feist, however, did not touch on the duration of copyright protection. Rather, the decision addressed the core question of copyrightability, *i.e.*, the "creative spark" a work must have to be eligible for copyright protection at all. Explaining the originality requirement, *Feist* trained on the Copyright Clause words "Authors" and "Writings." *Id.*, at 346–347, 111 S.Ct. 1282. The decision did not construe the "limited Times" for which a work may be protected, and the originality requirement has no bearing on that prescription.

More forcibly, petitioners contend that the CTEA's extension of existing copyrights does not "promote the Progress of Science" as contemplated by the preambular language of the Copyright Clause. Art. I, § 8, cl. 8. To sustain this objection, petitioners do not argue that the Clause's preamble is an independently enforceable limit on Congress' power. See 239 F.3d, at 378 (Petitioners acknowledge that "the preamble of the Copyright Clause is

17. Respondent notes that the CTEA's life-plus–70–years baseline term is expected to produce an average copyright duration of 95 years, and that this term "resembles some other long-accepted durational practices in the law, such as 99–year leases of real property and bequests within the rule against perpetuities." Brief for Respondent 27, n. 18. Whether such referents mark the outer boundary of "limited Times" is not before us today. JUSTICE BREYER suggests that the CTEA's baseline term extends beyond that typically permitted by the traditional rule against perpetuities. The traditional common-law rule looks to lives in being plus 21 years. Under that rule, the period before a bequest vests could easily equal or exceed the anticipated average copyright term under the CTEA. If, for example, the vesting period on a deed were defined with reference to the life of an infant, the sum of the measuring life plus 21 years could commonly add up to 95 years.

not a substantive limit on Congress' legislative power." (internal quotation marks omitted)). Rather, they maintain that the preambular language identifies the sole end to which Congress may legislate; accordingly, they conclude, the meaning of "limited Times" must be "determined in light of that specified end." Brief for Petitioners 19. The CTEA's extension of existing copyrights categorically fails to "promote the Progress of Science," petitioners argue, because it does not stimulate the creation of new works but merely adds value to works already created.

As petitioners point out, we have described the Copyright Clause as "both a grant of power and a limitation," Graham v. John Deere Co. of Kansas City, 383 U.S. 1, 5, 86 S.Ct. 684, 15 L.Ed.2d 545 (1966), and have said that "[t]he primary objective of copyright" is "[t]o promote the Progress of Science," Feist, 499 U.S., at 349, 111 S.Ct. 1282. The "constitutional command," we have recognized, is that Congress, to the extent it enacts copyright laws at all, create a "system" that "promote[s] the Progress of Science." Graham, 383 U.S., at 6, 86 S.Ct. 684.[18]

We have also stressed, however, that it is generally for Congress, not the courts, to decide how best to pursue the Copyright Clause's objectives. See Stewart v. Abend, 495 U.S., at 230, 110 S.Ct. 1750 ("Th[e] evolution of the duration of copyright protection tellingly illustrates the difficulties Congress faces.... [I]t is not our role to alter the delicate balance Congress has labored to achieve."); Sony, 464 U.S., at 429, 104 S.Ct. 774 ("[I]t is Congress that has been assigned the task of defining the scope of [rights] that should be granted to authors or to inventors in order to give the public appropriate access to their work product."); Graham, 383 U.S., at 6, 86 S.Ct. 684 ("Within the limits of the constitutional grant, the Congress may, of course, implement the stated purpose of the Framers by selecting the policy which in its judgment best effectuates the constitutional aim."). The justifications we earlier set out for Congress' enactment of the CTEA, provide a rational basis for the conclusion that the CTEA "promote[s] the Progress of Science."

18. Justice STEVENS' characterization of reward to the author as "a secondary consideration" of copyright law, understates the relationship between such rewards and the "Progress of Science." As we have explained, "[t]he economic philosophy behind the [Copyright] [C]lause ... is the conviction that encouragement of individual effort by personal gain is the best way to advance public welfare through the talents of authors and inventors." Mazer v. Stein, 347 U.S. 201, 219, 74 S.Ct. 460, 98 L.Ed. 630 (1954). Accordingly, "copyright law *celebrates* the profit motive, recognizing that the incentive to profit from the exploitation of copyrights will redound to the public benefit by resulting in the proliferation of knowledge.... The profit motive is the engine that ensures the progress of science." American Geophysical Union v. Texaco Inc., 802 F.Supp. 1, 27 (S.D.N.Y. 1992), *aff'd*, 60 F.3d 913 (C.A.2 1994). Rewarding authors for their creative labor and "promot[ing] ... Progress" are thus complementary; as James Madison observed, in copyright "[t]he public good fully coincides ... with the claims of individuals." The Federalist No. 43, p. 272 (C. Rossiter ed.1961). Justice BREYER's assertion that "copyright statutes must serve public, not private, ends" similarly misses the mark. The two ends are not mutually exclusive; copyright law serves public ends by providing individuals with an incentive to pursue private ones.

On the issue of copyright duration, Congress, from the start, has routinely applied new definitions or adjustments of the copyright term to both future works and existing works not yet in the public domain. Such consistent congressional practice is entitled to "very great weight, and when it is remembered that the rights thus established have not been disputed during a period of [over two] centur[ies], it is almost conclusive." Burrow–Giles Lithographic Co. v. Sarony, 111 U.S., at 57, 4 S.Ct. 279. Indeed, "[t]his Court has repeatedly laid down the principle that a contemporaneous legislative exposition of the Constitution when the founders of our Government and framers of our Constitution were actively participating in public affairs, acquiesced in for a long term of years, fixes the construction to be given [the Constitution's] provisions." Myers v. United States, 272 U.S. 52, 175, 47 S.Ct. 21, 71 L.Ed. 160 (1926). Congress' unbroken practice since the founding generation thus overwhelms petitioners' argument that the CTEA's extension of existing copyrights fails *per se* to "promote the Progress of Science."

Closely related to petitioners' preambular argument, or a variant of it, is their assertion that the Copyright Clause "imbeds a quid pro quo." Brief for Petitioners 23. They contend, in this regard, that Congress may grant to an "Autho[r]" an "exclusive Right" for a "limited Tim[e]," but only in exchange for a "Writin[g]." Congress' power to confer copyright protection, petitioners argue, is thus contingent upon an exchange: The author of an original work receives an "exclusive Right" for a "limited Tim[e]" in exchange for a dedication to the public thereafter. Extending an existing copyright without demanding additional consideration, petitioners maintain, bestows an unpaid-for benefit on copyright holders and their heirs, in violation of the *quid pro quo* requirement.

We can demur to petitioners' description of the Copyright Clause as a grant of legislative authority empowering Congress "to secure a bargain— this for that." Brief for Petitioners 16; see Mazer v. Stein, 347 U.S. 201, 219, 74 S.Ct. 460, 98 L.Ed. 630 (1954) ("The economic philosophy behind the clause empowering Congress to grant patents and copyrights is the conviction that encouragement of individual effort by personal gain is the best way to advance public welfare through the talents of authors and inventors in 'Science and useful Arts.' "). But the legislative evolution earlier recalled demonstrates what the bargain entails. Given the consistent placement of existing copyright holders in parity with future holders, the author of a work created in the last 170 years would reasonably comprehend, as the "this" offered her, a copyright not only for the time in place when protection is gained, but also for any renewal or extension legislated during that time.[21] Congress could rationally seek to "promote ... Prog-

---

21. Standard copyright assignment agreements reflect this expectation. See, e.g., A. Kohn & B. Kohn, Music Licensing 471(3d ed.1992–2002) (short form copyright assignment for musical composition, under which assignor conveys all rights to the work, "including the copyrights and proprietary rights therein and in any and all versions of said musical composition(s), and any renewals and extensions thereof (whether presently available *or subsequently available as a result of intervening legislation)*" (emphasis added)); 5

ress" by including in every copyright statute an express guarantee that authors would receive the benefit of any later legislative extension of the copyright term. Nothing in the Copyright Clause bars Congress from creating the same incentive by adopting the same position as a matter of unbroken practice. See Brief for Respondent 31–32.

* * * We note, furthermore, that patents and copyrights do not entail the same exchange, and that our references to a *quid pro quo* typically appear in the patent context. * * * [C]opyright gives the holder no monopoly on any knowledge. A reader of an author's writing may make full use of any fact or idea she acquires from her reading. See § 102(b). The grant of a patent, on the other hand, does prevent full use by others of the inventor's knowledge. See Brief for Respondent 22; Alfred Bell & Co. v. Catalda Fine Arts, 191 F.2d 99, 103, n. 16 (C.A.2 1951) (The monopoly granted by a copyright "is not a monopoly of knowledge. The grant of a patent does prevent full use being made of knowledge, but the reader of a book is not by the copyright laws prevented from making full use of any information he may acquire from his reading." (quoting W. Copinger, Law of Copyright 2 (7th ed.1936))). In light of these distinctions, one cannot extract from language in our patent decisions—language not trained on a grant's duration—genuine support for petitioners' bold view. Accordingly, we reject the proposition that a *quid pro quo* requirement stops Congress from expanding copyright's term in a manner that puts existing and future copyrights in parity.

* * * * For the several reasons stated, we find no Copyright Clause impediment to the CTEA's extension of existing copyrights.

III

Petitioners separately argue that the CTEA is a content-neutral regulation of speech that fails heightened judicial review under the First Amendment. We reject petitioners' plea for imposition of uncommonly strict scrutiny on a copyright scheme that incorporates its own speech-protective purposes and safeguards. The Copyright Clause and First Amendment were adopted close in time. This proximity indicates that, in the Framers' view, copyright's limited monopolies are compatible with free speech principles. Indeed, copyright's purpose is to *promote* the creation and publication of free expression. As *Harper & Row* observed: "[T]he Framers intended copyright itself to be the engine of free expression. By establishing a marketable right to the use of one's expression, copyright supplies the economic incentive to create and disseminate ideas." 471 U.S., at 558, 105 S.Ct. 2218.

M. Nimmer & D. Nimmer, Copyright § 21.11[B], p. 21–305 (2002) (short form copyright assignment under which assignor conveys all assets relating to the work, "including without limitation, copyrights and renewals and/or extensions thereof"); 6 *id.*, § 30.04[B][1], p. 30–325 (form composer-producer agreement under which composer "assigns to Producer all rights (copyrights, rights under copyright and otherwise, whether now or hereafter known) and all renewals and extensions (as may now or hereafter exist)").

In addition to spurring the creation and publication of new expression, copyright law contains built-in First Amendment accommodations. See *id.*, at 560, 105 S.Ct. 2218. First, it distinguishes between ideas and expression and makes only the latter eligible for copyright protection. Specifically, 17 U.S.C. § 102(b) provides: "In no case does copyright protection for an original work of authorship extend to any idea, procedure, process, system, method of operation, concept, principle, or discovery, regardless of the form in which it is described, explained, illustrated, or embodied in such work." As we said in *Harper & Row*, this "idea/expression dichotomy strike[s] a definitional balance between the First Amendment and the Copyright Act by permitting free communication of facts while still protecting an author's expression." 471 U.S., at 556, 105 S.Ct. 2218 (internal quotation marks omitted). Due to this distinction, every idea, theory, and fact in a copyrighted work becomes instantly available for public exploitation at the moment of publication. See Feist, 499 U.S., at 349–350, 111 S.Ct. 1282.

Second, the "fair use" defense allows the public to use not only facts and ideas contained in a copyrighted work, but also expression itself in certain circumstances. Codified at 17 U.S.C. § 107, the defense provides: "[T]he fair use of a copyrighted work, including such use by reproduction in copies ..., for purposes such as criticism, comment, news reporting, teaching (including multiple copies for classroom use), scholarship, or research, is not an infringement of copyright." The fair use defense affords considerable "latitude for scholarship and comment," Harper & Row, 471 U.S., at 560, 105 S.Ct. 2218, and even for parody, see Campbell v. Acuff–Rose Music, Inc., 510 U.S. 569, 114 S.Ct. 1164, 127 L.Ed.2d 500 (1994) (rap group's musical parody of Roy Orbison's "Oh, Pretty Woman" may be fair use).

The CTEA itself supplements these traditional First Amendment safeguards. First, it allows libraries, archives, and similar institutions to "reproduce" and "distribute, display, or perform in facsimile or digital form" copies of certain published works "during the last 20 years of any term of copyright ... for purposes of preservation, scholarship, or research" if the work is not already being exploited commercially and further copies are unavailable at a reasonable price. 17 U.S.C. § 108(h); see Brief for Respondent 36. Second, Title II of the CTEA, known as the Fairness in Music Licensing Act of 1998, exempts small businesses, restaurants, and like entities from having to pay performance royalties on music played from licensed radio, television, and similar facilities. 17 U.S.C. § 110(5)(B); see Brief for Representative F. James Sensenbrenner, Jr., et al. as *Amici Curiae* 5–6, n. 3.

* * * The First Amendment securely protects the freedom to make—or decline to make—one's own speech; it bears less heavily when speakers assert the right to make other people's speeches. To the extent such assertions raise First Amendment concerns, copyright's built-in free speech safeguards are generally adequate to address them. We recognize that the D.C. Circuit spoke too broadly when it declared copyrights "categorically immune from challenges under the First Amendment." 239 F.3d, at 375.

But when, as in this case, Congress has not altered the traditional contours of copyright protection, further First Amendment scrutiny is unnecessary. See *Harper & Row*, 471 U.S., at 560, 105 S.Ct. 2218; cf. San Francisco Arts & Athletics, Inc. v. United States Olympic Comm., 483 U.S. 522, 107 S.Ct. 2971, 97 L.Ed.2d 427 (1987).

IV

If petitioners' vision of the Copyright Clause held sway, it would do more than render the CTEA's duration extensions unconstitutional as to existing works. Indeed, petitioners' assertion that the provisions of the CTEA are not severable would make the CTEA's enlarged terms invalid even as to tomorrow's work. The 1976 Act's time extensions, which set the pattern that the CTEA followed, would be vulnerable as well.

As we read the Framers' instruction, the Copyright Clause empowers Congress to determine the intellectual property regimes that, overall, in that body's judgment, will serve the ends of the Clause. See *Graham*, 383 U.S., at 6, 86 S.Ct. 684 (Congress may "implement the stated purpose of the Framers by selecting the policy which *in its judgment* best effectuates the constitutional aim." (emphasis added)). Beneath the facade of their inventive constitutional interpretation, petitioners forcefully urge that Congress pursued very bad policy in prescribing the CTEA's long terms. The wisdom of Congress' action, however, is not within our province to second guess. Satisfied that the legislation before us remains inside the domain the Constitution assigns to the First Branch, we affirm the judgment of the Court of Appeals.

It is so ordered.

■ JUSTICE STEVENS, dissenting.

Writing for a unanimous Court in 1964, Justice Black stated that it is obvious that a State could not "extend the life of a patent beyond its expiration date," Sears, Roebuck & Co. v. Stiffel Co., 376 U.S. 225, 231, 84 S.Ct. 784, 11 L.Ed.2d 661 (1964). As I shall explain, the reasons why a State may not extend the life of a patent apply to Congress as well. If Congress may not expand the scope of a patent monopoly, it also may not extend the life of a copyright beyond its expiration date. Accordingly, insofar as the 1998 Sonny Bono Copyright Term Extension Act, 112 Stat. 2827, purported to extend the life of unexpired copyrights, it is invalid. Because the majority's contrary conclusion rests on the mistaken premise that this Court has virtually no role in reviewing congressional grants of monopoly privileges to authors, inventors and their successors, I respectfully dissent.

I

The authority to issue copyrights stems from the same Clause in the Constitution that created the patent power. It provides: "Congress shall have Power ... To promote the Progress of Science and useful Arts, by securing for limited Times to Authors and Inventors the exclusive Right to their respective Writings and Discoveries." Art. I, § 8, cl. 8.

It is well settled that the Clause is "both a grant of power and a limitation" and that Congress "may not overreach the restraints imposed by the stated constitutional purpose." Graham v. John Deere Co. of Kansas City, 383 U.S. 1, 5–6, 86 S.Ct. 684, 15 L.Ed.2d 545 (1966). As we have made clear in the patent context, that purpose has two dimensions. Most obviously the grant of exclusive rights to their respective writings and discoveries is intended to encourage the creativity of "Authors and Inventors." But the requirement that those exclusive grants be for "limited Times" serves the ultimate purpose of promoting the "Progress of Science and useful Arts" by guaranteeing that those innovations will enter the public domain as soon as the period of exclusivity expires * * *.

The issuance of a patent is appropriately regarded as a *quid pro quo*— the grant of a limited right for the inventor's disclosure and subsequent contribution to the public domain. See, *e.g.*, Pfaff v. Wells Electronics, Inc., 525 U.S. 55, 63, 119 S.Ct. 304, 142 L.Ed.2d 261 (1998) ("[T]he patent system represents a carefully crafted bargain that encourages both the creation and the public disclosure of new and useful advances in technology, in return for an exclusive monopoly for a limited period of time"). It would be manifestly unfair if, after issuing a patent, the Government as a representative of the public sought to modify the bargain by shortening the term of the patent in order to accelerate public access to the invention. The fairness considerations that underlie the constitutional protections against *ex post facto* laws and laws impairing the obligation of contracts would presumably disable Congress from making such a retroactive change in the public's bargain with an inventor without providing compensation for the taking. Those same considerations should protect members of the public who make plans to exploit an invention as soon as it enters the public domain from a retroactive modification of the bargain that extends the term of the patent monopoly. * * * *

II

We have recognized that these twin purposes of encouraging new works and adding to the public domain apply to copyrights as well as patents. Thus, with regard to copyrights on motion pictures, we have clearly identified the overriding interest in the "release to the public of the products of [the author's] creative genius." United States v. Paramount Pictures, Inc., 334 U.S. 131, 158, 68 S.Ct. 915, 92 L.Ed. 1260 (1948). And, as with patents, we have emphasized that the overriding purpose of providing a reward for authors' creative activity is to motivate that activity and "to allow the public access to the products of their genius after the limited period of exclusive control has expired." Sony Corp. of America v. Universal City Studios, Inc., 464 U.S. 417, 429, 104 S.Ct. 774, 78 L.Ed.2d 574 (1984). *Ex post facto* extensions of copyrights result in a gratuitous transfer of wealth from the public to authors, publishers, and their successors in interest. Such retroactive extensions do not even arguably serve either of the purposes of the Copyright/Patent Clause. The reasons why such extensions of the patent monopoly are unconstitutional apply to copyrights as well.

Respondent, however, advances four arguments in support of the constitutionality of such retroactive extensions: (1) the first Copyright Act enacted shortly after the Constitution was ratified applied to works that had already been produced; (2) later Congresses have repeatedly authorized extensions of copyrights and patents; (3) such extensions promote the useful arts by giving copyright holders an incentive to preserve and restore certain valuable motion pictures; and (4) as a matter of equity, whenever Congress provides a longer term as an incentive to the creation of new works by authors, it should provide an equivalent reward to the owners of all unexpired copyrights. None of these arguments is persuasive.

III

* * * *

The Copyright Act

Congress ... passed the first Copyright Act, 1 Stat. 124, in 1790. At that time there were a number of maps, charts, and books that had already been printed, some of which were copyrighted under state laws and some of which were arguably entitled to perpetual protection under the common law. The federal statute applied to those works as well as to new works. In some cases the application of the new federal rule reduced the pre-existing protections, and in others it may have increased the protection. What is significant is that the statute provided a general rule creating new federal rights that supplanted the diverse state rights that previously existed. It did not extend or attach to any of those pre-existing state and common-law rights: "That congress, in passing the act of 1790, did not legislate in reference to existing rights, appears clear." Wheaton v. Peters, 8 Pet. 591, 661, 8 L.Ed. 1055 (1834); see also Fox Film Corp. v. Doyal, 286 U.S. 123, 127, 52 S.Ct. 546, 76 L.Ed. 1010 (1932) ("As this Court has repeatedly said, the Congress did not sanction an existing right but created a new one"). Congress set in place a federal structure governing certain types of intellectual property for the new Republic. That Congress exercised its unquestionable constitutional authority to create a new federal system securing rights for authors and inventors in 1790 does not provide support for the proposition that Congress can *extend pre-existing* federal protections retroactively.

* * * Precisely put, the question presented by this case does not even implicate the 1790 Act, for that Act created, rather than extended, copyright protection. That this law applied to works already in existence says nothing about the First Congress' conception of their power to extend this newly created federal right. * * * [T]his Court should be especially wary of relying on Congress' creation of a new system to support the proposition that Congress unquestionably understood that it had constitutional authority to extend existing copyrights.

IV

Since the creation of federal patent and copyright protection in 1790, Congress has passed a variety of legislation, both providing specific relief for individual authors and inventors as well as changing the general statutes conferring patent and copyright privileges. Some of the changes did indeed, as the majority describes, extend existing protections retroactively. Other changes, however, did not do so. A more complete and comprehensive look at the history of congressional action under the Copyright/Patent Clause demonstrates that history, in this case, does not provide the " 'volume of logic,' " necessary to sustain the Sonny Bono Act's constitutionality.

Congress, aside from changing the process of applying for a patent in the 1793 Patent Act, did not significantly alter the basic patent and copyright systems for the next 40 years. During this time, however, Congress did consider many private bills. * * * Congress passed private bills either directly extending patents or allowing otherwise untimely applicants to apply for patent extensions for approximately 75 patents between 1790 and 1875. Of these 75 patents, at least 56 had already fallen into the public domain. The fact that this repeated practice was patently unconstitutional completely undermines the majority's reliance on this history as "significant."

Copyright legislation has a similar history. The federal Copyright Act was first amended in 1831. That amendment, like later amendments, not only authorized a longer term for new works, but also extended the terms of unexpired copyrights. Respondent argues that that historical practice effectively establishes the constitutionality of retroactive extensions of unexpired copyrights. Of course, the practice buttressess the presumption of validity that attaches to every Act of Congress. But, as our decision in INS v. Chadha, 462 U.S. 919, 103 S.Ct. 2764, 77 L.Ed.2d 317 (1983), demonstrates, the fact that Congress has repeatedly acted on a mistaken interpretation of the Constitution does not qualify our duty to invalidate an unconstitutional practice when it is finally challenged in an appropriate case. * * * For, as this Court has long recognized, "[i]t is obviously correct that no one acquires a vested or protected right in violation of the Constitution by long use, even when that span of time covers our entire national existence." Walz v. Tax Comm'n of City of New York, 397 U.S. 664, 678, 90 S.Ct. 1409, 25 L.Ed.2d 697 (1970).

* * * To be sure, Congress, at many times in its history, has retroactively extended the terms of existing copyrights and patents. This history, however, reveals a much more heterogeneous practice than respondent contends. It is replete with actions that were unquestionably unconstitutional. Though relevant, the history is not dispositive of the constitutionality of the Sonny Bono Act.

The general presumption that historic practice illuminates the constitutionality of congressional action is not controlling in this case. That presumption is strongest when the earliest acts of Congress are considered, for the overlap of identity between those who created the Constitution and those who first constituted Congress provides "contemporaneous and weighty evidence" of the Constitution's "true meaning." Wisconsin v. Pelican Ins. Co., 127 U.S. 265, 297, 8 S.Ct. 1370, 32 L.Ed. 239 (1888). But that strong presumption does not attach to congressional action in 1831, because no member of the 1831 Congress had been a delegate to the framing convention 44 years earlier. * * * *

V

Respondent also argues that the Act promotes the useful arts by providing incentives to restore old movies. For at least three reasons, the interest in preserving perishable copies of old copyrighted films does not justify a wholesale extension of existing copyrights. First, such restoration and preservation will not even arguably promote any new works by authors or inventors. And, of course, any original expression in the restoration and preservation of movies will receive new copyright protection. Second, however strong the justification for preserving such works may be, that justification applies equally to works whose copyrights have already expired. Yet no one seriously contends that the Copyright/Patent Clause would authorize the grant of monopoly privileges for works already in the public domain solely to encourage their restoration. Finally, even if this concern with aging movies would permit congressional protection, the remedy offered—a blanket extension of all copyrights—simply bears no relationship to the alleged harm.

VI

Finally, respondent relies on concerns of equity to justify the retroactive extension. If Congress concludes that a longer period of exclusivity is necessary in order to provide an adequate incentive to authors to produce new works, respondent seems to believe that simple fairness requires that the same lengthened period be provided to authors whose works have already been completed and copyrighted. This is a classic non sequitur. The reason for increasing the inducement to create something new simply does not apply to an already-created work. To the contrary, the equity argument actually provides strong support for petitioners. Members of the public were entitled to rely on a promised access to copyrighted or patented works at the expiration of the terms specified when the exclusive privileges were granted. On the other hand, authors will receive the full benefit of the exclusive terms that were promised as an inducement to their creativity, and have no equitable claim to increased compensation for doing nothing more.

One must indulge in two untenable assumptions to find support in the equitable argument offered by respondent—that the public interest in free access to copyrighted works is entirely worthless and that authors, as a class, should receive a windfall solely based on completed creative activity. Indeed, Congress has apparently indulged in those assumptions for under the series of extensions to copyrights, only one year's worth of creative work—that copyrighted in 1923—has fallen into the public domain during the last 80 years. But as our cases repeatedly and consistently emphasize, ultimate public access is the overriding purpose of the constitutional provision. See, *e.g.*, Sony Corp., 464 U.S., at 429, 104 S.Ct. 774. *Ex post facto* extensions of existing copyrights, unsupported by any consideration of the public interest, frustrate the central purpose of the Clause.

VII

The express grant of a perpetual copyright would unquestionably violate the textual requirement that the authors' exclusive rights be only "for limited Times." Whether the extraordinary length of the grants authorized by the 1998 Act are invalid because they are the functional equivalent of perpetual copyrights is a question that need not be answered in this case because the question presented by the certiorari petition merely challenges Congress' power to extend retroactively the terms of existing copyrights. Accordingly, there is no need to determine whether the deference that is normally given to congressional policy judgments may save from judicial review its decision respecting the appropriate length of the term. It is important to note, however, that a categorical rule prohibiting retroactive extensions would effectively preclude perpetual copyrights. More importantly, as the House of Lords recognized when it refused to amend the Statute of Anne in 1735, unless the Clause is construed to embody such a categorical rule, Congress may extend existing monopoly privileges *ad infinitum* under the majority's analysis.

By failing to protect the public interest in free access to the products of inventive and artistic genius—indeed, by virtually ignoring the central purpose of the Copyright/Patent Clause—the Court has quitclaimed to Congress its principal responsibility in this area of the law. Fairly read, the Court has stated that Congress' actions under the Copyright/Patent Clause are, for all intents and purposes, judicially unreviewable. That result cannot be squared with the basic tenets of our constitutional structure. It is not hyperbole to recall the trenchant words of Chief Justice John Marshall: "It is emphatically the province and duty of the judicial department to say what the law is." Marbury v. Madison, 1 Cranch 137, 177, 2 L.Ed. 60 (1803). We should discharge that responsibility....

I respectfully dissent.

■ JUSTICE BREYER, dissenting.

The Constitution's Copyright Clause grants Congress the power to "promote the Progress of Science ... by securing for limited Times to Authors ... the exclusive Right to their respective Writings." Art. I, § 8, cl. 8 (emphasis added). The statute before us, the 1998 Sonny Bono Copyright Term Extension Act, extends the term of most existing copyrights to 95 years and that of many new copyrights to 70 years after the author's death. The economic effect of this 20–year extension—the longest blanket extension since the Nation's founding—is to make the copyright term not limited, but virtually perpetual. Its primary legal effect is to grant the extended term not to authors, but to their heirs, estates, or corporate successors. And most importantly, its practical effect is not to promote, but to inhibit, the progress of "Science"—by which word the Framers meant learning or knowledge, E. Walterscheid, The Nature of the Intellectual Property Clause: A Study in Historical Perspective 125–126 (2002).

The majority believes these conclusions rest upon practical judgments that at most suggest the statute is unwise, not that it is unconstitutional. Legal distinctions, however, are often matters of degree. * * * And in this case the failings of degree are so serious that they amount to failings of constitutional kind. Although the Copyright Clause grants broad legislative power to Congress, that grant has limits. And in my view this statute falls outside them.

I

* * * * The Copyright Clause and the First Amendment seek related objectives—the creation and dissemination of information. When working in tandem, these provisions mutually reinforce each other, the first serving as an "engine of free expression," Harper & Row, Publishers, Inc. v. Nation Enterprises, 471 U.S. 539, 558, 105 S.Ct. 2218, 85 L.Ed.2d 588 (1985), the second assuring that government throws up no obstacle to its dissemination. At the same time, a particular statute that exceeds proper Copyright Clause bounds may set Clause and Amendment at cross-purposes, thereby depriving the public of the speech-related benefits that the Founders, through both, have promised.

Consequently, I would review plausible claims that a copyright statute seriously, and unjustifiably, restricts the dissemination of speech somewhat more carefully than reference to this Court's traditional Commerce Clause jurisprudence might suggest There is no need in this case to characterize that review as a search for " 'congruence and proportionality,' " or as some other variation of what this Court has called "intermediate scrutiny".... Rather, it is necessary only to recognize that this statute involves not pure economic regulation, but regulation of expression, and what may count as rational where economic regulation is at issue is not necessarily rational where we focus on expression—in a Nation constitutionally dedicated to the free dissemination of speech, information, learning, and culture. In this sense only, and where line-drawing among constitutional interests is at issue, I would look harder than does the majority at the statute's rationality—though less hard than precedent might justify * * *.

Thus, I would find that the statute lacks the constitutionally necessary rational support (1) if the significant benefits that it bestows are private, not public; (2) if it threatens seriously to undermine the expressive values that the Copyright Clause embodies; and (3) if it cannot find justification in any significant Clause-related objective. Where, after examination of the statute, it becomes difficult, if not impossible, even to dispute these characterizations, Congress' "choice is clearly wrong." Helvering v. Davis, 301 U.S. 619, 640, 57 S.Ct. 904, 81 L.Ed. 1307 (1937).

II

A

Because we must examine the relevant statutory effects in light of the Copyright Clause's own purposes, we should begin by reviewing the basic objectives of that Clause. The Clause authorizes a "tax on readers for the purpose of giving a bounty to writers." 56 Parl. Deb. (3d Ser.) (1841) 341, 350 (Lord Macaulay). Why? What constitutional purposes does the "bounty" serve?

The Constitution itself describes the basic Clause objective as one of "promot[ing] the Progress of Science," i.e., knowledge and learning. The Clause exists not to "provide a special private benefit," Sony, supra, at 429, 104 S.Ct. 774, but "to stimulate artistic creativity for the general public good," Twentieth Century Music Corp. v. Aiken, 422 U.S. 151, 156, 95 S.Ct. 2040, 45 L.Ed.2d 84 (1975). It does so by "motivat[ing] the creative activity of authors" through "the provision of a special reward." Sony, supra, at 429, 104 S.Ct. 774. The "reward" is a means, not an end. And that is why the copyright term is limited. It is limited so that its beneficiaries—the public—"will not be permanently deprived of the fruits of an artist's labors." Stewart v. Abend, 495 U.S. 207, 228, 110 S.Ct. 1750, 109 L.Ed.2d 184 (1990).

That is how the Court previously has described the Clause's objectives. * * * And, in doing so, the Court simply has reiterated the views of the Founders.

Madison, like Jefferson and others in the founding generation, warned against the dangers of monopolies. * * * * Madison noted that the Constitution had "limited them to two cases, the authors of Books, and of useful inventions." Madison on Monopolies 756. He thought that in those two cases monopoly is justified because it amounts to "compensation for" an actual community "benefit" and because the monopoly is "temporary"— the term originally being 14 years (once renewable). Ibid. Madison concluded that "under that limitation a sufficient recompence and encouragement may be given." Ibid. But he warned in general that monopolies must be "guarded with strictness against abuse." Ibid.

Many Members of the Legislative Branch have expressed themselves similarly. [Justice Breyer cited several passages from congressional committee reports from 1909 through 1988.] * * * *

For present purposes, then, we should take the following as well established: that copyright statutes must serve public, not private, ends; that they must seek "to promote the Progress" of knowledge and learning; and that they must do so both by creating incentives for authors to produce and by removing the related restrictions on dissemination after expiration of a copyright's "limited Tim[e]"—a time that (like "a limited monarch") is "restrain[ed]" and "circumscribe[d]," "not [left] at large," 2 S. Johnson, A Dictionary of the English Language 1151 (4th rev. ed. 1773). I would examine the statute's effects in light of these well-established constitutional purposes.

B

This statute, like virtually every copyright statute, imposes upon the public certain expression-related costs in the form of (1) royalties that may be higher than necessary to evoke creation of the relevant work, and (2) a requirement that one seeking to reproduce a copyrighted work must obtain the copyright holder's permission. The first of these costs translates into higher prices that will potentially restrict a work's dissemination. The second means search costs that themselves may prevent reproduction even where the author has no objection. Although these costs are, in a sense, inevitable concomitants of copyright protection, there are special reasons for thinking them especially serious here.

First, the present statute primarily benefits the holders of existing copyrights, *i.e.*, copyrights on works already created. And a Congressional Research Service (CRS) study prepared for Congress indicates that the added royalty-related sum that the law will transfer to existing copyright holders is large. E. Rappaport, CRS Report for Congress, Copyright Term Extension: Estimating the Economic Values (1998) (hereinafter CRS Report). In conjunction with official figures on copyright renewals, the CRS Report indicates that only about 2% of copyrights between 55 and 75 years old retain commercial value—*i.e.*, still generate royalties after that time. Brief for Petitioners 7 (estimate, uncontested by respondent, based on data from the CRS, Census Bureau, and Library of Congress). But books, songs, and movies of that vintage still earn about $400 million per year in royalties. CRS Report 8, 12, 15. Hence, (despite declining consumer interest in any given work over time) one might conservatively estimate that 20 extra years of copyright protection will mean the transfer of several billion extra royalty dollars to holders of existing copyrights—copyrights that, together, already will have earned many billions of dollars in royalty "reward." See *id.*, at 16.

The extra royalty payments will not come from thin air. Rather, they ultimately come from those who wish to read or see or hear those classic books or films or recordings that have survived. * * * *

A second, equally important, cause for concern arises out of the fact that copyright extension imposes a "permissions" requirement—not only upon potential users of "classic" works that still retain commercial value, but also upon potential users of any other work still in copyright. Again using CRS estimates, one can estimate that, by 2018, the number of such works 75 years of age or older will be about 350,000. See Brief for Petitioners 7. Because the Copyright Act of 1976 abolished the requirement that an owner must renew a copyright, such still-in-copyright works (of little or no commercial value) will eventually number in the millions. See Pub.L. 94–553, §§ 302–304, 90 Stat. 2572–2576; U.S. Dept. of Commerce, Bureau of Census, Statistical History of the United States: From Colonial Times to the Present 956 (1976) (hereinafter Statistical History).

The potential users of such works include not only movie buffs and aging jazz fans, but also historians, scholars, teachers, writers, artists, database operators, and researchers of all kinds—those who want to make the past accessible for their own use or for that of others. The permissions requirement can inhibit their ability to accomplish that task. Indeed, in an age where computer-accessible databases promise to facilitate research and learning, the permissions requirement can stand as a significant obstacle to realization of that technological hope.

The reason is that the permissions requirement can inhibit or prevent the use of old works (particularly those without commercial value): (1) because it may prove expensive to track down or to contract with the copyright holder, (2) because the holder may prove impossible to find, or (3) because the holder when found may deny permission either outright or through misinformed efforts to bargain. The CRS, for example, has found that the cost of seeking permission "can be prohibitive." CRS Report 4. And amici, along with petitioners, provide examples of the kinds of significant harm at issue.

Thus, the American Association of Law Libraries points out that the clearance process associated with creating an electronic archive, Documenting the American South, "consumed approximately a dozen man-hours" *per work*. Brief for American Association of Law Libraries et al. as *Amici Curiae* 20. The College Art Association says that the costs of obtaining permission for use of single images, short excerpts, and other short works can become prohibitively high; it describes the abandonment of efforts to include, e.g., campaign songs, film excerpts, and documents exposing "horrors of the chain gang" in historical works or archives; and it points to examples in which copyright holders in effect have used their control of copyright to try to control the content of historical or cultural works. Brief for College Art Association et al. as *Amici Curiae* 7–13. The National Writers Union provides similar examples. Brief for National Writers Union et al. as *Amici Curiae* 25–27. Petitioners point to music fees that may prevent youth or community orchestras, or church choirs, from performing early 20th-century music. Brief for Petitioners 3–5 * * * *

As I have said, to some extent costs of this kind accompany any copyright law, regardless of the length of the copyright term. But to extend that term, preventing works from the 1920's and 1930's from falling into the public domain, will dramatically increase the size of the costs just as—perversely—the likely benefits from protection diminish. The older the work, the less likely it retains commercial value, and the harder it will likely prove to find the current copyright holder. The older the work, the more likely it will prove useful to the historian, artist, or teacher. The older the work, the less likely it is that a sense of authors' rights can justify a copyright holder's decision not to permit reproduction, for the more likely it is that the copyright holder making the decision is not the work's creator, but, say, a corporation or a great-grandchild whom the work's creator never knew. Similarly, the costs of obtaining permission, now perhaps ranging in the millions of dollars, will multiply as the number of holders of affected copyrights increases from several hundred thousand to several million. * * *

The majority finds my description of these permissions-related harms overstated in light of Congress' inclusion of a statutory exemption, which, during the last 20 years of a copyright term, exempts "facsimile or digital" reproduction by a "library or archives" "for purposes of preservation, scholarship, or research," 17 U.S.C. § 108(h). This exemption, however, applies only where the copy is made for the special listed purposes; it simply permits a library (not any other subsequent users) to make "a copy" for those purposes; it covers only "published" works not "subject to normal commercial exploitation" and not obtainable, apparently not even as a used copy, at a "reasonable price"; and it insists that the library assure itself through "reasonable investigation" that these conditions have been met. 17 U.S.C. § 108(h). What database proprietor can rely on so limited an exemption—particularly when the phrase "reasonable investigation" is so open-ended and particularly if the database has commercial, as well as non-commercial, aspects?

* * * *

C

What copyright-related benefits might justify the statute's extension of copyright protection? First, no one could reasonably conclude that copyright's traditional economic rationale applies here. The extension will not act as an economic spur encouraging authors to create new works. * * * * No potential author can reasonably believe that he has more than a tiny chance of writing a classic that will survive commercially long enough for the copyright extension to matter. After all, if, after 55 to 75 years, only 2% of all copyrights retain commercial value, the percentage surviving after 75 years or more (a typical pre-extension copyright term)—must be far smaller. See supra, at 804; CRS Report 7 (estimating that, even after copyright renewal, about 3.8% of copyrighted books go out of print each year). And any remaining monetary incentive is diminished dramatically by the fact that the relevant royalties will not arrive until 75 years or more into the future, when, not the author, but distant heirs, or shareholders in a successor corporation, will receive them. Using assumptions about the time value of money provided us by a group of economists (including five Nobel prize winners), Brief for George A. Akerlof et al. as *Amici Curiae* 5–7, it seems fair to say that, for example, a 1% likelihood of earning $100 annually for 20 years, starting *75 years into the future*, is worth less than seven cents today. See *id.*, at 3a; see also CRS Report 5.

What potential Shakespeare, Wharton, or Hemingway would be moved by such a sum? What monetarily motivated Melville would not realize that he could do better for his grandchildren by putting a few dollars into an interest-bearing bank account? The Court itself finds no evidence to the contrary. It refers to testimony before Congress (1) that the copyright system's incentives encourage creation, and (2) (referring to Noah Webster) that income earned from one work can help support an artist who " 'continue[s] to create.' " But the first of these amounts to no more than a set of undeniably true propositions about the value of incentives *in general*. And the applicability of the second to *this* Act is mysterious. How will extension help today's Noah Webster create new works 50 years after his death? Or is that hypothetical Webster supposed to support himself with the extension's present discounted value, *i.e.*, a few pennies? Or (to change the metaphor) is the argument that Dumas *fils* would have written more books had Dumas *pére'* s Three Musketeers earned more royalties?

Regardless, even if this cited testimony were meant more specifically to tell Congress that somehow, somewhere, some potential author might be moved by the thought of great-grandchildren receiving copyright royalties a century hence, so might some potential author also be moved by the thought of royalties being paid for two centuries, five centuries, 1,000 years, " 'til the End of Time.' " And from a rational *economic perspective the time difference among these periods makes no real* difference. The present extension will produce a copyright period of protection that, even under conservative assumptions, is worth more than *99.8%* of protection in perpetuity (more than *99.99%* for a songwriter like Irving Berlin and a song like Alexander's Ragtime Band). The lack of a practically meaningful distinction from an author's *ex ante* perspective between (a) the statute's extended terms and (b) an infinite term makes this latest extension difficult to square with the Constitution's insistence on "limited Times." Cf. Tr. of Oral Arg. 34 (Solicitor General's related concession).

* * * *

In any event, the incentive-related numbers are far too small for Congress to have concluded rationally, even with respect to new works, that the extension's economic-incentive effect could justify the serious expression-related harms earlier described. And, of course, in respect to works already created—the source of many of the harms previously described—*the statute creates no economic incentive at all.* See *ante* (Stevens, J., dissenting).

Second, the Court relies heavily for justification upon international uniformity of terms. Although it can be helpful to look to international norms and legal experience in understanding American law, cf. Printz v. U.S., 521 U.S. 898, 977, 117 S.Ct. 2365, 138 L.Ed.2d 914 (1997) (Breyer, J., dissenting), in this case the justification based upon foreign rules is surprisingly weak. Those who claim that significant copyright-related benefits flow from greater international uniformity of terms point to the fact that the nations of the European Union have adopted a system of copyright terms uniform among themselves. And the extension before this Court implements a term of life plus 70 years that appears to conform with the European standard. But how does "uniformity" help to justify this statute?

Despite appearances, the statute does not create a uniform American–European term with respect to the lion's share of the economically significant works that it affects—*all* works made "for hire" and all existing works created prior to 1978. With respect to those works the American statute produces an extended term of 95 years while comparable European rights in "for hire" works last for periods that vary from 50 years to 70 years to life plus 70 years. Compare 17 U.S.C. §§ 302(c), 304(a)–(b) with Council Directive 93/98/EEC of 29 October 1993 Harmonizing the Term of Protection of Copyright and Certain Related Rights, Arts. 1–3, 1993 Official J. Eur. Cmty. 290 (hereinafter EU Council Directive 93/98). Neither does the statute create uniformity with respect to anonymous or pseudonymous works. Compare 17 U.S.C. §§ 302(c), 304(a)–(b) with EU Council Directive 93/98, Art. 1.

The statute does produce uniformity with respect to copyrights in new, post-1977 works attributed to natural persons. Compare 17 U.S.C. § 302(a) with EU Council Directive 93/98, Art. 1(1). But these works constitute only a subset (likely a minority) of works that retain commercial value after 75 years. And the fact that uniformity comes so late, if at all, means that bringing American law into conformity with this particular aspect of European law will neither encourage creation nor benefit the long-dead author in any other important way. * * * *

But if there is no incentive-related benefit, what is the benefit of the future uniformity that the statute only partially achieves? Unlike the Copyright Act of 1976, this statute does not constitute part of an American effort to conform to an important international treaty like the Berne Convention. See H.R.Rep. No. 94–1476, pp. 135–136 (1976), U.S.Code Cong. & Admin.News 1976, pp. 5659, 5751–52 (The 1976 Act's life-plus-fifty term was "required for adherence to the Berne Convention"); S.Rep. No. 94–473, p. 118 (1975) (same). Nor does European acceptance of the longer term seem to reflect more than special European institutional considerations, *i.e.*, the needs of, and the international politics surrounding, the development of the European Union. House Hearings 230 (statement of the Register of Copyrights); *id.*, at 396–398 (statement of J. Reichman). European and American copyright law have long coexisted despite important differences, including Europe's traditional respect for authors' "moral rights" and the absence in Europe of constitutional restraints that restrict copyrights to "limited Times." See, e.g., Kwall, *Copyright and the Moral Right: Is an American Marriage Possible?*, 38 Vand. L.Rev. 1, 1–3 (1985) (moral rights); House Hearings 187 (testimony of the Register of Copyrights) ("limited [T]imes").

In sum, the partial, future uniformity that the 1998 Act promises cannot reasonably be said to justify extension of the copyright term for new works. And concerns with uniformity cannot possibly justify the extension of the new term to older works, for the statute there creates no uniformity at all.

Third, several publishers and filmmakers argue that the statute provides incentives to *those who act as publishers* to republish and to redistribute older copyrighted works. This claim cannot justify this statute, however, because the rationale is inconsistent with the basic purpose of the Copyright Clause—as understood by the Framers and by this Court. The Clause assumes an initial grant of monopoly, designed primarily to encourage creation, followed by termination of the monopoly grant in order to promote dissemination of already-created works. It assumes that it is the *disappearance* of the monopoly grant, not its *perpetuation*, that will, on balance, promote the dissemination of works already in existence. * * * *

This view also finds textual support in the Copyright Clause's word "limited." * * * * It finds added textual support in the word "Authors," which is difficult to reconcile with a rationale that rests entirely upon incentives given to publishers perhaps long after the death of the work's creator. Cf. Feist Publications, Inc. v. Rural Telephone Service Co., 499 U.S. 340, 346–347, 111 S.Ct. 1282, 113 L.Ed.2d 358 (1991).

It finds empirical support in sources that underscore the wisdom of the Framers' judgment. See CRS Report 3 ("[N]ew, cheaper editions can be expected when works come out of copyright"). And it draws logical support from the endlessly self-perpetuating nature of the publishers' claim and the difficulty of finding any kind of logical stopping place were this Court to accept such a uniquely publisher-related rationale. * * * *

Fourth, the statute's legislative history suggests another possible justification. That history refers frequently to the financial assistance the statute will bring the entertainment industry, particularly through the promotion of exports. See, *e.g.*, S.Rep. No. 104–315, p. 3 (1996) ("The purpose of this bill is to ensure adequate copyright protection for American works in foreign nations and the continued economic benefits of a healthy surplus balance of trade"); 144 Cong. Rec., at H9951 (statement of Rep. Foley) (noting "the importance of this issue to America's creative community," "[w]hether it is Sony, BMI, Disney" or other companies). * * * * In doing so, however, Congress has exercised its commerce, not its copyright, power. I can find nothing in the Copyright Clause that would authorize Congress to enhance the copyright grant's monopoly power, likely leading to higher prices both at home and abroad, *solely* in order to produce higher foreign earnings. That objective is not a *copyright* objective. Nor, standing alone, is it related to any other objective more closely tied to the Clause itself. Neither can higher corporate profits alone justify the grant's enhancement. The Clause seeks public, not private, benefits.

Finally, the Court mentions as possible justifications "demographic, economic, and technological changes"—by which the Court apparently means the facts that today people communicate with the help of modern technology, live longer, and have children at a later age. The first fact seems to argue not for, but instead against, extension. The second fact seems already corrected for by the 1976 Act's life-plus-fifty term, which automatically grows with lifespans. Cf. Department of Health and Human Services, Centers for Disease Control and Prevention, Deaths: Final Data for 2000 (2002) (Table 8) (reporting a 4–year increase in expected lifespan between 1976 and 1998). And the third fact—that adults are having children later in life—is a makeweight at best, providing no explanation of why the 1976 Act's term of 50 years after an author's death—a longer term than was available to authors themselves for most of our Nation's history—is an insufficient potential bequest. The weakness of these final rationales simply underscores the conclusion that emerges from consideration of earlier attempts at justification: There is no legitimate, serious copyright-related justification for this statute.

III

The Court is concerned that our holding in this case not inhibit the broad decisionmaking leeway that the Copyright Clause grants Congress.

* * * * We cannot avoid the need to examine the statute carefully * * * * That degree of judicial vigilance—at the far outer boundaries of the Clause—is warranted if we are to avoid the monopolies and consequent restrictions of expression that the Clause, read consistently with the First Amendment, seeks to preclude. And that vigilance is all the more necessary in a new Century that will see intellectual property rights and the forms of expression that underlie them play an ever more important role in the Nation's economy and the lives of its citizens.

I do not share the Court's concern that my view of the 1998 Act could automatically doom the 1976 Act. Unlike the present statute, the 1976 Act thoroughly revised copyright law and enabled the United States to join the Berne Convention—an international treaty that requires the 1976 Act's basic life-plus-fifty term as a condition for substantive protections from a copyright's very inception, Berne Conv. Art. 7(1). Consequently, the balance of copyright-related harms and benefits there is far less one-sided. The same is true of the 1909 and 1831 Acts, which, in any event, provided for maximum terms of 56 years or 42 years while requiring renewal after 28 years, with most copyrighted works falling into the public domain after that 28–year period, well before the putative maximum terms had elapsed; Statistical History 956–957. Regardless, the law provides means to protect those who have reasonably relied upon prior copyright statutes. See Heckler v. Mathews, 465 U.S. 728, 746, 104 S.Ct. 1387, 79 L.Ed.2d 646 (1984). And, in any event, we are not here considering, and we need not consider, the constitutionality of other copyright statutes.

Neither do I share the Court's aversion to line-drawing in this case. Even if it is difficult to draw a single clear bright line, the Court could easily decide (as I would decide) that this particular statute simply goes too far. And such examples—of what goes too far—sometimes offer better constitutional guidance than more absolute-sounding rules. In any event, "this Court sits" in part to decide when a statute exceeds a constitutional boundary. * * * *

IV

This statute will cause serious expression-related harm. It will likely restrict traditional dissemination of copyrighted works. It will likely inhibit new forms of dissemination through the use of new technology. It threatens to interfere with efforts to preserve our Nation's historical and cultural heritage and efforts to use that heritage, say, to educate our Nation's children. It is easy to understand how the statute might benefit the private financial interests of corporations or heirs who own existing copyrights. But I cannot find any constitutionally legitimate, copyright-related way in which the statute will benefit the public. Indeed, in respect to existing works, the serious public harm and the virtually nonexistent public benefit could not be more clear. * * * * The statute falls outside the scope of legislative power that the Copyright Clause, read in light of the First Amendment, grants to Congress. I would hold the statute unconstitutional.

I respectfully dissent.

QUESTIONS

1. What limitations on the power of Congress, if any, are placed by the Constitutional phrase "for limited times"? What limitations on the power of Congress, if any, are placed by the Constitutional phrase "to promote the progress of science and useful arts"?

2. Do you believe that Justice Ginsburg applied too deferential a standard of judicial review of congressional action? What weight, if any, should be given to the fact, pointed out by Justice Breyer in his dissent, that copyright enforcement is often in tension with First Amendment values? Does Justice Ginsburg hint at *any* extension of the copyright term that she would find to be in excess of Congress's power?

3. Shortly after the Supreme Court decided the *Eldred* case, the New York Times wrote the following on its editorial page. Do you take issue with any of the views expressed here?

"The court's decision may make constitutional sense, but it does not serve the public well. * * * Artists naturally deserve to hold a property interest in their work, and so do the corporate owners of copyright. But the public has an equally strong interest in seeing the copyright lapse after a time, returning works to the public domain— the great democratic seedbed of artistic creation—where they can be used without paying royalties.

"In effect, the Supreme Court's decision makes it likely that we are seeing the beginning of the end of public domain and the birth of copyright perpetuity. Public domain has been a grand experiment, one that should not be allowed to die. The ability to draw freely on the entire creative output of humanity is one of the reasons we live in a time of such fruitful creative ferment."

4. Professor Lawrence Lessig, who presented the case for the petitioners before the Supreme Court, wrote the following (also in the New York Times) shortly after the decision. His purpose is to link the duration of copyright with a work's continuing commercial utilization—and otherwise to enrich the public domain. Professor Lessig wrote:

"Patent holders have to pay a fee every few years to maintain their patents. The same principle could be applied to copyright. Imagine requiring copyright holders to pay a tax 50 years after a work was published. The tax should be very small, maybe $50 a work. And when the tax was paid, the government would record that fact, including the name of the copyright holder paying the tax. That way artists and others who want to use a work would continue to have an easy way to identify the current copyright owner. But if a copyright owner fails to pay the tax for three years in a row, then the work will enter the public domain. Anyone would then be free to build upon and cultivate that part of our culture as he sees fit."

A proposal much like this is reflected in H.R. 2601, introduced by Congresswoman Lofgren on June 25, 2003, for published "United States

Works" (as defined in § 101)("Maintenance Fee"). See also W. Landes & R. Posner, *Indefinitely Renewable Copyright*, 70 U.Chi.L.Rev. 471 (2003).

Would you support this proposal? For one thing, would it be consistent with our existing international obligations? Which copyright owners are most likely to fail to pay the fees? What does that suggest about the works most likely to fall into the public domain?

Page 360: Add after first full paragraph on this page:

For decisions interpreting the "reliance party" provisions of the restoration statute, see, e.g., Dam Things from Denmark v. Russ Berrie & Co., 290 F.3d 548 (3d Cir.2002)(to find that defendant troll-doll manufacturer is a "reliance party" under § 104A, doll must be a "derivative work," which requires original non-trivial differences; it is insufficient for defendant to show "substantial similarity" under the infringement standard); *Hoepker v. Kruger*, 200 F.Supp.2d 340 (S.D.N.Y.2002) (the creator of a 1990 artwork incorporating an image from a German photograph whose U.S. copyright was restored in 1994 qualified as a reliance party, as did her licensees of museum gift shop items reproducing the artwork. As plaintiff photographer failed to serve defendants with a Notice of Intent to Enforce the restored copyright, his claim was dismissed; any future action, even if a NIE were properly filed against reliance parties, would be limited to a claim for "reasonable compensation" under § 104A(d)(3).)

Page 360: Add to end of Note on restored copyrights:

Luck's Music Library, Inc. v. Ashcroft

___ F.Supp.2d ___, 2004 WL 1278070 (D.D.C.2004).

■ RICARDO M. URBINA, UNITED STATES DISTRICT JUDGE.

MEMORANDUM OPINION GRANTING THE DEFENDANTS' MOTION TO DISMISS

I. INTRODUCTION

This case comes before the court on the defendants' motion to dismiss. The plaintiffs Luck's Music Library, Inc. ("Luck's Music") and Moviecraft, Inc. ("Moviecraft") (collectively, "the plaintiffs") bring suit alleging that Section 514 ("Section 514") of the Uruguay Round Agreements Act ("the URAA"), Pub. L. No. 103–465, amending 17 U.S.C. § 104A, is unconstitutional. Defendants John Ashcroft, Attorney General of the United States, and Marybeth Peters, Register of Copyrights (collectively, "the defendants") move to dismiss the instant case on the ground that the plaintiffs failed to state a claim on which relief can be granted. Because Section 514 does not overstep Congress' power under the Intellectual Property clause of the Constitution ("IP Clause") and does not violate the First Amendment, the court grants the defendants' motion to dismiss.

II. BACKGROUND

A. The Uruguay Round Agreements Act

Section 514 implements Article 18 of the Berne Convention for the Protection of Literary and Artistic Works ("the Convention").[1] S. REP. NO. 103–412, at 225 (Nov. 22, 1994). The Convention governs the international enforcement of copyright law. S. REP. NO. 100–352, at 2, (May 19, 1988). Since its entry into force in 1886, the Convention requires member countries to afford the same copyright protections to foreign copyright holders that they provide to their own citizens. Convention, Art. 5. The United States ratified the Convention in 1988. 134 CONG. REC. 32018 (Oct. 20, 1988).

Article 18 of the Convention provides that a member country must apply the protections in the Convention to all works that have not yet fallen into the public domain through the expiration of the copyright's term in its origin country.[2] Section 514 restores copyright to foreign copyright holders whose works remain protected in their origin country, but entered the public domain in the United States due to the (a) failure of the foreign copyright holder to comply with the United States' copyright formalities, (b) absence of prior subject-matter protection such as sound recordings fixed before 1972, or (c) failure of the United States to recognize copyrights from that country. 17 U.S.C. § 104A(h)(6).

. . .

B. Luck's Music

Luck's Music is a family-owned corporation that repackages and sells works already in the public domain. In particular, it sells and rents classical orchestral sheet music to more than 7,000 orchestras ranging from elementary to operatic and to 12,000 individuals worldwide. Much of Luck's Music's catalog of music consists of music composed and published in countries ineligible for copyright in the United States due to their refusal to provide reciprocal protection. For example, Russian works published in the former Soviet Union such as *Peter and the Wolf* and *Love for Three Oranges* by Prokofiev; *Symphony No. 5* and *Festive Overture* by Shostakovich; *Masquerade Suite* and *Sparticus Ballet* by Khatchaturian; *Russian Sailor's Dance* and *Red Poppy Ballet Suite* by Glier; *The Comedians*, *Piano Concerto*, and *Cello Concerto* by Kabalevsky; and *Soldier's Tales* and *Symphony of the Winds* by Stravinsky remained in the public domain in the

---

1. The URAA implemented the General Agreement on Tariffs and Trade 1994 ("GATT"). S. REP. NO. 103–412, at 3, (Nov. 22, 1994). Title V of the URAA implements the Agreement on Trade Related Aspects of Intellectual Property Rights ("TRIPs"), which requires compliance with the Articles 1–21 of the Berne Convention. *Id.*

2. Article 18 of the Berne Convention provides, in relevant part, that:

(1) This Convention shall apply to all works which, at the moment of its com-ing into force, have not yet fallen into the public domain in the country of origin through the expiry of the term of protection.

(2) If, however, through the expiry of the term of protection which was previously granted, a work has fallen into the public domain of the country where protection is claimed, that work shall not be protected anew[.]

United States. Works ineligible for copyright composed ten percent of Luck's Music's total inventory and netted average annual sales of $150,000.

Congress' passage of Section 514 restored copyright to these works. After the passage of Section 514, Luck's Music received several notices of intent to enforce copyright, demanding that Luck's Music cease and desist from selling 200–300 different works from Russian composers, including Prokofiev, Shostakovich, Khatchaturian, Giler, Kabalevsky, and Stravinsky. During the one-year grace period provided for under section 104A, Luck's Music was unable to sell its entire inventory of Russian works.

* * *

D. Procedural History

The plaintiffs filed their complaint on October 29, 2001, asking for declaratory and injunctive relief. On February 15, 2002, the defendants moved to dismiss the instant case for failure to state a claim on which relief can be granted. After filing briefs, the court granted the parties' joint request to stay the case pending the Supreme Court's ruling in *Eldred v. Reno*, a copyright case. After the Supreme Court decided *Eldred*, 537 U.S. 186, 154 L. Ed. 2d 683 (2003), both parties filed supplementary briefs addressing *Eldred*'s effect on the issues in the instant case. The court now turns to the defendants' motion to dismiss.

III. ANALYSIS

* * *

C. The Court Concludes That Section 514 Does Not Exceed Congress' Power Under the IP Clause

The plaintiffs claim that Section 514 oversteps the powers granted to Congress in Article I and violates the First Amendment. Specifically, the plaintiffs assert that the IP clause requires the public to have free access to copy and use works once they have fallen into the public domain. By enacting Section 514 and granting retroactive copyrights to various works, the plaintiffs argue, Congress violated the IP clause *Id.* The plaintiffs also assert that Congress' enactment of Section 514 rests outside the powers the IP clause grants because Section 514 grants retroactive copyrights to works that are not original and does not promote the progress of science and the useful arts. In turn, the defendants argue that the enactment of Section 514 falls within the authority of the IP clause, or, alternatively, that other powers in Article I grant Congress the power to enact Section 514. The court concludes that Section 514 does not violate the IP clause and, therefore does not address whether there are other constitutional powers through which Congress might pass Section 514. Because Section 514 is Constitutional, the plaintiff cannot prove any set of facts upon which relief can be granted.

1. Congress Has Traditionally Exercised Restorative Copyright Powers

The defendants seek to establish that Section 514 is constitutional by demonstrating a history of retroactive copyrighting based on previous acts and proclamations tracing back to the founding of the United States. The defendants assert that the Copyright Act of 1790 ("1790 Act"), 1 Stat. 124, established retroactive copyright, and several presidential declarations continued the tradition of restoring copyrights retroactively without constitutional challenge. In response, the plaintiffs argue that the 1790 Act simply codified a state-based statutory copyright, or, to the extent states did not have a copyright statute, common law copyright. The plaintiffs also contend that the presidential proclamations only applied to copyright holders who could not meet statutory formality requirements during times of war. The plaintiffs' arguments, however, are unpersuasive.

"To comprehend the scope of Congress' power under the [IP clause], 'a page of history is worth a volume of logic.'" *Eldred*, 537 U.S. at 200 (quoting *N.Y. Trust Co. v. Eisner*, 256 U.S. 345, 349, 65 L.Ed. 963 (1921)). A consistent congressional exercise of its power under the IP clause since the forming of the constitution "is entitled to very great weight." *Burrow-Giles Lithographic Co. v. Sarony*, 111 U.S. 53, 57, 28 L.Ed. 349 (1884). Thus, an unbroken practice of granting retroactive copyrights and removing works from the public domain since the founding of the Constitution would seriously impede the plaintiffs' argument that Section 514 violates an implicit public domain within the IP clause. *Id.*; *see also Eldred*, 537 U.S. 199–201, 154 L.Ed.2d 683 (citing an unbroken practice of extending copyrights in holding that the Copyright Term Extension Act is constitutional).

a. Congress Created Copyrights by Enacting the 1790 Act

The 1790 Act granted copyright protection to all books, maps and charts "already printed within these United States" at the time of enactment. 1 Stat. 124. The plaintiffs' interpretation that the 1790 Act merely codified existing copyright law requires the assumption that either all states had copyright statutes enacted or that a common-law of copyright existed in the United States. If neither of these bodies of law existed, then Congress' implementation of the 1790 Act would have created copyright law and granted retroactive copyrights to works already in the public domain. A review of state statutes before the ratification of the Constitution and the enactment of the 1790 Act reveals that the plaintiffs' argument is flawed.

Before the ratification of the Constitution, the Articles of Confederation granted any powers not expressly delegated to Congress to the States. Articles of Confederation, Art. II. Because the Articles of Confederation did not vest Congress with the power to protect intellectual properties, it fell to each state to pass its own copyright statute. Edward C. Walterscheid, The Nature of the Intellectual Property Clause: A Study in Historical Perspective, 31 (2002); *see also* 8 M. Nimmer and D. Nimmer, Nimmer on copyright, App. 7[B][1] (2003) (hereinafter Nimmer's Copyright) (reprinting the Continental Congress' recommendation that states pass intellectual property protection laws). Not all of the states, however, enacted statutory copyright laws. Lyman Ray Patterson, Copyright in Historical Perspective 183–184 (1968); 8 Nimmer's Copyright, App. 7[C] (reprinting the states' copyright statutes in Appendix 7). Delaware, Maryland and Pennsylvania never enacted copyright statutes. Bruce W. Bugbee, Genesis of American Patent and Copyright Law, (1967) at 123, 124. Accordingly, three of the original 13 states did not have any kind of copyright protection. *Id.* Thus, Congress' actions with the enactment of the 1790 Act created retroactive copyrights for works published by the citizens of these three states.

As noted, the plaintiffs argue that in cases where states did not have a copyright statute in effect, a common-law of copyright existed. By enabling the 1790 Act, the plaintiffs claim, Congress simply converted these common law rights into statutory law. The plaintiffs point out that British precedent, the foundation of American common law, supports their position. ([C]iting *Donaldson v. Beckett*, 98 Eng. Rep. 257 (H.L. 1774) and *Millar v. Taylor*, 98 Eng. Rep. 201 (K.B. 1769)).

Nearly two centuries ago, however, the Supreme Court ruled that a common law copyright did not exist in the United States. *Wheaton v. Peters.* 33 U.S. 591, 659–661, 8 L. Ed. 1055 (1834). In *Wheaton*, the Court interpreted the words "by securing" in the IP clause to mean that the Constitution gave Congress the power to create a new right through the 1790 Act. *Id.* at 662. The Court explained that "securing" had to refer to the creation of a new right, since the Constitution includes both copyright and patent law in the same clause, and patent law had no existing common law equivalent in England. *Id.* at 661. The Court further reasoned that any other interpretation would render the IP clause mere surplusage because the result would be a "vesting of a right already vested." *Id.* Thus, "Congress, . . . by [the 1790 Act], instead of sanctioning an existing right[,] created it." *Id.* Because not every state had a copyright statute and because no common law right to copyright existed, the plaintiffs' argument that the 1790 Act merely codified existing common law fails. *Id.*

b. The 1919 Amendments and the Emergency Act of 1941 Authorizing Restoration of Copyrights Demonstrates a Consistent Congressional Practice

The plaintiffs also argue that several presidential proclamations cited by the defendants as examples of continued tradition of Congress' restoration of copyrights are inadequate because the proclamations merely granted administrative extensions of time rather than restoring copyright to works already in the public domain as Section 514 does. The defendants, however, assert that the plaintiffs' arguments are "mere wordplay" because presidential proclamations did not simply extend time for complying with U.S. formalities regarding copyrights. Rather, the plaintiffs claim, the Congressionally authorized presidential proclamations "gave authors the opportunity to gain copyright protection for works that had fallen into and would otherwise have remained in the public domain[.]"

Congress has enacted two statutes allowing the president to exercise powers of copyright restoration through proclamations. *See* An Act to Amend Sections 8 and 21 of the Copyright Act, 41 Stat. 368 (1919) ("1919 Amendment"); Emergency Copyright Act of 1941, 55 Stat. 732 (1941)

("Emergency Act").[4] Both acts gave the president the power to restore copyrights to foreign authors for works published within a specific time period as long as the copyright holder complied with U.S. copyright formalities and reveal a Congressional practice of restoring copyrights. For instance, Presidents Wilson and Harding issued proclamations in 1920 and 1922 respectively that effectively restored copyright to British and German works published during World War I. Proclamations of Woodrow Wilson, 41 Stat. 1790 (1920); Proclamations of Warren Harding, 42 Stat. 2271–2278 (1922). Later proclamations restored copyrights to foreign works published on or after September 3, 1939 whose authors complied with U.S. copyright formalities. *E.g.*, Proclamation No. 2608, 3 C.F.R. § 2608 (1944) (restoring copyright to authors from the United Kingdom); Proclamation No. 2722, 3 C.F.R. § 2722 (1947) (France); Proclamation No. 2729, 2 C.F.R. § 2729 (1947) (New Zealand); Proclamation No. 2863, 3 C.F.R. § 2683 (1949) (Australia); Proclamation No. 2953, 3 C.F.R. § 2953 (1951) (Finland); Proclamation No. 3353, 3 C.F.R. § 3353 (Austria); Proclamation No. 3792, 3 C.F.R. § 3792 (1967) (Germany). In each case, before the president issued the proclamations, published works from those countries were automatically part of the public domain. *Nat'l Comic Pubs., Inc. v. Fawcett Pubs.*, 191 F.2d 594, 598 (2d Cir. 1951). Thus, these presidential proclamations allowed foreign authors to restore copyright to their works, which had fallen into the public domain in the United States.

4. The 1919 Amendment provides that:

all works made the subject of copyright by the laws of the United States first . . . published abroad after August 1, 1914, and before the date of the President's proclamation of peace, of which the author or proprietors are citizens or subjects of any foreign State or nation granting similar protection for works by citizens of the United States, the existence of which shall be determined by a copyright proclamation issued by the President of the United States, shall be entitled to the protection conferred by the copyright laws of the United States from and after the accomplishment, . . . of the conditions and formalities prescribed with respect to such works by the copyright laws of the Untied States:

Provided further, That nothing herein contained shall be construed to deprive any person of any right which he may have acquired by the republication of such foreign work in the United States prior to the approval of this Act.

41 Stat. at 369. The Emergency Act provides that:

That whenever the President shall find that the [copyright owners] of works first produced or published abroad and subject to copyright . . . are or may have been temporarily unable to comply with the conditions or formalities prescribed with respect to such works by the copyright laws of the United States, because of the disruptions or suspensions of facilities essential for such compliance, he may by proclamation grant such extension of time as he deems appropriate for the fulfillment of such conditions or formalities by [copyright owners].

Provided further, That no liability shall attach . . . for lawful uses made or acts done prior to the effective date of such proclamation in connection with such works, or in respect to the continuance for one year subsequent to such date of any business undertaking or enterprise lawfully undertaken prior to such date[.]

55 Stat. at 732.

The plaintiffs' argument that power vested by these statutes did not restore copyright but simply created an administrative extension of time does not account for the provisions within the 1919 Amendment and the Emergency Act that protected individuals who relied on the fact that these works were in the public domain before the proclamations restored their copyrights. 41 Stat. at 369; 55 Stat. at 732. Congress specifically provided these provisions to "protect the rights lawfully exercised by American users or publishers of copyrighted works[,] protection of which had lapsed [into the public domain]." H. REP. NO. 77–619, at 2 (July 21, 1941). Congress' intent, as shown in the House Report on the Emergency Act, was to allow restoration of retroactive copyrights. *Id.* Thus, Congress' past actions show a clear history of allowing retroactive copyrights, lending significant weight to the defendants' arguments. *Burrows-Giles Lithographic*, 111 U.S. at 57.

2. The Plaintiffs' Misplace Their Reliance on Caselaw Interpreting Patent Law

The plaintiffs next argue that the Constitution's IP clause has an implicit public domain limitation. Citing the patent case *Graham v. John Deere Co.*, 383 U.S. 1, 15 L.Ed.2d 545 (1966), the plaintiffs contend that the IP clause prevents Congress from granting copyright to works already in the public domain. The defendants argue that *Graham* is inapplicable here due to the nature of patents, which differs from the copyrights on the subject of retroactive protection. The court agrees with the defendants.

In *Graham*, the Supreme Court held that Congress could not grant a patent to an invention that entered the public domain before the inventor filed a patent application. *Graham*, 383 U.S. at 5–6. The Court stated that, "Congress may not authorize the issuance of patents whose effects are to remove existent knowledge from the public domain, or to restrict free access to materials already available." *Id.* Although *Graham* deals specifically with patents, the plaintiffs argue that since both patent and copyright stem from the IP clause in the Constitution, the court can apply the *Graham* reasoning to the instant copyright case.

While the plaintiffs are correct that "because the Clause empowering Congress to confer copyrights also authorizes patents, congressional practice with respect to patents inform [the Court's] inquiry [into copyright]," *Eldred*, 537 U.S. at 201, the differing scope of their protections creates noticeable differences between patent law and copyright law doctrines. *Alfred Bell & Co. v. Catalda Fine Arts*, 191 F.2d 99, 101–02 (2d Cir. 1951). Patent law provides the owner with the exclusive right to use a novel idea or invention. A copyright, however, gives protection "only to the expression of the idea—not the idea itself." *Mazer v. Stein*, 347 U.S. 201, 217, 98 L. Ed. 630 (1954). "While a copyright confers on its owner an exclusive right to reproduce the original work, a patent provides its owner with the far broader right to exclusive use of the novel invention or design for a time-specific period." *Demetriades*, 680 F.Supp. at 662. This "idea/expression dichotomy," underlines the fact that "the requisites for patent eligibility and review [are more] rigorous than the analogous provisions of copyright law." *Id.*

The *Graham* holding is inapplicable to the instant case because *Graham* concerns specific requirements unique to patent law. In *Graham*, the Court based its holding on the rigors of the patent statute's novelty requirement, which differs fundamentally from the copyright statute's requirements. *Bonito Boats, Inc. v. Thunder Craft Boats, Inc.,* 489 U.S. 141, 146–50, 103 L. Ed. 2d 118 (1989) (quoting and interpreting *Graham,* 383 U.S. at 6). In fact, the *Graham* court specifically noted that the copyright aspect of the IP clause was not relevant to the decision. *Graham,* 383 U.S. at 6 n.1. The plaintiffs' argument that a copyright cannot remove existing knowledge from the public domain borrows from the requirement that "the applicant for a patent must show that the idea is novel." The novelty requirement for patent protection, codified at 35 U.S.C. § 102, specifically excludes knowledge available to the public. *Bonito Boats,* 489 U.S. at 148.

In contrast, the copyright statute has no such novelty requirement. Given the lack of a novelty requirement in copyright law, the plaintiffs' claim that *Graham* precluded Congress from granting copyright to works already in the public domain lacks authority and rationale. Therefore, the court concludes that the plaintiffs' reliance on *Graham* is misplaced.

3. Section 514 Does Not Hinder the Promotion of Science

The plaintiffs also claim that Section 514 violates the preamble of the IP clause because it does not "promote the Progress of Science." They assert that a *quid pro quo* exists between the government's grants of exclusive rights to a work and the guarantee of public access after the copyright expires. Section 514, the plaintiffs contend, prevents this *quid pro quo* from occurring. The defendants argue, however, that the Constitution gives Congress the ultimate authority on the progression of science. Thus, the defendants assert that for Section 514 to pass constitutional muster, the court need only conclude that Congress acted rationally to promote science in enacting the statute.

Courts have not interpreted the phrase "To promote the Progress of Science and useful Arts," in the IP clause as constituting a limitation on the power of Congress. *Schnapper v. Foley,* 215 U.S. App. D.C. 59, 667 F.2d 102, 111–112 (D.C. Cir. 1981). Indeed, " 'the courts will not find that Congress has exceeded its power so long as the means adopted by Congress for achieving a constitutional end are "appropriate" and "plainly adapted" to achieving that end.' " *Id.* (quoting *Mitchell Bros. Film Group,* 604 F.2d at 860). Toward that end, the Supreme Court rejected the plaintiffs' argument that the extension of existing copyrights did not "promote the Progress of Science" on the grounds that Congress' action had a rational relationship to the progress of science. *Eldred,* 537 U.S. at 211.

Following this precedent, the court here determines that Section 514 bears a rational relation to the progression of science. Congress' rationale in enacting Section 514 was to secure the protection of copyrights in foreign countries for U.S. citizens. Given industry losses of $43 to $61 billion through piracy because of "inadequate [foreign] legal protection for United States intellectual property," the Senate noted that implementing Section 514 "is a significant opportunity to reduce the impact of copyright piracy on our world trade position." S. Rep. No. 100–352, at 2, (May 19, 1988). Accordingly, the court concludes that Congress' conception of Section 514 has a rational relationship to the promotion of science.

* * *

D. The Court Concludes That Section 514 Does Not Violate the First Amendment

Finally, the plaintiffs claim that Section 514 violates the First Amendment because it restricts the freedom of expression of works already in the public domain. The defendants argue—and the court agrees—that *Eldred* bars this argument.

The *Eldred* Court held that "the First Amendment securely protects the freedom to make ... one's own speech; it bears less heavily when speakers assert the right to make other people's speeches." *Eldred*, 537 U.S. at 221. In fact, by offering an economic incentive, "the Framers intended copyright itself to be the engine of free expression." *Harper & Row Publishers, Inc. v. Nation Enters.*, 471 U.S. 539, 558, 85 L.Ed.2d 588 (1985). For those instances when copyright protection raises First Amendment concerns, copyright law contains built-in accommodations for First Amendment speech such as through the idea/expression dichotomy and the fair use doctrine. *Eldred*, 537 U.S. at 219–21. When Congress "has not altered the traditional contours of copyright protection, further First Amendment scrutiny is unnecessary." *Id.* at 221 (citing *Harper & Row*, 471 U.S. at 560).

In the instant case, Congress has not altered the traditional contours of copyright protection by enacting Section 514. *See generally* 17 U.S.C. § 104A. Section 514 does not alter First Amendment accommodations such as the idea/expression dichotomy or the fair-use doctrine. *Id.* In fact, Section 514 supplements First Amendment protections by protecting parties who already have exploited the restored copyrighted work while in the public domain. *Id.* § 104A(d)(2). It allows parties to exploit a restored work indefinitely if no notice is provided, immunizes parties for acts prior to notification and allows a party to continue exploiting the copyrighted works for a year after notice. *Id.* In addition, Section 514 allows the continued exploitation of derivative works based on a restored copyright as long as the restored copyright holder receives reasonable compensation. *Id.* § 104A(d)(3). Given that Section 514 does not encroach on the traditional copyright protections and includes additional protections, further scrutiny under the First Amendment is unnecessary. *Eldred*, 537 U.S. at 221. Thus, the court grants the defendants' motion to dismiss on this basis as well.

QUESTIONS

1. Should a court show equal deference to Congress when it restores expired copyrights as when it extends existing viable ones? Why or why not?

2. Although the majority opinion in *Wheaton v. Peters* does state that the constitutional copyright clause's employment of the term "secured" did not mean reinforcement of a preexisting common law right, but rather the creation of a new right, the dissenting opinion in fact makes a more persuasive historical case to the contrary. What if *Wheaton* was wrong about the Framers' understanding of the nature of the "exclusive right?" Would/should that make a difference to the analysis of Congress' power to restore expired copyrights?

3. The *Luck's Music* court observes that Congress restored foreign copyrights to meet the U.S.'s obligation under art. 18 of the Berne Convention. The court does not, however, look to the constitution's "treaty power," art II, § 2, to validate Congress' action. What, if anything, might such reference have added to the analysis? Cf. Timothy R. Holbrook, *The Treaty Power and the Patent Clause: Are There Limits on the United States' Ability to Harmonize?*, 22 Cardozo Arts & Ent L.J. 1 (2004) (suggesting that Congress may not, in the name of international treaty compliance, elude some Constitutional constraints on its patent power, such as the requirement that the patent be vested in the Inventor).

C.   TERMINATION OF TRANSFERS

Page 378:   Insert the following after the Question:

Marvel Characters, Inc. v. Simon

310 F.3d 280 (2d Cir.2002).

■ McLAUGHLIN, CIRCUIT JUDGE.

This appeal requires us to examine the scope of the termination provision of the Copyright Act of 1976 (the "1976 Act"), 17 U.S.C. § 304(c). Section 304(c) grants authors (or if deceased, their statutory heirs) an inalienable right to terminate a grant in a copyright fifty-six years after the original grant "notwithstanding any agreement to the contrary." 17 U.S.C. § 304(c)(3),(5). The termination provision, however, has one salient exception: copyright grants in works created for hire cannot be terminated. 17 U.S.C. § 304(c).

The question of first impression raised here is whether a settlement agreement, entered into long after a work's creation, stipulating that a work was created for hire constitutes "any agreement to the contrary" under the 1976 Act. We conclude that it does and, therefore, reverse.

BACKGROUND

This being an appeal from a grant of summary judgment to plaintiff Marvel Comics, Inc. ("Marvel"), we view the deposition testimony, affidavits, and documentary evidence in the light most favorable to defendant Joseph H. Simon, the non-moving party. Roge v. NYP Holdings, Inc., 257 F.3d 164, 165 (2d Cir.2001).

I. Publication of Captain America Comics

In December 1940, Martin and Jean Goodman, doing business as Timely Publications and Timely Comics, Inc. (collectively "Timely") published the first issue of the now iconic Captain America Comics. Captain America, a.k.a. Steve Rogers, was an army-reject turned superhero who was charged with protecting America from all enemies, especially Nazi spies. Authorship of the comic book was attributed to Simon and Jack Kirby.

According to Simon, he created Captain America as an independent, freelance project before shopping it around to various publishers. Although there was no written agreement between the parties, Simon contends that he sold the Captain America story to Timely for a fixed page rate plus a twenty-five percent share of the profits of the comic books. Simon also maintains that he created the second through tenth issues of Captain America Comics on a freelance basis, and orally assigned his interest in Captain America Comics and the Captain America character (collectively the "Works") to Timely.

During 1941, Timely published the second through tenth issues of Captain America Comics. Shortly after their publication, Timely applied for and received certificates of registration of the copyrights for each issue of the Works. The Works were a tremendous success, and to this day continue to generate substantial revenue for Marvel, Timely's successor in interest.

* * * *

III. The Prior Actions

As the initial twenty-eight year term of copyright in the Captain America Works neared its completion, Simon commenced two separate lawsuits (the "Prior Actions") against the Goodmans and their affiliates.

In October 1966, Simon sued in New York State Supreme Court (the "State Action") claiming that, because he was the author of the Works, the Goodmans' exploitation of the Captain America character constituted unfair competition and misappropriation of his state law property rights. See Complaint, Joseph H. Simon v. Martin Goodman and Jean Goodman, individually and d/b/a Magazine Mgmt. Co., Krantz Films, Inc., R.K.O. Gen., Inc., and Weston Merch. Corp. (R. at 117). Simon sought an accounting, damages, and injunctive relief in the State Action. See id.

One year later, Simon filed a similar action against the Goodmans and their affiliates in the United States District Court for the Southern District of New York (the "Federal Action"). In this action, Simon sought a declaratory judgment that he, as the author of the Works, had the sole and exclusive right to the renewal term of the copyright in the Works. See Complaint, Joseph H. Simon v. Martin Goodman and Jean Goodman, individually and d/b/a Magazine Mgmt. Co. and Timely Comics, Inc. (R. at 142–48). He also sought injunctive relief to prohibit the Goodmans from applying for renewal registrations of the Works. See id. Simon was represented by counsel in the Prior Actions.

In both of the Prior Actions, the defendants denied that Simon was the sole author of the Works. In the State Action, the defendants specifically argued that Simon's contributions to the Works were made as an "employee for hire." See Defendants' Answer and Counterclaims (R. at 136–39). In the Federal Action, the defendants asserted a counterclaim for a judgment declaring that Timely owned the copyrights in the Works and therefore Simon should be enjoined from applying to renew such copyrights. See Defendants' Answer (R. at 150–55). While the Prior Actions were pending, Timely's successor in interest applied to the Copyright Office for renewal of the copyrights in the Works.

In November 1969, after two years of discovery, the parties to the Prior Actions entered into a settlement agreement (the "Settlement Agreement"). In the Settlement Agreement, Simon acknowledged that his contribution to the Works "was done as an employee for hire of the Goodmans." (R. at 185). Pursuant to this Settlement Agreement, Simon assigned "any and all right, title and interest he may have or control or which he has had or controlled in [the Works] (without warranty that he has had or controlled any such right, title or interest)" to the Goodmans and their affiliates. (R. at 179–80). The parties to both actions filed stipulations with the respective courts dismissing with prejudice "all claims and matters alleged, threatened, implied or set forth in any of the pleadings filed by [Simon]." (R. at 188–91).

IV.   The Copyright Act of 1976

The legislative purpose behind the 1909 Act's renewal right—to provide authors a second chance to benefit from their works—was dealt a serious blow by the Supreme Court's decision in Fred Fisher Music Co. v. M. Witmark & Sons, 318 U.S. 643, 63 S.Ct. 773, 87 L.Ed. 1055 (1943). See Woods, 60 F.3d at 982. In *Fisher Music*, the Supreme Court addressed the renewal rights in the ever-popular (not to mention mellifluous) song "When Irish Eyes Are Smiling." The Court held that renewal rights were assignable by an author during the initial copyright term, before the renewal right vested. See id., 318 U.S. at 656–59, 63 S.Ct. 773.

Not surprisingly, after *Fisher Music* publishers began to insist that authors assign both their initial and renewal rights to them in one transfer. The natural effect of this, of course, was to eliminate the author's renewal right under the 1909 Act. In 1976, Congress enacted a comprehensive revision of the Copyright Act. See Pub.L. No. 94–553 (1976)(codified at 17 U.S.C. §§ 101–810); see also Mills Music, Inc. v. Snyder, 469 U.S. 153, 159–62, 105 S.Ct. 638, 83 L.Ed.2d 556 (1985). Responding to the continual erosion of authors' rights subsequent to the 1909 Act, Congress extended the duration of copyrights then in their renewal terms for an additional nineteen years (the "extended renewal term"). See 17 U.S.C. § 304(b). More significantly, however, the 1976 Act gave new protections to authors. It allowed authors to terminate the rights of a grantee to whom the author had transferred rights in the original work. See 17 U.S.C. § 304(c) * * * [The Act afforded termination rights in works other than works made for hire; it also provided that "Termination of the grant may be effected notwithstanding any agreement to the contrary...."]

* * * *

V.   The Proceedings Below

In December 1999, recognizing an opportunity created by § 304(c) to reclaim his copyright in the Works, Simon filed Notices of Termination (the "Termination Notices") with the Copyright Office purporting to terminate his transfers of the copyrights to Timely pursuant to § 304(c). In the Termination Notices, Simon claimed that he independently created the Captain America character and authored the first issue in the Captain America comic book series, and that he was "neither an employee for hire nor a creator of a work for hire."

Thereafter, Marvel—as Timely's successor in interest in all rights, title, and interest to the Works by virtue of a series of assignments—commenced this action in the United States District Court for the Southern District of New York (Casey, J.) seeking a declaratory judgment that the Termination Notices were invalid and that Marvel remains the sole owner of the copyrights in the Works. Simon in turn filed a counterclaim for a declaratory judgment that: (1) he is the sole author of the Works; (2) the Termination Notices are valid; and (3) all copyrights in the Works revert to him on the effective date of the Notices of Termination. * * * *

Turning to the merits of Marvel's claims that the Termination Notices are invalid and Marvel is the sole owner of the copyright in the Works, the district court held that Marvel was entitled to summary judgment on these claims based on the plain language of the Settlement Agreement. The court found that Simon's unambiguous acknowledgment in the Settlement Agreement that he created the Works "for hire" prevented Simon from exercising the termination right under § 304(c).

This appeal followed.

DISCUSSION

* * * *

II.   The Preclusive Effect of the Prior Actions

* * * * On this appeal, Marvel contends that there is no meaningful distinction between the authorship issue raised in the Prior Actions and the termination right at issue in this case. Therefore, according to Marvel, res judicata bars Simon from asserting that he is the author of the Works in order to exercise his termination right under § 304(c). In contrast, Simon argues that the district court was correct in finding that neither res judicata nor collateral estoppel barred him from asserting that he was the Works' author because the factual issue of authorship was never fully and fairly litigated in the Prior Actions and is quite different from his present claim to termination rights in the Works. Simon is correct.

A.   Res judicata

* * * * Although they spring from the same set of underlying facts, the claims at issue in the Prior Actions and the claims asserted in the current action are plainly distinct. In the Prior Actions, Simon claimed that he was entitled to the renewal term of copyright for the Works. In the present suit, Simon claims that he is entitled to terminate Marvel's copyright in the Works and obtain the extended copyright term by virtue of § 304(c) of the 1976 Act. As the district court correctly recognized, neither the extended copyright term nor the termination right existed at the time of the Prior Actions. Indeed, the termination right is an entirely new and wholly separate right than the renewal right. Hence, the Prior Actions could not have resolved the question of whether Simon was entitled to termination rights in the extended copyright term. Nor could the Prior Actions have awarded the relief requested in this action—the right to terminate the grant to Marvel and obtain the right to the extended copyright term—as that relief was likewise unavailable at that time. * * * *

B.   Collateral Estoppel

* * * * Simon does not dispute that he raised the issue of the Works' authorship in the Prior Actions; nor does he contest that, by virtue of the stipulations of dismissal filed in the Prior Actions, he did not prevail on that issue. However, where a stipulation of settlement is "unaccompanied by findings," it does "not bind the parties on any issue ... which might arise in connection with another cause of action." * * *

Here, although the Settlement Agreement contained detailed findings on the authorship issue, neither of the stipulations filed in the Prior Actions contain any specific findings as to whether Simon authored the Works independently or whether the Captain America character was created as a work for hire. Nor do the stipulations reference the Settlement Agreement in any way. Therefore, the stipulations do not collaterally estop Simon from litigating the issue of authorship underlying his termination claim in this action.

III.   Application of Section 304(c) of the 1976 Act

Having concluded that Simon is not precluded from asserting that he is the author of the Works for purposes of exercising his statutory termination right, we turn, at length, to the issue of first impression presented by this case: whether an agreement made subsequent to a work's creation that declares that it is a work created for hire constitutes an "agreement to the contrary" under § 304(c)(5) of the 1976 Act. The district court never addressed this question. Instead, it simply assumed that because Simon had conceded in the unambiguous Settlement Agreement that the Works were created for hire, he could not now assert that he was the Works' author for purposes of exercising the termination right in this action. While the district court was undoubtedly correct that the Settlement Agreement is not ambiguous—a contention disputed by the amici curiae—this is not the relevant analysis on this issue. Instead, we must analyze the legislative intent and purpose of § 304(c) of the 1976 Act to determine its application to this case.

Simon contends that the district court's failure to give effect to § 304(c)'s mandate that authors can terminate copyright grants "notwithstanding any agreement to the contrary" contravenes the legislative intent and purpose of § 304(c). Further, because Simon has submitted testimony that he was not in fact an employee for hire when he created the Captain Marvel character, he maintains that a genuine issue of material fact exists regarding Marvel's claims that the Termination Notices are invalid and it is the sole owner of the copyright in the Works. Marvel's only response to Simon's contentions is that if Simon's reading of the statute is upheld, no litigation concerning a claim to authorship could ever be resolved by settlement. We find Simon's arguments persuasive and Marvel's prediction unfounded.

* * * * Here, whether § 304(c)(5)'s phrase "any agreement to the contrary" includes a settlement agreement stating that a work was created for hire is not clear from the text of the statute itself. Generally speaking, the Settlement Agreement is an agreement to the contrary. But without more specific or compelling evidence from the text, we find it necessary to go beyond the mere text and consider the legislative intent and purpose of § 304(c) to ascertain the statute's meaning.

The Supreme Court has elucidated the intent and purpose behind the termination provision of the 1976 Act:

> The principal purpose of the amendments in § 304 was to provide added benefits to authors. The ... concept of a termination right itself, w[as] obviously intended to make the rewards for the creativity of authors more substantial. More particularly, the termination right was expressly intended to relieve authors of the consequences of ill-advised and unremunerative grants that had been made before the author had a fair opportunity to appreciate the true value of his work product. That general purpose is plainly defined in the legislative history and, indeed, is fairly inferable from the text of § 304 itself.

Mills Music, 469 U.S. at 172–73, 105 S.Ct. 638 (footnote omitted) (interpreting the derivative works exception to the termination clause of § 304(c)). Furthermore, the legislative history of the termination provision reflects Congress's intent to protect authors from unequal bargaining positions. See H.R.Rep. No. 94–1476, at 124 (1976), reprinted in 1976 U.S.C.C.A.N. 5659, 5740 ("A provision of this sort is needed because of the unequal bargaining position of authors, resulting in part from the impossibility of determining a work's value until it has been exploited."); see also *Mills Music*, 469 U.S. at 173 n. 39, 105 S.Ct. 638. As these statements suggest, the clear Congressional purpose behind § 304(c) was to prevent authors from waiving their termination right by contract. *Accord Stewart*, 495 U.S. at 230, 110 S.Ct. 1750 ("The 1976 Copyright Act provides ... an inalienable termination right.").

When examining the legislative intent and purpose of § 304(c), it becomes clear that an agreement made after a work's creation stipulating that the work was created as a work for hire constitutes an "agreement to the contrary" which can be disavowed pursuant to the statute. Any other construction of § 304(c) would thwart the clear legislative purpose and intent of the statute. If an agreement between an author and publisher that a work was created for hire were outside the purview of § 304(c)(5), the termination provision would be rendered a nullity; litigation-savvy publishers would be able to utilize their superior bargaining position to compel authors to agree that a work was created for hire in order to get their works published. In effect, such an interpretation would likely repeat the result wrought by the *Fred Fisher* decision and provide a blueprint by which publishers could effectively eliminate an author's termination right. We conclude that Congress included the "notwithstanding any agreement to the contrary" language in the termination provision precisely to avoid such a result.

This view finds support in *Nimmer on Copyright*:

> The parties to a grant may not agree that a work shall be deemed one made "for hire" in order to avoid the termination provisions if a "for hire" relationship ... does not in fact exist between them. Such an avoidance device would be contrary to the statutory provision that "[t]ermination of the grant may be effected notwithstanding any agreement to the contrary." ... [I]t is the relationship that in fact exists between the parties, and not their description of that relationship, that is determinative.

3 Melville B. Nimmer & David Nimmer, *Nimmer on Copyright* § 11.02[A][2] (2000 ed.) (footnote omitted). This reading of the statute also explains why copyright grants in works created for hire are not subject to termination. See 17 U.S.C. § 304(c). Under the 1909 Act, the statutory author of a work created for hire was the employer-publisher. See, e.g., 17 U.S.C. § 26 (repealed 1976); *Cmty. for Creative Non–Violence*, 490 U.S. at 743–44 & n. 9, 109 S.Ct. 2166. Because an employer-publisher does not face the same potential unequal bargaining position as an individual author, it follows that an employer-publisher does not need the same protections as an individual author.

This reading of § 304(c) is also consistent with the way in which courts have interpreted the 1909 Act's "work for hire" provision. Courts engaging in such an analysis have focused on the actual relationship between the parties, rather than the language of their agreements, in determining authorship of the work. * * * *

Additionally, this Court has looked to agency law to determine whether a work is created "for hire" under the 1909 Act. See Aldon Accessories Ltd. v. Spiegel, Inc., 738 F.2d 548, 552 (2d Cir.1984). And under agency law, "[t]he manner in which the parties designate the relationship is not controlling, and if an act done by one person in behalf of another is in its essential nature one of agency, the one is the agent of such other notwithstanding that he or she is not so called. Conversely, the mere use of the word 'agent' by parties in their contract does not make one an agent who, in fact, is not such." 3 Am.Jur.2d Agency § 19 (2002) (footnotes omitted).

Contrary to Marvel's dire prediction about an expansive interpretation of § 304(c), we believe that parties will still be able to resolve their authorship disputes by settlement. If parties intend to preclude any future litigation regarding authorship by settling their claims, they need only comply with the requirements of collateral estoppel by filing a detailed stipulation of settlement, complete with sufficient factual findings on authorship, with the court. Furthermore, when the relationship between parties has deteriorated to the point of litigation, presumably all parties are represented by counsel. Accordingly, the need to protect "ill-advised" authors from publishers or other more sophisticated entities—the policy concern underlying § 304(c)—is no longer present.

In sum, we hold that an agreement made subsequent to a work's creation which retroactively deems it a "work for hire" constitutes an "agreement to the contrary" under § 304(c)(5) of the 1976 Act. Therefore, Simon is not bound by the statement in the Settlement Agreement that he created the Works as an employee for hire. Because Simon has proffered admissible evidence that he did not create the Works as an employee for hire, the district court's grant of summary judgment to Marvel was erroneous. It will be up to a jury to determine whether Simon was the author of the Works and, therefore, whether he can exercise § 304(c)'s termination right. See, e.g., Medforms, Inc. v. Healthcare Mgmt. Solutions, Inc., 290 F.3d 98, 110 (2d Cir.2002) (noting that authorship is a jury question).

IV.   Equitable Estoppel

* * * * Marvel's estoppel argument is unpersuasive for three reasons. First, the doctrine of equitable estoppel does not supersede § 304(c). It is plain that § 304(c) necessarily contemplates the likelihood that long-dormant copyright ownership issues will be awakened and litigated once the original fifty-six year copyright term expires. In fact, Congress's goal in providing authors with this termination right was to enable them to reclaim long lost copyright grants. As the district court correctly recognized, virtually every copyright holder could fashion a similar equitable estoppel argument in response to an author's legitimate exercise of his termination rights. See *Marvel Characters, Inc.*, 2002 WL 313865, at *4. Permitting such an exception, however, would contravene the plain language, intent, and purpose of § 304(c).

Second, Marvel's argument ignores the fact that the termination right did not come into existence until 1978, the effective date of the 1976 Act. Therefore, it is specious to argue that Simon should be estopped from raising a claim that did not come into existence until almost a decade after the Settlement Agreement.

Finally, Marvel cannot establish detriment for equitable estoppel purposes. Marvel has received the full economic benefit of the Works' twenty-eight year renewal term. Even if a jury concludes that Simon is the Works' author and can therefore terminate Marvel's copyright in the Works, Marvel can continue to exploit every Captain America property created prior to the effective date of termination. *See Mills Music*, 469 U.S. at 173, 105 S.Ct. 638 (noting that pre-termination derivative works may continue to be utilized under the terms of the terminated grant).

Accordingly, Simon is not equitably estopped from raising his purported authorship of the Works in this action.

CONCLUSION

For the foregoing reasons, the judgment of the district court is RE-VERSED. We hereby REMAND this action to the district court for further proceedings not inconsistent with this opinion.

QUESTIONS

1. Suppose Simon had co-authored Captain America with an employee of Marvel. Would Simon have been entitled to terminate under sec. 304(a)? Under sec. 203?

2. Suppose Simon had worked with many free-lance collaborators, that he had written the stories, but that another person had outlined the illustrations, while another colored them in, and yet another supplied the lettering for each cell of the strips. Who would be entitled to terminate and how, under sec. 304(c)? Under sec. 203?

CHAPTER 5

FORMALITIES

B. 1976 ACT SOLUTIONS AS TO PUBLICATION AND NOTICE

Page 398: Add the following to Question 1:

See Getaped.Com, Inc. v. Cangemi, 188 F.Supp.2d 398 (S.D.N.Y. 2002)(granting access to an internet website is not simply a "display" but also involves the distribution of "copies" and thus is a "publication"; this enables copyright owner to secure statutory damages by timely registration—after infringement but within post-publication grace period—under § 504(c)).

Add the following to Question 2:

See also John G. Danielson, Inc. v. Winchester–Conant Properties, Inc., 322 F.3d 26 (1st Cir.2003)(court incorporates the limited-publication doctrine developed under the 1909 Act in interpreting "publication" under the 1976 Act).

C. DEPOSIT AND REGISTRATION

Page 408: Add to end of first paragraph under "2. Registration a. Procedure":

The deposit copy must in fact be a copy of the work in which copyright is claimed. See Coles v. Wonder, 283 F.3d 798 (6th Cir.2002)(1990 registration of 1982 song was invalid when the deposited copy was a "reconstruction" of the song from memory and without direct reference to the original; defendant is therefore awarded summary judgment, for lack of jurisdiction).

Page 411: Add to end of first full paragraph:

Although registration is a prerequisite to a suit for copyright infringement of a U.S. work, non-registration or improper registration does not prevent an action alleging violation of the § 1201 provisions prohibiting circumvention of technological measures that protect access to or prevent copying of a copyrighted work. See *I.M.S. Inquiry Mgmt. v. Berkshire Info. Sys.*, 307 F.Supp.2d 521 (S.D.N.Y. 2004). (The court's analysis of the merits of the anti-circumvention claim in that case appears *infra* this Supplement, Chapter 8.)

Page 411: Add after the citation in Question 2:

See also Well–Made Toy Mfg. Corp. v. Goffa Intern'l Corp., 354 F.3d 112 (2d Cir. 2003), in which the plaintiff's 20–inch doll was registered with the

Copyright Office, but its 48–inch doll (allegedly a derivative work) was not; the defendant copied from the latter, larger doll. Although the plaintiff argued that copying from a derivative work based on a registered work is a basis for jurisdiction, the court ruled otherwise, and dismissed because of lack of registration of the 48–inch derivative work.

Page 412: Add the following at the end of Question 3:

On rehearing, the court held as before, that the registration of a journal as a compilation does not operate as a valid registration of an included article whose copyright is owned by another—but abandoned its earlier view that the owner of a particular exclusive right, rather than of the copyright itself, is not a "copyright owner," Morris v. Business Concepts, Inc., 283 F.3d 502 (2d Cir.2002). See also Xoom, Inc. v. Imageline, Inc., 323 F.3d 279 (4th Cir.2003)(after registering a compilation of clip-art images, plaintiff sues for infringement of certain individual images and of the underlying computer program that generated the images; court upholds jurisdiction concerning former but not latter).

Add the following after Question 5:

6. Author in 2003 mails her registration application to the Copyright Office, along with the proper fee, but processing of the application is delayed by the Office for six months, as a result of the continuing concern regarding possible anthrax contamination. Because of her perceived need for an immediate injunction, Author commences an infringement lawsuit in the second month of waiting and before the Copyright Office issues a registration certificate. The defendant has moved to dismiss for lack of jurisdiction. How should the court rule, after carefully perusing sections 410 and 411 of the Copyright Act? Compare Strategy Source, Inc. v. Lee, 233 F.Supp.2d 1 (D.D.C.2002), with International Kitchen Exhaust Cleaning Ass'n v. Power Washers of North America, 81 F.Supp.2d 70 (D.D.C. 2000).

7. National Geographic Magazine is famous for its striking photographs taken by some of the world's great free-lance photographers. Assume that in 1960, it publishes an issue containing the work of five different photographers (from whom it has taken copyright assignments) and registers the copyright in the magazine at that time. In 1988, National Geographic registers the renewal copyright in the magazine, but no action is taken—by National Geographic or by the individual photographers—to renew the copyright in the various individual photographs. The five photographers, or their offspring, have consulted you today, to ascertain whether they still own valid copyrights. (One of the potential infringers is National Geographic itself, which has placed all of its old issues—both text and photographs—onto a CD-rom.) See Faulkner v. National Geographic Soc'y, 211 F.Supp.2d 450 (S.D.N.Y.2002). (Recall that for photographs first published in 1964 through 1977, there will not be any need for a "voluntary" renewal in order to continue the copyright, which will be renewed "automatically.")

CHAPTER 6

EXCLUSIVE RIGHTS UNDER COPYRIGHT

A. THE RIGHT TO REPRODUCE THE WORK IN COPIES AND PHONORECORDS

1. THE RIGHT TO MAKE COPIES

Page 432: Add to end of note on Circumstantial Proof of Copying:

Even if plaintiff can show access, and though the works have much in common, a finding of copying does not always follow. In CBS Broadcasting, Inc. v. ABC, 2003 WL 23407514 (S.D.N.Y.2003), for example, the court rejected the claim that defendant's television show "I'm a Celebrity: Get Me Out of Here!" was copied from plaintiff's "Survivor" "reality" show. Both shows placed participants in hostile surroundings, and progressively eliminated them. Where "Survivor" built tension, however, "Celebrity" relied on humor. The court found independent generation of the "Celebrity" show:

> Defendants cannot dispute that they had access to Survivor in terms of viewing the broadcast, both in the UK and the U.S. Similarly, the extensive press coverage of Survivor makes clear that members of the television and entertainment industry, including defendant, had to be aware of the program.

> However, I'm persuaded by defendants' evidence of Celebrity's independent creation ... that defendants had the substantive elements of the program that eventually became Celebrity ... before the U.S. version of Survivor aired in May of 2000.

> In this respect, plaintiffs have not established that defendants copied from Survivor those elements of Celebrity that were in the pre-[existing] proposals. Rather, the evidence shows that both parties combined standard, unprotectable elements of reality shows, game shows and other television genres, and used them separately to create the programs.

The court also held that even if copying were shown, defendant would have copied no more than elements typical to the genre of "reality" participant-elimination shows.

112

Page 437: Add after *Ringgold v. Black Entertainment Television* (before *Ticketmaster*):

Compare *Newton v. Diamond*, 349 F.3d 591 (9th Cir. 2003) (holding that a sound recording that sampled 3 notes of a recorded musical composition has taken only a *de minimis* portion of the musical composition; the sampler had obtained a license to copy from the sound recording). (For a discussion whether the court correctly identified the contents of the musical composition, see *supra*, this Supplement, Chapter 2).

Page 443: Add the following after the *Kalpakian* decision:

Satava's Sculpture

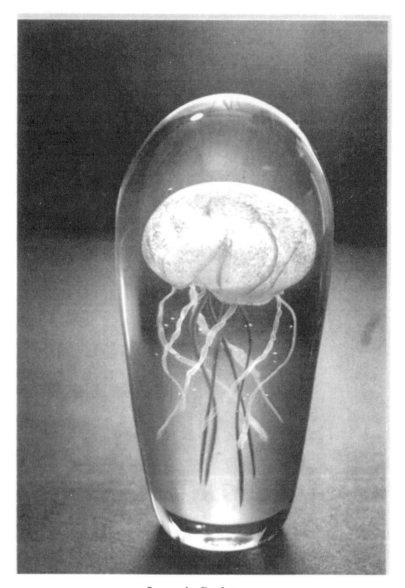

Lowry's Sculpture

[See Satava v. Lowry, 323 F.3d 805 (9th Cir.2003) (court finds no infringement of glass-in-glass sculpture of jellyfish, given their similarity to objects found in nature as well as the functional demands of creating such glass sculptures)].

Page 451: add to end of Question 1:

See also CBS Broadcasting, Inc. v. ABC, 2003 WL 23407514 (S.D.N.Y.2003) ("Survivor" may have created a genre of television shows, but "I'm a

Celebrity: Get Me Out of Here!''—if it copied at all–copied only stock devices, which it treated humorously, rather than the straightforward way in which "Survivor" presented them).

Page 489:   Insert the following after the *Kisch* case:

(Consult the Note *supra* in this Supplement at pp. 4–6. If you were to apply to the *Kisch* case the teachings of the Court of Appeals for the Ninth Circuit in the *Skyy Vodka* case, what would be the outcome?)

2.   The Right to Make Phonorecords

Page 507:   Add the following to the paragraph ending at the top of the page:

In Bridgeport Music, Inc. v. Dimension Films, 230 F.Supp.2d 830 (M.D.Tenn.2002), the court held that a three-note chord, played in a broken or "arpeggiated" fashion, can be sufficiently original to sustain copyright; but, even when repeatedly "looping" the chord through sampling on the defendant's recording, the taking is *de minimis* and not an infringement.

B.   The Right to Prepare Derivative Works

1.   The Scope of the Derivative Works Right

Page 522.   Add new Questions 6 and 7:

6.   Perceiving a market for motion pictures minus sex and/or violence and/or profanity, Sanifilms has set out to sanitize motion pictures and television programming. Sanifilms offers a variety of products. First, it purchases large quantities of videocassettes and edits each one to remove the offending scenes. It then resells the cassettes, as edited. Second, in a more high-tech offering, it sells Steven Clean 'Em, a device which, when hooked up to a DVD player will recognize sex and violence, and will allow the viewer to program the device to fast forward through such scenes. The program acts on the film as the film is being viewed, but does not store a copy in the viewer's DVD. Third, an enhanced version of Steven Clean 'Em is programmed to recognize obscene and profane vocabulary, and will, at the viewer's choice, substitute gentler locutions as the film or television program is running. Mort Mogul, a producer of racy screen fare, is distressed by these bowdlerizations, and asks you what means the copyright law might afford to prevent Sanifilms from purveying any of its products.

7.   WhenU.com distributes SaveNow, a program that resides on individual computer users' computer desktops. Entering a URL into the user's Internet browser can "trigger" the SaveNow software to deliver a "pop-up" advertisement, usually for a competitor of the business whose URL the user has entered. SaveNow will display that pop-up ad in a new window appearing on the user's computer screen. If a SaveNow user who has received a WhenU.com pop-up advertisement does not want to view the advertisement or the advertiser's website, the user can click on the visible portion of the window containing the website whose URL the user entered, and that website will move to the front of the screen display, with the pop-up ad moving behind the website window. Or, if the user recognizes that a different website has appeared on the screen, the user can close the pop-up website by clicking on its "x," or close, button. If the user clicks on the pop-up ad, the main browser window (containing the requested website) will be navigated to the website of the advertiser that was featured inside the pop-up advertisement. Businesses whose URL's WhenU uses as triggers for competitors' pop-up ads assert that the superimposition onto their websites of the pop-up ads creates a derivative work in violation of the copyright in the webpages. How should the court rule? See, e.g., 1–800 Contacts, Inc. v. WhenU.com, 309 F.Supp.2d 467 (S.D.N.Y. 2003); Wells Fargo & Co. v. WhenU.com, 293 F.Supp.2d 734 (E.D. Mich. 2003).

2.   MORAL RIGHTS

a.   FEDERAL LAW PROTECTION OF MORAL RIGHTS

Page 532:   Add this question after Question 2:

3.   Recall the "Sanifilms" question, on the previous page of this Supplement. Suppose you represent the Directors' Guild of America, which (although generally not speaking for owners of copyright) is even angrier than Mort Mogul. Can the Guild put a stop to Sanifilms' activities?

Page 538:   Add this question after Question 6:

7.   An insurance company agreed, in its policy with the owner of a building, to defend the owner against claims charging "the written publication of material that slanders or libels a person . . . or disparages a person's . . . goods, products or services." An earlier owner of the building had allowed an artist to paint a massive mural on the side of the building, but the present owner had covered the mural with an opaque whitewash, in order to facilitate the building's repair for a new owner. The artist brought an action against the present owner for a violation of his rights under the Visual Artists Rights Act. The owner has turned to its insurance company to defend the action, but the insurer has refused, claiming that the artist's lawsuit does not fall within the quoted language in the policy. Do you agree with the building owner or its insurance company? See Cort v. St. Paul Fire & Marine Ins. Cos., 311 F.3d 979 (9th Cir.2002).

Page 538: Add the following after Questions:

Pollara v. Seymour

344 F.3d 265 (2d Cir. 2003).

[The facts are summarized in Question 6 at page 537. The banner was prepared for a group named Gideon's Coalition, which advocates legal representation for the poor. It was placed behind a table at which Gideon representatives were to be seated for the purpose of soliciting funds for lobbying the state legislature for increased aid. The table was at a public plaza surrounded by New York State public buildings. The banner depicted a group of individuals approaching a lawyer while going passed closed doors labeled Public Defender, Legal Aid and Prisoners' Legal Services. At the direction of Gideon, artist Pollara painted the words: "Executive Budget Threatens Right to Counsel" and "Preserve the Right to Counsel—Now More Than Ever."]

■ JACOBS, CIRCUIT JUDGE:

* * * * VARA was enacted in 1990 as an amendment to the Copyright Act, to provide for the protection of the so-called "moral rights" of certain artists. *See Carter v. Helmsley-Spear ("Carter I"), 861 F.Supp. 303, 313 (S.D.N.Y.1994), vacated in part, rev'd in part on other grounds, Carter II, 71 F.3d 77 (2d Cir.1995).* "[M]oral rights afford protection for the author's personal, non-economic interests in receiving attribution for her work, and in preserving the work in the form in which it was created, even after its sale or licensing." *Id.* (quoting Jane C. Ginsburg, *Copyright in the 101st Congress: Commentary on the Visual Artists Rights Act and the Architectural Works Copyright Protection Act of 1990,* 14 Colum.-VLA J.L. & Arts 477, 478 (1990))....

Not every artist has rights under VARA, and not everything called "art" is protected by such rights. As the quoted text reflects, VARA confers rights only on artists who have produced works of "recognized stature," or whose "honor or reputation" is such that it would be prejudiced by the modification of a work. And VARA protects only things defined as "work[s] of visual art," *see id. § 106A(a)*—a definition that is "a critical underpinning of the limited scope of the [Act]." *H.R.Rep. No. 101–514,* at 1990 U.S.C.C.A.N. 6915, 6920–21; *see also id.* at 6919 (stating that the congressional debate "revealed a consensus that the bill's scope should be limited to certain carefully defined types of works and artists, and that if claims arising in other contexts are to be considered, they must be considered separately"); *id.* at 6921 (quoting Representative Edward Markey, cosponsor of the bill that became VARA, as stating that the "legislation covers only a very select group of artists").

Congress instructed courts to "use common sense and generally accepted standards of the artistic community in determining whether a particular work falls within the scope of the definition [of a 'work of visual art']," and explicitly stated that "whether a particular work falls within the definition should not depend on the medium or materials used." *Carter II,* 71 F.3d at 84 (quoting *H.R. Rep. 101–514,* 101st Cong., reprinted at 1990 U.S.C.C.A.N. 6915, 6921). Protection of a work under VARA will often depend, as it does here, upon the work's objective and evident purpose. VARA does not protect advertising, promotional, or utilitarian works, and does not protect works for hire, regardless of their artistic merit, their medium, or their value to the artist or the market. *See 17 U.S.C. § 101.* VARA may protect a sculpture that looks like a piece of furniture, but it

117

does not protect a piece of utilitarian furniture, whether or not it could arguably be called a sculpture. *See id.* Drawings and paintings are protected, but only if they do not advertise or promote. *Id.* Tellingly, only certain still photographs are protected, depending upon their intended use: Congress explicitly limited VARA's protection to works "intended for exhibition use only," as opposed to works intended for use in a publication or the photographer's photo album. *Id.* In each case, VARA's protections are limited depending on the purpose of the work.

The undisputed facts demonstrate that Pollara's banner falls outside the protections of the Act. The banner was created for the purpose of drawing attention to an information desk, as part of a lobbying effort, and the banner overtly promotes in word and picture a lobbying message. The banner was commissioned and paid for by Gideon, and Gideon determined in advance the banner's content, including its explicit textual message. Gideon's specification of content is insufficient on its own to make the banner a "work for hire," *see 17 U.S.C. § 101(1)* (defining a "work made for hire" for purposes of the Copyright Act as "a work prepared by an employee within the scope of his or her employment"); but the directions given by Gideon evidence the promotional and advertising purpose that bring the banner outside the scope of VARA. While Gideon's name did not appear on the banner, the banner's planned installation adjacent to Gideon's information table, and its explicit lobbying message leave no doubt as to the banner's purpose as promotional and advertising material for Gideon's lobbying effort.

Pollara argues that it is significant that the Banner was commissioned by a political advocacy organization, and that the banner had a political message. According to Pollara, the non-commercial nature of the banner distinguishes it from the sorts of commercial advertising materials that Congress intended to exclude from VARA's protections. Contrary to Pollara's position, however, the term "advertising" contains no such limitation. There is a lot of public interest advertising, including advertising for museums and art. There is political advertising. And "promotion" has an even broader exclusionary sweep. Congress chose to exclude from the scope of VARA all advertising and promotional materials, regardless of whether the thing being promoted or advertised was a commercial product or (as here) a particular advocacy group's lobbying efforts, and regardless of whether the work being used to promote or advertise might otherwise be called a painting, drawing, or sculpture. The banner in this case was created for the purpose of promoting and advertising, and we hold that it was therefore not a "work of visual art" subject to protection under VARA.[4]

---

4. The concurring opinion takes issue with this holding on the ground that "a work originally created for the purpose of promoting an event, product or cause" may "over time, achieve the status of a work of recognized stature...." Concurring Opinion, *in-* *fra,* at [2]. That may be so, but VARA only protects works of recognized stature that are "work[s] of visual art," *17 U.S.C. §§ 106A(a)(3), (d)(3),* and this term is defined to exclude promotional material, *see 17 U.S.C. § 101.* So even if (as the concurring

The district court politely found that the banner is "visually appealing and demonstrated a great deal of artistic ability and creativity," *Pollara II, 206 F.Supp.2d at 335,* but this finding, as the district court recognized, is beside the point. "It would be a dangerous undertaking for persons trained only in the law to constitute themselves final judges of the worth of pictorial illustrations, outside of the narrowest and most obvious limits." *Bleistein v. Donaldson Lithographing Co., 188 U.S. 239, 251, 23 S.Ct. 298, 47 L.Ed. 460 (1903).* We steer clear of an interpretation of VARA that would require courts to assess either the worth of a purported work of visual art, or the worth of the purpose for which the work was created. Congress chose to protect in VARA only a narrow subset of the many different forms and types of what can be called art, and expressly left unprotected works created for the primary purpose of promoting or advertising. Having concluded that the banner is such a work, our task is done.
* * * *

■ GLEESON, DISTRICT JUDGE, concurring.

I write separately because I would reach the same result as the majority, but for a different reason. Specifically, I would hold, as a matter of law, that Pollara's painting was not a work of recognized stature.

While the concept of "recognized stature" under VARA may give rise to some difficult cases, it seems clear that a work that has never been exhibited cannot, as a matter of law, be a work of recognized stature. The plain language of the provision suggests that the work must have attained a recognized stature by the time it is destroyed. As Professor Ginsburg has observed, "If a work has not been publicly displayed before its owner destroys it, how can the work be of 'recognized' stature?" Jane C. Ginsburg, *Copyright in the 101st Congress: Commentary on the Visual Artists Rights Act and the Architectural Works Copyright Protection Act of 1990,* 14 Colum.-VLA J.L. & Arts 477, 480 n. 19 (1990).

I respectfully disagree with the majority's ground for affirming—that Pollara's 300–square-foot mural was not, as a matter of law, a "work of visual art" within the meaning of *17 U.S.C. § 101.* VARA excludes from "work of visual art" status any "promotional ... *material.*" *17 U.S.C. § 101* (emphasis added). It does not state that all works that "promote" are not works of visual art. In short, I don't believe the exclusion supports the majority's statement that "Drawings and paintings are protected, but only if they do not advertise or promote." (Maj. Op. at 269.) That broad construction of the exclusion suggests that a painting commissioned to promote the Olympics, or a sculpture commissioned to promote AIDS awareness, could *never* receive protection under VARA. Also, there is

opinion posits) promotional material achieves recognized stature over time, the promotional material would not thereby become a "work of visual art." Similarly, Frank Gehry's Guggenheim Museum in Bilbao is a work, and it has recognized stature as art, but it could not be made to fit within the statute's definition of a "work of visual art." Buildings (as opposed to their design) are not subject to protection under the Copyright Act, *id.* at § 120(b), and are therefore excluded from VARA, *id.* at *§ 101* (defining "work of visual art" to exclude "any work not subject to copyright protection").

nothing in the statute that makes the purpose for which a work was created, or the manner in which it is first exhibited, dispositive in determining whether the work is "promotional material" at the time it is destroyed. Specifically, there is nothing that suggests that a work originally created for the purpose of promoting an event, product or cause could never, over time, achieve the status of a work of recognized stature, and thus be deserving of protection under VARA.

Accordingly, I believe that the promotional aspect of Pollara's mural creates, at most, a potential fact question as to whether the work was a "work of visual art" protected by VARA. That the impetus for the mural was to promote the Gideon Coalition's cause should no doubt be a factor in the determination whether the mural was merely promotional material. So should the fact that the Gideon Coalition supplied some text for the mural. The rest of the standard, *i.e.*, precisely how a factfinder should distinguish between a "work of visual art" and mere "promotional material," need not be decided here because the case can be so readily disposed of on other grounds.

QUESTION

Do you agree with the majority or concurring opinion with respect to the "promotional" nature of the Gideon banner? Do you agree with the concurring opinion that the banner could not, as a matter of law, be a "work of recognized stature"?

Page 543: Insert the following decision:

Phillips v. Pembroke Real Estate, Inc.

288 F.Supp.2d 89 (D. Mass. 2003).

■ PATTI B. SARIS, DISTRICT JUDGE.

INTRODUCTION

This case raises novel and important issues about the rights of artists under federal and state law to prevent the modification or destruction of their works of visual art. Plaintiff David Phillips, a well known sculptor, brings this action pursuant to the Visual Artists Rights Act, 17 U.S.C. § 106A (1990) ("VARA"), and the Massachusetts Art Preservation Act, Mass. Gen. Laws Ann. ch. 231, § 85S (1984) ("MAPA"). He seeks a preliminary injunction to prevent Defendant Pembroke Real Estate, Inc. from modifying Eastport Park, which Phillips helped design, and from altering his sculptures, which were specifically created for that public park.

The Court held an evidentiary hearing in which the Plaintiff Phillips; Ricardo Barreto, the Executive Director of the Urban Arts Institute at the Massachusetts College of Art; Konstantine Krekis, the Director of the Architect Resource Group at Pembroke, an arm of Fidelity Investments; and Michael Shaughnessy, a rigger and engineer, testified. The Court also took two views of the property.

The Court holds that federal law provides no protection for the placement of site-specific sculpture. However, under the broader protections of state law, Plaintiff has demonstrated a likelihood of success in showing that he has the right to prevent the alteration of his site-specific sculptures that would result from moving them to another location. There is no provision in the written contract between the artist and the purchaser waiving this right.

Based on the testimony, the views, and the submissions, the Court orders Pembroke not to destroy, alter, modify or move Phillips' sculpture along the northwest-southeast axis of the Park.

I. FACTUAL BACKGROUND

A. The Park

Eastport Park, in the South Boston Waterfront District of Boston, is located across from Boston Harbor. It is a public sculpture park with a nautical theme. Plaintiff's sculptures include a large, abstract sculpture entitled "Chords," a large bronze seashell, bronze hermit crabs, frogs and shrimp, and a bronze medallion with Zodiac signs crowning an S-shaped circular path. Three others also created art located in the Park. Judy McKie crafted bronze benches in the shape of fish; landscape architect Craig Halvorson (the designer of the park at Post Office Square) designed a pergola (an arbor on the new Congress Street side); and Japanese sculptor Susumu Shingu constructed towering kinetic sculptures. The Park contains large granite boulders and the paths are inlaid with granite paving stones. The plantings are scrubby to simulate a marine environment.

Pembroke, a Fidelity Investments company, leases the land upon which the Park is built from the Massachusetts Port Authority ("Massport"), which must approve any changes to the design of the Park. The Boston Redevelopment Authority ("BRA") must also approve changes. The Park must be open to the public free of charge 24 hours a day. According to the Boston Business Journal, this is the only privately-managed public park in the City of Boston.

The Park is roughly rectangular in area, and extends to the sidewalks running along Seaport Boulevard on the north, New Congress Street on the south, and D Street on the east side. The World Trade Center East Office building stands on the west side. The Park is currently in the midst of extensive construction known locally as "The Big Dig," which includes the development of new office buildings and the construction of a new convention center. Another park is being developed by Massport across D Street.

B. The Artist

Over the past twenty years, Phillips has earned numerous commissions for sculptures at universities, private companies and public spaces in Massachusetts, Connecticut, Washington, D.C., New York, Utah, Kofu and Tokyo, Japan, and Colombia, South America. His work is exhibited in galleries and museums in New York City, Maine, and elsewhere. He works primarily with stone and bronze forms that he integrates with the environment. In many sculptures, Phillips incorporates the designs of the stones

121

into the landscape. For example, in one private project in Ogunquit, Maine, he sought to extend the band of the rock into a bronze tributary in the ground that glistened in the sun like a nearby stream. Phillips frequently uses a spiral motif. Many of his works seek to seamlessly merge metals or polished stone with aged, naturally-shaped boulders. Some of his better-known local pieces include six large bronze frogs in the Boston Common Frog Pond Playground, sculpture at the Porter Square Subway Station in Cambridge, the "Water Strider Fountain" at the Christian Science Reflection Pond, and a sculpture at Quincy Square near Harvard Square, Cambridge. He has been featured in art magazines, in both the United States and Japan.

Phillips enjoys a national reputation and is particularly well known for his work in creating sculpture which is site-specific, meaning that it depends on the surrounding landscape. His 1993 promotional brochure describes his artistic vision: "It is Phillips' inherent reverence for natural beauty in this ecologically ravaged world that influences all his decisions, particularly when he recontextualizes a stone by replacing part of its form with a man-made surrogate or when he gracefully applies typical landscaping and architectural materials along with natural stone and traditional art materials into new equations of form and function."

C. Phillips' Work at the Park

Pembroke hired Phillips in 1999 to work on the Park in conjunction with the development of the World Trade Center East office building, which stands adjacent to the Park. Phillips' responsibilities were manifold. Phillips worked closely with Craig Halvorson, the renowned landscape architect, on the design of the Park. He had an oral agreement with Halvorson (but not Pembroke) to assist in the work at the design meetings as the artist who worked with the landscape specialists. For example, he helped design the repeated spirals on the axis running from the northwest corner towards the southeast.

In August of 1999, Pembroke and Phillips executed the Eastport Park Artwork Agreement, pursuant to which Phillips was responsible for creating approximately twenty-seven (27) sculptures for placement in the Park. They included fifteen (15) abstract sculptures, and twelve (12) realistic bronze sculptures of crabs, shrimp, and frogs. Pursuant to the East Port park Stonework Agreement with Pembroke executed in June of 1999, Phillips also selected and directed the placement of mosaic paving stones, granite feature strips, and rough stone walls at the base of the sculpture "Chords." He personally carved finished granite for "Chords," the centerpiece of the Park. Phillips worked with a stone mason to select and place the rough quarried stone covered with lichen from Maine. He also designed the granite path culminating in the bronze medallion, the "outpost sculptures," and the free flowing curve motifs. He specially selected the large granite stones that he used as part of his sculptures to reflect the large granite stones along Boston Harbor.

Phillips believes that his sculptures and related stone work are works of visual art specifically designed for Eastport Park and are meaningful only if they remain in Eastport Park.

D.   Re–Design of the Park

The Park was completed in the spring of 2000. In 2001, Pembroke decided to make certain changes to the Park, and hired London landscape artist Elizabeth Banks to direct the changes. Konstantine Krekis, the director of the Architectural Resource Group within Pembroke, was part of the original design team. Pembroke believed there were conceptual problems with the Park and wanted substantially more plants for better shade and simplified walkways. It also wanted to replace the river rock, which turned out to be a maintenance problem. Krekis summed up: "The aesthetic vision of the Park has changed." ...

Pembroke intends to donate, relocate or store Phillips' art. It hired a rigger and engineer to dismantle and store the art.

E.   Site–Specific Art

... [T]oday the concept of "site specificity" is the "rallying cry" of public artists who seek to create a piece that derives enhanced meaning from its environment. Much of modern sculpture does not exist separate from its context, but rather integrates its context with the work to form, ideally, a seamless whole.

Plaintiff's experts state that for site-specific art, the location of the work is a constituent element of the work. Daniel Ranalli, Professor of Art History and Director of the Graduate Program in Arts Administration at Boston University, stated: "Beginning at least with the last third of the 20th century, and continuing through the present, the notion of *sculpture* has undergone a radical redefinition. In essence, sculpture has come off its pedestal, functioning in the space in and around its site, and playing an integral role in *defining* that space."

Under this approach, because the location defines the art, site-specific sculpture is destroyed if it is moved from the site.... "This view contrasts with so-called 'plop-art' where a separately conceived art object is simply placed in a space." ...

[Plaintiff's expert] Barreto became aware of Phillips' work a decade ago from catalogs and Phillips' work in Porter Square. He believes that Phillips is "one of the most important artists in this area" and that he has a "national reputation." He testified that Phillips' art work in Eastport Park was discussed at a national meeting of the Public Art Network held in Portland, Oregon. According to Barreto, Phillips' sculptures at the Park form an integrated design that comprises a coherent whole. Phillips' placement of the paying stones around the "Chords" sculpture, the plinth (the raised platform) on which "Chords" sits; and the continuous line of bronze integrates the many pieces of "Chords." He also believes that the "repeated spirals" in the Park are a unifying design element throughout the Park, and teaches that the Park itself is a sculpture of the environment. However, he concedes that a park does not meet the traditional

123

definition of sculpture that involves an object with "formal elements" (although he notes that he instructs his students that a park like this is sculpture). Barreto testified that if Phillips' sculpture is moved, it will have an impact on his reputation as an artist because he will no longer have an important piece in an important location: his art will be "in exile."

III. ANALYSIS

. . .

B. Likelihood of Success

1. VARA

. . .

b. "Work of visual art"

The first question is whether Phillips' twenty-seven (27) sculptures constitute a single work of visual art or instead are discrete works of art that must be treated separately under VARA. A related issue is whether the Park as a whole should be treated as a work of visual art. While Defendant argues that the entire Park, and certain stone design elements within the Park, are not works of visual art under VARA, it does not dispute that the twenty-seven (27) abstract and realistic sculptures created by Phillips, including the bronze star chart medallion and "Chords," are sculptures within the meaning of 17 U.S.C. § 101.

Phillips takes the position that his artwork extends beyond these individual sculptures and includes the finished and rough-hewn granite and stone pavings and the stone walls that he designed and placed, including the "Chords" path and the medallion path (the "Stone Elements"). He also contends that all of his sculptures form one integrated, interrelated work of visual art. To place the sculptural elements in different alignments relative to one another, Plaintiff believes, would destroy sight lines and alter the deliberately-crafted spatial relationships among the paths, granite walls, and individual pieces of sculpture.

Congress has provided a "narrow definition of works of visual art." Carter II, 71 F.3d at 84. Legislative history indicates the reason Congress did so was to avoid conflict with other aspects of the Copyright Act, specifically sections applicable to movies and videos. See H.R. Rep. No. 101–514, at 9.

Despite the narrow definition, courts have held that works composed of a variety of pieces and in a variety of media may still constitute one work of "visual art" under VARA. Carter II, 71 F.3d at 83–84 (affirming district court holding that entire lobby of a building, composed of many separate sculptural and applied art elements, was a "single, indivisible whole" meeting the definition of "work of art" in VARA, but reversing on other grounds); English v. BFC & R East 11th St. LLC, 1997 U.S. Dist. LEXIS 19137, 1997 WL 746444, *3 (S.D.N.Y. 1997) (noting that Carter II offered support for contention that entire garden was a single work of visual art under VARA, but holding that VARA was inapplicable to artwork illegally placed on property); Pavia v. 1120 Ave. of the Americas Assoc., 901 F.Supp. 620, 627–28 (S.D.N.Y. 1995) (denying defendant's motion to dismiss on the grounds that plaintiff could establish that four separate bronze forms that had been separated by defendants were one "work of art").

The legislative history instructs courts to "use common sense and generally accepted standards of the artistic community in determining whether a particular work falls within the scope of the definition. Artists may work in a variety of media, and use any number of materials in creating their works. Therefore, whether a particular work falls within the definition should not depend on the medium or materials used." H.R. Rep. No. 101–514, at 6.

With this caselaw in mind, the Court finds that Plaintiff has a likelihood of proving that the sculptures along the northwest to southeast axis of the Park, including "Chords" and the medallion sculpture, as well as the Stone Elements, are one integrated "work of visual art." It begins with a spiral in the northwest corner along Seaport Boulevard, includes Plaintiff's "Chords" sculpture, and continues along a spiral path of mosaic paving stone, culminating in the bronze medallion. In determining that the sculptures along this axis, as well as the related Stone Elements, are one work of visual art, the Court relies on the integrated marine theme and recurring spirals, as well as the use of marine granite boulders and pavers. However, the remainder of the sculptures (like the six-foot bronze conch shell and miscellaneous whimsical sea creatures) that do not lie along the axis are not part of the same work of visual art. While these sculptures share the marine theme, the Court finds these pieces are individual free-standing pieces of sculpture, which are not integrated into the other pieces by spirals or granite.

One novel issue is whether a park can be a "work of visual art" under VARA. Phillips contends that the Eastport Park as a whole is one large integrated piece of "sculpture." He proclaims: "If any of Phillips' sculptures or any of the features of the Park are removed, there will be modification of Phillips' concept, and it will have an impact on the rest of his work. If this means that Eastport Park must be declared to be an inviolate work of art, then so be it."

The Court rejects Plaintiff's argument that the Park as a whole is a work of visual art. As Professor Barreto conceded, a park does not fit within the traditional definition of sculpture, and the definitions in VARA are to be construed narrowly. Conceivably, a sculptor could design a sculpture garden that includes multiple inter-related sculptural elements that form an integrated work of visual art. See, e.g., English v. BFC & R East 11th Street LLC, 1997 U.S. Dist. LEXIS 19137, 1997 WL 746444 at *3 (suggesting that the entire garden was a single work of art under VARA). However, here, many elements in the Park were not created by Phillips. These include the pergola, three bronze benches, several chairs, and two kinetic sculptures. Substantial areas of the Park are unrelated to Phillips' sculpture and not integrated with it (for example, the area adjacent to the pergola or the area near the office building). Phillips was also not responsible for the plantings or any of the landscape architecture apart from the stone elements. Mr. Halvorson is himself a renowned landscape architect, and he was the one hired to design the Park. As Mr. Halvorson points out, Phillips contributed ideas about the artistic vision of his artwork for the Park, and suggestions about how the Park design could provide a suitable setting and context for his work. While Phillips certainly assisted in designing the stone elements in the paths and walls and in placing his own sculptures, the Park as a whole is not an integrated work of art.

Therefore, I conclude that Plaintiff has not established a likelihood of success in proving that this Park as a whole is a work of visual art under VARA.

c. "Public Presentation" Exclusion

Plaintiff also argues that his work is so site-specific that moving it would be an intentional destruction or modification under VARA. Taking the sculpture from its current location and locating it on a private campus in Rhode Island not near the ocean, as Defendant has offered to do, would be like painting over the background landscape in the Mona Lisa.

Defendant contends that the "public presentation" exclusion in § 106A(c)(2) permits it to move Plaintiff's sculptures from their current placement to another, just as the statute would not prevent a curator from moving the Mona Lisa from one wall in the Louvre to another.

Section 106A(c)(2) has been interpreted to exclude from VARA's protection "site-specific" works, works that would be modified if they were moved. See Board of Managers of SOHO Int'l Arts Condo. v. City of New York, 2003 U.S. Dist. LEXIS 10221, 2003 WL 21403333, *10 (S.D.N.Y. 2003) (stating that the point of VARA "is not . . . to preserve a work of visual art *where* it is, but rather to preserve the work *as* it is"); aff'd on recons., Board of Managers of SOHO Int'l Arts Condo. v. City of New York, 2003 U.S. Dist. LEXIS 13201, 2003 WL 21767653, *3 (S.D.N.Y. 2003) ("Nowhere in VARA does the statute make any legal distinction between site-specific or free-standing works" in regards to "site-specific" art).

Plaintiff responds that VARA provides protection for a work of visual art that "has been incorporated in or made part of a building in such a way that removing the work from the building will cause the destruction, distortion, mutilation, or other modification of the work as described in section 106A(a) (3)," 17 U.S.C. § 113(d), and that art attached to real property that cannot be removed without destruction should have similar protection. Defendant's legal argument is more persuasive because it is rooted in the plain language of the exclusion in § 106A(c)(2) as well as the statute's legislative history. "Generally, the removal of a work from a specific location comes within the [presentation] exclusion because the location is a matter of presentation." H.R. Rep. No. 101–514, at 12. It is notable that the public presentation exception was crafted after the widely-publicized dispute between the General Services Administration and the artist Richard Serra over the removal of Serra's "site-specific" piece "Tilted Arc." See Serra v. United States Gen' 1 Serv. Admin., 847 F.2d

1045 (2d Cir. 1988) (rejecting Serra's argument that the removal of a government-owned artwork from federal property violates the free expression and due process rights of the artist). Despite "le droit moral," Congress adhered to "chacun a son gout" (each one to his taste) by declining to require the public presentation of art.

I conclude that an artist has no right to the placement or public presentation of his sculpture under the exception in § 106A(c)(2). Defendant is not obligated to display the works in the Park, as VARA provides no protection for a change in placement or presentation. However, under VARA, Defendant is under an obligation not to alter, modify or destroy the "works of visual art" as I have defined them.

2. MAPA

a. The Statute

The rarely-litigated Massachusetts Art Preservation Act ("MAPA") provides broader protection to artists than the federal statute. In MAPA, Mass. Gen. Laws Ann. ch. 231, § 85S(a) (1984), the Massachusetts legislature found:

> The physical alteration or destruction of fine art, which is an expression of the artist's personality, is detrimental to the artist's reputation, and artists therefore have an interest in protecting their works of fine art against such alteration or destruction; and that there is also a public interest in preserving the integrity of cultural and artistic creations.

"Fine art" is defined to mean "any original work of visual or graphic art of any media which shall include, but not limited to, any painting, print, drawing, sculpture, craft object, photograph, audio or video tape, film, hologram, or any combination thereof, of recognized quality." Section 85S(c) provides:

> No person, except an artist who owns or possesses a work of fine art which the artist has created, shall intentionally commit, or authorize the intentional commission of any physical defacement, mutilation, alteration, or destruction of a work of fine art. As used in this section, intentional physical defacement, mutilation, alteration, or destruction includes any such action taken deliberately or through gross negligence.

Section 85S(f) provides:

> In determining whether a work of fine art is of recognized quality, the court shall rely on the opinions of artists, art dealers, collectors of fine art, curators of art museums, restorers and conservators of fine art and other persons involved with the creation or marketing of fine art.

This right continues until the fiftieth anniversary of the death of the artist, and cannot be waived except by a written instrument signed by the artist. § 85S(g).

MAPA defines an artist to be "the natural person who actually creates a work of fine art but not to include such art as is created by an employee within the scope of his employment." § 85S(b). "In case of a joint creation of a work of art, each joint creator shall have the rights of an artist with respect to the work of fine art as a whole." Id.

The Act deals separately with "fine art [that] cannot be removed from a building without a substantial physical defacement, mutilation, alteration or destruction of such work." § 85S(h). As to these works, the rights and duties created under the Act are forfeited, "unless expressly reserved by an instrument in writing signed by the owner of such building and property recorded prior to the installation of such art." Id.

The Supreme Judicial Court of Massachusetts explained in Moakley v. Eastwick, 423 Mass. 52, 666 N.E.2d 505 (1996), the only reported decision construing the statute, that MAPA followed the lead of similar legislation in California and New York "in attempting to graft onto a generally inhospitable common law tradition the civil law concept of *droit moral* whereby a creative artist retains certain inalienable rights with respect to his or her creation before and after publication, display or sale." Id. at 509 (citing Vance R. Koven, Observations on the Massachusetts Art Preservation Act, 71 Mass. L. Rev. 101, 101 (1986)). To accomplish its ends, MAPA protects both an artist's "Right of Integrity," an artist's right not to have his or her creations altered, and an artist's "Right of Paternity," an artist's right to claim or disclaim authorship of a work of art. Id. at 508. MAPA is modeled on the California Art Preservation Act, Cal. Civ. Code § 987, enacted in 1979. Id.

b.   The Park

Defendant argues that the Park does not meet the definition of a work of "fine art." The definition of "fine art" in MAPA is significantly more expansive than the definition of "work of visual art" in VARA because it is not limited to the specific enumerated types of art (i.e., sculpture) and expressly includes art forms not covered by VARA, like audiotapes, videotapes, holograms, and films. Given the elasticity of the definition of "fine art," the Court concludes that a "park" can be a work of "visual art" under the statute.

However, Plaintiff has not demonstrated a likelihood of success in showing that the Park itself (as opposed to the sculptures in the Park) is of "recognized quality" as a work of "fine art." Plaintiff's experts testified primarily to the aesthetic merits of the sculptures within the Park and Phillips' reputation as an artist. Although Mr. Halvorson is a renowned landscape architect, and two experts (Barreto, Driscoll) believe the park design has meritorious quality, there is only conclusory evidence as to whether the quality of the Park design itself has been "recognized" by a cross-section of the artistic community or by artistic experts in the field. Cf. Martin, 192 F.3d at 612 (setting forth two-tiered test for "recognized stature" under VARA).

c.   Site–Specificity

Again, the predominant issue is whether the Massachusetts statute protects the placement of site-specific art. The analysis starts with the statutory language. MAPA defines fine art to include any "original work of visual or graphic art of any media." § 85S(b). One dictionary definition of "medium" is "the material or technique with which an artist works." Random House at 843. Under this definition, the question then becomes whether the location can be the medium with which the artist works.

The undisputed expert testimony is that in site-specific sculpture, the artist incorporates the environment as one of the media with which he works. I find that Phillips' sculpture has a marine theme that integrates the large granite stones of the Park with his sculptures and the granite sea walls of Boston Harbor into one inter-related visual work of art. Therefore, Phillips used the harborside location at Eastport Park as one medium of his art. To move Phillips' integrated work of visual art (i.e., the sculptures, boulders, and granite paths along the axis, which I described in the VARA discussion) to another location (particularly a non-marine one) would be to alter it physically.

Unlike VARA, MAPA contains no provision like the "public presenta-tion" exclusion, which exempts modifications from a change in placement from its protections. The statute does provide diminished protection for works of art that cannot be removed from a building without damaging the works, Mass. Gen. Laws Ann. ch. 231, § 85S(h)(1), but it does not preclude protection of art that cannot be removed from real estate without physical alteration. See Koven, 71 Mass. L. Rev. 101 at 108, n. 51 (nothing that "the statute actually only speaks to artwork attached to the building itself, thus leaving out of these special provisions artwork on the grounds but free-standing"). In contrast, the California Art Preservation Act, which is described as the model for MAPA, provides: "If a work of fine art cannot be removed from real property without substantial physical defacement, muti-lation, alteration, or destruction of such work, no action to preserve the integrity of the work of fine art may be brought under this section."[4] Cal. Civ. Code § 989(e). The failure to provide a parallel provision is a strong indication of legislative intent. See Moakley, 666 N.E.2d at 510 (interpret-ing failure of MAPA to provide for retrospectivity, as was done by statutes in California and other jurisdictions, as one indicator of legislative intent).

Given the broad definitions of "fine art" in the statute, the undisputed expert testimony that for site-specific art, the location of a piece is a constituent element of the art, and the absence of a "public presentation" exclusion in MAPA, the Plaintiff has a reasonable likelihood of success on this issue of first impression. Thus, I find that the environment of Phillips' integrated sculpture along the axis of the Park is a critical element of those works, and changing the location of the sculpture constitutes an alteration under § 85S(b) and § 85S(c).

d. Recognized Quality

Defendant does not dispute that the work of visual art is of recognized quality. Plaintiff submits affidavits from Professor Driscoll and Professor

---

4. It should also be noted that a sepa-rate California statute, intended to encourage art in public buildings, explicitly excludes "environmental landscaping placed about a state building" from its broad definition of "work of art." West's Ann. Cal. Gov. Code § 15813.1 (2003); Botello v. Shell Oil Co., 229 Cal. App. 3d 1130, 1137, 280 Cal. Rptr. 535 (Cal. Ct. App. 1991) (noting apparent intent of statute).

Ranalli, and the testimony of Mr. Barreto. In addition, Plaintiff has submitted various articles about the artwork: Pembroke Real Estate and the Drew Company Hold Grand Opening of World Trade Center East on South Boston Waterfront, High Profile Monthly, October–November 2000, at 32 (Ex. 17) (describing Eastport Park as a "sculpture Park featuring permanent exhibits by renowned artists"); Cambridge Arts Council, David Phillips: Quincy Square, at www.cambridgema.gov/ [approximately] CAC/public_art_tour/map_05_06.html (accessed by party on September 5, 2003) (Ex. 11) ("David Phillips is well known for his public sculpture and collaborating with landscape architects"); Linda Goodspeed, Artwork Finds a Place to Thrive in the Seaport Area, Boston Bus. J., Oct. 13–19, 2000 (page unavailable). I find that Plaintiff's has established a likelihood of success in proving that his sculptures are of "recognized quality."

3. First Amendment

Defendant makes an interesting but scantily-briefed claim that were this Court to find that Defendant must keep Phillips' artwork on its property, such action would violate Defendant's First Amendment right to be free from compelled artistic expression.

. . .

Defendant relies on Hurley v. Irish–American Gay, Lesbian & Bisexual Group of Boston, 515 U.S. 557, 574–75, 132 L. Ed. 2d 487, 115 S. Ct. 2338 (1995), a case involving the rights of a parade not to include certain groups, and Wooley v. Maynard, 430 U.S. 705, 713, 51 L. Ed. 2d 752, 97 S. Ct. 1428 (1977), a case involving a person's right not to display a state motto on his license plate, for the proposition that the First Amendment protects the right to be free from compelled expression.

Defendant's First Amendment claim fails for four reasons. First, Defendant, a highly sophisticated real estate development firm, agreed to place Plaintiff's sculpture in a public park and did not obtain a written waiver of MAPA rights—as it easily could have done under the law. Therefore, this was not compelled, but invited artistic expression. See Pruneyard Shopping Center v. Robins, 447 U.S. 74, 85–88, 64 L. Ed. 2d 741, 100 S. Ct. 2035 (1980) (rejecting a forced association claim by a shopping center into which the public was invited).

Second, Defendant has a diminished claim to First Amendment protection because it agreed to manage a public park and it voluntarily agreed that it would not alter the site without the permission of numerous government agencies, including Massport and the BRA. An owner of purely private property would have a stronger First Amendment interest in his own artistic expression—and the right to change his mind about artistic merit after purchasing art.

Third, Defendant has a right to regulate the time, place and manner of artistic expression in its park so long as its regulation is not content-based. Here, though, there is persuasive evidence that Defendant intended to eliminate Plaintiff's artwork because he exercised his First Amendment rights in bringing this action. See Serra, 847 F.2d at 1049–51 (noting right of government to place time, manner, and place restrictions on display of artwork); Mt. Healthy City School Dist. Bd. of Educ. v. Doyle, 429 U.S. 274, 284, 50 L.Ed.2d 471, 97 S.Ct. 568 (1977) (noting that even though teacher could have been discharged "for no reason whatsoever," teacher could establish right to reinstatement if discharge occurred because of exercise of constitutionally-protected First Amendment rights) . . .

Fourth, even if MAPA burdens protected speech, it serves a compelling state interest. MAPA states in its preamble that there is "a public interest in preserving the integrity of cultural and artistic creations." Mass. Gen. Laws Ann. ch. 231, § 85S(a). The legislative history to VARA indicates that the *droit moral* are also necessary to encourage artists in their arduous and often financially-unremunerative work by recognizing its special contribution to society. H.R. Rep. 101–514, at 2. MAPA is narrowly tailored in that parties can easily opt-out of its provisions through a contractual waiver. There has been no argument by Pembroke that MAPA is not a narrowly tailored means of serving this compelling state interest.

C.   Irreparable Injury

Phillips has demonstrated that he would suffer irreparable injury to his reputation if the construction proceeds. It is true that Mr. Shaughnessy—the skilled mover of the Tyrannosaurus Rex and the "Quest for Immortality: Treasures of Ancient Egypt" exhibit at the Boston Museum of Science—could store the art piece somewhere in South Boston without injuring it. However, the loss of Mr. Phillips' reputation is not quantifiable. "If the plaintiff suffers a substantial injury that is not accurately measurable or adequately compensable by money damages, irreparable harm is a natural sequel." Ross–Simons of Warwick, Inc. v. Baccarat, Inc., 102 F.3d 12, 19 (1st Cir. 1996).

D.   Balance of Hardships

At the outset of this litigation, Defendant stated that if it were not able to begin construction in the fall so that it could complete the renovations of the Park in spring 2004, it would have to pay an additional $120,000 in construction costs. Subsequent to that time, Defendant changed its plans for the Park, because of Plaintiff's assertion of his rights under VARA and MAPA. Pembroke's last-minute about-face required new approvals from the BRA and Massport and caused much of the delay in the court proceedings. The Court permitted the plantings and other Park modifications that did not affect Plaintiff's sculptures (i.e., the destruction of the pergola). No evidence has been presented as to any substantial costs that would result from delaying the remaining construction until next spring. The balance of hardships weighs in the Plaintiff's favor.

E.   Public Interest

Massachusetts noted in MAPA that there is "a public interest in preserving the integrity of cultural and artistic creations." Mass. Gen.

Laws Ann. ch. 231, § 85S § (a). This factor is not disputed by the Defendant.

. . .

ORDER

Defendant shall not alter, destroy, move or remove any of the sculptures along the northeast—southwest axis of the Park until the conclusion of this litigation or further order of the Court. With respect to the other sculptures, Defendant may move the sculptures but shall not destroy or alter them.

Page 543: Add the following after Question:

Postscript: Moral Right of Attribution

The materials on moral rights in this Casebook principally concern the moral right of "integrity," particularly as the derivative works right has, to some extent, afforded a U.S. law analog. The Lanham Act has also served as an important source of moral(ish) rights, not only with respect to the right of integrity, but also regarding the right to be recognized as the work's author, the attribution right. At least, some authors and performers had successfully invoked the Lanham Act to remedy the passing off of another's work as the author's, see, e.g., *King v. Innovation Books*, 976 F.2d 824 (2d Cir.1992) (over-attribution of motion picture to Stephen King), as well as the "reverse passing off" of the author's work by another as her own (i.e., plagiarism), see, e.g., *Smith v. Montoro*, 648 F.2d 602 (9th Cir.1981) (removal of actor's name from screen credits and substitution of another's). The Supreme Court's recent decision in *Dastar v. Twentieth Century Fox*, at page 1 of this supplement, however, appears to rule out Lanham Act assertions that miscrediting authorship is a "false designation of origin." See Williams v. UMG Recordings, Inc., 281 F.Supp.2d 1177 (C.D. Cal. 2003). The *Dastar* Court left open the possible recourse to other provisions of the Lanham Act, including "misrepresentation of the characteristics or qualities" of a product in "commercial advertising or promotion." Will such a claim redress the same acts as "false designation of origin?" What other sources of attribution rights might U.S. law afford? Can the U.S. still claim to be in compliance with its obligation under the Berne Convention to protect rights of attribution and integrity?

Decisions subsequent to *Dastar* tend to bear out some of the more ominous predictions about that ruling's impact. For example, in Williams v. UMG, 281 F.Supp.2d 1177 (C.D. Cal. 2003), the court rejected the Lanham Act claim of a director and screenwriter who asserted that his name had been wrongfully omitted from the film's credits. The court held that *Dastar* had effectively overruled the Ninth Circuit's "reverse passing off" precedents, and now "precludes plaintiff's Lanham Act claim." The court also declined to limit *Dastar*'s impact to Lanham Act claims involving copyright-expired or uncopyrighted works. See also Keane v. Fox, 297 F.Supp.2d 921 (S.D. Tex. 2004) (rejecting idea submission claim: "The Lanham Act does not create a cause of action for 'plagiarism,' that is, 'the use of otherwise unprotected works and inventions without attribution.' '')

C. The Right to Distribute

Page 544: Insert the following at the end of the textual Note:

See also Ortiz–Gonzalez v. Fonovisa, 277 F.3d 59 (1st Cir.2002)(even in the absence of infringement judgment against record manufacturer, the distributor of recordings can be held liable for unauthorized distribution of the recordings to the public; such distribution is a direct infringement in itself, not an act of contributory or vicarious infringement).

Page 548: Add to Question 2:

See Adobe Systems, Inc. v. Stargate Software Inc., 216 F.Supp.2d 1051 (N.D.Cal.2002), in which Adobe purports to "license" educational software to corporations which retransfer to others for ultimate acquisition by educational institutions or their students; the software is packaged with material containing references sometimes to "license" and sometimes to "purchase," along with restrictions on commercial re-sale. The defendant Stargate lawfully acquires the software and then re-sells it, invoking the first-sale doctrine. Does that doctrine apply on these facts?

D. Rights of Public Performance and Display

3. Performing Rights Societies

Page 576: Add the following to the Note ending at the top of the page:

The antitrust decrees and the judicial rate-setting apparatus have recently come into play in the internet context. In United States v. Broadcast Music, Inc., 316 F.3d 189 (2d Cir.2003), the Court of Appeals for the Second Circuit heard its first rate-setting case under the BMI consent decree. There, BMI on behalf of its songwriters and publishers was in a dispute about rates to be paid by MusicChoice, which supplies copyrighted music to "wholesalers" who then retransmit the music—through cable or satellite or over the internet—to private customers. The court of appeals concluded that "fair market value"—as measured by what customers pay to cable-satellite-internet providers of subscription music services—should be the basis for setting the license fees paid by MusicChoice to BMI.

4. The Right of Public Display

Page 580, add new Question 2:

2. Recall the pop-up advertisements described in Question 7, part B.1, *supra* this Supplement. Would a claim that superimposition of the pop-up

133

ads violates the public-display right of the website over which the pop-up ads appear fare any better? See U–Haul Int'l. v. WhenU.com, 279 F.Supp.2d 723 (E.D. Va. 2003).

5.   THE DIGITAL PERFORMANCE RIGHT IN SOUND RECORDINGS . . . AND ITS LIMITATIONS

Page 585:   Insert the following at the end of the textual Note:

The *Bonneville* decision was affirmed: 347 F.3d 485 (3d Cir.2003).

In July 2002, the Librarian of Congress, upon the recommendation of the Register of Copyrights, modified an earlier recommendation of a Copyright Arbitration Royalty Panel, in setting statutory compulsory-license royalty rates for the online streaming or webcasting of recorded music on the internet. The new rate—covering the period October 28, 1998 through December 31, 2002—was declared to be .07 cents per song per listener, both for internet-only webcasters and for radio broadcasters who simultaneously webcast. Certain smaller webcasters closed their businesses, claiming financial inability to pay the new rates. Congress moved quickly to address the issue, with the appropriate committees urging rate negotiations among the affected parties. An agreement was reached, which Congress promptly enacted into law, and President Bush signed the Small Webcaster Settlement Act on December 4, 2002. (P.L. 107–321) The statute provides that noncommercial and "small commercial" webcasters may negotiate with a record-industry representative to establish rates to be paid for digital performance rights. The new law added sections 114(f)(5) and 114(g)(2), (3) and (4) to the Copyright Act.

Page 594:   First full paragraph, add after second sentence:

The TEACH Act passed both Houses of Congress in October 2002 (see H.R. 2215 and S. 487 in the 107th Congress), and was signed into law by President Bush on November 2, 2002 (Public Law 107–273). For its full text, see Section 110(2) in the statutory appendix.

CHAPTER 7

FAIR USE

B. THE APPLICATION OF THE FAIR USE DOCTRINE TO THE CREATION OF NEW WORKS

Page 634: Add at the end of Question 3:

A recent decision of the Court of Appeals for the Ninth Circuit suggests that it might, see *Mattel, Inc. v. Walking Mountain Productions*, 353 F.3d 792 (9th Cir. 2003), excerpted immediately *infra*.

Page 635: Insert the following decision after the *Air Pirates* cartoon:

Mattel, Inc. v. Walking Mountain Productions
353 F.3d 792 (9th Cir. 2003).

[Defendant photographer Forsythe used a Barbie doll, often without clothes, in a series of 78 photographs, typically in the midst of kitchen appliances and other household objects. He called the photos "Food Chain Barbie." Some of the photos conveyed anxiety and distress on the part of the Barbie figure, while others conveyed sexuality. Forsythe described the message behind his photographic series as an attempt to "critique the objectification of women associated with [Barbie], and to lambaste the conventional beauty myth and the societal acceptance of women as objects because this is what Barbie embodies." He chose to parody Barbie in his photographs because he believed that "Barbie is the most enduring of those products that feed on the insecurities of our beauty and perfection-obsessed consumer culture." Forsythe claimed that, throughout his series of photographs, he attempted to communicate, through artistic expression, his serious message with an element of humor. His commercial success was limited, with sales of postcards and the like bringing in gross income of some $3600. Mattel sued for copyright infringement, and fair use was asserted as a defense. The district court granted the defendants' motion for summary judgment, and Mattel appealed.]

■ PREGERSON, CIRCUIT JUDGE:

* * * * Because Forsythe photographed the Barbie figure and reproduced those photographs, Mattel has established a prima facie case of copyright infringement.

Consistent with its policy goals, however, the Copyright Act recognizes certain statutory exceptions to protections on copyrights. At its core, the Act seeks to promote the progress of science and art by protecting artistic and scientific works while encouraging the development and evolution of new works. *See Campbell v. Acuff–Rose Music, Inc.,* 510 U.S. 569, 575–76, 114 S.Ct. 1164, 127 L.Ed.2d 500 (1994). Recognizing that science and art generally rely on works that came before them and rarely spring forth in a vacuum, the Act limits the rights of a copyright owner regarding works that build upon, reinterpret, and reconceive existing works. *See id.* at 575–77, 114 S.Ct. 1164 ("[F]ew, if any, things . . . are strictly new and original throughout. Every book in literature, science and art, borrows, and must necessarily borrow. . . .") (quoting *Emerson v. Davies,* 8 F. Cas. 615, 619(C.C.D.Mass.1845) (No. 4,436)). The fair use exception excludes from copyright restrictions certain works, such as those that criticize and comment on another work. *17 U.S.C. § 107. . . .*

. . . . Because we agree with the district court that no triable issues of fact exist on whether Forsythe's use of Mattel's Barbie constitutes fair use, we weigh the four *§ 107* fair use factors on appeal. We conclude that Forsythe's use of Mattel's copyrighted Barbie constitutes fair use and affirm the district court's grant of summary judgment.

A. *Purpose and Character of Use*

The "purpose and character of use" factor in the fair use inquiry asks "to what extent the new work is transformative" and does not simply "supplant [ ]" the original work and whether the work's purpose was for- or not-for-profit. *Campbell,* 510 U.S. at 579, 584, 114 S.Ct. 1164.

. . . . "[T]he threshold question [in the analysis of this first factor] . . . is whether a parodic character may reasonably be perceived." *Id.* at 582, 114 S.Ct. 1164. *See also Dr. Seuss,* 109 F.3d at 1400. Mattel argues that the district court erred in finding parody because a reasonable jury could conclude that Forsythe's works do not parody Mattel's Barbie. In support of this argument, Mattel offered into evidence a survey in which they presented individuals from the general public in a shopping mall with color photocopies of Forsythe's photographs and asked them what meaning they perceived. Relying on this survey, Mattel asserts that only some individuals may perceive parodic character.

. . . . Forsythe correctly points out that Mattel presents no case law in support of its contention that the parodic nature of a defendant's work should be assessed using surveys and opinion testimony. Forsythe is further correct that every court to address the issue whether a defendant's work qualifies as a parody has treated this question as one of law to be decided by the court. *E.g., Campbell,* 510 U.S. at 582–83, 114 S.Ct. 1164; *Leibovitz v. Paramount Pictures Corp.,* 137 F.3d 109, 114–15 (2d Cir.1998); *Dr. Seuss,* 109 F.3d at 1400–01.

We decline to consider Mattel's survey in assessing whether Forsythe's work can be reasonably perceived as a parody. Parody is an objectively defined rhetorical device. Further, because parody is "a form of social and literary criticism," it has "socially significant value as free speech under the First Amendment." *Dr. Seuss,* 109 F.3d at 1400. While individuals may disagree on the success or extent of a parody, parodic elements in a work will often justify fair use protection. . . . Use of surveys in assessing parody would allow majorities to determine the parodic nature of a work and possibly silence artistic creativity. Allowing majorities to determine whether a work is a parody would be greatly at odds with the purpose of the fair use exception and the Copyright Act. *See generally Campbell,* 510 U.S. at 583, 114 S.Ct. 1164.

. . . . We conclude that Forsythe's work may reasonably be perceived as a parody of Barbie.

Mattel, through impressive marketing, has established Barbie as "the ideal American woman" and a "symbol of American girlhood" for many. *Mattel, Inc. v. MCA Records, Inc.* ("*MCA*"), 296 F.3d 894, 898 (9th Cir.2002), *cert. denied,* 537 U.S. 1171, 123 S.Ct. 993, 154 L.Ed.2d 912 (2003). As abundantly evidenced in the record, Mattel's advertisements show these plastic dolls dressed in various outfits, leading glamorous lifestyles and engaged in exciting activities. To sell its product, Mattel uses associations of beauty, wealth, and glamour.

Forsythe turns this image on its head, so to speak, by displaying carefully positioned, nude, and sometimes frazzled looking Barbies in often ridiculous and apparently dangerous situations. His lighting, background, props, and camera angles all serve to create a context for Mattel's copyrighted work that transform Barbie's meaning. Forsythe presents the viewer with a different set of associations and a different context for this plastic figure. In some of Forsythe's photos, Barbie is about to be destroyed or harmed by domestic life in the form of kitchen appliances, yet continues displaying her well known smile, disturbingly oblivious to her predicament. As portrayed in some of Forsythe's photographs, the appliances are substantial and overwhelming, while Barbie looks defenseless. In other photographs, Forsythe conveys a sexualized perspective of Barbie by showing the nude doll in sexually suggestive contexts. It is not difficult to see the commentary that Forsythe intended or the harm that he perceived in Barbie's influence on gender roles and the position of women in society.

However one may feel about his message—whether he is wrong or right, whether his methods are powerful or banal—his photographs parody Barbie and everything Mattel's doll has come to signify. Undoubtedly, one could make similar statements through other means about society, gender roles, sexuality, and perhaps even social class. But Barbie, and all the associations she has acquired through Mattel's impressive marketing success, conveys these messages in a particular way that is ripe for social comment.[7]

---

7. Mattel strongly argues that Forsythe's work is not parody because he could have made his statements about consumerism, gender roles, and sexuality without using Barbie. Acceptance of this argument would severely and unacceptably limit the definition of parody. We do not make judgments about what objects an artist should choose for their art. For example, in *Camp-* *bell,* the Supreme Court found that hip-hop band 2–Live Crew's rendition of "Pretty Woman" was a parody because it targeted the original song and commented "on the naivete of the original of an earlier day, as a rejection of its sentiment that ignores the ugliness of street life and the debasement that it signifies." 510 U.S. at 583, 114 S.Ct. 1164. No doubt, 2–Live Crew could have cho-

.... By developing and transforming associations with Mattel's Barbie doll, Forsythe has created the sort of social criticism and parodic speech protected by the First Amendment and promoted by the Copyright Act. We find that this factor weighs heavily in favor of Forsythe.

Another element of the first factor analysis is whether the work's "purpose" was commercial or had a non-profit aim. *Campbell,* 510 U.S. at 584, 114 S.Ct. 1164. Clearly, Forsythe had a commercial expectation and presumably hoped to find a market for his art. However, as the Supreme Court noted in *Campbell,* even works involving comment and criticism "are generally conducted for profit in this country." *Id.* (quoting *Harper & Row,* 471 U.S. at 592, 105 S.Ct. 2218.) On balance, Forsythe's commercial expectation does not weigh much against him. Given the extremely transformative nature and parodic quality of Forsythe's work, its commercial qualities become less important. *Id.* at 579, 105 S.Ct. 2218 (recognizing that the more "transformative the new work, the less will be the significance of the other factors").

B.   *Nature of the copyrighted work*

The second factor in the fair use analysis "recognizes that creative works are 'closer to the core of intended copyright protection' than informational and functional works." *Dr. Seuss,* 109 F.3d at 1402 (quoting *Campbell,* 510 U.S. at 586, 114 S.Ct. 1164). Mattel's copyrighted Barbie figure and face can fairly be said to be a creative work. However, the creativity of Mattel's copyrighted Barbie is typical of cases where there are infringing parodies. *Campbell,* 510 U.S. at 586, 114 S.Ct. 1164 ("[P]arodies almost invariably copy publicly known, expressive works."). As we have recognized in the past, "this [nature of the copyrighted work] factor typically has not been terribly significant in the overall fair use balancing." *Dr. Seuss,* 109 F.3d at 1402. In any event, it may weigh slightly against Forsythe.

C.   *Amount and substantiality of the portion used.*

The third factor in the fair use analysis asks whether " 'the amount and substantiality of the portion used in relation to the copyrighted work as a whole,' are reasonable in relation to the purpose of copying." *Id.* (quoting 17 U.S.C. § 107(3)). We assess the "persuasiveness of a parodist's justification for the particular copying done," recognizing that the "extent of permissible copying varies with the purpose and character of the use." *Campbell,* 510 U.S. at 586–87, 114 S.Ct. 1164.

Mattel argues that Forsythe used the entirety of its copyrighted work and that this factor weighs against him. Mattel contends that Forsythe could have used less of the Barbie figure by, for example, limiting his photos to the Barbie heads.

sen another song to make such a statement. Parody only requires that "the plaintiff's copyrighted work is at least in part the target of the defendant's satire," not that the plain- tiff's work be the irreplaceable object for its form of social commentary. *Dr. Seuss,* 109 F.3d at 1400.

First, Forsythe did not simply copy the work "verbatim" with "little added or changed." *Id.* at 587–88, 114 S.Ct. 1164. A verbatim copy of Barbie would be an exact three dimensional reproduction of the doll. Forsythe did not display the entire Barbie head and body in his photographs. Parts of the Barbie figure are obscured or omitted depending on the angle at which the photos were taken and whether other objects obstructed a view of the Barbie figure.

Second, Mattel's argument that Forsythe could have taken a lesser portion of its work attempts to benefit from the somewhat unique nature of the copyrighted work in this case. Copyright infringement actions generally involve songs, video, or written works. *See, e.g., Elvis Presley Enters., Inc. v. Passport Video,* 349 F.3d 622 (9th Cir.2003) (use of copyrighted Elvis Presley-related video clips, photographs, and music); *Los Angeles News Serv.,* 305 F.3d at 924 (use of a few seconds of a copyrighted video footage by a news service); *Worldwide Church of God v. Phila. Church of God, Inc.,* 227 F.3d 1110 (9th Cir.2000) (reproduction and distribution by nonprofit organization of an entire copyrighted work), *cert. denied,* 532 U.S. 958, 121 S.Ct. 1486, 149 L.Ed.2d 373 (2001); *Dr. Seuss,* 109 F.3d at 1394 (use of Dr. Seuss's "Cat in the Hat" format in written work about the O.J. Simpson trial). Because parts of these works are naturally severable, the new work can easily choose portions of the original work and add to it.

Here because the copyrighted material is a doll design and the infringing work is a photograph containing that doll, Forsythe, short of severing the doll, must add to it by creating a context around it and capturing that context in a photograph. . . . In both Forsythe's use of the entire doll and his use of dismembered parts of the doll, portions of the old work are incorporated into the new work but emerge imbued with a different character.

Moreover, Forsythe was justified in the amount of Mattel's copyrighted work that he used in his photographs. Mattel's argument that Forsythe could have used a lesser portion of the Barbie doll is completely without merit and would lead to absurd results. We do not require parodic works to take the absolute minimum amount of the copyrighted work possible. . . . We conclude that the extent of Forsythe's copying of the Barbie figure and head was justifiable in light of his parodic purpose and medium used. This factor also weighs in his favor.

D. *Effect of the use upon potential market*

. . . . [Under the fourth factor,] [t]he less adverse effect that an alleged infringing use has on the copyright owner's expectation of gain, the less public benefit need be shown to justify the use. *Dr. Seuss,* 109 F.3d at 1403(quoting *MCA, Inc. v. Wilson,* 677 F.2d 180, 183 (2d Cir.1981)).

Mattel argues that Forsythe's work could lead to market harm by impairing the value of Barbie itself, Barbie derivatives, and licenses for use of the Barbie name and/or likeness to non-Mattel entities. Because of the parodic nature of Forsythe's work, however, it is highly unlikely that it will substitute for products in Mattel's markets or the markets of Mattel's licensees. In *Campbell,* the Court clearly stated, "as to parody pure and simple, it is more likely that the new work will not affect the market for the original in a way cognizable under this factor." *Campbell,* 510 U.S. at 591, 114 S.Ct. 1164. Nor is it likely that Mattel would license an artist to create a work that is so critical of Barbie. "[T]he unlikelihood that creators of imaginative works will license critical reviews or lampoons of their own productions removes such uses from the very notion of a potential licensing market." *Id.* at 592, 114 S.Ct. 1164.

As to Mattel's claim that Forsythe has impaired Barbie's value, this fourth factor does not recognize a decrease in value of a copyrighted work that may result from a particularly powerful critical work.... We recognize, however, that critical works may have another dimension beyond their critical aspects that may have effects on potential markets for the copyrighted work. *Id.* at 592, 114 S.Ct. 1164(recognizing that the new work "may have a more complex character, with effects not only in the arena of criticism but also in protectable markets for derivative works"). Thus, we look more generally, not only to the critical aspects of a work, but to the type of work itself in determining market harm. *Id.* at 593, 114 S.Ct. 1164 (looking beyond the critical aspect of 2 Live Crew's rap rendition of "Pretty Woman" to the derivative market for rap music). Given the nature of Forsythe's photographs, we decline Mattel's invitation to look to the licensing market for art in general. Forsythe's photographs depict nude and often sexualized figures, a category of artistic photography that Mattel is highly unlikely to license. "The existence of this potential market cannot be presumed." *Lewis Galoob Toys, Inc. v. Nintendo of Am., Inc.,* 964 F.2d 965, 972(9th Cir.1992), *cert. denied,* 507 U.S. 985, 113 S.Ct. 1582, 123 L.Ed.2d 149 (1993).

.... Forsythe's work could only reasonably substitute for a work in the market for adult-oriented artistic photographs of Barbie. We think it safe to assume that Mattel will not enter such a market or license others to do so. As the Court noted in *Campbell,* "the market for potential derivative uses includes only those that creators of original works would in general develop or license others to develop." 510 U.S. at 592, 114 S.Ct. 1164.

Finally, the public benefit in allowing artistic creativity and social criticism to flourish is great. The fair use exception recognizes this important limitation on the rights of the owners of copyrights. No doubt, Mattel would be less likely to grant a license to an artist that intends to create art that criticizes and reflects negatively on Barbie's image. It is not in the public's interest to allow Mattel complete control over the kinds of artistic works that use Barbie as a reference for criticism and comment.

Having balanced the four § 107 fair use factors, we hold that Forsythe's work constitutes fair use under § 107's exception. His work is a parody of Barbie and highly transformative. The amount of Mattel's figure that he used was justified. His infringement had no discernable impact on Mattel's market for derivative uses. Finally, the benefits to the public in allowing such use—allowing artistic freedom and expression and criticism of a cultural icon—are great. Allowing Forsythe's use serves the aims of the

Copyright Act by encouraging the very creativity and criticism that the Act protects. *Kelly*, 336 F.3d at 819–20. We affirm the district court on its grant of summary judgment on Mattel's copyright infringement claims.

[In what appears to be the largest fee award to a prevailing defendant in a copyright case, the court awarded Forsythe $1.8 million in attorneys' fees.]

QUESTION

Recall the observations of the same circuit court of appeals some 25 years earlier in the *Air Pirates* case, which also involved an iconic visual image (there, Mickey Mouse). The court adopted a fairly tough "conjure up" standard for defendants relying upon fair use, and particularly when considering the third statutory factor, at least where graphic works were involved. (Section 107 was only then in its first year of existence.) Can it accurately be said that the *Barbie* decision effectively overrules *Air Pirates* on that issue, and that the result in the earlier case would now be different?

Page 650: Add Note to follow Questions:

Although the Court's subsequent statements in *Campbell v. Acuff Rose*, *supra*, may have muted the importance of the factor that the *Harper & Row* court dubbed "undoubtedly the single most important element of fair use," in many cases that consideration remains determinative. The factor takes into consideration not only economic harm from lost or diverted sales, but destruction of the intellectual value of the work. For one, perhaps extreme, example, consider the following:

Chicago Bd. of Ed. v. Substance, 354 F.3d 624 (7th Cir. 2003) (Posner, J.). In the newspaper that he edited, Defendant Schmidt, a critic of standardized testing, published six of the "Chicago Academic Standards Exams" (CASE), a series of secure standardized tests then recently administered in public elementary schools.

> ... He did this because he thought them bad tests and that he could best demonstrate this by publishing them in full. His answer to the school board's complaint asserted that the unauthorized copying and publication of the tests were a fair use and therefore not a copyright infringement. ...
>
> [Schmidt] argues that the school board does not intend to sell the tests, and so Schmidt isn't eating into their market by publishing the tests. This is true, but irrelevant, because he is destroying the value of the tests and the fact that it's not a *market* value has no significance once the right to copyright unpublished works is conceded, as it must be. The [Schmidt] memorandum argues that expert testimony would establish that there is no educational value in publishing the exact same exam year after year. No one supposes there is; the argument rather is that *some* questions must be carried over to future years in order to validate the exam.... The memorandum's remaining argument is that expert witnesses can be found to testify that the CASE

tests are "dramatically inadequate." No doubt. But in so arguing the memorandum misunderstands the fair use privilege of criticism. It is not a privilege to criticize just bad works, and there is no right to copy copyrighted works promiscuously merely upon a showing that they are bad.

There is more than a suspicion that Schmidt simply does not like standardized tests. That is his right. But he does not have the right, as he believes he does (he claims a right to copy any test that an expert will testify is no good), to destroy the tests by publishing them indiscriminately, any more than a person who dislikes Michelangelo's statue of David has a right to take a sledgehammer to it. From the amicus curiae briefs filed in this case, moreover, it is apparent that many other teachers share Schmidt's unfavorable opinion of standardized tests. . . . So if Schmidt can publish six tests, other dissenters can each publish six other tests, and in no time all 44 will be published. The board will never be able to use the same question twice, and after a few years of Schmidtian tactics there will be such difficulty in inventing new questions without restructuring the curriculum that the board will have to abandon standardized testing. Which is Schmidt's goal.

If ever a "floodgates" argument had persuasive force, therefore, it is in this case. . . . If Schmidt wins this case, it is goodbye to standardized tests in the Chicago public school system; Schmidt, his allies, and the federal courts will have wrested control of educational policy from the Chicago public school authorities.

Page 653:   Add the following to Question 3:

For another example of quoting copyrighted material, without permission, in the context of an advertisement, see Los Angeles News Serv. v. CBS Broadcasting, Inc., 305 F.3d 924 (9th Cir.2002), in which Court TV used a few seconds of the plaintiff's footage of the beating of white truckdriver Reginald Denny in the Los Angeles riots, to promote Court TV's coverage of the trial of Denny's assailants. The court granted summary judgment for the defendant, finding fair use as a matter of law. Do you agree with the outcome?

Page 654: Add the following after the Questions:

Video Pipeline, Inc. v. Buena Vista Home Entertainment, Inc.

342 F.3d 191 (3d Cir. 2003).

■ AMBRO, CIRCUIT JUDGE:

In this copyright case we review the District Court's entry of a preliminary injunction against Video Pipeline, Inc.'s online display of "clip previews." A "clip preview," as we use the term, is an approximately two-minute segment of a movie, copied without authorization from the film's copyright holder, and used in the same way as an authorized movie "trailer." We reserve the term "trailer" for previews created by the copyright holder of a particular movie (or under the copyright holder's authority).

Video Pipeline challenges the injunction on the ground that its internet use of the clip previews is protected by the fair use doctrine and, alternatively, that appellees Buena Vista Home Entertainment, Inc. and Miramax Film Corp.[1] may not receive the benefits of copyright protection because they have engaged in copyright misuse. We reject both arguments, and affirm.

BACKGROUND

Video Pipeline compiles movie trailers onto videotape for home video retailers to display in their stores. To obtain the right to distribute the trailers used in the compilations, Video Pipeline enters into agreements with various entertainment companies. It entered into such an agreement, the Master Clip License Agreement ("License Agreement"), with Disney in 1988, and Disney thereafter provided Video Pipeline with over 500 trailers for its movies.

In 1997, Video Pipeline took its business to the web, where it operates VideoPipeline.net and VideoDetective.com. The company maintains a database accessible from Video Pipeline.net, which contains movie trailers Video Pipeline has received throughout the years. Video Pipeline's internet clients—retail web sites selling home videos—use VideoPipeline.net to display trailers to site visitors. The site visitors access trailers by clicking on a button labeled "preview" for a particular motion picture. The requested trailer is then "streamed" for the visitor to view (because it is streamed the trailer cannot be downloaded to or stored on the visitor's computer). The operators of the web sites from which the trailers are accessed—Video Pipeline's internet clients—pay a fee to have the trailers streamed based on the number of megabytes shown to site visitors. Video Pipeline has agreements to stream trailers with approximately 25 online retailers, including Yahoo!, Amazon, and Best Buy.

As noted, Video Pipeline also operates VideoDetective.com. On this web site, visitors can search for movies by title, actor, scene, genre, *etc.* When a search is entered, the site returns a list of movies and information about them, and allows the user to stream trailers from VideoPipeline.net. In addition to displaying trailers, VideoDetective.com includes a "Shop Now" button to link the user to a web site selling the requested video. Visitors to VideoDetective.com can also win prizes by playing "Can You Name that Movie?" after viewing a trailer on the site.

Video Pipeline included in its online database trailers it received under the License Agreement from Disney. Because the License Agreement did

---

1. Buena Vista holds an exclusive license to distribute Miramax and Walt Disney Pictures and Television home videos. Buena Vista, Miramax, and Walt Disney Pictures and Television are subsidiaries of The Walt Disney Co. Because of this connection and for simplicity's sake, we refer to the appellees collectively and individually as "Disney."

not permit this use, Disney requested that Video Pipeline remove the trailers from the database. It complied with that request.

On October 24, 2000, however, Video Pipeline filed a complaint in the District Court for the District of New Jersey seeking a declaratory judgment that its online use of the trailers did not violate federal copyright law. Disney shortly thereafter terminated the License Agreement.

Video Pipeline decided to replace some of the trailers it had removed at Disney's request from its database. In order to do so, it copied approximately two minutes from each of at least 62 Disney movies to create its own clip previews of the movies. (Again, to distinguish between the previews created under the copyright holder's authority and those created by Video Pipeline, we call the former "trailers" and the latter "clip previews" or "clips." We use the term "previews" generically.)

Video Pipeline stores the clip previews in its database and displays them on the internet in the same way it had displayed the Disney trailers. In content, however, the clip previews differ from the trailers. Each clip preview opens with a display of the Miramax or Disney trademark and the title of the movie, then shows one or two scenes from the first half of the movie, and closes with the title again. Disney's trailers, in contrast, are designed to entice sales from a target market by using techniques such as voice-over, narration, editing, and additional music. Video Pipeline's clip previews use none of these marketing techniques.

Disney also makes its trailers available online. It displays them on its own web sites in order to attract and to keep users there (a concept called "stickiness") and then takes advantage of the users' presence to advertise and sell other products. Disney has also entered into agreements to link its trailers with other businesses, and, for example, has such a link with the Apple Computer home page.

Video Pipeline amended its complaint to seek a declaratory judgment allowing it to use the clip previews. Disney filed a counterclaim alleging copyright infringement. The District Court entered a preliminary injunction, later revised, prohibiting Video Pipeline from displaying clip previews of Disney films on the internet. *See Video Pipeline, Inc. v. Buena Vista Home Entertainment, Inc.*, 192 F.Supp.2d 321 (D.N.J.2002). Video Pipeline appeals....

.... The District Court held that Video Pipeline's clip previews likely infringe Disney's exclusive rights under three of § 106's provisions: subsection (2), concerning derivative works; subsection (4), dealing with public performance of motion pictures; and subsection (5), relating to public display of individual images of a motion picture. ... As Video Pipeline's display of excerpts taken from the copyrighted movies clearly comes within the prohibition on public display of motion pictures, and images from a motion picture, we turn to whether Video Pipeline's use should nonetheless be countenanced on the ground that it falls within the "fair use" doctrine.

A.   Fair Use

[The fair use doctrine's] focus on copyright's purpose [to foster creative activity for the public good] makes relevant a comparison of the copy with the original: where the copier uses none of his own creative activity to transform the original work, holding the fair use doctrine inapplicable will not likely interfere with copyright's goal of encouraging creativity. Thus, in the typical fair use case, the analysis under each statutory factor concentrates on the copy and the original work from which it derives. In this case, however, our analysis of the four statutory factors will take into account where relevant Disney's original full-length films and its trailers. We examine in this way the fairness of the online display of the clip previews because, among other things, the statute directs our attention under factor four to the effect of the allegedly infringing uses on both the potential market for any derivative works (the parties do not dispute that Disney's trailers qualify as derivative works) and the potential market for the originals. *See Campbell,* 510 U.S. at 590.

1.   *Purpose and Character of the Use*

Once again, the first factor requires that we consider "the purpose and character of the use, including whether such use is of a commercial nature or is for nonprofit educational purposes." § 107(1). The District Court concluded that the purpose and character of Video Pipeline's clip previews weigh against finding fair use. We agree.

If a new work is used commercially rather than for a nonprofit purpose, its use will less likely qualify as fair. *Campbell,* 510 U.S. at 585, 114 S.Ct. 1164. As Video Pipeline charges a fee to stream the clip previews, its use of the copies is commercial (as the District Court found).

The commercial nature of the use does not by itself, however, determine whether the purpose and character of the use weigh for or against finding fair use. *Id.* at 583–84, 114 S.Ct. 1164. We look as well to any differences in character and purpose between the new use and the original. We consider whether the copy is "transformative" of the work it copied because it "alter [ed] the first with new expression, meaning, or message," or instead "whether the new work merely supersedes the objects of the original creation." *Id.* at 579, 114 S.Ct. 1164 (citations and alteration in original omitted).

Video Pipeline asserts that its use of the clip previews substantially transforms the full-length films from which they derive because the clips and the movies have different purposes. According to Video Pipeline, the original works have an aesthetic and entertainment purpose while the clip previews serve only to provide information about the movies to internet users or as advertisements for the company's retail web site clients.[5] To the

---

5. We note that the clip previews do not constitute mere "information" about the movies, as would, for example, a list of the names of the actors starring in a film, or a statement of the rating it received. Were Video Pipeline dealing only in this type of infor-mation, the fair use doctrine might not be implicated at all because copyright protection does not include facts and ideas, but only their expression. *See Harper & Row Publishers, Inc. v. Nation Enters.,* 471 U.S. 539, 547, 105 S.Ct. 2218, 85 L.Ed.2d 588 (1985); 17

extent that the character and purpose of the clip previews and the original full-length films diverge, however, the clips share the same character and purpose as Disney's derivative trailers. Whatever informational or promotional character and purpose the trailers possess, so do the clip previews. Consequently, the clips are likely to "supersede the objects of" Disney's derivatives. *Campbell,* 510 U.S. at 579, 114 S.Ct. 1164 (citations omitted). Although the clips are copied from Disney's original rather than its derivative works, it is highly relevant to our inquiry here that the clips will likely serve as substitutes for those derivatives.

Video Pipeline also urges us to take into account the functional character and purpose of the database in which it stores trailers and clip previews, apparently hoping we will discern no significant difference between its database and the internet search engine used in *Kelly v. Arriba Soft Corp.,* 336 F.3d 811 (9th Cir.2003).[7] In *Kelly,* Arriba Soft Corp.'s search engine located images on other web sites in response to a user's request and displayed the results in thumbnail-size pictures, with a link that would take the user to the web site on which the image was found. *Id.* at 815. The Court held that the display of the thumbnail images was a fair use. *Id.*

Video Pipeline's database does not, however, serve the same function as did Arriba Soft's search engine. As used with retailers' web sites, VideoPipeline.net does not improve access to authorized previews located on other web sites. Rather, it indexes and displays unauthorized copies of copyrighted works. VideoDetective.com does permit viewers to link to legitimate retailers' web sites, but a link to a legitimate seller of authorized copies does not here, if it ever would, make *prima facie* infringement a fair use.

Finally, we note that Video Pipeline's clip previews—to reiterate, approximately two-minute excerpts of full-length films with movie title and company trademark shown—do not add significantly to Disney's original

U.S.C. § 102(b). Regardless, the clips are part of—not information about—Disney's expressive creations. *See id.* at 569, 105 S.Ct. 2218 ("Any copyright infringer may claim to benefit the public by increasing public access to the copyrighted work.").

Additionally, it is not clear to us that the use of a copy—not accompanied by any creative expression on the part of the copier—as an advertisement for the original would qualify as a type of use intended to be recognized by the fair use doctrine. *See Campbell,* 510 U.S. at 578–79, 114 S.Ct. 1164 ("The enquiry [under the first factor] may be guided by the examples given in the preamble to § 107, looking to whether the use is for criticism, or comment, or news reporting, and the like . . . ."); *id.* at 585, 114 S.Ct. 1164 ("The use, for example, of a copyrighted work to advertise a product, even in a parody, will be entitled to less indulgence under the first factor of the fair use enquiry than the sale of a parody for its own sake, let alone one performed a single time by students in school.").

We need not resolve these issues, however, because (as we conclude in the text) the purpose and character of the use of the clip previews and that of Disney's derivative works—its trailers—are the same.

7. A database is a discrete collection of data (here, previews) set up for efficient retrieval. By comparison, a search engine refers to a system that locates data (or images, *etc.*) from other web sites; thus, a search engine will retrieve data that is not in the engine operator's control. VideoPipeline.net is a database, not a search engine.

expression. Video Pipeline itself asserts, and the District Court found, 192 F.Supp.2d at 337, that the clip previews "involved no new creative ingenuity." The Court did recognize that deciding which scene or scenes to include in a clip preview requires some creative choice. *Id.* But as Video Pipeline disclaims the use of any creative ingenuity, we have no difficulty viewing those decisions as involving creativity only in a theoretical, and most narrow, sense. Hence, it is dubious what "new expression, meaning, or message" Video Pipeline has brought to its copies. *Campbell,* 510 U.S. at 579, 114 S.Ct. 1164.

It is useful to compare the clip previews with a movie review, which might also display two-minute segments copied from a film. The movie reviewer does not simply display a scene from the movie under review but as well provides his or her own commentary and criticism. In so doing, the critic may add to the copy sufficient "new expression, message, or meaning" to render the use fair. *Id.* Here, in contrast, the fact that "a substantial portion," indeed almost all, "of the infringing work was copied verbatim from the copyrighted work" with no additional creative activity "reveal[s] a dearth of transformative character or purpose." *Id.* at 587, 114 S.Ct. 1164. Consequently, rejecting the fair use defense in this case will not likely "stifle the very creativity" that the Copyright Clause "is designed to foster." *Id.* at 577, 114 S.Ct. 1164.

With this context, the District Court correctly concluded that Video Pipeline's clip previews lack any significant transformative quality. Thus, the commercial nature of the clip previews weighs more strongly against Video Pipeline's use. *Campbell,* 510 U.S. at 580, 114 S.Ct. 1164 (If "the alleged infringer merely uses [the original work] to get attention or to avoid the drudgery in working up something fresh, the claim to fairness in borrowing from another's work diminishes accordingly (if it does not vanish), and other factors, like the extent of its commerciality, loom larger."). Given the shared character and purpose of the clip previews and the trailers (so that the clips will likely serve as a substitute for the trailers) and the absence of creative ingenuity in the creation of the clips, the first factor strongly weighs against fair use in this case.

2. *Nature of the Copyrighted Work*

The second statutory fair use factor directs courts to consider "the nature of the copyrighted work." § 107(2). "This factor calls for recognition that some works are closer to the core of intended copyright protection than others, with the consequence that fair use is more difficult to establish when the former works are copied." *Campbell,* 510 U.S. at 586, 114 S.Ct. 1164. Fictional, creative works come closer to this core than do primarily factual works. *Harper & Row Publishers, Inc. v. Nation Enters.,* 471 U.S. 539, 563, 105 S.Ct. 2218, 85 L.Ed.2d 588 (1985). The Disney movies at issue—including, for example, *Beauty and the Beast, Fantasia, Pretty Woman,* and *Dead Poet's Society*—are paradigms of creative, non-factual expression. And Disney's trailers share imaginative aspects with the originals....

3.   *Amount and Substantiality of the Work Copied*

The third factor requires an analysis of "the amount and substantiality of the portion used in relation to the copyrighted work as a whole." § 107(3). The District Court determined that this factor also weighed in Disney's favor. 192 F.Supp.2d at 340.

As Video Pipeline points out, its previews excerpt only about two minutes from movies that last one and a half to two hours. Quantitatively then, the portion taken is quite small.

But the third factor "calls for thought not only about the quantity of the materials used, but about their quality and importance, too." *Campbell,* 510 U.S. at 587, 114 S.Ct. 1164. The District Court found that the clip previews, "for the most part, were used to provide the potential customer with some idea of the plot of each motion picture, its overall tone, and a glimpse of its leading characters." 192 F.Supp.2d at 339. Although the plot, tone, and leading characters are, of course, significant aspects of the films, the two-minute "glimpse" provided by the clips is made up only of scenes taken from the first half of the Disney films. Disney has not claimed, for instance, that any of the clips "give away" the ending of a movie, or ruin other intended surprises for viewers of the full-length films. Moreover, as advertisements, the clip previews are meant to whet the customer's appetite, not to sate it; accordingly, they are not designed to reveal the "heart" of the movies. Simply put, we have no reason to believe that the two-minute clips manage in so brief a time, or even intend, to appropriate the "heart" of the movies. *Compare Harper & Row,* 471 U.S. at 564–55, 105 S.Ct. 2218 (weighing this factor against finding fair use because the alleged infringer "took what was essentially the heart of the book").

Because the clip previews copy a relatively small amount of the original full-length films and do not go to the "heart" of the movies, this factor, contrary to the District Court's determination, weighs in favor of finding fair Video Pipeline's display of its clips.

4.   *Effect on Potential Market or Value*

Finally, courts should evaluate "the effect of the use upon the potential market for or value of the copyrighted work." § 107(4). The District Court considered the question to be whether Video Pipeline's "use of the copyrighted work affects or materially impairs the marketability of the copyrighted motion pictures," and, finding the evidence equivocal, concluded that the fourth factor weighed neither for nor against finding a likelihood of fair use. 192 F.Supp.2d at 340, 343.

As mentioned above, this final factor "must take [into] account not only ... harm to the original but also ... harm to the market for derivative works." *Campbell,* 510 U.S. at 590, 114 S.Ct. 1164. Because the issues pertaining to the potential harm to the market for Disney's derivative trailers are more straightforward, we focus our analysis on this area and do not review the District Court's conclusion as to harm to the market for the original full-length films. It is in this context that we conclude that the fourth factor weighs in Disney's favor.

Video Pipeline argued in the District Court that no market exists, or could exist, for movie previews because no one "ever paid or will ever pay any money merely to see trailers." But in fact retail websites are paying Video Pipeline to display both trailers and clip previews. Moreover, Video Pipeline takes too narrow a view of the harm contemplated by this fourth factor. The statute directs us to consider "the effect of the use upon the . . . *value* of the copyrighted work," not only the effect upon the "market," however narrowly that term is defined. § 107(4); *see also Worldwide Church of God v. Philadelphia Church of God, Inc.,* 227 F.3d 1110, 1119 (9th Cir.2000) (drawing such a distinction). And the value "need not be limited to monetary rewards; compensation may take a variety of forms." *Id.; see also Sony Corp.,* 464 U.S. at 447 n. 28, 104 S.Ct. 774 (stating in a different context that the "copyright law does not require a copyright owner to charge a fee for the use of his works, and . . . the owner of a copyright may well have economic or noneconomic reasons for permitting certain kinds of copying to occur without receiving direct compensation from the copier").

Disney introduced evidence that it has entered an agreement to cross-link its trailers with the Apple Computer home page and that it uses on its own websites "the draw of the availability of authentic trailers to advertise, cross-market and cross-sell other products, and to obtain valuable marketing information from visitors who chose [*sic*] to register at the site or make a purchase there." App. 945; *see also Kelly,* 336 F.3d at 821 ("Kelly's images are related to several potential markets. One purpose of the photographs is to attract internet users to his web site, where he sells advertising space as well as books and travel packages. In addition, Kelly could sell or license his photographs to other web sites or to a stock photo database, which then could offer the images to its customers."). In light of Video Pipeline's commercial use of the clip previews and Disney's use of its trailers as described by the record evidence, we easily conclude that there is a sufficient market for, or other value in, movie previews such that the use of an infringing work could have a harmful effect cognizable under the fourth factor.

We have already determined that the clip previews lack transformative quality and that, though the clips are copies taken directly from the original full-length films rather than from the trailers, display of the clip previews would substitute for the derivative works. As a result, the clips, if Video Pipeline continues to stream them over the internet, will "serve[ ] as a market replacement" for the trailers, "making it likely that cognizable market harm to the [derivatives] will occur." *Campbell,* 510 U.S. at 591, 114 S.Ct. 1164. For instance, web sites wishing to show previews of Disney movies may choose to enter licensing agreements with Video Pipeline rather than Disney, as at least 25 have already done. And internet users searching for previews of Disney films may be drawn by the clip previews to web sites other than Disney's, depriving Disney of the opportunity to advertise and sell other products to those users.[10]

Consequently, " 'unrestricted and widespread conduct of the sort engaged in by [Video Pipeline] . . . would result in a substantially adverse impact on the potential market' for the [derivative works]." *Id.* at 590, 114 S.Ct. 1164 (quoting 3 M. Nimmer & D. Nimmer, *Nimmer on Copyright* § 13.05(A)(4) (1993)). We therefore hold that the District Court should have weighed this factor against recognizing the fair use defense in this case.

* * *

Three of the four statutory factors indicate that Video Pipeline's internet display of the clip previews will not qualify as a fair use. From our consideration of each of those factors, we cannot conclude that Video Pipeline's online display of its clip previews does anything but "infringe[ ] a work for personal profit." *Harper & Row,* 471 U.S. at 563, 105 S.Ct. 2218. The District Court therefore correctly held that Video Pipeline has failed to show that it will likely prevail on its fair use defense.

[For the court's treatment of the defense of copyright misuse, see Ch. 8H, *infra.*]

QUESTION

Passport Video has produced and is marketing a 16–hour video biography of Elvis Presley. The biography contains information about the life and professional career of Elvis, and has interviews (some 200) with those who knew him. It contains many excerpts from The King's television and motion picture performances, including copyrighted songs, as well as still photographs; these all have copyrights that are owned by others, and no licenses or permissions have been given to Passport. The clips run from a few seconds, the typical amount, to as long as a minute or so (for performances on the Ed Sullivan and Steve Allen television programs). In many instances, the clips and photos are accompanied by "voice-overs" that give pertinent information; in others, they (particularly the TV and film clips) are uninterrupted and unaccompanied by voice-over commentary. A number of the clips are repeated several times over the course of the biography. The copyright owners of the television programs and motion pictures, and of the still photographs and songs, have brought an action against Passport for infringement, and have sought injunctive relief. Passport relies on the defense of fair use. If you were the judge, how would you decide the case? See Elvis Presley Enterprises, Inc. v. Passport Video, 349 F.3d 622 (9th Cir. 2003).

---

10. Record evidence indicates that clip previews were streamed over the internet more than 30,000 times between November 2000 and April 2001.

Page 657: Insert at end of first full paragraph:

NXIVM Corp. v. Ross Institute

364 F.3d 471 (2d Cir. 2004).

■ JOHN W. WALKER, JR., CHIEF JUDGE:

NXIVM provides a course manual for the paid subscribers to its exclusive and expensive seminar training program known as "Executive Success." The 265-page manual contains a copyright notice on virtually every page and all seminar participants sign non-disclosure agreements, purporting to bar them from releasing the manuscript or proprietary techniques learned in the seminars to others. It is unpublished in the sense that it is not available to the general public. NXIVM claims to have developed a proprietary "technology" called "Rational Inquiry," a methodology to improve communication and decision-making.

Defendant Rick Ross runs nonprofit websites, *www.rickross.com* and *www.cultnews.com,* in connection with his work as a for-profit "cult deprogrammer." The websites provide information to the public about controversial groups, about which complaints of mind control have been lodged. Ross allegedly learned of NXIVM's activities in the course of his deprogramming services, obtaining the manuscript indirectly from defendant Stephanie Franco, a one-time NXIVM participant.

Two reports authored separately by defendants John Hochman and Paul Martin, self-styled experts on groups such as NXIVM, were commissioned by Ross; they analyze and critique the materials from the manual. The reports quote sections of the manual in support of their analyses and criticisms and were ultimately made available to the public through Ross's websites. One of the reports plainly acknowledges that NXIVM has "intellectual property rights" in its materials and that NXIVM makes an effort to keep its manual "confidential." This report seems to appreciate that its access to the copyrighted materials was unauthorized, although this is likely a disputed issue of fact.

[The district court upheld the defense of fair use, placing no weight upon the defendant's knowledge that its copy of the plaintiff's course manual was likely secured through unauthorized means. The two-judge majority in the court of appeals took issue with this particular point, concluding that the "propriety of the defendant's conduct" is properly to be given some—although not dispositive—weight as a subfactor under section 107(1), the purpose and *character* of the use.]

.... *Harper & Row* ["Fair use presupposes 'good faith' and 'fair dealing.'"] directs courts to consider a defendant's bad faith in applying the first statutory factor.... Thus, to the extent that Ross, Martin, or Hochman knew that his access to the manuscript was unauthorized or was derived from a violation of law or breach of duty, this consideration weighs in favor of plaintiffs.... The district court should have more fully and explicitly considered defendants' bad faith within its analysis of the first factor and did not. For the purposes of our analysis here, we assume defendants' bad faith and weigh this subfactor in favor of plaintiffs.

151

But just how much weight within the first factor should a court place on this subfactor of bad faith? Some courts have found *Harper & Row* to stand for the broad proposition that "[t]o invoke the fair use exception, an individual must possess an authorized copy of a literary work." *Atari Games Corp. v. Nintendo of Am. Inc.*, 975 F.2d 832, 843 (Fed.Cir.1992). Since we assume defendants' copy of the NXIVM manuscript was unauthorized, the rule enunciated in *Atari* would foreclose the fair use defense altogether based upon defendants' bad faith.

However, we read *Harper & Row*'s holding more narrowly than the broad proposition suggested by *Atari*. . . . . . Because the *Harper & Row* Court did not end its analysis of the fair use defense after considering and ascertaining the defendants' bad faith there, we believe that the bad faith of a defendant is not dispositive of a fair use defense. Instead, we agree with the court in *Religious Tech. Ctr. v. Netcom On–Line Communication Servs., Inc.*, 923 F.Supp. 1231, 1244 n. 14 (N.D.Cal.1995), that "[n]othing in *Harper & Row* indicates that [the defendants'] bad faith [is] itself conclusive of the fair use question, or even of the first factor." Moreover, "[a]fter *Campbell*, it is clear that a finding of bad faith, or a finding on any one of the four factors, cannot be considered dispositive." *Id.; see also Campbell*, 510 U.S. at 578, 114 S.Ct. 1164 (emphasizing that no single fair use factor is dispositive and warning against the application of "bright-line rules" in fair use analysis); 4 Melville B. Nimmer & David Nimmer, Nimmer on Copyright § 13.05[A][1][d] (2003)(noting that "knowing use of a purloined manuscript militates against a fair use defense," but not suggesting that bad faith is an absolute bar to fair use).

Thus, while the subfactor pertaining to defendants' good or bad faith must be weighed, and while it was error for the district court not to have fully and explicitly considered it, we find that even if the bad faith subfactor weighs in plaintiffs' favor, the first factor still favors defendants in light of the transformative nature of the secondary use as criticism. If no statutory factor can be dispositive after *Campbell*, neither can a single subfactor be, *a fortiori*. . . .

■ JACOBS, CIRCUIT JUDGE, concurring:

I concur in the majority opinion and subscribe in nearly all respects to its analysis, with the following further observations.

The majority opinion assumes that Dr. Ross and his co-defendants may have acquired the NXIVM training manual in bad faith, and observes that the district court did not explore this question. Even assuming such bad faith, the majority opinion nonetheless concludes that the defendants' quotation from the NXIVM original was a fair use protected by § 107. This is because Ross used the passages from NXIVM's manuals to criticize the original, *i.e.*, with a literary intention and effect that differed sufficiently from that of the original to be transformative. Accordingly, Dr. Ross' publication of the quoted material did not enter the marketplace as a potential substitute for NXIVM's original. In the majority's words, "[a]ll of the alleged harm arises from the biting criticism of [the defendant's] fair use, not from usurpation of the market" that properly belongs to the plaintiff. Maj. Op. at 482.

With all of this I completely agree. The fact that the defendants might have acted in bad faith in acquiring the plaintiff's material did not bar a finding of fair use. I would go somewhat further. The majority assumed, based on the Supreme Court's having said so in *Harper & Row Publishers, Inc. v. Nation Enters.*, 471 U.S. 539, 562–63, 105 S.Ct. 2218, 85 L.Ed.2d 588 (1985), that bad faith on the part of secondary users has a proper place in the fair use analysis. The Court's observation in *Harper & Row* was, however, a make-weight wholly unnecessary to the outcome; rejection of the fair use defense was compelled by the essential statutory considerations: the defendant took the "heart" of the plaintiff's book (the part the public was most interested in reading), and in so doing, usurped a significant part of its market.

The Supreme Court's most recent consideration of fair use in *Campbell v. Acuff–Rose Music, Inc.*, 510 U.S. 569, 585 n. 18, 114 S.Ct. 1164, 127 L.Ed.2d 500 (1994), treats as an open question whether the secondary user's good or bad faith is pertinent to the fair use inquiry (contrary to its observation in *Harper & Row*). . . . [The *Campbell* court stated:]

> [R]egardless of the weight one might place on the alleged infringer's state of mind, *compare Harper & Row,* 471 U.S. at 562[ ], 105 S.Ct. 2218 (fair use presupposes good faith and fair dealing) (quotation marks omitted), *with Folsom v. Marsh,* 9 F.Cas. 342, 349 (No. 4,901) (C.C.D.Mass.1841) (good faith does not bar a finding of infringement); [Pierre N.] Leval, [*Toward a Fair Use Standard,* 103 Harv. L.Rev. at] 1126–27 (good faith irrelevant to fair use analysis), we reject [the] argument that 2 Live Crew's request for permission to use the original should be weighed against a finding of fair use. *Even if good faith were central to fair use,* 2 Live Crew's actions do not necessarily suggest that they believed their version was not fair use. . . . If the use is otherwise fair, then no permission need be sought or granted.

Campbell, 510 U.S. at 585 n. 18, 114 S.Ct. 1164 (emphasis added). In opposition to *Harper & Row*'s assumption that "fair use presupposes good faith and fair dealing," the *Campbell* footnote highlighted the seemingly contrary inference of Justice Story's classic statement of the fair use principles in *Folsom*, as well as an often-cited study that questions whether good faith should be weighed in the balancing of "the social benefit of a transformative secondary use against injury to the incentives of authorship." Pierre N. Leval, *Toward a Fair Use Standard,* 103 Harv. L.Rev. 1105, 1126–27 (1990) ("Leval I"). *Campbell*'s contrary-to-fact phrasing— "[e]ven if good faith *were* central to fair use"—rather suggests that it should not.

So, even if *Harper & Row* did state in passing that fair use presupposes good faith, *Campbell* reopened the question. *See, e.g., Religious Tech. Ctr. v. Netcom On–Line Communication Servs., Inc.*, 923 F.Supp. 1231, 1244 n. 14 (N.D.Cal.1995) ("*Campbell* . . . hardly endorses the good faith requirement."). *Campbell*'s footnoted discussion questioning the pertinence of good faith reinforces the entire thrust of the decision, which requires that fair use be assessed primarily in light of whether the secondary work quotes the original with a transformative purpose and whether it usurps a market that properly belongs to the original author—issues as to which the defendant's good faith in accessing the plaintiff's original work does not matter.

II

... Fair use is not a doctrine that exists by sufferance, or that is earned by good works and clean morals; it is a right—codified in § 107 and recognized since shortly after the Statute of Anne—that is "necessary to fulfill copyright's very purpose, '[t]o promote the Progress of science and the useful arts....'" *Campbell,* 510 U.S. at 575, 114 S.Ct. 1164 (quoting U.S. Const., art. I, § 8, cl. 8).... A person who acquires the original work by crooked or unsavory means may expose himself to all sorts of civil claims and criminal charges; but the question of fair use itself should be decided on the basis of the transformative character and commercial effects of the secondary use. If the use satisfies the criteria of § 107, it is fair because it advances the utilitarian goals of copyright.

It might seem that it can never hurt to put bad faith at a disadvantage. But copyright is not about virtue; it is about the encouragement of creative output, including the output of transformative quotation. Its goals are not advanced if bad faith can defeat a fair use defense.... In *Campbell,* the Court affirmed that the fair use defense exists to further these same goals; it is not, as its label may connote, a privilege conferred on the well-intentioned. Fair play is no defense to infringement, *see, e.g., Folsom,* 9 F.Cas. at 349 (finding infringement despite having "no doubt [ ] that [defendant's copying was] deemed [by him] a perfectly lawful and justifi-able use of the plaintiff's work"), and bad faith should be no obstacle to fair use. Thus a hotelier who stocks each room with photocopies of a newly copyrighted translation of the Bible is not saved from infringement by his piety; similarly, a movie reviewer who critiques—and reveals—a surprise ending is not deprived of the fair use defense by his malice or spite. Nor should a book critic be denied the fair use protection because she gained access to a prepublication manuscript by deceit. Fair use is not a permitted infringement; it lies wholly outside the domain protected by the author's copyright.

Bad faith is a slippery concept in the copyright context. It (i) is difficult to define, (ii) may be impossible to detect, and (iii) given weight, may lead to the suppression of transformative works that are valuable to the expan-sion of public knowledge. In deciding whether to publish a work derived from copyrighted source material, a publisher ought to be able to make a judgment based solely on a comparison of the two works in light of market conditions, as indicated by the factors expressly set out in § 107. The goals of copyright are disserved if publishers (and editors) risk liability on the basis of the (often unknown or unsuspected) tactics and morals of authors who produce transformative works. Incremental risks drive up the cost of publication, thus the prudent publisher may elect to forgo a new work altogether if the good faith of the creator cannot be assured. And when bad faith *is* apparent or discovered, an otherwise transformative work will not be published at all—a result in tension (at least) with the public good that copyright exists to promote....

III

.... Certainly, no critic should need an author's permission to make such criticism, regardless of how he came by the original; nor should publication be inhibited by a publisher's anxiety or uncertainty about an author's ethics if his secondary work is transformative. The majority opinion thus properly affirms the district court's finding of fair use, notwithstanding the possibility that the defendant might have obtained the plaintiff's materials by an act of deception or otherwise in bad faith.

QUESTION

Do you agree with the concurring opinion that fair use is a "right" and not merely an infringement that is permitted when the defendant can prove satisfaction of the factors in section 107? Do you agree that the defendant's bad faith is altogether to be ignored in the fair use analysis, under both the text of section 107 and the pertinent Supreme Court jurisprudence? See generally Lloyd L. Weinreb, *Fair's Fair: A Comment on the Fair Use Doctrine*, 103 Harv. L. Rev. 1337 (1990).

Page 657: Add the following Problem to the end of the textual Note:

A custody proceeding has been initiated by Ms. W, who seeks custody of her three young children from a previous marriage. Her former husband, FH, is a party to the proceeding, and he has made a copy of—and seeks to introduce into evidence—an unpublished manuscript written by W's present husband, PH. The manuscript is an autobiography of PH, and it depicts his murder (when 17 years old) of his own father by a hammer beating, his tricking the juvenile justice system, and his securing his murdered father's estate. FH's purpose in introducing the manuscript is to convince the court of PH's unfitness (to say the least) as a custodian of the three children. PH has registered the copyright in the manuscript and has instituted an action for copyright infringement in the federal court, seeking an injunction against the use of the manuscript copy in the custody case. FH has raised the defense of fair use. How would you decide the infringement case? (Among other things, should it matter whether FH got possession of the manuscript by stealing it, or rather by being given it by PH's former attorney who had been holding it while seeking to get it published for PH?) See Bond v. Blum, 317 F.3d 385 (4th Cir.2003).

C. THE APPLICATION OF THE FAIR USE DOCTRINE TO NEW TECHNOLOGIES OF COPYING AND DISSEMINATION

Page 736–40: Substitute the following for the district court decision in *Kelly*:

Kelly v. Arriba Soft Corporation

336 F.3d 811 (9th Cir.2003).

■ T.G. NELSON, CIRCUIT JUDGE:

* * * * This case involves the application of copyright law to the vast world of the internet and internet search engines. The plaintiff, Leslie

Kelly, is a professional photographer who has copyrighted many of his images of the American West. Some of these images are located on Kelly's web site or other web sites with which Kelly has a license agreement. The defendant, Arriba Soft Corp., operates an internet search engine that displays its results in the form of small pictures rather than the more usual form of text. Arriba obtained its database of pictures by copying images from other web sites. By clicking on one of these small pictures, called "thumbnails," the user can then view a large version of that same picture within the context of the Arriba web page.

When Kelly discovered that his photographs were part of Arriba's search engine database, he brought a claim against Arriba for copyright infringement. The district court found that Kelly had established a prima facie case of copyright infringement based on Arriba's unauthorized reproduction and display of Kelly's works, but that this reproduction and display constituted a non-infringing "fair use" under Section 107 of the Copyright Act. Kelly appeals that decision, and we affirm in part and reverse in part. The creation and use of the thumbnails in the search engine is a fair use. However, the district court should not have decided whether the display of the larger image is a violation of Kelly's exclusive right to publicly display his works. Thus, we remand for further proceedings consistent with this opinion.

I.

The search engine at issue in this case is unconventional in that it displays the results of a user's query as "thumbnail" images. When a user wants to search the internet for information on a certain topic, he or she types a search term into a search engine, which then produces a list of web sites that have information relating to the search term. Normally, the list of results is in text format. The Arriba search engine, however, produces its list of results as small pictures.

To provide this functionality, Arriba developed a computer program that "crawls" the web looking for images to index. This crawler downloads full-sized copies of the images onto Arriba's server. The program then uses these copies to generate smaller, lower-resolution thumbnails of the images. Once the thumbnails are created, the program deletes the full-sized originals from the server. Although a user could copy these thumbnails to his computer or disk, he cannot increase the resolution of the thumbnail; any enlargement would result in a loss of clarity of the image.

The second component of the Arriba program occurs when the user double-clicks on the thumbnail. From January 1999 to June 1999, clicking on the thumbnail produced the "Images Attributes" page. This page used in-line linking to display the original full-sized image, surrounded by text describing the size of the image, a link to the original web site, the Arriba banner, and Arriba advertising. In-line linking allows one to import a graphic from a source website and incorporate it in one's own website, creating the appearance that the in-lined graphic is a seamless part of the second web page. The in-line link instructs the user's browser to retrieve the linked-to image from the source website and display it on the user's screen, but does so without leaving the linking document. Thus, the linking party can incorporate the linked image into its own content. As a result, although the image in Arriba's Images Attributes page came directly from the originating web site and was not copied onto Arriba's server, the user would not realize that the image actually resided on another web site.

From July 1999 until sometime after August 2000, the results page contained thumbnails accompanied by two links: "Source" and "Details." The "Details" link produced a screen similar to the Images Attributes page but with a thumbnail rather than the full-sized image. Alternatively, by clicking on the "Source" link or the thumbnail from the results page, the site produced two new windows on top of the Arriba page. The window in the forefront contained solely the full-sized image. This window partially obscured another window, which displayed a reduced-size version of the image's originating web page. Part of the Arriba web page was visible underneath both of these new windows.[4]

In January 1999, Arriba's crawler visited web sites that contained Kelly's photographs. The crawler copied thirty-five of Kelly's images to the Arriba database. Kelly had never given permission to Arriba to copy his images and objected when he found out that Arriba was using them. Arriba deleted the thumbnails of images that came from Kelly's own web sites and placed those sites on a list of sites that it would not crawl in the future. Several months later, Arriba received Kelly's complaint of copyright infringement, which identified other images of his that came from third-party web sites. Arriba subsequently deleted those thumbnails and placed those third-party sites on a list of sites that it would not crawl in the future.

The district court granted summary judgment in favor of Arriba. Kelly's motion for partial summary judgment asserted that Arriba's use of the thumbnail images violated his display, reproduction, and distribution rights.... The district court did not limit its decision to the thumbnail images alone. The court granted summary judgment to Arriba, finding that its use of both the thumbnail images and the full-size images was fair.... Kelly now appeals this decision.

II.

The district court's decision in this case involves two distinct actions by Arriba that warrant analysis. The first action consists of the reproduction of Kelly's images to create the thumbnails and the use of those thumbnails in Arriba's search engine. The second action involves the display of Kelly's larger images when the user clicks on the thumbnails. We conclude that, as to the first action, the district court correctly found that Arriba's use was fair. However, as to the second action, we conclude that

---

4. Currently, when a user clicks on the thumbnail, a window of the home page of the image appears on top of the Arriba page. There is no window just containing the image.

the district court should not have reached the issue because neither party moved for summary judgment as to the full-size images. . . .

A.

* * * * We now turn to the four fair use factors.

1. *Purpose and character of the use.*

. . . . There is no dispute that Arriba operates its web site for commercial purposes and that Kelly's images were part of Arriba's search engine database. As the district court found, while such use of Kelly's images was commercial, it was more incidental and less exploitative in nature than more traditional types of commercial use.[15] Arriba was neither using Kelly's images to directly promote its web site nor trying to profit by selling Kelly's images. Instead, Kelly's images were among thousands of images in Arriba's search engine database. Because the use of Kelly's images was not highly exploitative, the commercial nature of the use only slightly weighs against a finding of fair use.

The second part of the inquiry as to this factor involves the transformative nature of the use. We must determine if Arriba's use of the images merely superseded the object of the originals or instead added a further purpose or different character. We find that Arriba's use of Kelly's images for its thumbnails was transformative.

Despite the fact that Arriba made exact replications of Kelly's images, the thumbnails were much smaller, lower-resolution images that served an entirely different function than Kelly's original images. Kelly's images are artistic works used for illustrative purposes. His images are used to portray scenes from the American West in an esthetic manner. Arriba's use of Kelly's images in the thumbnails is unrelated to any esthetic purpose. Arriba's search engine functions as a tool to help index and improve access to images on the internet and their related web sites. In fact, users are unlikely to enlarge the thumbnails and use them for artistic purposes because the thumbnails are of much lower resolution than the originals; any enlargement results in a significant loss of clarity of the image, making them inappropriate as display material.

Kelly asserts that because Arriba reproduced his exact images and added nothing to them, Arriba's use cannot be transformative. It is true that courts have been reluctant to find fair use when an original work is merely retransmitted in a different medium. Those cases are inapposite, however, because the resulting use of the copyrighted work in those cases was the same as the original use. For instance, reproducing music CD's into computer MP3 format does not change the fact that both formats are used for entertainment purposes. Likewise, reproducing news footage into a

---

15. See, e.g., A & M Records, Inc. v. Napster, Inc., 239 F.3d 1004, 1015 (9th Cir. 2001) ("Commercial use is demonstrated by a showing that repeated and exploitative unauthorized copies of copyrighted works were made to save the expense of purchasing authorized copies.").

different format does not change the ultimate purpose of informing the public about current affairs.

Even in Infinity Broadcast Corp. v. Kirkwood [150 F.3d 104], where the retransmission of radio broadcasts over telephone lines was for the purpose of allowing advertisers and radio stations to check on the broadcast of commercials or on-air talent, there was nothing preventing listeners from subscribing to the service for entertainment purposes. Even though the intended purpose of the retransmission may have been different from the purpose of the original transmission, the result was that people could use both types of transmissions for the same purpose.

This case involves more than merely a retransmission of Kelly's images in a different medium. Arriba's use of the images serves a different function than Kelly's use-improving access to information on the internet versus artistic expression. Furthermore, it would be unlikely that anyone would use Arriba's thumbnails for illustrative or esthetic purposes because enlarging them sacrifices their clarity. Because Arriba's use is not superseding Kelly's use but, rather, has created a different purpose for the images, Arriba's use is transformative.

Comparing this case to two recent cases in the Ninth and First Circuits reemphasizes the functionality distinction. In Worldwide Church of God v. Philadelphia Church of God [227 F.3d 1110 (9th Cir. 2000)], we held that copying a religious book to create a new book for use by a different church was not transformative. The second church's use of the book merely superseded the object of the original book, which was to serve religious practice and education. The court noted that "where the use is for the same intrinsic purpose as [the copyright holder's] ... such use seriously weakens a claimed fair use."

On the other hand, in Nunez v. Caribbean International News Corp. [235 F.3d 18 (1st Cir. 2000)], the First Circuit found that copying a photograph that was intended to be used in a modeling portfolio and using it instead in a news article was a transformative use. By putting a copy of the photograph in the newspaper, the work was transformed into news, creating a new meaning or purpose for the work. The use of Kelly's images in Arriba's search engine is more analogous to the situation in Nunez because Arriba has created a new purpose for the images and is not simply superseding Kelly's purpose.

The Copyright Act was intended to promote creativity, thereby benefitting the artist and the public alike. To preserve the potential future use of artistic works for purposes of teaching, research, criticism, and news reporting, Congress made the fair use exception. Arriba's use of Kelly's images promotes the goals of the Copyright Act and the fair use exception. The thumbnails do not stifle artistic creativity because they are not used for illustrative or artistic purposes and therefore do not supplant the need for the originals. In addition, they benefit the public by enhancing information gathering techniques on the internet.

In Sony Computer Entertainment America, Inc. v. Bleem [214 F.3d 1022 (9th Cir.2000)], we held that when Bleem copied "screen shots" from Sony computer games and used them in its own advertising, it was a fair use. In finding that the first factor weighed in favor of Bleem, we noted that "comparative advertising redounds greatly to the purchasing public's benefit with very little corresponding loss to the integrity of Sony's copyrighted material." Similarly, this first factor weighs in favor of Arriba due to the public benefit of the search engine and the minimal loss of integrity to Kelly's images.

2.   *Nature of the copyrighted work.*

"Works that are creative in nature are closer to the core of intended copyright protection than are more fact-based works." Photographs used for illustrative purposes, such as Kelly's, are generally creative in nature. The fact that a work is published or unpublished also is a critical element of its nature. Published works are more likely to qualify as fair use because the first appearance of the artist's expression has already occurred. Kelly's images appeared on the internet before Arriba used them in its search image. When considering both of these elements, we find that this factor only slightly weighs in favor of Kelly.

3.   *Amount and substantiality of portion used.*

"While wholesale copying does not preclude fair use per se, copying an entire work militates against a finding of fair use." However, the extent of permissible copying varies with the purpose and character of the use. If the secondary user only copies as much as is necessary for his or her intended use, then this factor will not weigh against him or her.

This factor will neither weigh for nor against either party because, although Arriba did copy each of Kelly's images as a whole, it was reasonable to do so in light of Arriba's use of the images. It was necessary for Arriba to copy the entire image to allow users to recognize the image and decide whether to pursue more information about the image or the originating web site. If Arriba only copied part of the image, it would be more difficult to identify it, thereby reducing the usefulness of the visual search engine.

4.   *Effect of the use upon the potential market for or value of the copyrighted work.*

This last factor requires courts to consider "not only the extent of market harm caused by the particular actions of the alleged infringer, but also 'whether unrestricted and widespread conduct of the sort engaged in by the defendant ... would result in a substantially adverse impact on the potential market for the original.' " A transformative work is less likely to have an adverse impact on the market of the original than a work that merely supersedes the copyrighted work.

Kelly's images are related to several potential markets. One purpose of the photographs is to attract internet users to his web site, where he sells advertising space as well as books and travel packages. In addition, Kelly could sell or license his photographs to other web sites or to a stock photo database, which then could offer the images to its customers.

Arriba's use of Kelly's images in its thumbnails does not harm the market for Kelly's images or the value of his images. By showing the thumbnails on its results page when users entered terms related to Kelly's images, the search engine would guide users to Kelly's web site rather than away from it. Even if users were more interested in the image itself rather than the information on the web page, they would still have to go to Kelly's site to see the full-sized image. The thumbnails would not be a substitute for the full-sized images because when the thumbnails are enlarged, they lose their clarity. If a user wanted to view or download a quality image, he or she would have to visit Kelly's web site.[35] This would hold true whether the thumbnails are solely in Arriba's database or are more widespread and found in other search engine databases.

Arriba's use of Kelly's images also would not harm Kelly's ability to sell or license his full-sized images. Arriba does not sell or license its thumbnails to other parties. Anyone who downloaded the thumbnails would not be successful selling the full-sized images because of the low-resolution of the thumbnails. There would be no way to view, create, or sell a clear, full-sized image without going to Kelly's web sites. Therefore, Arriba's creation and use of the thumbnails does not harm the market for or value of Kelly's images. This factor weighs in favor of Arriba.

Having considered the four fair use factors and found that two weigh in favor of Arriba, one is neutral, and one weighs slightly in favor of Kelly, we conclude that Arriba's use of Kelly's images as thumbnails in its search engine is a fair use. * * * *

35. We do not suggest that the inferior display quality of a reproduction is in any way dispositive, or will always assist an alleged infringer in demonstrating fair use. In this case, however, it is extremely unlikely that users would download thumbnails for display purposes, as the quality full-size versions are easily accessible from Kelly's web sites.

In addition, we note that in the unique context of photographic images, the quality of the reproduction may matter more than in other fields of creative endeavor. The appearance of photographic images accounts for virtually their entire esthetic value.

CHAPTER 8

ENFORCEMENT OF COPYRIGHT

A. INJUNCTIONS

Page 751: Add to end of carry-over paragraph:

For an appellate court's amenability to the suggestion that injunctive relief may not always be appropriate, see Silverstein v. Penguin Putman, Inc., 368 F.3d 77 (2d Cir. 2004) (for facts, see Question 4, supra page 4 of this Supplement).

B. DAMAGES

Page 768: Add the following after Question 5:

6. The plaintiff in a copyright infringement action is a sculptor, who several years ago designed and mounted a large sculpture in a public setting in the city. Two years ago, the City Symphony Orchestra widely distributed a brochure announcing the details of its forthcoming musical season. Among a number of photographs of city sights contained in the brochure is a conspicuous photograph of the plaintiff's sculpture, which was duplicated by the Orchestra without securing permission. The sculptor can prove that, in the musical season that followed the distribution of the brochure, the Orchestra's gross box office income was $3 million. As counsel to the sculptor, explain to him whether he will be able to recover any of that amount as a remedy for infringement. See Mackie v. Rieser, 296 F.3d 909 (9th Cir.2002).

7. Residential Designers Inc. (RDI), an architecture firm, has prepared the building plans of a new and highly dramatic house, to be built in an affluent suburban development. It is paid $10,000 by the homeowner. Bill and Barbara Schemer, who also live in the development, were able to get the RDI plans and to have their own architect make a "knock-off" plan for their own house; their house has been built, they have moved in, and they are presently living there. RDI has brought an action against the Schemers for copyright infringement. (Assume that the RDI plans are copyrightable and that the Schemers' building their house from the RDI plans constitutes infringement.) RDI has made a claim for profits as measured by the present market value of the house minus the Schemers' cost of building it. The Schemers assert that although they may be presently liable for damages, roughly $10,000, they cannot be liable for profits until they sell their house in the future and make some. As judge, what is your ruling? See Associated Residential Design, LLC v. Molotky, 226 F.Supp.2d 1251 (D.Nev.2002).

C. Costs and Attorney's Fees

Page 779: Insert the following after the Note on *Fogerty v. Fantasy* :

See Gonzales v. Transfer Technologies, Inc., 301 F.3d 608 (7th Cir. 2002), in which the district court had awarded the minimum statutory damages of $750 for each of four infringed t-shirt images. On appeal, the court did not set aside that award as inadequate or an abuse of discretion. However, speaking for the court with respect to the award of attorneys' fees, Circuit Judge Posner said that, in the interest of deterrence, "the prevailing party in a copyright case in which the monetary stakes are small should have a presumptive entitlement to an award of attorneys' fees." You will note that this is consistent with the Supreme Court decision in the *Fogerty* case. But is it sound? Shouldn't deterrence, and making copyright lawsuits affordable, be more properly addressed through the calibration of the award of statutory damages (at least in those cases in which the plaintiff asks for them)?

F. Individual, Vicarious and Contributory Liability

1. General Principles

Page 789: Add the following to the Questions:

3. National Geographic Magazine has placed all of the content (text and photographs) of all of its issues onto a CD–Rom, which it distributes widely. No permission has been secured from the various photographers, many of whom are the present owners of copyright in their photos. The photographers have sued National Geographic for infringement, and are also making a claim of contributory infringement against the Kodak Company. Kodak has placed advertising for its own camera-related products on the CD–Roms; in addition, the Kodak website carries advertising for the National Geographic CD–Rom. Does either of these activities by Kodak expose it to substantial claims for contributory infringement by the photographers? *See Faulkner v. National Geog. Soc'y*, 211 F.Supp.2d 450 (S.D.N.Y.2002).

Page 795: Add the following after the Questions:

Metro–Goldwyn–Mayer Studios, Inc. v. Grokster, Ltd.

259 F.Supp.2d 1029 (C.D.Cal.2003), *appeal pending*.

■ Wilson, District J.

I. INTRODUCTION

Plaintiffs bring these actions for copyright infringement under 17 U.S.C. §§ 501, et seq. The Court has jurisdiction pursuant to 28 U.S.C.

§ 1331. Plaintiffs and Defendants StreamCast Networks, Inc. and Grokster, Ltd. ("Defendants") filed cross-motions for summary judgment with regard to contributory and vicarious infringement. Plaintiffs contend that Defendants' conduct renders them liable for copyright infringement committed by users of Defendants' software. Defendants argue, however, that they merely provide software to users over whom they have no control, and thus that no liability may accrue to them under copyright law.

Both parties believe that there are no disputed issues of fact material to Defendants' liability, and thus that there are no factual disputes requiring a trial. Instead, both sides maintain that the only question before the Court (as to liability) is a legal one: whether Defendants' materially undisputed conduct gives rise to copyright liability.

For the reasons stated herein, the Court GRANTS Defendants' Motions for Summary Judgment and DENIES Plaintiffs' Motion for Summary Judgment with respect to Defendants Grokster and StreamCast.

II. FACTUAL/PROCEDURAL BACKGROUND

A. *General Background*

These cases arise from the free exchange of copyrighted music, movies and other digital media over the Internet. When the actions were originally filed, Defendants Grokster, Ltd. ("Grokster"), StreamCast Networks, Inc. (formerly known as MusicCity Networks, Inc.) ("StreamCast"), and Kazaa BV (formerly known as Consumer Empowerment BV) ("Kazaa BV"), distributed software that enabled users to exchange digital media via a peer-to-peer transfer network. In the *Metro–Goldwyn–Mayer v. Grokster* case, CV–01–8541, Plaintiffs are organizations in the motion picture and music recording industries, and bring this action against Defendants for copyright infringement, pursuant to 17 U.S.C. §§ 501, et seq. In the *Lieber v. Consumer Empowerment* case, CV–01–9923, Plaintiffs are professional songwriters and music publishers bringing a class action against the same Defendants for copyright infringement, although their Complaint lists separate causes of action for contributory infringement and vicarious infringement. The cases have been consolidated for discovery and pretrial purposes.

Each Defendant distributes free software, which users can download free of charge. Although Grokster, StreamCast and Kazaa BV independently branded, marketed and distributed their respective software, all three platforms initially were powered by the same FastTrack networking technology. The FastTrack technology was developed by Defendants Niklas Zennström and Janus Friis, who also launched Kazaa BV. FastTrack was then licensed to Kazaa BV, Grokster and StreamCast for use in each company's file-sharing software. As a result, users of these software platforms essentially were connected to the same peer-to-peer network and were able to exchange files seamlessly.

However, StreamCast no longer uses the FastTrack technology. Rather, StreamCast now employs the "open" (i.e., not proprietary) Gnutella technology, and distributes its own software—Morpheus—instead of a branded version of the Kazaa Media Desktop. Grokster, meanwhile, continues to distribute a branded version of the Kazaa Media Desktop, which operates on the same FastTrack technology as the Sharman/Kazaa software.

B. *Operation of the StreamCast (Morpheus) and Grokster Software*

Although novel in important respects, both the Grokster and Morpheus platforms operate in a manner conceptually analogous to the Napster system described at length by the district court in *A & M Records, Inc. v. Napster, Inc.*, 114 F.Supp.2d 896 (N.D.Cal.2000).

In both cases, the software can be transferred to the user's computer, or "downloaded," from servers operated by Defendants. Once installed, a user may elect to "share" certain files located on the user's computer, including, for instance, music files, video files, software applications, e-books and text files. When launched on the user's computer, the software automatically connects to a peer-to-peer network (FastTrack in Grokster's case; Gnutella in the case of Morpheus), and makes any shared files available for transfer to any other user currently connected to the same peer-to-peer network.

Both the Morpheus and Grokster software provide a range of means through which a user may search through the respective pool of shared files. For instance, a user can select to search only among audio files, and then enter a keyword, title, or artist search. Once a search commences, the software displays a list (or partial list) of users who are currently sharing files that match the search criteria, including data such as the estimated time required to transfer each file.

The user may then click on a specific listing to initiate a direct transfer from the source computer to the requesting user's computer. When the transfer is complete, the requesting user and source user have identical copies of the file, and the requesting user may also start sharing the file with others. Multiple transfers to other users ("uploads"), or from other users ("downloads"), may occur simultaneously to and from a single user's computer.

Both platforms include other incidental features, such as facilities for organizing, viewing and playing media files, and for communicating with other users.

C. *Limitations of this Order*

Because Plaintiffs principally seek prospective injunctive relief, the Court at this time considers only whether the current versions of Grokster's and StreamCast's products and services subject either party to liability. This Order does not reach the question whether either Defendant is liable for damages arising from past versions of their software, or from other past activities.

Additionally, it is important to reiterate that the instant motions concern only the software operated by Defendants StreamCast (the Morpheus software) and Grokster (the Grokster software). Defendant Sharman

Networks, proprietor of the Kazaa.com website and Kazaa Media Desktop, is not a party to these Motions. Accordingly, the Court offers no opinion in this Order as to Sharman's potential liability.

* * * *

IV. DISCUSSION

Plaintiffs argue that Defendants are liable for both contributory and vicarious copyright infringement. As a threshold matter, in order to find either contributory or vicarious infringement liability, Plaintiffs must demonstrate that Defendants' end-users are themselves engaged in direct copyright infringement. A & M Records, Inc. v. Napster, Inc., 239 F.3d 1004, 1013 n. 2 (9th Cir.2001) (*"Napster"*) (citation omitted) ("Secondary liability for copyright infringement does not exist in the absence of direct infringement by a third party.").

A. *Direct Infringement*

* * * * [I]t is undisputed that at least some of the individuals who use Defendants' software are engaged in direct copyright infringement of Plaintiffs' copyrighted works. In *Napster*, the Ninth Circuit explained: "[T]he evidence establishes that a majority of Napster users use the service to download and upload copyrighted music. . . . And by doing that, it constitutes—the uses constitute direct infringement of plaintiffs' musical compositions, recordings." *Napster*, 239 F.3d at 1013–14 (quoting transcript from district court proceedings) (internal quotation marks omitted).

Just as in *Napster*, many of those who use Defendants' software do so to download copyrighted media files, including those owned by Plaintiffs, (*see, e.g.*, Pls.' Statement of Uncontroverted Facts ("Pls.' SUF") 3(j), 3(t); Griffin Depo. 278:5–10 and Ex. 291), and thereby infringe Plaintiffs' rights of reproduction and distribution. *See Napster*, 239 F.3d at 1014 (citations omitted). Thus, for purposes of these motions, Plaintiffs have established direct infringement of their copyrighted works by some end-users of Defendants' software.

B. *Contributory Infringement*

Under the doctrine of contributory copyright infringement, one is liable for contributory infringement if "with knowledge of the infringing activity, [he/she] induces, causes or materially contributes to the infringing conduct of another[.]" *Napster*, 239 F.3d at 1019 (citations and internal quotation marks omitted).

There are two factors that come into play in determining liability for contributory infringement: (1) knowledge, and (2) material contribution. The secondary infringer must "know, or have reason to know of [the] direct infringement." Adobe Systems Inc. v. Canus Prods., Inc., 173 F.Supp.2d 1044, 1048 (C.D.Cal.2001) (citations and internal quotation marks omitted). Furthermore, with regard to the second element, "liability [for contributory infringement] exists if the defendant engages in personal conduct that encourages or assists the infringement." *Napster*, 239 F.3d at 1019 (citation and internal quotation marks omitted).

1. Knowledge of Infringing Activity

In order to be held liable for contributory infringement, the secondary infringer must know or have reason to know of the direct infringement. *See Napster*, 239 F.3d at 1020. Evidence of actual knowledge of *specific acts* of infringement is required for contributory infringement liability. *Id.* at 1021.

In *Sony Corp. of America v. Universal City Studios, Inc.*, 464 U.S. 417, 104 S.Ct. 774, 78 L.Ed.2d 574 (1984), sale of video cassette recorders ("VCR"s) did not subject Sony to contributory copyright liability, even though Sony knew as a general matter that the machines could be used, and were being used, to infringe the plaintiffs' copyrighted works. Because video tape recorders were capable of both infringing and "substantial noninfringing uses," generic or "constructive" knowledge of infringing activity was insufficient to warrant liability based on the mere retail of Sony's products. *See id.* at 442. "[T]he sale of copying equipment, like the sale of other articles of commerce, does not constitute contributory infringement" if the product is "capable of substantial noninfringing uses." *Id.*

Here, it is undisputed that there are substantial noninfringing uses for Defendants' software—e.g., distributing movie trailers, free songs or other non-copyrighted works; using the software in countries where it is legal; or sharing the works of Shakespeare.... For instance, StreamCast has adduced evidence that the Morpheus program is regularly used to facilitate and search for public domain materials, government documents, media content for which distribution is authorized, media content as to which the rights owners do not object to distribution, and computer software for which distribution is permitted.... The same is true of Grokster's software....

Furthermore, as the Supreme Court has explained, the existence of substantial noninfringing uses turns not only on a product's *current* uses, but also on potential *future* noninfringing uses. *See Sony*, 464 U.S. at 442; *see also Napster*, 239 F.3d at 1020–21. Plaintiffs do not dispute that Defendants' software is being used, and could be used, for substantial noninfringing purposes.

In light of *Sony*, the Ninth Circuit in *Napster* refused to "impute the requisite level of knowledge to Napster merely because peer-to-peer file-sharing technology may be used to infringe plaintiffs' copyrights." 239 F.3d at 1020–21. Just as Sony could not be held liable for contributory infringement simply because it sold video tape recorders that could be used unlawfully, Napster would not be liable simply because it distributed software that could be used to infringe copyrights. "[A]bsent any specific information which identifies infringing activity, a computer system operator cannot be liable for contributory infringement merely because the structure of the system allows for the exchange of copyrighted material." *Napster*, 239 F.3d at 1021 (citing *Sony*, 464 U.S. at 436, 442–43).

Rather, liability for contributory infringement accrues where a defendant has actual—not merely constructive—knowledge of the infringement at a time during which the defendant materially contributes to that infringement. *See Napster*, 239 F.3d at 1020–22.

In other words, as the Ninth Circuit explained, defendants are liable for contributory infringement only if they (1) have specific knowledge of infringement at a time at which they contribute to the infringement, and (2) fail to act upon that information. *See Napster*, 239 F.3d at 1021 (citation omitted) ("We agree that if a computer system operator learns of specific infringing material available on his system and fails to purge such material from the system, the operator knows of and contributes to direct infringement.").

With respect to Napster's "actual knowledge" of infringement, the court cited: (1) a document authored by one of Napster's founders mentioning "the need to remain ignorant of users' real names and IP addresses 'since they are exchanging pirated music' "; and (2) the fact that the Recording Industry Association of America notified Napster of more than 12,000 infringing files on its system, some of which were still available. *Id.* at 1020, n. 5 (citation and internal quotation marks omitted).

In this case, Plaintiffs point to a massive volume of similar evidence, including documents suggesting that both Defendants marketed themselves as "the next Napster," that various searches were performed by Defendants' executives for copyrighted song titles or artists, that various internal documents reveal Defendants were aware that their users were infringing copyrights, and that Plaintiffs sent Defendants thousands of notices regarding alleged infringement. * * * In other words, Defendants clearly know that many if not most of those individuals who download their software subsequently use it to infringe copyrights.

However, Defendants correctly point out that in order to be liable under a theory of contributory infringement, they must have actual knowledge of infringement at a time when they can use that knowledge to stop the particular infringement. In other words, Plaintiffs' notices of infringing conduct are irrelevant if they arrive when Defendants do nothing to facilitate, and cannot do anything to stop, the alleged infringement.

This distinction is illustrated by *Religious Tech. Center v. Netcom On-Line Communication Servs., Inc.*, 907 F.Supp. 1361 (N.D.Cal.1995) ("*Netcom*"), a case informing the Ninth Circuit decision in *Napster*. The *Netcom* court distinguished a line of cases cited by the plaintiff, which concerned a landlord's liability for contributory infringement in the landlord-tenant context. These cases held "that there is no contributory infringement by the lessors of premises that are later used for infringement unless the lessor had knowledge of the intended use at the time of the signing of the lease." *Id.* at 1373 (citation and footnote omitted).

In other words, once the lease is signed, the landlord has no control over his/her tenant's use of the premises for infringing activities. Thus, any knowledge of the infringement that the landlord acquires after the tenant is in control is insufficient to establish contributory infringement liability, because there is nothing the landlord does to facilitate the infringement, or could do to stop it. In contrast, the *Netcom* court explained that "Netcom not only leases space but also serves as an access provider, which includes the storage and transmission of information necessary to facilitate [the end user's] postings to [an Internet newsgroup]. Unlike a landlord, Netcom retains some control over[ ] the use of its system." *Id.* at 1373–74.

It was critical to the court that the allegedly infringing messages were transmitted to Netcom, briefly resided on servers controlled by Netcom, and then were distributed by Netcom to other Internet systems. See *id.* "With an easy software modification Netcom could identify postings that contain particular words or come from particular individuals[,]" and delete those postings from its system (thereby preventing their propagation). Id. at 1376. Furthermore, Netcom was able to suspend user accounts—as it had done on at least 1,000 occasions—and preclude any access and distribution by a particular user through Netcom servers. *Id.*

Accordingly, the relevant time frame for purposes of assessing contributory infringement covered the entire "relationship" between Netcom and its users. Thus, the contributory infringement claim was to be decided not based on Netcom's knowledge at the time it entered into the relevant user agreement, but rather based on any knowledge acquired or possessed while Netcom contributed to the alleged infringement—i.e., "when Netcom provided its services to allow [the end user] to infringe plaintiffs' copyrights." *Id.* at 1374 (citation omitted). The Netcom court denied summary judgment because there was "a genuine issue as to whether Netcom knew of any infringement [ ] before it was too late to do anything about it." *Id.*

Here, it is undisputed that Defendants are generally aware that many of their users employ Defendants' software to infringe copyrighted works. (*See, e.g.*, Grokster's Mot. at 15 ("[Grokster] is of course aware as a general matter that some of its users are infringing copyrights.").) The question, however, is whether *actual knowledge of specific infringement* accrues at a time when either Defendant materially contributes to the alleged infringement, and can therefore do something about it.

2. Material Contribution to the Infringing Activity of Another

As noted *supra*, "liability [for contributory infringement] exists if the defendant engages in personal conduct that encourages or assists the infringement." *Napster*, 239 F.3d at 1019 (citation and internal quotation marks omitted). To be liable for contributory infringement, Defendants must "materially contribute[ ]" to the infringing activity. *Id.* (citations and internal quotation marks omitted).

The original formulation of this doctrine "stems from the notion that one who *directly contributes* to another's infringement should be held accountable." Fonovisa, Inc. v. Cherry Auction, Inc., 76 F.3d 259, 264 (9th Cir.1996) (emphasis added) (citations omitted). Traditionally, one is liable for contributory infringement if, "with knowledge of the infringing activity, [he or she] induces, causes or materially contributes to the infringing conduct of another[.]" Gershwin Publ'g Corp. v. Columbia Artists Mgmt., Inc., 443 F.2d 1159, 1162 (2d Cir.1971) (cited by *Fonovisa*, 76 F.3d at 264).

The Ninth Circuit concluded in *Napster* that "liability exists if the defendant engages in personal conduct that encourages or assists the infringement." 239 F.3d at 1019 (citation and internal quotation marks omitted).

In concluding that Napster materially contributed to the infringement, the Ninth Circuit relied on the district court's finding that "without the support services defendant provides, Napster users could not find and download the music they want with the ease of which defendant boasts." *Napster*, 239 F.3d at 1022 (quoting A & M Records, Inc. v. Napster, 114 F.Supp.2d at 919–20) (internal quotation marks omitted).

The district court explained that "Napster is an integrated service designed to enable users to locate and download MP3 music files." A & M Records v. Napster, 114 F.Supp.2d at 920. Furthermore, the Ninth Circuit agreed with the district court that because Napster provided the "site and facilities" for direct infringement, Napster materially contributed to the infringement. *Napster*, 239 F.3d at 1022.

In reaching this conclusion, the *Napster* court followed the reasoning of *Fonovisa, Inc. v. Cherry Auction, Inc.*, 76 F.3d 259, an earlier Ninth Circuit case. In *Fonovisa*, the defendant operated a swap meet where many of the vendors sold counterfeit goods. *Id.* at 260. In concluding that the plaintiff's allegations supported its claim for contributory infringement against the defendant swap meet operator, the court found significant that the defendant did more than provide the space for vendors to sell their goods. The defendant provided other services—utilities, parking, advertising, plumbing, customers—which enabled the infringement to occur in large quantities. *Id.* at 264.

The court further explained that the defendant did not have to directly promote the infringing products to be held liable—it was enough that the defendant provided "the site and facilities for known infringing activity [.]" *Id.* While the defendant attempted to persuade the court that it provided rental space alone, the court explained that the defendant swap meet operator "actively str[ove] to provide the environment and the market for counterfeit sales to thrive. Its participation in the sales cannot be termed 'passive,' as [the defendant] would prefer." *Id.*

While Napster provided its software free of charge, the district court explained, and the Ninth Circuit agreed, that Napster was no different than the swap meet operator in *Fonovisa*—"The swap meet provided services like parking, booth space, advertising, and clientele. [Citation.] Here, Napster, Inc. supplies the proprietary software, search engine, servers, and means of establishing a connection between users' computers." A & M Records v. Napster, 114 F.Supp.2d at 920; *see also Napster*, 239 F.3d at 1022 ("The district court correctly applied the reasoning from *Fonovisa*, and properly found that Napster materially contributes to direct infringement.").

Furthermore, in addition to the software, Napster provided a network—the "site and facilities" for the infringement to take place. Napster hosted a central list of the files available on each user's computer, and thus served as the axis of the file-sharing network's wheel. When Napster closed down, the Napster file-sharing network disappeared with it.

As noted *supra*, the court in *Netcom* reached similar conclusions. Netcom was distinct from a landlord because it was also an "access provider," and because it stored and transmitted the allegedly infringing newsgroup posts at issue in the case. *Netcom*, 907 F.Supp. at 1373–74. Netcom's services were "necessary to facilitate" the infringing postings of which Netcom allegedly had been notified. *Id.* If Plaintiffs could prove Netcom's knowledge of these postings, Netcom would be liable "for contributory infringement since its failure to simply cancel [the end user's] infringing message and thereby stop an infringing copy from being distributed worldwide constitutes substantial participation in [the end user's] public distribution of the message." *Id.* at 1374 (citation omitted) (quoted in *Napster*, 239 F.3d at 1022).

Thus, here, the critical question is whether Grokster and StreamCast do anything, aside from distributing software, to actively facilitate—or whether they could do anything to stop—their users' infringing activity.

Plaintiffs argue that Defendants, like Napster, do much to facilitate the actual exchange of copyrighted files, and thus materially contribute to the infringement. In their original Motion, Plaintiffs—who lumped together the activities of Grokster and StreamCast with those of Kazaa BV—asserted that these Defendants provide the "means, environment, and support . . . that enable users to . . . locate, distribute and copy" copyrighted works. (Pls.'s MSJ at 21.)

As Plaintiffs' own Proposed Statement of Uncontroverted Facts reflects, however, the facts are somewhat distinct—though materially undisputed—with respect to each Defendant.

a.   Grokster

Grokster currently distributes a branded version of the Kazaa Media Desktop, originally licensed by Consumer Empowerment BV (and now controlled by Sharman). (See D. Rung Decl. ¶ 3.) Grokster does not have access to the source code for the application, and cannot alter it in any way. (D. Rung Decl. ¶ 3.) Grokster's primary ability to affect its users' experience derives from its ability to configure a "start page" and provide advertising automatically retrieved by the Grokster client software. (D. Rung Decl. ¶ 3.)

Grokster does not operate a centralized file-sharing network like that seen in *Napster*. Rather, the Grokster-licensed Kazaa Media Desktop software employs FastTrack networking technology, which is licensed by Sharman and is not owned by Grokster.

One of the central features distinguishing FastTrack-based software from other peer-to-peer technology is the dynamic, or variable use of "supernodes." A "node" is an end-point on the Internet, typically a user's computer. A "supernode" is a node that has a heightened function, accumulating information from numerous other nodes. (Smith Opp. Decl. ¶ ¶ 70–71.) An individual node using FastTrack-based software automatically self-selects its own supernode status; a user's node may be a supernode one day and not on the following day, depending on resource needs and availability of the network.(Smith Opp. Decl. ¶ 72.)

This creates a two-tiered organizational structure, with groups of nodes clustered around a single supernode. When a user starts his/her software, the user's computer finds a supernode and accesses the network. The process of locating a supernode has varied over time. The undisputed evidence is that the Grokster software is preset with a list of "root supernodes," each of which functions principally to connect users to the network by directing them to active supernodes. While Grokster may briefly have had some control over a root supernode, Plaintiffs do not dispute that Grokster no longer operates such a supernode. Thus, the technical process of locating and connecting to a supernode—and the FastTrack network—currently occurs essentially independently of Defendant Grokster.

Once a user is connected to the network, his/her search queries and results are relayed among supernodes, maximizing the breadth of the search pool and minimizing redundancy in search traffic. This also reflects a critical distinction from Napster. Napster utilized, in effect, a single "supernode" owned and operated by Napster. The company's central servers indexed files from, and passed search queries and results among, all Napster users. All Napster search traffic went through, and relied upon, Napster.

When users search for and initiate transfers of files using the Grokster client, they do so without any information being transmitted to or through any computers owned or controlled by Grokster. (*Id*. at ¶ 6.)

b.   StreamCast

Certain versions of StreamCast's Morpheus product prior to March 2002 were, like Grokster today, based on the FastTrack technology. However, the current iteration of StreamCast's Morpheus is distinct in important respects from Grokster's software. First, Morpheus is now a proprietary program owned and controlled exclusively by StreamCast. In other words, StreamCast, unlike Grokster, has access to the source code for its software, and can modify the software at will. Second, Morpheus is based on the open-source Gnutella peer-to-peer platform and does not employ a proprietary protocol such as FastTrack.

Gnutella is a "true" peer-to-peer network, featuring even more decentralization than FastTrack. A user connects to the Gnutella network (comprised of all users of Gnutella-based software, including not only Morpheus but that distributed by companies such as "LimeWire," "Bear-Share," "Gnucleus" and others) by contacting another user who is already connected. This initial connection is usually performed automatically after the user's computer contacts one of many publicly available directories of those currently connected to the Gnutella network. (Smith Opp. Decl. ¶ ¶ 32–33.) Plaintiffs do not dispute that StreamCast does not itself operate any of these directories or compensate those who do for their use by Morpheus users. (See Smith Depo. T. 509:15–509:22; 510:18–511:2.)

Instead of using supernodes, search requests on the Gnutella network are passed from user to user until a match is found or the search request expires. (Gribble Opp. Decl. ¶ ¶ 27–31.) When a user selects a file, the transfer is initiated directly between the two users. (Gribble Opp. Decl. ¶ ¶ 32–33.)

c.   Analysis

Plaintiffs appear reluctant to acknowledge a seminal distinction between Grokster/StreamCast and Napster: neither Grokster nor StreamCast provides the "site and facilities" for direct infringement. *Napster*, 239 F.3d at 1022. Neither StreamCast nor Grokster facilitates the exchange of files between users in the way Napster did. Users connect to the respective networks, select which files to share, send and receive searches, and download files, all with no material involvement of Defendants. If either Defendant closed their doors and deactivated all computers within their control, users of their products could continue sharing files with little or no interruption. (*See, e.g.*, Gribble Decl. ¶ ¶ 7, 13, 18, 21, 23, 27, 32, and 34; D. Rung Decl. ¶ 6.)

In contrast, Napster indexed the files contained on each user's computer, and each and every search request passed through Napster's servers. *Napster*, 239 F.3d at 1012. Napster provided the "site and facilities" for the alleged infringement, *id.* at 1022, affording it perfect knowledge and complete control over the infringing activity of its users. If Napster deactivated its computers, users would no longer be able to share files through the Napster network.

The evidence of contributory infringement cited by Plaintiffs with respect to these Defendants is not material. For instance, in their Statement of Uncontroverted Facts, Plaintiffs propose the following fact: "Defendants' systems enable, and provide an infrastructure for, users to search for, reproduce and distribute copyrighted sound recordings, motion pictures and other types of works without the authorization of the copyright owner." (Pls.' SUF 4(b)). If established by the record, the fact that Defendants provide an "infrastructure" for file-sharing would be of obvious significance in light of the *Napster* cases.

Plaintiffs, however, present no admissible evidence to create a genuine dispute regarding this fact. Rather, characteristic of the evidence cited are (1) a handful of isolated technical support e-mails from Grokster and StreamCast employees sent in response to users who encountered difficulties playing copyrighted media files; and (2) evidence of previously unmoderated discussion forums in which some Grokster users searched for, and discussed the propriety of exchanging, copyrighted files. (*See* Pls.' SUF 4(b); *see also* Pls.' SUF 4(p).)

As an initial matter, the record indicates that Defendants have undertaken efforts to avoid assisting users who seek to use their software for improper purposes. More critically, technical assistance and other incidental services are not "material" to the alleged infringement. To be liable for contributory infringement, "[p]articipation in the infringement must be substantial. The authorization or assistance must bear a direct relationship to the infringing acts, and the contributory infringer must have acted in concert with the direct infringer." Marvullo v. Gruner & Jahr, 105 F.Supp.2d 225, 230 (S.D.N.Y.2000) (citation omitted); *accord* Arista Records, Inc. v. MP3Board, Inc., 2002 U.S. Dist. LEXIS 16165, at *16 (S.D.N.Y. Aug. 28, 2002). Here, the technical assistance was rendered after the alleged infringement took place, was routine and non-specific in nature, and, in most cases, related to use of *other companies'* software (e.g., third-party media player software).

The only "technical assistance" that would bear on this analysis would be that which suggests Defendants somehow facilitate or contribute to the actual exchange of files. Plaintiffs cite no such evidence. Indeed, Plaintiffs cite two e-mails to Defendant Grokster in which users complained that copyrighted files they had attempted to download contained computer viruses. (D. Rung Depo. Ex. 64, 66.) In both cases, Grokster responded with a "stock" statement explaining that Grokster has no "control over who uses the system or what is shared through it," and could not block the files. (*Id.*) This, despite the fact that the files at issue were viruses that presumably could have posed a risk to Grokster's users.

    * * * *

Defendants distribute and support software, the users of which can and do choose to employ it for both lawful and unlawful ends. Grokster and StreamCast are not significantly different from companies that sell home video recorders or copy machines, both of which can be and are used to infringe copyrights. While Defendants, like Sony or Xerox, may know that their products will be used illegally by some (or even many) users, and may provide support services and refinements that indirectly support such use, liability for contributory infringement does not lie "merely because peer-to-peer file-sharing technology may be used to infringe plaintiffs' copyrights." *Napster*, 239 F.3d at 1020–21 (citation omitted). Absent evidence of active and substantial contribution to the infringement itself, Defendants cannot be liable.

Because there are no disputed issues of fact material to this analysis, summary judgment is granted for Defendants.

C. *Vicarious Infringement*

The doctrine of vicarious infringement, an expansion of traditional respondeat superior, extends liability for copyright infringement to "cases in which a defendant 'has a right and ability to supervise the infringing activity and also has a direct financial interest in such activities.'" *Napster*, 239 F.3d at 1022 (quoting *Fonovisa*, 76 F.3d at 262 (citation omitted)).

There are two elements required for vicarious infringement: (1) financial benefit, and (2) the defendant's right and ability to supervise the infringing conduct. As opposed to contributory infringement, one can be liable for vicarious infringement without knowledge of the infringement.

Adobe Systems, 173 F.Supp.2d at 1049 (citation omitted) ("Lack of knowledge of the infringement is irrelevant.").

1. Financial Benefit

To be liable for vicarious infringement, a defendant must have a "direct financial interest in the infringing activity." *Napster*, 239 F.3d at 1023 (citing A & M Records, Inc. v. Napster, Inc., 114 F.Supp.2d 896, 921–22). The Ninth Circuit held in *Fonovisa* that financial benefit may be shown "where infringing performances enhance the attractiveness of the venue to potential customers." 76 F.3d at 263. Further, "[f]inancial benefit exists where the availability of infringing material 'acts as a "draw" for customers.'" *Napster*, 239 F.3d at 1023 (quoting *Fonovisa*, 76 F.3d at 263–64).

Here, it is clear that Defendants derive a financial benefit from the infringing conduct. The ability to trade copyrighted songs and other copyrighted works certainly is a "draw" for many users of Defendants' software. As a result, Defendants have a user base in the tens of millions. (Pls.' SUF 5(a).)

* * * * While those who use Defendants' software do not pay for the product, Defendants derive substantial revenue from advertising. For example, StreamCast had $1.8 million in revenue in 2001 from advertising. (SUF 5(b); Griffin Depo. 446:1–14.) And as of July of 2002, StreamCast had $2 million in revenue and projects $5.7 million by the end of the year. (Griffin Depo. 455:7, 456:2–3.) Grokster also derives substantial revenue from advertising. (D.Rung.Depo.140:21–141:1.) The more individuals who download the software, the more advertising revenue Defendants collect. And because a substantial number of users download the software to acquire copyrighted material, a significant proportion of Defendants' advertising revenue depends upon the infringement. Defendants thus derive a financial benefit from the infringement.

2. Right and Ability to Supervise the Infringing Conduct

As noted *supra*, vicarious liability arose from the agency doctrine of respondeat superior. *See Gershwin*, 443 F.2d at 1162. The doctrine ultimately was expanded to include other situations where a defendant has the "right and ability to supervise the infringing activity" of another. *Fonovisa*, 76 F.3d at 262 (citing *Gershwin*, 443 F.2d at 1162).

In *Fonovisa*, the Ninth Circuit held that the plaintiff's complaint alleged sufficient control. 76 F.3d at 263. The court concluded that the defendant swap meet operator had the right to supervise (or "police") the infringing conduct for the following reasons: the defendant had the right to terminate vendors for any reason; the defendant promoted the swap meet; the defendant controlled the access of customers to the booth area; the defendant patrolled the small booth area; the defendant could control direct infringers through its rules and regulations; and the defendant promoted the show. *Id.* at 262–63.

The Ninth Circuit identified similar influence and control in *Napster*. Most notably, Napster had the "right and ability to supervise its users' conduct[,]'' including the central indices of files being shared and exchanged. *Napster*, 239 F.3d at 1023 (citing district court opinion). Moreover, Napster users were required to register with Napster, and access to the file-sharing system depended upon a user's valid registration. *Id.* at 1011–12, 23–24. As a result, Napster possessed—and frequently exercised—the power to terminate access for users who violated company policies or applicable law. *Id.* at 1023. The "ability to block infringers' access to a particular environment for any reason whatsoever is evidence of the right and ability to supervise" the infringing conduct. *Id.* Together, the centralized search indices and mandatory registration system gave Napster both "knowledge" of what was being exchanged, and an ability to police those exchanges. Similarly, in a case involving vicarious liability for operation of a peer-to-peer file-sharing network, a district court in Illinois explained that the defendant had "the right and ability to supervise" the infringing conduct because the defendant had the ability to terminate users and control access to the system. In re: Aimster Copyright Litig., 2002 U.S. Dist. LEXIS 17054, at *50–*51 (N.D.Ill. Sep. 4, 2002).

Defendants argue principally that they do not have the ability to control the infringement as did these other defendants. Because they have no ability to supervise or control the file-sharing networks, or to restrict access to them, Defendants maintain that they cannot police what is being traded as Napster could. Plaintiffs contend, however, that the software itself could be altered to prevent users from sharing copyrighted files. Indeed, Napster was obligated to exercise its "right to police" to the fullest extent, which included implementing new client software filtering mechanisms. See *Napster*, 239 F.3d at 1023–24.

Plaintiffs note that Defendants' software already includes optional screens for pornographic/obscene file names, and that it could just as easily screen out copyrighted song titles. Likewise, they note that the software searches "meta data"—information beyond the filename contained in the file itself, including artist, title, album, etc.—and that an effective "meta data" screen could likewise be implemented quite easily. Finally, Plaintiffs contend that Defendants could with relative ease employ emerging "digital fingerprinting" technology that would block out a substantial percentage of copyrighted songs. Defendants dispute the feasibility and efficacy of these remedies.

However, whether these safeguards are practicable is immaterial to this analysis, as the obligation to "police" arises only where a defendant has the "right and ability" to supervise *the infringing conduct*. See *Napster*, 239 F.3d at 1023; *Fonovisa*, 76 F.3d at 262.

* * * * Defendants provide software that communicates across networks that are entirely outside Defendants control. In the case of Grokster, the network is the propriety FastTrack network, which is clearly not controlled by Defendant Grokster. In the case of StreamCast, the network is Gnutella, the open-source nature of which apparently places it outside the control of any single entity.

While the parties dispute what Defendants feasibly could do to alter their software, here, unlike in *Napster*, there is no admissible evidence before the Court indicating that Defendants have the ability to supervise and control the infringing conduct (all of which occurs *after* the product has passed to end-users). The doctrine of vicarious infringement does not contemplate liability based upon the fact that a product could be made such that it is less susceptible to unlawful use, where no control over the user of the product exists.

Accordingly, there are no genuine issues of fact material to this claim, and summary judgment is appropriate.

V. CONCLUSION

The Court is not blind to the possibility that Defendants may have intentionally structured their businesses to avoid secondary liability for copyright infringement, while benefitting financially from the illicit draw of their wares. While the Court need not decide whether steps could be taken to reduce the susceptibility of such software to unlawful use, assuming such steps could be taken, additional legislative guidance may be well-counseled.

To justify a judicial remedy, however, Plaintiffs invite this Court to expand existing copyright law beyond its well-drawn boundaries. * * * *

In re Aimster Copyright Litigation

334 F.3d 643 (7th Cir.2003).

POSNER, Circuit J.

Owners of copyrighted popular music filed a number of closely related suits, which were consolidated and transferred to the Northern District of Illinois by the Multidistrict Litigation Panel, against John Deep and corporations that are controlled by him and need not be discussed separately. The numerous plaintiffs, who among them appear to own most subsisting copyrights on American popular music, claim that Deep's "Aimster" Internet service (recently renamed "Madster") is a contributory and vicarious infringer of these copyrights. The district judge entered a broad preliminary injunction, which had the effect of shutting down the Aimster service until the merits of the suit are finally resolved, from which Deep appeals. Aimster is one of a number of enterprises (the former Napster is the best known) that have been sued for facilitating the swapping of digital copies of popular music, most of it copyrighted, over the Internet. (For an illuminating discussion, see Tim Wu, "When Code Isn't Law," 89 Va. L.Rev. 679 (2003), esp. 723–41; and with special reference to Aimster, see Alec Klein, "Going Napster One Better; Aimster Says Its File–Sharing Software Skirts Legal Quagmire," Wash. Post, Feb. 25, 2001, p. A1.) To simplify exposition, we refer to the appellant as "Aimster" and to the appellees (the plaintiffs) as the recording industry.

177

Teenagers and young adults who have access to the Internet like to swap computer files containing popular music. If the music is copyrighted, such swapping, which involves making and transmitting a digital copy of the music, infringes copyright. The swappers, who are ignorant or more commonly disdainful of copyright and in any event discount the likelihood of being sued or prosecuted for copyright infringement, are the direct infringers. But firms that facilitate their infringement, even if they are not themselves infringers because they are not making copies of the music that is shared, may be liable to the copyright owners as contributory infringers. Recognizing the impracticability or futility of a copyright owner's suing a multitude of individual infringers ("chasing individual consumers is time consuming and is a teaspoon solution to an ocean problem," Randal C. Picker, "Copyright as Entry Policy: The Case of Digital Distribution," 47 Antitrust Bull. 423, 442 (2002)), the law allows a copyright holder to sue a contributor to the infringement instead, in effect as an aider and abettor. * * *

The district judge ruled that the recording industry had demonstrated a likelihood of prevailing on the merits should the case proceed to trial. He so ruled with respect to vicarious as well as contributory infringement; we begin with the latter, the more familiar charge.

The Aimster system has the following essential components: proprietary software that can be downloaded free of charge from Aimster's Web site; Aimster's server (a server is a computer that provides services to other computers, in this case personal computers owned or accessed by Aimster's users, over a network), which hosts the Web site and collects and organizes information obtained from the users but does not make copies of the swapped files themselves and that also provides the matching service described below; computerized tutorials instructing users of the software on how to use it for swapping computer files; and "Club Aimster," a related Internet service owned by Deep that users of Aimster's software can join for a fee and use to download the "top 40" popular-music files more easily than by using the basic, free service. The "AIM" in "Aimster" stands for AOL instant-messaging service. Aimster is available only to users of such services (of which AOL's is the most popular) because Aimster users can swap files only when both are online and connected in a chat room enabled by an instant-messaging service.

Someone who wants to use Aimster's basic service for the first time to swap files downloads the software from Aimster's Web site and then registers on the system by entering a user name (it doesn't have to be his real name) and a password at the Web site. Having done so, he can designate any other registrant as a "buddy" and can communicate directly with all his buddies when he and they are online, attaching to his communications (which are really just emails) any files that he wants to share with the buddies. All communications back and forth are encrypted by the sender by means of encryption software furnished by Aimster as part of the software package downloadable at no charge from the Web site, and are decrypted by the recipient using the same Aimsterfurnished software package. If the user does not designate a buddy or buddies, then *all* the users of the Aimster system become his buddies; that is, he can send or receive from any of them.

Users list on their computers the computer files they are willing to share. (They needn't list them separately, but can merely designate a folder in their computer that contains the files they are willing to share.) A user who wants to make a copy of a file goes online and types the name of the file he wants in his "Search For" field. Aimster's server searches the computers of those users of its software who are online and so are available to be searched for files they are willing to share, and if it finds the file that has been requested it instructs the computer in which it is housed to transmit the file to the recipient via the Internet for him to download into his computer. Once he has done this he can if he wants make the file available for sharing with other users of the Aimster system by listing it as explained above. In principle, therefore, the purchase of a single CD could be levered into the distribution within days or even hours of millions of identical, near-perfect (depending on the compression format used) copies of the music recorded on the CD—hence the recording industry's anxiety about file-sharing services oriented toward consumers of popular music. But because copies of the songs reside on the computers of the users and not on Aimster's own server, Aimster is not a direct infringer of the copyrights on those songs. Its function is similar to that of a stock exchange, which is a facility for matching offers rather than a repository of the things being exchanged (shares of stock). But unlike transactions on a stock exchange, the consummated "transaction" in music files does not take place in the facility, that is, in Aimster's server.

What we have described so far is a type of Internet file-sharing system that might be created for innocuous purposes such as the expeditious exchange of confidential business data among employees of a business firm.... The fact that copyrighted materials might sometimes be shared between users of such a system without the authorization of the copyright owner or a fair use privilege would not make the firm a contributory infringer. Otherwise AOL's instant-messaging system, which Aimster piggybacks on, might be deemed a contributory infringer. For there is no doubt that some of the attachments that AOL's multitudinous subscribers transfer are copyrighted, and such distribution is an infringement unless authorized by the owner of the copyright. The Supreme Court made clear in the *Sony* decision that the producer of a product that has substantial noninfringing uses is not a contributory infringer merely because some of the uses actually made of the product (in that case a machine, the predecessor of today's videocassette recorders, for recording television programs on tape) are infringing. Sony Corp. of America, Inc. v. Universal City Studios, Inc., 464 U.S. 417 (1984); see also Vault Corp. v. Quaid Software Ltd., 847 F.2d 255, 262–67 (5th Cir.1988). How much more the Court held is the principal issue that divides the parties; and let us try to resolve it, recognizing of course that the Court must have the last word.

Sony's Betamax video recorder was used for three principal purposes, as Sony was well aware (a fourth, playing home movies, involved no copying). The first, which the majority opinion emphasized, was time shifting, that is, recording a television program that was being shown at a time inconvenient for the owner of the Betamax for later watching at a convenient time. The second was "library building," that is, making copies of programs to retain permanently. The third was skipping commercials by taping a program before watching it and then, while watching the tape, using the fast-forward button on the recorder to skip over the commercials. The first use the Court held was a fair use (and hence not infringing) because it enlarged the audience for the program. The copying involved in the second and third uses was unquestionably infringing to the extent that the programs copied were under copyright and the taping of them was not authorized by the copyright owners—but not all fell in either category. Subject to this qualification, building a library of taped programs was infringing because it was the equivalent of borrowing a copyrighted book from a public library, making a copy of it for one's personal library, then returning the original to the public library. The third use, commercial-skipping, amounted to creating an unauthorized derivative work, see WGN Continental Broadcasting Co. v. United Video, Inc., 693 F.2d 622, 625 (7th Cir.1982); Gilliam v. American Broadcasting Cos., 538 F.2d 14, 17–19, 23 (2d Cir.1976); cf. Ty, Inc. v. GMA Accessories, Inc., 132 F.3d 1167, 1173 (7th Cir.1997), namely a commercial-free copy that would reduce the copyright owner's income from his original program, since "free" television programs are financed by the purchase of commercials by advertisers.

Thus the video recorder was being used for a mixture of infringing and noninfringing uses and the Court thought that Sony could not demix them because once Sony sold the recorder it lost all control over its use. Sony Corp. of America, Inc. v. Universal City Studios, Inc., supra, 464 U.S at 438. The court ruled that "the sale of copying equipment, like the sale of other articles of commerce, does not constitute contributory infringement if the product is widely used for legitimate, unobjectionable purposes. Indeed, it need merely be capable of substantial noninfringing uses. The question is thus whether the Betamax is capable of commercially significant non-infringing uses. In order to resolve that question, we need not explore *all* the different potential uses of the machine and determine whether or not they would constitute infringement. Rather, we need only consider whether on the basis of the facts as found by the district court a significant number of them would be non-infringing. Moreover, in order to resolve this case we need not give precise content to the question of how much use is commercially significant. For one potential use of the Betamax plainly satisfies this standard, however it is understood: private, noncommercial timeshifting in the home." Id. at 441.

In our case the recording industry, emphasizing the reference to "articles of commerce" in the passage just quoted and elsewhere in the Court's opinion (see id. at 440; cf. 35 U.S.C. § 271(c)), and emphasizing as well the Court's evident concern that the copyright holders were trying to lever their copyright monopolies into a monopoly over video recorders,

Sony Corp. of America, Inc. v. Universal City Studios, Inc., *supra*, 464 U.S at 441–42 and n. 21, and also remarking Sony's helplessness to prevent infringing uses of its recorders once it sold them, argues that *Sony* is inapplicable to services. With regard to services, the industry argues, the test is merely whether the provider knows it's being used to infringe copyright. The industry points out that the provider of a service, unlike the seller of a product, has a continuing relation with its customers and therefore should be able to prevent, or at least limit, their infringing copyright by monitoring their use of the service and terminating them when it is discovered that they are infringing. * * * [W]e agree with the recording industry that the ability of a service provider to prevent its customers from infringing is a factor to be considered in determining whether the provider is a contributory infringer. Congress so recognized in the Digital Millennium Copyright Act, which we discuss later in this opinion.

It is not necessarily a controlling factor, however, as the recording industry believes. If a service facilitates both infringing and noninfringing uses, as in the case of AOL's instant-messaging service, and the detection and prevention of the infringing uses would be highly burdensome, the rule for which the recording industry is contending could result in the shutting down of the service or its annexation by the copyright owners (contrary to the clear import of the *Sony* decision), because the provider might find it impossible to estimate its potential damages liability to the copyright holders and would anyway face the risk of being enjoined. The fact that the recording industry's argument if accepted might endanger AOL's instant-messaging service ... is not only alarming; it is paradoxical, since subsidiaries of AOL's parent company (AOL Time Warner), such as Warner Brothers Records and Atlantic Recording Corporation, are among the plaintiffs in this case and music chat rooms are among the facilities offered by AOL's instant-messaging service.

We also reject the industry's argument that *Sony* provides no defense to a charge of contributory infringement when, in the words of the industry's brief, there is anything "more than a mere showing that a product may be used for infringing purposes." Although the fact was downplayed in the majority opinion, it was apparent that the Betamax was being used for infringing as well as noninfringing purposes—even the majority acknowledged that 25 percent of Betamax users were fast forwarding through commercials, id. at 452 n. 36—yet Sony was held not to be a contributory infringer. The Court was unwilling to allow copyright holders to prevent infringement effectuated by means of a new technology at the price of possibly denying noninfringing consumers the benefit of the technology. We therefore agree with Professor Goldstein that the Ninth Circuit erred in A & M Records, Inc. v. Napster, Inc., 239 F.3d 1004, 1020 (9th Cir.2001), in suggesting that actual knowledge of specific infringing uses is a sufficient condition for deeming a facilitator a contributory infringer. 2 Paul Goldstein, Copyright § 6.1.2, p. 6:12–1 (2d ed.2003)

The recording industry's hostility to the *Sony* decision is both understandable, given the amount of Internet enabled infringement of music copyrights, and manifest—the industry in its brief offers five reasons for confining its holding to its specific facts. But it is being articulated in the wrong forum.

Equally, however, we reject Aimster's argument that to prevail the recording industry must prove it has actually lost money as a result of the copying that its service facilitates. It is true that the Court in *Sony* emphasized that the plaintiffs had failed to show that they had sustained substantial harm from the Betamax. Id. at 450–54, 456. But the Court did so in the context of assessing the argument that time shifting of television programs was fair use rather than infringement. One reason time shifting was fair use, the Court believed, was that it wasn't hurting the copyright owners because it was enlarging the audience for their programs. But a copyright owner who can prove infringement need not show that the infringement caused him a financial loss. Granted, without such a showing he cannot obtain compensatory damages; but he can obtain statutory damages, or an injunction, just as the owner of physical property can obtain an injunction against a trespasser without proving that the trespass has caused him a financial loss.

What is true is that when a supplier is offering a product or service that has noninfringing as well as infringing uses, some estimate of the respective magnitudes of these uses is necessary for a finding of contributory infringement. The Court's action in striking the cost benefit tradeoff in favor of Sony came to seem prescient when it later turned out that the principal use of video recorders was to allow people to watch at home movies that they bought or rented rather than to tape television programs. * * * An enormous new market thus opened for the movie industry—which by the way gives point to the Court's emphasis on potential as well as actual noninfringing uses. But the balancing of costs and benefits is necessary only in a case in which substantial noninfringing uses, present or prospective, are demonstrated.

We also reject Aimster's argument that because the Court said in *Sony* that mere "constructive knowledge" of infringing uses is not enough for contributory infringement, 464 U.S. at 439, and the encryption feature of Aimster's service prevented Deep from knowing what songs were being copied by the users of his system, he lacked the knowledge of infringing uses that liability for contributory infringement requires. Willful blindness is knowledge, in copyright law (where indeed it may be enough that the defendant *should* have known of the direct infringement, Casella v. Morris, 820 F.2d 362, 365 (11th Cir.1987); 2 Goldstein, *supra*, § 6.1, p. 6:6), as it is in the law generally. See, e.g., Louis Vuitton S.A. v. Lee, 875 F.2d 584, 590 (7th Cir.1989) (contributory trademark infringement). One who, knowing or strongly suspecting that he is involved in shady dealings, takes steps to make sure that he does not acquire full or exact knowledge of the nature and extent of those dealings is held to have a criminal intent, United States v. Giovannetti, 919 F.2d 1223, 1228 (7th Cir.1990), because a deliberate effort to avoid guilty knowledge is all that the law requires to establish a guilty state of mind. * * * [N]o more can Deep [escape liability] by using encryption software to prevent himself from learning what surely he strongly suspects to be the case: that the users of his service—maybe *all* the users of his service—are copyright infringers.

This is not to say that the provider of an encrypted instant-messaging service or encryption software is *ipso facto* a contributory infringer should his buyers use the service to infringe copyright, merely because encryption, like secrecy generally, facilitates unlawful transactions. * * * * Our point is only that a service provider that would otherwise be a contributory infringer does not obtain immunity by using encryption to shield itself from actual knowledge of the unlawful purposes for which the service is being used.

We also do not buy Aimster's argument that since the Supreme Court distinguished, in the long passage from the *Sony* opinion that we quoted earlier, between actual and potential noninfringing uses, all Aimster has to show in order to escape liability for contributory infringement is that its file-sharing system could be used in noninfringing ways, which obviously it could be. Were that the law, the seller of a product or service used solely to facilitate copyright infringement, though it was capable in principle of noninfringing uses, would be immune from liability for contributory infringement. That would be an extreme result, and one not envisaged by the *Sony* majority. * * * * [The *Sony* decision is] not inconsistent with imposing liability on the seller of a product or service that ... is capable of noninfringing uses but in fact is used only to infringe. To the recording industry, a single known infringing use brands the facilitator as a contributory infringer. To the Aimsters of this world, a single noninfringing use provides complete immunity from liability. Neither is correct.

To situate Aimster's service between these unacceptable poles, we need to say just a bit more about it. In explaining how to use the Aimster software, the tutorial gives as its only examples of file sharing the sharing of copyrighted music, including copyrighted music that the recording industry had notified Aimster was being infringed by Aimster's users. The tutorial is the invitation to infringement that the Supreme Court found was missing in *Sony*. In addition, membership in Club Aimster enables the member for a fee of $4.95 a month to download with a single click the music most often shared by Aimster users, which turns out to be music copyrighted by the plaintiffs. Because Aimster's software is made available free of charge and Aimster does not sell paid advertising on its Web site, Club Aimster's monthly fee is the only means by which Aimster is financed and so the club cannot be separated from the provision of the free software. When a member of the club clicks on "play" next to the name of a song on the club's Web site, Aimster's server searches through the computers of the Aimster users who are online until it finds one who has listed the song as available for sharing, and it then effects the transmission of the file to the computer of the club member who selected it. Club Aimster lists only the 40 songs that are currently most popular among its members; invariably these are under copyright.

The evidence that we have summarized does not exclude the *possibility* of substantial noninfringing uses of the Aimster system, but the evidence is sufficient, especially in a preliminary-injunction proceeding, which is summary in character, to shift the burden of production to Aimster to demonstrate that its service has substantial noninfringing uses.... As it might:

1. Not all popular music is copyrighted. Apart from music on which the copyright has expired (not much of which, however, is of interest to the teenagers and young adults interested in swapping music), start-up bands and performers may waive copyright in the hope that it will encourage the playing of their music and create a following that they can convert to customers of their subsequent works.

* * * *

5. Someone might own a popular-music CD that he was particularly fond of, but he had not downloaded it into his computer and now he finds himself out of town but with his laptop and he wants to listen to the CD, so he uses Aimster's service to download a copy. This might be a fair use rather than a copyright infringement, by analogy to the time shifting approved as fair use in the *Sony* case. Recording Industry Ass'n of America v. Diamond Multimedia Systems, Inc., 180 F.3d 1072, 1079 (9th Cir.1999) * * * *

All ... of our examples of actually or arguably noninfringing uses of Aimster's service are possibilities, but as should be evident from our earlier discussion the question is how probable they are. It is not enough, as we have said, that a product or service be physically capable, as it were, of a noninfringing use. Aimster has failed to produce any evidence that its service has ever been used for a noninfringing use, let alone evidence concerning the frequency of such uses. In the words of the district judge, "defendants here have provided no evidence whatsoever (besides the unsupported declaration of Deep) that Aimster is *actually* used for any of the stated non-infringing purposes. Absent is any indication from real-life Aimster users that their primary use of the system is to transfer non-copyrighted files to their friends or identify users of similar interests and share information. Absent is any indication that even a single business without a network administrator uses Aimster to exchange business records as Deep suggests." In re Aimster Copyright Litigation, 252 F.Supp.2d 634, 653 (N.D.Ill.2002) (emphasis in original).

We have to assume for purposes of deciding this appeal that no such evidence exists; its absence, in combination with the evidence presented by the recording industry, justified the district judge in concluding that the industry would be likely to prevail in a full trial on the issue of contributory infringement. Because Aimster failed to show that its service is ever used for any purpose other than to infringe the plaintiffs' copyrights, the question (as yet unsettled, see Wu, supra, at 708 and nn. 95 and 98) of the net effect of Napsterlike services on the music industry's income is irrelevant to this case. If the *only* effect of a service challenged as contributory infringement is to enable copyrights to be infringed, the magnitude of the resulting loss, even whether there is a net loss, becomes irrelevant to liability.

Even when there are noninfringing uses of an Internet file-sharing service, moreover, if the infringing uses are substantial then to avoid liability as a contributory infringer the provider of the service must show that it would have been disproportionately costly for him to eliminate or at least reduce substantially the infringing uses. Aimster failed to make that showing too * * * *

[The court next concluded that Aimster's liability as a *vicarious* infringer was less clear, but that the issue did not have to be resolved, given the finding regarding contributory liability.]

We turn now to Aimster's defenses under the Online Copyright Infringement Liability Limitation Act, Title II of the Digital Millennium Copyright Act (DMCA), 17 U.S.C. § 512; see 2 Goldstein, *supra*, § 6.3. The DMCA is an attempt to deal with special problems created by the so-called digital revolution. One of these is the vulnerability of Internet service providers such as AOL to liability for copyright infringement as a result of file swapping among their subscribers. Although the Act was not passed with Napster-type services in mind, the definition of Internet service provider is broad ("a provider of online services or network access, or the operator of facilities therefor," 17 U.S.C. § 512(k)(1)(B)), and, as the district judge ruled, Aimster fits it. See 2 Goldstein, *supra*, § 6.3.1, p. 6:27. The Act provides a series of safe harbors for Internet service providers and related entities, but none in which Aimster can moor. The Act does not abolish contributory infringement. The common element of its safe harbors is that the service provider must do what it can reasonably be asked to do to prevent the use of its service by "repeat infringers." 17 U.S.C. § 512(i)(1)(A). Far from doing anything to discourage repeat infringers of the plaintiffs' copyrights, Aimster invited them to do so, showed them how they could do so with ease using its system, and by teaching its users how to encrypt their unlawful distribution of copyrighted materials disabled itself from doing anything to prevent infringement.

This completes our discussion of the merits of Aimster's appeal. But the fact that the recording industry is likely to win this case if it is ever tried is not by itself a sufficient basis for the issuance of a preliminary injunction. A court asked to issue such an injunction must also consider which party will suffer the greater harm as a result of a ruling for or against issuance. * * * * The only harm that is relevant to the decision to grant a preliminary injunction is irreparable harm, since if it is reparable by an award of damages at the end of trial there is no need for preliminary relief. The recording industry's harm should the preliminary injunction be dissolved would undoubtedly be irreparable. The industry's damages from Aimster's contributory infringement cannot be reliably estimated and Aimster would in any event be unlikely ever to have the resources to pay them. Aimster's irreparable harm from the grant of the injunction is, if anything, less, because of the injunction bond of $500,000 that the industry was required to post and that Aimster does not contend is inadequate. (Even without the bond, the recording industry would undoubtedly be good for any damages that Aimster may have sustained from being temporarily shut down, though, bond or no bond, there is still the measurement problem.) Even if the irreparable harms are deemed the same, since the plaintiffs have a stronger case on the merits than Aimster does the judge was right to grant the injunction.

Aimster objects to the injunction's breadth. * * * * We are not impressed by Aimster's argument that the district court had an independent duty, rooted in the free-speech clause of the First Amendment, to make sure that the impact of the injunction on communications over the Internet is no greater than is absolutely necessary to provide the recording industry with the legal protection to which it is entitled while the case wends its way to a conclusion. Copyright law and the principles of equitable relief are quite complicated enough without the superimposition of First Amendment case law on them; and we have been told recently by the Supreme Court not only that "copyright law contains built-in First Amendment accommodations" but also that, in any event, the First Amendment "bears less heavily when speakers assert the right to make other people's speeches." Eldred v. Ashcroft, 123 S.Ct. 769, 788–89 (2003). Or, we add, to copy, or enable the copying of, other people's music.

AFFIRMED.

QUESTIONS

1. Do you agree with the *Grokster* court's application of the "knowledge" and "material contribution" components of the test for contributory liability? Is the court's analysis consistent with *Sony, Fonovisa* and *Napster*? Is the court taking factual elements that were *sufficient* to establish contributory liability in *Fonovisa* and *Napster* and making them *necessary* elements, perhaps somewhat too strictly?

2. Is the *Sony* standard "*merely capable* of substantial non-infringing use" (emphasis supplied), or in fact substantially used for non-infringing ends? How substantial is "substantial?" Recall that, on the record in *Sony*, the primary use of the video tape recorder at the time was to time-shift. After *Napster*, an entrepreneur's knowledge that the product *can* be used to infringe does not suffice to establish contributory liability; does it make sense to say that, by contrast, an entrepreneur's expectation that the product *could* be used for legitimate purposes suffices to refute liability?

3. Recall that a defendant who deliberately "turns a blind eye" to the infringements it has enabled can also be held contributorily liable, as can one who "incites" end-users to infringe, see e.g., *Sega Enters. Ltd. v. MAPHIA*, 948 F.Supp. 923 (N.D. Cal.1996). Does either characterization apply to Morpheus's and Grokster's enterprises?

4. Recall the *Grokster* court's statement that "The doctrine of vicarious infringement does not contemplate liability based upon the fact that a product could be made such that it is less susceptible to unlawful use, where no control over the user of the product exists." But if the entrepreneur knows that the primary attraction of its product (as well, perhaps, as the primary purpose) is to facilitate infringement, then *shouldn't* the entrepreneur be obliged to design the product in a way that will permit the entrepreneur to intervene to prevent infringements? Why or why not?

5. The facts in the *Aimster* case fall somewhere between those in *Napster* and those in *Grokster*. Do you believe that the *Aimster* court would have issued a preliminary injunction had the *Grokster* facts been before it? (The possible differences across the circuits are of particular interest in an internet age, when the principles of *in personam* jurisdiction may allow the plaintiff a wide range of choices of forum.) See Metro–Goldwyn–Mayer Studios Inc. v. Grokster, Ltd., 243 F.Supp.2d 1073 (C.D.Cal.2003), at the earlier jurisdictional stage of the case set forth above, in which the court upheld the "specific" long-arm jurisdiction of California over a defendant providing peer-to-peer software to at least 2 million Californians, and also upheld jurisdiction through the discrete federal basis provided in Federal Rule of Civil Procedure 4(k)(2) (permitting the aggregation of nation-wide contacts when the claim arises under a federal statute).

2. Secondary Liability of Internet Service Providers

Page 806: Add the following after the Questions:

Ellison v. Robertson, 357 F.3d 1072 (9th Cir. 2004). The well-known science fiction writer Harlan Ellison sued website operators, host service providers, and AOL. Acting out of well-meaning, but misguided, enthusiasm to spread the word of Ellison's works, several of Ellison's fans had scanned and posted his works to newsgroups carried on AOL. Upon being advised that this kind of display of their affection for Ellison's work was in fact deleterious to the author's ability to make a living by selling his books, most of the fans removed their postings, and AOL ultimately blocked access to the rest. But Ellison claimed that thousands of downloads had already occurred, harming his market.[1] The hosts, having complied with the statutory notice and take down scheme, were not liable in damages; the fans were likely to be either judgment proof or hostile or both. That left AOL, a very large, and presumably wealthy, access provider. But, as an access provider, AOL would have been immune from liability for damages, were its services limited to "intermediate and transient storage" of the infringing material under sec. 512(a). Ellison, however, posited that AOL should disqualified from the § 512 "safe harbors" because AOL had not provided an effective means for copyright owners to notify the service of infringements. Ellison also contended that the § 512(a) immunity for "mere conduit" access providers should not apply because the infringing

---

1. Harlan Ellison devotes a portion of his webpage to the lawsuit, in which he has described internet-based copyright infringement as "Rampant. Out of control. Pandemic." Ellison asserts the scope of infringement covers "Hundreds of writers' stories, entire books, the work of a lifetime, everyone from Isaac Asimov to Roger Zelazny." *See* Ellison Webderland, Harlan Ellison Fights for Creators' Rights, *available at http://harlanellison.com/KICK/* (last visited July 6, 2004).

material that AOL transited did not simply pass through AOL's system; AOL in fact harbored the newsgroups' content for some 14 days. The district court granted summary judgment for AOL; the Ninth Circuit affirmed on the later ground but reversed and remanded regarding AOL's notification procedures.

IV. AOL and the Safe Harbors from Liability Under the DMCA

A. Threshold Eligibility Under § 512(i) for OCILLA's Safe Harbors

To be eligible for any of the four safe harbor limitations of liability, a service provider must meet the conditions for eligibility set forth in OCILLA. 17 U.S.C. § 512(i). The safe harbor limitations of liability only apply to a service provider that:

(A) has adopted and reasonably implemented, and informs subscribers and account holders of the service provider's system or network of, a policy that provides for the termination in appropriate circumstances of subscribers and account holders of the service provider's system or network who are repeat infringers; and

(B) accommodates and does not interfere with standard technical measures.

17 U.S.C. § 512(i)(1). If a service provider does not meet these threshold requirements, it is not entitled to invoke OCILLA's safe harbor limitations on liability. 17 U.S.C. § 512(i)(1).

We hold that the district court erred in concluding on summary judgment that AOL satisfied the requirements of § 512(i). There is at least a triable issue of material fact regarding AOL's eligibility for the safe harbor limitations of liability in this case. Section 512(i)(1)(A) requires service providers to: (1) adopt a policy that provides for the termination of service access for repeat copyright infringers in appropriate circumstances; (2) implement that policy in a reasonable manner; and (3) inform its subscribers of the policy. It is difficult to conclude as a matter of law, as the district court did, that AOL had "reasonably implemented" a policy against repeat infringers. There is ample evidence in the record that suggests that AOL did not have an effective notification procedure in place at the time the alleged infringing activities were taking place. Although AOL did notify the Copyright Office of its correct e-mail address before Ellison's attorney attempted to contact AOL and did post its correct e-mail address on the AOL website with a brief summary of its policy as to repeat infringers, AOL also: (1) changed the e-mail address to which infringement notifications were supposed to have been sent; and (2) failed to provide for forwarding of messages sent to the old address or notification that the e-mail address was inactive. *See Ellison*, 189 F.Supp.2d at 1057–58. AOL should have closed the old e-mail account or forwarded the e-mails sent to the old account to the new one. Instead, AOL allowed notices of potential copyright infringement to fall into a vacuum and to go unheeded; that fact is sufficient for a reasonable jury to conclude that AOL had not reasonably implemented its policy against repeat infringers.

B. AOL and the Limitation of Liability Under § 512(a)

If after remand a jury finds AOL eligible under § 512(i) to assert OCILLA's safe harbor limitations of liability, the court need not revisit whether AOL qualifies for the limitation of liability provided by § 512(a).

The first safe harbor in OCILLA pertains to "transitory digital network communications." 17 U.S.C. § 512(a)....

Whether AOL functioned as a conduit service provider in this case presents pure questions of law: was the fourteen day period during which AOL stored and retained the infringing material "transient" and "intermediate" within the meaning of § 512(a)?; was "no ... copy ... maintained on the system or network ... for a longer period than is reasonably necessary for the transmission, routing, or provision of connections?" The district court appropriately answered these questions in the affirmative. In doing so, the court relied upon on the legislative history indicating that Congress intended the relevant language of § 512(a) to codify the result of *Netcom*, 907 F.Supp. at 1361 (provider that stored Usenet messages for 11 days not liable for direct infringement merely for "installing and maintaining a system whereby software automatically forwards messages received from subscribers onto the Usenet, and temporarily stores copies on its system"), and to extend it to claims for secondary liability. We affirm the district court's ruling that AOL is eligible for the safe harbor limitation of liability of § 512(a).

QUESTIONS

1. How "transient" is retention of material for two weeks? What is the difference in fact and in legal consequences between this kind of storage, and the "system caching" set out in § 512(b)?

2. Ellison alleged that AOL was contributorily and vicariously liable for its users' postings; the Ninth circuit rejected the vicarious liability claim, on the ground that AOL did not derive a direct financial benefit from the users' infringements. On the other hand, the court found a prima facie contributory infringement claim (subject to the § 512 safe harbors) because AOL's Usenet service supplied a material contribution, and AOL should have known of the infringing activity (and would have known had it implemented an effective notification system). But might Ellison also have asserted AOL's direct liability for copyright infringement? Why or why not?

Recording Industry Association of America, Inc. v. Verizon Internet Services, Inc.

351 F.3d 1229 (D.C. Cir. 2003).

■ GINSBURG, CHIEF JUDGE: This case concerns the Recording Industry Association of America's use of the subpoena provision of the Digital

Millennium Copyright Act, 17 U.S.C. § 512(h), to identify internet users the RIAA believes are infringing the copyrights of its members. The RIAA served two subpoenas upon Verizon Internet Services in order to discover the names of two Verizon subscribers who appeared to be trading large numbers of .mp3 files of copyrighted music via "peer-to-peer" (P2P) file sharing programs, such as KaZaA. Verizon refused to comply with the subpoenas on various legal grounds.

The district court rejected Verizon's statutory and constitutional challenges to § 512(h) and ordered the internet service provider (ISP) to disclose to the RIAA the names of the two subscribers. On appeal Verizon presents three alternative arguments for reversing the orders of the district court: (1) § 512(h) does not authorize the issuance of a subpoena to an ISP acting solely as a conduit for communications the content of which is determined by others; if the statute does authorize such a subpoena, then the statute is unconstitutional because (2) the district court lacked Article III jurisdiction to issue a subpoena with no underlying "case or controversy" pending before the court; and (3) § 512(h) violates the First Amendment because it lacks sufficient safeguards to protect an internet user's ability to speak and to associate anonymously. Because we agree with Verizon's interpretation of the statute, we reverse the orders of the district court enforcing the subpoenas and do not reach either of Verizon's constitutional arguments.

I.   Background

Individuals with a personal computer and access to the internet began to offer digital copies of recordings for download by other users, an activity known as file sharing, in the late 1990's using a program called Napster. Although recording companies and music publishers successfully obtained an injunction against Napster's facilitating the sharing of files containing copyrighted recordings, *see A & M Records, Inc. v. Napster, Inc.*, 284 F.3d 1091 (9th Cir. 2002); *A & M Records, Inc. v. Napster, Inc.*, 239 F.3d 1004 (9th Cir. 2001), millions of people in the United States and around the world continue to share digital .mp3 files of copyrighted recordings using P2P computer programs such as KaZaA, Morpheus, Grokster, and eDonkey. *See* John Borland, *File Swapping Shifts Up a Gear* (May 27, 2003), *available at* http://news.com.com/2100–1026–1009742.html, (last visited December 2, 2003). Unlike Napster, which relied upon a centralized communication architecture to identify the .mp3 files available for download, the current generation of P2P file sharing programs allow an internet user to search directly the .mp3 file libraries of other users; no web site is involved. *See* Douglas Lichtman & William Landes, *Indirect Liability for Copyright Infringement: An Economic Perspective*, 16 HARV. J. LAW & TECH. 395, 403, 408–09 (2003). To date, owners of copyrights have not been able to stop the use of these decentralized programs. *See Metro–Goldwyn–Mayer Studios, Inc. v. Grokster, Ltd.*, 259 F.Supp.2d 1029 (C.D. Cal. 2003) (holding Grokster not contributorily liable for copyright infringement by users of its P2P file sharing program).

The RIAA now has begun to direct its anti-infringement efforts against individual users of P2P file sharing programs. In order to pursue apparent infringers the RIAA needs to be able to identify the individuals who are sharing and trading files using P2P programs. The RIAA can readily obtain the screen name of an individual user, and using the Internet Protocol (IP) address associated with that screen name, can trace the user to his ISP. Only the ISP, however, can link the IP address used to access a P2P program with the name and address of a person—the ISP's customer—who can then be contacted or, if need be, sued by the RIAA.

The RIAA has used the subpoena provisions of § 512(h) of the Digital Millennium Copyright Act (DMCA) to compel ISPs to disclose the names of subscribers whom the RIAA has reason to believe are infringing its members' copyrights. *See* 17 U.S.C. § 512(h)(1) (copyright owner may "request the clerk of any United States district court to issue a subpoena to [an ISP] for identification of an alleged infringer"). Some ISPs have complied with the RIAA's § 512(h) subpoenas and identified the names of the subscribers sought by the RIAA. The RIAA has sent letters to and filed lawsuits against several hundred such individuals, each of whom allegedly made available for download by other users hundreds or in some cases even thousands of .mp3 files of copyrighted recordings. Verizon refused to comply with and instead has challenged the validity of the two § 512(h) subpoenas it has received.

A copyright owner (or its agent, such as the RIAA) must file three items along with its request that the Clerk of a district court issue a subpoena: (1) a "notification of claimed infringement" identifying the copyrighted work(s) claimed to have been infringed and the infringing material or activity, and providing information reasonably sufficient for the ISP to locate the material, all as further specified in § 512(c)(3)(A); (2) the proposed subpoena directed to the ISP; and (3) a sworn declaration that the purpose of the subpoena is "to obtain the identity of an alleged infringer and that such information will only be used for the purpose of protecting" rights under the copyright laws of the United States. 17 U.S.C. § § 512(h)(2)(A)-(C). If the copyright owner's request contains all three items, then the Clerk "shall expeditiously issue and sign the proposed subpoena and return it to the requester for delivery to the [ISP]." 17 U.S.C. § 512(h)(4). Upon receipt of the subpoena the ISP is "authorized and ordered" to disclose to the copyright owner the identity of the alleged infringer. *See* 17 U.S.C. § § 512(h)(3), (5).

On July 24, 2002 the RIAA served Verizon with a subpoena issued pursuant to § 512(h), seeking the identity of a subscriber whom the RIAA believed to be engaged in infringing activity. The subpoena was for "information sufficient to identify the alleged infringer of the sound recordings described in the attached notification." The "notification of claimed infringement" identified the IP address of the subscriber and about 800 sound files he offered for trading; expressed the RIAA's "good faith belief" the file sharing activity of Verizon's subscriber constituted infringement of its members' copyrights; and asked for Verizon's "immediate assistance in stopping this unauthorized activity." "Specifically, we request that you remove or disable access to the infringing sound files via your system."

When Verizon refused to disclose the name of its subscriber, the RIAA filed a motion to compel production pursuant to Federal Rule of Civil Procedure 45(c)(2)(B) and § 512(h)(6) of the Act. In opposition to that motion, Verizon argued § 512(h) does not apply to an ISP acting merely as a conduit for an individual using a P2P file sharing program to exchange files. The district court rejected Verizon's argument based upon "the language and structure of the statute, as confirmed by the purpose and history of the legislation," and ordered Verizon to disclose to the RIAA the name of its subscriber. *In re Verizon Internet Servs., Inc.*, 240 F.Supp.2d 24, 45 (D.D.C. 2003) (*Verizon I*).

. . .

Verizon appealed . . .

II. Analysis

. . .

The issue is whether § 512(h) applies to an ISP acting only as a conduit for data transferred between two internet users, such as persons sending and receiving e-mail or, as in this case, sharing P2P files. Verizon contends § 512(h) does not authorize the issuance of a subpoena to an ISP that transmits infringing material but does not store any such material on its servers. The RIAA argues § 512(h) on its face authorizes the issuance of a subpoena to an "[internet] service provider" without regard to whether the ISP is acting as a conduit for user-directed communications. We conclude from both the terms of § 512(h) and the overall structure of § 512 that, as Verizon contends, a subpoena may be issued only to an ISP engaged in storing on its servers material that is infringing or the subject of infringing activity.

A. Subsection 512(h) by its Terms

. . .

Section 512 creates four safe harbors, each of which immunizes ISPs from liability for copyright infringement under certain highly specified conditions. Subsection 512(a), entitled "Transitory digital network communications," provides a safe harbor "for infringement of copyright by reason of the [ISP's] transmitting, routing, or providing connections for" infringing material, subject to certain conditions, including that the transmission is initiated and directed by an internet user. *See* 17 U.S.C. § § 512(a)(1)-(5). Subsection 512(b), "System caching," provides immunity from liability "for infringement of copyright by reason of the intermediate and temporary storage of material on a system or network controlled or operated by or for the [ISP]," § 512(b)(1), as long as certain conditions regarding the transmission and retrieval of the material created by the ISP are met. *See* 17 U.S.C. § § 512(b)(2)(A)-(E). Subsection 512(c), "Information residing on systems or networks at the direction of users," creates a safe harbor from liability "for infringement of copyright by reason of the storage at the direction of a user of material that resides on a system or network controlled or operated by or for the service provider," as long as the ISP meets certain conditions regarding its lack of knowledge concerning, financial benefit from, and expeditious efforts to remove or deny access to, material that is infringing or that is claimed to be the subject of infringing activity. *See* 17 U.S.C. § § 512(c)(1)(A)-(C). Finally, § 512(d), "Information location tools," provides a safe harbor from liability "for infringement of copyright by reason of the provider referring or linking users to an online location containing infringing material or infringing activity, by using information location tools" such as "a directory, index, reference, pointer, or hypertext link," subject to the same conditions as in § § 512(c)(1)(A)-(C). *See* 17 U.S.C. §§ 512(d)(1)-(3).

Notably present in §§ 512(b)-(d), and notably absent from § 512(a), is the so-called notice and take-down provision. It makes a condition of the ISP's protection from liability for copyright infringement that "upon notification of claimed infringement as described in [§ 512](c)(3)," the ISP "responds expeditiously to remove, or disable access to, the material that is claimed to be infringing." *See* 17 U.S.C. § § 512(b)(2)(E), 512(c)(1)(C), and 512(d)(3).

Verizon argues that § 512(h) by its terms precludes the Clerk of Court from issuing a subpoena to an ISP acting as a conduit for P2P communications because a § 512(h) subpoena request cannot meet the requirement in § 512(h)(2)(A) that a proposed subpoena contain "a copy of a notification [of claimed infringement, as] described in [§ 512](c)(3)(A)." In particular, Verizon maintains the two subpoenas obtained by the RIAA fail to meet the requirements of § 512(c)(3)(A)(iii) in that they do not—because Verizon is not storing the infringing material on its server—and can not, identify material "to be removed or access to which is to be disabled" by Verizon. Here Verizon points out that § 512(h)(4) makes satisfaction of the notification requirement of § 512(c)(3)(A) a condition precedent to issuance of a subpoena: "If the notification filed satisfies the provisions of [§ 512](c)(3)(A)" and the other content requirements of § 512(h)(2) are met, then "the clerk shall expeditiously issue and sign the proposed subpoena . . . for delivery" to the ISP.

Infringing material obtained or distributed via P2P file sharing is located in the computer (or in an off-line storage device, such as a compact disc) of an individual user. No matter what information the copyright owner may provide, the ISP can neither "remove" nor "disable access to" the infringing material because that material is not stored on the ISP's servers. Verizon can not remove or disable one user's access to infringing material resident on another user's computer because Verizon does not control the content on its subscribers' computers.

The RIAA contends an ISP can indeed "disable access" to infringing material by terminating the offending subscriber's internet account. This argument is undone by the terms of the Act, however. As Verizon notes, the Congress considered disabling an individual's access to infringing

193

material and disabling access to the internet to be different remedies for the protection of copyright owners, the former blocking access to the infringing material on the offender's computer and the latter more broadly blocking the offender's access to the internet (at least via his chosen ISP). *Compare* 17 U.S.C. § 512(j)(1)(A)(i) (authorizing injunction restraining ISP "from providing access to infringing material") *with* 17 U.S.C. § 512(j)(1)(A)(ii) (authorizing injunction restraining ISP "from providing access to a subscriber or account holder . . . who is engaging in infringing activity . . . by terminating the accounts of the subscriber or account holder"). "Where different terms are used in a single piece of legislation, the court must presume that Congress intended the terms have different meanings." *Transbrasil S.A. Linhas Aereas v. Dep't of Transp.*, 253 U.S. App. D.C. 31, 791 F.2d 202, 205 (D.C. Cir. 1986). These distinct statutory remedies establish that terminating a subscriber's account is not the same as removing or disabling access by others to the infringing material resident on the subscriber's computer.

The RIAA points out that even if, with respect to an ISP functioning as a conduit for user-directed communications, a copyright owner cannot satisfy the requirement of § 512(c)(3)(A)(iii) by identifying material to be removed by the ISP, a notification is effective under § 512(c)(3)(A) if it "includes substantially" the required information; that standard is satisfied, the RIAA maintains, because the ISP can identify the infringer based upon the information provided by the copyright owner pursuant to § § 512(c)(3)(A)(i)-(ii) and (iv)-(vi). According to the RIAA, the purpose of § 512(h) being to identify infringers, a notice should be deemed sufficient so long as the ISP can identify the infringer from the IP address in the subpoena.

Nothing in the Act itself says how we should determine whether a notification "includes substantially" all the required information; both the Senate and House Reports, however, state the term means only that "technical errors . . . such as misspelling a name" or "supplying an outdated area code" will not render ineffective an otherwise complete § 512(c)(3)(A) notification. S. Rep. No. 105–190, at 47 (1998); H.R. Rep. No. 105–551 (II), at 56 (1998). Clearly, however, the defect in the RIAA's notification is not a mere technical error; nor could it be thought "insubstantial" even under a more forgiving standard. The RIAA's notification identifies absolutely no material Verizon could remove or access to which it could disable, which indicates to us that § 512(c)(3)(A) concerns means of infringement other than P2P file sharing.

Finally, the RIAA argues the definition of "[internet] service provider" in § 512(k)(1)(B) makes § 512(h) applicable to an ISP regardless what function it performs with respect to infringing material—transmitting it per § 512(a), caching it per § 512(b), hosting it per § 512(c), or locating it per § 512(d).

This argument borders upon the silly. The details of this argument need not burden the Federal Reporter, for the specific provisions of § 512(h), which we have just rehearsed, make clear that however broadly "[internet] service provider" is defined in § 512(k)(1)(B), a subpoena may issue to an ISP only under the prescribed conditions regarding notification. Define all the world as an ISP if you like, the validity of a § 512(h) subpoena still depends upon the copyright holder having given the ISP, however defined, a notification effective under § 512(c)(3)(A). And as we have seen, any notice to an ISP concerning its activity as a mere conduit does not satisfy the condition of § 512(c)(3)(A)(iii) and is therefore ineffective.

In sum, we agree with Verizon that § 512(h) does not by its terms authorize the subpoenas issued here. A § 512(h) subpoena simply cannot meet the notice requirement of § 512(c)(3)(A)(iii).

B. Structure

Verizon also argues the subpoena provision, § 512(h), relates uniquely to the safe harbor in § 512(c) for ISPs engaged in storing copyrighted material and does not apply to the transmitting function addressed by the safe harbor in § 512(a). Verizon's claim is based upon the "three separate cross-references" in § 512(h) to the notification described in § 512(c)(3)(A). First, as we have seen, § 512(h)(2)(A) requires the copyright owner to file, along with its request for a subpoena, the notification described in § 512(c)(3)(A). Second, and again as we have seen, § 512(h)(4) requires that the notification satisfy "the provisions of [§ 512](c)(3)(A)" as a condition precedent to the Clerk's issuing the requested subpoena. Third, § 512(h)(5) conditions the ISP's obligation to identify the alleged infringer upon "receipt of a notification described in [§ 512](c)(3)(A)." We agree that the presence in § 512(h) of three separate references to § 512(c) and the absence of any reference to § 512(a) suggests the subpoena power of § 512(h) applies only to ISPs engaged in storing copyrighted material and not to those engaged solely in transmitting it on behalf of others.

As the RIAA points out in response, however, because §§ 512(b) and (d) also require a copyright owner to provide a "notification ... as described in [§ 512](c)(3)," the cross-references to § 512(c)(3)(A) in § 512(h) can not confine the operation of § 512(h) solely to the functions described in § 512(c), but must also include, at a minimum, the functions described in §§ 512(b) and (d). Therefore, according to the RIAA, because Verizon is mistaken in stating that "the takedown notice described in [§ 512](c)(3)(A) ... applies exclusively to the particular functions described in [§ 512](c) of the statute," the subpoena power in § 512(h) is not linked exclusively to § 512(c) but rather applies to all the ISP functions, wherever they may be described in § § 512(a)-(d).

Although the RIAA's conclusion is a non-sequitur with respect to § 512(a), we agree with the RIAA that Verizon overreaches by claiming the notification described in § 512(c)(3)(A) applies only to the functions identified in § 512(c). As Verizon correctly notes, however, the ISP activities described in §§ 512(b) and (d) are storage functions. As such, they are, like the ISP activities described in § 512(c) and unlike the transmission functions listed in § 512(a), susceptible to the notice and take down regime of

§§ 512(b)-(d), of which the subpoena power of § 512(h) is an integral part. We think it clear, therefore, that the cross-references to § 512(c)(3) in §§ 512(b)-(d) demonstrate that § 512(h) applies to an ISP storing infringing material on its servers in any capacity—whether as a temporary cache of a web page created by the ISP per § 512(b), as a web site stored on the ISP's server per § 512(c), or as an information locating tool hosted by the ISP per § 512(d)—and does not apply to an ISP routing infringing material to or from a personal computer owned and used by a subscriber.

The storage activities described in the safe harbors of §§ 512(b)-(d) are subject to § 512(c)(3), including the notification described in § 512(c)(3)(A). By contrast, as we have already seen, an ISP performing a function described in § 512(a), such as transmitting e-mails, instant messages, or files sent by an internet user from his computer to that of another internet user, cannot be sent an effective § 512(c)(3)(A) notification. Therefore, the references to § 512(c)(3) in §§ 512(b) and (d) lead inexorably to the conclusion that § 512(h) is structurally linked to the storage functions of an ISP and not to its transmission functions, such as those listed in § 512(a).

C.   Legislative History

In support of its claim that § 512(h) can—and should—be read to reach P2P technology, the RIAA points to congressional testimony and news articles available to the Congress prior to passage of the DMCA. These sources document the threat to copyright owners posed by bulletin board services (BBSs) and file transfer protocol (FTP) sites, which the RIAA says were precursors to P2P programs.

We need not, however, resort to investigating what the 105th Congress may have known because the text of § 512(h) and the overall structure of § 512 clearly establish, as we have seen, that § 512(h) does not authorize the issuance of a subpoena to an ISP acting as a mere conduit for the transmission of information sent by others. Legislative history can serve to inform the court's reading of an otherwise ambiguous text; it cannot lead the court to contradict the legislation itself. *See Ratzlaf v. United States*, 510 U.S. 135, 147–48, 126 L. Ed. 2d 615, 114 S. Ct. 655 (1994) ("We do not resort to legislative history to cloud a statutory text that is clear").

In any event, not only is the statute clear (albeit complex), the legislative history of the DMCA betrays no awareness whatsoever that internet users might be able directly to exchange files containing copyrighted works. That is not surprising; P2P software was "not even a glimmer in anyone's eye when the DMCA was enacted." *In re Verizon I*, 240 F.Supp.2d at 38. Furthermore, such testimony as was available to the Congress prior to passage of the DMCA concerned "hackers" who established unauthorized FTP or BBS sites on the servers of ISPs, *see Balance of Responsibilities on the Internet and the Online Copyright Liability Limitation Act: Hearing on H.R. 2180 Before the House Subcomm. on Courts and Intellectual Property, Comm. on the Judiciary*, 105th Cong. (1997) (statement of Ken Wasch, President, Software Publishers Ass'n); rogue ISPs that posted FTP sites on their servers, thereby making files of copyrighted musical works available for download, *see* Complaint, *Geffen Records, Inc. v. Arizona Bizness Network*, No. CIV. 98–0794, at P 1 (D. Ariz. May 5, 1998) *available at* http://www.riaa.com/news/newsletter/pdf/geffencomplaint.pdf, (last visited December 2, 2003); and BBS subscribers using dial-up technology to connect to a BBS hosted by an ISP. The Congress had no reason to foresee the application of § 512(h) to P2P file sharing, nor did they draft the DMCA broadly enough to reach the new technology when it came along. Had the Congress been aware of P2P technology, or anticipated its development, § 512(h) might have been drafted more generally. Be that as it may, contrary to the RIAA's claim, nothing in the legislative history supports the issuance of a § 512(h) subpoena to an ISP acting as a conduit for P2P file sharing.

D. Purpose of the DMCA

Finally, the RIAA argues Verizon's interpretation of the statute "would defeat the core objectives" of the Act. More specifically, according to the RIAA there is no policy justification for limiting the reach of § 512(h) to situations in which the ISP stores infringing material on its system, considering that many more acts of copyright infringement are committed in the P2P realm, in which the ISP merely transmits the material for others, and that the burden upon an ISP required to identify an infringing subscriber is minimal.

We are not unsympathetic either to the RIAA's concern regarding the widespread infringement of its members' copyrights, or to the need for legal tools to protect those rights. It is not the province of the courts, however, to rewrite the DMCA in order to make it fit a new and unforeseen internet architecture, no matter how damaging that development has been to the music industry or threatens being to the motion picture and software industries. The plight of copyright holders must be addressed in the first instance by the Congress; only the "Congress has the constitutional authority and the institutional ability to accommodate fully the varied permutations of competing interests that are inevitably implicated by such new technology." *See Sony Corp. v. Universal City Studios, Inc.*, 464 U.S. 417, 431, 78 L.Ed.2d 574, 104 S.Ct. 774 (1984).

. . .

QUESTION

The district court accepted the structural argument that the court of appeals branded as "border[ing] upon the silly." The district court held:

The textual definition of "service provider" in subsection (k) leaves no doubt, therefore, that the subpoena power in subsection (h) applies to all service providers, regardless of the functions a service provider may perform under the four categories set out in subsections (a) through (d). The broad definition in subsection (k)(1)(B)—"a provider of online services or network access"—expressly applies to the term "service provider" as used in subsection (h), since the narrow definition found in subsection (k)(1)(A) is applicable only to the term as used in subsection (a). By the plain text of the statute, moreover, the term "service provider" as employed in subsection (h) encompasses those entities defined in subsection (k)(1)(A), which explicitly includes "service providers" under subsection (a) such as Verizon (an "entity offering the transmission, routing, or providing of connections for digital online communications"). In short, Verizon contends that it has only provided an Internet connection, and thus is within subsection (a) of the DMCA; but the definition of "service provider" in subsection (k) applicable to the subpoena authority under subsection (h) squarely includes subsection (a) entities such as Verizon that are "providing . . . connections for digital online communications." Given the broad definition of "service provider" in subsection (k)(1)(B), and the use of that defined term throughout subsection (h), the Court must, under well-established statutory construction tools, read these provisions together, as a whole. See United States v. Wilson, 290 F.3d 347, 355 (D.C.Cir. 2002) ("It is the 'classic judicial task' of construing related statutory provisions 'to make sense in combination.' ") (quoting United States v. Fausto, 484 U.S. 439, 453, 108 S.Ct. 668, 98 L.Ed.2d 830 (1988)). Applying the statutory definition of "service provider" leaves no doubt whatsoever, then, that the DMCA subpoena authority reaches a subsection (a) service provider such as Verizon contends it is here.

Each court is categorically convinced of its conclusion: which exercise in statutory construction do you find more persuasive?

G. TECHNOLOGICAL PROTECTION MEASURES

Page 816: Insert following:

The *Streambox* decision offered one of the first analyses of "circumventing" conduct, holding that emulation of the "secret handshake" exchanged between the Real player and server met the statutory definition of "to circumvent." In the following decision, a different court rejected the claim that the unauthorized inputting of a password constituted circumvention.

I.M.S. Inquiry Management Systems, Ltd. v. Berkshire Information Systems, Inc.

307 F.Supp.2d 521 (S.D.N.Y. 2004).

■ BUCHWALD, JUDGE

. . .

I.M.S., a Canadian Corporation, is engaged in the service of providing advertising tracking information to publishers, advertisers, and others. I.M.S. operates a web-based service known as "e-Basket", which is used by I.M.S.'s clients to track magazine advertising. e-Basket is available exclusively to I.M.S. clients. Each I.M.S. client is issued a unique user identification and password which allows the client to access the e-Basket service and information in I.M.S.'s computers through an I.M.S. website. The e-Basket content is selected by I.M.S. and arranged into categories and subcategories, a process which involves substantial creativity, time and effort. According to I.M.S., the e-Basket service contains copyrightable subject matter.

Berkshire has introduced and operates a competing tracking service called "Marketshareinfo.com". I.M.S. alleges that in or around March of 2002, Berkshire, or an agent thereof, intentionally and without authorization accessed I.M.S.'s e-Basket service, and gathered and copied content therefrom for use in Marketshareinfo.com. Specifically, Berkshire's unauthorized access spanned eight different webpages of e-Basket content, including that which would ordinarily be used by I.M.S. clients. Through its unauthorized access, I.M.S. contends that Berkshire copied roughly eighty-five percent of I.M.S.'s report formats. Marketshareinfo.com was launched after Berkshire accessed e-Basket, and I.M.S. alleges that Marketshareinfo.com incorporates original copyrightable elements of e-Basket, including the selection and arrangement of informational category headings and I.M.S.-compiled market data.

To gain access to e-Basket, I.M.S. alleges that Berkshire obtained a user identification and password issued to a third party . . .

V. DIGITAL MILLENNIUM COPYRIGHT ACT

. . . Plaintiff claims that defendant, by accessing I.M.S.'s computer system through the unauthorized use of a password issued to a party other than defendant, violated the DMCA's bar on circumventing a technological measure that effectively controls access to protected work. . . .

Defendant challenges whether the facts as alleged manifest a "circumvention" as that term is defined in the subsection. According to defendant, the DMCA was passed to combat unauthorized disabling of digital walls which otherwise safeguard copyrighted materials available on the Internet and the decryption of encrypted content, such as that found on a DVD. Defendant argues that it is not accused of having "hacked" into plaintiff's website, and that "the disconnect between the harm the statute is designed to address and the acts of which plaintiff complains" warrants dismissal of this claim.

Whether accessing copyrighted work by unauthorized use of an otherwise legitimate, owner-issued password qualifies as circumvention under the DMCA appears to be a question of first impression in this Circuit and in all others.

A. Was An Effective Technological Measure In Place?

. . .

I.M.S.'s password protection fits within th[e statutory] definition. In order to gain access to the e-Basket service, a user in the ordinary course of operation needs to enter a password, which is the application of information. Indeed, the Second Circuit in [Universal City Studios, Inc. v. Corley, 273 F.3d 429 (2d Cir.2001)] confirmed that "the DMCA ... backed with legal sanctions the efforts of copyright owners to protect their works from piracy behind digital walls such as encryption codes or password protections." *Universal Studios*, 273 F.3d at 435 (emphasis added).

B.   Was The Technological Measure Circumvented?

It is of course the case, as defendant propounds, that the DMCA addresses activity such as decryption, descrambling, deactivation and impairment, and that these are all forms of circumvention under the subsection commonly involving technologically-sophisticated maneuvers. One might associate these activities with the breaking and entering (or hacking) into computer systems.

On the other hand, other actions proscribed by the DMCA, connote broader application of the anti-circumvention prohibition, such as the terms "avoid" and "bypass". These actions are far more open-ended and mundane, and do not necessarily involve some kind of tech-based execution. Notwithstanding this, defendant argues that it has not even committed any act of avoidance or bypass, as it is accused of confronting IMS's password-controlled access in the way precisely intended: "All [I.M.S.] accuses Berkshire of doing is using IMS's own customer's valid password and user [identification] to view IMS's e-Basket system exactly as the customer itself might have done."

We agree that plaintiff's allegations do not evince circumvention as that term is used in the DMCA. Circumvention requires either descrambling, decrypting, avoiding, bypassing, removing, deactivating or impairing a technological measure qua technological measure. In the instant matter, defendant is not said to have avoided or bypassed the deployed technological measure in the measure's gatekeeping capacity. The Amended Complaint never accuses defendant of accessing the e-Basket system without first entering a plaintiff-generated password.

More precisely and accurately, what defendant avoided and bypassed was permission to engage and move through the technological measure from the measure's author. Unlike the CFAA [Computer Fraud and Abuse Act, 18 U.S.C. §§ 1030 et seq.], a cause of action under the DMCA does not accrue upon unauthorized and injurious access alone; rather, the DMCA "targets the circumvention of digital walls guarding copyrighted material." *Universal Studios*, 273 F.3d 429, 443 (emphasis in original).

Although whether an activity qualified as circumvention was not the question posed to the court, *Universal Studios* is instructive as a matter of reference. There, the offending circumvention was a DVD decryption program, DeCSS, which enabled the viewing of movies without using a DVD player. The security device that prevented access to DVD movies without a DVD player, CSS, was described "in its basic function ... [as] a lock on a homeowner's door, a combination of a safe, or a security device attached to a store's products." Likewise, "in its basic function, [DeCSS, the decryption program] is like a skeleton key that can open a locked door, a combination that can open a safe, or a device that can neutralize the security device attached to a store's products. DeCSS enables anyone to gain access to a DVD movie without using a DVD player."

Defendant is alleged to have accessed plaintiff's protected website without plaintiff's authorization. Defendant did not surmount or puncture or evade any technological measure to do so; instead, it used a password intentionally issued by plaintiff to another entity. As an analogy to *Universal Studios*, the password defendant used to enter plaintiff's webservice was the DVD player, not the DeCSS decryption code, or some alternate avenue of access not sponsored by the copyright owner (like a skeleton key, or neutralizing device). Plaintiff, however, did not authorize defendant to utilize the DVD player. Plaintiff authorized someone else to use the DVD player, and defendant borrowed it without plaintiff's permission. Whatever the impropriety of defendant's conduct, the DMCA and the anti-circumvention provision at issue do not target this sort of activity.

QUESTIONS

1. In *321 Studios v. Metro Goldwyn Mayer Studios*, 307 F.Supp.2d 1085 (N.D. Cal. 2004), the manufacturer of a device designed to decrypt DVDs asserted that the decryption software did not "circumvent" the encryption because "its software does not avoid, bypass, remove, deactivate, or otherwise impair a technological measure, but that it simply uses the authorized key to unlock the encryption." The court rejected this contention: "While 321's software does use the authorized key to access the DVD, it does not have authority to use this key, as licensed DVD players do, and it therefore avoids and bypasses CSS." Might the same be said of a third party who uses an authorized user's password? Does it matter if the authorized user allowed a friend to use her password?

2. Jack Ripper operates the Happy Hacker website. He has posted an article analyzing and criticizing sec. 1201 of the DMCA, to which he has appended UnZip, a downloadable computer program that he has written. Jack's article asserts that UnZip guesses the passwords subscribers use to access MP3 files distributed by the licensed digital music download service, MegaRights. In effect, UnZip keeps trying passwords until one works. A password will work if it corresponds to an actual MegaRights subscriber password, and if that subscriber is not currently online with MegaRights. Has Jack violated § 1201(a)?

Page 816, after *RealNetworks v. Streambox*, insert the following:

Lexmark Int'l., Inc. v. Static Control Components, Inc., 253 F.Supp.2d 943 (E.D.Ky.2003). This controversy involved an application of 1201(a)(2) to a context probably unanticipated when Congress banned trafficking in devices primarily designed to circumvent access controls. The plaintiff produces printers and printer cartridges. To ensure that only printer cartridges of its manufacture can be used in its printers, Lexmark conditions the ability of the computer chip in the cartridge to communicate with the computer program in the printer by adding an access control to the printer program. A cartridge manufactured or recycled by a third party will not be able to work with the printer unless it exchanges the "secret handshake" information that allows the cartridge and the printer to perform together. Static Controls discovered the secret handshake information and then, according to the court, copied the printer and cartridge programs so that its recycled cartridges would work with Lexmark printers. Lexmark was granted a preliminary injunction against the distribution of the cartridges, which the court found to be access-circumvention devices in violation of the statute. The court's conclusions of law state:

> 70. The authentication sequence that occurs between Lexmark's printers and the microchips contained on authorized Lexmark toner cartridges constitutes a "technological measure" that "controls access" to a copyrighted work. This authentication sequence requires the application of information and the application of a process to gain access to Lexmark's copyrighted Toner Loading Programs and Printer Engine Programs.

> 71. Lexmark's authentication sequence effectively "controls access" to the Toner Loading Programs and the Printer Engine Program because it controls the consumer's ability to make use of these programs. *See [Sony Computer Enter. Am. Inc. v.] GameMasters,* 87 F.Supp.2d [976, 987 (N.D. Cal.1999)] (Sony's PlayStation console contained a technological measure that controlled a consumer's ability to make use of copyrighted computer programs).

> **A. SCC's SMARTEK Microchips Circumvent the Technological Measure that Controls Access to Lexmark's Copyrighted Toner Loading Programs**

> 72. SCC admits that its SMARTEK microchips avoid or bypass Lexmark's authentication sequence. The SMARTEK microchips mimic the technology for calculating and transmitting a MAC [Message Authentication Code] from Lexmark's toner cartridges to Lexmark's T–Series printers and circumvents the authentication sequence. As a result, the SMARTEK microchips are able to deceive the Lexmark T–Series printers into thinking that the SMARTEK microchips are, in fact, original microchips contained on authorized Lexmark toner cartridges. After the SMARTEK microchips bypass the authentication sequence, the printers access, without Lexmark's authority, the copyrighted Toner Loading Programs.

> 73. Lexmark has demonstrated that SCC's SMARTEK microchips satisfy all three tests for liability under section 1201(a)(2).

> 74. SCC's SMARTEK microchips satisfy the first independent test for liability because SCC acknowledges that it specifically developed the SMARTEK microchips to circumvent the authentication sequence that controls access to Lexmark's copyrighted Toner Loading Programs.

75. SCC's SMARTEK microchips satisfy the second independent test for liability because SCC acknowledges that its SMARTEK microchips have no commercial purpose other than to circumvent the authentication sequence that controls access to Lexmark's copyrighted Toner Loading Programs.

76. SCC's SMARTEK microchips satisfy the third independent test for liability because SCC markets the SMARTEK microchips as being capable of circumventing the access control protections provided by the original microchips on Lexmark's T–Series toner cartridges.

* * *

C. SCC's Actions do not Fall under any of the Exceptions to Section 1201(a)(2)

1. SCC's Manufacture, Distribution and Sale of its SMARTEK Microchips Fall within the Plain Language of the DMCA

82. Because the language of the DMCA is clear, it is unnecessary to consider the legislative history or the policy arguments raised by SCC to determine congressional intent or the scope of the DMCA. *See Elcom,* 203 F.Supp.2d at 1124. In addition, SCC does not cite to any portion of the legislative history that indicates that "the literal application of [the] statute will produce a result demonstrably at odds with the intentions of its drafters." *Koenig Sporting Goods,* 203 F.3d at 988.

83. The protections provided by the DMCA are not, and were never intended to be, as limited as SCC asserts. The DMCA is clear that the right to protect against unauthorized access is a right separate and distinct from the right to protect against violations of exclusive copyright rights such as reproduction and distribution. Section 1201(b) prohibits trafficking in devices that circumvent measures that "effectively protect[] a right of a copyright owner under this title." 17 U.S.C. § 1201(b)(1)(A). In contrast, section 1201(a)(2) more broadly prohibits trafficking in devices that circumvent measures that "effectively control[] access to a work protected under this title." 17 U.S.C. § 1201(a)(2)(A).

84. If the DMCA were only intended to protect copyrighted works from digital piracy, that goal was accomplished through section 1201(b); SCC's argument would render section 1201(a)(2) mere surplusage. Section 1201(a) creates, and section 1201(a)(2) protects, a right of "access," the violation of which is the "electronic equivalent [of] breaking into a castle." 3 Nimmer § 12A.03[D][1] at 12A–29.

85. The few cases that have applied the DMCA are in accord. *See, e.g., RealNetworks, Inc.,* 2000 U.S. Dist. LEXIS 1889 at *3 (the plaintiff's "Secret Handshake" was species of access control governed by section 1201(a)(2)); *GameMasters,* 87 F.Supp.2d at 987

(enjoining sale of device that circumvented technological measure that prevented access to software embedded in Sony's PlayStation console, even though the device did not facilitate piracy).

86.   The DMCA is not limited to the protection of "copies of works (such as books, CD's and motion pictures) that have an independent market value." The DMCA broadly prohibits trafficking in a product or device that circumvents "a technological measure that effectively controls access *to a work protected under this title.*" 17 U.S.C. § 1201(a)(2)(A), (B) (emphasis added).

87.   Lexmark's Toner Loading Programs and Printer Engine Program are works protected under the Copyright Act.

88.   Quite simply, if a work is entitled to protection under the Copyright Act, trafficking in a device that circumvents a technological measure that controls access to such work constitutes a violation under section 1201(a). The few cases decided under the DMCA prove that section 1201(a) applies to the very type of computer software that Lexmark seeks to protect, and the very type of access-protection regime Lexmark has employed to protect it.

89.   The authentication sequence employed by Lexmark in this case is similar to the technological measure employed by Sony in the *Gamemasters* case that prevented access to the copyrighted computer software that operates with Sony's PlayStation video game console. The console employs a technological measure that verifies whether a CD–ROM game inserted into the console is "an authorized, legitimate [Sony] product licensed for distribution in the same geographical territory of the console's sale." *Gamemasters,* 87 F.Supp.2d at 981. If the console cannot verify that the game is, in fact, such an authorized product, the console will not operate and the game will not play. *Id.* The *Gamemasters* court found that Sony was likely to succeed on the merits of its 1201(a)(2)(A) claim, and thus granted injunctive relief, because the defendant's "GameEnhancer" device circumvented the access control measure on the console "that ensures the console operates only when encrypted data is read from an authorized CD–ROM [video game]." *Id.* at 987.

90.   The access control measure upheld by the *Gamemasters* court is, as a technical matter, virtually identical to, and as a legal matter, indistinguishable from, the access control measure employed by Lexmark in the instant case. Like the PlayStation console, the Lexmark printer employs a technological measure— the authentication sequence—that verifies whether the toner cartridge inserted into the printer is authorized ..., or a Lexmark remanufactured cartridge, but it is not an unauthorized third-party refilled ... cartridge. If the printer cannot verify that the cartridge is, in fact, such a product, the Printer Engine Program will not operate and will not "play" the Toner Loading Program.

SCC's SMARTEK microchips, like the "GameEnhancer" device in
Gamemasters, circumvents the access control measure on the
Lexmark printer "that ensures the [printer] operates only when
encrypted data is read from an authorized [toner cartridge]."
Thus, the allegations in Lexmark's complaint are hardly, as SCC
claims, "novel."

**Chamberlain Group, Inc v. Skylink Technologies, Inc., 292
F.Supp.2d 1040 (N.D. Ill. 2003).** Chamberlain, a manufacturer of
garage door openers alleged that its competitor, Skylink, had violated
§ 1201(a)(2) by marketing a transmitter that circumvented Chamberlain's "rolling code" in order to activate Chamberlain's opener.

Chamberlain notes that it never expressly authorized the
circumvention of its GDOs and argues that under copyright and
patent infringement law, implied authorization—more accurately,
implied license—constitutes an affirmative defense. Chamberlain
has not provided any authority for its assumption that the patent
law or copyright statute sets forth the proper analysis for a DMCA
claim. ... [I]t is clear that to the extent Skylink was authorized
to decrypt, descramble, avoid, bypass, remove, deactivate, or impair Chamberlain's GDOs, it cannot be held liable under the
DMCA.

Skylink argues that in order for the Model 39 transmitter to
operate the Chamberlain GDO, the homeowner must store the
transmitter's signal into the GDO's memory. By doing so, Skylink
reasons, the homeowner "must by definition have authorized
access by the Skylink transmitter to operate the Chamberlain
GDO." In addition, Skylink reasons, the homeowners themselves
are authorized to access the Chamberlain GDO because Chamberlain does not place any restrictions on the type of transmitters
they are permitted to use.

... Chamberlain admits that the packaging for its Security+
GDO does not include "any restrictions on a consumer's ability to
buy a replacement transmitter or additional transmitter."

Chamberlain concedes that it never warned customers against
using unauthorized transmitters but explains that it did not do so
because it had no idea that other transmitters could be made to
operate its rolling code GDOs. Chamberlain's failure to anticipate
such technology, however, does not refute the fact that homeowners have a reasonable expectation of using the technology now
that it is available....

... [T]here is a history in the GDO industry of universal
transmitters being marketed and sold to allow homeowners an
alternative means to access any brand of GDO. In fact, Chamberlain itself markets and sells a universal remote under the brand
name "Clicker." Chamberlain did not advise its customers that no

other universal transmitter would work on its Security+ line, let alone prohibit them from using such products.

   . . .

Chamberlain next reiterates its argument raised in support of its summary judgment motion that under *Universal City Studios, Inc. v. Reimerdes,* 111 F.Supp.2d 294, 317 (S.D.N.Y. 2000), customers do not obtain implied authorization to circumvent the rolling code security measure simply by purchasing the GDO.... *Reimerdes* is distinguishable from this case: "The plaintiff in *Reimerdes* did in fact authorize certain circumvention of its technological protective measure pursuant to a license. It did not authorize circumvention by means of non-licensed software." *See also Lexmark Int'l, Inc. v. Static Control Components, Inc.,* 253 F.Supp.2d 943, 947–48 (E.D. Ky. 2003) (plaintiff explicitly restricted the use of third-party toner cartridge refills for customers opting to buy toner cartridges at a discount under a shrinkwrap agreement). Chamberlain places no such limitations on the type of transmitter a homeowner can utilize to access his or her own garage.

In addition, a homeowner has a legitimate expectation that he or she will be able to access the garage even if the original transmitter is misplaced or malfunctions. Chamberlain disagrees, but "it is rather curious why Chamberlain would take such an extreme position, considering that, if marketed as such, few homeowners would be inclined to purchase such a product." Under Chamberlain's theory, any customer who loses his or her Chamberlain transmitter, but manages to operate the opener either with a non-Chamberlain transmitter or by some other means of circumventing the rolling code, has violated the DMCA. In this court's view, the statute does not require such a conclusion. GDO transmitters are similar to television remote controls in that consumers of both products may need to replace them at some point due to damage or loss, and may program them to work with other devices manufactured by different companies. In both cases, consumers have a reasonable expectation that they can replace the original product with a competing, universal product without violating federal law....

QUESTIONS

1. Are printers and printer cartridges, or garage-door openers, "works protected under this title [17]", as referred to in § 1201(a)(2)(A)? But printers and printer cartridges and garage-door openers require computer programs in order to function. If the computer programs are "works protected under this title," i.e., if they meet standards of originality and non-merger, must it therefore follow that technological measures protecting access to computer programs that themselves control products that are not "works protected under this title" must be protected against circumvention under sec. 1201(a)? Is it possible to distinguish the *RealNetworks v.*

Streambox and *Gamemasters* decisions? Cf. sec. 109(b)(1)(B)(i) (scope of rental right in copies of computer programs).

2. Examine the text of sec. 1202(f), the reverse engineering exception. Had Static Controls circumvented the Lexmark access protection in order to create an independently-produced computer program for its cartridges that would interoperate with the computer program in Lexmark's printer, would Static Control's circumvention have been excused? Would Static Control's distribution of compatible cartridges also be excused? Recall that, in order to work with the printer program, the cartridges would have to circumvent the access control each time the printer functions are engaged.

3. If Chamberlain clearly marked all its garage-door openers that they are to be used only with Chamberlain's transmitters, would all conditions prerequisite to § 1201(a)(2) liability then be met? Does the court's opinion offer any other grounds for distinguishing or refuting *Lexmark*?

Page 831: Insert before Questions:

United States v. Elcom, Ltd., 203 F.Supp.2d 1111 (N.D.Cal.2002). In this prosecution of an employee of a Russian company charged with distributing over the Internet devices designed to circumvent the access protection used on Adobe e-books, the court, following the Second Circuit's analysis in *Corley*, rejected a variety of challenges to the constitutionality of the DMCA.

First, the court found no merit to defendant's contention that section 1201(a)(2) was unconstitutionally vague. On the contrary, the court found the scope of the prohibited activity to be quite clear, covering all trafficking in circumvention devices, whatever the purpose to which a user might put that tool. Turning to the first amendment challenges, the court largely echoed *Corley*'s distinction between computer code as speech and as conduct, and held that Congress could regulate the latter, given an important state interest, which the court found to be present. Like the *Corley* court, the *Elcom* court did not find that the DMCA burdened more speech than necessary to achieve the objective.

> Defendant's arguments are not persuasive. First, the DMCA does not "eliminate" fair use. Although certain fair uses may become more difficult, no fair use has been prohibited. Lawful possessors of copyrighted works may continue to engage in each and every fair use authorized by law. It may, however, have become more difficult for such uses to occur with regard to technologically protected digital works, but the fair uses themselves have not been eliminated or prohibited.

> * * * A flaw in defendant's argument is that it presumes that the only available version of a public domain work is an electronic, technology-protected, version. If a work is in the public domain, any person may make use of that expression, for whatever purposes desired. To the extent that a publisher has taken a public domain work and made it available in electronic form, and in the course of doing so has also imposed use restrictions on the electronic version, the publisher has

not gained any lawfully protected intellectual property interest in the work. The publisher has only gained a technological protection against copying that particular electronic version of the work. * * *

Publishing a public domain work in a restricted format does not thereby remove the work from the public domain, even if it does allow the publisher to control that particular electronic copy. If this is an evil in the law, the remedy is for Congress to prohibit use or access restrictions from being imposed upon public domain works. Or perhaps, if left to the market, the consuming public could decline to purchase public domain works packaged with use restrictions.

In addition, the alternatives proposed by defendant—enacting more severe penalties for copyright infringement—may not be as effective at preventing widespread copyright infringement and electronic piracy as is banning the trafficking in or the marketing of the tools that allow piracy to thrive. Congress certainly could have approached the problem by targeting the infringers, rather than those who traffic in the tools that enable the infringement to occur. However, it is already unlawful to infringe, yet piracy of intellectual property has reached epidemic proportions. Pirates are world-wide, and locating and prosecuting each could be both impossible and ineffective, as new pirates arrive on the scene. But, pirates and other infringers require tools in order to bypass the technological measures that protect against unlawful copying. Thus, targeting the tool sellers is a reasoned, and reasonably tailored, approach to "remedying the evil" targeted by Congress. In addition, because tools that circumvent copyright protection measures for the purpose of allowing fair use can also be used to enable infringement, it is reasonably necessary to ban the sale of all circumvention tools in order to achieve the objectives of preventing widespread copyright infringement and electronic piracy in digital media. Banning the sale of all circumvention tools thus does not substantially burden more speech than is necessary.

Finally, the court addressed a different objection to Congress' power to enact the DMCA, drawn not from the first amendment, but from the structure of Congress' Article I, section 8, clause 8 powers:

Defendant's final challenge is that Congress exceeded its authority in enacting the DMCA and that, as a result, the statute is unconstitutional. The federal government is one of enumerated powers and Congress may exercise only those powers granted to it. [Citations omitted.] The Constitution contains several express grants of power to Congress, among them the Intellectual Property Clause and the Commerce Clause.

Under the Intellectual Property Clause, Congress is empowered "to promote the Progress of Science and the useful Arts, by securing for limited Times to Authors and Inventors the exclusive Right to their respective Writings and Discoveries." U.S. Const., art. I, § 8 cl. 8. This power, while broad, is not unlimited. More than a century ago, the Supreme Court held that Congress could not exercise its Intellectual

Property power to grant exclusive rights in matters other than "writings" or "discoveries" such that the Trademark Act of 1876 was not a proper exercise of Congress' Intellectual Property power. The Trade–Mark Cases, 100 U.S. 82, 93–94, 25 L.Ed. 550, 1879 Dec. Comm'r Pat. 619 (1879). Congress may not, for example, grant exclusive rights to writings that do not constitute original works of authorship. Feist Publ'ns v. Rural Tel. Serv. Co., 499 U.S. 340, 111 S.Ct. 1282, 113 L.Ed.2d 358 (1991). Similarly, the Intellectual Property Clause limits Congress' powers so that patents may only be granted in new inventions that are not obvious in view of the existing art and Congress may not authorize the issuance of a patent whose effects are to remove existing knowledge from the public domain. Graham v. John Deere Co. of Kan. City, 383 U.S. 1, 6, 86 S.Ct. 684, 15 L.Ed.2d 545 (1966).

Under the Commerce Clause, Congress' power is quite broad. Congress may regulate the use of the channels of interstate commerce; may regulate and protect the instrumentalities of interstate commerce, including persons or things in interstate commerce; and may regulate those activities having a substantial relation to, or which substantially affect, interstate commerce. Lopez, 514 U.S. at 558–59. Once again, however, the power is not unlimited and Congress does not have the authority to legislate matters that are of such a local character that there is too remote a connection to interstate commerce. Id. at 559. Both parties also agree that, as broad as Congress' Commerce Power is, Congress may not use that power in such a way as to override or circumvent another constitutional restraint. Ry. Labor Executives' Ass'n v. Gibbons, 455 U.S. 457, 102 S.Ct. 1169, 71 L.Ed.2d 335 (1982) (striking down an act by Congress under the Commerce Clause that violated the Bankruptcy Clause's uniformity requirement).

Defendant argues that Congress exceeded its powers under the Intellectual Property Clause in enacting the DMCA. The government responds that Congress used its Commerce Power to regulate trafficking in devices for gain. Thus, the issue presented is whether the DMCA was within Congress' Commerce Power, generally, and if so, whether Congress was nevertheless prohibited from enacting the DMCA because of other restraints on Congress' power imposed by the Intellectual Property Clause.

With regard to the first issue, Congress plainly has the power to enact the DMCA under the Commerce Clause. "The commerce power 'is the power to regulate; that is, to prescribe the rule by which commerce is to be governed. This power, like all others vested in Congress, is complete in itself, may be exercised to its utmost extent, and acknowledges no limitations, other than are prescribed by the Constitution.'" Lopez, 514 U.S. at 553 (citing Gibbons v. Ogden, 22 U.S. 1, 9 Wheat. 1, 196, 6 L.Ed. 23 (1824)). The DMCA prohibits conduct that has a substantial effect on commerce between the states and commerce with foreign nations. Trafficking in or the marketing of circumvention devices "for gain," as proscribed by Sections 1201(b) and 1204, has a direct effect on interstate commerce. To the extent that circumvention devices enable wrongdoers to engage in on-line piracy by unlawfully copying and distributing copyrighted works of authorship, the sale of such devices has a direct effect on suppressing the market for legitimate copies of the works. Accordingly, there is a rational basis for concluding that the regulated activity sufficiently affects interstate commerce to establish that Congress had authority under the Commerce Clause to enact the legislation. *Lopez*, 514 U.S. at 557; United States v. Moghadam, 175 F.3d 1269, 1276–77 (11th Cir. 1999) (finding the anti-bootlegging statute to have a sufficient connection to interstate and foreign commerce to meet the *Lopez* test).

The more difficult question, however, is whether Congress was nevertheless precluded from enacting the DMCA by restraints imposed by the Intellectual Property Clause. The Eleventh Circuit was presented with this same issue in the context of the anti-bootlegging statute in *Moghadam*, 175 F.3d 1269. The statute in that case prohibited persons from making unauthorized recordings of live performances, in effect, granting copyright-like protection to live performances. The defendant challenged the constitutionality of the statute, contending that the Intellectual Property power extended only to "writings" and "inventions," and that a live performance was not a "writing." The government argued that the statute was a valid exercise of Congress' Commerce Power. In a well-reasoned opinion, the Eleventh Circuit first analyzed Supreme Court precedents that could be read to conflict with each other—The Trade–Mark Cases, 100 U.S. 82, 25 L.Ed. 550 (1879), Heart of Atlanta Motel, Inc. v. United States, 379 U.S. 241, 85 S.Ct. 348, 13 L.Ed.2d 258 (1964), and Railway Labor Executives' Association v. Gibbons, 455 U.S. 457, 102 S.Ct. 1169, 71 L.Ed.2d 335 (1982)—and then resolved the tension in those cases to decide the case before it.

> We note that there is some tension between the former line of cases (*Heart of Atlanta Motel*, the *Trade-Mark Cases* and *Authors League [of America, Inc. v. Oman*, 790 F.2d 220 (2d Cir.1986)]) and the *Railway Labor Executives* case. The former cases suggest that in some circumstances the Commerce Clause can be used by Congress to accomplish something that the [Intellectual Property Clause] might not allow. But the *Railway Labor Executives* case suggests that in some circumstances the Commerce Clause cannot be used to eradicate a limitation placed upon Congressional power in another grant of power.

Moghadam, 175 F.3d at 1279–80. The court then resolved the tension as follows:

> We take as a given that there are some circumstances, as illustrated by *Railway Labor Executives*, in which the Commerce Clause cannot be used by Congress to eradicate a limitation placed upon Congress in another grant of power. For the reasons that follow, we hold that the instant case is not one such circumstance. We hold that the [Intellectual Property] Clause does not envision

that Congress is positively forbidden from extending copyright-like protection under other constitutional clauses, such as the Commerce Clause, to works of authorship that may not meet the fixation requirement inherent in the term "Writings." The grant itself is stated in positive terms, and does not imply any negative pregnant that suggests that the term "Writings" operates as a ceiling on Congress' ability to legislate pursuant to other grants. Extending quasi-copyright protection to unfixed live musical performances is in no way inconsistent with the [Intellectual Property] Clause, even if that Clause itself does not expressly authorize such protection. Quite the contrary, extending such protection actually complements and is in harmony with the existing scheme that Congress has set up under the [Intellectual Property] Clause. A live musical performance clearly satisfies the originality requirement. Extending quasi-copyright protection also furthers the purpose of the [Intellectual Property] Clause to promote the progress of the useful arts by securing some exclusive rights to the creative author. . . .

For the foregoing reasons, we conclude that extending copyright-like protection in the instant case is not fundamentally inconsistent with the fixation requirement of the [Intellectual Property] Clause. By contrast, the nonuniform bankruptcy statute at issue in *Railway Labor Executives* was irreconcilably inconsistent with the uniformity requirement of the Bankruptcy Clause of the Constitution.

Id., 175 F.3d at 1280–81.

Accordingly, *Moghadam* provides an instructive guide and analytical framework for resolving the constitutional question posed. If the statute passed by Congress "is not fundamentally inconsistent with" the Intellectual Property clause and is otherwise within Congress' Commerce Power to enact, then the statute is not an unconstitutional exercise of congressional power. On the other hand, if the statute is "irreconcilably inconsistent" with a requirement of another constitutional provision, then the enactment exceeds congressional authority even if otherwise authorized by the Commerce Clause. With this teaching in mind, the court turns to the DMCA and the Intellectual Property Clause.

The first issue is to determine whether the DMCA is "not fundamentally inconsistent" with the purpose of the Intellectual Property Clause. The purpose of the Intellectual Property Clause is to promote the useful arts and sciences. Thus, the government is empowered to grant exclusive rights to inventors and authors in their respective inventions and original works of authorship, for limited times. This allows the inventor/author a reasonable time in which to reap the economic fruits of his or her inventive or creative labor. As a result of this economic incentive, people are encouraged to engage in inventive and originally expressive endeavors, thereby promoting the arts and sciences. In addition, because the grant of property rights is to be of limited duration, the public will generally benefit, once the exclusive rights expire and the invention or expression becomes dedicated to the public. * * *

The second half of the analysis is to determine whether the DMCA is nevertheless "irreconcilably inconsistent" with a limitation contained within the Intellectual Property Clause. Here, defendant and the amici curiae make several arguments, some of which have already been addressed. Defendant and the amici curiae contend that the DMCA is irreconcilably inconsistent with the Intellectual Property Clause because: 1) the Act eliminates fair use; 2) the Act allows publishers to recapture works from the public domain and obtain copyright-like protection in those works; and 3) the Act violates the "limited times" clause by effectively granting copyright owners perpetual rights to protect their works.

The first two contentions have been addressed, and rejected, above. While the DMCA may make certain fair uses more difficult for digital works of authorship published with use restrictions, fair use has not been eliminated. Similarly, the argument that Congress' ban on the sale of circumvention tools has the effect of allowing publishers to claim copyright-like protection in public domain works is tenuous and unpersuasive. Nothing within the DMCA grants any rights to anyone in any public domain work. A public domain work remains in the public domain and any person may make use of the public domain work for any purpose.

Finally, the DMCA does not allow a copyright owner to effectively prevent an ebook from ever entering the public domain, despite the expiration of the copyright. See Amici EFF Brief at 16. Upon the expiration of the copyright, there is no longer any protectable intellectual property right in the work's expression. The expression may be copied, quoted, republished in new format and sold, without any legally enforceable restriction on the use of the expression. The publisher/copyright owner has no right to prevent any user from using the work any way the user prefers. At best, the publisher has a technological measure embedded within the digital product precluding certain uses of that particular copy of the work and, in many cases, the user/purchaser has acquiesced in this restriction when purchasing/licensing the work. See End User License Agreements, O'Connell Decl. Exhs. A–D. The essence of a copyright is the legally enforceable exclusive rights to reproduce and distribute copies of an original work of authorship, to make derivative works, and to perform the work publicly, for a limited period of time. 17 U.S.C. § § 106, 302–303. None of those rights is extended beyond the statutory term merely by prohibiting the trafficking in or marketing of devices primarily designed to circumvent use restrictions on works in electronic form.

Accordingly, the DMCA does not run afoul of any restraint on Congress' power imposed by the Intellectual Property Clause. Section

1201(b) of the DMCA was within Congress' Commerce Power to enact, and because it is not irreconcilably inconsistent with any provision of the Intellectual Property Clause, Congress did not exceed its constitutional authority in enacting the law.

Page 831: *Replace* Question 3 with the following:

3. The *Elcom* court found support for the DMCA in the commerce clause, then considered whether there was a conflict between the objectives of that clause and the patent-copyright clause. The court did not address whether the patent-copyright clause itself furnished support for anticircumvention legislation. Had the court done so, and found authority within the patent-copyright clause, then there would have been no conflict with the commerce clause, though that clause might supply an additional basis for the legislation. Is the patent-copyright clause not only consonant with anticircumvention legislation, but also supportive of it? Consider, in this context, what the phrase "by *securing* . . . the exclusive right" might/should mean.

Page 831: Add as new Question 4:

4. Is CSS an access control, or a copy control? Consider the response of the district court in *321 Studios v. Metro Goldwyn Mayer Studios*, 307 F.Supp.2d 1085 (N.D. Cal. 2004), an action unsuccessfully brought by the manufacturer of a device designed to decrypt DVDs (allegedly in order to permit consumers to make "back up copies") seeking a declaration that the device was either permissible under § 1201, or that § 1201 was unconstitutional:

> While 321 is technically correct that CSS controls access to encrypted DVDs, the purpose of this access control is to control copying of those DVDs, since encrypted DVDs cannot be copied unless they are accessed. 321 claims that CSS does not prevent copying, since it does not prevent copying the encrypted data on the DVD. However, as 321 admits "that copying is not particularly useful," as any copy made without circumventing CSS could not be accessed or viewed. It is clear to this Court CSS is a copy control system, and therefore § 1201(b)(1) does apply.

Does it make any difference whether the manufacturer or distributor of a circumvention device has violated § 1201(a)(2) or § 1201(b)?

Page 835: Insert after note on *Kelly v. Arriba*:

Gordon v. Nextel Comms., 345 F.3d 922 (6th Cir. 2003). Gordon brought suit against Nextel Communications and Nextel's advertising agency, Mullen Advertising, Inc., for using in a television commercial for Nextel's two-way text messaging several of Gordon's dental illustrations from which the copyright notice had been removed, allegedly in violation of § 1202. The district court granted summary judgment on the basis that Gordon failed to present any evidence that defendants intentionally removed or altered the copyright information or that these defendants knew that the copyright information had been removed. The Sixth Circuit affirmed.

A section 1202(b)(1) violation occurs when a person (i) without authority of the copyright owner or the law (ii) intentionally removes or alters any copyright management information (iii) knowing or having reasonable grounds to know that it will induce, enable, facilitate, or conceal an infringement of the federal copyright laws. Although Gordon failed to introduce evidence that Nextel or Mullen was aware of any infringement until they received the cease and desist letter from Gordon's counsel, he argues that because the copyright information is absent from the illustrations, Crossroads must have removed it, and that Nextel and Mullen are liable for Crossroads' actions. . . .

[Kevin] McCarthy [Crossroads' art director] admits that he used the rental poster, scanned and enlarged a portion of it, and made the framed pictures that were used as the set decorations. McCarthy admits that he removed the information, and there is no suggestion that the removal was unintentional.

[But] Gordon submitted no proof that the removal of the copyright notice was done with the requisite "reason to know that the removal would induce, enable, facilitate, or conceal an infringement." 17 U.S.C. § 1202(b). Rather, when Crossroads obtained the poster from the prop company, its personnel believed that the poster had been cleared for use in television commercials. As a result, the defendants assert, there is no evidence that Crossroads had any reason to know that the removal would facilitate or conceal an infringement. . . .

QUESTION

In light of *Kelly* and *Nextel*, what would a § 1202 plaintiff have to show to make out a violation? How well-founded should a defendant's belief be that the material from which she removed the copyright management information had been cleared for use? Even if this belief is well-founded, is it relevant? *Whose* infringement would the putative licensee's notice-removal "induce, enable, facilitate, or conceal"? The licensee's or that of downstream users deprived of the copyright management information?

H.   OVERENFORCEMENT: COPYRIGHT MISUSE

Page 837: Add following Question:

Video Pipeline, Inc. v. Buena Vista Home Entertainment, Inc.

342 F.3d 191 (3d Cir. 2003).

[The facts of the case are set forth at page 142–50 of this Supplement. There, the court of appeals rejected the declaratory plaintiff's reliance on the fair use doctrine. In the passages below, the court addresses the declaratory plaintiff's invoking of the copyright misuse doctrine.]

Video Pipeline further contends that Disney has misused its copyright and, as a result, should not receive the protection of copyright law. Video Pipeline points to certain licensing agreements that Disney has entered into with three companies and sought to enter into with a number of other companies operating web sites. Each of these licensing agreements provides that Disney, the licensor, will deliver trailers by way of hyperlinks for display on the licensee's web site. The Agreements further state:

> The Website in which the Trailers are used may not be derogatory to or critical of the entertainment industry or of [Disney] (and its officers, directors, agents, employees, affiliates, divisions and subsidiaries) or of any motion picture produced or distributed by [Disney] ... [or] of the materials from which the Trailers were taken or of any person involved with the production of the Underlying Works. Any breach of this paragraph will render this license null and void and Licensee will be liable to all parties concerned for defamation and copyright infringement, as well as breach of contract....

As Video Pipeline sees it, such licensing agreements seek to use copyright law to suppress criticism and, in so doing, misuse those laws, triggering the copyright misuse doctrine.

Neither the Supreme Court nor this Court has affirmatively recognized the copyright misuse doctrine. *See Dun & Bradstreet Software Servs., Inc. v. Grace Consulting, Inc.,* 307 F.3d 197, 221 (3d Cir.2002). There is, however, a well-established patent misuse doctrine, *see, e.g., Morton Salt Co. v. G.S. Suppiger Co.,* 314 U.S. 488, 62 S.Ct. 402, 86 L.Ed. 363 (1942); *W.L. Gore & Assocs., Inc. v. Carlisle Corp.,* 529 F.2d 614 (3d Cir.1976), and, as noted below, other courts of appeals have extended the doctrine to the copyright context.

The misuse doctrine extends from the equitable principle that courts "may appropriately withhold their aid where the plaintiff is using the right asserted contrary to the public interest." *Morton Salt,* 314 U.S. at 492, 62 S.Ct. 402. Misuse is not cause to invalidate the copyright or patent, but instead "precludes its enforcement during the period of misuse." *Practice Management Info. Corp. v. American Med. Assoc.,* 121 F.3d 516, 520 n. 9 (9th Cir.1997) (citing *Lasercomb America, Inc. v. Reynolds,* 911 F.2d 970, 979 n.22 (4th Cir.1990)). To defend on misuse grounds, the alleged infringer need not be subject to the purported misuse. *Morton Salt,* 314 U.S. at 494, 62 S.Ct. 402 ("It is the adverse effect upon the public interest of a successful infringement suit in conjunction with the patentee's course of conduct which disqualifies him to maintain the suit, regardless of whether the particular defendant has suffered from the misuse of the patent."); *Lasercomb,* 911 F.2d at 979 ("[T]he fact that appellants here were not parties to one of Lasercomb's standard license agreements is inapposite to their copyright misuse defense. The question is whether Lasercomb is using its copyright in a manner contrary to public policy, which question we have answered in the affirmative.").

Misuse often exists where the patent or copyright holder has engaged in some form of anti-competitive behavior. *See, e.g., Morton Salt,* 314 U.S. at 492, 62 S.Ct. 402 (explaining that public policy "forbids the use of the patent to secure an exclusive right or limited monopoly not granted by the Patent Office"); *Practice Management,* 121 F.3d at 521 (finding copyright misuse where license to use copyrighted good prohibited licensee from using competing goods); *Lasercomb,* 911 F.2d at 979 (holding the copyright holder misused its copyright by including in licensing agreements a provision that neither the licensee company nor its officers, employees, *et al.,* could develop competing goods for the term of the agreement, ninety-nine years).

More on point, however, is the underlying policy rationale for the misuse doctrine set out in the Constitution's Copyright and Patent Clause: "to promote the Progress of Science and useful Arts." Const. Art. I, § 8, cl. 8; *see also Morton Salt,* 314 U.S. at 494, 62 S.Ct. 402 ("The patentee, like these other holders of an exclusive privilege granted in furtherance of a public policy [trademark and copyright holders], may not claim protection of his grant by the courts where it is being used to subvert that policy."); *Lasercomb,* 911 F.2d at 978 ("The question is ... whether the copyright is being used in a manner violative of the public policy embodied in the grant of a copyright."). The "ultimate aim" of copyright law is "to stimulate artistic creativity for the general public good." *Sony Corp.,* 464 U.S. at 432, 104 S.Ct. 774; *see also Eldred v. Ashcroft,* 537 U.S. 186, 123 S.Ct. 769, 787, 154 L.Ed.2d 683 (2003) ("[C]opyright's purpose is to *promote* the creation and publication of free expression.") (emphasis in original). Put simply, our Constitution emphasizes the purpose and value of copyrights and patents. Harm caused by their misuse undermines their usefulness.

Anti-competitive licensing agreements may conflict with the purpose behind a copyright's protection by depriving the public of the would-be competitor's creativity. The fair use doctrine and the refusal to copyright facts and ideas also address applications of copyright protection that would otherwise conflict with a copyright's constitutional goal. *See Eldred,* 123 S.Ct. at 789; *Campbell,* 510 U.S. at 575 & n. 5, 114 S.Ct. 1164. But it is possible that a copyright holder could leverage its copyright to restrain the creative expression of another without engaging in anti-competitive behavior or implicating the fair use and idea/expression doctrines.

For instance, the concurring opinion, written for a majority of the judges, in *Rosemont Enters., Inc. v. Random House, Inc.,* 366 F.2d 303 (2d Cir.1966), concluded that pursuant to the unclean hands doctrine the District Court should not have entered a preliminary injunction against an alleged copyright infringer where the copyright holder sought to use his copyright "to restrict the dissemination of information." *Id.* at 311 (Lumbard, C.J., concurring). In *Rosemont Enters.,* a corporation acting for the publicity-shy Howard Hughes purchased the copyright to an article about Hughes solely to bring an infringement suit to enjoin the publication of a forthcoming biography on Hughes. *Id.* at 313. ...

Although *Rosemont Enters.* did not concern an anti-competitive licensing agreement as in the typical misuse case, it focused—as do the misuse cases—on the copyright holder's attempt to disrupt a copyright's goal to increase the store of creative expression for the public good. 366 F.2d at 311 ("It would be contrary to the public interest to permit any man to buy up the copyright to anything written about himself and to use his copyright ownership to restrain other[s] from publishing biographical material concerning him."); *Lasercomb,* 911 F.2d at 978 ("[T]he company is required to forego utilization of the creative abilities of all its officers, directors and employees in the area of [computer assisted design and computer assisted manufacture] die-making software. Of yet greater concern, these creative abilities are withdrawn from the public."). A copyright holder's attempt to restrict expression that is critical of it (or of its copyrighted good, or the industry in which it operates, *etc.*) may, in context, subvert—as do anti-competitive restrictions—a copyright's policy goal to encourage the creation and dissemination to the public of creative activity.

The licensing agreements in this case do seek to restrict expression by licensing the Disney trailers for use on the internet only so long as the web sites on which the trailers will appear do not derogate Disney, the entertainment industry, *etc.* But we nonetheless cannot conclude on this record that the agreements are likely to interfere with creative expression to such a degree that they affect in any significant way the policy interest in increasing the public store of creative activity. The licensing agreements do not, for instance, interfere with the licensee's opportunity to express such criticism on other web sites or elsewhere. There is no evidence that the public will find it any more difficult to obtain criticism of Disney and its interests, or even that the public is considerably less likely to come across this criticism, if it is not displayed on the same site as the trailers. Moreover, if a critic wishes to comment on Disney's works, the fair use doctrine may be implicated regardless of the existence of the licensing agreements.

Finally, copyright law, and the misuse doctrine in particular, should not be interpreted to require Disney, if it licenses its trailers for display on any web sites but its own, to do so willy-nilly regardless of the content displayed with its copyrighted works. Indeed such an application of the misuse doctrine would likely decrease the public's access to Disney's works because it might as a result refuse to license at all online display of its works.

Thus, while we extend the patent misuse doctrine to copyright, and recognize that it might operate beyond its traditional anti-competition context, we hold it inapplicable here. On this record Disney's licensing agreements do not interfere significantly with copyright policy (while holding to the contrary might, in fact, do so). The District Court therefore correctly held that Video Pipeline will not likely succeed on its copyright misuse defense.

217

QUESTIONS

1.   Although Disney (even Disney) is not equivalent to an arm of the U.S. government, might there be a plausible claim of a First Amendment violation when Disney uses its copyrights—privileges granted by the federal government—to inhibit free speech on matters of public moment, as it arguably has done through its licenses in the present case? On the other hand, should not Disney—or any copyright owner—be fully free to select its licensees, either because of their present attitudes toward Disney and the entertainment industries or because of their promises about future attitudes?

2.   Once the copyright misuse doctrine is cut loose from its moorings as an adjunct to antitrust enforcement, are courts given too much authority to decline enforcement simply because of the "unclean hands" (as perceived by particular judges) of the copyright owner? Is this a salutary development? Is it consistent with the move toward ignoring the unclean hands of the defendant in infringement and fair use analyses?

CHAPTER 9

FEDERAL PREEMPTION OF STATE LAW

C. COPYRIGHT PREEMPTION UNDER SECTION 301 OF THE 1976 ACT

2. RIGHTS EQUIVALENT TO COPYRIGHT

Page 880: Add after Question 2:

3. Review the legislative history of the 1976 Act with respect to Section 301 and the intended preemption (or non-preemption) of the state tort of misappropriation. (See Casebook pp. 861–65.) To what extent, as a matter of text and of policy, does it appear that Congress intended to preempt state misappropriation law? Assume that the author of a compilation of poetry learns that another has, without consent, fully duplicated the compilation and placed his own name on it as author. There is clearly a copyright infringement. Is the author free, instead, to sue in a state court, asserting a tort of misappropriation? If there is a concern about preemption, can that concern be put to rest by framing the state action as one for "reverse passing off," i.e., marketing the plaintiff's compilation under the defendant's name? Does the express misrepresentation with regard to authorship supply the crucial "extra element"? Can any concern about the viability of such a state tort be put to rest merely by asserting the "reverse passing off" claim as a federal statutory claim under Section 43(a) of the Lanham Act? Consult Section 301(d). See Video Pipeline, Inc. v. Buena Vista Home Entertainment, Inc., 210 F.Supp.2d 552 (D.N.J.2002); Silverstein v. Penguin Putnam, Inc., 2003 WL 1797848 (S.D.N.Y.2003), *rev'd and remanded on other grounds* 368 F.3d 77 (2d Cir.2004).

Page 887: Add the following after Question 4:

The issues raised in Questions 3 and 4 are addressed by the Court of Appeals for the Federal Circuit (applying the law of the First Circuit, where the dispute arose) in Bowers v. Baystate Technologies, Inc., 320 F.3d 1317 (Fed.Cir.2003). The court majority held that there was no preemption of an action to enforce a contract, embodied in a shrinkwrap license, barring reverse engineering (and thus the fair use) of a computer template that gathers embedded instructions to operate a program for use in design (i.e., a CAD program). Relying in part on the *ProCD* decision, the court held that contracts, which affect only the two parties to it, may waive statutory rights. It also pointed out, however, that the calculation of damages for contract breach and copyright infringement must avoid duplication. The dissenting judge concluded that, apart from Section 301, state law must not be permitted to frustrate the federal policy of allowable copying as manifested in the fair use doctrine; although a freely negotiated waiver of fair use rights would not be preempted, a waiver contained in a non-negotiated shrinkwrap license should not be enforced.

Page 891:   Add to Question 2:

See Kabehie v. Zoland, 102 Cal.App.4th 513, 125 Cal.Rptr.2d 721 (2002), which holds that not all contract actions inherently contain an "extra element" that is sufficient to avoid preemption under Section 301; there is preemption if the promise that is sought to be enforced is one not to copy, prepare derivative works, etc. The court collects and discusses the cases at 102 Cal.App.4th 525–29, in support of both what the court regards as the majority view (preemption as a fact-specific inquiry) and the minority view (all breach of contract actions are non-preempted).

Page 896:   After the *Computer Associates* case, insert:

[Accord, with respect to state trade-secret claims, Dun & Bradstreet Software Serv., Inc. v. Grace Consulting, Inc., 307 F.3d 197 (3d Cir.2002).]

Page 900:   Add to Question 4(b):

A fashion model owns the copyright in her photographs, which she licenses to a company that manufactures and markets hair products. The latter company has continued to use the photographs after the end of the license period set forth in its contract with the model. She sues for a violation of her right of publicity, as well as for breach of contract. The defendant asserts that both state claims are preempted. How would you decide the dispute? See Toney v. L'Oreal USA, Inc., 64 U.S.P.Q.2d 1857 (N.D.Ill.2002). As to the publicity claim, the court acknowledged that its decision was contrary to most of the other decided cases (finding no preemption): Downing v. Abercrombie & Fitch, 265 F.3d 994 (9th Cir. 2001); Brown v. Ames, 201 F.3d 654 (5th Cir.2000); Landham v. Lewis Galoob Toys, Inc., 227 F.3d 619 (6th Cir.2000).

Page 911:   Add new Question 8:

8. Although the recent *Dastar v. Twentieth Century Fox* decision by the Supreme Court (see *supra* this Supplement, page 1) limits attribution rights only under the Lanham Act, do the Court's views about the role of the Copyright Act and the Copyright Clause of the Constitution narrow, in effect, the authority of the States to accord attribution rights by statute or common law?

CHAPTER 10

INTERNATIONAL DIMENSIONS OF COPYRIGHT

D. U.S.-BASED COPYRIGHT ACTIONS WITH AN INTERNATIONAL DIMENSION

3. WHEN U.S. COURTS EXERCISE JURISDICTION

Page 951: Add to the discussion of the *iCraveTV* case:

In addition to considering whether a federal court has "subject matter" jurisdiction to hear a case arguably involving U.S. law, it is necessary for the court to find that the court has personal jurisdiction over the defendant, for example through service of process personally in the state or at a place of business in the state. In an internet age, when transmissions to a U.S. audience of scores or millions of recipients can be accomplished without ever physically leaving foreign shores, U.S. courts are handling an increasing number of cases in which the foreign defendant claims a lack of personal jurisdiction. An example is Graduate Mgt. Admission Council v. Raju, 241 F.Supp.2d 589 (E.D.Va.2003). There, the defendant—the operator of a website in India—carried on its website the text of questions from GMAT examinations, whose copyright is owned by the Virginia plaintiff. The federal court, although holding that jurisdiction could not properly be asserted under the Virginia state long-arm statute because of lack of sufficient business activities within the state, found that there was an independent source of federal *in personam* jurisdiction under Federal Rule of Civil Procedure 4(k)(2). The court also held that the proper substantive law governing the claim was U.S. copyright law.

Similarly, in Metro–Goldwyn–Mayer Studios v. Grokster, Ltd., 243 F.Supp.2d 1073 (C.D.Cal.2003), the Central District of California upheld the assertion of jurisdiction in a contributory infringement claim against KaZaA, an Australian–Vanuatan entrepreneur of peer-to-peer file-sharing software that facilitates the copying of music and motion picture files. The court held that the extensive downloading engaged in by California residents using the KaZaA software met minimum contacts and fairness standards. The court also upheld California's jurisdiction on the theory that KaZaA had "targeted" California movie studios for economic harm. Finally, the court offered Fed. R. Civ. Pro. 4(k)(2) as an alternative basis for jurisdiction. Because the scope of the U.S. plaintiffs' claims were limited to downloads facilitated in the U.S. (rather than worldwide), U.S. law would apply.

*

THE COPYRIGHT ACT OF 1976

Public Law 94–553, 90 Stat. 2541,
as amended through November 1, 2001
TITLE 17—COPYRIGHTS

CHAPTER 1—SUBJECT MATTER AND SCOPE OF COPYRIGHT

§ 101. Definitions

Except as otherwise provided in this title, as used in this title, the following terms and their variant forms mean the following:

An "anonymous work" is a work on the copies or phonorecords of which no natural person is identified as author.

An "architectural work" is the design of a building as embodied in any tangible medium of expression, including a building, architectural plans, or drawings. The work includes the overall form as well as the arrangement and composition of spaces and elements in the design, but does not include individual standard features.

"Audiovisual works" are works that consist of a series of related images which are intrinsically intended to be shown by the use of machines or devices such as projectors, viewers, or electronic equipment, together with accompanying sounds, if any, regardless of the nature of the material objects, such as films or tapes, in which the works are embodied.

The "Berne Convention" is the Convention for the Protection of Literary and Artistic Works, signed at Berne, Switzerland, on September 9, 1886, and all acts, protocols, and revisions thereto.*

The "best edition" of a work is the edition, published in the United States at any time before the date of deposit, that the Library of Congress determines to be most suitable for its purposes.

---

* Section 2 of the Berne Convention Implementation Act of 1988, Pub. L. No. 100–568, 102 Stat. 2853 (Oct. 31, 1988), provides the following declarations:

The Congress makes the following declarations:

  (1) The Convention for the Protection of Literary and Artistic Works, signed at Berne, Switzerland, on September 9, 1886, and all acts, protocols, and revisions thereto (hereafter in this Act referred to as the "Berne Convention") are not self-executing under the Constitution and laws of the United States.

  (2) The obligations of the United States under the Berne Convention may be performed only pursuant to appropriate domestic law.

  (3) The amendments made by this Act, together with the law as it exists on the date of the enactment of this Act, satisfy the obligations of the United States in adhering to the Berne Convention and no further rights or interests shall be recognized or created for that purpose.

A person's "children" are that person's immediate offspring, whether legitimate or not, and any children legally adopted by that person.

A "collective work" is a work, such as a periodical issue, anthology, or encyclopedia, in which a number of contributions, constituting separate and independent works in themselves, are assembled into a collective whole.

A "compilation" is a work formed by the collection and assembling of preexisting materials or of data that are selected, coordinated, or arranged in such a way that the resulting work as a whole constitutes an original work of authorship. The term "compilation" includes collective works.

A "computer program" is a set of statements or instructions to be used directly or indirectly in a computer in order to bring about a certain result.

"Copies" are material objects, other than phonorecords, in which a work is fixed by any method now known or later developed, and from which the work can be perceived, reproduced, or otherwise communicated, either directly or with the aid of a machine or device. The term "copies" includes the material object, other than a phonorecord, in which the work is first fixed.

"Copyright owner", with respect to any one of the exclusive rights comprised in a copyright, refers to the owner of that particular right.

A work is "created" when it is fixed in a copy or phonorecord for the first time; where a work is prepared over a period of time, the portion of it that has been fixed at any particular time constitutes the work as of that time, and where the work has been prepared in different versions, each version constitutes a separate work.

A "derivative work" is a work based upon one or more preexisting works, such as a translation, musical arrangement, dramatization, fictionalization, motion picture version, sound recording, art reproduction, abridgment, condensation, or any other form in which a work may be recast, transformed, or adapted. A work consisting of editorial revisions, annotations, elaborations, or other modifications, which, as a whole, represent an original work of authorship, is a "derivative work".

A "device", "machine", or "process" is one now known or later developed.

A "digital transmission" is a transmission in whole or in part in a digital or other non-analog format.

To "display" a work means to show a copy of it, either directly or by means of a film, slide, television image, or any other device or process or, in the case of a motion picture or other audiovisual work, to show individual images nonsequentially.

An "establishment" is a store, shop, or any similar place of business open to the general public for the primary purpose of selling goods or services in which the majority of the gross square feet of space that is nonresidential is used for that purpose, and in which nondramatic musical works are performed publicly.

A "food service or drinking establishment" is a restaurant, inn, bar, tavern, or any other similar place of business in which the public or patrons assemble for the primary purpose of being served food or drink, in which the majority of the gross square feet of space that is nonresidential is used for that purpose, and in which nondramatic musical works are performed publicly.

The term "financial gain" includes receipt, or expectation of receipt, of anything of value, including the receipt of other copyrighted works.

A work is "fixed" in a tangible medium of expression when its embodiment in a copy or phonorecord, by or under the authority of the author, is sufficiently permanent or stable to permit it to be perceived, reproduced, or otherwise communicated for a period of more than transitory duration. A work consisting of sounds, images, or both, that are being transmitted, is "fixed" for purposes of this title if a fixation of the work is being made simultaneously with its transmission.

The "Geneva Phonograms Convention" is the Convention for the Protection of Producers of Phonograms Against Unauthorized Duplication of Their Phonograms, concluded at Geneva, Switzerland, on October 29, 1971.

The "gross square feet of space" of an establishment means the entire interior space of that establishment, and any adjoining outdoor space used to serve patrons, whether on a seasonal basis or otherwise.

The terms "including" and "such as" are illustrative and not limitative.

An "international agreement" is—

(1) the Universal Copyright Convention;

(2) the Geneva Phonograms Convention;

(3) the Berne Convention;

(4) the WTO Agreement;

(5) the WIPO Copyright Treaty*;

(6) the WIPO Performances and Phonograms Treaty**; and

(7) any other copyright treaty to which the United States is a party.

A "joint work" is a work prepared by two or more authors with the intention that their contributions be merged into inseparable or interdependent parts of a unitary whole.

"Literary works" are works, other than audiovisual works, expressed in words, numbers, or other verbal or numerical symbols or indicia, regardless of the nature of the material objects, such as books, periodicals,

---

* This provision takes effect upon entry into force of the WIPO Copyright Treaty with respect to the United States, as provided by § 105(b)(1) of Act Oct. 28, 1998, Pub. L. 105–304.

** This provision takes effect upon entry into force of the WIPO Performances and Phonograms Treaty with respect to the United States, as provided by § 105(b)(2) of Act Oct. 28, 1998, Pub. L. 105–304.

manuscripts, phonorecords, film, tapes, disks, or cards, in which they are embodied.

"Motion pictures" are audiovisual works consisting of a series of related images which, when shown in succession, impart an impression of motion, together with accompanying sounds, if any.

To "perform" a work means to recite, render, play, dance, or act it, either directly or by means of any device or process or, in the case of a motion picture or other audiovisual work, to show its images in any sequence or to make the sounds accompanying it audible.

A "performing rights society" is an association, corporation, or other entity that licenses the public performance of nondramatic musical works on behalf of copyright owners of such works, such as the American Society of Composers, Authors and Publishers (ASCAP), Broadcast Music, Inc. (BMI), and SESAC, Inc.

"Phonorecords" are material objects in which sounds, other than those accompanying a motion picture or other audiovisual work, are fixed by any method now known or later developed, and from which the sounds can be perceived, reproduced, or otherwise communicated, either directly or with the aid of a machine or device. The term "phonorecords" includes the material object in which the sounds are first fixed.

"Pictorial, graphic, and sculptural works" include two-dimensional and three-dimensional works of fine, graphic, and applied art, photographs, prints and art reproductions, maps, globes, charts, diagrams, models, and technical drawings, including architectural plans. Such works shall include works of artistic craftsmanship insofar as their form but not their mechanical or utilitarian aspects are concerned; the design of a useful article, as defined in this section, shall be considered a pictorial, graphic, or sculptural work only if, and only to the extent that, such design incorporates pictorial, graphic, or sculptural features that can be identified separately from, and are capable of existing independently of, the utilitarian aspects of the article.

For purposes of section 513, a "proprietor" is an individual, corporation, partnership, or other entity, as the case may be, that owns an establishment or a food service or drinking establishment, except that no owner or operator of a radio or television station licensed by the Federal Communications Commission, cable system or satellite carrier, cable or satellite carrier service or programmer, provider of online services or network access or the operator of facilities therefor, telecommunications company, or any other such audio or audiovisual service or programmer now known or as may be developed in the future, commercial subscription music service, or owner or operator of any other transmission service, shall under any circumstances be deemed to be a proprietor.

A "pseudonymous work" is a work on the copies or phonorecords of which the author is identified under a fictitious name.

"Publication" is the distribution of copies or phonorecords of a work to the public by sale or other transfer of ownership, or by rental, lease, or lending. The offering to distribute copies or phonorecords to a group of persons for purposes of further distribution, public performance, or public display, constitutes publication. A public performance or display of a work does not of itself constitute publication.

To perform or display a work "publicly" means—

(1) to perform or display it at a place open to the public or at any place where a substantial number of persons outside of a normal circle of a family and its social acquaintances is gathered; or

(2) to transmit or otherwise communicate a performance or display of the work to a place specified by clause (1) or to the public, by means of any device or process, whether the members of the public capable of receiving the performance or display receive it in the same place or in separate places and at the same time or at different times.

"Registration", for purposes of sections 205(c)(2), 405, 406, 410(d), 411, 412, and 506(e), means a registration of a claim in the original or the renewed and extended term of copyright.

"Sound recordings" are works that result from the fixation of a series of musical, spoken, or other sounds, but not including the sounds accompanying a motion picture or other audiovisual work, regardless of the nature of the material objects, such as disks, tapes, or other phonorecords, in which they are embodied.

"State" includes the District of Columbia and the Commonwealth of Puerto Rico, and any territories to which this title is made applicable by an Act of Congress.

A "transfer of copyright ownership" is an assignment, mortgage, exclusive license, or any other conveyance, alienation, or hypothecation of a copyright or of any of the exclusive rights comprised in a copyright, whether or not it is limited in time or place of effect, but not including a nonexclusive license.

A "transmission program" is a body of material that, as an aggregate, has been produced for the sole purpose of transmission to the public in sequence and as a unit.

To "transmit" a performance or display is to communicate it by any device or process whereby images or sounds are received beyond the place from which they are sent.

A "treaty party" is a country or intergovernmental organization other than the United States that is a party to an international agreement.

The "United States", when used in a geographical sense, comprises the several States, the District of Columbia and the Commonwealth of Puerto Rico, and the organized territories under the jurisdiction of the United States Government.

For purposes of section 411, a work is a "United States work" only if—

(1) in the case of a published work, the work is first published—

(A) in the United States;

(B) simultaneously in the United States and another treaty party or parties, whose law grants a term of copyright protection that is the same as or longer than the term provided in the United States;

(C) simultaneously in the United States and a foreign nation that is not a treaty party; or

(D) in a foreign nation that is not a treaty party, and all of the authors of the work are nationals, domiciliaries, or habitual residents of, or in the case of an audiovisual work legal entities with headquarters in, the United States;

(2) in the case of an unpublished work, all the authors of the work are nationals, domiciliaries, or habitual residents of the United States, or, in the case of an unpublished audiovisual work, all the authors are legal entities with headquarters in the United States; or

(3) in the case of a pictorial, graphic, or sculptural work incorporated in a building or structure, the building or structure is located in the United States.

A "useful article" is an article having an intrinsic utilitarian function that is not merely to portray the appearance of the article or to convey information. An article that is normally a part of a useful article is considered a "useful article".

The author's "widow" or "widower" is the author's surviving spouse under the law of the author's domicile at the time of his or her death, whether or not the spouse has later remarried.

The "WIPO Copyright Treaty" is the WIPO Copyright Treaty concluded at Geneva, Switzerland, on December 20, 1996.*

The "WIPO Performances and Phonograms Treaty" is the WIPO Performances and Phonograms Treaty concluded at Geneva, Switzerland, on December 20, 1996.**

A "work of visual art" is—

(1) a painting, drawing, print or sculpture, existing in a single copy, in a limited edition of 200 copies or fewer that are signed and consecutively numbered by the author, or, in the case of a sculpture, in multiple cast, carved, or fabricated sculptures of 200 or fewer that are consecutively numbered by the author and bear the signature or other identifying mark of the author; or

(2) a still photographic image produced for exhibition purposes only, existing in a single copy that is signed by the author, or in a

---

* This provision takes effect upon entry into force of the WIPO Copyright Treaty with respect to the United States, as provided by § 105(b)(1) of Act Oct. 28, 1998, Pub. L. 105–304.

** This provision takes effect upon entry into force of the WIPO Performances and Phonograms Treaty with respect to the United States, as provided by § 105(b)(2) of Act Oct. 28, 1998, Pub. L. 105–304.

limited edition of 200 copies or fewer that are signed and consecutively numbered by the author.

A work of visual art does not include—

(A)(i) any poster, map, globe, chart, technical drawing, diagram, model, applied art, motion picture or other audiovisual work, book, magazine, newspaper, periodical, data base, electronic information service, electronic publication, or similar publication;

(ii) any merchandising item or advertising, promotional, descriptive, covering, or packaging material or container;

(iii) any portion or part of any item described in clause (i) or (ii);

(B) any work made for hire; or

(C) any work not subject to copyright protection under this title.

A "work of the United States Government" is a work prepared by an officer or employee of the United States Government as part of that person's official duties.

A "work made for hire" is—

(1) a work prepared by an employee within the scope of his or her employment; or

(2) a work specially ordered or commissioned for use as a contribution to a collective work, as a part of a motion picture or other audiovisual work, as a translation, as a supplementary work, as a compilation, as an instructional text, as a test, as answer material for a test, or as an atlas, if the parties expressly agree in a written instrument signed by them that the work shall be considered a work made for hire. For the purpose of the foregoing sentence, a "supplementary work" is a work prepared for publication as a secondary adjunct to a work by another author for the purpose of introducing, concluding, illustrating, explaining, revising, commenting upon, or assisting in the use of the other work, such as forewords, afterwords, pictorial illustrations, maps, charts, tables, editorial notes, musical arrangements, answer material for tests, bibliographies, appendixes, and indexes, and an "instructional text" is a literary, pictorial, or graphic work prepared for publication and with the purpose of use in systematic instructional activities.

In determining whether any work is eligible to be considered a work made for hire under paragraph (2), neither the amendment contained in section 1011(d) of the Intellectual Property and Communications Omnibus Reform Act of 1999, as enacted by section 1000(a)(9) of Public Law 106–113, nor the deletion of the words added by that amendment—

(A) shall be considered or otherwise given any legal significance, or

(B) shall be interpreted to indicate congressional approval or disapproval of, or acquiescence in, any judicial determination, by the courts or the Copyright Office. Paragraph (2) shall be interpreted as if both section 2(a)(1) of the Work Made For Hire and Copyright Corrections Act of 2000 and section 1011(d) of the Intellectual Property and Communications Omnibus Reform Act of 1999, as enacted by section 1000(a)(9) of Public Law 106–113, were never enacted, and without regard to any inaction or awareness by the Congress at any time of any judicial determinations.

The terms "WTO Agreement" and "WTO member country" have the meanings given those terms in paragraphs (9) and (10), respectively, of section 2 of the Uruguay Round Agreements Act.

§ 102. Subject matter of copyright: In general

(a) Copyright protection subsists, in accordance with this title, in original works of authorship fixed in any tangible medium of expression, now known or later developed, from which they can be perceived, reproduced, or otherwise communicated, either directly or with the aid of a machine or device. Works of authorship include the following categories:

(1) literary works;

(2) musical works, including any accompanying words;

(3) dramatic works, including any accompanying music;

(4) pantomimes and choreographic works;

(5) pictorial, graphic, and sculptural works;

(6) motion pictures and other audiovisual works;

(7) sound recordings; and

(8) architectural works.

(b) In no case does copyright protection for an original work of authorship extend to any idea, procedure, process, system, method of operation, concept, principle, or discovery, regardless of the form in which it is described, explained, illustrated, or embodied in such work.

§ 103. Subject matter of copyright: Compilations and derivative works

(a) The subject matter of copyright as specified by section 102 includes compilations and derivative works, but protection for a work employing preexisting material in which copyright subsists does not extend to any part of the work in which such material has been used unlawfully.

(b) The copyright in a compilation or derivative work extends only to the material contributed by the author of such work, as distinguished from the preexisting material employed in the work, and does not imply any exclusive right in the preexisting material. The copyright in such work is independent of, and does not affect or enlarge the scope, duration, ownership, or subsistence of, any copyright protection in the preexisting material.

§ 104.   Subject matter of copyright: National origin

(a) Unpublished Works. The works specified by sections 102 and 103, while unpublished, are subject to protection under this title without regard to the nationality or domicile of the author.

(b) Published Works. The works specified by sections 102 and 103, when published, are subject to protection under this title if—

(1) on the date of first publication, one or more of the authors is a national or domiciliary of the United States, or is a national, domiciliary, or sovereign authority of a treaty party, or is a stateless person, wherever that person may be domiciled; or

(2) the work is first published in the United States or in a foreign nation that, on the date of first publication, is a treaty party; or

(3) the work is a sound recording that was first fixed in a treaty party; or

(4) the work is a pictorial, graphic, or sculptural work that is incorporated in a building or other structure, or an architectural work that is embodied in a building and the building or structure is located in the United States or a treaty party; or

(5) the work is first published by the United Nations or any of its specialized agencies, or by the Organization of American States; or

(6) the work comes within the scope of a Presidential proclamation. Whenever the President finds that a particular foreign nation extends, to works by authors who are nationals or domiciliaries of the United States or to works that are first published in the United States, copyright protection on substantially the same basis as that on which the foreign nation extends protection to works of its own nationals and domiciliaries and works first published in that nation, the President may by proclamation extend protection under this title to works of which one or more of the authors is, on the date of first publication, a national, domiciliary, or sovereign authority of that nation, or which was first published in that nation. The President may revise, suspend, or revoke any such proclamation or impose any conditions or limitations on protection under a proclamation.

For purposes of paragraph (2), a work that is published in the United States or a treaty party within 30 days after publication in a foreign nation that is not a treaty party shall be considered to be first published in the United States or such treaty party, as the case may be.

(c) Effect of Berne Convention. No right or interest in a work eligible for protection under this title may be claimed by virtue of, or in reliance upon, the provisions of the Berne Convention, or the adherence of the United States thereto. Any rights in a work eligible for protection under this title that derive from this title, other Federal or State statutes, or the common law, shall not be expanded or reduced by virtue of, or in reliance upon, the provisions of the Berne Convention, or the adherence of the United States thereto.

(d) Effect of Phonograms Treaties. Notwithstanding the provisions of subsection (b), no works other than sound recordings shall be eligible for protection under this title solely by virtue of the adherence of the United States to the Geneva Phonograms Convention or the WIPO Performances and Phonograms Treaty.*

§ 104A. Copyright in restored works

(a) Automatic Protection and Term.—

(1) Term.—

(A) Copyright subsists, in accordance with this section, in restored works, and vests automatically on the date of restoration.

(B) Any work in which copyright is restored under this section shall subsist for the remainder of the term of copyright that the work would have otherwise been granted in the United States if the work never entered the public domain in the United States.

(2) Exception. Any work in which the copyright was ever owned or administered by the Alien Property Custodian and in which the restored copyright would be owned by a government or instrumentality thereof, is not a restored work.

(b) Ownership of Restored Copyright. A restored work vests initially in the author or initial rightholder of the work as determined by the law of the source country of the work.

(c) Filing of Notice of Intent to Enforce Restored Copyright Against Reliance Parties. On or after the date of restoration, any person who owns a copyright in a restored work or an exclusive right therein may file with the Copyright Office a notice of intent to enforce that person's copyright or exclusive right or may serve such a notice directly on a reliance party. Acceptance of a notice by the Copyright Office is effective as to any reliance parties but shall not create a presumption of the validity of any of the facts stated therein. Service on a reliance party is effective as to that reliance party and any other reliance parties with actual knowledge of such service and of the contents of that notice.

(d) Remedies for Infringement of Restored Copyrights.—

(1) Enforcement of copyright in restored works in the absence of a reliance party. As against any party who is not a reliance party, the remedies provided in chapter 5 of this title shall be available on or after the date of restoration of a restored copyright with respect to an act of infringement of the restored copyright that is commenced on or after the date of restoration.

(2) Enforcement of copyright in restored works as against reliance parties. As against a reliance party, except to the extent

---

* This provision takes effect upon entry into force of the WIPO Performances and Phonograms Treaty with respect to the United States, as provided by § 105(b)(2) of Act Oct. 28, 1998, Pub. L. 105–304.

provided in paragraphs (3) and (4), the remedies provided in chapter 5 of this title shall be available, with respect to an act of infringement of a restored copyright, on or after the date of restoration of the restored copyright if the requirements of either of the following subparagraphs are met:

(A)(i) The owner of the restored copyright (or such owner's agent) or the owner of an exclusive right therein (or such owner's agent) files with the Copyright Office, during the 24–month period beginning on the date of restoration, a notice of intent to enforce the restored copyright; and

(ii)(I) the act of infringement commenced after the end of the 12–month period beginning on the date of publication of the notice in the Federal Register;

(II) the act of infringement commenced before the end of the 12–month period described in subclause (I) and continued after the end of that 12–month period, in which case remedies shall be available only for infringement occurring after the end of that 12–month period; or

(III) copies or phonorecords of a work in which copyright has been restored under this section are made after publication of the notice of intent in the Federal Register.

(B)(i) The owner of the restored copyright (or such owner's agent) or the owner of an exclusive right therein (or such owner's agent) serves upon a reliance party a notice of intent to enforce a restored copyright; and

(ii)(I) the act of infringement commenced after the end of the 12–month period beginning on the date the notice of intent is received;

(II) the act of infringement commenced before the end of the 12–month period described in subclause (I) and continued after the end of that 12–month period, in which case remedies shall be available only for the infringement occurring after the end of that 12–month period; or

(III) copies or phonorecords of a work in which copyright has been restored under this section are made after receipt of the notice of intent.

In the event that notice is provided under both subparagraphs (A) and (B), the 12–month period referred to in such subparagraphs shall run from the earlier of publication or service of notice.

(3) Existing derivative works.—

(A) In the case of a derivative work that is based upon a restored work and is created—

(i) before the date of the enactment of the Uruguay Round Agreements Act, if the source country of the restored work is an eligible country on such date, or

(ii) before the date on which the source country of the restored work becomes an eligible country, if that country is not an eligible country on such date of enactment,

a reliance party may continue to exploit that derivative work for the duration of the restored copyright if the reliance party pays to the owner of the restored copyright reasonable compensation for conduct which would be subject to a remedy for infringement but for the provisions of this paragraph.

(B) In the absence of an agreement between the parties, the amount of such compensation shall be determined by an action in United States district court, and shall reflect any harm to the actual or potential market for or value of the restored work from the reliance party's continued exploitation of the work, as well as compensation for the relative contributions of expression of the author of the restored work and the reliance party to the derivative work.

(4) Commencement of infringement for reliance parties. For purposes of section 412, in the case of reliance parties, infringement shall be deemed to have commenced before registration when acts which would have constituted infringement had the restored work been subject to copyright were commenced before the date of restoration.

(e) Notices of Intent to Enforce a Restored Copyright.—

(1) Notices of intent filed with the copyright office.—

(A)(i) A notice of intent filed with the Copyright Office to enforce a restored copyright shall be signed by the owner of the restored copyright or the owner of an exclusive right therein, who files the notice under subsection (d)(2)(A)(i) (hereafter in this paragraph referred to as the "owner"), or by the owner's agent, shall identify the title of the restored work, and shall include an English translation of the title and any other alternative titles known to the owner by which the restored work may be identified, and an address and telephone number at which the owner may be contacted. If the notice is signed by an agent, the agency relationship must have been constituted in a writing signed by the owner before the filing of the notice. The Copyright Office may specifically require in regulations other information to be included in the notice, but failure to provide such other information shall not invalidate the notice or be a basis for refusal to list the restored work in the Federal Register.

(ii) If a work in which copyright is restored has no formal title, it shall be described in the notice of intent in detail sufficient to identify it.

(iii) Minor errors or omissions may be corrected by further notice at any time after the notice of intent is filed. Notices of corrections for such minor errors or omissions shall be accepted after the period established in subsection (d)(2)(A)(i). Notices shall be published in the Federal Register pursuant to subparagraph (B).

(B)(i) The Register of Copyrights shall publish in the Federal Register, commencing not later than 4 months after the date of restoration for a particular nation and every 4 months thereafter for a period of 2 years, lists identifying restored works and the ownership thereof if a notice of intent to enforce a restored copyright has been filed.

(ii) Not less than 1 list containing all notices of intent to enforce shall be maintained in the Public Information Office of the Copyright Office and shall be available for public inspection and copying during regular business hours pursuant to sections 705 and 708.

(C) The Register of Copyrights is authorized to fix reasonable fees based on the costs of receipt, processing, recording, and publication of notices of intent to enforce a restored copyright and corrections thereto.

(D)(i) Not later than 90 days before the date the Agreement on Trade–Related Aspects of Intellectual Property referred to in section 101(d)(15) of the Uruguay Round Agreements Act enters into force with respect to the United States, the Copyright Office shall issue and publish in the Federal Register regulations governing the filing under this subsection of notices of intent to enforce a restored copyright.

(ii) Such regulations shall permit owners of restored copyrights to file simultaneously for registration of the restored copyright.

(2) Notices of intent served on a reliance party.—

(A) Notices of intent to enforce a restored copyright may be served on a reliance party at any time after the date of restoration of the restored copyright.

(B) Notices of intent to enforce a restored copyright served on a reliance party shall be signed by the owner or the owner's agent, shall identify the restored work and the work in which the restored work is used, if any, in detail sufficient to identify them, and shall include an English translation of the title, any other alternative titles known to the owner by which the work may be identified, the use or uses to which the owner objects, and an address and telephone number at which the reliance party may contact the owner. If the notice is signed by an agent, the agency relationship must have been constituted in writing and signed by the owner before service of the notice.

(3) Effect of material false statements. Any material false statement knowingly made with respect to any restored copyright identified in any notice of intent shall make void all claims and assertions made with respect to such restored copyright.

(f) Immunity from Warranty and Related Liability.—

(1) In general. Any person who warrants, promises, or guarantees that a work does not violate an exclusive right granted in section 106 shall not be liable for legal, equitable, arbitral, or administrative relief if the warranty, promise, or guarantee is breached by virtue of the restoration of copyright under this section, if such warranty, promise, or guarantee is made before January 1, 1995.

(2) Performances. No person shall be required to perform any act if such performance is made infringing by virtue of the restoration of copyright under the provisions of this section, if the obligation to perform was undertaken before January 1, 1995.

(g) Proclamation of Copyright Restoration. Whenever the President finds that a particular foreign nation extends, to works by authors who are nationals or domiciliaries of the United States, restored copyright protection on substantially the same basis as provided under this section, the President may by proclamation extend restored protection provided under this section to any work—

(1) of which one or more of the authors is, on the date of first publication, a national, domiciliary, or sovereign authority of that nation; or

(2) which was first published in that nation.

The President may revise, suspend, or revoke any such proclamation or impose any conditions or limitations on protection under such a proclamation.

(h) Definitions. For purposes of this section and section 109(a):

(1) The term "date of adherence or proclamation" means the earlier of the date on which a foreign nation which, as of the date the WTO Agreement enters into force with respect to the United States, is not a nation adhering to the Berne Convention or a WTO member country, becomes—

(A) a nation adhering to the Berne Convention;

(B) a WTO member country;

(C) a nation adhering to the WIPO Copyright Treaty;

(D) a nation adhering to the WIPO Performances and Phonograms Treaty; or

(E) subject to a Presidential proclamation under subsection (g).

(2) The "date of restoration" of a restored copyright is—

(A) January 1, 1996, if the source country of the restored work is a nation adhering to the Berne Convention or a WTO member country on such date, or

(B) the date of adherence or proclamation, in the case of any other source country of the restored work.

(3) The term "eligible country" means a nation, other than the United States, that—

(A) becomes a WTO member country after the date of the enactment of the Uruguay Round Agreements Act;

(B) on such date of enactment is, or after such date of enactment becomes, a nation adhering to the Berne Convention;

(C) adheres to the WIPO Copyright Treaty;

(D) adheres to the WIPO Performances and Phonograms Treaty; or

(E) after such date of enactment becomes subject to a proclamation under subsection (g).

(4) The term "reliance party" means any person who—

(A) with respect to a particular work, engages in acts, before the source country of that work becomes an eligible country, which would have violated section 106 if the restored work had been subject to copyright protection, and who, after the source country becomes an eligible country, continues to engage in such acts;

(B) before the source country of a particular work becomes an eligible country, makes or acquires 1 or more copies or phonorecords of that work; or

(C) as the result of the sale or other disposition of a derivative work covered under subsection (d)(3), or significant assets of a person described in subparagraph (A) or (B), is a successor, assignee, or licensee of that person.

(5) The term "restored copyright" means copyright in a restored work under this section.

(6) The term "restored work" means an original work of authorship that—

(A) is protected under subsection (a);

(B) is not in the public domain in its source country through expiration of term of protection;

(C) is in the public domain in the United States due to—

(i) noncompliance with formalities imposed at any time by United States copyright law, including failure of renewal, lack of proper notice, or failure to comply with any manufacturing requirements;

(ii) lack of subject matter protection in the case of sound recordings fixed before February 15, 1972; or

(iii) lack of national eligibility;

(D) has at least one author or rightholder who was, at the time the work was created, a national or domiciliary of an eligible country, and if published, was first published in an eligible country and not published in the United States during the 30–day period following publication in such eligible country; and

(E) if the source country for the work is an eligible country solely by virtue of its adherence to the WIPO Performances and Phonograms Treaty, is a sound recording.

(7) The term "rightholder" means the person—

(A) who, with respect to a sound recording, first fixes a sound recording with authorization, or

(B) who has acquired rights from the person described in subparagraph (A) by means of any conveyance or by operation of law.

(8) The "source country" of a restored work is—

(A) a nation other than the United States;

(B) in the case of an unpublished work—

(i) the eligible country in which the author or rightholder is a national or domiciliary, or, if a restored work has more than 1 author or rightholder, of which the majority of foreign authors or rightholders are nationals or domiciliaries; or

(ii) if the majority of authors or rightholders are not foreign, the nation other than the United States which has the most significant contacts with the work; and

(C) in the case of a published work—

(i) the eligible country in which the work is first published, or

(ii) if the restored work is published on the same day in 2 or more eligible countries, the eligible country which has the most significant contacts with the work.

§ 105. Subject matter of copyright: United States Government works

Copyright protection under this title is not available for any work of the United States Government, but the United States Government is not precluded from receiving and holding copyrights transferred to it by assignment, bequest, or otherwise.

§ 106. Exclusive rights in copyrighted works

Subject to sections 107 through 122, the owner of copyright under this title has the exclusive rights to do and to authorize any of the following:

(1) to reproduce the copyrighted work in copies or phonorecords;

(2) to prepare derivative works based upon the copyrighted work;

(3) to distribute copies or phonorecords of the copyrighted work to the public by sale or other transfer of ownership, or by rental, lease, or lending;

(4) in the case of literary, musical, dramatic, and choreographic works, pantomimes, and motion pictures and other audiovisual works, to perform the copyrighted work publicly;

(5) in the case of literary, musical, dramatic, and choreographic works, pantomimes, and pictorial, graphic, or sculptural works, including the individual images of a motion picture or other audiovisual work, to display the copyrighted work publicly; and

(6) in the case of sound recordings, to perform the copyrighted work publicly by means of a digital audio transmission.

§ 106A. Rights of certain authors to attribution and integrity

(a) Rights of Attribution and Integrity. Subject to section 107 and independent of the exclusive rights provided in section 106, the author of a work of visual art—

(1) shall have the right—

(A) to claim authorship of that work, and

(B) to prevent the use of his or her name as the author of any work of visual art which he or she did not create;

(2) shall have the right to prevent the use of his or her name as the author of the work of visual art in the event of a distortion, mutilation, or other modification of the work which would be prejudicial to his or her honor or reputation; and

(3) subject to the limitations set forth in section 113(d), shall have the right—

(A) to prevent any intentional distortion, mutilation, or other modification of that work which would be prejudicial to his or her honor or reputation, and any intentional distortion, mutilation, or modification of that work is a violation of that right, and

(B) to prevent any destruction of a work of recognized stature, and any intentional or grossly negligent destruction of that work is a violation of that right.

(b) Scope and Exercise of Rights. Only the author of a work of visual art has the rights conferred by subsection (a) in that work, whether or not the author is the copyright owner. The authors of a joint work of visual art are coowners of the rights conferred by subsection (a) in that work.

(c) Exceptions. (1) The modification of a work of visual art which is the result of the passage of time or the inherent nature of the materials is not a distortion, mutilation, or other modification described in subsection (a)(3)(A).

(2) The modification of a work of visual art which is the result of conservation, or of the public presentation, including lighting and placement, of the work is not a destruction, distortion, mutilation, or other modification described in subsection (a)(3) unless the modification is caused by gross negligence.

(3) The rights described in paragraphs (1) and (2) of subsection (a) shall not apply to any reproduction, depiction, portrayal, or other use of a work in, upon, or in any connection with any item described in subparagraph (A) or (B) of the definition of "work of visual art" in section 101, and any such reproduction, depiction, portrayal, or other use of a work is not a destruction, distortion, mutilation, or other modification described in paragraph (3) of subsection (a).

(d) Duration of Rights. (1) With respect to works of visual art created on or after the effective date [June 1, 1991] set forth in section 610(a) of the Visual Artists Rights Act of 1990, the rights conferred by subsection (a) shall endure for a term consisting of the life of the author.

(2) With respect to works of visual art created before the effective date [June 1, 1991] set forth in section 610(a) of the Visual Artists Rights Act of 1990, but title to which has not, as of such effective date, been transferred from the author, the rights conferred by subsection (a) shall be coextensive with, and shall expire at the same time as, the rights conferred by section 106.

(3) In the case of a joint work prepared by two or more authors, the rights conferred by subsection (a) shall endure for a term consisting of the life of the last surviving author.

(4) All terms of the rights conferred by subsection (a) run to the end of the calendar year in which they would otherwise expire.

(e) Transfer and Waiver. (1) The rights conferred by subsection (a) may not be transferred, but those rights may be waived if the author expressly agrees to such waiver in a written instrument signed by the author. Such instrument shall specifically identify the work, and uses of that work, to which the waiver applies, and the waiver shall apply only to the work and uses so identified. In the case of a joint work prepared by two or more authors, a waiver of rights under this paragraph made by one such author waives such rights for all such authors.

(2) Ownership of the rights conferred by subsection (a) with respect to a work of visual art is distinct from ownership of any copy of that work, or of a copyright or any exclusive right under a copyright in that work. Transfer of ownership of any copy of a work of visual art, or of a copyright or any exclusive right under a copyright, shall not constitute a waiver of the rights conferred by subsection (a). Except as may otherwise be agreed by the author in a written instrument signed

by the author, a waiver of the rights conferred by subsection (a) with respect to a work of visual art shall not constitute a transfer of ownership of any copy of that work, or of ownership of a copyright or of any exclusive right under a copyright in that work.

§ 107. Limitations on exclusive rights: Fair use

Notwithstanding the provisions of sections 106 and 106A, the fair use of a copyrighted work, including such use by reproduction in copies or phono-records or by any other means specified by that section, for purposes such as criticism, comment, news reporting, teaching (including multiple copies for classroom use), scholarship, or research, is not an infringement of copyright. In determining whether the use made of a work in any particu-lar case is a fair use the factors to be considered shall include—

(1) the purpose and character of the use, including whether such use is of a commercial nature or is for nonprofit educational purposes;

(2) the nature of the copyrighted work;

(3) the amount and substantiality of the portion used in relation to the copyrighted work as a whole; and

(4) the effect of the use upon the potential market for or value of the copyrighted work.

The fact that a work is unpublished shall not itself bar a finding of fair use if such finding is made upon consideration of all the above factors.

§ 108. Limitations on exclusive rights: Reproduction by libraries and archives

(a) Except as otherwise provided in this title and notwithstanding the provisions of section 106, it is not an infringement of copyright for a library or archives, or any of its employees acting within the scope of their employment, to reproduce no more than one copy or phonorecord of a work, except as provided in subsections (b) and (c), or to distribute such copy or phonorecord, under the conditions specified by this section, if—

(1) the reproduction or distribution is made without any purpose of direct or indirect commercial advantage;

(2) the collections of the library or archives are (i) open to the public, or (ii) available not only to researchers affiliated with the library or archives or with the institution of which it is a part, but also to other persons doing research in a specialized field; and

(3) the reproduction or distribution of the work includes a notice of copyright that appears on the copy or phonorecord that is repro-duced under the provisions of this section, or includes a legend stating that the work may be protected by copyright if no such notice can be found on the copy or phonorecord that is reproduced under the provisions of this section.

(b) The rights of reproduction and distribution under this section apply to three copies or phonorecords of an unpublished work duplicated solely for purposes of preservation and security or for deposit for research use in another library or archives of the type described by clause (2) of subsection (a), if—

(1) the copy or phonorecord reproduced is currently in the collections of the library or archives; and

(2) any such copy or phonorecord that is reproduced in digital format is not otherwise distributed in that format and is not made available to the public in that format outside the premises of the library or archives.

(c) The right of reproduction under this section applies to three copies or phonorecords of a published work duplicated solely for the purpose of replacement of a copy or phonorecord that is damaged, deteriorating, lost, or stolen, or if the existing format in which the work is stored has become obsolete, if—

(1) the library or archives has, after a reasonable effort, determined that an unused replacement cannot be obtained at a fair price; and

(2) any such copy or phonorecord that is reproduced in digital format is not made available to the public in that format outside the premises of the library or archives in lawful possession of such copy.

For purposes of this subsection, a format shall be considered obsolete if the machine or device necessary to render perceptible a work stored in that format is no longer manufactured or is no longer reasonably available in the commercial marketplace.

(d) The rights of reproduction and distribution under this section apply to a copy, made from the collection of a library or archives where the user makes his or her request or from that of another library or archives, of no more than one article or other contribution to a copyrighted collection or periodical issue, or to a copy or phonorecord of a small part of any other copyrighted work, if—

(1) the copy or phonorecord becomes the property of the user, and the library or archives has had no notice that the copy or phonorecord would be used for any purpose other than private study, scholarship, or research; and

(2) the library or archives displays prominently, at the place where orders are accepted, and includes on its order form, a warning of copyright in accordance with requirements that the Register of Copyrights shall prescribe by regulation.

(e) The rights of reproduction and distribution under this section apply to the entire work, or to a substantial part of it, made from the collection of a library or archives where the user makes his or her request or from that of another library or archives, if the library or archives has first determined, on the basis of a reasonable investigation, that a copy or phonorecord of the copyrighted work cannot be obtained at a fair price, if—

(1) the copy or phonorecord becomes the property of the user, and the library or archives has had no notice that the copy or phonorecord would be used for any purpose other than private study, scholarship, or research; and

(2) the library or archives displays prominently, at the place where orders are accepted, and includes on its order form, a warning of copyright in accordance with requirements that the Register of Copyrights shall prescribe by regulation.

(f) Nothing in this section—

(1) shall be construed to impose liability for copyright infringement upon a library or archives or its employees for the unsupervised use of reproducing equipment located on its premises: *Provided,* That such equipment displays a notice that the making of a copy may be subject to the copyright law;

(2) excuses a person who uses such reproducing equipment or who requests a copy or phonorecord under subsection (d) from liability for copyright infringement for any such act, or for any later use of such copy or phonorecord, if it exceeds fair use as provided by section 107;

(3) shall be construed to limit the reproduction and distribution by lending of a limited number of copies and excerpts by a library or archives of an audiovisual news program, subject to clauses (1), (2), and (3) of subsection (a); or

(4) in any way affects the right of fair use as provided by section 107, or any contractual obligations assumed at any time by the library or archives when it obtained a copy or phonorecord of a work in its collections.

(g) The rights of reproduction and distribution under this section extend to the isolated and unrelated reproduction or distribution of a single copy or phonorecord of the same material on separate occasions, but do not extend to cases where the library or archives, or its employee—

(1) is aware or has substantial reason to believe that it is engaging in the related or concerted reproduction or distribution of multiple copies or phonorecords of the same material, whether made on one occasion or over a period of time, and whether intended for aggregate use by one or more individuals or for separate use by the individual members of a group; or

(2) engages in the systematic reproduction or distribution of single or multiple copies or phonorecords of material described in subsection (d): *Provided,* That nothing in this clause prevents a library or archives from participating in interlibrary arrangements that do not have, as their purpose or effect, that the library or archives receiving such copies or phonorecords for distribution does so in such aggregate quantities as to substitute for a subscription to or purchase of such work.

(h)(1) For purposes of this section, during the last 20 years of any term of copyright of a published work, a library or archives, including a nonprofit educational institution that functions as such, may reproduce, distribute, display, or perform in facsimile or digital form a copy or phonorecord of such work, or portions thereof, for purposes of preservation, scholarship, or research, if such library or archives has first determined, on the basis of a reasonable investigation, that none of the conditions set forth in subparagraphs (A), (B), and (C) of paragraph (2) apply.

(2) No reproduction, distribution, display, or performance is authorized under this subsection if—

(A) the work is subject to normal commercial exploitation;

(B) a copy or phonorecord of the work can be obtained at a reasonable price; or

(C) the copyright owner or its agent provides notice pursuant to regulations promulgated by the Register of Copyrights that either of the conditions set forth in subparagraphs (A) and (B) applies.

(3) The exemption provided in this subsection does not apply to any subsequent uses by users other than such library or archives.

(i) The rights of reproduction and distribution under this section do not apply to a musical work, a pictorial, graphic or sculptural work, or a motion picture or other audiovisual work other than an audiovisual work dealing with news, except that no such limitation shall apply with respect to rights granted by subsections (b) and (c), or with respect to pictorial or graphic works published as illustrations, diagrams, or similar adjuncts to works of which copies are reproduced or distributed in accordance with subsections (d) and (e).

§ 109. Limitations on exclusive rights: Effect of transfer of particular copy or phonorecord

(a) Notwithstanding the provisions of section 106(3), the owner of a particular copy or phonorecord lawfully made under this title, or any person authorized by such owner, is entitled, without the authority of the copyright owner, to sell or otherwise dispose of the possession of that copy or phonorecord. Notwithstanding the preceding sentence, copies or phonorecords of works subject to restored copyright under section 104A that are manufactured before the date of restoration of copyright or, with respect to reliance parties, before publication or service of notice under section 104A(e), may be sold or otherwise disposed of without the authorization of the owner of the restored copyright for purposes of direct or indirect commercial advantage only during the 12-month period beginning on—

(1) the date of the publication in the Federal Register of the notice of intent filed with the Copyright Office under section 104A(d)(2)(A), or

(2) the date of the receipt of actual notice served under section 104A(d)(2)(B), whichever occurs first.

(b)(1)(A) Notwithstanding the provisions of subsection (a), unless authorized by the owners of copyright in the sound recording or the owner of copyright in a computer program (including any tape, disk, or other medium embodying such program), and in the case of a sound recording in the musical works embodied therein, neither the owner of a particular phonorecord nor any person in possession of a particular copy of a computer program (including any tape, disk, or other medium embodying such program), may, for the purposes of direct or indirect commercial advantage, dispose of, or authorize the disposal of, the possession of that phonorecord or computer program (including any tape, disk, or other medium embodying such program) by rental, lease, or lending, or by any other act or practice in the nature of rental, lease, or lending. Nothing in the preceding sentence shall apply to the rental, lease, or lending of a phonorecord for nonprofit purposes by a nonprofit library or nonprofit educational institution. The transfer of possession of a lawfully made copy of a computer program by a nonprofit educational institution to another nonprofit educational institution or to faculty, staff, and students does not constitute rental, lease, or lending for direct or indirect commercial purposes under this subsection.

(B) This subsection does not apply to—

(i) a computer program which is embodied in a machine or product and which cannot be copied during the ordinary operation or use of the machine or product; or

(ii) a computer program embodied in or used in conjunction with a limited purpose computer that is designed for playing video games and may be designed for other purposes.

(C) Nothing in this subsection affects any provision of chapter 9 of this title.

(2)(A) Nothing in this subsection shall apply to the lending of a computer program for nonprofit purposes by a nonprofit library, if each copy of a computer program which is lent by such library has affixed to the packaging containing the program a warning of copyright in accordance with requirements that the Register of Copyrights shall prescribe by regulation.

(B) Not later than three years after the date of the enactment of the Computer Software Rental Amendments Act of 1990, and at such times thereafter as the Register of Copyrights considers appropriate, the Register of Copyrights, after consultation with representatives of copyright owners and librarians, shall submit to the Congress a report stating whether this paragraph has achieved its intended purpose of maintaining the integrity of the copyright system while providing nonprofit libraries the capability to fulfill their function. Such report shall advise the Congress as to any information or recommendations that the Register of Copyrights considers necessary to carry out the purposes of this subsection.

(3) Nothing in this subsection shall affect any provision of the antitrust laws. For purposes of the preceding sentence, "antitrust laws" has the meaning given that term in the first section of the Clayton Act and includes section 5 of the Federal Trade Commission Act to the extent that section relates to unfair methods of competition.

(4) Any person who distributes a phonorecord or a copy of a computer program (including any tape, disk, or other medium embodying such program) in violation of paragraph (1) is an infringer of copyright under section 501 of this title and is subject to the remedies set forth in sections 502, 503, 504, 505, and 509. Such violation shall not be a criminal offense under section 506 or cause such person to be subject to the criminal penalties set forth in section 2319 of title 18.

(c) Notwithstanding the provisions of section 106(5), the owner of a particular copy lawfully made under this title, or any person authorized by such owner, is entitled, without the authority of the copyright owner, to display that copy publicly, either directly or by the projection of no more than one image at a time, to viewers present at the place where the copy is located.

(d) The privileges prescribed by subsections (a) and (c) do not, unless authorized by the copyright owner, extend to any person who has acquired possession of the copy or phonorecord from the copyright owner, by rental, lease, loan, or otherwise, without acquiring ownership of it.

(e) Notwithstanding the provisions of sections 106(4) and 106(5), in the case of an electronic audiovisual game intended for use in coin-operated equipment, the owner of a particular copy of such a game lawfully made under this title, is entitled, without the authority of the copyright owner of the game, to publicly perform or display that game in coin-operated equipment, except that this subsection shall not apply to any work of authorship embodied in the audiovisual game if the copyright owner of the electronic audiovisual game is not also the copyright owner of the work of authorship.

§ 110. Limitations on exclusive rights: Exemption of certain performances and displays

Notwithstanding the provisions of section 106, the following are not infringements of copyright:

(1) performance or display of a work by instructors or pupils in the course of face-to-face teaching activities of a nonprofit educational institution, in a classroom or similar place devoted to instruction, unless, in the case of a motion picture or other audiovisual work, the performance, or the display of individual images, is given by means of a copy that was not lawfully made under this title, and that the person responsible for the performance knew or had reason to believe was not lawfully made;

(2) except with respect to a work produced or marketed primarily for performance or display as part of mediated instructional activities transmitted via digital networks, or a performance or display that is given by means of a copy or phonorecord that is not lawfully made and acquired under this title, and the transmitting government body or accredited nonprofit educational institution knew or had reason to believe was not lawfully made and acquired, the performance of a nondramatic literary or musical work or reasonable and limited portions of any other work, or display of a work in an amount comparable to that which is typically displayed in the course of a live classroom session, by or in the course of a transmission, if—

(A) the performance or display is made by, at the direction of, or under the actual supervision of an instructor as an integral part of a class session offered as a regular part of the systematic mediated instructional activities of a governmental body or an accredited nonprofit educational institution;

(B) the performance or display is directly related and of material assistance to the teaching content of the transmission;

(C) the transmission is made solely for, and, to the extent technologically feasible, the reception of such transmission is limited to—

(i) students officially enrolled in the course for which the transmission is made; or

(ii) officers or employees of governmental bodies as a part of their official duties or employment; and

(D) the transmitting body or institution—

(i) institutes policies regarding copyright, provides informational materials to faculty, students, and relevant staff members that accurately describe, and promote compliance with, the laws of the United States relating to copyright, and provides notice to students that materials used in connection with the course may be subject to copyright protection; and

(ii) in the case of digital transmissions—

(I) applies technological measures that reasonably prevent—

(aa) retention of the work in accessible form by recipients of the transmission from the transmitting body or institution for longer than the class session; and

(bb) unauthorized further dissemination of the work in accessible form by such recipients to others; and

(II) does not engage in conduct that could reasonably be expected to interfere with technological measures used by copyright owners to prevent such retention or unauthorized further dissemination;

(3) performance of a nondramatic literary or musical work or of a dramatico-musical work of a religious nature, or display of a work, in the course of services at a place of worship or other religious assembly;

(4) performance of a nondramatic literary or musical work otherwise than in a transmission to the public, without any purpose of direct or indirect commercial advantage and without payment of any fee or other compensation for the performance to any of its performers, promoters, or organizers, if—

(A) there is no direct or indirect admission charge; or

(B) the proceeds, after deducting the reasonable costs of producing the performance, are used exclusively for educational, religious, or charitable purposes and not for private financial gain, except where the copyright owner has served notice of objection to the performance under the following conditions:

(i) the notice shall be in writing and signed by the copyright owner or such owner's duly authorized agent; and

(ii) the notice shall be served on the person responsible for the performance at least seven days before the date of the performance, and shall state the reasons for the objection; and

(iii) the notice shall comply, in form, content, and manner of service, with requirements that the Register of Copyrights shall prescribe by regulation;

(5)(A) except as provided in subparagraph (B), communication of a transmission embodying a performance or display of a work by the public reception of the transmission on a single receiving apparatus of a kind commonly used in private homes, unless—

(i) a direct charge is made to see or hear the transmission; or

(ii) the transmission thus received is further transmitted to the public;

(B) communication by an establishment of a transmission or retransmission embodying a performance or display of a nondramatic musical work intended to be received by the general public, originated by a radio or television broadcast station licensed as such by the Federal Communications Commission, or, if an audiovisual transmission, by a cable system or satellite carrier, if—

(i) in the case of an establishment other than a food service or drinking establishment, either the establishment in which the communication occurs has less than 2,000 gross square feet of space (excluding space used for customer parking and for no other purpose), or the establishment in which the communication occurs has 2,000 or more gross square feet of space (excluding space used for customer parking and for no other purpose) and—

(I) if the performance is by audio means only, the performance is communicated by means of a total of not more than 6 loudspeakers, of which not more than 4 loudspeakers are located in any 1 room or adjoining outdoor space; or

(II) if the performance or display is by audiovisual means, any visual portion of the performance or display is communicated by means of a total of not more than 4 audiovisual devices, of which not more than 1 audiovisual device is located in any 1 room, and no such audiovisual device has a diagonal screen size greater than 55 inches, and any audio portion of the performance or display is communicated by means of a total of not more than 6 loudspeakers, of which not more than 4 loudspeakers are located in any 1 room or adjoining outdoor space;

(ii) in the case of a food service or drinking establishment, either the establishment in which the communication occurs has less than 3,750 gross square feet of space (excluding space used for customer parking and for no other purpose), or the establishment in which the communication occurs has 3,750 gross square feet of space or more (excluding space used for customer parking and for no other purpose) and—

(I) if the performance is by audio means only, the performance is communicated by means of a total of not more than 6 loudspeakers, of which not more than 4 loudspeakers are located in any 1 room or adjoining outdoor space; or

(II) if the performance or display is by audiovisual means, any visual portion of the performance or display is communicated by means of a total of not more than 4 audiovisual devices, of which not more than 1 audiovisual device is located in any 1 room, and no such audiovisual device has a diagonal screen size greater than 55 inches, and any audio portion of the performance or display is communicated by means of a total of not more than 6 loudspeakers, of which not more than 4 loudspeakers are located in any 1 room or adjoining outdoor space;

(iii) no direct charge is made to see or hear the transmission or retransmission;

(iv) the transmission or retransmission is not further transmitted beyond the establishment where it is received; and

(v) the transmission or retransmission is licensed by the copyright owner of the work so publicly performed or displayed;

(6) performance of a nondramatic musical work by a governmental body or a nonprofit agricultural or horticultural organization, in the course of an annual agricultural or horticultural fair or exhibition conducted by such body or organization; the exemption provided by this clause shall extend to any liability for copyright infringement that would otherwise be imposed on such body or organization, under doctrines of vicarious liability or related infringement, for a performance by a concessionnaire, business establishment, or other person at such fair or exhibition, but shall not excuse any such person from liability for the performance;

(7) performance of a nondramatic musical work by a vending establishment open to the public at large without any direct or indirect admission charge, where the sole purpose of the performance is to promote the retail sale of copies or phonorecords of the work, or of the audiovisual or other devices utilized in such performance, and the performance is not transmitted beyond the place where the establishment is located and is within the immediate area where the sale is occurring;

(8) performance of a nondramatic literary work, by or in the course of a transmission specifically designed for and primarily directed to blind or other handicapped persons who are unable to read normal printed material as a result of their handicap, or deaf or other handicapped persons who are unable to hear the aural signals accompanying a transmission of visual signals, if the performance is made without any purpose of direct or indirect commercial advantage and its transmission is made through the facilities of: (i) a governmental body; or (ii) a noncommercial educational broadcast station (as defined in section 397 of title 47); or (iii) a radio subcarrier authorization (as defined in 47 CFR 73.293–73.295 and 73.593–73.595); or (iv) a cable system (as defined in section 111 (f));

(9) performance on a single occasion of a dramatic literary work published at least ten years before the date of the performance, by or in the course of a transmission specifically designed for and primarily directed to blind or other handicapped persons who are unable to read normal printed material as a result of their handicap, if the performance is made without any purpose of direct or indirect commercial advantage and its transmission is made through the facilities of a radio subcarrier authorization referred to in clause (8) (iii), *Provided*, That the provisions of this clause shall not be applicable to more than one performance of the same work by the same performers or under the auspices of the same organization; and

(10) notwithstanding paragraph (4), the following is not an infringement of copyright: performance of a nondramatic literary or musical work in the course of a social function which is organized and

promoted by a nonprofit veterans' organization or a nonprofit fraternal organization to which the general public is not invited, but not including the invitees of the organizations, if the proceeds from the performance, after deducting the reasonable costs of producing the performance, are used exclusively for charitable purposes and not for financial gain. For purposes of this section the social functions of any college or university fraternity or sorority shall not be included unless the social function is held solely to raise funds for a specific charitable purpose.

The exemptions provided under paragraph (5) shall not be taken into account in any administrative, judicial, or other governmental proceeding to set or adjust the royalties payable to copyright owners for the public performance or display of their works. Royalties payable to copyright owners for any public performance or display of their works other than such performances or displays as are exempted under paragraph (5) shall not be diminished in any respect as a result of such exemption.

In paragraph (2), the term "mediated instructional activities" with respect to the performance or display of a work by digital transmission under this section refers to activities that use such work as an integral part of the class experience, controlled by or under the actual supervision of the instructor and analogous to the type of performance or display that would take place in a live classroom setting. The term does not refer to activities that use, in 1 or more class sessions of a single course, such works as textbooks, course packs, or other material in any media, copies or phonorecords of which are typically purchased or acquired by the students in higher education for their independent use and retention or are typically purchased or acquired for elementary and secondary students for their possession and independent use.

For purposes of paragraph (2), accreditation—

(A) with respect to an institution providing post-secondary education, shall be as determined by a regional or national accrediting agency recognized by the Council on Higher Education Accreditation or the United States Department of Education; and

(B) with respect to an institution providing elementary or secondary education, shall be as recognized by the applicable state certification or licensing procedures.

For purposes of paragraph (2), no governmental body or accredited nonprofit educational institution shall be liable for infringement by reason of the transient or temporary storage of material carried out through the automatic technical process of a digital transmission of the performance or display of that material as authorized under paragraph (2). No such material stored on the system or network controlled or operated by the transmitting body or institution under this paragraph shall be maintained on such system or network in a manner ordinarily accessible to anyone other than anticipated recipients. No such copy shall be maintained on the system or network in a manner ordinarily accessible to such anticipated recipients for a longer period than is reasonably necessary to facilitate the transmissions for which it was made.

§ 111. Limitations on exclusive rights: Secondary transmissions

(a) Certain Secondary Transmissions Exempted. The secondary transmission of a performance or display of a work embodied in a primary transmission is not an infringement of copyright if—

(1) the secondary transmission is not made by a cable system, and consists entirely of the relaying, by the management of a hotel, apartment house, or similar establishment, of signals transmitted by a broadcast station licensed by the Federal Communications Commission, within the local service area of such station, to the private lodgings of guests or residents of such establishment, and no direct charge is made to see or hear the secondary transmission; or

(2) the secondary transmission is made solely for the purpose and under the conditions specified by clause (2) of section 110; or

(3) the secondary transmission is made by any carrier who has no direct or indirect control over the content or selection of the primary transmission or over the particular recipients of the secondary transmission, and whose activities with respect to the secondary transmission consist solely of providing wires, cables, or other communications channels for the use of others: *Provided,* That the provisions of this clause extend only to the activities of said carrier with respect to secondary transmissions and do not exempt from liability the activities of others with respect to their own primary or secondary transmissions;

(4) the secondary transmission is made by a satellite carrier for private home viewing pursuant to a statutory license under section 119; or

(5) the secondary transmission is not made by a cable system but is made by a governmental body, or other nonprofit organization, without any purpose of direct or indirect commercial advantage, and without charge to the recipients of the secondary transmission other than assessments necessary to defray the actual and reasonable costs of maintaining and operating the secondary transmission service.

(b) Secondary Transmission of Primary Transmission to Controlled Group. Notwithstanding the provisions of subsections (a) and (c), the secondary transmission to the public of a performance or display of a work embodied in a primary transmission is actionable as an act of infringement under section 501, and is fully subject to the remedies provided by sections 502 through 506 and 509, if the primary transmission is not made for reception by the public at large but is controlled and limited to reception by particular members of the public: *Provided, however,* That such secondary transmission is not actionable as an act of infringement if—

(1) the primary transmission is made by a broadcast station licensed by the Federal Communications Commission; and

(2) the carriage of the signals comprising the secondary transmission is required under the rules, regulations, or authorizations of the Federal Communications Commission; and

(3) the signal of the primary transmitter is not altered or changed in any way by the secondary transmitter.

(c) Secondary Transmissions by Cable Systems.

(1) Subject to the provisions of clauses (2), (3), and (4) of this subsection and section 114(d), secondary transmissions to the public by a cable system of a performance or display of a work embodied in a primary transmission made by a broadcast station licensed by the Federal Communications Commission or by an appropriate governmental authority of Canada or Mexico shall be subject to statutory licensing upon compliance with the requirements of subsection (d) where the carriage of the signals comprising the secondary transmission is permissible under the rules, regulations, or authorizations of the Federal Communications Commission.

(2) Notwithstanding the provisions of clause (1) of this subsection, the willful or repeated secondary transmission to the public by a cable system of a primary transmission made by a broadcast station licensed by the Federal Communications Commission or by an appropriate governmental authority of Canada or Mexico and embodying a performance or display of a work is actionable as an act of infringement under section 501, and is fully subject to the remedies provided by sections 502 through 506 and 509, in the following cases:

(A) where the carriage of the signals comprising the secondary transmission is not permissible under the rules, regulations, or authorizations of the Federal Communications Commission; or

(B) where the cable system has not deposited the statement of account and royalty fee required by subsection (d).

(3) Notwithstanding the provisions of clause (1) of this subsection and subject to the provisions of subsection (e) of this section, the secondary transmission to the public by a cable system of a performance or display of a work embodied in a primary transmission made by a broadcast station licensed by the Federal Communications Commission or by an appropriate governmental authority of Canada or Mexico is actionable as an act of infringement under section 501, and is fully subject to the remedies provided by sections 502 through 506 and sections 509 and 510, if the content of the particular program in which the performance or display is embodied, or any commercial advertising or station announcements transmitted by the primary transmitter during, or immediately before or after, the transmission of such program, is in any way willfully altered by the cable system through changes, deletions, or additions, except for the alteration, deletion, or substitution of commercial advertisements performed by those engaged in television commercial advertising market research: *Provided,* That the research company has obtained the prior consent of the advertiser

who has purchased the original commercial advertisement, the television station broadcasting that commercial advertisement, and the cable system performing the secondary transmission: *And provided further,* That such commercial alteration, deletion, or substitution is not performed for the purpose of deriving income from the sale of that commercial time.

(4) Notwithstanding the provisions of clause (1) of this subsection, the secondary transmission to the public by a cable system of a performance or display of a work embodied in a primary transmission made by a broadcast station licensed by an appropriate governmental authority of Canada or Mexico is actionable as an act of infringement under section 501, and is fully subject to the remedies provided by sections 502 through 506 and section 509, if (A) with respect to Canadian signals, the community of the cable system is located more than 150 miles from the United States–Canadian border and is also located south of the forty-second parallel of latitude, or (B) with respect to Mexican signals, the secondary transmission is made by a cable system which received the primary transmission by means other than direct interception of a free space radio wave emitted by such broadcast television station, unless prior to April 15, 1976, such cable system was actually carrying, or was specifically authorized to carry, the signal of such foreign station on the system pursuant to the rules, regulations, or authorizations of the Federal Communications Commission.

(d) Statutory License for Secondary Transmissions by Cable Systems.

(1) A cable system whose secondary transmissions have been subject to statutory licensing under subsection (c) shall, on a semiannual basis, deposit with the Register of Copyrights, in accordance with requirements that the Register shall prescribe by regulation—

(A) a statement of account, covering the six months next preceding, specifying the number of channels on which the cable system made secondary transmissions to its subscribers, the names and locations of all primary transmitters whose transmissions were further transmitted by the cable system, the total number of subscribers, the gross amounts paid to the cable system for the basic service of providing secondary transmissions of primary broadcast transmitters, and such other data as the Register of Copyrights may from time to time prescribe by regulation. In determining the total number of subscribers and the gross amounts paid to the cable system for the basic service of providing secondary transmissions of primary broadcast transmitters, the cable system shall not include subscribers and amounts collected from subscribers receiving secondary transmissions for private home viewing pursuant to section 119. Such statement shall also include a special statement of account covering any nonnetwork television programming that was carried by the cable system in whole or in part beyond the local service area of the primary transmitter, under rules, regulations, or authorizations of the Federal Communications Commission permitting the substitution or addition of signals under certain circumstances, together with logs showing the times, dates, stations, and programs involved in such substituted or added carriage; and

(B) except in the case of a cable system whose royalty is specified in subclause (C) or (D), a total royalty fee for the period covered by the statement, computed on the basis of specified percentages of the gross receipts from subscribers to the cable service during said period for the basic service of providing secondary transmissions of primary broadcast transmitters, as follows:

(i) 0.675 of 1 per centum of such gross receipts for the privilege of further transmitting any nonnetwork programming of a primary transmitter in whole or in part beyond the local service area of such primary transmitter, such amount to be applied against the fee, if any, payable pursuant to paragraphs (ii) through (iv);

(ii) 0.675 of 1 per centum of such gross receipts for the first distant signal equivalent;

(iii) 0.425 of 1 per centum of such gross receipts for each of the second, third, and fourth distant signal equivalents;

(iv) 0.2 of 1 per centum of such gross receipts for the fifth distant signal equivalent and each additional distant signal equivalent thereafter;

and in computing the amounts payable under paragraph (ii) through (iv), above, any fraction of a distant signal equivalent shall be computed at its fractional value and, in the case of any cable system located partly within and partly without the local service area of a primary transmitter, gross receipts shall be limited to those gross receipts derived from subscribers located without the local service area of such primary transmitter; and

(C) if the actual gross receipts paid by subscribers to a cable system for the period covered by the statement for the basic service of providing secondary transmissions of primary broadcast transmitters total $80,000 or less, gross receipts of the cable system for the purpose of this subclause shall be computed by subtracting from such actual gross receipts the amount by which $80,000 exceeds such actual gross receipts, except that in no case shall a cable system's gross receipts be reduced to less than $3,000. The royalty fee payable under this subclause shall be 0.5 of 1 per centum, regardless of the number of distant signal equivalents, if any; and

(D) if the actual gross receipts paid by subscribers to a cable system for the period covered by the statement, for the basic service of providing secondary transmissions of primary broadcast transmitters, are more than $80,000 but less than $160,000, the royalty fee payable under this subclause shall be

(i) 0.5 of 1 per centum of any gross receipts up to $80,000; and

(ii) 1 per centum of any gross receipts in excess of $80,000 but less than $160,000, regardless of the number of distant signal equivalents, if any.

(2) The Register of Copyrights shall receive all fees deposited under this section and, after deducting the reasonable costs incurred by the Copyright Office under this section, shall deposit the balance in the Treasury of the United States, in such manner as the Secretary of the Treasury directs. All funds held by the Secretary of the Treasury shall be invested in interest-bearing United States securities for later distribution with interest by the Librarian of Congress in the event no controversy over distribution exists, or by a copyright arbitration royalty panel in the event a controversy over such distribution exists.

(3) The royalty fees thus deposited shall, in accordance with the procedures provided by clause (4), be distributed to those among the following copyright owners who claim that their works were the subject of secondary transmissions by cable systems during the relevant semiannual period:

(A) any such owner whose work was included in a secondary transmission made by a cable system of a nonnetwork television program in whole or in part beyond the local service area of the primary transmitter; and

(B) any such owner whose work was included in a secondary transmission identified in a special statement of account deposited under clause (1) (A); and

(C) any such owner whose work was included in nonnetwork programming consisting exclusively of aural signals carried by a cable system in whole or in part beyond the local service area of the primary transmitter of such programs.

(4) The royalty fees thus deposited shall be distributed in accordance with the following procedures:

(A) During the month of July in each year, every person claiming to be entitled to statutory license fees for secondary transmissions shall file a claim with the Librarian of Congress, in accordance with requirements that the Librarian of Congress shall prescribe by regulation. Notwithstanding any provisions of the antitrust laws, for purposes of this clause any claimants may agree among themselves as to the proportionate division of statutory licensing fees among them, may lump their claims together and file them jointly or as a single claim, or may designate a common agent to receive payment on their behalf.

(B) After the first day of August of each year, the Librarian of Congress shall, upon the recommendation of the Register of Copyrights, determine whether there exists a controversy concerning the distribution of royalty fees. If the Librarian determines that no such controversy exists, the Librarian shall, after deducting reasonable administrative costs under this section, distribute such fees to the copyright owners entitled to such fees, or to their designated agents. If the Librarian finds the existence of a controversy, the Librarian shall, pursuant to chapter 8 of this title, convene a copyright arbitration royalty panel to determine the distribution of royalty fees.

(C) During the pendency of any proceeding under this subsection, the Librarian of Congress shall withhold from distribution an amount sufficient to satisfy all claims with respect to which a controversy exists, but shall have discretion to proceed to distribute any amounts that are not in controversy.

(e) Nonsimultaneous Secondary Transmissions by Cable Systems.

(1) Notwithstanding those provisions of the second paragraph of subsection (f) relating to nonsimultaneous secondary transmissions by a cable system, any such transmissions are actionable as an act of infringement under section 501, and are fully subject to the remedies provided by sections 502 through 506 and sections 509 and 510, unless—

(A) the program on the videotape is transmitted no more than one time to the cable system's subscribers; and

(B) the copyrighted program, episode, or motion picture videotape, including the commercials contained within such program, episode, or picture, is transmitted without deletion or editing; and

(C) an owner or officer of the cable system

(i) prevents the duplication of the videotape while in the possession of the system,

(ii) prevents unauthorized duplication while in the possession of the facility making the videotape for the system if the system owns or controls the facility, or takes reasonable precautions to prevent such duplication if it does not own or control the facility,

(iii) takes adequate precautions to prevent duplication while the tape is being transported, and

(iv) subject to clause (2), erases or destroys, or causes the erasure or destruction of, the videotape; and

(D) within forty-five days after the end of each calendar quarter, an owner or officer of the cable system executes an affidavit attesting

(i) to the steps and precautions taken to prevent duplication of the videotape, and

(ii) subject to clause (2), to the erasure or destruction of all videotapes made or used during such quarter; and

(E) such owner or officer places or causes each such affidavit, and affidavits received pursuant to clause (2)(C), to be placed in a file, open to public inspection, at such system's main office in the community where the transmission is made or in the nearest community where such system maintains an office; and

(F) the nonsimultaneous transmission is one that the cable system would be authorized to transmit under the rules, regulations, and authorizations of the Federal Communications Commission in effect at the time of the nonsimultaneous transmission if the transmission had been made simultaneously, except that this subclause shall not apply to inadvertent or accidental transmissions.

(2) If a cable system transfers to any person a videotape of a program nonsimultaneously transmitted by it, such transfer is actionable as an act of infringement under section 501, and is fully subject to the remedies provided by sections 502 through 506 and 509, except that, pursuant to a written, nonprofit contract providing for the equitable sharing of the costs of such videotape and its transfer, a videotape nonsimultaneously transmitted by it, in accordance with clause (1), may be transferred by one cable system in Alaska to another system in Alaska, by one cable system in Hawaii permitted to make such nonsimultaneous transmissions to another such cable system in Hawaii, or by one cable system in Guam, the Northern Mariana Islands, or the Trust Territory of the Pacific Islands, to another cable system in any of those three territories, if—

(A) each such contract is available for public inspection in the offices of the cable systems involved, and a copy of such contract is filed, within thirty days after such contract is entered into, with the Copyright Office (which Office shall make each such contract available for public inspection); and

(B) the cable system to which the videotape is transferred complies with clause (1)(A), (B), (C)(i), (iii), and (iv), and (D) through (F); and

(C) such system provides a copy of the affidavit required to be made in accordance with clause (1)(D) to each cable system making a previous nonsimultaneous transmission of the same videotape.

(3) This subsection shall not be construed to supersede the exclusivity protection provisions of any existing agreement, or any such agreement hereafter entered into, between a cable system and a television broadcast station in the area in which the cable system is located, or a network with which such station is affiliated.

(4) As used in this subsection, the term "videotape", and each of its variant forms, means the reproduction of the images and sounds of a program or programs broadcast by a television broadcast station licensed by the Federal Communications Commission, regardless of the nature of the material objects, such as tapes or films, in which the reproduction is embodied.

(f) Definitions. As used in this section, the following terms and their variant forms mean the following:

A "primary transmission" is a transmission made to the public by the transmitting facility whose signals are being received and further transmitted by the secondary transmission service, regardless of where or when the performance or display was first transmitted.

A "secondary transmission" is the further transmitting of a primary transmission simultaneously with the primary transmission, or nonsimultaneously with the primary transmission if by a "cable system" not located in whole or in part within the boundary of the forty-eight contiguous States, Hawaii, or Puerto Rico: *Provided, however,* That a nonsimultaneous further transmission by a cable system located in Hawaii of a primary transmission shall be deemed to be a secondary transmission if the carriage of the television broadcast signal comprising such further transmission is permissible under the rules, regulations, or authorizations of the Federal Communications Commission.

A "cable system" is a facility, located in any State, Territory, Trust Territory, or Possession, that in whole or in part receives signals transmitted or programs broadcast by one or more television broadcast stations licensed by the Federal Communications Commission, and makes secondary transmissions of such signals or programs by wires, cables, microwave, or other communications channels to subscribing members of the public who pay for such service. For purposes of determining the royalty fee under subsection (d)(1), two or more cable systems in contiguous communities under common ownership or control or operating from one headend shall be considered as one system.

The "local service area of a primary transmitter", in the case of a television broadcast station, comprises the area in which such station is entitled to insist upon its signal being retransmitted by a cable system pursuant to the rules, regulations, and authorizations of the Federal Communications Commission in effect on April 15, 1976, or such station's television market as defined in section 76.55(e) of title 47, Code of Federal Regulations (as in effect on September 18, 1993), or any modifications to such television market made, on or after September 18, 1993, pursuant to section 76.55(e) or 76.59 of title 47 of the Code of Federal Regulations, or in the case of a television broadcast station licensed by an appropriate governmental authority of Canada or Mexico, the area in which it would be entitled to insist upon its signal being retransmitted if it were a television broadcast station subject to such rules, regulations, and authorizations. In the case of a low power television station, as defined by the rules and regulations of the Federal Communications Commission, the "local service area of a primary transmitter" comprises the area within 35 miles of the transmitter site, except that in the case of such a station located in a standard metropolitan statistical area which has one of the 50 largest populations of all standard metropolitan statistical areas (based on the 1980 decennial census of population taken by the Secretary of Commerce), the number of miles shall be 20 miles. The "local service area of a primary transmitter", in the case of a radio broadcast station, comprises the primary service area of such station, pursuant to the rules and regulations of the Federal Communications Commission.

A "distant signal equivalent" is the value assigned to the secondary transmission of any nonnetwork television programming carried by a cable system in whole or in part beyond the local service area of the primary transmitter of such programming. It is computed by assigning a value of one to each independent station and a value of one-quarter to each network station and noncommercial educational station for the nonnetwork programming so carried pursuant to the rules, regulations, and authorizations of the Federal Communications Commission. The foregoing values for independent, network, and noncommercial educational stations are subject, however, to the following exceptions and limitations. Where the rules and regulations of the Federal Communications Commission require a cable system to omit the further transmission of a particular program and such rules and regulations also permit the substitution of another program embodying a performance or display of a work in place of the omitted transmission, or where such rules and regulations in effect on the date of enactment of this Act permit a cable system, at its election, to effect such deletion and substitution of a nonlive program or to carry additional programs not transmitted by primary transmitters within whose local service area the cable system is located, no value shall be assigned for the substituted or additional program; where the rules, regulations, or authorizations of the Federal Communications Commission in effect on the date of enactment of this Act permit a cable system, at its election, to omit the further transmission of a particular program and such rules, regulations, or authorizations also permit the substitution of another program embodying a performance or display of a work in place of the omitted transmission, the value assigned for the substituted or additional program shall be, in the case of a live program, the value of one full distant signal equivalent multiplied by a fraction that has as its numerator the number of days in the year in which such substitution occurs and as its denominator the number of days in the year. In the case of a station carried pursuant to the late-night or specialty programming rules of the Federal Communications Commission, or a station carried on a part-time basis where full-time carriage is not possible because the cable system lacks the activated channel capacity to retransmit on a full-time basis all signals which it is authorized to carry, the values for independent, network, and noncommercial educational stations set forth above, as the case may be, shall be multiplied by a fraction which is equal to the ratio of the broadcast hours of such station carried by the cable system to the total broadcast hours of the station.

A "network station" is a television broadcast station that is owned or operated by, or affiliated with, one or more of the television networks in the United States providing nationwide transmissions, and that transmits a substantial part of the programming supplied by such networks for a substantial part of that station's typical broadcast day.

An "independent station" is a commercial television broadcast station other than a network station.

A "noncommercial educational station" is a television station that is a noncommercial educational broadcast station as defined in section 397 of title 47.

§ 112. Limitations on exclusive rights: Ephemeral recordings

(a)(1) Notwithstanding the provisions of section 106, and except in the case of a motion picture or other audiovisual work, it is not an infringement of copyright for a transmitting organization entitled to transmit to the public a performance or display of a work, under a license, including a statutory license under section 114(f), or transfer of the copyright or under the limitations on exclusive rights in sound recordings specified by section 114 (a) or for a transmitting organization that is a broadcast radio or television station licensed as such by the Federal Communications Commission and that makes a broadcast transmission of a performance of a sound recording in a digital format on a nonsubscription basis, to make no more than one copy or phonorecord of a particular transmission program embodying the performance or display, if—

> (A) the copy or phonorecord is retained and used solely by the transmitting organization that made it, and no further copies or phonorecords are reproduced from it; and

> (B) the copy or phonorecord is used solely for the transmitting organization's own transmissions within its local service area, or for purposes of archival preservation or security; and

> (C) unless preserved exclusively for archival purposes, the copy or phonorecord is destroyed within six months from the date the transmission program was first transmitted to the public.

(2) In a case in which a transmitting organization entitled to make a copy or phonorecord under paragraph (1) in connection with the transmission to the public of a performance or display of a work is prevented from making such copy or phonorecord by reason of the application by the copyright owner of technical measures that prevent the reproduction of the work, the copyright owner shall make available to the transmitting organization the necessary means for permitting the making of such copy or phonorecord as permitted under that paragraph, if it is technologically feasible and economically reasonable for the copyright owner to do so. If the copyright owner fails to do so in a timely manner in light of the transmitting organization's reasonable business requirements, the transmitting organization shall not be liable for a violation of section 1201(a)(1) of this title for engaging in

such activities as are necessary to make such copies or phonorecords as permitted under paragraph (1) of this subsection.

(b) Notwithstanding the provisions of section 106, it is not an infringement of copyright for a governmental body or other nonprofit organization entitled to transmit a performance or display of a work, under section 110(2) or under the limitations on exclusive rights in sound recordings specified by section 114(a), to make no more than thirty copies or phonorecords of a particular transmission program embodying the performance or display, if—

(1) no further copies or phonorecords are reproduced from the copies or phonorecords made under this clause; and

(2) except for one copy or phonorecord that may be preserved exclusively for archival purposes, the copies or phonorecords are destroyed within seven years from the date the transmission program was first transmitted to the public.

(c) Notwithstanding the provisions of section 106, it is not an infringement of copyright for a governmental body or other nonprofit organization to make for distribution no more than one copy or phonorecord, for each transmitting organization specified in clause (2) of this subsection, of a particular transmission program embodying a performance of a nondramatic musical work of a religious nature, or of a sound recording of such a musical work, if—

(1) there is no direct or indirect charge for making or distributing any such copies or phonorecords; and

(2) none of such copies or phonorecords is used for any performance other than a single transmission to the public by a transmitting organization entitled to transmit to the public a performance of the work under a license or transfer of the copyright; and

(3) except for one copy or phonorecord that may be preserved exclusively for archival purposes, the copies or phonorecords are all destroyed within one year from the date the transmission program was first transmitted to the public.

(d) Notwithstanding the provisions of section 106, it is not an infringement of copyright for a governmental body or other nonprofit organization entitled to transmit a performance of a work under section 110(8) to make no more than ten copies or phonorecords embodying the performance, or to permit the use of any such copy or phonorecord by any governmental body or nonprofit organization entitled to transmit a performance of a work under section 110(8), if—

(1) any such copy or phonorecord is retained and used solely by the organization that made it, or by a governmental body or nonprofit organization entitled to transmit a performance of a work under section 110(8), and no further copies or phonorecords are reproduced from it; and

(2) any such copy or phonorecord is used solely for transmissions authorized under section 110(8), or for purposes of archival preservation or security; and

(3) the governmental body or nonprofit organization permitting any use of any such copy or phonorecord by any governmental body or nonprofit organization under this subsection does not make any charge for such use.

(e) Statutory License. (1) A transmitting organization entitled to transmit to the public a performance of a sound recording under the limitation on exclusive rights specified by section 114(d)(1)(C)(iv) or under a statutory license in accordance with section 114(f) is entitled to a statutory license, under the conditions specified by this subsection, to make no more than 1 phonorecord of the sound recording (unless the terms and conditions of the statutory license allow for more), if the following conditions are satisfied:

(A) The phonorecord is retained and used solely by the transmitting organization that made it, and no further phonorecords are reproduced from it.

(B) The phonorecord is used solely for the transmitting organization's own transmissions originating in the United States under a statutory license in accordance with section 114(f) or the limitation on exclusive rights specified by section 114(d)(1)(C)(iv).

(C) Unless preserved exclusively for purposes of archival preservation, the phonorecord is destroyed within 6 months from the date the sound recording was first transmitted to the public using the phonorecord.

(D) Phonorecords of the sound recording have been distributed to the public under the authority of the copyright owner or the copyright owner authorizes the transmitting entity to transmit the sound recording, and the transmitting entity makes the phonorecord under this subsection from a phonorecord lawfully made and acquired under the authority of the copyright owner.

(2) Notwithstanding any provision of the antitrust laws, any copyright owners of sound recordings and any transmitting organizations entitled to a statutory license under this subsection may negotiate and agree upon royalty rates and license terms and conditions for making phonorecords of such sound recordings under this section and the proportionate division of fees paid among copyright owners, and may designate common agents to negotiate, agree to, pay, or receive such royalty payments.

(3) No later than 30 days after the date of the enactment of the Digital Millennium Copyright Act, the Librarian of Congress shall cause notice to be published in the Federal Register of the initiation of voluntary negotiation proceedings for the purpose of determining reasonable terms and rates of royalty payments for the activities specified by paragraph (1) of this subsection during the period beginning on the

date of the enactment of such Act and ending on December 31, 2000, or such other date as the parties may agree. Such rates shall include a minimum fee for each type of service offered by transmitting organizations. Any copyright owners of sound recordings or any transmitting organizations entitled to a statutory license under this subsection may submit to the Librarian of Congress licenses covering such activities with respect to such sound recordings. The parties to each negotiation proceeding shall bear their own costs.

(4) In the absence of license agreements negotiated under paragraph (2), during the 60–day period commencing 6 months after publication of the notice specified in paragraph (3), and upon the filing of a petition in accordance with section 803(a)(1), the Librarian of Congress shall, pursuant to chapter 8, convene a copyright arbitration royalty panel to determine and publish in the Federal Register a schedule of reasonable rates and terms which, subject to paragraph (5), shall be binding on all copyright owners of sound recordings and transmitting organizations entitled to a statutory license under this subsection during the period beginning on the date of the enactment of the Digital Millennium Copyright Act and ending on December 31, 2000, or such other date as the parties may agree. Such rates shall include a minimum fee for each type of service offered by transmitting organizations. The copyright arbitration royalty panel shall establish rates that most clearly represent the fees that would have been negotiated in the marketplace between a willing buyer and a willing seller. In determining such rates and terms, the copyright arbitration royalty panel shall base its decision on economic, competitive, and programming information presented by the parties, including—

(A) whether use of the service may substitute for or may promote the sales of phonorecords or otherwise interferes with or enhances the copyright owner's traditional streams of revenue; and

(B) the relative roles of the copyright owner and the transmitting organization in the copyrighted work and the service made available to the public with respect to relative creative contribution, technological contribution, capital investment, cost, and risk.

In establishing such rates and terms, the copyright arbitration royalty panel may consider the rates and terms under voluntary license agreements negotiated as provided in paragraphs (2) and (3). The Librarian of Congress shall also establish requirements by which copyright owners may receive reasonable notice of the use of their sound recordings under this section, and under which records of such use shall be kept and made available by transmitting organizations entitled to obtain a statutory license under this subsection.

(5) License agreements voluntarily negotiated at any time between 1 or more copyright owners of sound recordings and 1 or more transmitting organizations entitled to obtain a statutory license under this subsection shall be given effect in lieu of any determination by a

copyright arbitration royalty panel or decision by the Librarian of Congress.

(6) Publication of a notice of the initiation of voluntary negotiation proceedings as specified in paragraph (3) shall be repeated, in accordance with regulations that the Librarian of Congress shall prescribe, in the first week of January 2000, and at 2–year intervals thereafter, except to the extent that different years for the repeating of such proceedings may be determined in accordance with paragraph (3). The procedures specified in paragraph (4) shall be repeated, in accordance with regulations that the Librarian of Congress shall prescribe, upon filing of a petition in accordance with section 803(a)(1), during a 60–day period commencing on July 1, 2000, and at 2–year intervals thereafter, except to the extent that different years for the repeating of such proceedings may be determined in accordance with paragraph (3). The procedures specified in paragraph (4) shall be concluded in accordance with section 802.

(7)(A) Any person who wishes to make a phonorecord of a sound recording under a statutory license in accordance with this subsection may do so without infringing the exclusive right of the copyright owner of the sound recording under section 106(1)—

> (i) by complying with such notice requirements as the Librarian of Congress shall prescribe by regulation and by paying royalty fees in accordance with this subsection; or

> (ii) if such royalty fees have not been set, by agreeing to pay such royalty fees as shall be determined in accordance with this subsection.

> (B) Any royalty payments in arrears shall be made on or before the 20th day of the month next succeeding the month in which the royalty fees are set.

(8) If a transmitting organization entitled to make a phonorecord under this subsection is prevented from making such phonorecord by reason of the application by the copyright owner of technical measures that prevent the reproduction of the sound recording, the copyright owner shall make available to the transmitting organization the necessary means for permitting the making of such phonorecord as permitted under this subsection, if it is technologically feasible and economically reasonable for the copyright owner to do so. If the copyright owner fails to do so in a timely manner in light of the transmitting organization's reasonable business requirements, the transmitting organization shall not be liable for a violation of section 1201(a)(1) of this title for engaging in such activities as are necessary to make such phonorecords as permitted under this subsection.

(9) Nothing in this subsection annuls, limits, impairs, or otherwise affects in any way the existence or value of any of the exclusive rights of the copyright owners in a sound recording, except as otherwise provided in this subsection, or in a musical work, including the

exclusive rights to reproduce and distribute a sound recording or musical work, including by means of a digital phonorecord delivery, under section 106(1), 106(3), and 115, and the right to perform publicly a sound recording or musical work, including by means of a digital audio transmission, under sections 106(4) and 106(6).

(f)(1) Notwithstanding the provisions of section 106, and without limiting the application of subsection (b), it is not an infringement of copyright for a governmental body or other nonprofit educational institution entitled under section 110(2) to transmit a performance or display to make copies or phonorecords of a work that is in digital form and, solely to the extent permitted in paragraph (2), of a work that is in analog form, embodying the performance or display to be used for making transmissions authorized under section 110(2), if—

(A) such copies or phonorecords are retained and used solely by the body or institution that made them, and no further copies or phonorecords are reproduced from them, except as authorized under section 110(2); and

(B) such copies or phonorecords are used solely for transmissions authorized under section 110(2).

(2) This subsection does not authorize the conversion of print or other analog versions of works into digital formats, except that such conversion is permitted hereunder, only with respect to the amount of such works authorized to be performed or displayed under section 110(2), if—

(A) no digital version of the work is available to the institution; or

(B) the digital version of the work that is available to the institution is subject to technological protection measures that prevent its use for section 110(2).

(g) The transmission program embodied in a copy or phonorecord made under this section is not subject to protection as a derivative work under this title except with the express consent of the owners of copyright in the preexisting works employed in the program.

§ 113. Scope of exclusive rights in pictorial, graphic, and sculptural works

(a) Subject to the provisions of subsections (b) and (c) of this section, the exclusive right to reproduce a copyrighted pictorial, graphic, or sculptural work in copies under section 106, includes the right to reproduce the work in or on any kind of article, whether useful or otherwise.

(b) This title does not afford, to the owner of copyright in a work that portrays a useful article as such, any greater or lesser rights with respect to the making, distribution, or display of the useful article so portrayed than those afforded to such works under the law, whether title 17 or the common law or statutes of a State, in effect on December 31, 1977, as held applicable and construed by a court in an action brought under this title.

(c) In the case of a work lawfully reproduced in useful articles that have been offered for sale or other distribution to the public, copyright does not include any right to prevent the making, distribution, or display of pictures or photographs of such articles in connection with advertisements or commentaries related to the distribution or display of such articles, or in connection with news reports.

(d)(1) In a case in which—

> (A) a work of visual art has been incorporated in or made part of a building in such a way that removing the work from the building will cause the destruction, distortion, mutilation, or other modification of the work as described in section 106A(a)(3), and

> (B) the author consented to the installation of the work in the building either before the effective date set forth in section 610(a) of the Visual Artists Rights Act of 1990, or in a written instrument executed on or after such effective date that is signed by the owner of the building and the author and that specifies that installation of the work may subject the work to destruction, distortion, mutilation, or other modification, by reason of its removal, then the rights conferred by paragraphs (2) and (3) of section 106A(a) shall not apply.

(2) If the owner of a building wishes to remove a work of visual art which is a part of such building and which can be removed from the building without the destruction, distortion, mutilation, or other modification of the work as described in section 106A(a)(3), the author's rights under paragraphs (2) and (3) of section 106A(a) shall apply unless—

> (A) the owner has made a diligent, good faith attempt without success to notify the author of the owner's intended action affecting the work of visual art, or

> (B) the owner did provide such notice in writing and the person so notified failed, within 90 days after receiving such notice, either to remove the work or to pay for its removal.

For purposes of subparagraph (A), an owner shall be presumed to have made a diligent, good faith attempt to send notice if the owner sent such notice by registered mail to the author at the most recent address of the author that was recorded with the Register of Copyrights pursuant to paragraph (3). If the work is removed at the expense of the author, title to that copy of the work shall be deemed to be in the author.

(3) The Register of Copyrights shall establish a system of records whereby any author of a work of visual art that has been incorporated in or made part of a building, may record his or her identity and address with the Copyright Office. The Register shall also establish procedures under which any such author may update the information

so recorded, and procedures under which owners of buildings may record with the Copyright Office evidence of their efforts to comply with this subsection.

§ 114. Scope of exclusive rights in sound recordings

(a) The exclusive rights of the owner of copyright in a sound recording are limited to the rights specified by clauses (1), (2), (3) and (6) of section 106, and do not include any right of performance under section 106(4).

(b) The exclusive right of the owner of copyright in a sound recording under clause (1) of section 106 is limited to the right to duplicate the sound recording in the form of phonorecords or copies that directly or indirectly recapture the actual sounds fixed in the recording. The exclusive right of the owner of copyright in a sound recording under clause (2) of section 106 is limited to the right to prepare a derivative work in which the actual sounds fixed in the sound recording are rearranged, remixed, or otherwise altered in sequence or quality. The exclusive rights of the owner of copyright in a sound recording under clauses (1) and (2) of section 106 do not extend to the making or duplication of another sound recording that consists entirely of an independent fixation of other sounds, even though such sounds imitate or simulate those in the copyrighted sound recording. The exclusive rights of the owner of copyright in a sound recording under clauses (1), (2), and (3) of section 106 do not apply to sound recordings included in educational television and radio programs (as defined in section 397 of title 47) distributed or transmitted by or through public broadcasting entities (as defined by section 118(g)): *Provided,* That copies or phonorecords of said programs are not commercially distributed by or through public broadcasting entities to the general public.

(c) This section does not limit or impair the exclusive right to perform publicly, by means of a phonorecord, any of the works specified by section 106(4).

(d) **Limitations on Exclusive Right.** Notwithstanding the provisions of section 106(6)—

(1) **Exempt transmissions and retransmissions.** The performance of a sound recording publicly by means of a digital audio transmission, other than as a part of an interactive service, is not an infringement of section 106(6) if the performance is part of—

(A) a nonsubscription broadcast transmission;

(B) a retransmission of a nonsubscription broadcast transmission: *Provided,* That, in the case of a retransmission of a radio station's broadcast transmission—

(i) the radio station's broadcast transmission is not willfully or repeatedly retransmitted more than a radius of 150 miles from the site of the radio broadcast transmitter, however—

269

(I) the 150 mile limitation under this clause shall not apply when a nonsubscription broadcast transmission by a radio station licensed by the Federal Communications Commission is retransmitted on a non-subscription basis by a terrestrial broadcast station, terrestrial translator, or terrestrial repeater licensed by the Federal Communications Commission; and

(II) in the case of a subscription retransmission of a non-subscription broadcast retransmission covered by subclause (I), the 150 mile radius shall be measured from the transmitter site of such broadcast retransmitter;

(ii) the retransmission is of radio station broadcast transmissions that are—

(I) obtained by the retransmitter over the air;

(II) not electronically processed by the retransmitter to deliver separate and discrete signals; and

(III) retransmitted only within the local communities served by the retransmitter;

(iii) the radio station's broadcast transmission was being retransmitted to cable systems (as defined in section 111(f)) by a satellite carrier on January 1, 1995, and that retransmission was being retransmitted by cable systems as a separate and discrete signal, and the satellite carrier obtains the radio station's broadcast transmission in an analog format: *Provided,* That the broadcast transmission being retransmitted may embody the programming of no more than one radio station; or

(iv) the radio station's broadcast transmission is made by a noncommercial educational broadcast station funded on or after January 1, 1995, under section 396(k) of the Communications Act of 1934 (47 U.S.C. 396(k)), consists solely of noncommercial educational and cultural radio programs, and the retransmission, whether or not simultaneous, is a nonsubscription terrestrial broadcast retransmission; or

(C) a transmission that comes within any of the following categories—

(i) a prior or simultaneous transmission incidental to an exempt transmission, such as a feed received by and then retransmitted by an exempt transmitter: *Provided,* That such incidental transmissions do not include any subscription transmission directly for reception by members of the public;

(ii) a transmission within a business establishment, confined to its premises or the immediately surrounding vicinity;

(iii) a retransmission by any retransmitter, including a multichannel video programming distributor as defined in section 602(12) of the Communications Act of 1934 (47 U.S.C. 522 (12)), of a transmission by a transmitter licensed to publicly perform the sound recording as a part of that transmission, if the retransmission is simultaneous with the licensed transmission and authorized by the transmitter; or

(iv) a transmission to a business establishment for use in the ordinary course of its business: *Provided,* That the business recipient does not retransmit the transmission outside of its premises or the immediately surrounding vicinity, and that the transmission does not exceed the sound recording performance complement. Nothing in this clause shall limit the scope of the exemption in clause (ii).

(2) Statutory licensing of certain transmissions. The performance of a sound recording publicly by means of a subscription digital audio transmission not exempt under paragraph (1), an eligible nonsubscription transmission, or a transmission not exempt under paragraph (1) that is made by a preexisting satellite digital audio radio service shall be subject to statutory licensing, in accordance with subsection (f) if—

(A)(i) the transmission is not part of an interactive service;

(ii) except in the case of a transmission to a business establishment, the transmitting entity does not automatically and intentionally cause any device receiving the transmission to switch from one program channel to another; and

(iii) except as provided in section 1002(e), the transmission of the sound recording is accompanied, if technically feasible, by the information encoded in that sound recording, if any, by or under the authority of the copyright owner of that sound recording, that identifies the title of the sound recording, the featured recording artist who performs on the sound recording, and related information, including information concerning the underlying musical work and its writer;

(B) in the case of a subscription transmission not exempt under paragraph (1) that is made by a preexisting subscription service in the same transmission medium used by such service on July 31, 1998, or in the case of a transmission not exempt under paragraph (1) that is made by a preexisting satellite digital audio radio service—

(i) the transmission does not exceed the sound recording performance complement; and

(ii) the transmitting entity does not cause to be published by means of an advance program schedule or prior announcement the titles of the specific sound recordings or phonorecords embodying such sound recordings to be transmitted; and

(C) in the case of an eligible nonsubscription transmission or a subscription transmission not exempt under paragraph (1) that is made by a new subscription service or by a preexisting subscription service other than in the same transmission medium used by such service on July 31, 1998—

(i) the transmission does not exceed the sound recording performance complement, except that this requirement shall not apply in the case of a retransmission of a broadcast transmission if the retransmission is made by a transmitting entity that does not have the right or ability to control the programming of the broadcast station making the broadcast transmission, unless—

(I) the broadcast station makes broadcast transmissions—

(aa) in digital format that regularly exceed the sound recording performance complement; or

(bb) in analog format, a substantial portion of which, on a weekly basis, exceed the sound recording performance complement; and

(II) the sound recording copyright owner or its representative has notified the transmitting entity in writing that broadcast transmissions of the copyright owner's sound recordings exceed the sound recording performance complement as provided in this clause;

(ii) the transmitting entity does not cause to be published, or induce or facilitate the publication, by means of an advance program schedule or prior announcement, the titles of the specific sound recordings to be transmitted, the phonorecords embodying such sound recordings, or, other than for illustrative purposes, the names of the featured recording artists, except that this clause does not disqualify a transmitting entity that makes a prior announcement that a particular artist will be featured within an unspecified future time period, and in the case of a retransmission of a broadcast transmission by a transmitting entity that does not have the right or ability to control the programming of the broadcast transmission, the requirement of this clause shall not apply to a prior oral announcement by the broadcast station, or to an advance program schedule published, induced, or facilitated by the broadcast station, if the transmitting entity does not have actual knowledge and has not received written notice from the copyright owner or its representative that the broadcast station publishes or induces or facilitates the publication of such advance program schedule, or if such advance program schedule is a schedule of classical music programming published by the broadcast station in the same manner as published by that broadcast station on or before September 30, 1998;

(iii) the transmission—

(I) is not part of an archived program of less than 5 hours duration;

(II) is not part of an archived program of 5 hours or greater in duration that is made available for a period exceeding 2 weeks;

(III) is not part of a continuous program which is of less than 3 hours duration; or

(IV) is not part of an identifiable program in which performances of sound recordings are rendered in a predetermined order, other than an archived or continuous program, that is transmitted at—

(aa) more than 3 times in any 2–week period that have been publicly announced in advance, in the case of a program of less than 1 hour in duration, or

(bb) more than 4 times in any 2–week period that have been publicly announced in advance, in the case of a program of 1 hour or more in duration, except that the requirement of this subclause shall not apply in the case of a retransmission of a broadcast transmission by a transmitting entity that does not have the right or ability to control the programming of the broadcast transmission, unless the transmitting entity is given notice in writing by the copyright owner of the sound recording that the broadcast station makes broadcast transmissions that regularly violate such requirement;

(iv) the transmitting entity does not knowingly perform the sound recording, as part of a service that offers transmissions of visual images contemporaneously with transmissions of sound recordings, in a manner that is likely to cause confusion, to cause mistake, or to deceive, as to the affiliation, connection, or association of the copyright owner or featured recording artist with the transmitting entity or a particular product or service advertised by the transmitting entity, or as to the origin, sponsorship, or approval by the copyright owner or featured recording artist of the activities of the transmitting entity other than the performance of the sound recording itself;

(v) the transmitting entity cooperates to prevent, to the extent feasible without imposing substantial costs or burdens, a transmission recipient or any other person or entity from automatically scanning the transmitting entity's transmissions alone or together with transmissions by other transmitting entities in order to select a particular sound recording to be transmitted to the transmission recipient, except that the requirement of this clause shall not apply to a satellite digital audio service that is in operation, or that is licensed by the Federal Communications Commission, on or before July 31, 1998;

(vi) the transmitting entity takes no affirmative steps to cause or induce the making of a phonorecord by the transmission recipient, and if the technology used by the transmitting entity enables the transmitting entity to limit the making by the transmission recipient of phonorecords of the transmission directly in a digital format, the transmitting entity sets such technology to limit such making of phonorecords to the extent permitted by such technology;

(vii) phonorecords of the sound recording have been distributed to the public under the authority of the copyright owner or the copyright owner authorizes the transmitting entity to transmit the sound recording, and the transmitting entity makes the transmission from a phonorecord lawfully made under the authority of the copyright owner, except that the requirement of this clause shall not apply to a retransmission of a broadcast transmission by a transmitting entity that does not have the right or ability to control the programming of the broadcast transmission, unless the transmitting entity is given notice in writing by the copyright owner of the sound recording that the broadcast station makes broadcast transmissions that regularly violate such requirement;

(viii) the transmitting entity accommodates and does not interfere with the transmission of technical measures that are widely used by sound recording copyright owners to identify or protect copyrighted works, and that are technically feasible of being transmitted by the transmitting entity without imposing substantial costs on the transmitting entity or resulting in perceptible aural or visual degradation of the digital signal, except that the requirement of this clause shall not apply to a satellite digital audio service that is in operation, or that is licensed under the authority of the Federal Communications Commission, on or before July 31, 1998, to the extent that such service has designed, developed, or made commitments to procure equipment or technology that is not compatible with such technical measures before such technical measures are widely adopted by sound recording copyright owners; and

(ix) the transmitting entity identifies in textual data the sound recording during, but not before, the time it is performed, including the title of the sound recording, the title of the phonorecord embodying such sound recording, if any, and the featured recording artist, in a manner to permit it to be displayed to the transmission recipient by the device or technology intended for receiving the service provided by the transmitting entity, except that the obligation in this clause shall not take effect until 1 year after the date of the enactment of the Digital Millennium Copyright Act and shall not apply in the case of a retransmission of a broadcast transmission by a transmitting entity that does not have the right or ability to control the programming of the broadcast transmission, or in the case in which devices or technology intended for receiving the service provided by the transmitting entity that have the capability to display such textual data are not common in the marketplace.

(3) Licenses for transmissions by interactive services.

(A) No interactive service shall be granted an exclusive license under section 106(6) for the performance of a sound recording publicly by means of digital audio transmission for a period in excess of 12 months, except that with respect to an exclusive license granted to an interactive service by a licensor that holds the copyright to 1,000 or fewer sound recordings, the period of such license shall not exceed 24 months: *Provided, however,* That the grantee of such exclusive license shall be ineligible to receive another exclusive license for the performance of that sound recording for a period of 13 months from the expiration of the prior exclusive license.

(B) The limitation set forth in subparagraph (A) of this paragraph shall not apply if—

(i) the licensor has granted and there remain in effect licenses under section 106(6) for the public performance of sound recordings by means of digital audio transmission by at least 5 different interactive services; *Provided, however,* That each such license must be for a minimum of 10 percent of the copyrighted sound recordings owned by the licensor that have been licensed to interactive services, but in no event less than 50 sound recordings; or

(ii) the exclusive license is granted to perform publicly up to 45 seconds of a sound recording and the sole purpose of the performance is to promote the distribution or performance of that sound recording.

(C) Notwithstanding the grant of an exclusive or nonexclusive license of the right of public performance under section 106(6), an interactive service may not publicly perform a sound recording unless a license has been granted for the public performance of any copyrighted musical work contained in the sound recording: *Provided,* That such license to publicly perform the copyrighted musical work may be granted either by a performing rights society representing the copyright owner or by the copyright owner.

(D) The performance of a sound recording by means of a retransmission of a digital audio transmission is not an infringement of section 106(6) if—

(i) the retransmission is of a transmission by an interactive service licensed to publicly perform the sound recording to a particular member of the public as part of that transmission; and

(ii) the retransmission is simultaneous with the licensed transmission, authorized by the transmitter, and limited to that particular member of the public intended by the interactive service to be the recipient of the transmission.

(E) For the purposes of this paragraph—

(i) a "licensor" shall include the licensing entity and any other entity under any material degree of common ownership, management, or control that owns copyrights in sound recordings; and

(ii) a "performing rights society" is an association or corporation that licenses the public performance of nondramatic musical works on behalf of the copyright owner, such as the American Society of Composers, Authors and Publishers, Broadcast Music, Inc., and SESAC, Inc.

(4) Rights not otherwise limited.

(A) Except as expressly provided in this section, this section does not limit or impair the exclusive right to perform a sound recording publicly by means of a digital audio transmission under section 106(6).

(B) Nothing in this section annuls or limits in any way—

(i) the exclusive right to publicly perform a musical work, including by means of a digital audio transmission, under section 106(4);

(ii) the exclusive rights in a sound recording or the musical work embodied therein under sections 106(1), 106(2) and 106(3); or

(iii) any other rights under any other clause of section 106, or remedies available under this title as such rights or remedies exist either before or after the date of enactment of the Digital Performance Right in Sound Recordings Act of 1995.

(C) Any limitations in this section on the exclusive right under section 106(6) apply only to the exclusive right under section 106(6) and not to any other exclusive rights under section 106. Nothing in this section shall be construed to annul, limit, impair or otherwise affect in any way the ability of the owner of a copyright in a sound recording to exercise the rights under sections 106(1), 106(2) and 106(3), or to obtain the remedies available under this title pursuant to such rights, as such rights and remedies exist either before or after the date of enactment of the Digital Performance Right in Sound Recordings Act of 1995.

(e) Authority for Negotiations.

(1) Notwithstanding any provision of the antitrust laws, in negotiating statutory licenses in accordance with subsection (f), any copyright owners of sound recordings and any entities performing sound recordings affected by this section may negotiate and agree upon the royalty rates and license terms and conditions for the performance of such sound recordings and the proportionate division of fees paid among copyright owners, and may designate common agents on a nonexclusive basis to negotiate, agree to, pay, or receive payments.

(2) For licenses granted under section 106(6), other than statutory licenses, such as for performances by interactive services or performances that exceed the sound recording performance complement—

(A) copyright owners of sound recordings affected by this section may designate common agents to act on their behalf to grant licenses and receive and remit royalty payments: *Provided,* That each copyright owner shall establish the royalty rates and material license terms and conditions unilaterally, that is, not in agreement, combination, or concert with other copyright owners of sound recordings; and

(B) entities performing sound recordings affected by this section may designate common agents to act on their behalf to obtain licenses and collect and pay royalty fees: *Provided,* That each entity performing sound recordings shall determine the royalty rates and material license terms and conditions unilaterally, that is, not in agreement, combination, or concert with other entities performing sound recordings.

(f) Licenses for Certain Nonexempt Transmissions.

(1)(A) No later than 30 days after the enactment of the Digital Performance Right in Sound Recordings Act of 1995, the Librarian of Congress shall cause notice to be published in the Federal Register of the initiation of voluntary negotiation proceedings for the purpose of determining reasonable terms and rates of royalty payments for subscription transmissions by preexisting subscription services and transmissions by preexisting satellite digital audio radio services specified by subsection (d)(2) of this section during the period beginning on the effective date of such Act and ending on December 31, 2001, or, if a copyright arbitration royalty panel is convened, ending 30 days after the Librarian issues and publishes in the Federal Register an order adopting the determination of the copyright arbitration royalty panel or an order setting the terms and rates (if the Librarian rejects the panel's determination). Such terms and rates shall distinguish among the different types of digital audio transmission services then in operation. Any copyright owners of sound recordings, preexisting subscription services, or preexisting satellite digital audio radio services may submit to the Librarian of Congress licenses covering such subscription transmissions with respect to such sound recordings. The parties to each negotiation proceeding shall bear their own costs.

(B) In the absence of license agreements negotiated under subparagraph (A), during the 60–day period commencing 6 months after publication of the notice specified in subparagraph (A), and upon the filing of a petition in accordance with section 803(a)(1), the Librarian of Congress shall, pursuant to chapter 8, convene a copyright arbitration royalty panel to determine and publish in the Federal Register a schedule of rates and terms which, subject to paragraph (3), shall be binding on all copyright owners of sound recordings and entities performing sound recordings affected by this paragraph. In establishing rates and terms for preexisting subscription services and preexisting satellite digital audio radio services, in addition to the objectives set forth in section 801(b)(1), the copyright arbitration royalty panel may consider the rates and terms for comparable types of subscription digital audio transmission services and comparable circumstances under voluntary license agreements negotiated as provided in subparagraph (A).

(C)(i) Publication of a notice of the initiation of voluntary negotiation proceedings as specified in subparagraph (A) shall be repeated, in accordance with regulations that the Librarian of Congress shall prescribe—

(I) no later than 30 days after a petition is filed by any copyright owners of sound recordings, any preexisting subscription services, or any preexisting satellite digital audio radio services indicating that a new type of subscription digital audio transmission service on which sound recordings are performed is or is about to become operational; and

(II) in the first week of January 2001, and at 5–year intervals thereafter.

(ii) The procedures specified in subparagraph (B) shall be repeated, in accordance with regulations that the Librarian of Congress shall prescribe, upon filing of a petition in accordance with section 803(a)(1) during a 60–day period commencing—

(I) 6 months after publication of a notice of the initiation of voluntary negotiation proceedings under subparagraph (A) pursuant to a petition under clause (i)(I) of this subparagraph; or

(II) on July 1, 2001, and at 5–year intervals thereafter.

(iii) The procedures specified in subparagraph (B) shall be concluded in accordance with section 802.

(2)(A) No later than 30 days after the date of the enactment of the Digital Millennium Copyright Act, the Librarian of Congress shall cause notice to be published in the Federal Register of the initiation of voluntary negotiation proceedings for the purpose of determining reasonable terms and rates of royalty payments for public performances of sound recordings by means of eligible nonsubscription transmissions and transmissions by new subscription services specified by subsection (d)(2) during the period beginning on the date of the enactment of such Act and ending on December 31, 2000, or such other date as the parties may agree. Such rates and terms shall distinguish among the different types of eligible nonsubscription transmission services and new subscription services then in operation and shall include a minimum fee for each such type of service. Any copyright owners of sound recordings or any entities performing sound recordings affected by this paragraph may submit to the Librarian of Congress licenses covering such eligible nonsubscription transmissions and new subscription services with respect to such sound recordings. The parties to each negotiation proceeding shall bear their own costs.

(B) In the absence of license agreements negotiated under subparagraph (A), during the 60–day period commencing 6 months after publication of the notice specified in subparagraph (A), and upon the filing of a petition in accordance with section 803(a)(1), the Librarian of Congress shall, pursuant to chapter 8, convene a copyright arbitration royalty panel to determine and publish in the Federal Register a schedule of rates and terms which, subject to paragraph (3), shall be binding on all copyright owners of sound recordings and entities performing sound recordings affected by this paragraph during the period beginning on the date of the enactment of the Digital Millennium Copyright Act and ending on December 31, 2000, or such other date as the parties may agree. Such rates and terms shall distinguish among the different types of eligible nonsubscription transmission services then in operation and shall include a minimum fee for each such type of service, such differences to be based on criteria including, but not limited to, the quantity and nature of the use of sound recordings and the degree to which use of the service may substitute for or may promote the purchase of phonorecords by consumers. In establishing rates and terms for transmissions by eligible nonsubscription services and new subscription services, the copyright arbitration royalty panel shall establish rates and terms that most clearly represent the rates and terms that would have been negotiated in the marketplace between a willing buyer and a willing seller. In determining such rates and terms, the copyright arbitration royalty panel shall base its decision on economic, competitive and programming information presented by the parties, including—

(i) whether use of the service may substitute for or may promote the sales of phonorecords or otherwise may interfere with or may enhance the sound recording copyright owner's other streams of revenue from its sound recordings; and

(ii) the relative roles of the copyright owner and the transmitting entity in the copyrighted work and the service made available to the public with respect to relative creative contribution, technological contribution, capital investment, cost, and risk.

In establishing such rates and terms, the copyright arbitration royalty panel may consider the rates and terms for comparable types of digital audio transmission services and comparable circumstances under voluntary license agreements negotiated under subparagraph (A).

(C)(i) Publication of a notice of the initiation of voluntary negotiation proceedings as specified in subparagraph (A) shall be repeated in accordance with regulations that the Librarian of Congress shall prescribe—

(I) no later than 30 days after a petition is filed by any copyright owners of sound recordings or any eligible nonsubscription service or new subscription service indicating that a new type of eligible nonsubscription service or new subscription service on which sound recordings are performed is or is about to become operational; and

(II) in the first week of January 2000, and at 2–year intervals thereafter, except to the extent that different years for the repeating of such proceedings may be determined in accordance with subparagraph (A).

(ii) The procedures specified in subparagraph (B) shall be repeated, in accordance with regulations that the Librarian of Congress shall prescribe, upon filing of a petition in accordance with section 803(a)(1) during a 60–day period commencing—

(I) 6 months after publication of a notice of the initiation of voluntary negotiation proceedings under subparagraph (A) pursuant to a petition under clause (i)(I); or

(II) on July 1, 2000, and at 2–year intervals thereafter, except to the extent that different years for the repeating of such proceedings may be determined in accordance with subparagraph (A).

(iii) The procedures specified in subparagraph (B) shall be concluded in accordance with section 802.

(3) License agreements voluntarily negotiated at any time between 1 or more copyright owners of sound recordings and 1 or more entities performing sound recordings shall be given effect in lieu of any determination by a copyright arbitration royalty panel or decision by the Librarian of Congress.

(4)(A) The Librarian of Congress shall also establish requirements by which copyright owners may receive reasonable notice of the use of their sound recordings under this section, and under which records of such use shall be kept and made available by entities performing sound recordings.

(B) Any person who wishes to perform a sound recording publicly by means of a transmission eligible for statutory licensing under this subsection may do so without infringing the exclusive right of the copyright owner of the sound recording—

(i) by complying with such notice requirements as the Librarian of Congress shall prescribe by regulation and by paying royalty fees in accordance with this subsection; or

(ii) if such royalty fees have not been set, by agreeing to pay such royalty fees as shall be determined in accordance with this subsection.

(C) Any royalty payments in arrears shall be made on or before the twentieth day of the month next succeeding the month in which the royalty fees are set.

(5)(A) Notwithstanding section 112(e) and the other provisions of this subsection, the receiving agent may enter into agreements for the reproduction and performance of sound recordings under section 112(e) and this section by any 1 or more small commercial webcasters or noncommercial webcasters during the period beginning on October 28, 1998, and ending on December 31, 2004, that, once published in the Federal Register pursuant to subparagraph (B), shall be binding on all copyright owners of sound recordings and other persons entitled to payment under this section, in lieu of any determination by a copyright arbitration royalty panel or decision by the Librarian of Congress. Any such agreement for small commercial webcasters shall include provisions for payment of royalties on the basis of a percentage of revenue or expenses, or both, and include a minimum fee. Any such agreement may include other terms and conditions, including requirements by which copyright owners may receive notice of the use of their sound recordings and under which records of such use shall be kept and made available by small commercial webcasters or noncommercial webcasters. The receiving agent shall be under no obligation to negotiate any such agreement. The receiving agent shall have no obligation to any copyright owner of sound recordings or any other person entitled to payment under this section in negotiating any such agreement, and no liability to any copyright owner of sound recordings or any other person entitled to payment under this section for having entered into such agreement.

(B) The Copyright Office shall cause to be published in the Federal Register any agreement entered into pursuant to subparagraph (A). Such publication shall include a statement containing the substance of subparagraph (C). Such agreements shall not be included in the Code of Federal Regulations. Thereafter, the terms of such agreement shall be available, as an option, to any small commercial webcaster or noncommercial webcaster meeting the eligibility conditions of such agreement.

(C) Neither subparagraph (A) nor any provisions of any agreement entered into pursuant to subparagraph (A), including any rate structure, fees, terms, conditions, or notice and recordkeeping requirements set forth therein, shall be admissible as evidence or otherwise taken into account in any administrative, judicial, or other government proceeding involving the setting or adjustment of the royalties payable for the public performance or reproduction in ephemeral phonorecords or copies of sound recordings, the determination of terms or conditions related thereto, or the establishment of notice or recordkeeping requirements by the Librarian of Congress under paragraph (4) or section 112(e)(4). It is the intent of Congress that any royalty rates, rate structure, definitions, terms, conditions, or notice and recordkeeping requirements, included in such agreements shall be considered as a compromise motivated by the unique business, economic and political circumstances of small webcasters, copyright owners, and performers rather than as matters that would have been negotiated in the marketplace between a willing buyer and a willing seller, or otherwise meet the objectives set forth in section 801(b).

(D) Nothing in the Small Webcaster Settlement Act of 2002 or any agreement entered into pursuant to subparagraph (A) shall be taken into account by the United States Court of Appeals for the District of Columbia Circuit in its review of the determination by the Librarian of Congress of July 8, 2002, of rates and terms for the digital performance of sound recordings and ephemeral recordings, pursuant to sections 112 and 114.

(E) As used in this paragraph—

(i) the term "noncommercial webcaster" means a webcaster that—

(I) is exempt from taxation under section 501 of the Internal Revenue Code of 1986 (26 U.S.C. 501);

(II) has applied in good faith to the Internal Revenue Service for exemption from taxation under section 501 of the Internal Revenue Code and has a commercially reasonable expectation that such exemption shall be granted; or

(III) is operated by a State or possession or any governmental entity or subordinate thereof, or by the United States or District of Columbia, for exclusively public purposes;

(ii) the term "receiving agent" shall have the meaning given that term in section 261.2 of title 37, Code of Federal Regulations, as published in the Federal Register on July 8, 2002; and

(iii) the term "webcaster" means a person or entity that has obtained a compulsory license under section 112 or 114 and the implementing regulations therefor to make eligible nonsubscription transmissions and ephemeral recordings.

(F) The authority to make settlements pursuant to subparagraph (A) shall expire December 15, 2002, except with respect to noncommercial webcasters for whom the authority shall expire May 31, 2003.

(g) Proceeds from Licensing of Transmissions.

(1) Except in the case of a transmission licensed under a statutory license in accordance with subsection (f) of this section—

(A) a featured recording artist who performs on a sound recording that has been licensed for a transmission shall be entitled to receive payments from the copyright owner of the sound recording in accordance with the terms of the artist's contract; and

(B) a nonfeatured recording artist who performs on a sound recording that has been licensed for a transmission shall be entitled to receive payments from the copyright owner of the sound recording in accordance with the terms of the nonfeatured recording artist's applicable contract or other applicable agreement.

(2) An agent designated to distribute receipts from the licensing of transmissions in accordance with subsection (f) shall distribute such receipts as follows:

(A) 50 percent of the receipts shall be paid to the copyright owner of the exclusive right under section 106(6) of this title to publicly perform a sound recording by means of a digital audio transmission.

(B) 2 ½ percent of the receipts shall be deposited in an escrow account managed by an independent administrator jointly appointed by copyright owners of sound recordings and the American Federation of Musicians (or any successor entity) to be distributed to nonfeatured musicians (whether or not members of the American Federation of Musicians) who have performed on sound recordings.

(C) 2 ½ percent of the receipts shall be deposited in an escrow account managed by an independent administrator jointly appointed by copyright owners of sound recordings and the American Federation of Television and Radio Artists (or any successor entity) to be distributed to nonfeatured vocalists (whether or not members of the American Federation of Television and Radio Artists) who have performed on sound recordings.

(D) 45 percent of the receipts shall be paid, on a per sound recording basis, to the recording artist or artists featured on such sound recording (or the persons conveying rights in the artists' performance in the sound recordings).

(3) A nonprofit agent designated to distribute receipts from the licensing of transmissions in accordance with subsection (f) may deduct from any of its receipts, prior to the distribution of such receipts to any person or entity entitled thereto other than copyright owners and performers who have elected to receive royalties from another designated agent and have notified such nonprofit agent in writing of such election, the reasonable costs of such agent incurred after November 1, 1995, in—

(A) the administration of the collection, distribution, and calculation of the royalties;

(B) the settlement of disputes relating to the collection and calculation of the royalties; and

(C) the licensing and enforcement of rights with respect to the making of ephemeral recordings and performances subject to licensing under section 112 and this section, including those incurred in participating in negotiations or arbitration proceedings under section 112 and this section, except that all costs incurred relating to the section 112 ephemeral recordings right may only be deducted from the royalties received pursuant to section 112.

(4) Notwithstanding paragraph (3), any designated agent designated to distribute receipts from the licensing of transmissions in accordance with subsection (f) may deduct from any of its receipts, prior to the distribution of such receipts, the reasonable costs identified in paragraph (3) of such agent incurred after November 1, 1995, with respect to such copyright owners and performers who have entered with such agent a contractual relationship that specifies that such costs may be deducted from such royalty receipts.

(h) Licensing to Affiliates.

(1) If the copyright owner of a sound recording licenses an affiliated entity the right to publicly perform a sound recording by means of a digital audio transmission under section 106(6), the copyright owner shall make the licensed sound recording available under section 106(6) on no less favorable terms and conditions to all bona fide entities that offer similar services, except that, if there are material differences in the scope of the requested license with respect to the type of service,

the particular sound recordings licensed, the frequency of use, the number of subscribers served, or the duration, then the copyright owner may establish different terms and conditions for such other services.

(2) The limitation set forth in paragraph (1) of this subsection shall not apply in the case where the copyright owner of a sound recording licenses—

(A) an interactive service; or

(B) an entity to perform publicly up to 45 seconds of the sound recording and the sole purpose of the performance is to promote the distribution or performance of that sound recording.

(i) No Effect on Royalties for Underlying Works. License fees payable for the public performance of sound recordings under section 106(6) shall not be taken into account in any administrative, judicial, or other governmental proceeding to set or adjust the royalties payable to copyright owners of musical works for the public performance of their works. It is the intent of Congress that royalties payable to copyright owners of musical works for the public performance of their works shall not be diminished in any respect as a result of the rights granted by section 106(6).

(j) Definitions. As used in this section, the following terms have the following meanings:

(1) An "affiliated entity" is an entity engaging in digital audio transmissions covered by section 106(6), other than an interactive service, in which the licensor has any direct or indirect partnership or any ownership interest amounting to 5 percent or more of the outstanding voting or non-voting stock.

(2) An "archived program" is a predetermined program that is available repeatedly on the demand of the transmission recipient and that is performed in the same order from the beginning, except that an archived program shall not include a recorded event or broadcast transmission that makes no more than an incidental use of sound recordings, as long as such recorded event or broadcast transmission does not contain an entire sound recording or feature a particular sound recording.

(3) A "broadcast" transmission is a transmission made by a terrestrial broadcast station licensed as such by the Federal Communications Commission.

(4) A "continuous program" is a predetermined program that is continuously performed in the same order and that is accessed at a point in the program that is beyond the control of the transmission recipient.

(5) A "digital audio transmission" is a digital transmission as defined in section 101, that embodies the transmission of a sound

recording. This term does not include the transmission of any audiovisual work.

(6) An "eligible nonsubscription transmission" is a noninteractive nonsubscription digital audio transmission not exempt under subsection (d)(1) that is made as part of a service that provides audio programming consisting, in whole or in part, of performances of sound recordings, including retransmissions of broadcast transmissions, if the primary purpose of the service is to provide to the public such audio or other entertainment programming, and the primary purpose of the service is not to sell, advertise, or promote particular products or services other than sound recordings, live concerts, or other music-related events.

(7) An "interactive service" is one that enables a member of the public to receive a transmission of a program specially created for the recipient, or on request, a transmission of a particular sound recording, whether or not as part of a program, which is selected by or on behalf of the recipient. The ability of individuals to request that particular sound recordings be performed for reception by the public at large, or in the case of a subscription service, by all subscribers of the service, does not make a service interactive, if the programming on each channel of the service does not substantially consist of sound recordings that are performed within 1 hour of the request or at a time designated by either the transmitting entity or the individual making such request. If an entity offers both interactive and noninteractive services (either concurrently or at different times), the noninteractive component shall not be treated as part of an interactive service.

(8) A "new subscription service" is a service that performs sound recordings by means of noninteractive subscription digital audio transmissions and that is not a preexisting subscription service or a preexisting satellite digital audio radio service.

(9) A "nonsubscription" transmission is any transmission that is not a subscription transmission.

(10) A "preexisting satellite digital audio radio service" is a subscription satellite digital audio radio service provided pursuant to a satellite digital audio radio service license issued by the Federal Communications Commission on or before July 31, 1998, and any renewal of such license to the extent of the scope of the original license, and may include a limited number of sample channels representative of the subscription service that are made available on a nonsubscription basis in order to promote the subscription service.

(11) A "preexisting subscription service" is a service that performs sound recordings by means of noninteractive audio-only subscription digital audio transmissions, which was in existence and was making such transmissions to the public for a fee on or before July 31, 1998, and may include a limited number of sample channels represen-

tative of the subscription service that are made available on a nonsubscription basis in order to promote the subscription service.

(12) A "retransmission" is a further transmission of an initial transmission, and includes any further retransmission of the same transmission. Except as provided in this section, a transmission qualifies as a "retransmission" only if it is simultaneous with the initial transmission. Nothing in this definition shall be construed to exempt a transmission that fails to satisfy a separate element required to qualify for an exemption under section 114(d)(1).

(13) The "sound recording performance complement" is the transmission during any 3–hour period, on a particular channel used by a transmitting entity, of no more than—

(A) 3 different selections of sound recordings from any one phonorecord lawfully distributed for public performance or sale in the United States, if no more than 2 such selections are transmitted consecutively; or

(B) 4 different selections of sound recordings—

(i) by the same featured recording artist; or

(ii) from any set or compilation of phonorecords lawfully distributed together as a unit for public performance or sale in the United States,

if no more than three such selections are transmitted consecutively:

Provided, That the transmission of selections in excess of the numerical limits provided for in clauses (A) and (B) from multiple phonorecords shall nonetheless qualify as a sound recording performance complement if the programming of the multiple phonorecords was not willfully intended to avoid the numerical limitations prescribed in such clauses.

(14) A "subscription" transmission is a transmission that is controlled and limited to particular recipients, and for which consideration is required to be paid or otherwise given by or on behalf of the recipient to receive the transmission or a package of transmissions including the transmission.

(15) A "transmission" is either an initial transmission or a retransmission.

§ 115. Scope of exclusive rights in nondramatic musical works: Compulsory license for making and distributing phonorecords

In the case of nondramatic musical works, the exclusive rights provided by clauses (1) and (3) of section 106, to make and to distribute phonorecords of such works, are subject to compulsory licensing under the conditions specified by this section.

(a) Availability and Scope of Compulsory License.

(1) When phonorecords of a nondramatic musical work have been distributed to the public in the United States under the authority of the copyright owner, any other person, including those who make phonorecords or digital phonorecord deliveries, may, by complying with the provisions of this section, obtain a compulsory license to make and distribute phonorecords of the work. A person may obtain a compulsory license only if his or her primary purpose in making phonorecords is to distribute them to the public for private use, including by means of a digital phonorecord delivery. A person may not obtain a compulsory license for use of the work in the making of phonorecords duplicating a sound recording fixed by another, unless:

(i) such sound recording was fixed lawfully; and

(ii) the making of the phonorecords was authorized by the owner of copyright in the sound recording or, if the sound recording was fixed before February 15, 1972, by any person who fixed the sound recording pursuant to an express license from the owner of the copyright in the musical work or pursuant to a valid compulsory license for use of such work in a sound recording.

(2) A compulsory license includes the privilege of making a musical arrangement of the work to the extent necessary to conform it to the style or manner of interpretation of the performance involved, but the arrangement shall not change the basic melody or fundamental character of the work, and shall not be subject to protection as a derivative work under this title, except with the express consent of the copyright owner.

(b) Notice of Intention to Obtain Compulsory License.

(1) Any person who wishes to obtain a compulsory license under this section shall, before or within thirty days after making, and before distributing any phonorecords of the work, serve notice of intention to do so on the copyright owner. If the registration or other public records of the Copyright Office do not identify the copyright owner and include an address at which notice can be served, it shall be sufficient to file the notice of intention in the Copyright Office. The notice shall comply, in form, content, and manner of service, with requirements that the Register of Copyrights shall prescribe by regulation.

(2) Failure to serve or file the notice required by clause (1) forecloses the possibility of a compulsory license and, in the absence of a negotiated license, renders the making and distribution of phonorecords actionable as acts of infringement under section 501 and fully subject to the remedies provided by sections 502 through 506 and 509.

(c) Royalty Payable under Compulsory License.

(1) To be entitled to receive royalties under a compulsory license, the copyright owner must be identified in the registration or other

public records of the Copyright Office. The owner is entitled to royalties for phonorecords made and distributed after being so identified, but is not entitled to recover for any phonorecords previously made and distributed.

(2) Except as provided by clause (1), the royalty under a compulsory license shall be payable for every phonorecord made and distributed in accordance with the license. For this purpose, and other than as provided in paragraph (3), a phonorecord is considered "distributed" if the person exercising the compulsory license has voluntarily and permanently parted with its possession. With respect to each work embodied in the phonorecord, the royalty shall be either two and three-fourths cents, or one-half of one cent per minute of playing time or fraction thereof, whichever amount is larger.***

(3)(A) A compulsory license under this section includes the right of the compulsory licensee to distribute or authorize the distribution of a phonorecord of a nondramatic musical work by means of a digital transmission which constitutes a digital phonorecord delivery, regardless of whether the digital transmission is also a public performance of the sound recording under section 106(6) of this title or of any nondramatic musical work embodied therein under section 106(4) of this title. For every digital phonorecord delivery by or under the authority of the compulsory licensee—

    (i) on or before December 31, 1997, the royalty payable by the compulsory licensee shall be the royalty prescribed under paragraph (2) and chapter 8 of this title; and

    (ii) on or after January 1, 1998, the royalty payable by the compulsory licensee shall be the royalty prescribed under subparagraphs (B) through (F) and chapter 8 of this title.

(B) Notwithstanding any provision of the antitrust laws, any copyright owners of nondramatic musical works and any persons entitled to obtain a compulsory license under subsection (a)(1) may negotiate and agree upon the terms and rates of royalty payments under this paragraph and the proportionate division of fees paid among copyright owners, and may designate common agents to negotiate, agree to, pay or receive such royalty payments. Such authority to negotiate the terms and rates of royalty payments includes, but is not limited to, the authority to negotiate the year during which the royalty rates prescribed under subparagraphs (B) through (F) and chapter 8 of this title shall next be determined.

(C) During the period of June 30, 1996, through December 31, 1996, the Librarian of Congress shall cause notice to be published in the Federal Register of the initiation of voluntary negotiation proceedings for the purpose of determining reasonable terms and rates of royalty payments for the activities specified by subpara-

*** The current royalty rate is set as provided in 37 C.F.R. § 255.3.

graph (A) during the period beginning January 1, 1998, and ending on the effective date of any new terms and rates established pursuant to subparagraph (C), (D) or (F), or such other date (regarding digital phonorecord deliveries) as the parties may agree. Such terms and rates shall distinguish between (i) digital phonorecord deliveries where the reproduction or distribution of a phonorecord is incidental to the transmission which constitutes the digital phonorecord delivery, and (ii) digital phonorecord deliveries in general. Any copyright owners of nondramatic musical works and any persons entitled to obtain a compulsory license under subsection (a)(1) may submit to the Librarian of Congress licenses covering such activities. The parties to each negotiation proceeding shall bear their own costs.

(D) In the absence of license agreements negotiated under subparagraphs (B) and (C), upon the filing of a petition in accordance with section 803(a)(1), the Librarian of Congress shall, pursuant to chapter 8, convene a copyright arbitration royalty panel to determine a schedule of rates and terms which, subject to subparagraph (E), shall be binding on all copyright owners of nondramatic musical works and persons entitled to obtain a compulsory license under subsection (a)(1) during the period beginning January 1, 1998, and ending on the effective date of any new terms and rates established pursuant to subparagraph (C), (D) or (F), or such other date (regarding digital phonorecord deliveries) as may be determined pursuant to subparagraphs (B) and (C). Such terms and rates shall distinguish between (i) digital phonorecord deliveries where the reproduction or distribution of a phonorecord is incidental to the transmission which constitutes the digital phonorecord delivery, and (ii) digital phonorecord deliveries in general. In addition to the objectives set forth in section 801(b)(1), in establishing such rates and terms, the copyright arbitration royalty panel may consider rates and terms under voluntary license agreements negotiated as provided in subparagraphs (B) and (C). The royalty rates payable for a compulsory license for a digital phonorecord delivery under this section shall be established de novo and no precedential effect shall be given to the amount of the royalty payable by a compulsory licensee for digital phonorecord deliveries on or before December 31, 1997. The Librarian of Congress shall also establish requirements by which copyright owners may receive reasonable notice of the use of their works under this section, and under which records of such use shall be kept and made available by persons making digital phonorecord deliveries.

(E)(i) License agreements voluntarily negotiated at any time between one or more copyright owners of nondramatic musical works and one or more persons entitled to obtain a compulsory license under subsection (a)(1) shall be given effect in lieu of any determination by the Librarian of Congress. Subject to clause (ii), the royalty rates determined pursuant to subparagraph (C), (D) or (F) shall be given effect in lieu of any contrary royalty rates specified in a contract pursuant to which a recording artist who is the author of a nondramatic musical work grants a license under that person's exclusive rights in the musical work under paragraphs (1) and (3) of section 106 or commits another person to grant a license in that musical work under paragraphs (1) and (3) of section 106, to a person desiring to fix in a tangible medium of expression a sound recording embodying the musical work.

(ii) The second sentence of clause (i) shall not apply to—

(I) a contract entered into on or before June 22, 1995 and not modified thereafter for the purpose of reducing the royalty rates determined pursuant to subparagraph (C), (D) or (F) or of increasing the number of musical works within the scope of the contract covered by the reduced rates, except if a contract entered into on or before June 22, 1995, is modified thereafter for the purpose of increasing the number of musical works within the scope of the contract, any contrary royalty rates specified in the contract shall be given effect in lieu of royalty rates determined pursuant to subparagraph (C), (D) or (F) for the number of musical works within the scope of the contract as of June 22, 1995; and

(II) a contract entered into after the date that the sound recording is fixed in a tangible medium of expression substantially in a form intended for commercial release, if at the time the contract is entered into, the recording artist retains the right to grant licenses as to the musical work under paragraphs (1) and (3) of section 106.

(F) The procedures specified in subparagraphs (C) and (D) shall be repeated and concluded, in accordance with regulations that the Librarian of Congress shall prescribe, in each fifth calendar year after 1997, except to the extent that different years for the repeating and concluding of such proceedings may be determined in accordance with subparagraphs (B) and (C).

(G) Except as provided in section 1002(e) of this title, a digital phonorecord delivery licensed under this paragraph shall be accompanied by the information encoded in the sound recording, if any, by or under the authority of the copyright owner of that sound recording, that identifies the title of the sound recording, the featured recording artist who performs on the sound recording, and related information, including information concerning the underlying musical work and its writer.

(H)(i) A digital phonorecord delivery of a sound recording is actionable as an act of infringement under section 501, and is fully subject to the remedies provided by sections 502 through 506 and section 509, unless—

    (I) the digital phonorecord delivery has been authorized by the copyright owner of the sound recording; and

    (II) the owner of the copyright in the sound recording or the entity making the digital phonorecord delivery has obtained a compulsory license under this section or has otherwise been authorized by the copyright owner of the musical work to distribute or authorize the distribution, by means of a digital phonorecord delivery, of each musical work embodied in the sound recording.

    (ii) Any cause of action under this subparagraph shall be in addition to those available to the owner of the copyright in the nondramatic musical work under subsection (c)(6) and section 106(4) and the owner of the copyright in the sound recording under section 106(6).

    (I) The liability of the copyright owner of a sound recording for infringement of the copyright in a nondramatic musical work embodied in the sound recording shall be determined in accordance with applicable law, except that the owner of a copyright in a sound recording shall not be liable for a digital phonorecord delivery by a third party if the owner of the copyright in the sound recording does not license the distribution of a phonorecord of the nondramatic musical work.

    (J) Nothing in section 1008 shall be construed to prevent the exercise of the rights and remedies allowed by this paragraph, paragraph (6), and chapter 5 in the event of a digital phonorecord delivery, except that no action alleging infringement of copyright may be brought under this title against a manufacturer, importer or distributor of a digital audio recording device, a digital audio recording medium, an analog recording device, or an analog recording medium, or against a consumer, based on the actions described in such section.

    (K) Nothing in this section annuls or limits

    (i) the exclusive right to publicly perform a sound recording or the musical work embodied therein, including by means of a digital transmission, under sections 106(4) and 106(6),

    (ii) except for compulsory licensing under the conditions specified by this section, the exclusive rights to reproduce and distribute the sound recording and the musical work embodied therein under sections 106(1) and 106(3), including by means of a digital phonorecord delivery, or (iii) any other rights under any other provision of section 106, or remedies available under this title, as such rights or remedies exist either before or after the date of enactment of the Digital Performance Right in Sound Recordings Act of 1995.

(L) The provisions of this section concerning digital phonorecord deliveries shall not apply to any exempt transmissions or retransmissions under section 114(d)(1). The exemptions created in section 114(d)(1) do not expand or reduce the rights of copyright owners under section 106(1) through (5) with respect to such transmissions and retransmissions.

(4) A compulsory license under this section includes the right of the maker of a phonorecord of a nondramatic musical work under subsection (a)(1) to distribute or authorize distribution of such phonorecord by rental, lease, or lending (or by acts or practices in the nature of rental, lease, or lending). In addition to any royalty payable under clause (2) and chapter 8 of this title, a royalty shall be payable by the compulsory licensee for every act of distribution of a phonorecord by or in the nature of rental, lease, or lending, by or under the authority of the compulsory licensee. With respect to each nondramatic musical work embodied in the phonorecord, the royalty shall be a proportion of the revenue received by the compulsory licensee from every such act of distribution of the phonorecord under this clause equal to the proportion of the revenue received by the compulsory licensee from distribution of the phonorecord under clause (2) that is payable by a compulsory licensee under that clause and under chapter 8. The Register of Copyrights shall issue regulations to carry out the purpose of this clause.

(5) Royalty payments shall be made on or before the twentieth day of each month and shall include all royalties for the month next preceding. Each monthly payment shall be made under oath and shall comply with requirements that the Register of Copyrights shall prescribe by regulation. The Register shall also prescribe regulations under which detailed cumulative annual statements of account, certified by a certified public accountant, shall be filed for every compulsory license under this section. The regulations covering both the monthly and the annual statements of account shall prescribe the form, content, and manner of certification with respect to the number of records made and the number of records distributed.

(6) If the copyright owner does not receive the monthly payment and the monthly and annual statements of account when due, the owner may give written notice to the licensee that, unless the default is remedied within thirty days from the date of the notice, the compulsory license will be automatically terminated. Such termination renders either the making or the distribution, or both, of all phonorecords for which the royalty has not been paid, actionable as acts of infringement under section 501 and fully subject to the remedies provided by sections 502 through 506 and 509.

(d) Definition. As used in this section, the following term has the following meaning: A "digital phonorecord delivery" is each individual delivery of a phonorecord by digital transmission of a sound recording which results in a specifically identifiable reproduction by or for any transmission recipient of a phonorecord of that sound recording, regardless of whether the digital transmission is also a public performance of the sound recording or any nondramatic musical work embodied therein. A digital phonorecord delivery does not result from a real-time, non-interactive subscription transmission of a sound recording where no reproduction of the sound recording or the musical work embodied therein is made from the inception of the transmission through to its receipt by the transmission recipient in order to make the sound recording audible.

§ 116. Negotiated licenses for public performances by means of coin-operated phonorecord players

(a) **Applicability of Section.** This section applies to any nondramatic musical work embodied in a phonorecord.

(b) **Negotiated Licenses.**

(1) **Authority for negotiations**. Any owners of copyright in works to which this section applies and any operators of coin-operated phonorecord players may negotiate and agree upon the terms and rates of royalty payments for the performance of such works and the proportionate division of fees paid among copyright owners, and may designate common agents to negotiate, agree to, pay, or receive such royalty payments.

(2) **Arbitration.** Parties not subject to such a negotiation, may determine, by arbitration in accordance with the provisions of chapter 8, the terms and rates and the division of fees described in paragraph (1).

(c) **License Agreements Superior to Copyright Arbitration Royalty Panel Determinations.** License agreements between one or more copyright owners and one or more operators of coin-operated phonorecord players, which are negotiated in accordance with subsection (b), shall be given effect in lieu of any otherwise applicable determination by a copyright arbitration royalty panel.

(d) **Definitions.** As used in this section, the following terms mean the following:

(1) A "coin-operated phonorecord player" is a machine or device that—

(A) is employed solely for the performance of nondramatic musical works by means of phonorecords upon being activated by the insertion of coins, currency, tokens, or other monetary units or their equivalent;

(B) is located in an establishment making no direct or indirect charge for admission;

(C) is accompanied by a list which is comprised of the titles of all the musical works available for performance on it, and is affixed to the phonorecord player or posted in the establishment in a prominent position where it can be readily examined by the public; and

(D) affords a choice of works available for performance and permits the choice to be made by the patrons of the establishment in which it is located.

(2) An "operator" is any person who, alone or jointly with others—

(A) owns a coin-operated phonorecord player;

(B) has the power to make a coin-operated phonorecord player available for placement in an establishment for purposes of public performance; or

(C) has the power to exercise primary control over the selection of the musical works made available for public performance on a coin-operated phonorecord player.

§ 117. Limitations on exclusive rights: Computer programs

(a) **Making of Additional Copy or Adaptation by Owner of Copy.** Notwithstanding the provisions of section 106, it is not an infringement for the owner of a copy of a computer program to make or authorize the making of another copy or adaptation of that computer program provided:

(1) that such a new copy or adaptation is created as an essential step in the utilization of the computer program in conjunction with a machine and that it is used in no other manner, or

(2) that such new copy or adaptation is for archival purposes only and that all archival copies are destroyed in the event that continued possession of the computer program should cease to be rightful.

(b) **Lease, Sale, or Other Transfer of Additional Copy or Adaptation.** Any exact copies prepared in accordance with the provisions of this section may be leased, sold, or otherwise transferred, along with the copy from which such copies were prepared, only as part of the lease, sale, or other transfer of all rights in the program. Adaptations so prepared may be transferred only with the authorization of the copyright owner.

(c) **Machine Maintenance or Repair.** Notwithstanding the provisions of section 106, it is not an infringement for the owner or lessee of a machine to make or authorize the making of a copy of a computer program if such copy is made solely by virtue of the activation of a machine that lawfully contains an authorized copy of the computer program, for purposes only of maintenance or repair of that machine, if—

(1) such new copy is used in no other manner and is destroyed immediately after the maintenance or repair is completed; and

(2) with respect to any computer program or part thereof that is not necessary for that machine to be activated, such program or part

thereof is not accessed or used other than to make such new copy by virtue of the activation of the machine.

(d) Definitions. For purposes of this section—

(1) the "maintenance" of a machine is the servicing of the machine in order to make it work in accordance with its original specifications and any changes to those specifications authorized for that machine; and

(2) the "repair" of a machine is the restoring of the machine to the state of working in accordance with its original specifications and any changes to those specifications authorized for that machine.

§ 118. Scope of exclusive rights: Use of certain works in connection with noncommercial broadcasting

(a) The exclusive rights provided by section 106 shall, with respect to the works specified by subsection (b) and the activities specified by subsection (d), be subject to the conditions and limitations prescribed by this section.

(b) Notwithstanding any provision of the antitrust laws, any owners of copyright in published nondramatic musical works and published pictorial, graphic, and sculptural works and any public broadcasting entities, respectively, may negotiate and agree upon the terms and rates of royalty payments and the proportionate division of fees paid among various copyright owners, and may designate common agents to negotiate, agree to, pay, or receive payments.

(1) Any owner of copyright in a work specified in this subsection or any public broadcasting entity may submit to the Librarian of Congress proposed licenses covering such activities with respect to such works. The Librarian of Congress shall proceed on the basis of the proposals submitted as well as any other relevant information. The Librarian of Congress shall permit any interested party to submit information relevant to such proceedings.

(2) License agreements voluntarily negotiated at any time between one or more copyright owners and one or more public broadcasting entities shall be given effect in lieu of any determination by the Librarian of Congress: *Provided*, That copies of such agreements are filed in the Copyright Office within thirty days of execution in accordance with regulations that the Register of Copyrights shall prescribe.

(3) In the absence of license agreements negotiated under paragraph (2), the Librarian of Congress shall, pursuant to chapter 8, convene a copyright arbitration royalty panel to determine and publish in the Federal Register a schedule of rates and terms which, subject to paragraph (2), shall be binding on all owners of copyright in works specified by this subsection and public broadcasting entities, regardless of whether such copyright owners have submitted proposals to the Librarian of Congress. In establishing such rates and terms the copyright arbitration royalty panel may consider the rates for comparable

circumstances under voluntary license agreements negotiated as provided in paragraph (2). The Librarian of Congress shall also establish requirements by which copyright owners may receive reasonable notice of the use of their works under this section, and under which records of such use shall be kept by public broadcasting entities.

(c) The initial procedure specified in subsection (b) shall be repeated and concluded between June 30 and December 31, 1997, and at five-year intervals thereafter, in accordance with regulations that the Librarian of Congress shall prescribe.

(d) Subject to the terms of any voluntary license agreements that have been negotiated as provided by subsection (b)(2), a public broadcasting entity may, upon compliance with the provisions of this section, including the rates and terms established by a copyright arbitration royalty panel under subsection (b)(3), engage in the following activities with respect to published nondramatic musical works and published pictorial, graphic, and sculptural works:

(1) performance or display of a work by or in the course of a transmission made by a noncommercial educational broadcast station referred to in subsection (g); and

(2) production of a transmission program, reproduction of copies or phonorecords of such a transmission program, and distribution of such copies or phonorecords, where such production, reproduction, or distribution is made by a nonprofit institution or organization solely for the purpose of transmissions specified in paragraph (1); and

(3) the making of reproductions by a governmental body or a nonprofit institution of a transmission program simultaneously with its transmission as specified in paragraph (1), and the performance or display of the contents of such program under the conditions specified by paragraph (1) of section 110, but only if the reproductions are used for performances or displays for a period of no more than seven days from the date of the transmission specified in paragraph (1), and are destroyed before or at the end of such period. No person supplying, in accordance with paragraph (2), a reproduction of a transmission program to governmental bodies or nonprofit institutions under this paragraph shall have any liability as a result of failure of such body or institution to destroy such reproduction: *Provided,* That it shall have notified such body or institution of the requirement for such destruction pursuant to this paragraph: *And provided further,* That if such body or institution itself fails to destroy such reproduction it shall be deemed to have infringed.

(e) Except as expressly provided in this subsection, this section shall have no applicability to works other than those specified in subsection (b). Owners of copyright in nondramatic literary works and public broadcasting entities may, during the course of voluntary negotiations, agree among themselves, respectively, as to the terms and rates of royalty payments without liability under the antitrust laws. Any such terms and rates of royalty payments shall be effective upon filing in the Copyright Office, in accordance with regulations that the Register of Copyrights shall prescribe.

(f) Nothing in this section shall be construed to permit, beyond the limits of fair use as provided by section 107, the unauthorized dramatization of a nondramatic musical work, the production of a transmission program drawn to any substantial extent from a published compilation of pictorial, graphic, or sculptural works, or the unauthorized use of any portion of an audiovisual work.

(g) As used in this section, the term "public broadcasting entity" means a noncommercial educational broadcast station as defined in section 397 of title 47 and any nonprofit institution or organization engaged in the activities described in paragraph (2) of subsection (d).

§ 119. Limitations on exclusive rights: Secondary transmissions of superstations and network stations for private home viewing

(a) Secondary Transmissions by Satellite Carriers.

(1) Superstations and PBS satellite feed. Subject to the provisions of paragraphs (3), (4), and (6) of this subsection and section 114(d), secondary transmissions of a performance or display of a work embodied in a primary transmission made by a superstation or by the Public Broadcasting Service satellite feed shall be subject to statutory licensing under this section if the secondary transmission is made by a satellite carrier to the public for private home viewing, with regard to secondary transmissions the satellite carrier is in compliance with the rules, regulations, or authorizations of the Federal Communications Commission governing the carriage of television broadcast station signals, and the carrier makes a direct or indirect charge for each retransmission service to each household receiving the secondary transmission or to a distributor that has contracted with the carrier for direct or indirect delivery of the secondary transmission to the public for private home viewing. In the case of the Public Broadcasting Service satellite feed, the statutory license shall be effective until January 1, 2002.

(2) Network stations.

(A) In general. Subject to the provisions of subparagraphs (B) and (C) of this paragraph and paragraphs (3), (4), (5), and (6) of this subsection and section 114(d), secondary transmissions of a performance or display of a work embodied in a primary transmission made by a network station shall be subject to statutory licensing under this section if the secondary transmission is made by a satellite carrier to the public for private home viewing, with regard to secondary transmissions the satellite carrier is in compliance with the rules, regulations, or authorizations of the Federal Communications Commission governing the carriage of television broadcast station signals, and the carrier makes a direct or indirect charge for such retransmission service to each subscriber receiving the secondary transmission.

(B) Secondary transmissions to unserved households.

(i) In general. The statutory license provided for in subparagraph (A) shall be limited to secondary transmissions of the signals of no more than two network stations in a single day for each television network to persons who reside in unserved households.

(ii) Accurate determinations of eligibility.

(I) Accurate predictive model. In determining presumptively whether a person resides in an unserved household under subsection (d)(10)(A), a court shall rely on the Individual Location Longley–Rice model set forth by the Federal Communications Commission in Docket No. 98–201, as that model may be amended by the Commission over time under section 339(c)(3) of the Communications Act of 1934 to increase the accuracy of that model.

(II) Accurate measurements. For purposes of site measurements to determine whether a person resides in an unserved household under subsection (d)(10)(A), a court shall rely on section 339(c)(4) of the Communications Act of 1934.

(iii) C-band exemption to unserved households.

(I) In general. The limitations of clause (i) shall not apply to any secondary transmissions by C-band services of network stations that a subscriber to C-band service received before any termination of such secondary transmissions before October 31, 1999.

(II) Definition. In this clause the term "C-band service" means a service that is licensed by the Federal Communications Commission and operates in the Fixed Satellite Service under part 25 of title 47 of the Code of Federal Regulations.

(C) Submission of subscriber lists to networks. A satellite carrier that makes secondary transmissions of a primary transmission made by a network station pursuant to subparagraph (A) shall, 90 days after commencing such secondary transmissions, submit to the network that owns or is affiliated with the network station a list identifying (by name and street address, including county and zip code) all subscribers to which the satellite carrier makes secondary transmissions of that primary transmission. Thereafter, on the 15th of each month, the satellite carrier shall submit to the network a list identifying (by name and street address, including county and zip code) any persons who have been added or dropped as such subscribers since the last submission under this subparagraph. Such subscriber information submitted by a satellite carrier may be used only for purposes of monitoring compliance by the satellite carrier with this subsection. The submission requirements of this subparagraph shall apply to a satellite carrier only if the network to whom the submissions are to be made places on file with the Register of Copyrights a document identifying the name and address of the person to whom such submissions are to be made. The Register shall maintain for public inspection a file of all such documents.

(3) Noncompliance with reporting and payment requirements. Notwithstanding the provisions of paragraphs (1) and (2), the willful or repeated secondary transmission to the public by a satellite carrier of a primary transmission made by a superstation or a network station and embodying a performance or display of a work is actionable as an act of infringement under section 501, and is fully subject to the remedies provided by sections 502 through 506 and 509, where the satellite carrier has not deposited the statement of account and royalty fee required by subsection (b), or has failed to make the submissions to networks required by paragraph (2)(C).

(4) Willful alterations. Notwithstanding the provisions of paragraphs (1) and (2), the secondary transmission to the public by a satellite carrier of a performance or display of a work embodied in a primary transmission made by a superstation or a network station is actionable as an act of infringement under section 501, and is fully subject to the remedies provided by sections 502 through 506 and sections 509 and 510, if the content of the particular program in which the performance or display is embodied, or any commercial advertising or station announcement transmitted by the primary transmitter during, or immediately before or after, the transmission of such program, is in any way willfully altered by the satellite carrier through changes, deletions, or additions, or is combined with programming from any other broadcast signal.

(5) Violation of territorial restrictions on statutory license for network stations.

(A) Individual violations. The willful or repeated secondary transmission by a satellite carrier of a primary transmission made by a network station and embodying a performance or display of a work to a subscriber who does not reside in an unserved household is actionable as an act of infringement under section 501 and is fully subject to the remedies provided by sections 502 through 506 and 509, except that—

(i) no damages shall be awarded for such act of infringement if the satellite carrier took corrective action by promptly withdrawing service from the ineligible subscriber, and

(ii) any statutory damages shall not exceed $5 for such subscriber for each month during which the violation occurred.

(B) Pattern of violations. If a satellite carrier engages in a willful or repeated pattern or practice of delivering a primary transmission made by a network station and embodying a performance or display of a work to subscribers who do not reside in unserved households, then in addition to the remedies set forth in subparagraph (A)—

(i) if the pattern or practice has been carried out on a substantially nationwide basis, the court shall order a permanent injunction barring the secondary transmission by the satellite carrier, for private home viewing, of the primary transmissions of any primary network station affiliated with the same network, and the court may order statutory damages of not to exceed $250,000 for each 6–month period during which the pattern or practice was carried out; and

(ii) if the pattern or practice has been carried out on a local or regional basis, the court shall order a permanent injunction barring the secondary transmission, for private home viewing in that locality or region, by the satellite carrier of the primary transmissions of any primary network station affiliated with the same network, and the court may order statutory damages of not to exceed $250,000 for each 6–month period during which the pattern or practice was carried out.

(C) Previous subscribers excluded. Subparagraphs (A) and (B) do not apply to secondary transmissions by a satellite carrier to persons who subscribed to receive such secondary transmissions from the satellite carrier or a distributor before November 16, 1988.

(D) Burden of proof. In any action brought under this paragraph, the satellite carrier shall have the burden of proving that its secondary transmission of a primary transmission by a network station is for private home viewing to an unserved household.

(E) Exception. The secondary transmission by a satellite carrier of a performance or display of a work embodied in a primary transmission made by a network station to subscribers who do not reside in unserved households shall not be an act of infringement if—

(i) the station on May 1, 1991, was retransmitted by a satellite carrier and was not on that date owned or operated by or affiliated with a television network that offered interconnected program service on a regular basis for 15 or more hours per week to at least 25 affiliated television licensees in 10 or more States;

(ii) as of July 1, 1998, such station was retransmitted by a satellite carrier under the statutory license of this section; and

(iii) the station is not owned or operated by or affiliated with a television network that, as of January 1, 1995, offered interconnected program service on a regular basis for 15 or more hours per week to at least 25 affiliated television licensees in 10 or more States.

(6) Discrimination by a satellite carrier. Notwithstanding the provisions of paragraph (1), the willful or repeated secondary transmission to the public by a satellite carrier of a performance or display of a work embodied in a primary transmission made by a superstation or a network station is actionable as an act of infringement under section 501, and is fully subject to the remedies provided by sections 502 through 506 and 509, if the satellite carrier unlawfully discriminates against a distributor.

(7) Geographic limitation on secondary transmissions. The statutory license created by this section shall apply only to secondary transmissions to households located in the United States.

(8) Transitional signal intensity measurement procedures.

(A) In general. Subject to subparagraph (C), upon a challenge by a network station regarding whether a subscriber is an unserved household within the predicted Grade B Contour of the station, the satellite carrier shall, within 60 days after the receipt of the challenge—

(i) terminate service to that household of the signal that is the subject of the challenge, and within 30 days thereafter notify the network station that made the challenge that service to that household has been terminated; or

(ii) conduct a measurement of the signal intensity of the subscriber's household to determine whether the household is an unserved household after giving reasonable notice to the network station of the satellite carrier's intent to conduct the measurement.

(B) Effect of measurement. If the satellite carrier conducts a signal intensity measurement under subparagraph (A) and the measurement indicates that—

(i) the household is not an unserved household, the satellite carrier shall, within 60 days after the measurement is conducted, terminate the service to that household of the signal that is the subject of the challenge, and within 30 days thereafter notify the network station that made the challenge that service to that household has been terminated; or

(ii) the household is an unserved household, the station challenging the service shall reimburse the satellite carrier for the costs of the signal measurement within 60 days after receipt of the measurement results and a statement of the costs of the measurement.

(C) Limitation on measurements.

(i) Notwithstanding subparagraph (A), a satellite carrier may not be required to conduct signal intensity measurements during any calendar year in excess of 5 percent of the number of subscribers within the network station's local market that have subscribed to the service as of the effective date of the Satellite Home Viewer Act of 1994.

(ii) If a network station challenges whether a subscriber is an unserved household in excess of 5 percent of the subscribers within the network station's local market within a calendar year, subparagraph (A) shall not apply to challenges in excess of such 5 percent, but the station may conduct its own signal intensity measurement of the subscriber's household after giving reasonable notice to the satellite carrier of the network station's intent to conduct the measurement. If such measurement indicates that the household is not an unserved household, the carrier shall, within 60 days after receipt of the measurement, terminate service to the household of the signal that is the subject of the challenge and within 30 days thereafter notify the network station that made the challenge that service has been terminated. The carrier shall also, within 60 days after receipt of the measurement and a statement of the costs of the measurement, reimburse the network station for the cost it incurred in conducting the measurement.

(D) Outside the predicted grade b contour.

(i) If a network station challenges whether a subscriber is an unserved household outside the predicted Grade B Contour of the station, the station may conduct a measurement of the signal intensity of the subscriber's household to determine whether the household is an unserved household after giving reasonable notice to the satellite carrier of the network station's intent to conduct the measurement.

(ii) If the network station conducts a signal intensity measurement under clause (i) and the measurement indicates that—

(I) the household is not an unserved household, the station shall forward the results to the satellite carrier who shall, within 60 days after receipt of the measurement, terminate the service to the household of the signal that is the subject of the challenge, and shall reimburse the station for the costs of the measurement within 60 days after receipt of the measurement results and a statement of such costs; or

(II) the household is an unserved household, the station shall pay the costs of the measurement.

(9) Loser pays for signal intensity measurement; recovery of measurement costs in a civil action. In any civil action filed relating to the eligibility of subscribing households as unserved households—

(A) a network station challenging such eligibility shall, within 60 days after receipt of the measurement results and a statement of such costs, reimburse the satellite carrier for any signal intensity measurement that is conducted by that carrier in response to a challenge by the network station and that establishes the household is an unserved household; and

(B) a satellite carrier shall, within 60 days after receipt of the measurement results and a statement of such costs, reimburse the network station challenging such eligibility for any signal intensity measurement that is conducted by that station and that establishes the household is not an unserved household.

(10) Inability to conduct measurement. If a network station makes a reasonable attempt to conduct a site measurement of its signal at a subscriber's household and is denied access for the purpose of conducting the measurement, and is otherwise unable to conduct a measurement, the satellite carrier shall within 60 days notice thereof, terminate service of the station's network to that household.

(11) Service to recreational vehicles and commercial trucks.

(A) Exemption.

(i) In general. For purposes of this subsection, and subject to clauses (ii) and (iii), the term "unserved household" shall include—

(I) recreational vehicles as defined in regulations of the Secretary of Housing and Urban Development under section 3282.8 of title 24 of the Code of Federal Regulations; and

(II) commercial trucks that qualify as commercial motor vehicles under regulations of the Secretary of Transportation under section 383.5 of title 49 of the Code of Federal Regulations.

(ii) Limitation. Clause (i) shall apply only to a recreational vehicle or commercial truck if any satellite carrier that proposes to make a secondary transmission of a network station to the operator of such a recreational vehicle or commercial truck complies with the documentation requirements under subparagraphs (B) and (C).

(iii) Exclusion. For purposes of this subparagraph, the terms "recreational vehicle" and "commercial truck" shall not include any fixed dwelling, whether a mobile home or otherwise.

(B) Documentation requirements. A recreational vehicle or commercial truck shall be deemed to be an unserved household beginning 10 days after the relevant satellite carrier provides to the network that owns or is affiliated with the network station that will be secondarily transmitted to the recreational vehicle or commercial truck the following documents:

(i) Declaration. A signed declaration by the operator of the recreational vehicle or commercial truck that the satellite dish is permanently attached to the recreational vehicle or commercial truck, and will not be used to receive satellite programming at any fixed dwelling.

(ii) Registration. In the case of a recreational vehicle, a copy of the current State vehicle registration for the recreational vehicle.

(iii) Registration and license. In the case of a commercial truck, a copy of—

(I) the current State vehicle registration for the truck; and

(II) a copy of a valid, current commercial driver's license, as defined in regulations of the Secretary of Transportation under section 383 of title 49 of the Code of Federal Regulations, issued to the operator.

(C) Updated documentation requirements. If a satellite carrier wishes to continue to make secondary transmissions to a recreational vehicle or commercial truck for more than a 2–year period, that carrier shall provide each network, upon request, with updated documentation in the form described under subparagraph (B) during the 90 days before expiration of that 2–year period.

(12) Statutory license contingent on compliance with FCC rules and remedial steps. Notwithstanding any other provision of this section, the willful or repeated secondary transmission to the public by a satellite carrier of a primary transmission embodying a performance or display of a work made by a broadcast station licensed by the Federal Communications Commission is actionable as an act of infringement under section 501, and is fully subject to the remedies provided by sections 502 through 506 and 509, if, at the time of such transmission, the satellite carrier is not in compliance with the rules, regulations, and authorizations of the Federal Communications Commission concerning the carriage of television broadcast station signals.

(b) Statutory License for Secondary Transmissions for Private Home Viewing.

(1) Deposits with the Register of Copyrights. A satellite carrier whose secondary transmissions are subject to statutory licensing under subsection (a) shall, on a semiannual basis, deposit with the Register of Copyrights, in accordance with requirements that the Register shall prescribe by regulation—

(A) a statement of account, covering the preceding 6–month period, specifying the names and locations of all superstations and network stations whose signals were retransmitted, at any time during that period, to subscribers for private home viewing as described in subsections (a)(1) and (a)(2), the total number of subscribers that received such retransmissions, and such other data as the Register of Copyrights may from time to time prescribe by regulation; and

(B) a royalty fee for that 6–month period, computed by—

(i) multiplying the total number of subscribers receiving each secondary transmission of a superstation during each calendar month by 17.5 cents per subscriber in the case of superstations that as retransmitted by the satellite carrier include any program which, if delivered by any cable system in the United States, would be subject to the syndicated exclusivity rules of the Federal Communications Commission, and 14 cents per subscriber in the case of superstations that are syndex-proof as defined in section 258.2 of title 37, Code of Federal Regulations;

(ii) multiplying the number of subscribers receiving each secondary transmission of a network station or the Public Broadcasting Service satellite feed during each calendar month by 6 cents; and

(iii) adding together the totals computed under clauses (i) and (ii).

(2) Investment of fees. The Register of Copyrights shall receive all fees deposited under this section and, after deducting the reasonable costs incurred by the Copyright Office under this section (other than the costs deducted under paragraph (4)), shall deposit the balance in the Treasury of the United States, in such manner as the Secretary of the Treasury directs. All funds held by the Secretary of the Treasury shall be invested in interest-bearing securities of the United States for later distribution with interest by the Librarian of Congress as provided by this title.

(3) Persons to whom fees are distributed. The royalty fees deposited under paragraph (2) shall, in accordance with the procedures provided by paragraph (4), be distributed to those copyright owners whose works were included in a secondary transmission for private home viewing made by a satellite carrier during the applicable 6–month accounting period and who file a claim with the Librarian of Congress under paragraph (4).

(4) Procedures for distribution. The royalty fees deposited under paragraph (2) shall be distributed in accordance with the following procedures:

(A) Filing of claims for fees. During the month of July in each year, each person claiming to be entitled to statutory license fees for secondary transmissions for private home viewing shall file a claim with the Librarian of Congress, in accordance with requirements that the Librarian of Congress shall prescribe by regulation. For purposes of this paragraph, any claimants may agree among themselves as to the proportionate division of statutory license fees among them, may lump their claims together and file them jointly or as a single claim, or may designate a common agent to receive payment on their behalf.

(B) Determination of controversy; distributions. After the first day of August of each year, the Librarian of Congress shall determine whether there exists a controversy concerning the distribution of royalty fees. If the Librarian of Congress determines that no such controversy exists, the Librarian of Congress shall, after deducting reasonable administrative costs under this paragraph, distribute such fees to the copyright owners entitled to receive them, or to their designated agents. If the Librarian of Congress finds the existence of a controversy, the Librarian of Congress shall, pursuant to chapter 8 of this title, convene a copyright arbitration royalty panel to determine the distribution of royalty fees.

(C) Withholding of fees during controversy. During the pendency of any proceeding under this subsection, the Librarian of Congress shall withhold from distribution an amount sufficient to satisfy all claims with respect to which a controversy exists, but shall have discretion to proceed to distribute any amounts that are not in controversy.

(c) Adjustment of Royalty Fees.

(1) Applicability and determination of royalty fees. The rate of the royalty fee payable under subsection (b)(1)(B) shall be effective unless a royalty fee is established under paragraph (2) or (3) of this subsection.

(2) Fee set by voluntary negotiation.

(A) Notice of initiation of proceedings. On or before July 1, 1996, the Librarian of Congress shall cause notice to be published in the Federal Register of the initiation of voluntary negotiation proceedings for the purpose of determining the royalty fee to be paid by satellite carriers under subsection (b)(1)(B).

(B) Negotiations. Satellite carriers, distributors, and copyright owners entitled to royalty fees under this section shall negotiate in good faith in an effort to reach a voluntary agreement or voluntary agreements for the payment of royalty fees. Any such satellite carriers, distributors, and copyright owners may at any time negotiate and agree to the royalty fee, and may designate common agents to negotiate, agree to, or pay such fees. If the parties fail to identify common agents, the Librarian of Congress shall do so, after requesting recommendations from the parties to the negotiation proceeding. The parties to each negotiation proceeding shall bear the entire cost thereof.

(C) Agreements binding on parties; filing of agreements. Voluntary agreements negotiated at any time in accordance with this paragraph shall be binding upon all satellite carriers, distributors, and copyright owners that are parties thereto. Copies of such agreements shall be filed with the Copyright Office within 30 days after execution in accordance with regulations that the Register of Copyrights shall prescribe.

(D) Period agreement is in effect. The obligation to pay the royalty fees established under a voluntary agreement which has been filed with the Copyright Office in accordance with this paragraph shall become effective on the date specified in the agreement, and shall remain in effect until December 31, 1999, or in accordance with the terms of the agreement, whichever is later.

(3) Fee set by compulsory arbitration.

(A) Notice of initiation of proceedings. On or before January 1, 1997, the Librarian of Congress shall cause notice to be published in the Federal Register of the initiation of arbitration proceedings for the purpose of determining a reasonable royalty fee to be paid under subsection (b)(1)(B) by satellite carriers who are not parties to a voluntary agreement filed with the Copyright Office in accordance with paragraph (2). Such arbitration proceeding shall be conducted under chapter 8.

(B) Establishment of royalty fees. In determining royalty fees under this paragraph, the copyright arbitration royalty panel appointed under chapter 8 shall establish fees for the retransmission of network stations and superstations that most clearly represent the fair market value of secondary transmissions. In determining the fair market value, the panel shall base its decision on economic, competitive, and programming information presented by the parties, including—

(i) the competitive environment in which such programming is distributed, the cost of similar signals in similar private and compulsory license marketplaces, and any special features and conditions of the retransmission marketplace;

(ii) the economic impact of such fees on copyright owners and satellite carriers; and

(iii) the impact on the continued availability of secondary transmissions to the public.

(C) Period during which decision of arbitration panel or order of librarian effective. The obligation to pay the royalty fee established under a determination which—

(i) is made by a copyright arbitration royalty panel in an arbitration proceeding under this paragraph and is adopted by the Librarian of Congress under section 802(f), or

(ii) is established by the Librarian of Congress under section 802(f), shall become effective as provided in section 802(g), or July 1, 1997, whichever is later.

(D) Persons subject to royalty fee. The royalty fee referred to in subparagraph (C) shall be binding on all satellite carriers, distributors, and copyright owners, who are not party to a voluntary agreement filed with the Copyright Office under paragraph (2).

(4) Reduction.

(A) Superstation. The rate of the royalty fee in effect on January 1, 1998, payable in each case under subsection (b)(1)(B)(i) shall be reduced by 30 percent.

(B) Network and public broadcasting satellite feed. The rate of the royalty fee in effect on January 1, 1998, payable under subsection (b)(1)(B)(ii) shall be reduced by 45 percent.

(5) Public broadcasting service as agent. For purposes of section 802, with respect to royalty fees paid by satellite carriers for retransmitting the Public Broadcasting Service satellite feed, the Public Broadcasting Service shall be the agent for all public television copyright claimants and all Public Broadcasting Service member stations.

(d) Definitions. As used in this section—

(1) Distributor. The term "distributor" means an entity which contracts to distribute secondary transmissions from a satellite carrier and, either as a single channel or in a package with other programming, provides the secondary transmission either directly to individual subscribers for private home viewing or indirectly through other program distribution entities.

(2) Network station. The term "network station" means—

(A) a television broadcast station, including any translator station or terrestrial satellite station that rebroadcasts all or substantially all of the programming broadcast by a network station, that is owned or operated by, or affiliated with, one or more of the television networks in the United States which offer an interconnected program service on a regular basis for 15 or more hours per week to at least 25 of its affiliated television licensees in 10 or more States; or

(B) a noncommercial educational broadcast station (as defined in section 397 of the Communications Act of 1934).

(3) Primary network station. The term "primary network station" means a network station that broadcasts or rebroadcasts the basic programming service of a particular national network.

(4) Primary transmission. The term "primary transmission" has the meaning given that term in section 111(f) of this title.

(5) Private home viewing. The term "private home viewing" means the viewing, for private use in a household by means of satellite reception equipment which is operated by an individual in that household and which serves only such household, of a secondary transmission delivered by a satellite carrier of a primary transmission of a television station licensed by the Federal Communications Commission.

(6) Satellite carrier. The term "satellite carrier" means an entity that uses the facilities of a satellite or satellite service licensed by the Federal Communications Commission and operates in the Fixed–Satellite Service under part 25 of title 47 of the Code of Federal Regulations or the Direct Broadcast Satellite Service under part 100 of title 47 of the Code of Federal Regulations to establish and operate a channel of communications for point-to-multipoint distribution of television station signals, and that owns or leases a capacity or service on a satellite in order to provide such point-to-multipoint distribution, except to the extent that such entity provides such distribution pursuant to tariff under the Communications Act of 1934, other than for private home viewing.

(7) Secondary transmission. The term "secondary transmission" has the meaning given that term in section 111(f) of this title.

(8) Subscriber. The term "subscriber" means an individual who receives a secondary transmission service for private home viewing by means of a secondary transmission from a satellite carrier and pays a fee for the service, directly or indirectly, to the satellite carrier or to a distributor.

(9) Superstation. The term "superstation"—

(A) means a television broadcast station, other than a network station, licensed by the Federal Communications Commission that is secondarily transmitted by a satellite carrier; and

(B) except for purposes of computing the royalty fee, includes the Public Broadcasting Service satellite feed.

(10) Unserved household. The term "unserved household", with respect to a particular television network, means a household that—

(A) cannot receive, through the use of a conventional, stationary, outdoor rooftop receiving antenna, an over-the-air signal of a primary network station affiliated with that network of Grade B intensity as defined by the Federal Communications Commission under section 73.683(a) of title 47 of the Code of Federal Regulations, as in effect on January 1, 1999;

(B) is subject to a waiver granted under regulations established under section 339(c)(2) of the Communications Act of 1934;

(C) is a subscriber to whom subsection (e) applies;

(D) is a subscriber to whom subsection (a)(11) applies; or

(E) is a subscriber to whom the exemption under subsection (a)(2)(B)(iii) applies.

(11) Local market. The term "local market" has the meaning given such term under section 122(j).

(12) Public broadcasting service satellite feed. The term "Public Broadcasting Service satellite feed" means the national satellite feed distributed and designated for purposes of this section by the Public Broadcasting Service consisting of educational and informational programming intended for private home viewing, to which the Public Broadcasting Service holds national terrestrial broadcast rights.

(e) Moratorium on Copyright Liability. Until December 31, 2004, a subscriber who does not receive a signal of Grade A intensity (as defined in the regulations of the Federal Communications Commission under section 73.683(a) of title 47 of the Code of Federal Regulations, as in effect on January 1, 1999, or predicted by the Federal Communications Commission using the Individual Location Longley–Rice methodology described by the Federal Communications Commission in Docket No. 98–201) of a local network television broadcast station shall remain eligible to receive signals of network stations affiliated with the same network, if that subscriber had satellite service of such network signal terminated after July 11, 1998, and before October 31, 1999, as required by this section, or received such service on October 31, 1999.

§ 120. Scope of exclusive rights in architectural works

(a) Pictorial Representations Permitted. The copyright in an architectural work that has been constructed does not include the right to prevent the making, distributing, or public display of pictures, paintings, photographs, or other pictorial representations of the work, if the building in which the work is embodied is located in or ordinarily visible from a public place.

(b) Alterations to and Destruction of Buildings. Notwithstanding the provisions of section 106(2), the owners of a building embodying an architectural work may, without the consent of the author or copyright owner of the architectural work, make or authorize the making of alterations to such building, and destroy or authorize the destruction of such building.

§ 121. Limitations on exclusive rights: reproduction for blind or other people with disabilities

(a) Notwithstanding the provisions of section 106, it is not an infringement of copyright for an authorized entity to reproduce or to distribute copies or phonorecords of a previously published, nondramatic literary work if such copies or phonorecords are reproduced or distributed in specialized formats exclusively for use by blind or other persons with disabilities.

(b)(1) Copies or phonorecords to which this section applies shall—

(A) not be reproduced or distributed in a format other than a specialized format exclusively for use by blind or other persons with disabilities;

(B) bear a notice that any further reproduction or distribution in a format other than a specialized format is an infringement; and

(C) include a copyright notice identifying the copyright owner and the date of the original publication.

(2) The provisions of this subsection shall not apply to standardized, secure, or norm-referenced tests and related testing material, or to computer programs, except the portions thereof that are in conventional human language (including descriptions of pictorial works) and displayed to users in the ordinary course of using the computer programs.

(c) For purposes of this section, the term—

(1) "authorized entity" means a nonprofit organization or a governmental agency that has a primary mission to provide specialized services relating to training, education, or adaptive reading or information access needs of blind or other persons with disabilities;

(2) "blind or other persons with disabilities" means individuals who are eligible or who may qualify in accordance with the Act entitled "An Act to provide books for the adult blind", approved March 3, 1931 (2 U.S.C. 135a; 46 Stat. 1487) to receive books and other publications produced in specialized formats; and

(3) "specialized formats" means braille, audio, or digital text which is exclusively for use by blind or other persons with disabilities.

§ 122. Limitations on exclusive rights; secondary transmissions by satellite carriers within local markets

(a) Secondary Transmissions of Television Broadcast Stations by Satellite Carriers. A secondary transmission of a performance or display of a work embodied in a primary transmission of a television broadcast station into the station's local market shall be subject to statutory licensing under this section if—

(1) the secondary transmission is made by a satellite carrier to the public;

(2) with regard to secondary transmissions, the satellite carrier is in compliance with the rules, regulations, or authorizations of the Federal Communications Commission governing the carriage of television broadcast station signals; and

(3) the satellite carrier makes a direct or indirect charge for the secondary transmission to—

(A) each subscriber receiving the secondary transmission; or

(B) a distributor that has contracted with the satellite carrier for direct or indirect delivery of the secondary transmission to the public.

(b) Reporting Requirements.

(1) Initial lists. A satellite carrier that makes secondary transmissions of a primary transmission made by a network station under subsection (a) shall, within 90 days after commencing such secondary transmissions, submit to the network that owns or is affiliated with the network station a list identifying (by name in alphabetical order and street address, including county and zip code) all subscribers to which the satellite carrier makes secondary transmissions of that primary transmission under subsection (a).

(2) Subsequent lists. After the list is submitted under paragraph (1), the satellite carrier shall, on the 15th of each month, submit to the network a list identifying (by name in alphabetical order and street address, including county and zip code) any subscribers who have been added or dropped as subscribers since the last submission under this subsection.

(3) Use of subscriber information. Subscriber information submitted by a satellite carrier under this subsection may be used only for the purposes of monitoring compliance by the satellite carrier with this section.

(4) Requirements of networks. The submission requirements of this subsection shall apply to a satellite carrier only if the network to which the submissions are to be made places on file with the Register of Copyrights a document identifying the name and address of the person to whom such submissions are to be made. The Register of Copyrights shall maintain for public inspection a file of all such documents.

(c) No Royalty Fee Required. A satellite carrier whose secondary transmissions are subject to statutory licensing under subsection (a) shall have no royalty obligation for such secondary transmissions.

(d) Noncompliance with Reporting and Regulatory Requirements. Notwithstanding subsection (a), the willful or repeated secondary transmission to the public by a satellite carrier into the local market of a television broadcast station of a primary transmission embodying a performance or display of a work made by that television broadcast station is actionable as an act of infringement under section 501, and is fully subject to the remedies provided under sections 502 through 506 and 509, if the satellite carrier has not complied with the reporting requirements of subsection (b) or with the rules, regulations, and authorizations of the Federal Communications Commission concerning the carriage of television broadcast signals.

(e) Willful Alterations. Notwithstanding subsection (a), the secondary transmission to the public by a satellite carrier into the local market of a television broadcast station of a performance or display of a work embodied in a primary transmission made by that television broadcast station is actionable as an act of infringement under section 501, and is fully subject to the remedies provided by sections 502 through 506 and sections 509 and 510, if the content of the particular program in which the performance or display is embodied, or any commercial advertising or station announcement transmitted by the primary transmitter during, or immediately before or after, the transmission of such program, is in any way willfully altered by the satellite carrier through changes, deletions, or additions, or is combined with programming from any other broadcast signal.

(f) Violation of Territorial Restrictions on Statutory License for Television Broadcast Stations.

(1) Individual violations. The willful or repeated secondary transmission to the public by a satellite carrier of a primary transmission embodying a performance or display of a work made by a television broadcast station to a subscriber who does not reside in that station's local market, and is not subject to statutory licensing under section 119 or a private licensing agreement, is actionable as an act of infringement under section 501 and is fully subject to the remedies provided by sections 502 through 506 and 509, except that—

(A) no damages shall be awarded for such act of infringement if the satellite carrier took corrective action by promptly withdrawing service from the ineligible subscriber; and

(B) any statutory damages shall not exceed $5 for such subscriber for each month during which the violation occurred.

(2) Pattern of violations. If a satellite carrier engages in a willful or repeated pattern or practice of secondarily transmitting to the public a primary transmission embodying a performance or display of a work made by a television broadcast station to subscribers who do not reside in that station's local market, and are not subject to statutory licensing under section 119 or a private licensing agreement, then in addition to the remedies under paragraph (1)—

(A) if the pattern or practice has been carried out on a substantially nationwide basis, the court—

(i) shall order a permanent injunction barring the secondary transmission by the satellite carrier of the primary transmissions of that television broadcast station (and if such television broadcast station is a network station, all other television broadcast stations affiliated with such network); and

(ii) may order statutory damages not exceeding $250,000 for each 6–month period during which the pattern or practice was carried out; and

(B) if the pattern or practice has been carried out on a local or regional basis with respect to more than one television broadcast station, the court—

(i) shall order a permanent injunction barring the secondary transmission in that locality or region by the satellite carrier of the primary transmissions of any television broadcast station; and

(ii) may order statutory damages not exceeding $250,000 for each 6–month period during which the pattern or practice was carried out.

(g) Burden of Proof. In any action brought under subsection (f), the satellite carrier shall have the burden of proving that its secondary transmission of a primary transmission by a television broadcast station is made only to subscribers located within that station's local market or subscribers being served in compliance with section 119 or a private licensing agreement.

(h) Geographic Limitations on Secondary Transmissions. The statutory license created by this section shall apply to secondary transmissions to locations in the United States.

(i) Exclusivity with Respect to Secondary Transmissions of Broadcast Stations by Satellite to Members of the Public. No provision of section 111 or any other law (other than this section and section 119) shall be construed to contain any authorization, exemption, or license through which secondary transmissions by satellite carriers of programming contained in a primary transmission made by a television broadcast station may be made without obtaining the consent of the copyright owner.

(j) Definitions. In this section—

(1) Distributor. The term "distributor" means an entity which contracts to distribute secondary transmissions from a satellite carrier and, either as a single channel or in a package with other programming, provides the secondary transmission either directly to individual subscribers or indirectly through other program distribution entities.

(2) Local market.

(A) In general. The term "local market", in the case of both commercial and noncommercial television broadcast stations, means the designated market area in which a station is located, and—

(i) in the case of a commercial television broadcast station, all commercial television broadcast stations licensed to a community within the same designated market area are within the same local market; and

(ii) in the case of a noncommercial educational television broadcast station, the market includes any station that is licensed to a community within the same designated market area as the noncommercial educational television broadcast station.

(B) County of license. In addition to the area described in subparagraph (A), a station's local market includes the county in which the station's community of license is located.

(C) Designated market area. For purposes of subparagraph (A), the term "designated market area" means a designated market area, as determined by Nielsen Media Research and published in the 1999–2000 Nielsen Station Index Directory and Nielsen Station Index United States Television Household Estimates or any successor publication.

(3) Network station; satellite carrier; secondary transmission. The terms "network station", "satellite carrier", and "secondary transmission" have the meanings given such terms under section 119(d).

(4) Subscriber. The term "subscriber" means a person who receives a secondary transmission service from a satellite carrier and pays a fee for the service, directly or indirectly, to the satellite carrier or to a distributor.

(5) Television broadcast station. The term "television broadcast station"—

(A) means an over-the-air, commercial or noncommercial television broadcast station licensed by the Federal Communications Commission under subpart E of part 73 of title 47, Code of Federal Regulations, except that such term does not include a low-power or translator television station; and

(B) includes a television broadcast station licensed by an appropriate governmental authority of Canada or Mexico if the station broadcasts primarily in the English language and is a network station as defined in section 119(d)(2)(A).

CHAPTER 2—COPYRIGHT LAW

§ 201. Ownership of copyright

(a) **Initial Ownership.** Copyright in a work protected under this title vests initially in the author or authors of the work. The authors of a joint work are coowner of copyright in the work.

(b) **Works Made for Hire.** In the case of a work made for hire, the employer or other person for whom the work was prepared is considered the author for purposes of this title, and, unless the parties have expressly agreed otherwise in a written instrument signed by them, owns all of the rights comprised in the copyright.

(c) **Contributions to Collective Works.** Copyright in each separate contribution to a collective work is distinct from copyright in the collective work as a whole, and vests initially in the author of the contribution. In the absence of an express transfer of the copyright or of any rights under it, the owner of copyright in the collective work is presumed to have acquired only the privilege of reproducing and distributing the contribution as part of that particular collective work, any revision of that collective work, and any later collective work in the same series.

(d) **Transfer of Ownership.**

(1) The ownership of a copyright may be transferred in whole or in part by any means of conveyance or by operation of law, and may be bequeathed by will or pass as personal property by the applicable laws of intestate succession.

(2) Any of the exclusive rights comprised in a copyright, including any subdivision of any of the rights specified by section 106, may be transferred as provided by clause (1) and owned separately. The owner of any particular exclusive right is entitled, to the extent of that right, to all of the protection and remedies accorded to the copyright owner by this title.

(e) **Involuntary Transfer.** When an individual author's ownership of a copyright, or of any of the exclusive rights under a copyright, has not previously been transferred voluntarily by that individual author, no action by any governmental body or other official or organization purporting to seize, expropriate, transfer, or exercise rights of ownership with respect to the copyright, or any of the exclusive rights under a copyright, shall be given effect under this title, except as provided under title 11.

§ 202. Ownership of copyright as distinct from ownership of material object

Ownership of a copyright, or of any of the exclusive rights under a copyright, is distinct from ownership of any material object in which the work is embodied. Transfer of ownership of any material object, including the copy or phonorecord in which the work is first fixed, does not of itself convey any rights in the copyrighted work embodied in the object; nor, in the absence of an agreement, does transfer of ownership of a copyright or of any exclusive rights under a copyright convey property rights in any material object.

§ 203. Termination of transfers and licenses granted by the author

(a) Conditions for Termination. In the case of any work other than a work made for hire, the exclusive or nonexclusive grant of a transfer or license of copyright or of any right under a copyright, executed by the author on or after January 1, 1978, otherwise than by will, is subject to termination under the following conditions:

(1) In the case of a grant executed by one author, termination of the grant may be effected by that author or, if the author is dead, by the person or persons who, under clause (2) of this subsection, own and are entitled to exercise a total of more than one-half of that author's termination interest. In the case of a grant executed by two or more authors of a joint work, termination of the grant may be effected by a majority of the authors who executed it; if any of such authors is dead, the termination interest of any such author may be exercised as a unit by the person or persons who, under clause (2) of this subsection, own and are entitled to exercise a total of more than one-half of that author's interest.

(2) Where an author is dead, his or her termination interest is owned, and may be exercised, as follows:

(A) The widow or widower owns the author's entire termination interest unless there are any surviving children or grandchildren of the author, in which case the widow or widower owns one-half of the author's interest.

(B) The author's surviving children, and the surviving children of any dead child of the author, own the author's entire termination interest unless there is a widow or widower, in which case the ownership of one-half of the author's interest is divided among them.

(C) The rights of the author's children and grandchildren are in all cases divided among them and exercised on a per stirpes basis according to the number of such author's children represented; the share of the children of a dead child in a termination interest can be exercised only by the action of a majority of them.

(D) In the event that the author's widow or widower, children, and grandchildren are not living, the author's executor, administrator, personal representative, or trustee shall own the author's entire termination interest.

(3) Termination of the grant may be effected at any time during a period of five years beginning at the end of thirty-five years from the date of execution of the grant; or, if the grant covers the right of publication of the work, the period begins at the end of thirty-five years from the date of publication of the work under the grant or at the end of forty years from the date of execution of the grant, whichever term ends earlier.

(4) The termination shall be effected by serving an advance notice in writing, signed by the number and proportion of owners of termination interests required under clauses (1) and (2) of this subsection, or by their duly authorized agents, upon the grantee or the grantee's successor in title.

(A) The notice shall state the effective date of the termination, which shall fall within the five-year period specified by clause (3) of this subsection, and the notice shall be served not less than two or more than ten years before that date. A copy of the notice shall be recorded in the Copyright Office before the effective date of termination, as a condition to its taking effect.

(B) The notice shall comply, in form, content, and manner of service, with requirements that the Register of Copyrights shall prescribe by regulation.

(5) Termination of the grant may be effected notwithstanding any agreement to the contrary, including an agreement to make a will or to make any future grant.

(b) Effect of Termination. Upon the effective date of termination, all rights under this title that were covered by the terminated grants revert to the author, authors, and other persons owning termination interests under clauses (1) and (2) of subsection (a), including those owners who did not join in signing the notice of termination under clause (4) of subsection (a), but with the following limitations:

(1) A derivative work prepared under authority of the grant before its termination may continue to be utilized under the terms of the grant after its termination, but this privilege does not extend to the preparation after the termination of other derivative works based upon the copyrighted work covered by the terminated grant.

(2) The future rights that will revert upon termination of the grant become vested on the date the notice of termination has been served as provided by clause (4) of subsection (a). The rights vest in the author, authors, and other persons named in, and in the proportionate shares provided by, clauses (1) and (2) of subsection (a).

(3) Subject to the provisions of clause (4) of this subsection, a further grant, or agreement to make a further grant, of any right covered by a terminated grant is valid only if it is signed by the same number and proportion of the owners, in whom the right has vested under clause (2) of this subsection, as are required to terminate the grant under clauses (1) and (2) of subsection (a). Such further grant or agreement is effective with respect to all of the persons in whom the right it covers has vested under clause (2) of this subsection, including those who did not join in signing it. If any person dies after rights under a terminated grant have vested in him or her, that person's legal representatives, legatees, or heirs at law represent him or her for purposes of this clause.

(4) A further grant, or agreement to make a further grant, of any right covered by a terminated grant is valid only if it is made after the effective date of the termination. As an exception, however, an agreement for such a further grant may be made between the persons provided by clause (3) of this subsection and the original grantee or such grantee's successor in title, after the notice of termination has been served as provided by clause (4) of subsection (a).

(5) Termination of a grant under this section affects only those rights covered by the grants that arise under this title, and in no way affects rights arising under any other Federal, State, or foreign laws.

(6) Unless and until termination is effected under this section, the grant, if it does not provide otherwise, continues in effect for the term of copyright provided by this title.

§ 204. Execution of transfers of copyright ownership

(a) A transfer of copyright ownership, other than by operation of law, is not valid unless an instrument of conveyance, or a note or memorandum of the transfer, is in writing and signed by the owner of the rights conveyed or such owner's duly authorized agent.

(b) A certificate of acknowledgment is not required for the validity of a transfer, but is prima facie evidence of the execution of the transfer if—

(1) in the case of a transfer executed in the United States, the certificate is issued by a person authorized to administer oaths within the United States; or

(2) in the case of a transfer executed in a foreign country, the certificate is issued by a diplomatic or consular officer of the United States, or by a person authorized to administer oaths whose authority is proved by a certificate of such an officer.

§ 205. Recordation of transfers and other documents

(a) Conditions for Recordation. Any transfer of copyright ownership or other document pertaining to a copyright may be recorded in the Copyright Office if the document filed for recordation bears the actual signature of the person who executed it, or if it is accompanied by a sworn or official certification that it is a true copy of the original, signed document.

(b) Certificate of Recordation. The Register of Copyrights shall, upon receipt of a document as provided by subsection (a) and of the fee provided by section 708, record the document and return it with a certificate of recordation.

(c) Recordation as Constructive Notice. Recordation of a document in the Copyright Office gives all persons constructive notice of the facts stated in the recorded document, but only if—

(1) the document, or material attached to it, specifically identifies the work to which it pertains so that, after the document is indexed by the Register of Copyrights, it would be revealed by a reasonable search under the title or registration number of the work; and

(2) registration has been made for the work.

(d) Priority between Conflicting Transfers. As between two conflicting transfers, the one executed first prevails if it is recorded, in the manner required to give constructive notice under subsection (c), within one month after its execution in the United States or within two months after its execution outside the United States, or at any time before recordation in such manner of the later transfer. Otherwise the later transfer prevails if recorded first in such manner, and if taken in good faith, for valuable consideration or on the basis of a binding promise to pay royalties, and without notice of the earlier transfer.

(e) Priority between Conflicting Transfer of Ownership and Nonexclusive License. A nonexclusive license, whether recorded or not, prevails over a conflicting transfer of copyright ownership if the license is evidenced by a written instrument signed by the owner of the rights licensed or such owner's duly authorized agent, and if

(1) the license was taken before execution of the transfer; or

(2) the license was taken in good faith before recordation of the transfer and without notice of it.

CHAPTER 3—DURATION OF COPYRIGHT

§ 301. Preemption with respect to other laws

(a) On and after January 1, 1978, all legal or equitable rights that are equivalent to any of the exclusive rights within the general scope of copyright as specified by section 106 in works of authorship that are fixed in a tangible medium of expression and come within the subject matter of copyright as specified by sections 102 and 103, whether created before or after that date and whether published or unpublished, are governed exclusively by this title. Thereafter, no person is entitled to any such right or equivalent right in any such work under the common law or statutes of any State.

(b) Nothing in this title annuls or limits any rights or remedies under the common law or statutes of any State with respect to—

(1) subject matter that does not come within the subject matter of copyright as specified by sections 102 and 103, including works of authorship not fixed in any tangible medium of expression; or

(2) any cause of action arising from undertakings commenced before January 1, 1978;

(3) activities violating legal or equitable rights that are not equivalent to any of the exclusive rights within the general scope of copyright as specified by section 106; or

(4) State and local landmarks, historic preservation, zoning, or building codes, relating to architectural works protected under section 102(a)(8).

(c) With respect to sound recordings fixed before February 15, 1972, any rights or remedies under the common law or statutes of any State shall not be annulled or limited by this title until February 15, 2067. The preemptive provisions of subsection (a) shall apply to any such rights and remedies pertaining to any cause of action arising from undertakings commenced on and after February 15, 2067. Notwithstanding the provisions of section 303, no sound recording fixed before February 15, 1972, shall be subject to copyright under this title before, on, or after February 15, 2067.

(d) Nothing in this title annuls or limits any rights or remedies under any other Federal statute.

(e) The scope of Federal preemption under this section is not affected by the adherence of the United States to the Berne Convention or the satisfaction of obligations of the United States thereunder.

(f)(1) On or after the effective date [June 1, 1991] set forth in section 610(a) of the Visual Artists Rights Act of 1990, all legal or equitable rights that are equivalent to any of the rights conferred by section 106A with respect to works of visual art to which the rights conferred by section 106A apply are governed exclusively by section 106A and section 113(d) and the provisions of this title relating to such sections. Thereafter, no person is entitled to any such right or equivalent right in any work of visual art under the common law or statutes of any State.

(2) Nothing in paragraph (1) annuls or limits any rights or remedies under the common law or statutes of any State with respect to—

(A) any cause of action from undertakings commenced before the effective date set forth in section 610(a) of the Visual Artists Rights Act of 1990;

(B) activities violating legal or equitable rights that are not equivalent to any of the rights conferred by section 106A with respect to works of visual art; or

(C) activities violating legal or equitable rights which extend beyond the life of the author.

§ 302. Duration of copyright: Works created on or after January 1, 1978

(a) In General. Copyright in a work created on or after January 1, 1978, subsists from its creation and, except as provided by the following subsections, endures for a term consisting of the life of the author and 70 years after the author's death.

(b) Joint Works. In the case of a joint work prepared by two or more authors who did not work for hire, the copyright endures for a term consisting of the life of the last surviving author and 70 years after such last surviving author's death.

(c) Anonymous Works, Pseudonymous Works, and Works Made for Hire. In the case of an anonymous work, a pseudonymous work, or a work made for hire, the copyright endures for a term of 95 years from the year of its first publication, or a term of 120 years from the year of its creation, whichever expires first. If, before the end of such term, the identity of one or more of the authors of an anonymous or pseudonymous work is revealed in the records of a registration made for that work under subsections (a) or (d) of section 408, or in the records provided by this subsection, the copyright in the work endures for the term specified by subsection (a) or (b), based on the life of the author or authors whose identity has been revealed. Any person having an interest in the copyright in an anonymous or pseudonymous work may at any time record, in records to be maintained by the Copyright Office for that purpose, a statement identifying one or more authors of the work; the statement shall also identify the person filing it, the nature of that person's interest, the source of the information recorded, and the particular work affected, and shall comply in form and content with requirements that the Register of Copyrights shall prescribe by regulation.

(d) Records Relating to Death of Authors. Any person having an interest in a copyright may at any time record in the Copyright Office a statement of the date of death of the author of the copyrighted work, or a statement that the author is still living on a particular date. The statement shall identify the person filing it, the nature of that person's interest, and the source of the information recorded, and shall comply in form and content with requirements that the Register of Copyrights shall prescribe by regulation. The Register shall maintain current records of information relating to the death of authors of copyrighted works, based on such recorded statements and, to the extent the Register considers practicable, on data contained in any of the records of the Copyright Office or in other reference sources.

(e) Presumption as to Author's Death. After a period of 95 years from the year of first publication of a work, or a period of 120 years from the year of its creation, whichever expires first, any person who obtains from the Copyright Office a certified report that the records provided by subsection (d) disclose nothing to indicate that the author of the work is living, or died less than 70 years before, is entitled to the benefit of a presumption that the author has been dead for at least 70 years. Reliance in good faith upon this presumption shall be a complete defense to any action for infringement under this title.

§ 303. Duration of copyright: Works created but not published or copyrighted before January 1, 1978

(a) Copyright in a work created before January 1, 1978, but not theretofore in the public domain or copyrighted, subsists from January 1, 1978, and endures for the term provided by section 302. In no case, however, shall the term of copyright in such a work expire before December 31, 2002; and, if the work is published on or before December 31, 2002, the term of copyright shall not expire before December 31, 2047.

(b) The distribution before January 1, 1978, of a phonorecord shall not for any purpose constitute a publication of the musical work embodied therein.

§ 304. Duration of copyright: Subsisting copyrights

(a) Copyrights in Their First Term on January 1, 1978.

(1)(A) Any copyright, in the first term of which is subsisting on January 1, 1978, shall endure for 28 years from the date it was originally secured.

(B) In the case of—

(i) any posthumous work or of any periodical, cyclopedic, or other composite work upon which the copyright was originally secured by the proprietor thereof, or

(ii) any work copyrighted by a corporate body (otherwise than as assignee or licensee of the individual author) or by an employer for whom such work is made for hire,

the proprietor of such copyright shall be entitled to a renewal and extension of the copyright in such work for the further term of 67 years.

(C) In the case of any other copyrighted work, including a contribution by an individual author to a periodical or to a cyclopedic or other composite work—

(i) the author of such work, if the author is still living,

(ii) the widow, widower, or children of the author, if the author is not living,

(iii) the author's executors, if such author, widow, widower, or children are not living, or

(iv) the author's next of kin, in the absence of a will of the author, shall be entitled to a renewal and extension of the copyright in such work for a further term of 67 years.

(2)(A) At the expiration of the original term of copyright in a work specified in paragraph (1)(B) of this subsection, the copyright shall endure for a renewed and extended further term of 67 years, which—

(i) if an application to register a claim to such further term has been made to the Copyright Office within 1 year before the expiration of the original term of copyright, and the claim is registered, shall vest, upon the beginning of such further term, in the proprietor of the copyright who is entitled to claim the renewal of copyright at the time the application is made; or

(ii) if no such application is made or the claim pursuant to such application is not registered, shall vest, upon the beginning of such further term, in the person or entity that was the proprietor of the copyright as of the last day of the original term of copyright.

(B) At the expiration of the original term of copyright in a work specified in paragraph (1)(C) of this subsection, the copyright shall endure for a renewed and extended further term of 67 years, which—

(i) if an application to register a claim to such further term has been made to the Copyright Office within 1 year before the expiration of the original term of copyright, and the claim is registered, shall vest, upon the beginning of such further term, in any person who is entitled under paragraph

(1)(C) to the renewal and extension of the copyright at the time the application is made; or

(ii) if no such application is made or the claim pursuant to such application is not registered, shall vest, upon the beginning of such further term, in any person entitled under paragraph (1)(C), as of the last day of the original term of copyright, to the renewal and extension of the copyright.

(3)(A) An application to register a claim to the renewed and extended term of copyright in a work may be made to the Copyright Office—

(i) within 1 year before the expiration of the original term of copyright by any person entitled under paragraph (1)(B) or (C) to such further term of 67 years; and

(ii) at any time during the renewed and extended term by any person in whom such further term vested, under paragraph (2)(A) or (B), or by any successor or assign of such person, if the application is made in the name of such person.

(B) Such an application is not a condition of the renewal and extension of the copyright in a work for a further term of 67 years.

(4)(A) If an application to register a claim to the renewed and extended term of copyright in a work is not made within 1 year before the expiration of the original term of copyright in a work, or if the claim pursuant to such application is not registered, then a derivative work prepared under authority of a grant of a transfer or license of the copyright that is made before the expiration of the original term of copyright may continue to be used under the terms of the grant during the renewed and extended term of copyright without infringing the copyright, except that such use does not extend to the preparation during such renewed and extended term of other derivative works based upon the copyrighted work covered by such grant.

(B) If an application to register a claim to the renewed and extended term of copyright in a work is made within 1 year before its expiration, and the claim is registered, the certificate of such registration shall constitute prima facie evidence as to the validity of the copyright during its renewed and extended term and of the facts stated in the certificate. The evidentiary weight to be accorded the certificates of a registration of a renewed and extended term of copyright made after the end of that 1–year period shall be within the discretion of the court.*

* **Editor's note**: Congress, in revising section 304(a) effective June 26, 1992, stated the following with respect to the effective date of this new renewal provision: "The amendments made by this section shall apply only to those copyrights secured between January 1, 1964, and December 31, 1977. Copyrights secured before January 1, 1964, shall be governed by the provisions of section 304(a) of title 17, United States Code, as in effect on the day before the effective date of this section." Pub. L. 102–307, § 102(g)(2). The text of section 304(a) as enacted in 1976, which thus governs works that were in their

(b) Copyrights in Their Renewal Term at the Time of the Effective Date of the Sonny Bono Copyright Term Extension Act. Any copyright still in its renewal term at the time that the Sonny Bono Copyright Term Extension Act becomes effective shall have a copyright term of 95 years from the date copyright was originally secured.

(c) Termination of Transfers and Licenses Covering Extended Renewal Term. In the case of any copyright subsisting in either its first or renewal term on January 1, 1978, other than a copyright in a work made for hire, the exclusive or nonexclusive grant of a transfer or license of the renewal copyright or any right under it, executed before January 1, 1978, by any of the persons designated by subsection (a)(1)(C) of this section, otherwise than by will, is subject to termination under the following conditions:

(1) In the case of a grant executed by a person or persons other than the author, termination of the grant may be effected by the surviving person or persons who executed it. In the case of a grant executed by one or more of the authors of the work, termination of the grant may be effected, to the extent of a particular author's share in the ownership of the renewal copyright, by the author who executed it or, if such author is dead, by the person or persons who, under clause (2) of this subsection, own and are entitled to exercise a total of more than one-half of that author's termination interest.

(2) Where an author is dead, his or her termination interest is owned, and may be exercised, as follows:

(A) The widow or widower owns the author's entire termination interest unless there are any surviving children or grand-

first term of copyright prior to January 1, 1964, and which thus would have to be renewed before the end of 1991, was as follows:

(a) Copyrights in their first term on January 1, 1978. Any copyright, the first term of which is subsisting on January 1, 1978, shall endure for twenty–eight years from the date it was originally secured: *Provided,* That in the case of any posthumous work or of any periodical, cyclopedic, or other composite work upon which the copyright was originally secured by the proprietor thereof, or of any work copyrighted by a corporate body (otherwise than as assignee or licensee of the individual author) or by an employer for whom such work is made for hire, the proprietor of such copyright shall be entitled to a renewal and extension of the copyright in such work for the further term of forty–seven years when application for such renewal and extension shall have been made to the Copyright Office and duly registered therein within one year prior to the expiration of the original

term of copyright: *And provided further,* That in the case of any other copyrighted work, including a contribution by an individual author to a periodical or to a cyclopedic or other composite work, the author of such work, if still living, or the widow, widower, or children of the author, if the author be not living, or if such author, widow, widower, or children be not living, then the author's executors, or in the absence of a will, his or her next of kin shall be entitled to a renewal and extension of the copyright in such work for a further term of forty–seven years when application for such renewal and extension shall have been made to the Copyright Office and duly registered therein within one year prior to the expiration of the original term of copyright: *And provided further,* That in default of the registration of such application for renewal and extension, the copyright in any work shall terminate at the expiration of twenty–eight years from the date copyright was originally secured.

children of the author, in which case the widow or widower owns one-half of the author's interest.

(B) The author's surviving children, and the surviving children of any dead child of the author, own the author's entire termination interest unless there is a widow or widower, in which case the ownership of one-half of the author's interest is divided among them.

(C) The rights of the author's children and grandchildren are in all cases divided among them and exercised on a per stirpes basis according to the number of such author's children represented; the share of the children of a dead child in a termination interest can be exercised only by the action of a majority of them.

(D) In the event that the author's widow or widower, children, and grandchildren are not living, the author's executor, administrator, personal representative, or trustee shall own the author's entire termination interest.

(3) Termination of the grant may be effected at any time during a period of five years beginning at the end of fifty-six years from the date copyright was originally secured, or beginning on January 1, 1978, whichever is later.

(4) The termination shall be effected by serving an advance notice in writing upon the grantee or the grantee's successor in title. In the case of a grant executed by a person or persons other than the author, the notice shall be signed by all of those entitled to terminate the grant under clause (1) of this subsection, or by their duly authorized agents. In the case of a grant executed by one or more of the authors of the work, the notice as to any one author's share shall be signed by that author or his or her duly authorized agent or, if that author is dead, by the number and proportion of the owners of his or her termination interest required under clauses (1) and (2) of this subsection, or by their duly authorized agents.

(A) The notice shall state the effective date of the termination, which shall fall within the five-year period specified by clause (3) of this subsection, or, in the case of a termination under subsection (d), within the five-year period specified by subsection (d)(2), and the notice shall be served not less than two or more than ten years before that date. A copy of the notice shall be recorded in the Copyright Office before the effective date of termination, as a condition to its taking effect.

(B) The notice shall comply, in form, content, and manner of service, with requirements that the Register of Copyrights shall prescribe by regulation.

(5) Termination of the grant may be effected notwithstanding any agreement to the contrary, including an agreement to make a will or to make any future grant.

(6) In the case of a grant executed by a person or persons other than the author, all rights under this title that were covered by the terminated grant revert, upon the effective date of termination, to all of those entitled to terminate the grant under clause (1) of this subsection. In the case of a grant executed by one or more of the authors of the work, all of a particular author's rights under this title that were covered by the terminated grant revert, upon the effective date of termination, to that author or, if that author is dead, to the persons owning his or her termination interest under clause (2) of this subsection, including those owners who did not join in signing the notice of termination under clause (4) of this subsection. In all cases the reversion of rights is subject to the following limitations:

(A) A derivative work prepared under authority of the grant before its termination may continue to be utilized under the terms of the grant after its termination, but this privilege does not extend to the preparation after the termination of other derivative works based upon the copyrighted work covered by the terminated grant.

(B) The future rights that will revert upon termination of the grant become vested on the date the notice of termination has been served as provided by clause (4) of this subsection.

(C) Where the author's rights revert to two or more persons under clause (2) of this subsection, they shall vest in those persons in the proportionate shares provided by that clause. In such a case, and subject to the provisions of subclause (D) of this clause, a further grant, or agreement to make a further grant, of a particular author's share with respect to any right covered by a terminated grant is valid only if it is signed by the same number and proportion of the owners, in whom the right has vested under this clause, as are required to terminate the grant under clause (2) of this subsection. Such further grant or agreement is effective with respect to all of the persons in whom the right it covers has vested under this subclause, including those who did not join in signing it. If any person dies after rights under a terminated grant have vested in him or her, that person's legal representatives, legatees, or heirs at law represent him or her for purposes of this subclause.

(D) A further grant, or agreement to make a further grant, of any right covered by a terminated grant is valid only if it is made after the effective date of the termination. As an exception, however, an agreement for such a further grant may be made between the author or any of the persons provided by the first sentence of clause (6) of this subsection, or between the persons provided by subclause (C) of this clause, and the original grantee or such grantee's successor in title, after the notice of termination has been served as provided by clause (4) of this subsection.

(E) Termination of a grant under this subsection affects only those rights covered by the grant that arise under this title, and in

329

no way affects rights arising under any other Federal, State, or foreign laws.

(F) Unless and until termination is effected under this subsection, the grant, if it does not provide otherwise, continues in effect for the remainder of the extended renewal term.

(d) Termination Rights Provided in Subsection (c) Which Have Expired on or before the Effective Date of the Sonny Bono Copyright Term Extension Act. In the case of any copyright other than a work made for hire, subsisting in its renewal term on the effective date of the Sonny Bono Copyright Term Extension Act for which the termination right provided in subsection (c) has expired by such date, where the author or owner of the termination right has not previously exercised such termination right, the exclusive or nonexclusive grant of a transfer or license of the renewal copyright or any right under it, executed before January 1, 1978, by any of the persons designated in subsection (a)(1)(C) of this section, other than by will, is subject to termination under the following conditions:

(1) The conditions specified in subsections (c)(1), (2), (4), (5), and (6) of this section apply to terminations of the last 20 years of copyright term as provided by the amendments made by the Sonny Bono Copyright Term Extension Act.

(2) Termination of the grant may be effected at any time during a period of 5 years beginning at the end of 75 years from the date copyright was originally secured.

§ 305. Duration of copyright: Terminal date

All terms of copyright provided by sections 302 through 304 run to the end of the calendar year in which they would otherwise expire.

CHAPTER 4—COPYRIGHT NOTICE, DEPOSIT, AND REGISTRATION

§ 401. Notice of copyright: Visually perceptible copies

(a) **General Provisions.** Whenever a work protected under this title is published in the United States or elsewhere by authority of the copyright owner, a notice of copyright as provided by this section may be placed on publicly distributed copies from which the work can be visually perceived, either directly or with the aid of a machine or device.

(b) **Form of Notice.** If a notice appears on the copies, it shall consist of the following three elements:

(1) the symbol © (the letter C in a circle), or the word "Copyright", or the abbreviation "Copr."; and

(2) the year of first publication of the work; in the case of compilations or derivative works incorporating previously published material, the year date of first publication of the compilation or derivative work is sufficient. The year date may be omitted where a pictorial, graphic, or sculptural work, with accompanying text matter, if any, is reproduced in or on greeting cards, postcards, stationery, jewelry, dolls, toys, or any useful articles; and

(3) the name of the owner of copyright in the work, or an abbreviation by which the name can be recognized, or a generally known alternative designation of the owner.

(c) **Position of Notice.** The notice shall be affixed to the copies in such manner and location as to give reasonable notice of the claim of copyright. The Register of Copyrights shall prescribe by regulation, as examples, specific methods of affixation and positions of the notice on various types of works that will satisfy this requirement, but these specifications shall not be considered exhaustive.

(d) **Evidentiary Weight of Notice.** If a notice of copyright in the form and position specified by this section appears on the published copy or copies to which a defendant in a copyright infringement suit had access, then no weight shall be given to such a defendant's interposition of a defense based on innocent infringement in mitigation of actual or statutory damages, except as provided in the last sentence of section 504(c)(2).

§ 402. Notice of copyright: Phonorecords of sound recordings

(a) General Provisions. Whenever a sound recording protected under this title is published in the United States or elsewhere by authority of the copyright owner, a notice of copyright as provided by this section may be placed on publicly distributed phonorecords of the sound recording.

(b) Form of Notice. If a notice appears on the phonorecords, it shall consist of the following three elements:

(1) the symbol ℗ ; and

(2) the year of first publication of the sound recording; and

(3) the name of the owner of copyright in the sound recording, or an abbreviation by which the name can be recognized, or a generally known alternative designation of the owner; if the producer of the sound recording is named on the phonorecord labels or containers, and if no other name appears in conjunction with the notice, the producer's name shall be considered a part of the notice.

(c) Position of Notice. The notice shall be placed on the surface of the phonorecord, or on the phonorecord label or container, in such manner and location as to give reasonable notice of the claim of copyright.

(d) Evidentiary Weight of Notice. If a notice of copyright in the form and position specified by this section appears on the published phonorecord or phonorecords to which a defendant in a copyright infringement suit had access, then no weight shall be given to such a defendant's interposition of a defense based on innocent infringement in mitigation of actual or statutory damages, except as provided in the last sentence of section 504(c)(2).

§ 403. Notice of copyright: Publications incorporating United States Government works

Sections 401(d) and 402(d) shall not apply to a work published in copies or phonorecords consisting predominantly of one or more works of the United States Government unless the notice of copyright appearing on the published copies or phonorecords to which a defendant in the copyright infringement suit had access includes a statement identifying, either affirmatively or negatively, those portions of the copies or phonorecords embodying any work or works protected under this title.

§ 404. Notice of copyright: Contributions to collective works

(a) A separate contribution to a collective work may bear its own notice of copyright, as provided by sections 401 through 403. However, a single notice applicable to the collective work as a whole is sufficient to invoke the provisions of section 401(d) or 402(d), as applicable with respect to the separate contributions it contains (not including advertisements inserted on behalf of persons other than the owner of copyright in the collective work), regardless of the ownership of copyright in the contributions and whether or not they have been previously published.

(b) With respect to copies and phonorecords publicly distributed by authority of the copyright owner before the effective date of the Berne Convention Implementation Act of 1988, where the person named in a single notice applicable to a collective work as a whole is not the owner of copyright in a separate contribution that does not bear its own notice, the case is governed by the provisions of section 406(a).

§ 405. Notice of copyright: Omission of notice on certain copies and phonorecords

(a) **Effect of Omission on Copyright.** With respect to copies and phonorecords publicly distributed by authority of the copyright owner before the effective date of the Berne Convention Implementation Act of 1988, the omission of the copyright notice described in sections 401 through 403 from copies or phonorecords publicly distributed by authority of the copyright owner does not invalidate the copyright in a work if—

(1) the notice has been omitted from no more than a relatively small number of copies or phonorecords distributed to the public; or

(2) registration for the work has been made before or is made within five years after the publication without notice, and a reasonable effort is made to add notice to all copies or phonorecords that are distributed to the public in the United States after the omission has been discovered; or

(3) the notice has been omitted in violation of an express requirement in writing that, as a condition of the copyright owner's authorization of the public distribution of copies or phonorecords, they bear the prescribed notice.

(b) **Effect of Omission on Innocent Infringers.** Any person who innocently infringes a copyright, in reliance upon an authorized copy or phonorecord from which the copyright notice has been omitted and which was publicly distributed by authority of the copyright owner before the effective date of the Berne Convention Implementation Act of 1988, incurs no liability for actual or statutory damages under section 504 for any infringing acts committed before receiving actual notice that registration for the work has been made under section 408, if such person proves that he or she was misled by the omission of notice. In a suit for infringement in such a case the court may allow or disallow recovery of any of the infringer's profits attributable to the infringement, and may enjoin the continuation of the infringing undertaking or may require, as a condition for permitting the continuation of the infringing undertaking, that the infringer pay the copyright owner a reasonable license fee in an amount and on terms fixed by the court.

333

(c) Removal of Notice. Protection under this title is not affected by the removal, destruction, or obliteration of the notice, without the authorization of the copyright owner, from any publicly distributed copies or phonorecords.

§ 406. Notice of copyright: Error in name or date on certain copies and phonorecords

(a) Error in Name. With respect to copies and phonorecords publicly distributed by authority of the copyright owner before the effective date of the Berne Convention Implementation Act of 1988, where the person named in the copyright notice on copies or phonorecords publicly distributed by authority of the copyright owner is not the owner of copyright, the validity and ownership of the copyright are not affected. In such a case, however, any person who innocently begins an undertaking that infringes the copyright has a complete defense to any action for such infringement if such person proves that he or she was misled by the notice and began the undertaking in good faith under a purported transfer or license from the person named therein, unless before the undertaking was begun-

(1) registration for the work had been made in the name of the owner of copyright; or

(2) a document executed by the person named in the notice and showing the ownership of the copyright had been recorded.

The person named in the notice is liable to account to the copyright owner for all receipts from transfers or licenses purportedly made under the copyright by the person named in the notice.

(b) Error in Date. When the year date in the notice on copies or phonorecords distributed before the effective date of the Berne Convention Implementation Act of 1988 by authority of the copyright owner is earlier than the year in which publication first occurred, any period computed from the year of first publication under section 302 is to be computed from the year in the notice. Where the year date is more than one year later than the year in which publication first occurred, the work is considered to have been published without any notice and is governed by the provisions of section 405.

(c) Omission of Name or Date. Where copies or phonorecords publicly distributed before the effective date of the Berne Convention Implementation Act of 1988 by authority of the copyright owner contain no name or no date that could reasonably be considered a part of the notice, the work is considered to have been published without any notice and is governed by the provisions of section 405 as in effect on the day before the effective date of the Berne Convention Implementation Act of 1988.

§ 407. Deposit of copies or phonorecords for Library of Congress

(a) Except as provided by subsection (c), and subject to the provisions of subsection (e), the owner of copyright or of the exclusive right of publication in a work published in the United States shall deposit, within three months after the date of such publication—

(1) two complete copies of the best edition; or

(2) if the work is a sound recording, two complete phonorecords of the best edition, together with any printed or other visually perceptible material published with such phonorecords.

Neither the deposit requirements of this subsection nor the acquisition provisions of subsection (e) are conditions of copyright protection.

(b) The required copies or phonorecords shall be deposited in the Copyright Office for the use or disposition of the Library of Congress. The Register of Copyrights shall, when requested by the depositor and upon payment of the fee prescribed by section 708, issue a receipt for the deposit.

(c) The Register of Copyrights may by regulation exempt any categories of material from the deposit requirements of this section, or require deposit of only one copy or phonorecord with respect to any categories. Such regulations shall provide either for complete exemption from the deposit requirements of this section, or for alternative forms of deposit aimed at providing a satisfactory archival record of a work without imposing practical or financial hardships on the depositor, where the individual author is the owner of copyright in a pictorial, graphic, or sculptural work and (i) less than five copies of the work have been published, or (ii) the work has been published in a limited edition consisting of numbered copies, the monetary value of which would make the mandatory deposit of two copies of the best edition of the work burdensome, unfair, or unreasonable.

(d) At any time after publication of a work as provided by subsection(a), the Register of Copyrights may make written demand for the required deposit on any of the persons obligated to make the deposit under subsection (a). Unless deposit is made within three months after the demand is received, the person or persons on whom the demand was made are liable—

(1) to a fine of not more than $250 for each work; and

(2) to pay into a specially designated fund in the Library of Congress the total retail price of the copies or phonorecords demanded, or, if no retail price has been fixed, the reasonable cost to the Library of Congress of acquiring them; and

(3) to pay a fine of $2,500, in addition to any fine or liability imposed under clauses (1) and (2), if such person willfully or repeatedly fails or refuses to comply with such a demand.

(e) With respect to transmission programs that have been fixed and transmitted to the public in the United States but have not been published, the Register of Copyrights shall, after consulting with the Librarian of Congress and other interested organizations and officials, establish regulations governing the acquisition, through deposit or otherwise, of copies or phonorecords of such programs for the collections of the Library of Congress.

(1) The Librarian of Congress shall be permitted, under the standards and conditions set forth in such regulations, to make a fixation of a transmission program directly from a transmission to the public, and to reproduce one copy or phonorecord from such fixation for archival purposes.

(2) Such regulations shall also provide standards and procedures by which the Register of Copyrights may make written demand, upon the owner of the right of transmission in the United States, for the deposit of a copy or phonorecord of a specific transmission program. Such deposit may, at the option of the owner of the right of transmission in the United States, be accomplished by gift, by loan for purposes of reproduction, or by sale at a price not to exceed the cost of reproducing and supplying the copy or phonorecord. The regulations established under this clause shall provide reasonable periods of not less than three months for compliance with a demand, and shall allow for extensions of such periods and adjustments in the scope of the demand or the methods for fulfilling it, as reasonably warranted by the circumstances. Willful failure or refusal to comply with the conditions prescribed by such regulations shall subject the owner of the right of transmission in the United States to liability for an amount, not to exceed the cost of reproducing and supplying the copy or phonorecord in question, to be paid into a specially designated fund in the Library of Congress.

(3) Nothing in this subsection shall be construed to require the making or retention, for purposes of deposit, of any copy or phonorecord of an unpublished transmission program, the transmission of which occurs before the receipt of a specific written demand as provided by clause (2).

(4) No activity undertaken in compliance with regulations prescribed under clauses (1) and (2) of this subsection shall result in liability if intended solely to assist in the acquisition of copies or phonorecords under this subsection.

§ 408. Copyright registration in general

(a) **Registration Permissive.** At any time during the subsistence of the first term of copyright in any published or unpublished work in which the copyright was secured before January 1, 1978, and during the subsistence of any copyright secured on or after that date, the owner of copyright or of any exclusive right in the work may obtain registration of the copyright claim by delivering to the Copyright Office the deposit specified by this section, together with the application and fee specified by sections 409 and 708. Such registration is not a condition of copyright protection.

(b) **Deposit for Copyright Registration.** Except as provided by subsection (c), the material deposited for registration shall include—

(1) in the case of an unpublished work, one complete copy or phonorecord;

(2) in the case of a published work, two complete copies or phonorecords of the best edition;

(3) in the case of a work first published outside the United States, one complete copy or phonorecord as so published;

(4) in the case of a contribution to a collective work, one complete copy or phonorecord of the best edition of the collective work.

Copies or phonorecords deposited for the Library of Congress under section 407 may be used to satisfy the deposit provisions of this section, if they are accompanied by the prescribed application and fee, and by any additional identifying material that the Register may, by regulation, require. The Register shall also prescribe regulations establishing requirements under which copies or phonorecords acquired for the Library of Congress under subsection (e) of section 407, otherwise than by deposit, may be used to satisfy the deposit provisions of this section.

(c) Administrative Classification and Optional Deposit.

(1) The Register of Copyrights is authorized to specify by regulation the administrative classes into which works are to be placed for purposes of deposit and registration, and the nature of the copies or phonorecords to be deposited in the various classes specified. The regulations may require or permit, for particular classes, the deposit of identifying material instead of copies or phonorecords, the deposit of only one copy or phonorecord where two would normally be required, or a single registration for a group of related works. This administrative classification of works has no significance with respect to the subject matter of copyright or the exclusive rights provided by this title.

(2) Without prejudice to the general authority provided under clause (1), the Register of Copyrights shall establish regulations specifically permitting a single registration for a group of works by the same individual author, all first published as contributions to periodicals, including newspapers, within a twelve-month period, on the basis of a single deposit, application, and registration fee, under the following conditions—

(A) if the deposit consists of one copy of the entire issue of the periodical, or of the entire section in the case of a newspaper, in which each contribution was first published; and

(B) if the application identifies each work separately, including the periodical containing it and its date of first publication.

(3) As an alternative to separate renewal registrations under subsection (a) of section 304, a single renewal registration may be made for a group of works by the same individual author, all first published as contributions to periodicals, including newspapers, upon the filing of a single application and fee, under all of the following conditions:

(A) the renewal claimant or claimants, and the basis of claim or claims under section 304(a), is the same for each of the works; and

(B) the works were all copyrighted upon their first publication, either through separate copyright notice and registration or by virtue of a general copyright notice in the periodical issue as a whole; and

(C) the renewal application and fee are received not more than twenty-eight or less than twenty-seven years after the thirty-first day of December of the calendar year in which all of the works were first published; and

(D) the renewal application identifies each work separately, including the periodical containing it and its date of first publication.

(d) Corrections and Amplifications. The Register may also establish, by regulation, formal procedures for the filing of an application for supplementary registration, to correct an error in a copyright registration or to amplify the information given in a registration. Such application shall be accompanied by the fee provided by section 708, and shall clearly identify the registration to be corrected or amplified. The information contained in a supplementary registration augments but does not supersede that contained in the earlier registration.

(e) Published Edition of Previously Registered Work. Registration for the first published edition of a work previously registered in unpublished form may be made even though the work as published is substantially the same as the unpublished version.

§ 409. Application for copyright registration

The application for copyright registration shall be made on a form prescribed by the Register of Copyrights and shall include—

(1) the name and address of the copyright claimant;

(2) in the case of a work other than an anonymous or pseudonymous work, the name and nationality or domicile of the author or authors, and, if one or more of the authors is dead, the dates of their deaths;

(3) if the work is anonymous or pseudonymous, the nationality or domicile of the author or authors;

(4) in the case of a work made for hire, a statement to this effect;

(5) if the copyright claimant is not the author, a brief statement of how the claimant obtained ownership of the copyright;

(6) the title of the work, together with any previous or alternative titles under which the work can be identified;

(7) the year in which creation of the work was completed;

(8) if the work has been published, the date and nation of its first publication;

(9) in the case of a compilation or derivative work, an identification of any preexisting work or works that it is based on or incorporates, and a brief, general statement of the additional material covered by the copyright claim being registered;

(10) in the case of a published work containing material of which copies are required by section 601 to be manufactured in the United States, the names of the persons or organizations who performed the processes specified by subsection (c) of section 601 with respect to that material, and the places where those processes were performed; and

(11) any other information regarded by the Register of Copyrights as bearing upon the preparation or identification of the work or the existence, ownership, or duration of the copyright.

If an application is submitted for the renewed and extended term provided for in section 304(a)(3)(A) and an original term registration has not been made, the Register may request information with respect to the existence, ownership, or duration of the copyright for the original term.

§ 410.   Registration of claim and issuance of certificate

(a) When, after examination, the Register of Copyrights determines that, in accordance with the provisions of this title, the material deposited constitutes copyrightable subject matter and that the other legal and formal requirements of this title have been met, the Register shall register the claim and issue to the applicant a certificate of registration under the seal of the Copyright Office. The certificate shall contain the information given in the application, together with the number and effective date of the registration.

(b) In any case in which the Register of Copyrights determines that, in accordance with the provisions of this title, the material deposited does not constitute copyrightable subject matter or that the claim is invalid for any other reason, the Register shall refuse registration and shall notify the applicant in writing of the reasons for such refusal.

(c) In any judicial proceedings the certificate of a registration made before or within five years after first publication of the work shall constitute *prima facie* evidence of the validity of the copyright and of the facts stated in the certificate. The evidentiary weight to be accorded the certificate of a registration made thereafter shall be within the discretion of the court.

(d) The effective date of a copyright registration is the day on which an application, deposit, and fee, which are later determined by the Register of Copyrights or by a court of competent jurisdiction to be acceptable for registration, have all been received in the Copyright Office.

§ 411. Registration and infringement actions

(a) Except for an action brought for a violation of the rights of the author under section 106A(a), and subject to the provisions of subsection (b), no action for infringement of the copyright in any United States work shall be instituted until registration of the copyright claim has been made in accordance with this title. In any case, however, where the deposit, application, and fee required for registration have been delivered to the Copyright Office in proper form and registration has been refused, the applicant is entitled to institute an action for infringement if notice thereof, with a copy of the complaint, is served on the Register of Copyrights. The Register may, at his or her option, become a party to the action with respect to the issue of registrability of the copyright claim by entering an appearance within sixty days after such service, but the Register's failure to become a party shall not deprive the court of jurisdiction to determine that issue.

(b) In the case of a work consisting of sounds, images, or both, the first fixation of which is made simultaneously with its transmission, the copyright owner may, either before or after such fixation takes place, institute an action for infringement under section 501, fully subject to the remedies provided by sections 502 through 506 and sections 509 and 510, if, in accordance with requirements that the Register of Copyrights shall prescribe by regulation, the copyright owner—

(1) serves notice upon the infringer, not less than 48 hours before such fixation, identifying the work and the specific time and source of its first transmission, and declaring an intention to secure copyright in the work; and

(2) makes registration for the work, if required by subsection (a), within three months after its first transmission.

§ 412. Registration as prerequisite to certain remedies for infringement

In any action under this title, other than an action brought for a violation of the rights of the author under section 106A(a) or an action instituted under section 411(b), no award of statutory damages or of attorney's fees, as provided by sections 504 and 505, shall be made for—

(1) any infringement of copyright in an unpublished work commenced before the effective date of its registration; or

(2) any infringement of copyright commenced after first publication of the work and before the effective date of its registration, unless such registration is made within three months after the first publication of the work.

CHAPTER 5—COPYRIGHT INFRINGEMENT AND REMEDIES

§ 501. Infringement of copyright

(a) Anyone who violates any of the exclusive rights of the copyright owner as provided by sections 106 through 122 or of the author as provided in section 106A(a), or who imports copies or phonorecords into the United States in violation of section 602, is an infringer of the copyright or right of the author, as the case may be. For purposes of this chapter (other than section 506), any reference to copyright shall be deemed to include the rights conferred by section 106A(a). As used in this subsection, the term "anyone" includes any State, any instrumentality of a State, and any officer or employee of a State or instrumentality of a State acting in his or her official capacity. Any State, and any such instrumentality, officer, or employee, shall be subject to the provisions of this title in the same manner and to the same extent as any nongovernmental entity.

(b) The legal or beneficial owner of an exclusive right under a copyright is entitled, subject to the requirements of section 411, to institute an action for any infringement of that particular right committed while he or she is the owner of it. The court may require such owner to serve written notice of the action with a copy of the complaint upon any person shown, by the records of the Copyright Office or otherwise, to have or claim an interest in the copyright, and shall require that such notice be served upon any person whose interest is likely to be affected by a decision in the case. The court may require the joinder, and shall permit the intervention, of any person having or claiming an interest in the copyright.

(c) For any secondary transmission by a cable system that embodies a performance or a display of a work which is actionable as an act of infringement under subsection (c) of section 111, a television broadcast station holding a copyright or other license to transmit or perform the same version of that work shall, for purposes of subsection (b) of this section, be treated as a legal or beneficial owner if such secondary transmission occurs within the local service area of that television station.

(d) For any secondary transmission by a cable system that is actionable as an act of infringement pursuant to section 111(c)(3), the following shall also have standing to sue: (i) the primary transmitter whose transmission has been altered by the cable system; and (ii) any broadcast station within whose local service area the secondary transmission occurs.

(e) With respect to any secondary transmission that is made by a satellite carrier of a performance or display of a work embodied in a primary transmission and is actionable as an act of infringement under section 119(a)(5), a network station holding a copyright or other license to transmit or perform the same version of that work shall, for purposes of subsection (b) of this section, be treated as a legal or beneficial owner if such secondary transmission occurs within the local service area of that station.

(f)(1) With respect to any secondary transmission that is made by a satellite carrier of a performance or display of a work embodied in a primary transmission and is actionable as an act of infringement under section 122, a television broadcast station holding a copyright or other license to transmit or perform the same version of that work shall, for purposes of subsection (b) of this section, be treated as a legal or beneficial owner if such secondary transmission occurs within the local market of that station.

(2) A television broadcast station may file a civil action against any satellite carrier that has refused to carry television broadcast signals, as required under section 122(a)(2), to enforce that television broadcast station's rights under section 338(a) of the Communications Act of 1934.

§ 502. Remedies for infringement: Injunctions

(a) Any court having jurisdiction of a civil action arising under this title may, subject to the provisions of section 1498 of title 28, grant temporary and final injunctions on such terms as it may deem reasonable to prevent or restrain infringement of a copyright.

(b) Any such injunction may be served anywhere in the United States on the person enjoined; it shall be operative throughout the United States and shall be enforceable, by proceedings in contempt or otherwise, by any United States court having jurisdiction of that person. The clerk of the court granting the injunction shall, when requested by any other court in which enforcement of the injunction is sought, transmit promptly to the other court a certified copy of all the papers in the case on file in such clerk's office.

§ 503. Remedies for infringement: Impounding and disposition of infringing articles

(a) At any time while an action under this title is pending, the court may order the impounding, on such terms as it may deem reasonable, of all copies or phonorecords claimed to have been made or used in violation of the copyright owner's exclusive rights, and of all plates, molds, matrices, masters, tapes, film negatives, or other articles by means of which such copies or phonorecords may be reproduced.

(b) As part of a final judgment or decree, the court may order the destruction or other reasonable disposition of all copies or phonorecords found to have been made or used in violation of the copyright owner's exclusive rights, and of all plates, molds, matrices, masters, tapes, film negatives, or other articles by means of which such copies or phonorecords may be reproduced.

§ 504. Remedies for infringement: Damages and profits

(a) **In General.** Except as otherwise provided by this title, an infringer of copyright is liable for either—

(1) the copyright owner's actual damages and any additional profits of the infringer, as provided by subsection (b); or

(2) statutory damages, as provided by subsection (c).

(b) **Actual Damages and Profits.** The copyright owner is entitled to recover the actual damages suffered by him or her as a result of the infringement, and any profits of the infringer that are attributable to the infringement and are not taken into account in computing the actual damages. In establishing the infringer's profits, the copyright owner is required to present proof only of the infringer's gross revenue, and the infringer is required to prove his or her deductible expenses and the elements of profit attributable to factors other than the copyrighted work.

(c) **Statutory Damages.**

(1) Except as provided by clause (2) of this subsection, the copyright owner may elect, at any time before final judgment is rendered, to recover, instead of actual damages and profits, an award of statutory damages for all infringements involved in the action, with respect to any one work, for which any one infringer is liable individually, or for which any two or more infringers are liable jointly and severally, in a sum of not less than $750 or more than $30,000 as the court considers just. For the purposes of this subsection, all the parts of a compilation or derivative work constitute one work.

(2) In a case where the copyright owner sustains the burden of proving, and the court finds, that infringement was committed willfully, the court in its discretion may increase the award of statutory damages to a sum of not more than $150,000. In a case where the infringer sustains the burden of proving, and the court finds, that such infringer was not aware and had no reason to believe that his or her acts constituted an infringement of copyright, the court in its discretion may reduce the award of statutory damages to a sum of not less than $200. The court shall remit statutory damages in any case where an infringer believed and had reasonable grounds for believing that his

or her use of the copyrighted work was a fair use under section 107, if the infringer was: (i) an employee or agent of a nonprofit educational institution, library, or archives acting within the scope of his or her employment who, or such institution, library, or archives itself, which infringed by reproducing the work in copies or phonorecords; or (ii) a public broadcasting entity which or a person who, as a regular part of the nonprofit activities of a public broadcasting entity (as defined in subsection (g) of section 118) infringed by performing a published nondramatic literary work or by reproducing a transmission program embodying a performance of such a work.

(d) Additional Damages in Certain Cases. In any case in which the court finds that a defendant proprietor of an establishment who claims as a defense that its activities were exempt under section 110(5) did not have reasonable grounds to believe that its use of a copyrighted work was exempt under such section, the plaintiff shall be entitled to, in addition to any award of damages under this section, an additional award of two times the amount of the license fee that the proprietor of the establishment concerned should have paid the plaintiff for such use during the preceding period of up to 3 years.

§ 505. Remedies for infringement: Costs and attorney's fees

In any civil action under this title, the court in its discretion may allow the recovery of full costs by or against any party other than the United States or an officer thereof. Except as otherwise provided by this title, the court may also award a reasonable attorney's fee to the prevailing party as part of the costs.

§ 506. Criminal offenses

(a) Criminal Infringement. Any person who infringes a copyright willfully either—

(1) for purposes of commercial advantage or private financial gain, or

(2) by the reproduction or distribution, including by electronic means, during any 180–day period, of 1 or more copies or phonorecords of 1 or more copyrighted works, which have a total retail value of more than $1,000,

shall be punished as provided under section 2319 of title 18, United States Code.* For purposes of this subsection, evidence of reproduction or distribution of a copyrighted work, by itself, shall not be sufficient to establish willful infringement.

* 18 U.S.C. § 2319 (Act of May 24, 1982—Pub. L. 97–180, amended Oct. 28, 1992, Pub. L. 102–561, 106 Stat. 4233; Dec. 16, 1997; Pub. L. 105–147.) reads as follows:

§ 2319. Criminal infringement of a copyright

(a) Whoever violates section 506(a) (relating to criminal offenses of title 17) shall be punished as provided in subsections (b) and (c) of this section and such penalties shall be in addition to any other provisions of title 17 or any other law.

(b) Any person who commits an offense under section 506(a)(1) of title 17—

(b) Forfeiture and Destruction. When any person is convicted of any violation of subsection (a), the court in its judgment of conviction shall, in addition to the penalty therein prescribed, order the forfeiture and destruction or other disposition of all infringing copies or phonorecords and all implements, devices, or equipment used in the manufacture of such infringing copies or phonorecords.

(c) Fraudulent Copyright Notice. Any person who, with fraudulent intent, places on any article a notice of copyright or words of the same purport that such person knows to be false, or who, with fraudulent intent, publicly distributes or imports for public distribution any article bearing such notice or words that such person knows to be false, shall be fined not more than $2,500.

(d) Fraudulent Removal of Copyright Notice. Any person who, with fraudulent intent, removes or alters any notice of copyright appearing on a copy of a copyrighted work shall be fined not more than $2,500.

(1) shall be imprisoned not more than 5 years, or fined in the amount set forth in this title, or both, if the offense consists of the reproduction or distribution including by electronic means, during any 180–day period, of at l[e]ast 10 copies or phonorecords, of 1 or more copyrighted works, which have a total retail value of more than $2,500;

(2) shall be imprisoned not more than 10 years, or fined in the amount set forth in this title, or both, if the offense is a second or subsequent offense under paragraph (1); and

(3) shall be imprisoned not more than 1 year, or fined in the amount set forth in this title, or both, in any other case.

(c) Any person who commits an offense under section 506(a)(2) of title 17, United States Code—

(1) shall be imprisoned not more than 3 years, or fined in the amount set forth in this title, or both, if the offense consists of the reproduction or distribution of 10 or more copies or phonorecords of 1 or more copyrighted works, which have a total retail value of $ 2,500 or more;

(2) shall be imprisoned not more than 6 years, or fined in the amount set forth in this title, or both, if the offense is a second or subsequent offense under paragraph (1); and

(3) shall be imprisoned not more than 1 year, or fined in the amount set forth in this title, or both, if the offense consists of the reproduction or distribution of 1 or more copies or phonorecords of 1 or more copyrighted works, which have a total retail value of more than $ 1,000.

(d)(1) During preparation of the presentence report pursuant to Rule 32(c) of the Federal Rules of Criminal Procedure, victims of the offense shall be permitted to submit, and the probation officer shall receive, a victim impact statement that identifies the victim of the offense and the extent and scope of the injury and loss suffered by the victim, including the estimated economic impact of the offense on that victim.

(2) Persons permitted to submit victim impact statements shall include—

(A) producers and sellers of legitimate works affected by conduct involved in the offense;

(B) holders of intellectual property rights in such works; and

(C) the legal representatives of such producers, sellers, and holders.

(e) As used in this section—

(1) the terms "phonorecord" and "copies" have, respectively, the meanings set forth in section 101 (relating to definitions) of title 17; and

(2) the terms "reproduction" and "distribution" refer to the exclusive rights of a copyright owner under clauses (1) and (3) respectively of section 106 (relating to exclusive rights in copyrighted works), as limited by sections 107 through 120, of title 17.

(e) False Representation. Any person who knowingly makes a false representation of a material fact in the application for copyright registration provided for by section 409, or in any written statement filed in connection with the application, shall be fined not more than $2,500.

(f) Rights of Attribution and Integrity. Nothing in this section applies to infringement of the rights conferred by section 106A(a).

§ 507. Limitations on actions

(a) Criminal Proceedings. Except as expressly provided otherwise in this title, no criminal proceeding shall be maintained under the provisions of this title unless it is commenced within 5 years after the cause of action arose.

(b) Civil Actions. No civil action shall be maintained under the provisions of this title unless it is commenced within three years after the claim accrued.

§ 508. Notification of filing and determination of actions

(a) Within one month after the filing of any action under this title, the clerks of the courts of the United States shall send written notification to the Register of Copyrights setting forth, as far as is shown by the papers filed in the court, the names and addresses of the parties and the title, author, and registration number of each work involved in the action. If any other copyrighted work is later included in the action by amendment, answer, or other pleading, the clerk shall also send a notification concerning it to the Register within one month after the pleading is filed.

(b) Within one month after any final order or judgment is issued in the case, the clerk of the court shall notify the Register of it, sending with the notification a copy of the order or judgment together with the written opinion, if any, of the court.

(c) Upon receiving the notifications specified in this section, the Register shall make them a part of the public records of the Copyright Office.

§ 509. Seizure and forfeiture

(a) All copies or phonorecords manufactured, reproduced, distributed, sold, or otherwise used, intended for use, or possessed with intent to use in violation of section 506 (a), and all plates, molds, matrices, masters, tapes, film negatives, or other articles by means of which such copies or phonorecords may be reproduced, and all electronic, mechanical, or other devices for manufacturing, reproducing, or assembling such copies or phonorecords may be seized and forfeited to the United States.

(b) The applicable procedures relating to

       (i) the seizure, summary and judicial forfeiture, and condemnation of vessels, vehicles, merchandise, and baggage for violations of the customs laws contained in title 19,

(ii) the disposition of such vessels, vehicles, merchandise, and baggage or the proceeds from the sale thereof,

(iii) the remission or mitigation of such forfeiture,

(iv) the compromise of claims, and

(v) the award of compensation to informers in respect of such forfeitures, shall apply to seizures and forfeitures incurred, or alleged to have been incurred, under the provisions of this section, insofar as applicable and not inconsistent with the provisions of this section; except that such duties as are imposed upon any officer or employee of the Treasury Department or any other person with respect to the seizure and forfeiture of vessels, vehicles, merchandise, and baggage under the provisions of the customs laws contained in title 19 shall be performed with respect to seizure and forfeiture of all articles described in subsection (a) by such officers, agents, or other persons as may be authorized or designated for that purpose by the Attorney General.

§ 510. Remedies for alteration of programming by cable systems

(a) In any action filed pursuant to section 111(c)(3), the following remedies shall be available:

(1) Where an action is brought by a party identified in subsections (b) or (c) of section 501, the remedies provided by sections 502 through 505, and the remedy provided by subsection (b) of this section; and

(2) When an action is brought by a party identified in subsection (d) of section 501, the remedies provided by sections 502 and 505, together with any actual damages suffered by such party as a result of the infringement, and the remedy provided by subsection (b) of this section.

(b) In any action filed pursuant to section 111(c)(3), the court may decree that, for a period not to exceed thirty days, the cable system shall be deprived of the benefit of a statutory license for one or more distant signals carried by such cable system.

§ 511. Liability of States, instrumentalities of States, and State officials for infringement of copyright

(a) **In General.** Any State, any instrumentality of a State, and any officer or employee of a State or instrumentality of a State acting in his or her official capacity, shall not be immune, under the Eleventh Amendment of the Constitution of the United States or under any other doctrine of sovereign immunity, from suit in Federal Court by any person, including any governmental or nongovernmental entity, for a violation of any of the exclusive rights of a copyright owner provided by sections 106 through 122, for importing copies of phonorecords in violation of section 602, or for any other violation under this title.

(b) Remedies. In a suit described in subsection (a) for a violation described in that subsection, remedies (including remedies both at law and in equity) are available for the violation to the same extent as such remedies are available for such a violation in a suit against any public or private entity other than a State, instrumentality of a State, or officer or employee of a State acting in his or her official capacity. Such remedies include impounding and disposition of infringing articles under section 503, actual damages and profits and statutory damages under section 504, costs and attorney's fees under section 505, and the remedies provided in section 510.

§ 512. Limitations on liability relating to material online

(a) Transitory Digital Network Communications. A service provider shall not be liable for monetary relief, or, except as provided in subsection (j), for injunctive or other equitable relief, for infringement of copyright by reason of the provider's transmitting, routing, or providing connections for, material through a system or network controlled or operated by or for the service provider, or by reason of the intermediate and transient storage of that material in the course of such transmitting, routing, or providing connections, if—

(1) the transmission of the material was initiated by or at the direction of a person other than the service provider;

(2) the transmission, routing, provision of connections, or storage is carried out through an automatic technical process without selection of the material by the service provider;

(3) the service provider does not select the recipients of the material except as an automatic response to the request of another person;

(4) no copy of the material made by the service provider in the course of such intermediate or transient storage is maintained on the system or network in a manner ordinarily accessible to anyone other than anticipated recipients, and no such copy is maintained on the system or network in a manner ordinarily accessible to such anticipated recipients for a longer period than is reasonably necessary for the transmission, routing, or provision of connections; and

(5) the material is transmitted through the system or network without modification of its content.

(b) System Caching.

(1) **Limitation on liability.** A service provider shall not be liable for monetary relief, or, except as provided in subsection (j), for injunctive or other equitable relief, for infringement of copyright by reason of the intermediate and temporary storage of material on a system or network controlled or operated by or for the service provider in a case in which—

(A) the material is made available online by a person other than the service provider;

(B) the material is transmitted from the person described in subparagraph (A) through the system or network to a person other than the person described in subparagraph (A) at the direction of that other person; and

(C) the storage is carried out through an automatic technical process for the purpose of making the material available to users of the system or network who, after the material is transmitted as described in subparagraph (B), request access to the material from the person described in subparagraph (A), if the conditions set forth in paragraph (2) are met.

(2) Conditions. The conditions referred to in paragraph (1) are that—

(A) the material described in paragraph (1) is transmitted to the subsequent users described in paragraph (1)(C) without modification to its content from the manner in which the material was transmitted from the person described in paragraph (1)(A);

(B) the service provider described in paragraph (1) complies with rules concerning the refreshing, reloading, or other updating of the material when specified by the person making the material available online in accordance with a generally accepted industry standard data communications protocol for the system or network through which that person makes the material available, except that this subparagraph applies only if those rules are not used by the person described in paragraph (1)(A) to prevent or unreasonably impair the intermediate storage to which this subsection applies;

(C) the service provider does not interfere with the ability of technology associated with the material to return to the person described in paragraph (1)(A) the information that would have been available to that person if the material had been obtained by the subsequent users described in paragraph (1)(C) directly from that person, except that this subparagraph applies only if that technology—

(i) does not significantly interfere with the performance of the provider's system or network or with the intermediate storage of the material;

(ii) is consistent with generally accepted industry standard communications protocols; and

(iii) does not extract information from the provider's system or network other than the information that would have been available to the person described in paragraph (1)(A) if the subsequent users had gained access to the material directly from that person;

(D) if the person described in paragraph (1)(A) has in effect a condition that a person must meet prior to having access to the material, such as a condition based on payment of a fee or provision of a password or other information, the service provider permits access to the stored material in significant part only to users of its system or network that have met those conditions and only in accordance with those conditions; and

(E) if the person described in paragraph (1)(A) makes that material available online without the authorization of the copyright owner of the material, the service provider responds expeditiously to remove, or disable access to, the material that is claimed to be infringing upon notification of claimed infringement as described in subsection (c)(3), except that this subparagraph applies only if—

(i) the material has previously been removed from the originating site or access to it has been disabled, or a court has ordered that the material be removed from the originating site or that access to the material on the originating site be disabled; and

(ii) the party giving the notification includes in the notification a statement confirming that the material has been removed from the originating site or access to it has been disabled or that a court has ordered that the material be removed from the originating site or that access to the material on the originating site be disabled.

(c) Information Residing on Systems or Networks at Direction of Users.

(1) In general. A service provider shall not be liable for monetary relief, or, except as provided in subsection (j), for injunctive or other equitable relief, for infringement of copyright by reason of the storage at the direction of a user of material that resides on a system or network controlled or operated by or for the service provider, if the service provider—

(A)(i) does not have actual knowledge that the material or an activity using the material on the system or network is infringing;

(ii) in the absence of such actual knowledge, is not aware of facts or circumstances from which infringing activity is apparent; or

(iii) upon obtaining such knowledge or awareness, acts expeditiously to remove, or disable access to, the material;

(B) does not receive a financial benefit directly attributable to the infringing activity, in a case in which the service provider has the right and ability to control such activity; and

(C) upon notification of claimed infringement as described in paragraph (3), responds expeditiously to remove, or disable access to, the material that is claimed to be infringing or to be the subject of infringing activity.

(2) Designated agent. The limitations on liability established in this subsection apply to a service provider only if the service provider has designated an agent to receive notifications of claimed infringement described in paragraph (3), by making available through its service, including on its website in a location accessible to the public, and by providing to the Copyright Office, substantially the following information:

(A) the name, address, phone number, and electronic mail address of the agent.

(B) other contact information which the Register of Copyrights may deem appropriate.

The Register of Copyrights shall maintain a current directory of agents available to the public for inspection, including through the Internet, in both electronic and hard copy formats, and may require payment of a fee by service providers to cover the costs of maintaining the directory.

(3) Elements of notification.

(A) To be effective under this subsection, a notification of claimed infringement must be a written communication provided to the designated agent of a service provider that includes substantially the following:

(i) A physical or electronic signature of a person authorized to act on behalf of the owner of an exclusive right that is allegedly infringed.

(ii) Identification of the copyrighted work claimed to have been infringed, or, if multiple copyrighted works at a single online site are covered by a single notification, a representative list of such works at that site.

(iii) Identification of the material that is claimed to be infringing or to be the subject of infringing activity and that is to be removed or access to which is to be disabled, and information reasonably sufficient to permit the service provider to locate the material.

(iv) Information reasonably sufficient to permit the service provider to contact the complaining party, such as an address, telephone number, and, if available, an electronic mail address at which the complaining party may be contacted.

(v) A statement that the complaining party has a good faith belief that use of the material in the manner complained of is not authorized by the copyright owner, its agent, or the law.

(vi) A statement that the information in the notification is accurate, and under penalty of perjury, that the complaining party is authorized to act on behalf of the owner of an exclusive right that is allegedly infringed.

(B)(i) Subject to clause (ii), a notification from a copyright owner or from a person authorized to act on behalf of the copyright owner that fails to comply substantially with the provisions of subparagraph (A) shall not be considered under paragraph (1)(A) in determining whether a service provider has actual knowledge or is aware of facts or circumstances from which infringing activity is apparent.

(ii) In a case in which the notification that is provided to the service provider's designated agent fails to comply substantially with all the provisions of subparagraph (A) but substantially complies with clauses (ii), (iii), and (iv) of subparagraph (A), clause (i) of this subparagraph applies only if the service provider promptly attempts to contact the person making the notification or takes other reasonable steps to assist in the receipt of notification that substantially complies with all the provisions of subparagraph (A).

(d) Information Location Tools. A service provider shall not be liable for monetary relief, or, except as provided in subsection (j), for injunctive or other equitable relief, for infringement of copyright by reason of the provider referring or linking users to an online location containing infringing material or infringing activity, by using information location tools, including a directory, index, reference, pointer, or hypertext link, if the service provider—

(1)(A) does not have actual knowledge that the material or activity is infringing;

(B) in the absence of such actual knowledge, is not aware of facts or circumstances from which infringing activity is apparent; or

(C) upon obtaining such knowledge or awareness, acts expeditiously to remove, or disable access to, the material;

(2) does not receive a financial benefit directly attributable to the infringing activity, in a case in which the service provider has the right and ability to control such activity; and

(3) upon notification of claimed infringement as described in subsection (c)(3), responds expeditiously to remove, or disable access to, the material that is claimed to be infringing or to be the subject of infringing activity, except that, for purposes of this paragraph, the information described in subsection (c)(3)(A)(iii) shall be identification of the reference or link, to material or activity claimed to be infringing, that is to be removed or access to which is to be disabled, and information reasonably sufficient to permit the service provider to locate that reference or link.

(e) Limitation on Liability of Nonprofit Educational Institutions. (1) When a public or other nonprofit institution of higher education is a service provider, and when a faculty member or graduate student who is an employee of such institution is performing a teaching or research function, for the purposes of subsections (a) and (b) such faculty member or graduate student shall be considered to be a person other than the institution, and for the purposes of subsections (c) and (d) such faculty member's or graduate student's knowledge or awareness of his or her infringing activities shall not be attributed to the institution, if—

(A) such faculty member's or graduate student's infringing activities do not involve the provision of online access to instructional materials that are or were required or recommended, within the preceding 3–year period, for a course taught at the institution by such faculty member or graduate student;

(B) the institution has not, within the preceding 3–year period, received more than 2 notifications described in subsection (c)(3) of claimed infringement by such faculty member or graduate student, and such notifications of claimed infringement were not actionable under subsection (f); and

(C) the institution provides to all users of its system or network informational materials that accurately describe, and promote compliance with, the laws of the United States relating to copyright.

(2) For the purposes of this subsection, the limitations on injunctive relief contained in subsections (j)(2) and (j)(3), but not those in (j)(1), shall apply.

(f) Misrepresentations. Any person who knowingly materially misrepresents under this section—

(1) that material or activity is infringing, or

(2) that material or activity was removed or disabled by mistake or misidentification,

shall be liable for any damages, including costs and attorneys' fees, incurred by the alleged infringer, by any copyright owner or copyright owner's authorized licensee, or by a service provider, who is injured by such misrepresentation, as the result of the service provider relying upon such misrepresentation in removing or disabling access to the material or activity claimed to be infringing, or in replacing the removed material or ceasing to disable access to it.

(g) Replacement of Removed or Disabled Material and Limitation on Other Liability.

(1) No liability for taking down generally. Subject to paragraph (2), a service provider shall not be liable to any person for any claim based on the service provider's good faith disabling of access to, or removal of, material or activity claimed to be infringing or based on facts or circumstances from which infringing activity is apparent,

353

regardless of whether the material or activity is ultimately determined to be infringing.

(2) Exception. Paragraph (1) shall not apply with respect to material residing at the direction of a subscriber of the service provider on a system or network controlled or operated by or for the service provider that is removed, or to which access is disabled by the service provider, pursuant to a notice provided under subsection (c)(1)(C), unless the service provider—

(A) takes reasonable steps promptly to notify the subscriber that it has removed or disabled access to the material;

(B) upon receipt of a counter notification described in paragraph (3), promptly provides the person who provided the notification under subsection (c)(1)(C) with a copy of the counter notification, and informs that person that it will replace the removed material or cease disabling access to it in 10 business days; and

(C) replaces the removed material and ceases disabling access to it not less than 10, nor more than 14, business days following receipt of the counter notice, unless its designated agent first receives notice from the person who submitted the notification under subsection (c)(1)(C) that such person has filed an action seeking a court order to restrain the subscriber from engaging in infringing activity relating to the material on the service provider's system or network.

(3) Contents of counter notification. To be effective under this subsection, a counter notification must be a written communication provided to the service provider's designated agent that includes substantially the following:

(A) A physical or electronic signature of the subscriber.

(B) Identification of the material that has been removed or to which access has been disabled and the location at which the material appeared before it was removed or access to it was disabled.

(C) A statement under penalty of perjury that the subscriber has a good faith belief that the material was removed or disabled as a result of mistake or misidentification of the material to be removed or disabled.

(D) The subscriber's name, address, and telephone number, and a statement that the subscriber consents to the jurisdiction of Federal District Court for the judicial district in which the address is located, or if the subscriber's address is outside of the United States, for any judicial district in which the service provider may be found, and that the subscriber will accept service of process from the person who provided notification under subsection (c)(1)(C) or an agent of such person.

(4) Limitation on other liability. A service provider's compliance with paragraph (2) shall not subject the service provider to liability for copyright infringement with respect to the material identified in the notice provided under subsection (c)(1)(C).

(h) Subpoena to Identify Infringer.

(1) Request. A copyright owner or a person authorized to act on the owner's behalf may request the clerk of any United States district court to issue a subpoena to a service provider for identification of an alleged infringer in accordance with this subsection.

(2) Contents of request. The request may be made by filing with the clerk—

(A) a copy of a notification described in subsection (c)(3)(A);

(B) a proposed subpoena; and

(C) a sworn declaration to the effect that the purpose for which the subpoena is sought is to obtain the identity of an alleged infringer and that such information will only be used for the purpose of protecting rights under this title.

(3) Contents of subpoena. The subpoena shall authorize and order the service provider receiving the notification and the subpoena to expeditiously disclose to the copyright owner or person authorized by the copyright owner information sufficient to identify the alleged infringer of the material described in the notification to the extent such information is available to the service provider.

(4) Basis for granting subpoena. If the notification filed satisfies the provisions of subsection (c)(3)(A), the proposed subpoena is in proper form, and the accompanying declaration is properly executed, the clerk shall expeditiously issue and sign the proposed subpoena and return it to the requester for delivery to the service provider.

(5) Actions of service provider receiving subpoena. Upon receipt of the issued subpoena, either accompanying or subsequent to the receipt of a notification described in subsection (c)(3)(A), the service provider shall expeditiously disclose to the copyright owner or person authorized by the copyright owner the information required by the subpoena, notwithstanding any other provision of law and regardless of whether the service provider responds to the notification.

(6) Rules applicable to subpoena. Unless otherwise provided by this section or by applicable rules of the court, the procedure for issuance and delivery of the subpoena, and the remedies for noncompliance with the subpoena, shall be governed to the greatest extent practicable by those provisions of the Federal Rules of Civil Procedure governing the issuance, service, and enforcement of a subpoena *duces tecum*.

(i) Conditions for Eligibility.

(1) Accommodation of technology. The limitations on liability established by this section shall apply to a service provider only if the service provider—

(A) has adopted and reasonably implemented, and informs subscribers and account holders of the service provider's system or network of, a policy that provides for the termination in appropriate circumstances of subscribers and account holders of the service provider's system or network who are repeat infringers; and

(B) accommodates and does not interfere with standard technical measures.

(2) Definition. As used in this subsection, the term "standard technical measures" means technical measures that are used by copyright owners to identify or protect copyrighted works and—

(A) have been developed pursuant to a broad consensus of copyright owners and service providers in an open, fair, voluntary, multi-industry standards process;

(B) are available to any person on reasonable and nondiscriminatory terms; and

(C) do not impose substantial costs on service providers or substantial burdens on their systems or networks.

(j) Injunctions. The following rules shall apply in the case of any application for an injunction under section 502 against a service provider that is not subject to monetary remedies under this section:

(1) Scope of relief. (A) With respect to conduct other than that which qualifies for the limitation on remedies set forth in subsection (a), the court may grant injunctive relief with respect to a service provider only in one or more of the following forms:

(i) An order restraining the service provider from providing access to infringing material or activity residing at a particular online site on the provider's system or network.

(ii) An order restraining the service provider from providing access to a subscriber or account holder of the service provider's system or network who is engaging in infringing activity and is identified in the order, by terminating the accounts of the subscriber or account holder that are specified in the order.

(iii) Such other injunctive relief as the court may consider necessary to prevent or restrain infringement of copyrighted material specified in the order of the court at a particular online location, if such relief is the least burdensome to the service provider among the forms of relief comparably effective for that purpose.

(B) If the service provider qualifies for the limitation on remedies described in subsection (a), the court may only grant injunctive relief in one or both of the following forms:

(i) An order restraining the service provider from providing access to a subscriber or account holder of the service provider's system or network who is using the provider's service to engage in infringing activity and is identified in the order, by terminating the accounts of the subscriber or account holder that are specified in the order.

(ii) An order restraining the service provider from providing access, by taking reasonable steps specified in the order to block access, to a specific, identified, online location outside the United States.

(2) **Considerations.** The court, in considering the relevant criteria for injunctive relief under applicable law, shall consider—

(A) whether such an injunction, either alone or in combination with other such injunctions issued against the same service provider under this subsection, would significantly burden either the provider or the operation of the provider's system or network;

(B) the magnitude of the harm likely to be suffered by the copyright owner in the digital network environment if steps are not taken to prevent or restrain the infringement;

(C) whether implementation of such an injunction would be technically feasible and effective, and would not interfere with access to noninfringing material at other online locations; and

(D) whether other less burdensome and comparably effective means of preventing or restraining access to the infringing material are available.

(3) **Notice and ex parte orders.** Injunctive relief under this subsection shall be available only after notice to the service provider and an opportunity for the service provider to appear are provided, except for orders ensuring the preservation of evidence or other orders having no material adverse effect on the operation of the service provider's communications network.

(k) **Definitions.**

(1) **Service provider.** (A) As used in subsection (a), the term "service provider" means an entity offering the transmission, routing, or providing of connections for digital online communications, between or among points specified by a user, of material of the user's choosing, without modification to the content of the material as sent or received.

(B) As used in this section, other than subsection (a), the term "service provider" means a provider of online services or network access, or the operator of facilities therefor, and includes an entity described in subparagraph (A).

(2) Monetary relief. As used in this section, the term "monetary relief" means damages, costs, attorneys' fees, and any other form of monetary payment.

(l) **Other Defenses Not Affected.** The failure of a service provider's conduct to qualify for limitation of liability under this section shall not bear adversely upon the consideration of a defense by the service provider that the service provider's conduct is not infringing under this title or any other defense.

(m) Protection of Privacy. Nothing in this section shall be construed to condition the applicability of subsections (a) through (d) on—

> (1) a service provider monitoring its service or affirmatively seeking facts indicating infringing activity, except to the extent consistent with a standard technical measure complying with the provisions of subsection (i); or

> (2) a service provider gaining access to, removing, or disabling access to material in cases in which such conduct is prohibited by law.

(n) Construction. Subsections (a), (b), (c), and (d) describe separate and distinct functions for purposes of applying this section. Whether a service provider qualifies for the limitation on liability in any one of those subsections shall be based solely on the criteria in that subsection, and shall not affect a determination of whether that service provider qualifies for the limitations on liability under any other such subsection.

§ 513. Determination of reasonable license fees for individual proprietors

In the case of any performing rights society subject to a consent decree which provides for the determination of reasonable license rates or fees to be charged by the performing rights society, notwithstanding the provisions of that consent decree, an individual proprietor who owns or operates fewer than 7 non-publicly traded establishments in which nondramatic musical works are performed publicly and who claims that any license agreement offered by that performing rights society is unreasonable in its license rate or fee as to that individual proprietor, shall be entitled to determination of a reasonable license rate or fee as follows:

> (1) The individual proprietor may commence such proceeding for determination of a reasonable license rate or fee by filing an application in the applicable district court under paragraph (2) that a rate disagreement exists and by serving a copy of the application on the performing rights society. Such proceeding shall commence in the applicable district court within 90 days after the service of such copy, except that such 90-day requirement shall be subject to the administrative requirements of the court.

> (2) The proceeding under paragraph (1) shall be held, at the individual proprietor's election, in the judicial district of the district court with jurisdiction over the applicable consent decree or in that place of holding court of a district court that is the seat of the Federal

circuit (other than the Court of Appeals for the Federal Circuit) in which the proprietor's establishment is located.

(3) Such proceeding shall be held before the judge of the court with jurisdiction over the consent decree governing the performing rights society. At the discretion of the court, the proceeding shall be held before a special master or magistrate judge appointed by such judge. Should that consent decree provide for the appointment of an advisor or advisors to the court for any purpose, any such advisor shall be the special master so named by the court.

(4) In any such proceeding, the industry rate shall be presumed to have been reasonable at the time it was agreed to or determined by the court. Such presumption shall in no way affect a determination of whether the rate is being correctly applied to the individual proprietor.

(5) Pending the completion of such proceeding, the individual proprietor shall have the right to perform publicly the copyrighted musical compositions in the repertoire of the performing rights society by paying an interim license rate or fee into an interest bearing escrow account with the clerk of the court, subject to retroactive adjustment when a final rate or fee has been determined, in an amount equal to the industry rate, or, in the absence of an industry rate, the amount of the most recent license rate or fee agreed to by the parties.

(6) Any decision rendered in such proceeding by a special master or magistrate judge named under paragraph (3) shall be reviewed by the judge of the court with jurisdiction over the consent decree governing the performing rights society. Such proceeding, including such review, shall be concluded within 6 months after its commencement.

(7) Any such final determination shall be binding only as to the individual proprietor commencing the proceeding, and shall not be applicable to any other proprietor or any other performing rights society, and the performing rights society shall be relieved of any obligation of nondiscrimination among similarly situated music users that may be imposed by the consent decree governing its operations.

(8) An individual proprietor may not bring more than one proceeding provided for in this section for the determination of a reasonable license rate or fee under any license agreement with respect to any one performing rights society.

(9) For purposes of this section, the term "industry rate" means the license fee a performing rights society has agreed to with, or which has been determined by the court for, a significant segment of the music user industry to which the individual proprietor belongs.

CHAPTER 6—MANUFACTURING REQUIREMENTS AND IMPORTATION

§ 601. Manufacture, importation, and public distribution of certain copies

(a) Prior to July 1, 1986, and except as provided by subsection (b), the importation into or public distribution in the United States of copies of a work consisting preponderantly of nondramatic literary material that is in the English language and is protected under this title is prohibited unless the portions consisting of such material have been manufactured in the United States or Canada.

(b) The provisions of subsection (a) do not apply—

(1) where, on the date when importation is sought or public distribution in the United States is made, the author of any substantial part of such material is neither a national nor a domiciliary of the United States or, if such author is a national of the United States, he or she has been domiciled outside the United States for a continuous period of at least one year immediately preceding that date; in the case of a work made for hire, the exemption provided by this clause does not apply unless a substantial part of the work was prepared for an employer or other person who is not a national or domiciliary of the United States or a domestic corporation or enterprise;

(2) where the United States Customs Service is presented with an import statement issued under the seal of the Copyright Office, in which case a total of no more than two thousand copies of any one such work shall be allowed entry; the import statement shall be issued upon request to the copyright owner or to a person designated by such owner at the time of registration for the work under section 408 or at any time thereafter;

(3) where importation is sought under the authority or for the use, other than in schools, of the Government of the United States or of any State or political subdivision of a State;

(4) where importation, for use and not for sale, is sought—

(A) by any person with respect to no more than one copy of any work at any one time;

(B) by any person arriving from outside the United States, with respect to copies forming part of such person's personal baggage; or

(C) by an organization operated for scholarly, educational, or religious purposes and not for private gain, with respect to copies intended to form a part of its library;

(5) where the copies are reproduced in raised characters for the use of the blind; or

(6) where, in addition to copies imported under clauses (3) and (4) of this subsection, no more than two thousand copies of any one such work, which have not been manufactured in the United States or Canada, are publicly distributed in the United States; or

(7) where, on the date when importation is sought or public distribution in the United States is made—

(A) the author of any substantial part of such material is an individual and receives compensation for the transfer or license of the right to distribute the work in the United States; and

(B) the first publication of the work has previously taken place outside the United States under a transfer or license granted by such author to a transferee or licensee who was not a national or domiciliary of the United States or a domestic corporation or enterprise; and

(C) there has been no publication of an authorized edition of the work of which the copies were manufactured in the United States; and

(D) the copies were reproduced under a transfer or license granted by such author or by the transferee or licensee of the right of first publication as mentioned in subclause (B), and the transferee or the licensee of the right of reproduction was not a national or domiciliary of the United States or a domestic corporation or enterprise.

(c) The requirement of this section that copies be manufactured in the United States or Canada is satisfied if—

(1) in the case where the copies are printed directly from type that has been set, or directly from plates made from such type, the setting of the type and the making of the plates have been performed in the United States or Canada; or

(2) in the case where the making of plates by a lithographic or photoengraving process is a final or intermediate step preceding the printing of the copies, the making of the plates has been performed in the United States or Canada; and

(3) in any case, the printing or other final process of producing multiple copies and any binding of the copies have been performed in the United States or Canada.

(d) Importation or public distribution of copies in violation of this section does not invalidate protection for a work under this title. However, in any civil action or criminal proceeding for infringement of the exclusive rights to reproduce and distribute copies of the work, the infringer has a complete defense with respect to all of the nondramatic literary material comprised in the work and any other parts of the work in which the exclusive rights to reproduce and distribute copies are owned by the same person who owns such exclusive rights in the nondramatic literary material, if the infringer proves—

(1) that copies of the work have been imported into or publicly distributed in the United States in violation of this section by or with the authority of the owner of such exclusive rights; and

(2) that the infringing copies were manufactured in the United States or Canada in accordance with the provisions of subsection (c); and

(3) that the infringement was commenced before the effective date of registration for an authorized edition of the work, the copies of which have been manufactured in the United States or Canada in accordance with the provisions of subsection (c).

(e) In any action for infringement of the exclusive rights to reproduce and distribute copies of a work containing material required by this section to be manufactured in the United States or Canada, the copyright owner shall set forth in the complaint the names of the persons or organizations who performed the processes specified by subsection (c) with respect to that material, and the places where those processes were performed.

§ 602. Infringing importation of copies or phonorecords

(a) Importation into the United States, without the authority of the owner of copyright under this title, of copies or phonorecords of a work that have been acquired outside the United States is an infringement of the exclusive right to distribute copies or phonorecords under section 106, actionable under section 501. This subsection does not apply to—

(1) importation of copies or phonorecords under the authority or for the use of the Government of the United States or of any State or political subdivision of a State, but not including copies or phonorecords for use in schools, or copies of any audiovisual work imported for purposes other than archival use;

(2) importation, for the private use of the importer and not for distribution, by any person with respect to no more than one copy or phonorecord of any one work at any one time, or by any person arriving from outside the United States with respect to copies or phonorecords forming part of such person's personal baggage; or

(3) importation by or for an organization operated for scholarly, educational, or religious purposes and not for private gain, with respect to no more than one copy of an audiovisual work solely for its archival purposes, and no more than five copies or phonorecords of any other work for its library lending or archival purposes, unless the importation of such copies or phonorecords is part of an activity consisting of

systematic reproduction or distribution, engaged in by such organization in violation of the provisions of section 108(g)(2).

(b) In a case where the making of the copies or phonorecords would have constituted an infringement of copyright if this title had been applicable, their importation is prohibited. In a case where the copies or phonorecords were lawfully made, the United States Customs Service has no authority to prevent their importation unless the provisions of section 601 are applicable. In either case, the Secretary of the Treasury is authorized to prescribe, by regulation, a procedure under which any person claiming an interest in the copyright in a particular work may, upon payment of a specified fee, be entitled to notification by the Customs Service of the importation of articles that appear to be copies or phonorecords of the work.

§ 603. Importation prohibitions: Enforcement and disposition of excluded articles

(a) The Secretary of the Treasury and the United States Postal Service shall separately or jointly make regulations for the enforcement of the provisions of this title prohibiting importation.

(b) These regulations may require, as a condition for the exclusion of articles under section 602—

(1) that the person seeking exclusion obtain a court order enjoining importation of the articles; or

(2) that the person seeking exclusion furnish proof, of a specified nature and in accordance with prescribed procedures, that the copyright in which such person claims an interest is valid and that the importation would violate the prohibition in section 602; the person seeking exclusion may also be required to post a surety bond for any injury that may result if the detention or exclusion of the articles proves to be unjustified.

(c) Articles imported in violation of the importation prohibitions of this title are subject to seizure and forfeiture in the same manner as property imported in violation of the customs revenue laws. Forfeited articles shall be destroyed as directed by the Secretary of the Treasury or the court, as the case may be.

CHAPTER 7—COPYRIGHT OFFICE

§ 701. The Copyright Office: General responsibilities and organization

(a) All administrative functions and duties under this title, except as otherwise specified, are the responsibility of the Register of Copyrights as director of the Copyright Office of the Library of Congress. The Register of Copyrights, together with the subordinate officers and employees of the Copyright Office, shall be appointed by the Librarian of Congress, and shall act under the Librarian's general direction and supervision.

(b) In addition to the functions and duties set out elsewhere in this chapter, the Register of Copyrights shall perform the following functions:

(1) Advise Congress on national and international issues relating to copyright, other matters arising under this title, and related matters.

(2) Provide information and assistance to Federal departments and agencies and the Judiciary on national and international issues relating to copyright, other matters arising under this title, and related matters.

(3) Participate in meetings of international intergovernmental organizations and meetings with foreign government officials relating to copyright, other matters arising under this title, and related matters, including as a member of United States delegations as authorized by the appropriate Executive branch authority.

(4) Conduct studies and programs regarding copyright, other matters arising under this title, and related matters, the administration of the Copyright Office, or any function vested in the Copyright Office by law, including educational programs conducted cooperatively with foreign intellectual property offices and international intergovernmental organizations.

(5) Perform such other functions as Congress may direct, or as may be appropriate in furtherance of the functions and duties specifically set forth in this title.

(c) The Register of Copyrights shall adopt a seal to be used on and after January 1, 1978, to authenticate all certified documents issued by the Copyright Office.

(d) The Register of Copyrights shall make an annual report to the Librarian of Congress of the work and accomplishments of the Copyright Office during the previous fiscal year. The annual report of the Register of Copyrights shall be published separately and as a part of the annual report of the Librarian of Congress.

(e) Except as provided by section 706(b) and the regulations issued thereunder, all actions taken by the Register of Copyrights under this title are subject to the provisions of the Administrative Procedure Act of June 11, 1946, as amended (c. 324, 60 Stat. 237, title 5, United States Code, Chapter 5, Subchapter II and Chapter 7).

(f) The Register of Copyrights shall be compensated at the rate of pay in effect for level III of the Executive Schedule under section 5314 of title 5. The Librarian of Congress shall establish not more than four positions for Associate Registers of Copyrights, in accordance with the recommendations of the Register of Copyrights. The Librarian shall make appointments to such positions after consultation with the Register of Copyrights. Each Associate Register of Copyrights shall be paid at a rate not to exceed the maximum annual rate of basic pay payable for GS–18 of the General Schedule under section 5332 of title 5.

§ 702. Copyright Office regulations

The Register of Copyrights is authorized to establish regulations not inconsistent with law for the administration of the functions and duties made the responsibility of the Register under this title. All regulations established by the Register under this title are subject to the approval of the Librarian of Congress.

§ 703. Effective date of actions in Copyright Office

In any case in which time limits are prescribed under this title for the performance of an action in the Copyright Office, and in which the last day of the prescribed period falls on a Saturday, Sunday, holiday, or other nonbusiness day within the District of Columbia or the Federal Government, the action may be taken on the next succeeding business day, and is effective as of the date when the period expired.

§ 704. Retention and disposition of articles deposited in Copyright Office

(a) Upon their deposit in the Copyright Office under sections 407 and 408, all copies, phonorecords, and identifying material, including those deposited in connection with claims that have been refused registration, are the property of the United States Government.

(b) In the case of published works, all copies, phonorecords, and identifying material deposited are available to the Library of Congress for its collections, or for exchange or transfer to any other library. In the case of unpublished works, the Library is entitled, under regulations that the Register of Copyrights shall prescribe, to select any deposits for its collections or for transfer to the National Archives of the United States or to a Federal records center, as defined in section 2901 of title 44.

(c) The Register of Copyrights is authorized, for specific or general categories of works, to make a facsimile reproduction of all or any part of the material deposited under section 408, and to make such reproduction a part of the Copyright Office records of the registration, before transferring such material to the Library of Congress as provided by subsection (b), or before destroying or otherwise disposing of such material as provided by subsection (d).

(d) Deposits not selected by the Library under subsection (b), or identifying portions or reproductions of them, shall be retained under the control of the Copyright Office, including retention in Government storage facilities, for the longest period considered practicable and desirable by the Register of Copyrights and the Librarian of Congress. After that period it is within the joint discretion of the Register and the Librarian to order their destruction or other disposition; but, in the case of unpublished works, no deposit shall be knowingly or intentionally destroyed or otherwise disposed of during its term of copyright unless a facsimile reproduction of the entire deposit has been made a part of the Copyright Office records as provided by subsection (c).

(e) The depositor of copies, phonorecords, or identifying material under section 408, or the copyright owner of record, may request retention, under the control of the Copyright Office, of one or more of such articles for the full term of copyright in the work. The Register of Copyrights shall prescribe, by regulation, the conditions under which such requests are to be made and granted, and shall fix the fee to be charged under section 708(a)(10) if the request is granted.

§ 705. Copyright Office records: Preparation, maintenance, public inspection, and searching

(a) The Register of Copyrights shall ensure that records of deposits, registrations, recordations, and other actions taken under this title are maintained, and that indexes of such records are prepared.

(b) Such records and indexes, as well as the articles deposited in connection with completed copyright registrations and retained under the control of the Copyright Office, shall be open to public inspection.

(c) Upon request and payment of the fee specified by section 708, the Copyright Office shall make a search of its public records, indexes, and deposits, and shall furnish a report of the information they disclose with respect to any particular deposits, registrations, or recorded documents.

§ 706. Copies of Copyright Office records

(a) Copies may be made of any public records or indexes of the Copyright Office; additional certificates of copyright registration and copies of any public records or indexes may be furnished upon request and payment of the fees specified by section 708.

(b) Copies or reproductions of deposited articles retained under the control of the Copyright Office shall be authorized or furnished only under the conditions specified by the Copyright Office regulations.

§ 707. Copyright Office forms and publications

(a) **Catalog of Copyright Entries.** The Register of Copyrights shall compile and publish at periodic intervals catalogs of all copyright registrations. These catalogs shall be divided into parts in accordance with the various classes of works, and the Register has discretion to determine, on the basis of practicability and usefulness, the form and frequency of publication of each particular part.

(b) **Other Publications.** The Register shall furnish, free of charge upon request, application forms for copyright registration and general informational material in connection with the functions of the Copyright Office. The Register also has the authority to publish compilations of information, bibliographies, and other material he or she considers to be of value to the public.

(c) **Distribution of Publications.** All publications of the Copyright Office shall be furnished to depository libraries as specified under section 1905 of title 44, and, aside from those furnished free of charge, shall be offered for sale to the public at prices based on the cost of reproduction and distribution.

§ 708. Copyright Office fees*

(a) **Fees.** Fees shall be paid to the Register of Copyrights—

(1) on filing each application under section 408 for registration of a copyright claim or for a supplementary registration, including the issuance of a certificate of registration if registration is made;

(2) on filing each application for registration of a claim for renewal of a subsisting copyright under section 304(a), including the issuance of a certificate of registration if registration is made;

(3) for the issuance of a receipt for a deposit under section 407;

(4) for the recordation, as provided by section 205, of a transfer of copyright ownership or other document;

(5) for the filing, under section 115(b), of a notice of intention to obtain a compulsory license;

(6) for the recordation, under section 302(c), of a statement revealing the identity of an author of an anonymous or pseudonymous work,

---

* **Editors' Note**: For the current fee amounts, see Copyright Office Regulations, 37 C.F.R. § 201.3, set forth at Appendix C of the casebook supplement.

or for the recordation, under section 302(d), of a statement relating to the death of an author;

(7) for the issuance, under section 706, of an additional certificate of registration;

(8) for the issuance of any other certification; and

(9) for the making and reporting of a search as provided by section 705, and for any related services.

The Register of Copyrights is authorized to fix fees for other services, including the cost of preparing copies of Copyright Office records, whether or not such copies are certified, based on the cost of providing the service.

(b) Adjustment of Fees. The Register of Copyrights may, by regulation, adjust the fees for the services specified in paragraphs (1) through (9) of subsection (a) in the following manner.

(1) The Register shall conduct a study of the costs incurred by the Copyright Office for the registration of claims, the recordation of documents, and the provision of services. The study shall also consider the timing of any adjustment in fees and the authority to use such fees consistent with the budget.

(2) The Register may, on the basis of the study under paragraph (1), and subject to paragraph (5), adjust fees to not more than that necessary to cover the reasonable costs incurred by the Copyright Office for the services described in paragraph (1), plus a reasonable inflation adjustment to account for any estimated increase in costs.

(3) Any fee established under paragraph (2) shall be rounded off to the nearest dollar, or for a fee less than $12, rounded off to the nearest 50 cents.

(4) Fees established under this subsection shall be fair and equitable and give due consideration to the objectives of the copyright system.

(5) If the Register determines under paragraph (2) that fees should be adjusted, the Register shall prepare a proposed fee schedule and submit the schedule with the accompanying economic analysis to the Congress. The fees proposed by the Register may be instituted after the end of 120 days after the schedule is submitted to the Congress unless, within that 120–day period, a law is enacted stating in substance that the Congress does not approve the schedule.

(c) The fees prescribed by or under this section are applicable to the United States Government and any of its agencies, employees, or officers, but the Register of Copyrights has discretion to waive the requirement of this subsection in occasional or isolated cases involving relatively small amounts.

(d)(1) Except as provided in paragraph (2), all fees received under this section shall be deposited by the Register of Copyrights in the Treasury of the United States and shall be credited to the appropriations for necessary expenses of the Copyright Office. Such fees that are collected shall remain available until expended. The Register may, in accordance with regulations that he or she shall prescribe, refund any sum paid by mistake or in excess of the fee required by this section.

(2) In the case of fees deposited against future services, the Register of Copyrights shall request the Secretary of the Treasury to invest in interest-bearing securities in the United States Treasury any portion of the fees that, as determined by the Register, is not required to meet current deposit account demands. Funds from such portion of fees shall be invested in securities that permit funds to be available to the Copyright Office at all times if they are determined to be necessary to meet current deposit account demands. Such investments shall be in public debt securities with maturities suitable to the needs of the Copyright Office, as determined by the Register of Copyrights, and bearing interest at rates determined by the Secretary of the Treasury, taking into consideration current market yields on outstanding marketable obligations of the United States of comparable maturities.

(3) The income on such investments shall be deposited in the Treasury of the United States and shall be credited to the appropriations for necessary expenses of the Copyright Office.

§ 709. Delay in delivery caused by disruption of postal or other services

In any case in which the Register of Copyrights determines, on the basis of such evidence as the Register may by regulation require, that a deposit, application, fee, or any other material to be delivered to the Copyright Office by a particular date, would have been received in the Copyright Office in due time except for a general disruption or suspension of postal or other transportation or communications services, the actual receipt of such material in the Copyright Office within one month after the date on which the Register determines that the disruption or suspension of such services has terminated, shall be considered timely.

CHAPTER 8—COPYRIGHT ARBITRATION ROYALTY PANELS

§ 801. Copyright arbitration royalty panels: Establishment and purpose

(a) Establishment. The Librarian of Congress, upon the recommendation of the Register of Copyrights, is authorized to appoint and convene copyright arbitration royalty panels.

(b) Purposes. Subject to the provisions of this chapter, the purposes of the copyright arbitration royalty panels shall be as follows:

(1) To make determinations concerning the adjustment of reasonable copyright royalty rates as provided in sections 114, 115, 116, and 119, and to make determinations as to reasonable terms and rates of royalty payments as provided in section 118. The rates applicable under sections 114(f)(1)(B), 115, and 116 shall be calculated to achieve the following objectives:

(A) To maximize the availability of creative works to the public;

(B) To afford the copyright owner a fair return for his creative work and the copyright user a fair income under existing economic conditions;

(C) To reflect the relative roles of the copyright owner and the copyright user in the product made available to the public with respect to relative creative contribution, technological contribution, capital investment, cost, risk, and contribution to the opening of new markets for creative expression and media for their communication;

(D) To minimize any disruptive impact on the structure of the industries involved and on generally prevailing industry practices.

(2) To make determinations concerning the adjustment of the copyright royalty rates in section 111 solely in accordance with the following provisions:

(A) The rates established by section 111(d)(1)(B) may be adjusted to reflect (i) national monetary inflation or deflation or (ii) changes in the average rates charged cable subscribers for the basic service of providing secondary transmissions to maintain the real constant dollar level of the royalty fee per subscriber which existed as of the date of enactment of this Act: Provided, That if the average rates charged cable system subscribers for the basic service of providing secondary transmissions are changed so that the average rates exceed national monetary inflation, no change in the rates established by section 111(d)(1)(B) shall be permitted: *And provided further,* That no increase in the royalty fee shall be permitted based on any reduction in the average number of distant signal equivalents per subscriber. The copyright arbitration royalty panels may consider all factors relating to the maintenance of such level of payments including, as an extenuating factor, whether the industry has been restrained by subscriber rate regulating authorities from increasing the rates for the basic service of providing secondary transmissions.

(B) In the event that the rules and regulations of the Federal Communications Commission are amended at any time after April 15, 1976, to permit the carriage by cable systems of additional television broadcast signals beyond the local service area of the primary transmitters of such signals, the royalty rates established by section 111(d)(1)(B) may be adjusted to insure that the rates for the additional distant signal equivalents resulting from such carriage are reasonable in the light of the changes effected by the amendment to such rules and regulations. In determining the reasonableness of rates proposed following an amendment of Federal Communications Commission rules and regulations, the copyright arbitration royalty panels shall consider, among other factors, the economic impact on copyright owners and users: *Provided,* That no adjustment in royalty rates shall be made under this subclause with respect to any distant signal equivalent or fraction thereof represented by (i) carriage of any signal permitted under the rules and regulations of the Federal Communications Commission in effect on April 15, 1976, or the carriage of a signal of the same type (that is, independent, network, or noncommercial educational) substituted for such permitted signal, or (ii) a television broadcast signal first carried after April 15, 1976, pursuant to an individual waiver of the rules and regulations of the Federal Communications Commission, as such rules and regulations were in effect on April 15,1976.

(C) In the event of any change in the rules and regulations of the Federal Communications Commission with respect to syndicated and sports program exclusivity after April 15, 1976, the rates established by section 111(d)(1)(B) may be adjusted to assure that such rates are reasonable in light of the changes to such rules and regulations, but any such adjustment shall apply only to the affected television broadcast signals carried on those systems affected by the change.

(D) The gross receipts limitations established by section 111(d)(1)(C) and (D) shall be adjusted to reflect national monetary inflation or deflation or changes in the average rates charged cable system subscribers for the basic service of providing secondary transmissions to maintain the real constant dollar value of the exemption provided by such section; and the royalty rate specified therein shall not be subject to adjustment.

(3) To distribute royalty fees deposited with the Register of Copyrights under sections 111, 116, 119(b), and 1003, and to determine, in cases where controversy exists, the distribution of such fees.

(c) Rulings. The Librarian of Congress, upon the recommendation of the Register of Copyrights, may, before a copyright arbitration royalty panel is convened, make any necessary procedural or evidentiary rulings that would apply to the proceedings conducted by such panel, including—

(1) authorizing the distribution of those royalty fees collected under sections 111, 119, and 1005 that the Librarian has found are not subject to controversy; and

(2) accepting or rejecting royalty claims filed under sections 111, 119, and 1007 on the basis of timeliness or the failure to establish the basis for a claim.

(d) Support and Reimbursement of Arbitration Panels. The Librarian of Congress, upon the recommendation of the Register of Copyrights, shall provide the copyright arbitration royalty panels with the necessary administrative services related to proceedings under this chapter, and shall reimburse the arbitrators presiding in distribution proceedings at such intervals and in such manner as the Librarian shall provide by regulation. Each such arbitrator is an independent contractor acting on behalf of the United States, and shall be hired pursuant to a signed agreement between the Library of Congress and the arbitrator. Payments to the arbitrators shall be considered reasonable costs incurred by the Library of Congress and the Copyright Office for purposes of section 802(h)(1).

§ 802. Membership and proceedings of copyright arbitration royalty panels

(a) Composition of Copyright Arbitration Royalty Panels. A copyright arbitration royalty panel shall consist of 3 arbitrators selected by the Librarian of Congress pursuant to subsection (b).

(b) Selection of Arbitration Panel. Not later than 10 days after publication of a notice in the Federal Register initiating an arbitration proceeding under section 803, and in accordance with procedures specified by the Register of Copyrights, the Librarian of Congress shall, upon the recommendation of the Register of Copyrights, select 2 arbitrators from lists provided by professional arbitration associations. Qualifications of the arbitrators shall include experience in conducting arbitration proceedings and facilitating the resolution and settlement of disputes, and any qualifications which the Librarian of Congress, upon the recommendation of the Register of Copyrights, shall adopt by regulation. The 2 arbitrators so selected shall, within 10 days after their selection, choose a third arbitrator from the same lists, who shall serve as the chairperson of the arbitrators. If such 2 arbitrators fail to agree upon the selection of a third arbitrator, the

Librarian of Congress shall promptly select the third arbitrator. The Librarian of Congress, upon the recommendation of the Register of Copyrights, shall adopt regulations regarding standards of conduct which shall govern arbitrators and the proceedings under this chapter.

(c) Arbitration Proceedings. Copyright arbitration royalty panels shall conduct arbitration proceedings, subject to subchapter II of chapter 5 of title 5, for the purpose of making their determinations in carrying out the purposes set forth in section 801. The arbitration panels shall act on the basis of a fully documented written record, prior decisions of the Copyright Royalty Tribunal, prior copyright arbitration panel determinations, and rulings by the Librarian of Congress under section 801(c). Any copyright owner who claims to be entitled to royalties under section 111, 112, 114, 116, or 119, any transmitting organization entitled to a statutory license under section 112(g), any person entitled to a statutory license under section 114(d), any person entitled to a compulsory license under section 115, or any interested copyright party who claims to be entitled to royalties under section 1006, may submit relevant information and proposals to the arbitration panels in proceedings applicable to such copyright owner or interested copyright party, and any other person participating in arbitration proceedings may submit such relevant information and proposals to the arbitration panel conducting the proceedings. In ratemaking proceedings, the parties to the proceedings shall bear the entire cost thereof in such manner and proportion as the arbitration panels shall direct. In distribution proceedings, the parties shall bear the cost in direct proportion to their share of the distribution.

(d) Procedures. Effective on the date of the enactment of the Copyright Royalty Tribunal Reform Act of 1993, the Librarian of Congress shall adopt the rules and regulations set forth in chapter 3 of title 37 of the Code of Federal Regulations to govern proceedings under this chapter. Such rules and regulations shall remain in effect unless and until the Librarian, upon the recommendation of the Register of Copyrights, adopts supplemental or superseding regulations under subchapter II of chapter 5 of title 5.

(e) Report to the Librarian of Congress. Not later than 180 days after publication of the notice in the Federal Register initiating an arbitration proceeding, the copyright arbitration royalty panel conducting the proceeding shall report to the Librarian of Congress its determination concerning the royalty fee or distribution of royalty fees, as the case may be. Such report shall be accompanied by the written record, and shall set forth the facts that the arbitration panel found relevant to its determination.

(f) Action by Librarian of Congress. Within 90 days after receiving the report of a copyright arbitration royalty panel under subsection (e), the Librarian of Congress, upon the recommendation of the Register of Copyrights, shall adopt or reject the determination of the arbitration panel. The Librarian shall adopt the determination of the arbitration panel unless the Librarian finds that the determination is arbitrary or contrary to the applicable provisions of this title. If the Librarian rejects the determination of the arbitration panel, the Librarian shall, before the end of an additional 30–day period, and after full examination of the record created in the arbitration proceeding, issue an order setting the royalty fee or distribution of fees, as the case may be. The Librarian shall cause to be published in the Federal Register the determination of the arbitration panel, and the decision of the Librarian (including an order issued under the preceding sentence). The Librarian shall also publicize such determination and decision in such other manner as the Librarian considers appropriate. The Librarian shall also make the report of the arbitration panel and the accompanying record available for public inspection and copying.

(g) Judicial Review. Any decision of the Librarian of Congress under subsection (f) with respect to a determination of an arbitration panel may be appealed, by any aggrieved party who would be bound by the determination, to the United States Court of Appeals for the District of Columbia Circuit, within 30 days after the publication of the decision in the Federal Register. If no appeal is brought within such 30–day period, the decision of the Librarian is final, and the royalty fee or determination with respect to the distribution of fees, as the case may be, shall take effect as set forth in the decision. When this title provides that the royalty rates or terms that were previously in effect are to expire on a specified date, any adjustment by the Librarian of those rates or terms shall be effective as of the day following the date of expiration of the rates or terms that were previously in effect, even if the Librarian's decision is rendered on a later date. The pendency of an appeal under this paragraph shall not relieve persons obligated to make royalty payments under sections 111, 112, 114, 115, 116, 118, 119, or 1003 who would be affected by the determination on appeal to deposit the statement of account and royalty fees specified in those sections. The court shall have jurisdiction to modify or vacate a decision of the Librarian only if it finds, on the basis of the record before the Librarian, that the Librarian acted in an arbitrary manner. If the court modifies the decision of the Librarian, the court shall have jurisdiction to enter its own determination with respect to the amount or distribution of royalty fees and costs, to order the repayment of any excess fees, and to order the payment of any underpaid fees, and the interest pertaining respectively thereto, in accordance with its final judgment. The court may further vacate the decision of the arbitration panel and remand the case to the Librarian for arbitration proceedings in accordance with subsection (c).

(h) Administrative Matters.

(1) Deduction of costs of library of congress and copyright office from royalty fees. The Librarian of Congress and the Register of Copyrights may, to the extent not otherwise provided under this title, deduct from royalty fees deposited or collected under this title the reasonable costs incurred by the Library of Congress and the Copyright Office under this chapter. Such deduction may be made before the fees are distributed to any copyright claimants. In addition, all funds made available by an appropriations Act as offsetting collections and available for deductions under this subsection shall remain available until expended. In ratemaking proceedings, the reasonable costs of the Librarian of Congress and the Copyright Office shall be borne by the parties to the proceedings as directed by the arbitration panels under subsection (c).

(2) Positions required for administration of compulsory licensing. Section 307 of the Legislative Branch Appropriations Act, 1994, shall not apply to employee positions in the Library of Congress that are required to be filled in order to carry out section 111, 112, 114, 115, 116, 118, or 119 or chapter 10.

§ 803. Institution and conclusion of proceedings

(a)(1) With respect to proceedings under section 801(b)(1) concerning the adjustment of royalty rates as provided in sections 112, 114, 115, and 116, and with respect to proceedings under subparagraphs (A) and (D) of section 801(b)(2), during the calendar years specified in the schedule set forth in paragraphs (2), (3), (4), and (5), any owner or user of a copyrighted work whose royalty rates are specified by this title, established by the Copyright Royalty Tribunal before the date of the enactment of the Copyright Royalty Tribunal Reform Act of 1993, or established by a copyright arbitration royalty panel after such date of enactment, may file a petition with the Librarian of Congress declaring that the petitioner requests an adjustment of the rate. The Librarian of Congress shall, upon the recommendation of the Register of Copyrights, make a determination as to whether the petitioner has such a significant interest in the royalty rate in which an adjustment is requested. If the Librarian determines that the petitioner has such a significant interest, the Librarian shall cause notice of this determination, with the reasons therefor, to be published in the Federal Register, together with the notice of commencement of proceedings under this chapter.

(2) In proceedings under section 801(b)(2)(A) and (D), a petition described in paragraph (1) may be filed during 1995 and in each subsequent fifth calendar year.

(3) In proceedings under section 801(b)(1) concerning the adjustment of royalty rates as provided in section 115, a petition described in paragraph (1) may be filed in 1997 and in each subsequent tenth calendar year or as prescribed in section 115(c)(3)(D).

(4)(A) In proceedings under section 801(b)(1) concerning the adjustment of royalty rates as provided in section 116, a petition described in paragraph (1) may be filed at any time within 1 year after negotiated licenses authorized by section 116 are terminated or expire and are not replaced by subsequent agreements.

(B) If a negotiated license authorized by section 116 is terminated or expires and is not replaced by another such license agreement which provides permission to use a quantity of musical works not substantially smaller than the quantity of such works performed on coin-operated phonorecord players during the 1–year period ending March 1, 1989, the Librarian of Congress shall, upon petition filed under paragraph (1) within 1 year after such termination or expiration, convene a copyright arbitration royalty panel. The arbitration panel shall promptly establish an interim royalty rate or rates for the public performance by means of a coin-operated phonorecord player of non-dramatic musical works embodied in phonorecords which had been subject to the terminated or expired negotiated license agreement. Such rate or rates shall be the same as the last such rate or rates and shall remain in force until the conclusion of proceedings by the arbitration panel, in accordance with section 802, to adjust the royalty rates applicable to such works, or until superseded by a new negotiated license agreement, as provided in section 116(b).

(5) With respect to proceedings under section 801(b)(1) concerning the determination of reasonable terms and rates of royalty payments as provided in section 112 or 114, the Librarian of Congress shall proceed when and as provided by those sections.

(b) With respect to proceedings under subparagraph (B) or (C) of section 801(b)(2), following an event described in either of those subsections, any owner or user of a copyrighted work whose royalty rates are specified by section 111, or by a rate established by the Copyright Royalty Tribunal or the Librarian of Congress, may, within twelve months, file a petition with the Librarian declaring that the petitioner requests an adjustment of the rate. In this event the Librarian shall proceed as in subsection (a) of this section. Any change in royalty rates made by the Copyright Royalty Tribunal or the Librarian of Congress pursuant to this subsection may be reconsidered in 1980, 1985, and each fifth calendar year thereafter, in accordance with the provisions in section 801(b)(2)(B) or (C), as the case may be.

(c) With respect to proceedings under section 801(b)(1), concerning the determination of reasonable terms and rates of royalty payments as provided in section 118, the Librarian of Congress shall proceed when and as provided by that section.

(d) With respect to proceedings under section 801(b)(3) or (4), concerning the distribution of royalty fees in certain circumstances under section 111, 116, 119, or 1007, the Librarian of Congress shall, upon a determination that a controversy exists concerning such distribution, cause to be published in the Federal Register notice of commencement of proceedings under this chapter.

CHAPTER 9—PROTECTION OF SEMICONDUCTOR CHIP PRODUCTS

Pub.L. 98–620, 98 Stat. 3347 (1984)

§ 901. Definitions

(a) As used in this chapter—

(1) a "semiconductor chip product" is the final or intermediate form of any product—

(A) having two or more layers of metallic, insulating, or semiconductor material, deposited or otherwise placed on, or etched away or otherwise removed from, a piece of semiconductor material in accordance with a predetermined pattern; and

(B) intended to perform electronic circuitry functions;

(2) a "mask work" is a series of related images, however fixed or encoded—

(A) having or representing the predetermined, three-dimensional pattern of metallic, insulating, or semiconductor material present or removed from the layers of a semiconductor chip product; and

(B) in which series the relation of the images to one another is that each image has the pattern of the surface of one form of the semiconductor chip product;

(3) a mask work is "fixed" in a semiconductor chip product when its embodiment in the product is sufficiently permanent or stable to permit the mask work to be perceived or reproduced from the product for a period of more than transitory duration;

(4) to "distribute" means to sell, or to lease, bail, or otherwise transfer, or to offer to sell, lease, bail, or otherwise transfer;

(5) to "commercially exploit" a mask work is to distribute to the public for commercial purposes a semiconductor chip product embodying the mask work; except that such term includes an offer to sell or transfer a semiconductor chip product only when the offer is in writing and occurs after the mask work is fixed in the semiconductor chip product;

(6) the "owner" of a mask work is the person who created the mask work, the legal representative of that person if that person is deceased or under a legal incapacity, or a party to whom all the rights under this chapter of such person or representative are transferred in accordance with section 903(b); except that, in the case of a work made within the scope of a person's employment, the owner is the employer for whom the person created the mask work or a party to whom all the rights under this chapter of the employer are transferred in accordance with section 903(b);

(7) an "innocent purchaser" is a person who purchases a semiconductor chip product in good faith and without having notice of protection with respect to the semiconductor chip product;

(8) having "notice of protection" means having actual knowledge that, or reasonable grounds to believe that, a mask work is protected under this chapter; and

(9) an "infringing semiconductor chip product" is a semiconductor chip product which is made, imported, or distributed in violation of the exclusive rights of the owner of a mask work under this chapter.

(b) For purposes of this chapter, the distribution or importation of a product incorporating a semiconductor chip product as a part thereof is a distribution or importation of that semiconductor chip product.

§ 902.　Subject matter of protection

(a)(1) Subject to the provisions of subsection (b), a mask work fixed in a semiconductor chip product, by or under the authority of the owner of the mask work, is eligible for protection under this chapter if—

(A) on the date on which the mask work is registered under section 908, or is first commercially exploited anywhere in the world, whichever occurs first, the owner of the mask work is (i) a national or domiciliary of the United States, (ii) a national, domiciliary, or sovereign authority of a foreign nation that is a party to a treaty affording protection to mask works to which the United States is also a party, or (iii) a stateless person, wherever that person may be domiciled;

(B) the mask work is first commercially exploited in the United States; or

(C) the mask work comes within the scope of a Presidential proclamation issued under paragraph (2).

(2) Whenever the President finds that a foreign nation extends, to mask works of owners who are nationals or domiciliaries of the United States protection (A) on substantially the same basis as that on which the foreign nation extends protection to mask works of its own nationals and domiciliaries and mask works first commercially exploited in that nation, or (B) on substantially the same basis as provided in this chapter, the President may by proclamation extend protection under this chapter to mask works (i) of owners who are, on the date on which the mask works are registered under section 908, or the date on which the mask works are first commercially exploited anywhere in the world, whichever occurs first, nationals, domiciliaries, or sovereign authorities of that nation, or (ii) which are first commercially exploited in that nation. The President may revise, suspend, or revoke any such proclamation or impose any conditions or limitations on protection extended under any such proclamation.

(b) Protection under this chapter shall not be available for a mask work that—

(1) is not original; or

(2) consists of designs that are staple, commonplace, or familiar in the semiconductor industry, or variations of such designs, combined in a way that, considered as a whole, is not original.

(c) In no case does protection under this chapter for a mask work extend to any idea, procedure, process, system, method of operation, concept, principle, or discovery, regardless of the form in which it is described, explained, illustrated, or embodied in such work.

§ 903. Ownership, transfer, licensing, and recordation

(a) The exclusive rights in a mask work subject to protection under this chapter belong to the owner of the mask work.

(b) The owner of the exclusive rights in a mask work may transfer all of those rights, or license all or less than all of those rights, by any written instrument signed by such owner or a duly authorized agent of the owner. Such rights may be transferred or licensed by operation of law, may be bequeathed by will, and may pass as personal property by the applicable laws of intestate succession.

(c)(1) Any document pertaining to a mask work may be recorded in the Copyright Office if the document filed for recordation bears the actual signature of the person who executed it, or if it is accompanied by a sworn or official certification that it is a true copy of the original, signed document. The Register of Copyrights shall, upon receipt of the document and the fee specified pursuant to section 908(d), record the document and return it with a certificate of recordation. The recordation of any transfer or license under this paragraph gives all persons constructive notice of the facts stated in the recorded document concerning the transfer or license.

(2) In any case in which conflicting transfers of the exclusive rights in a mask work are made, the transfer first executed shall be

void as against a subsequent transfer which is made for a valuable consideration and without notice of the first transfer, unless the first transfer is recorded in accordance with paragraph (1) within three months after the date on which it is executed, but in no case later than the day before the date of such subsequent transfer.

(d) Mask works prepared by an officer or employee of the United States Government as part of that person's official duties are not protected under this chapter, but the United States Government is not precluded from receiving and holding exclusive rights in mask works transferred to the Government under subsection (b).

§ 904. Duration of protection

(a) The protection provided for a mask work under this chapter shall commence on the date on which the mask work is registered under section 908, or the date on which the mask work is first commercially exploited anywhere in the world, whichever occurs first.

(b) Subject to subsection (c) and the provisions of this chapter, the protection provided under this chapter to a mask work shall end ten years after the date on which such protection commences under subsection (a).

(c) All terms of protection provided in this section shall run to the end of the calendar year in which they would otherwise expire.

§ 905. Exclusive rights in mask works

The owner of a mask work provided protection under this chapter has the exclusive rights to do and to authorize any of the following:

(1) to reproduce the mask work by optical, electronic, or any other means;

(2) to import or distribute a semiconductor chip product in which the mask work is embodied; and

(3) to induce or knowingly to cause another person to do any of the acts described in paragraphs (1) and (2).

§ 906. Limitation on exclusive rights: reverse engineering; first sale

(a) Notwithstanding the provisions of section 905, it is not an infringement of the exclusive rights of the owner of a mask work for—

(1) a person to reproduce the mask work solely for the purpose of teaching, analyzing, or evaluating the concepts or techniques embodied in the mask work or the circuitry, logic flow, or organization of components used in the mask work; or

(2) a person who performs the analysis or evaluation described in paragraph (1) to incorporate the results of such conduct in an original mask work which is made to be distributed.

(b) Notwithstanding the provisions of section 905(2), the owner of a particular semiconductor chip product made by the owner of the mask work, or by any person authorized by the owner of the mask work, may import, distribute, or otherwise dispose of or use, but not reproduce, that particular semiconductor chip product without the authority of the owner of the mask work.

§ 907. Limitation on exclusive rights: innocent infringement

(a) Notwithstanding any other provision of this chapter, an innocent purchaser of an infringing semiconductor chip product—

(1) shall incur no liability under this chapter with respect to the importation or distribution of units of the infringing semiconductor chip product that occurs before the innocent purchaser has notice of protection with respect to the mask work embodied in the semiconductor chip product; and

(2) shall be liable only for a reasonable royalty on each unit of the infringing semiconductor chip product that the innocent purchaser imports or distributes after having notice of protection with respect to the mask work embodied in the semiconductor chip product.

(b) The amount of the royalty referred to in subsection (a)(2) shall be determined by the court in a civil action for infringement unless the parties resolve the issue by voluntary negotiation, mediation, or binding arbitration.

(c) The immunity of an innocent purchaser from liability referred to in subsection (a)(1) and the limitation of remedies with respect to an innocent purchaser referred to in subsection (a)(2) shall extend to any person who directly or indirectly purchases an infringing semiconductor chip product from an innocent purchaser.

(d) The provisions of subsections (a), (b), and (c) apply only with respect to those units of an infringing semiconductor chip product that an innocent purchaser purchased before having notice of protection with respect to the mask work embodied in the semiconductor chip product.

§ 908. Registration of claims of protection

(a) The owner of a mask work may apply to the Register of Copyrights for registration of a claim of protection in a mask work. Protection of a mask work under this chapter shall terminate if application for registration of a claim of protection in the mask work is not made as provided in this chapter within two years after the date on which the mask work is first commercially exploited anywhere in the world.

(b) The Register of Copyrights shall be responsible for all administrative functions and duties under this chapter. Except for section 708, the provisions of chapter 7 of this title relating to the general responsibilities, organization, regulatory authority, actions, records, and publications of the Copyright Office shall apply to this chapter, except that the Register of

Copyrights may make such changes as may be necessary in applying those provisions to this chapter.

(c) The application for registration of a mask work shall be made on a form prescribed by the Register of Copyrights. Such form may require any information regarded by the Register as bearing upon the preparation or identification of the mask work, the existence or duration of protection of the mask work under this chapter, or ownership of the mask work. The application shall be accompanied by the fee set pursuant to subsection (d) and the identifying material specified pursuant to such subsection.

(d) The Register of Copyrights shall by regulation set reasonable fees for the filing of applications to register claims of protection in mask works under this chapter, and for other services relating to the administration of this chapter or the rights under this chapter, taking into consideration the cost of providing those services, the benefits of a public record, and statutory fee schedules under this title. The Register shall also specify the identifying material to be deposited in connection with the claim for registration.

(e) If the Register of Copyrights, after examining an application for registration, determines, in accordance with the provisions of this chapter, that the application relates to a mask work which is entitled to protection under this chapter, then the Register shall register the claim of protection and issue to the applicant a certificate of registration of the claim of protection under the seal of the Copyright Office. The effective date of registration of a claim of protection shall be the date on which an application, deposit of identifying material, and fee, which are determined by the Register of Copyrights or by a court of competent jurisdiction to be acceptable for registration of the claim, have all been received in the Copyright Office.

(f) In any action for infringement under this chapter, the certificate of registration of a mask work shall constitute prima facie evidence (1) of the facts stated in the certificate, and (2) that the applicant issued the certificate has met the requirements of this chapter, and the regulations issued under this chapter, with respect to the registration of claims.

(g) Any applicant for registration under this section who is dissatisfied with the refusal of the Register of Copyrights to issue a certificate of registration under this section may seek judicial review of that refusal by bringing an action for such review in an appropriate United States district court not later than sixty days after the refusal. The provisions of chapter 7 of title 5 shall apply to such judicial review. The failure of the Register of Copyrights to issue a certificate of registration within four months after an application for registration is filed shall be deemed to be a refusal to issue a certificate of registration for purposes of this subsection and section 910(b)(2), except that, upon a showing of good cause, the district court may shorten such four-month period.

§ 909. Mask work notice

(a) The owner of a mask work provided protection under this chapter may affix notice to the mask work, and to masks and semiconductor chip products embodying the mask work, in such manner and location as to give reasonable notice of such protection. The Register of Copyrights shall prescribe by regulation, as examples, specific methods of affixation and positions of notice for purposes of this section, but these specifications shall not be considered exhaustive. The affixation of such notice is not a condition of protection under this chapter, but shall constitute prima facie evidence of notice of protection.

(b) The notice referred to in subsection (a) shall consist of—

(1) the words "mask work", the symbol *M*, or the symbol Ⓜ ; and

(2) the name of the owner or owners of the mask work or an abbreviation by which the name is recognized or is generally known.

§ 910. Enforcement of exclusive rights

(a) Except as otherwise provided in this chapter, any person who violates any of the exclusive rights of the owner of a mask work under this chapter, by conduct in or affecting commerce, shall be liable as an infringer of such rights. As used in this subsection, the term "any person" includes any State, any instrumentality of a State, and any officer or employee of a State or instrumentality of a State acting in his or her official capacity. Any State, and any such instrumentality, officer, or employee, shall be subject to the provisions of this chapter in the same manner and to the same extent as any nongovernmental entity.

(b)(1) The owner of a mask work protected under this chapter, or the exclusive licensee of all rights under this chapter with respect to the mask work, shall, after a certificate of registration of a claim of protection in that mask work has been issued under section 908, be entitled to institute a civil action for any infringement with respect to the mask work which is committed after the commencement of protection of the mask work under section 904(a).

(2) In any case in which an application for registration of a claim of protection in a mask work and the required deposit of identifying material and fee have been received in the Copyright Office in proper form and registration of the mask work has been refused, the applicant is entitled to institute a civil action for infringement under this chapter with respect to the mask work if notice of the action, together with a copy of the complaint, is served on the Register of Copyrights, in accordance with the Federal Rules of Civil Procedure. The Register may, at his or her option, become a party to the action with respect to the issue of whether the claim of protection is eligible for registration by entering an appearance within sixty days after such service, but the failure of the Register to become a party to the action shall not deprive the court of jurisdiction to determine that issue.

(c)(1) The Secretary of the Treasury and the United States Postal Service shall separately or jointly issue regulations for the enforcement of the rights set forth in section 905 with respect to importation. These regulations may require, as a condition for the exclusion of articles from the United States, that the person seeking exclusion take any one or more of the following actions:

(A) Obtain a court order enjoining, or an order of the International Trade Commission under section 337 of the Tariff Act of 1930 excluding, importation of the articles.

(B) Furnish proof that the mask work involved is protected under this chapter and that the importation of the articles would infringe the rights in the mask work under this chapter.

(C) Post a surety bond for any injury that may result if the detention or exclusion of the articles proves to be unjustified.

(2) Articles imported in violation of the rights set forth in section 905 are subject to seizure and forfeiture in the same manner as property imported in violation of the customs laws. Any such forfeited articles shall be destroyed as directed by the Secretary of the Treasury or the court, as the case may be, except that the articles may be returned to the country of export whenever it is shown to the satisfaction of the Secretary of the Treasury that the importer had no reasonable grounds for believing that his or her acts constituted a violation of the law.

§ 911. Civil actions

(a) Any court having jurisdiction of a civil action arising under this chapter may grant temporary restraining orders, preliminary injunctions, and permanent injunctions on such terms as the court may deem reasonable to prevent or restrain infringement of the exclusive rights in a mask work under this chapter.

(b) Upon finding an infringer liable, to a person entitled under section 910(b)(1) to institute a civil action, for an infringement of any exclusive right under this chapter, the court shall award such person actual damages suffered by the person as a result of the infringement. The court shall also award such person the infringer's profits that are attributable to the infringement and are not taken into account in computing the award of actual damages. In establishing the infringer's profits, such person is required to present proof only of the infringer's gross revenue, and the infringer is required to prove his or her deductible expenses and the elements of profit attributable to factors other than the mask work.

(c) At any time before final judgment is rendered, a person entitled to institute a civil action for infringement may elect, instead of actual damages and profits as provided by subsection (b), an award of statutory damages for all infringements involved in the action, with respect to any one mask work for which any one infringer is liable individually, or for which any two or more infringers are liable jointly and severally, in an amount not more than $250,000 as the court considers just.

(d) An action for infringement under this chapter shall be barred unless the action is commenced within three years after the claim accrues.

(e)(1) At any time while an action for infringement of the exclusive rights in a mask work under this chapter is pending, the court may order the impounding, on such terms as it may deem reasonable, of all semiconductor chip products, and any drawings, tapes, masks, or other products by means of which such products may be reproduced, that are claimed to have been made, imported, or used in violation of those exclusive rights. Insofar as practicable, applications for orders under this paragraph shall be heard and determined in the same manner as an application for a temporary restraining order or preliminary injunction.

(2) As part of a final judgment or decree, the court may order the destruction or other disposition of any infringing semiconductor chip products, and any masks, tapes, or other articles by means of which such products may be reproduced.

(f) In any civil action arising under this chapter, the court in its discretion may allow the recovery of full costs, including reasonable attorneys' fees, to the prevailing party.

(g)(1) Any State, any instrumentality of a State, and any officer or employee of a State or instrumentality of a State acting in his or her official capacity, shall not be immune, under the Eleventh Amendment of the Constitution of the United States or under any other doctrine of sovereign immunity, from suit in Federal court by any person, including any governmental or nongovernmental entity, for a violation of any of the exclusive rights of the owner of a mask work under this chapter, or for any other violation under this chapter.

(2) In a suit described in paragraph (1) for a violation described in that paragraph, remedies (including remedies both at law and in equity) are available for the violation to the same extent as such remedies are available for such a violation in a suit against any public or private entity other than a State, instrumentality of a State, or officer or employee of a State acting in his or her official capacity. Such remedies include actual damages and profits under subsection (b), statutory damages under subsection (c), impounding and disposition of infringing articles under subsection (e), and costs and attorney's fees under subsection (f).

§ 912. Relation to other laws

(a) Nothing in this chapter shall affect any right or remedy held by any person under chapters 1 through 8 or 10 of this title, or under title 35.

(b) Except as provided in section 908(b) of this title, references to "this title" or "title 17" in chapters 1 through 8 or 10 of this title shall be deemed not to apply to this chapter.

(c) The provisions of this chapter shall preempt the laws of any State to the extent those laws provide any rights or remedies with respect to a mask work which are equivalent to those rights or remedies provided by this chapter, except that such preemption shall be effective only with respect to actions filed on or after January 1, 1986.

(d) Notwithstanding subsection (c), nothing in this chapter shall detract from any rights of a mask work owner, whether under Federal law (exclusive of this chapter) or under the common law or the statutes of a State, heretofore or hereafter declared or enacted, with respect to any mask work first commercially exploited before July 1, 1983.

§ 913. Transitional provisions

(a) No application for registration under section 908 may be filed, and no civil action under section 910 or other enforcement proceeding under this chapter may be instituted, until sixty days after the date of the enactment of this chapter.

(b) No monetary relief under section 911 may be granted with respect to any conduct that occurred before the date of the enactment of this chapter, except as provided in subsection (d).

(c) Subject to subsection (a), the provisions of this chapter apply to all mask works that are first commercially exploited or are registered under this chapter, or both, on or after the date of the enactment of this chapter.

(d)(1) Subject to subsection (a), protection is available under this chapter to any mask work that was first commercially exploited on or after July 1, 1983, and before the date of the enactment of this chapter, if a claim of protection in the mask work is registered in the Copyright Office before July 1, 1985, under section 908.

(2) In the case of any mask work described in paragraph (1) that is provided protection under this chapter, infringing semiconductor chip product units manufactured before the date of the enactment of this chapter may, without liability under sections 910 and 911, be imported into or distributed in the United States, or both, until two years after the date of registration of the mask work under section 908, but only if the importer or distributor, as the case may be, first pays or offers to pay the reasonable royalty referred to in section 907(a)(2) to the mask work owner, on all such units imported or distributed, or both, after the date of the enactment of this chapter.

(3) In the event that a person imports or distributes infringing semiconductor chip product units described in paragraph (2) of this subsection without first paying or offering to pay the reasonable royalty specified in such paragraph, or if the person refuses or fails to make such payment, the mask work owner shall be entitled to the relief provided in sections 910 and 911.

§ 914. International transitional provisions

(a) Notwithstanding the conditions set forth in subparagraphs (A) and (C) of section 902(a)(1) with respect to the availability of protection under this chapter to nationals, domiciliaries, and sovereign authorities of a foreign nation, the Secretary of Commerce may, upon the petition of any person, or upon the Secretary's own motion, issue an order extending protection under this chapter to such foreign nationals, domiciliaries, and sovereign authorities if the Secretary finds—

(1) that the foreign nation is making good faith efforts and reasonable progress toward—

(A) entering into a treaty described in section 902(a)(1)(A); or

(B) enacting or implementing legislation that would be in compliance with subparagraph (A) or (B) of section 902(a)(2); and

(2) that the nationals, domiciliaries, and sovereign authorities of the foreign nation, and persons controlled by them, are not engaged in the misappropriation, or unauthorized distribution or commercial exploitation, of mask works; and

(3) that issuing the order would promote the purposes of this chapter and international comity with respect to the protection of mask works.

(b) While an order under subsection (a) is in effect with respect to a foreign nation, no application for registration of a claim for protection in a mask work under this chapter may be denied solely because the owner of the mask work is a national, domiciliary, or sovereign authority of that foreign nation, or solely because the mask work was first commercially exploited in that foreign nation.

(c) Any order issued by the Secretary of Commerce under subsection (a) shall be effective for such a period as the Secretary designates in the order, except that no such order may be effective after that date on which the authority of the Secretary of Commerce terminates under subsection (e). The effective date of any such order shall also be designated in the order. In the case of an order issued upon the petition of a person, such effective date may be no earlier than the date on which the Secretary receives such petition.

(d)(1) Any order issued under this section shall terminate if—

(A) the Secretary of Commerce finds that any of the conditions set forth in paragraphs (1), (2), and (3) of subsection (a) no longer exist; or

(B) mask works of nationals, domiciliaries, and sovereign authorities of that foreign nation or mask works first commercially exploited in that foreign nation become eligible for protection under subparagraph (A) or (C) of section 902(a)(1).

(2) Upon the termination or expiration of an order issued under this section, registrations of claims of protection in mask works made pursuant to that order shall remain valid for the period specified in section 904.

(e) The authority of the Secretary of Commerce under this section shall commence on the date of the enactment of this chapter, and shall terminate on July 1, 1995.

(f)(1) The Secretary of Commerce shall promptly notify the Register of Copyrights and the Committees on the Judiciary of the Senate and the House of Representatives of the issuance or termination of any order under this section, together with a statement of the reasons for such action. The Secretary shall also publish such notification and statement of reasons in the Federal Register.

(2) Two years after the date of the enactment of this chapter, the Secretary of Commerce, in consultation with the Register of Copyrights, shall transmit to the Committees on the Judiciary of the Senate and the House of Representatives a report on the actions taken under this section and on the current status of international recognition of mask work protection. The report shall include such recommendation for modifications of the protection accorded under this chapter to mask works owned by nationals, domiciliaries, or sovereign authorities of foreign nations as the Secretary, in consultation with the Register of Copyrights, considers would promote the purposes of this chapter and international comity with respect to mask work protection. Not later than July 1, 1994, the Secretary of Commerce, in consultation with the Register of Copyrights, shall transmit to the Committees on the Judiciary of the Senate and the House of Representatives a report updating the matters contained in the report transmitted under the preceding sentence.

CHAPTER 10—DIGITAL AUDIO RECORDING DEVICES AND MEDIA

Pub.L. 102–563, 106 Stat. 4237 (Oct. 28, 1992)

Subchapter A—Definitions

Subchapter A—Definitions

§ 1001. Definitions

As used in this chapter, the following terms have the following meanings:

(1) A "digital audio copied recording" is a reproduction in a digital recording format of a digital musical recording, whether that reproduction is made directly from another digital musical recording or indirectly from a transmission.

(2) A "digital audio interface device" is any machine or device that is designed specifically to communicate digital audio information and related interface data to a digital audio recording device through a nonprofessional interface.

(3) A "digital audio recording device" is any machine or device of a type commonly distributed to individuals for use by individuals, whether or not included with or as part of some other machine or device, the digital recording function of which is designed or marketed for the primary purpose of, and that is capable of, making a digital audio copied recording for private use, except for—

(A) professional model products, and

(B) dictation machines, answering machines, and other audio recording equipment that is designed and marketed primarily for the creation of sound recordings resulting from the fixation of nonmusical sounds.

(4)(A) A "digital audio recording medium" is any material object in a form commonly distributed for use by individuals, that is primarily marketed or most commonly used by consumers for the purpose of making digital audio copied recordings by use of a digital audio recording device.

(B) Such term does not include any material object—

(i) that embodies a sound recording at the time it is first distributed by the importer or manufacturer; or

(ii) that is primarily marketed and most commonly used by consumers either for the purpose of making copies of motion pictures or other audiovisual works or for the purpose of making copies of nonmusical literary works, including computer programs or data bases.

(5)(A) A "digital musical recording" is a material object—

(i) in which are fixed, in a digital recording format, only sounds, and material, statements, or instructions incidental to those fixed sounds, if any, and

(ii) from which the sounds and material can be perceived, reproduced, or otherwise communicated, either directly or with the aid of a machine or device.

(B) A "digital musical recording" does not include a material object—

(i) in which the fixed sounds consist entirely of spoken word recordings, or

(ii) in which one or more computer programs are fixed, except that a digital musical recording may contain statements or instructions constituting the fixed sounds and incidental material, and statements or instructions to be used directly or indirectly in order to bring about the perception, reproduction, or communication of the fixed sounds and incidental material.

(C) For purposes of this paragraph—

(i) a "spoken word recording" is a sound recording in which are fixed only a series of spoken words, except that the spoken words may be accompanied by incidental musical or other sounds, and

(ii) the term "incidental" means related to and relatively minor by comparison.

(6) "Distribute" means to sell, lease, or assign a product to consumers in the United States, or to sell, lease, or assign a product in the United States for ultimate transfer to consumers in the United States.

(7) An "interested copyright party" is—

(A) the owner of the exclusive right under section 106(1) of this title to reproduce a sound recording of a musical work that has been embodied in a digital musical recording or analog musical recording lawfully made under this title that has been distributed;

(B) the legal or beneficial owner of, or the person that controls, the right to reproduce in a digital musical recording or analog musical recording a musical work that has been embodied in a digital musical recording or analog musical recording lawfully made under this title that has been distributed;

(C) a featured recording artist who performs on a sound recording that has been distributed; or

(D) any association or other organization—

(i) representing persons specified in subparagraph (A), (B), or (C), or

(ii) engaged in licensing rights in musical works to music users on behalf of writers and publishers.

(8) To "manufacture" means to produce or assemble a product in the United States. A "manufacturer" is a person who manufactures.

(9) A "music publisher" is a person that is authorized to license the reproduction of a particular musical work in a sound recording.

(10) A "professional model product" is an audio recording device that is designed, manufactured, marketed, and intended for use by recording professionals in the ordinary course of a lawful business, in accordance with such requirements as the Secretary of Commerce shall establish by regulation.

(11) The term "serial copying" means the duplication in a digital format of a copyrighted musical work or sound recording from a digital reproduction of a digital musical recording. The term "digital reproduction of a digital musical recording" does not include a digital musical recording as distributed, by authority of the copyright owner, for ultimate sale to consumers.

(12) The "transfer price" of a digital audio recording device or a digital audio recording medium—

(A) is, subject to subparagraph (B)—

(i) in the case of an imported product, the actual entered value at United States Customs (exclusive of any freight, insurance, and applicable duty), and

(ii) in the case of a domestic product, the manufacturer's transfer price (FOB the manufacturer, and exclusive of any direct sales taxes or excise taxes incurred in connection with the sale); and

391

(B) shall, in a case in which the transferor and transferee are related entities or within a single entity, not be less than a reasonable arms-length price under the principles of the regulations adopted pursuant to section 482 of the Internal Revenue Code of 1986, or any successor provision to such section.

(13) A "writer" is the composer or lyricist of a particular musical work.

Subchapter B—Copying Controls

§ 1002.   Incorporation of copying controls

(a) Prohibition on Importation, Manufacture, and Distribution. No person shall import, manufacture, or distribute any digital audio recording device or digital audio interface device that does not conform to—

(1) the Serial Copy Management System;

(2) a system that has the same functional characteristics as the Serial Copy Management System and requires that copyright and generation status information be accurately sent, received, and acted upon between devices using the system's method of serial copying regulation and devices using the Serial Copy Management System; or

(3) any other system certified by the Secretary of Commerce as prohibiting unauthorized serial copying.

(b) Development of Verification Procedure. The Secretary of Commerce shall establish a procedure to verify, upon the petition of an interested party, that a system meets the standards set forth in subsection (a)(2).

(c) Prohibition on Circumvention of the System. No person shall import, manufacture, or distribute any device, or offer or perform any service, the primary purpose or effect of which is to avoid, bypass, remove, deactivate, or otherwise circumvent any program or circuit which implements, in whole or in part, a system described in subsection (a).

(d) Encoding of Information on Digital Musical Recordings.

(1) Prohibition on encoding inaccurate information. No person shall encode a digital musical recording of a sound recording with inaccurate information relating to the category code, copyright status, or generation status of the source material for the recording.

(2) Encoding of copyright status not required. Nothing in this chapter requires any person engaged in the importation or manufacture of digital musical recordings to encode any such digital musical recording with respect to its copyright status.

(e) Information Accompanying Transmission in Digital Format. Any person who transmits or otherwise communicates to the public any sound recording in digital format is not required under this chapter to transmit or otherwise communicate the information relating to the copyright status of the sound recording. Any such person who does transmit or otherwise communicate such copyright status information shall transmit or communicate such information accurately.

Subchapter C—Royalty Payments

§ 1003.   Obligation to make royalty payments

(a) Prohibition on Importation and Manufacture. No person shall import into and distribute, or manufacture and distribute, any digital audio recording device or digital audio recording medium unless such person records the notice specified by this section and subsequently deposits the statements of account and applicable royalty payments for such device or medium specified in section 1004.

(b) Filing of Notice. The importer or manufacturer of any digital audio recording device or digital audio recording medium, within a product category or utilizing a technology with respect to which such manufacturer or importer has not previously filed a notice under this subsection, shall file with the Register of Copyrights a notice with respect to such device or medium, in such form and content as the Register shall prescribe by regulation.

(c) Filing of Quarterly and Annual Statements of Account.—

    (1) Generally. Any importer or manufacturer that distributes any digital audio recording device or digital audio recording medium that it manufactured or imported shall file with the Register of Copyrights, in such form and content as the Register shall prescribe by regulation, such quarterly and annual statements of account with respect to such distribution as the Register shall prescribe by regulation.

    (2) Certification, verification, and confidentiality. Each such statement shall be certified as accurate by an authorized officer or principal of the importer or manufacturer. The Register shall issue regulations to provide for the verification and audit of such statements and to protect the confidentiality of the information contained in such statements. Such regulations shall provide for the disclosure, in confidence, of such statements to interested copyright parties.

    (3) Royalty payments. Each such statement shall be accompanied by the royalty payments specified in section 1004.

§ 1004.   Royalty payments

(a) Digital Audio Recording Devices.

    (1) Amount of payment. The royalty payment due under section 1003 for each digital audio recording device imported into and distributed in the United States, or manufactured and distributed in the United States, shall be 2 percent of the transfer price. Only the first person to manufacture and distribute or import and distribute such device shall be required to pay the royalty with respect to such device.

(2) Calculation for devices distributed with other devices. With respect to a digital audio recording device first distributed in combination with one or more devices, either as a physically integrated unit or as separate components, the royalty payment shall be calculated as follows:

(A) If the digital audio recording device and such other devices are part of a physically integrated unit, the royalty payment shall be based on the transfer price of the unit, but shall be reduced by any royalty payment made on any digital audio recording device included within the unit that was not first distributed in combination with the unit.

(B) If the digital audio recording device is not part of a physically integrated unit and substantially similar devices have been distributed separately at any time during the preceding 4 calendar quarters, the royalty payment shall be based on the average transfer price of such devices during those 4 quarters.

(C) If the digital audio recording device is not part of a physically integrated unit and substantially similar devices have not been distributed separately at any time during the preceding 4 calendar quarters, the royalty payment shall be based on a constructed price reflecting the proportional value of such device to the combination as a whole.

(3) Limits on royalties. Notwithstanding paragraph (1) or (2), the amount of the royalty payment for each digital audio recording device shall not be less than $1 nor more than the royalty maximum. The royalty maximum shall be $8 per device, except that in the case of a physically integrated unit containing more than 1 digital audio recording device, the royalty maximum for such unit shall be $12. During the 6th year after the effective date of this chapter, and not more than once each year thereafter, any interested copyright party may petition the Librarian of Congress to increase the royalty maximum and, if more than 20 percent of the royalty payments are at the relevant royalty maximum, the Librarian of Congress shall prospectively increase such royalty maximum with the goal of having no more than 10 percent of such payments at the new royalty maximum; however the amount of any such increase as a percentage of the royalty maximum shall in no event exceed the percentage increase in the Consumer Price Index during the period under review.

(b) Digital Audio Recording Media. The royalty payment due under section 1003 for each digital audio recording medium imported into and distributed in the United States, or manufactured and distributed in the United States, shall be 3 percent of the transfer price. Only the first person to manufacture and distribute or import and distribute such medium shall be required to pay the royalty with respect to such medium.

§ 1005. Deposit of royalty payments and deduction of expenses

The Register of Copyrights shall receive all royalty payments deposited under this chapter and, after deducting the reasonable costs incurred by the Copyright Office under this chapter, shall deposit the balance in the Treasury of the United States as offsetting receipts, in such manner as the Secretary of the Treasury directs. All funds held by the Secretary of the Treasury shall be invested in interest-bearing United States securities for later distribution with interest under section 1007. The Register may, in the Register's discretion, 4 years after the close of any calendar year, close out the royalty payments account for that calendar year, and may treat any funds remaining in such account and any subsequent deposits that would otherwise be attributable to that calendar year as attributable to the succeeding calendar year.

§ 1006. Entitlement to royalty payments

(a) **Interested Copyright Parties.** The royalty payments deposited pursuant to section 1005 shall, in accordance with the procedures specified in section 1007, be distributed to any interested copyright party—

    (1) whose musical work or sound recording has been—

        (A) embodied in a digital musical recording or an analog musical recording lawfully made under this title that has been distributed, and

        (B) distributed in the form of digital musical recordings or analog musical recordings or disseminated to the public in transmissions, during the period to which such payments pertain; and

    (2) who has filed a claim under section 1007.

(b) **Allocation of Royalty Payments to Groups.** The royalty payments shall be divided into 2 funds as follows:

    (1) **The sound recordings fund.** 66 2/3 percent of the royalty payments shall be allocated to the Sound Recordings Fund. 2 5/8 percent of the royalty payments allocated to the Sound Recordings Fund shall be placed in an escrow account managed by an independent administrator jointly appointed by the interested copyright parties described in section 1001(7)(A) and the American Federation of Musicians (or any successor entity) to be distributed to nonfeatured musicians (whether or not members of the American Federation of Musicians or any successor entity) who have performed on sound recordings distributed in the United States. 1 3/8 percent of the royalty payments allocated to the Sound Recordings Fund shall be placed in an escrow account managed by an independent administrator jointly appointed by the interested copyright parties described in section 1001(7)(A) and the American Federation of Television and Radio Artists (or any successor entity) to be distributed to nonfeatured vocalists (whether or not members of the American Federation of Television and Radio Artists or any successor entity) who have performed on sound recordings distributed in the United States. 40 percent of the remaining royalty payments in the Sound Recordings Fund shall be distributed to the

interested copyright parties described in section 1001(7)(C), and 60 percent of such remaining royalty payments shall be distributed to the interested copyright parties described in section 1001(7)(A).

(2) The Musical Works Fund.

(A) 33 ⅓ percent of the royalty payments shall be allocated to the Musical Works Fund for distribution to interested copyright parties described in section 1001(7)(B).

(B)(i) Music publishers shall be entitled to 50 percent of the royalty payments allocated to the Musical Works Fund.

(ii) Writers shall be entitled to the other 50 percent of the royalty payments allocated to the Musical Works Fund.

(c) **Allocation of Royalty Payments Within Groups.** If all interested copyright parties within a group specified in subsection (b) do not agree on a voluntary proposal for the distribution of the royalty payments within each group, the Librarian of Congress shall convene a copyright arbitration royalty panel which shall, pursuant to the procedures specified under section 1007(c), allocate royalty payments under this section based on the extent to which, during the relevant period—

(1) for the Sound Recordings Fund, each sound recording was distributed in the form of digital musical recordings or analog musical recordings; and

(2) for the Musical Works Fund, each musical work was distributed in the form of digital musical recordings or analog musical recordings or disseminated to the public in transmissions.

§ 1007. Procedures for distributing royalty payments

(a) Filing of Claims and Negotiations.

(1) **Filing of claims.** During the first 2 months of each calendar year after calendar year 1992, every interested copyright party seeking to receive royalty payments to which such party is entitled under section 1006 shall file with the Librarian of Congress a claim for payments collected during the preceding year in such form and manner as the Librarian of Congress shall prescribe by regulation.

(2) **Negotiations.** Notwithstanding any provision of the antitrust laws, for purposes of this section interested copyright parties within each group specified in section 1006(b) may agree among themselves to the proportionate division of royalty payments, may lump their claims together and file them jointly or as a single claim, or may designate a common agent, including any organization described in section 1001(7)(D), to negotiate or receive payment on their behalf; except that no agreement under this subsection may modify the allocation of royalties specified in section 1006(b).

(b) **Distribution of Payments in the Absence of a Dispute.** After the period established for the filing of claims under subsection (a), in each year after 1992, the Librarian of Congress shall determine whether there exists a controversy concerning the distribution of royalty payments under section 1006(c). If the Librarian of Congress determines that no such controversy exists, the Librarian of Congress shall, within 30 days after such determination, authorize the distribution of the royalty payments as set forth in the agreements regarding the distribution of royalty payments entered into pursuant to subsection (a), after deducting its reasonable administrative costs under this section.

(c) Resolution of Disputes. If the Librarian of Congress finds the existence of a controversy, the Librarian shall, pursuant to chapter 8 of this title, convene a copyright arbitration royalty panel to determine the distribution of royalty payments. During the pendency of such a proceeding, the Librarian of Congress shall withhold from distribution an amount sufficient to satisfy all claims with respect to which a controversy exists, but shall, to the extent feasible, authorize the distribution of any amounts that are not in controversy. The Librarian of Congress shall, before authorizing the distribution of such royalty payments, deduct the reasonable administrative costs incurred by the Librarian under this section.

Subchapter D—Prohibition on Certain Infringement Actions, Remedies, and Arbitration

§ 1008. Prohibition on certain infringement actions

No action may be brought under this title alleging infringement of copyright based on the manufacture, importation, or distribution of a digital audio recording device, a digital audio recording medium, an analog recording device, or an analog recording medium, or based on the noncommercial use by a consumer of such a device or medium for making digital musical recordings or analog musical recordings.

§ 1009. Civil remedies

(a) Civil Actions. Any interested copyright party injured by a violation of section 1002 or 1003 may bring a civil action in an appropriate United States district court against any person for such violation.

(b) Other Civil Actions. Any person injured by a violation of this chapter may bring a civil action in an appropriate United States district court for actual damages incurred as a result of such violation.

(c) Powers of the Court. In an action brought under subsection (a), the court—

(1) may grant temporary and permanent injunctions on such terms as it deems reasonable to prevent or restrain such violation;

(2) in the case of a violation of section 1002, or in the case of an injury resulting from a failure to make royalty payments required by section 1003, shall award damages under subsection (d);

(3) in its discretion may allow the recovery of costs by or against any party other than the United States or an officer thereof; and

(4) in its discretion may award a reasonable attorney's fee to the prevailing party.

(d) Award of Damages.

(1) Damages for section 1002 or 1003 violations.

(A) Actual damages.

(i) In an action brought under subsection (a), if the court finds that a violation of section 1002 or 1003 has occurred, the court shall award to the complaining party its actual damages if the complaining party elects such damages at any time before final judgment is entered.

(ii) In the case of section 1003, actual damages shall constitute the royalty payments that should have been paid under section 1004 and deposited under section 1005. In such a case, the court, in its discretion, may award an additional amount of not to exceed 50 percent of the actual damages.

(B) Statutory damages for section 1002 violations.

(i) Device. A complaining party may recover an award of statutory damages for each violation of section 1002(a) or (c) in the sum of not more than $2,500 per device involved in such violation or per device on which a service prohibited by section 1002(c) has been performed, as the court considers just.

(ii) Digital musical recording. A complaining party may recover an award of statutory damages for each violation of section 1002(d) in the sum of not more than $25 per digital musical recording involved in such violation, as the court considers just.

(iii) Transmission. A complaining party may recover an award of damages for each transmission or communication that violates section 1002(e) in the sum of not more than $10,000, as the court considers just.

(2) Repeated violations. In any case in which the court finds that a person has violated section 1002 or 1003 within 3 years after a final judgment against that person for another such violation was entered, the court may increase the award of damages to not more than double the amounts that would otherwise be awarded under paragraph (1), as the court considers just.

(3) Innocent violations of section 1002. The court in its discretion may reduce the total award of damages against a person violating section 1002 to a sum of not less than $250 in any case in which the court finds that the violator was not aware and had no reason to believe that its acts constituted a violation of section 1002.

(e) Payment of Damages. Any award of damages under subsection (d) shall be deposited with the Register pursuant to section 1005 for distribution to interested copyright parties as though such funds were royalty payments made pursuant to section 1003.

(f) Impounding of Articles. At any time while an action under subsection (a) is pending, the court may order the impounding, on such terms as it deems reasonable, of any digital audio recording device, digital musical recording, or device specified in section 1002(c) that is in the custody or control of the alleged violator and that the court has reasonable cause to believe does not comply with, or was involved in a violation of, section 1002.

(g) Remedial Modification and Destruction of Articles. In an action brought under subsection (a), the court may, as part of a final judgment or decree finding a violation of section 1002, order the remedial modification or the destruction of any digital audio recording device, digital musical recording, or device specified in section 1002(c) that—

(1) does not comply with, or was involved in a violation of, section 1002, and

(2) is in the custody or control of the violator or has been impounded under subsection (f).

§ 1010. Arbitration of certain disputes

(a) Scope of Arbitration. Before the date of first distribution in the United States of a digital audio recording device or a digital audio interface device, any party manufacturing, importing, or distributing such device, and any interested copyright party may mutually agree to binding arbitration for the purpose of determining whether such device is subject to section 1002, or the basis on which royalty payments for such device are to be made under section 1003.

(b) Initiation of Arbitration Proceedings. Parties agreeing to such arbitration shall file a petition with the Librarian of Congress requesting the commencement of an arbitration proceeding. The petition may include the names and qualifications of potential arbitrators. Within 2 weeks after receiving such a petition, the Librarian of Congress shall cause notice to be published in the Federal Register of the initiation of an arbitration proceeding. Such notice shall include the names and qualifications of 3 arbitrators chosen by the Librarian of Congress from a list of available arbitrators obtained from the American Arbitration Association or such similar organization as the Librarian of Congress shall select, and from potential arbitrators listed in the parties' petition. The arbitrators selected under this subsection shall constitute an Arbitration Panel.

(c) Stay of Judicial Proceedings. Any civil action brought under section 1009 against a party to arbitration under this section shall, on application of one of the parties to the arbitration, be stayed until completion of the arbitration proceeding.

(d) Arbitration Proceeding. The Arbitration Panel shall conduct an arbitration proceeding with respect to the matter concerned, in accordance with such procedures as it may adopt. The Panel shall act on the basis of a fully documented written record. Any party to the arbitration may submit relevant information and proposals to the Panel. The parties to the proceeding shall bear the entire cost thereof in such manner and proportion as the Panel shall direct.

(e) Report to the Librarian of Congress. Not later than 60 days after publication of the notice under subsection (b) of the initiation of an arbitration proceeding, the Arbitration Panel shall report to the Librarian of Congress its determination concerning whether the device concerned is subject to section 1002, or the basis on which royalty payments for the device are to be made under section 1003. Such report shall be accompanied by the written record, and shall set forth the facts that the Panel found relevant to its determination.

(f) Action by the Librarian of Congress. Within 60 days after receiving the report of the Arbitration Panel under subsection (e), the Librarian of Congress shall adopt or reject the determination of the Panel. The Librarian of Congress shall adopt the determination of the Panel unless the Librarian of Congress finds that the determination is clearly erroneous. If the Librarian of Congress rejects the determination of the Panel, the Librarian of Congress shall, before the end of that 60–day period, and after full examination of the record created in the arbitration proceeding, issue an order setting forth the Librarian's decision and the reasons therefor. The Librarian of Congress shall cause to be published in the Federal Register the determination of the Panel and the decision of the Librarian of Congress under this subsection with respect to the determination (including any order issued under the preceding sentence).

(g) Judicial Review. Any decision of the Librarian of Congress under subsection (f) with respect to a determination of the Arbitration Panel may be appealed, by a party to the arbitration, to the United States Court of Appeals for the District of Columbia Circuit, within 30 days after the publication of the decision in the Federal Register. The pendency of an appeal under this subsection shall not stay the decision of the Librarian of Congress. The court shall have jurisdiction to modify or vacate a decision of the Librarian of Congress only if it finds, on the basis of the record before the Librarian of Congress, that the Arbitration Panel or the Librarian of Congress acted in an arbitrary manner. If the court modifies the decision of the Librarian of Congress, the court shall have jurisdiction to enter its own decision in accordance with its final judgment. The court may further vacate the decision of the Librarian of Congress and remand the case for arbitration proceedings as provided in this section.

CHAPTER 11—SOUND RECORDINGS AND MUSIC VIDEOS

Pub.L. 103–465, 108 Stat. 4974 (Dec. 8, 1994)

Sec.
1101. Unauthorized fixation and trafficking in sound recordings and music videos

§ 1101. Unauthorized fixation and trafficking in sound recordings and music videos

(a) Unauthorized Acts. Anyone who, without the consent of the performer or performers involved—

(1) fixes the sounds or sounds and images of a live musical performance in a copy or phonorecord, or reproduces copies or phonorecords of such a performance from an unauthorized fixation,

(2) transmits or otherwise communicates to the public the sounds or sounds and images of a live musical performance, or

(3) distributes or offers to distribute, sells or offers to sell, rents or offers to rent, or traffics in any copy or phonorecord fixed as described in paragraph (1), regardless of whether the fixations occurred in the United States, shall be subject to the remedies provided in *sections 502 through 505,* to the same extent as an infringer of copyright.

(b) Definition. As used in this section, the term "traffic in" means transport, transfer, or otherwise dispose of, to another, as consideration for anything of value, or make or obtain control of with intent to transport, transfer, or dispose of.

(c) Applicability. This section shall apply to any act or acts that occur on or after the date of the enactment of the Uruguay Round Agreements Act.

(d) State Law Not Preempted. Nothing in this section may be construed to annul or limit any rights or remedies under the common law or statutes of any State.

CHAPTER 12—COPYRIGHT PROTECTION AND MANAGEMENT SYSTEMS

Pub.L. 105–304, 112 Stat. 2863 (Oct. 28, 1998)

§ 1201. Circumvention of copyright protection systems

(a) Violations Regarding Circumvention of Technological Measures. (1)(A) No person shall circumvent a technological measure that effectively controls access to a work protected under this title. The prohibition contained in the preceding sentence shall take effect at the end of the 2–year period beginning on the date of the enactment of this chapter.

(B) The prohibition contained in subparagraph (A) shall not apply to persons who are users of a copyrighted work which is in a particular class of works, if such persons are, or are likely to be in the succeeding 3–year period, adversely affected by virtue of such prohibition in their ability to make noninfringing uses of that particular class of works under this title, as determined under subparagraph (C).

(C) During the 2–year period described in subparagraph (A), and during each succeeding 3–year period, the Librarian of Congress, upon the recommendation of the Register of Copyrights, who shall consult with the Assistant Secretary for Communications and Information of the Department of Commerce and report and comment on his or her views in making such recommendation, shall make the determination in a rulemaking proceeding for purposes of subparagraph (B) of whether persons who are users of a copyrighted work are, or are likely to be in the succeeding 3–year period, adversely affected by the prohibition under subparagraph (A) in their ability to make noninfringing uses under this title of a particular class of copyrighted works. In conducting such rulemaking, the Librarian shall examine—

(i) the availability for use of copyrighted works;

(ii) the availability for use of works for nonprofit archival, preservation, and educational purposes;

(iii) the impact that the prohibition on the circumvention of technological measures applied to copyrighted works has on criticism, comment, news reporting, teaching, scholarship, or research;

(iv) the effect of circumvention of technological measures on the market for or value of copyrighted works; and

(v) such other factors as the Librarian considers appropriate.

(D) The Librarian shall publish any class of copyrighted works for which the Librarian has determined, pursuant to the rulemaking conducted under subparagraph (C), that noninfringing uses by persons who are users of a copyrighted work are, or are likely to be, adversely affected, and the prohibition contained in subparagraph (A) shall not apply to such users with respect to such class of works for the ensuing 3–year period.

(E) Neither the exception under subparagraph (B) from the applicability of the prohibition contained in subparagraph (A), nor any determination made in a rulemaking conducted under subparagraph (C), may be used as a defense in any action to enforce any provision of this title other than this paragraph.

(2) No person shall manufacture, import, offer to the public, provide, or otherwise traffic in any technology, product, service, device, component, or part thereof, that—

(A) is primarily designed or produced for the purpose of circumventing a technological measure that effectively controls access to a work protected under this title;

(B) has only limited commercially significant purpose or use other than to circumvent a technological measure that effectively controls access to a work protected under this title; or

(C) is marketed by that person or another acting in concert with that person with that person's knowledge for use in circumventing a technological measure that effectively controls access to a work protected under this title.

(3) As used in this subsection—

(A) to "circumvent a technological measure" means to descramble a scrambled work, to decrypt an encrypted work, or otherwise to avoid, bypass, remove, deactivate, or impair a technological measure, without the authority of the copyright owner; and

(B) a technological measure "effectively controls access to a work" if the measure, in the ordinary course of its operation, requires the application of information, or a process or a treatment, with the authority of the copyright owner, to gain access to the work.

(b) Additional Violations. (1) No person shall manufacture, import, offer to the public, provide, or otherwise traffic in any technology, product, service, device, component, or part thereof, that—

(A) is primarily designed or produced for the purpose of circumventing protection afforded by a technological measure that

403

effectively protects a right of a copyright owner under this title in a work or a portion thereof;

(B) has only limited commercially significant purpose or use other than to circumvent protection afforded by a technological measure that effectively protects a right of a copyright owner under this title in a work or a portion thereof; or

(C) is marketed by that person or another acting in concert with that person with that person's knowledge for use in circumventing protection afforded by a technological measure that effectively protects a right of a copyright owner under this title in a work or a portion thereof.

(2) As used in this subsection—

(A) to "circumvent protection afforded by a technological measure" means avoiding, bypassing, removing, deactivating, or otherwise impairing a technological measure; and

(B) a technological measure "effectively protects a right of a copyright owner under this title" if the measure, in the ordinary course of its operation, prevents, restricts, or otherwise limits the exercise of a right of a copyright owner under this title.

(c) Other Rights, Etc., Not Affected. (1) Nothing in this section shall affect rights, remedies, limitations, or defenses to copyright infringement, including fair use, under this title.

(2) Nothing in this section shall enlarge or diminish vicarious or contributory liability for copyright infringement in connection with any technology, product, service, device, component, or part thereof.

(3) Nothing in this section shall require that the design of, or design and selection of parts and components for, a consumer electronics, telecommunications, or computing product provide for a response to any particular technological measure, so long as such part or component, or the product in which such part or component is integrated, does not otherwise fall within the prohibitions of subsection (a)(2) or (b)(1).

(4) Nothing in this section shall enlarge or diminish any rights of free speech or the press for activities using consumer electronics, telecommunications, or computing products.

(d) Exemption for Nonprofit Libraries, Archives, and Educational Institutions. (1) A nonprofit library, archives, or educational institution which gains access to a commercially exploited copyrighted work solely in order to make a good faith determination of whether to acquire a copy of that work for the sole purpose of engaging in conduct permitted under this title shall not be in violation of subsection (a)(1)(A). A copy of a work to which access has been gained under this paragraph—

(A) may not be retained longer than necessary to make such good faith determination; and

(B) may not be used for any other purpose.

(2) The exemption made available under paragraph (1) shall only apply with respect to a work when an identical copy of that work is not reasonably available in another form.

(3) A nonprofit library, archives, or educational institution that willfully for the purpose of commercial advantage or financial gain violates paragraph (1)—

(A) shall, for the first offense, be subject to the civil remedies under section 1203; and

(B) shall, for repeated or subsequent offenses, in addition to the civil remedies under section 1203, forfeit the exemption provided under paragraph (1).

(4) This subsection may not be used as a defense to a claim under subsection (a)(2) or (b), nor may this subsection permit a nonprofit library, archives, or educational institution to manufacture, import, offer to the public, provide, or otherwise traffic in any technology, product, service, component, or part thereof, which circumvents a technological measure.

(5) In order for a library or archives to qualify for the exemption under this subsection, the collections of that library or archives shall be—

(A) open to the public; or

(B) available not only to researchers affiliated with the library or archives or with the institution of which it is a part, but also to other persons doing research in a specialized field.

(e) Law Enforcement, Intelligence, and Other Government Activities. This section does not prohibit any lawfully authorized investigative, protective, information security, or intelligence activity of an officer, agent, or employee of the United States, a State, or a political subdivision of a State, or a person acting pursuant to a contract with the United States, a State, or a political subdivision of a State. For purposes of this subsection, the term "information security" means activities carried out in order to identify and address the vulnerabilities of a government computer, computer system, or computer network.

(f) Reverse Engineering. (1) Notwithstanding the provisions of subsection (a)(1)(A), a person who has lawfully obtained the right to use a copy of a computer program may circumvent a technological measure that effectively controls access to a particular portion of that program for the sole purpose of identifying and analyzing those elements of the program that are necessary to achieve interoperability of an independently created computer program with other programs, and that have not previously been readily available to the person engaging in the circumvention, to the extent any such acts of identification and analysis do not constitute infringement under this title.

(2) Notwithstanding the provisions of subsections (a)(2) and (b), a person may develop and employ technological means to circumvent a technological measure, or to circumvent protection afforded by a technological measure, in order to enable the identification and analysis under paragraph (1), or for the purpose of enabling interoperability of an independently created computer program with other programs, if such means are necessary to achieve such interoperability, to the extent that doing so does not constitute infringement under this title.

(3) The information acquired through the acts permitted under paragraph (1), and the means permitted under paragraph (2), may be made available to others if the person referred to in paragraph (1) or (2), as the case may be, provides such information or means solely for the purpose of enabling interoperability of an independently created computer program with other programs, and to the extent that doing so does not constitute infringement under this title or violate applicable law other than this section.

(4) For purposes of this subsection, the term "interoperability" means the ability of computer programs to exchange information, and of such programs mutually to use the information which has been exchanged.

(g) Encryption Research.

(1) Definitions. For purposes of this subsection—

(A) the term "encryption research" means activities necessary to identify and analyze flaws and vulnerabilities of encryption technologies applied to copyrighted works, if these activities are conducted to advance the state of knowledge in the field of encryption technology or to assist in the development of encryption products; and

(B) the term "encryption technology" means the scrambling and descrambling of information using mathematical formulas or algorithms.

(2) Permissible acts of encryption research. Notwithstanding the provisions of subsection (a)(1)(A), it is not a violation of that subsection for a person to circumvent a technological measure as applied to a copy, phonorecord, performance, or display of a published work in the course of an act of good faith encryption research if—

(A) the person lawfully obtained the encrypted copy, phonorecord, performance, or display of the published work;

(B) such act is necessary to conduct such encryption research;

(C) the person made a good faith effort to obtain authorization before the circumvention; and

(D) such act does not constitute infringement under this title or a violation of applicable law other than this section, including section 1030 of title 18 and those provisions of title 18 amended by the Computer Fraud and Abuse Act of 1986.

(3) Factors in determining exemption. In determining whether a person qualifies for the exemption under paragraph (2), the factors to be considered shall include—

(A) whether the information derived from the encryption research was disseminated, and if so, whether it was disseminated in a manner reasonably calculated to advance the state of knowledge or development of encryption technology, versus whether it was disseminated in a manner that facilitates infringement under this title or a violation of applicable law other than this section, including a violation of privacy or breach of security;

(B) whether the person is engaged in a legitimate course of study, is employed, or is appropriately trained or experienced, in the field of encryption technology; and

(C) whether the person provides the copyright owner of the work to which the technological measure is applied with notice of the findings and documentation of the research, and the time when such notice is provided.

(4) Use of technological means for research activities. Notwithstanding the provisions of subsection (a)(2), it is not a violation of that subsection for a person to—

(A) develop and employ technological means to circumvent a technological measure for the sole purpose of that person performing the acts of good faith encryption research described in paragraph (2); and

(B) provide the technological means to another person with whom he or she is working collaboratively for the purpose of conducting the acts of good faith encryption research described in paragraph (2) or for the purpose of having that other person verify his or her acts of good faith encryption research described in paragraph (2).

(5) Report to Congress. Not later than 1 year after the date of the enactment of this chapter, the Register of Copyrights and the Assistant Secretary for Communications and Information of the Department of Commerce shall jointly report to the Congress on the effect this subsection has had on—

(A) encryption research and the development of encryption technology;

(B) the adequacy and effectiveness of technological measures designed to protect copyrighted works; and

(C) protection of copyright owners against the unauthorized access to their encrypted copyrighted works.

The report shall include legislative recommendations, if any.

(h) Exceptions Regarding Minors. In applying subsection (a) to a component or part, the court may consider the necessity for its intended and actual incorporation in a technology, product, service, or device, which—

(1) does not itself violate the provisions of this title; and

(2) has the sole purpose to prevent the access of minors to material on the Internet.

(i) Protection of Personally Identifying Information.

(1) Circumvention permitted. Notwithstanding the provisions of subsection (a)(1)(A), it is not a violation of that subsection for a person to circumvent a technological measure that effectively controls access to a work protected under this title, if—

(A) the technological measure, or the work it protects, contains the capability of collecting or disseminating personally identifying information reflecting the online activities of a natural person who seeks to gain access to the work protected;

(B) in the normal course of its operation, the technological measure, or the work it protects, collects or disseminates personally identifying information about the person who seeks to gain access to the work protected, without providing conspicuous notice of such collection or dissemination to such person, and without providing such person with the capability to prevent or restrict such collection or dissemination;

(C) the act of circumvention has the sole effect of identifying and disabling the capability described in subparagraph (A), and has no other effect on the ability of any person to gain access to any work; and

(D) the act of circumvention is carried out solely for the purpose of preventing the collection or dissemination of personally identifying information about a natural person who seeks to gain access to the work protected, and is not in violation of any other law.

(2) Inapplicability to certain technological measures.

This subsection does not apply to a technological measure, or a work it protects, that does not collect or disseminate personally identifying information and that is disclosed to a user as not having or using such capability.

(j) Security Testing.

(1) Definition. For purposes of this subsection, the term ''security testing'' means accessing a computer, computer system, or computer network, solely for the purpose of good faith testing, investigating, or correcting, a security flaw or vulnerability, with the authorization of the owner or operator of such computer, computer system, or computer network.

(2) Permissible acts of security testing. Notwithstanding the provisions of subsection (a)(1)(A), it is not a violation of that subsection for a person to engage in an act of security testing, if such act does not constitute infringement under this title or a violation of applicable law other than this section, including section 1030 of title 18 and those provisions of title 18 amended by the Computer Fraud and Abuse Act of 1986.

(3) Factors in determining exemption. In determining whether a person qualifies for the exemption under paragraph (2), the factors to be considered shall include—

(A) whether the information derived from the security testing was used solely to promote the security of the owner or operator of such computer, computer system or computer network, or shared directly with the developer of such computer, computer system, or computer network; and

(B) whether the information derived from the security testing was used or maintained in a manner that does not facilitate infringement under this title or a violation of applicable law other than this section, including a violation of privacy or breach of security.

(4) Use of technological means for security testing. Notwithstanding the provisions of subsection (a)(2), it is not a violation of that subsection for a person to develop, produce, distribute or employ technological means for the sole purpose of performing the acts of security testing described in subsection (2), provided such technological means does not otherwise violate section (a)(2).

(k) Certain Analog Devices and Certain Technological Measures.

(1) Certain analog devices.

(A) Effective 18 months after the date of the enactment of this chapter, no person shall manufacture, import, offer to the public, provide or otherwise traffic in any—

(i) VHS format analog video cassette recorder unless such recorder conforms to the automatic gain control copy control technology;

(ii) 8mm format analog video cassette camcorder unless such camcorder conforms to the automatic gain control technology;

(iii) Beta format analog video cassette recorder, unless such recorder conforms to the automatic gain control copy control technology, except that this requirement shall not apply until there are 1,000 Beta format analog video cassette recorders sold in the United States in any one calendar year after the date of the enactment of this chapter;

(iv) 8mm format analog video cassette recorder that is not an analog video cassette camcorder, unless such recorder conforms to the automatic gain control copy control technology, except that this requirement shall not apply until there are 20,000 such recorders sold in the United States in any one calendar year after the date of the enactment of this chapter; or

(v) analog video cassette recorder that records using an NTSC format video input and that is not otherwise covered under clauses (i) through (iv), unless such device conforms to the automatic gain control copy control technology.

(B) Effective on the date of the enactment of this chapter, no person shall manufacture, import, offer to the public, provide or otherwise traffic in—

(i) any VHS format analog video cassette recorder or any 8mm format analog video cassette recorder if the design of the model of such recorder has been modified after such date of enactment so that a model of recorder that previously conformed to the automatic gain control copy control technology no longer conforms to such technology; or

(ii) any VHS format analog video cassette recorder, or any 8mm format analog video cassette recorder that is not an 8mm analog video cassette camcorder, if the design of the model of such recorder has been modified after such date of enactment so that a model of recorder that previously conformed to the four-line colorstripe copy control technology no longer conforms to such technology.

Manufacturers that have not previously manufactured or sold a VHS format analog video cassette recorder, or an 8mm format analog cassette recorder, shall be required to conform to the four-line colorstripe copy control technology in the initial model of any such recorder manufactured after the date of the enactment of this chapter, and thereafter to continue conforming to the four-line colorstripe copy control technology. For purposes of this subparagraph, an analog video cassette recorder "conforms to" the four-line colorstripe copy control technology if it records a signal that, when played back by the playback function of that recorder in the normal viewing mode, exhibits, on a reference display device, a display containing distracting visible lines through portions of the viewable picture.

(2) Certain encoding restrictions. No person shall apply the automatic gain control copy control technology or colorstripe copy control technology to prevent or limit consumer copying except such copying—

(A) of a single transmission, or specified group of transmissions, of live events or of audiovisual works for which a member of the public has exercised choice in selecting the transmissions, including the content of the transmissions or the time of receipt of such transmissions, or both, and as to which such member is charged a separate fee for each such transmission or specified group of transmissions;

(B) from a copy of a transmission of a live event or an audiovisual work if such transmission is provided by a channel or service where payment is made by a member of the public for such channel or service in the form of a subscription fee that entitles the member of the public to receive all of the programming contained in such channel or service;

(C) from a physical medium containing one or more prerecorded audiovisual works; or

(D) from a copy of a transmission described in subparagraph (A) or from a copy made from a physical medium described in subparagraph (C).

In the event that a transmission meets both the conditions set forth in subparagraph (A) and those set forth in subparagraph (B), the transmission shall be treated as a transmission described in subparagraph (A).

(3) Inapplicability. This subsection shall not—

(A) require any analog video cassette camcorder to conform to the automatic gain control copy control technology with respect to any video signal received through a camera lens;

(B) apply to the manufacture, importation, offer for sale, provision of, or other trafficking in, any professional analog video cassette recorder; or

(C) apply to the offer for sale or provision of, or other trafficking in, any previously owned analog video cassette recorder, if such recorder was legally manufactured and sold when new and not subsequently modified in violation of paragraph (1)(B).

(4) Definitions. For purposes of this subsection:

(A) An "analog video cassette recorder" means a device that records, or a device that includes a function that records, on electromagnetic tape in an analog format the electronic impulses produced by the video and audio portions of a television program, motion picture, or other form of audiovisual work.

(B) An "analog video cassette camcorder" means an analog video cassette recorder that contains a recording function that operates through a camera lens and through a video input that may be connected with a television or other video playback device.

(C) An analog video cassette recorder "conforms" to the automatic gain control copy control technology if it—

(i) detects one or more of the elements of such technology and does not record the motion picture or transmission protected by such technology; or

(ii) records a signal that, when played back, exhibits a meaningfully distorted or degraded display.

411

(D) The term "professional analog video cassette recorder" means an analog video cassette recorder that is designed, manufactured, marketed, and intended for use by a person who regularly employs such a device for a lawful business or industrial use, including making, performing, displaying, distributing, or transmitting copies of motion pictures on a commercial scale.

(E) The terms "VHS format," "8mm format," "Beta format," "automatic gain control copy control technology," "colorstripe copy control technology," "four-line version of the colorstripe copy control technology," and "NTSC" have the meanings that are commonly understood in the consumer electronics and motion picture industries as of the date of the enactment of this chapter.

(5) Violations. Any violation of paragraph (1) of this subsection shall be treated as a violation of subsection (b)(1) of this section. Any violation of paragraph (2) of this subsection shall be deemed an "act of circumvention" for the purposes of section 1203(c)(3)(A) of this chapter.

§ 1202.   Integrity of copyright management information

(a) False Copyright Management Information. No person shall knowingly and with the intent to induce, enable, facilitate, or conceal infringement—

(1) provide copyright management information that is false, or

(2) distribute or import for distribution copyright management information that is false.

(b) Removal or Alteration of Copyright Management Information. No person shall, without the authority of the copyright owner or the law

(1) intentionally remove or alter any copyright management information,

(2) distribute or import for distribution copyright management information knowing that the copyright management information has been removed or altered without authority of the copyright owner or the law, or

(3) distribute, import for distribution, or publicly perform works, copies of works, or phonorecords, knowing that copyright management information has been removed or altered without authority of the copyright owner or the law,

knowing, or, with respect to civil remedies under section 1203, having reasonable grounds to know, that it will induce, enable, facilitate, or conceal an infringement of any right under this title.

(c) Definition. As used in this section, the term "copyright management information" means any of the following information conveyed in connection with copies or phonorecords of a work or performances or displays of a work, including in digital form, except that such term does not include any personally identifying information about a user of a work or of a copy, phonorecord, performance, or display of a work:

(1) The title and other information identifying the work, including the information set forth on a notice of copyright.

(2) The name of, and other identifying information about, the author of a work.

(3) The name of, and other identifying information about, the copyright owner of the work, including the information set forth in a notice of copyright.

(4) With the exception of public performances of works by radio and television broadcast stations, the name of, and other identifying information about, a performer whose performance is fixed in a work other than an audiovisual work.

(5) With the exception of public performances of works by radio and television broadcast stations, in the case of an audiovisual work, the name of, and other identifying information about, a writer, performer, or director who is credited in the audiovisual work.

(6) Terms and conditions for use of the work.

(7) Identifying numbers or symbols referring to such information or links to such information.

(8) Such other information as the Register of Copyrights may prescribe by regulation, except that the Register of Copyrights may not require the provision of any information concerning the user of a copyrighted work.

(d) Law Enforcement, Intelligence, and Other Government Activities. This section does not prohibit any lawfully authorized investigative, protective, information security, or intelligence activity of an officer, agent, or employee of the United States, a State, or a political subdivision of a State, or a person acting pursuant to a contract with the United States, a State, or a political subdivision of a State. For purposes of this subsection, the term "information security" means activities carried out in order to identify and address the vulnerabilities of a government computer, computer system, or computer network.

(e) Limitations on Liability.

(1) Analog transmissions. In the case of an analog transmission, a person who is making transmissions in its capacity as a broadcast station, or as a cable system, or someone who provides programming to such station or system, shall not be liable for a violation of subsection (b) if—

(A) avoiding the activity that constitutes such violation is not technically feasible or would create an undue financial hardship on such person; and

(B) such person did not intend, by engaging in such activity, to induce, enable, facilitate, or conceal infringement of a right under this title.

(2) Digital transmissions.

(A) If a digital transmission standard for the placement of copyright management information for a category of works is set in a voluntary, consensus standard-setting process involving a representative cross-section of broadcast stations or cable systems and copyright owners of a category of works that are intended for public performance by such stations or systems, a person identified in paragraph (1) shall not be liable for a violation of subsection (b) with respect to the particular copyright management information addressed by such standard if—

(i) the placement of such information by someone other than such person is not in accordance with such standard; and

(ii) the activity that constitutes such violation is not intended to induce, enable, facilitate, or conceal infringement of a right under this title.

(B) Until a digital transmission standard has been set pursuant to subparagraph (A) with respect to the placement of copyright management information for a category of works, a person identified in paragraph (1) shall not be liable for a violation of subsection (b) with respect to such copyright management information, if the activity that constitutes such violation is not intended to induce, enable, facilitate, or conceal infringement of a right under this title, and if—

(i) the transmission of such information by such person would result in a perceptible visual or aural degradation of the digital signal; or

(ii) the transmission of such information by such person would conflict with—

(I) an applicable government regulation relating to transmission of information in a digital signal;

(II) an applicable industry-wide standard relating to the transmission of information in a digital signal that was adopted by a voluntary consensus standards body prior to the effective date of this chapter; or

(III) an applicable industry-wide standard relating to the transmission of information in a digital signal that was adopted in a voluntary, consensus standards-setting process open to participation by a representative cross-section of broadcast stations or cable systems and copyright owners of a category of works that are intended for public performance by such stations or systems.

(3) Definitions. As used in this subsection—

(A) the term "broadcast station" has the meaning given that term in section 3 of the Communications Act of 1934 (47 U.S.C. 153); and

(B) the term "cable system" has the meaning given that term in section 602 of the Communications Act of 1934 (47 U.S.C. 522).

§ 1203. Civil remedies

(a) Civil Actions. Any person injured by a violation of section 1201 or 1202 may bring a civil action in an appropriate United States district court for such violation.

(b) Powers of the Court. In an action brought under subsection (a), the court—

(1) may grant temporary and permanent injunctions on such terms as it deems reasonable to prevent or restrain a violation, but in no event shall impose a prior restraint on free speech or the press protected under the 1st amendment to the Constitution;

(2) at any time while an action is pending, may order the impounding, on such terms as it deems reasonable, of any device or product that is in the custody or control of the alleged violator and that the court has reasonable cause to believe was involved in a violation;

(3) may award damages under subsection (c);

(4) in its discretion may allow the recovery of costs by or against any party other than the United States or an officer thereof;

(5) in its discretion may award reasonable attorney's fees to the prevailing party; and

(6) may, as part of a final judgment or decree finding a violation, order the remedial modification or the destruction of any device or product involved in the violation that is in the custody or control of the violator or has been impounded under paragraph (2).

(c) Award of Damages.

(1) In general. Except as otherwise provided in this title, a person committing a violation of section 1201 or 1202 is liable for either—

(A) the actual damages and any additional profits of the violator, as provided in paragraph (2), or

(B) statutory damages, as provided in paragraph (3).

(2) Actual damages. The court shall award to the complaining party the actual damages suffered by the party as a result of the violation, and any profits of the violator that are attributable to the violation and are not taken into account in computing the actual damages, if the complaining party elects such damages at any time before final judgment is entered.

(3) Statutory damages. (A) At any time before final judgment is entered, a complaining party may elect to recover an award of statutory damages for each violation of section 1201 in the sum of not less than $200 or more than $2,500 per act of circumvention, device, product, component, offer, or performance of service, as the court considers just.

(B) At any time before final judgment is entered, a complaining party may elect to recover an award of statutory damages for each violation of section 1202 in the sum of not less than $2,500 or more than $25,000.

(4) Repeated violations. In any case in which the injured party sustains the burden of proving, and the court finds, that a person has violated section 1201 or 1202 within three years after a final judgment was entered against the person for another such violation, the court may increase the award of damages up to triple the amount that would otherwise be awarded, as the court considers just.

(5) Innocent violations.

(A) In general. The court in its discretion may reduce or remit the total award of damages in any case in which the violator sustains the burden of proving, and the court finds, that the violator was not aware and had no reason to believe that its acts constituted a violation.

(B) Nonprofit library, archives, educational institutions, or public broadcasting entities.

(i) Definition. In this subparagraph, the term "public broadcasting entity" has the meaning given such term under section 118(g).

(ii) In general. In the case of a nonprofit library, archives, educational institution, or public broadcasting entity, the court shall remit damages in any case in which the library, archives, educational institution, or public broadcasting entity sustains the burden of proving, and the court finds, that the library, archives, educational institution, or public broadcasting entity was not aware and had no reason to believe that its acts constituted a violation.

§ 1204. Criminal offenses and penalties

(a) In General. Any person who violates section 1201 or 1202 willfully and for purposes of commercial advantage or private financial gain—

(1) shall be fined not more than $500,000 or imprisoned for not more than 5 years, or both, for the first offense; and

(2) shall be fined not more than $1,000,000 or imprisoned for not more than 10 years, or both, for any subsequent offense.

(b) Limitation for Nonprofit Library, Archives, Educational Institution, or Public Broadcasting Entity. Subsection (a) shall not apply to a nonprofit library, archives, educational institution, or public broadcasting entity (as defined under section 118(g)).

(c) Statute of Limitations. No criminal proceeding shall be brought under this section unless such proceeding is commenced within five years after the cause of action arose.

§ 1205. Savings clause

Nothing in this chapter abrogates, diminishes, or weakens the provisions of, nor provides any defense or element of mitigation in a criminal prosecution or civil action under, any Federal or State law that prevents the violation of the privacy of an individual in connection with the individual's use of the Internet.

CHAPTER 13—PROTECTION
OF ORIGINAL DESIGNS

Pub.L. 105–304, 112 Stat. 2905 (Oct. 28, 1998)

§ 1301. Designs protected

(a) Designs protected.

(1) In general. The designer or other owner of an original design of a useful article which makes the article attractive or distinctive in appearance to the purchasing or using public may secure the protection provided by this chapter upon complying with and subject to this chapter.

(2) Vessel hulls. The design of a vessel hull, including a plug or mold, is subject to protection under this chapter, notwithstanding section 1302(4).

(b) Definitions. For the purpose of this chapter, the following terms have the following meanings:

(1) A design is "original" if it is the result of the designer's creative endeavor that provides a distinguishable variation over prior work pertaining to similar articles which is more than merely trivial and has not been copied from another source.

(2) A "useful article" is a vessel hull, including a plug or mold, which in normal use has an intrinsic utilitarian function that is not merely to portray the appearance of the article or to convey information. An article which normally is part of a useful article shall be deemed to be a useful article.

(3) A "vessel" is a craft—

(A) that is designed and capable of independently steering a course on or through water through its own means of propulsion; and

(B) that is designed and capable of carrying and transporting one or more passengers.

(4) A "hull" is the frame or body of a vessel, including the deck of a vessel, exclusive of masts, sails, yards, and rigging.

(5) A "plug" means a device or model used to make a mold for the purpose of exact duplication, regardless of whether the device or model has an intrinsic utilitarian function that is not only to portray the appearance of the product or to convey information.

(6) A "mold" means a matrix or form in which a substance for material is used, regardless of whether the matrix or form has an intrinsic utilitarian function that is not only to portray the appearance of the product or to convey information.

§ 1302. Designs not subject to protection

Protection under this chapter shall not be available for a design that is—

(1) not original;

(2) staple or commonplace, such as a standard geometric figure, a familiar symbol, an emblem, or a motif, or another shape, pattern, or configuration which has become standard, common, prevalent, or ordinary;

(3) different from a design excluded by paragraph (2) only in insignificant details or in elements which are variants commonly used in the relevant trades;

(4) dictated solely by a utilitarian function of the article that embodies it; or

(5) embodied in a useful article that was made public by the designer or owner in the United States or a foreign country more than 2 years before the date of the application for registration under this chapter.

§ 1303. Revisions, adaptations, and rearrangements

Protection for a design under this chapter shall be available notwithstanding the employment in the design of subject matter excluded from protection under section 1302 if the design is a substantial revision, adaptation, or rearrangement of such subject matter. Such protection shall be independent of any subsisting protection in subject matter employed in the design, and shall not be construed as securing any right to subject matter excluded from protection under this chapter or as extending any subsisting protection under this chapter.

§ 1304. Commencement of protection

The protection provided for a design under this chapter shall commence upon the earlier of the date of publication of the registration under section 1313(a) or the date the design is first made public as defined by section 1310(b).

§ 1305. Term of protection

(a) **In General.** Subject to subsection (b), the protection provided under this chapter for a design shall continue for a term of 10 years beginning on the date of the commencement of protection under section 1304.

(b) **Expiration.** All terms of protection provided in this section shall run to the end of the calendar year in which they would otherwise expire.

(c) **Termination of Rights.** Upon expiration or termination of protection in a particular design under this chapter, all rights under this chapter in the design shall terminate, regardless of the number of different articles in which the design may have been used during the term of its protection.

§ 1306. Design notice

(a) **Contents of Design Notice.** (1) Whenever any design for which protection is sought under this chapter is made public under section 1310(b), the owner of the design shall, subject to the provisions of section 1307, mark it or have it marked legibly with a design notice consisting of—

    (A) the words "Protected Design", the abbreviation "Prot'd Des.", or ⓓ , or the symbol " *D* ";

    (B) the year of the date on which protection for the design commenced; and

    (C) the name of the owner, an abbreviation by which the name can be recognized, or a generally accepted alternative designation of the owner.

Any distinctive identification of the owner may be used for purposes of subparagraph (C) if it has been recorded by the Administrator before the design marked with such identification is registered.

(2) After registration, the registration number may be used instead of the elements specified in subparagraphs (B) and (C) of paragraph (1).

(b) Location of Notice. The design notice shall be so located and applied as to give reasonable notice of design protection while the useful article embodying the design is passing through its normal channels of commerce.

(c) Subsequent Removal of Notice. When the owner of a design has complied with the provisions of this section, protection under this chapter shall not be affected by the removal, destruction, or obliteration by others of the design notice on an article.

§ 1307. Effect of omission of notice

(a) Actions with Notice. Except as provided in subsection (b), the omission of the notice prescribed in section 1306 shall not cause loss of the protection under this chapter or prevent recovery for infringement under this chapter against any person who, after receiving written notice of the design protection, begins an undertaking leading to infringement under this chapter.

(b) Actions without Notice. The omission of the notice prescribed in section 1306 shall prevent any recovery under section 1323 against a person who began an undertaking leading to infringement under this chapter before receiving written notice of the design protection. No injunction shall be issued under this chapter with respect to such undertaking unless the owner of the design reimburses that person for any reasonable expenditure or contractual obligation in connection with such undertaking that was incurred before receiving written notice of the design protection, as the court in its discretion directs. The burden of providing written notice of design protection shall be on the owner of the design.

§ 1308. Exclusive rights

The owner of a design protected under this chapter has the exclusive right to—

(1) make, have made, or import, for sale or for use in trade, any useful article embodying that design; and

(2) sell or distribute for sale or for use in trade any useful article embodying that design.

§ 1309. Infringement

(a) Acts of Infringement. Except as provided in subsection (b), it shall be infringement of the exclusive rights in a design protected under this chapter for any person, without the consent of the owner of the design, within the United States and during the term of such protection, to—

(1) make, have made, or import, for sale or for use in trade, any infringing article as defined in subsection (e); or

(2) sell or distribute for sale or for use in trade any such infringing article.

(b) Acts of Sellers and Distributors. A seller or distributor of an infringing article who did not make or import the article shall be deemed to have infringed on a design protected under this chapter only if that person—

(1) induced or acted in collusion with a manufacturer to make, or an importer to import such article, except that merely purchasing or giving an order to purchase such article in the ordinary course of business shall not of itself constitute such inducement or collusion; or

(2) refused or failed, upon the request of the owner of the design, to make a prompt and full disclosure of that person's source of such article, and that person orders or reorders such article after receiving notice by registered or certified mail of the protection subsisting in the design.

(c) Acts without Knowledge. It shall not be infringement under this section to make, have made, import, sell, or distribute, any article embodying a design which was created without knowledge that a design was protected under this chapter and was copied from such protected design.

(d) Acts in Ordinary Course of Business. A person who incorporates into that person's product of manufacture an infringing article acquired from others in the ordinary course of business, or who, without knowledge of the protected design embodied in an infringing article, makes or processes the infringing article for the account of another person in the ordinary course of business, shall not be deemed to have infringed the rights in that design under this chapter except under a condition contained in paragraph (1) or (2) of subsection (b). Accepting an order or reorder from the source of the infringing article shall be deemed ordering or reordering within the meaning of subsection (b)(2).

(e) Infringing Article Defined. As used in this section, an "infringing article" is any article the design of which has been copied from a design protected under this chapter, without the consent of the owner of the protected design. An infringing article is not an illustration or picture of a protected design in an advertisement, book, periodical, newspaper, photograph, broadcast, motion picture, or similar medium. A design shall not be deemed to have been copied from a protected design if it is original and not substantially similar in appearance to a protected design.

(f) Establishing Originality. The party to any action or proceeding under this chapter who alleges rights under this chapter in a design shall have the burden of establishing the design's originality whenever the opposing party introduces an earlier work which is identical to such design, or so similar as to make prima facie showing that such design was copied from such work.

(g) Reproduction for Teaching or Analysis. It is not an infringement of the exclusive rights of a design owner for a person to reproduce the design in a useful article or in any other form solely for the purpose of teaching, analyzing, or evaluating the appearance, concepts, or techniques embodied in the design, or the function of the useful article embodying the design.

§ 1310. Application for registration

(a) Time Limit for Application for Registration. Protection under this chapter shall be lost if application for registration of the design is not made within 2 years after the date on which the design is first made public.

(b) When Design Is Made Public. A design is made public when an existing useful article embodying the design is anywhere publicly exhibited, publicly distributed, or offered for sale or sold to the public by the owner of the design or with the owner's consent.

(c) Application by Owner of Design. Application for registration may be made by the owner of the design.

(d) Contents of Application. The application for registration shall be made to the Administrator and shall state—

(1) the name and address of the designer or designers of the design;

(2) the name and address of the owner if different from the designer;

(3) the specific name of the useful article embodying the design;

(4) the date, if any, that the design was first made public, if such date was earlier than the date of the application;

(5) affirmation that the design has been fixed in a useful article; and

(6) such other information as may be required by the Administrator.

The application for registration may include a description setting forth the salient features of the design, but the absence of such a description shall not prevent registration under this chapter.

(e) Sworn Statement. The application for registration shall be accompanied by a statement under oath by the applicant or the applicant's duly authorized agent or representative, setting forth, to the best of the applicant's knowledge and belief—

(1) that the design is original and was created by the designer or designers named in the application;

(2) that the design has not previously been registered on behalf of the applicant or the applicant's predecessor in title; and

(3) that the applicant is the person entitled to protection and to registration under this chapter.

If the design has been made public with the design notice prescribed in section 1306, the statement shall also describe the exact form and position of the design notice.

(f) Effect of Errors. (1) Error in any statement or assertion as to the utility of the useful article named in the application under this section, the design of which is sought to be registered, shall not affect the protection secured under this chapter.

(2) Errors in omitting a joint designer or in naming an alleged joint designer shall not affect the validity of the registration, or the actual ownership or the protection of the design, unless it is shown that the error occurred with deceptive intent.

(g) Design Made in Scope of Employment. In a case in which the design was made within the regular scope of the designer's employment and individual authorship of the design is difficult or impossible to ascribe and the application so states, the name and address of the employer for whom the design was made may be stated instead of that of the individual designer.

(h) Pictorial Representation of Design. The application for registration shall be accompanied by two copies of a drawing or other pictorial representation of the useful article embodying the design, having one or more views, adequate to show the design, in a form and style suitable for reproduction, which shall be deemed a part of the application.

(i) Design in More than One Useful Article. If the distinguishing elements of a design are in substantially the same form in different useful articles, the design shall be protected as to all such useful articles when protected as to one of them, but not more than one registration shall be required for the design.

(j) Application for More than One Design. More than one design may be included in the same application under such conditions as may be prescribed by the Administrator. For each design included in an application the fee prescribed for a single design shall be paid.

§ 1311. Benefit of earlier filing date in foreign country

An application for registration of a design filed in the United States by any person who has, or whose legal representative or predecessor or successor in title has, previously filed an application for registration of the same design in a foreign country which extends to designs of owners who are citizens of the United States, or to applications filed under this chapter, similar protection to that provided under this chapter shall have that same effect as if filed in the United States on the date on which the application was first filed in such foreign country, if the application in the United States is filed within 6 months after the earliest date on which any such foreign application was filed.

§ 1312. Oaths and acknowledgments

(a) In General. Oaths and acknowledgments required by this chapter—

(1) may be made—

(A) before any person in the United States authorized by law to administer oaths; or

(B) when made in a foreign country, before any diplomatic or consular officer of the United States authorized to administer oaths, or before any official authorized to administer oaths in the foreign country concerned, whose authority shall be proved by a certificate of a diplomatic or consular officer of the United States; and

(2) shall be valid if they comply with the laws of the State or country where made.

(b) Written Declaration in Lieu of Oath. (1) The Administrator may by rule prescribe that any document which is to be filed under this chapter in the Office of the Administrator and which is required by any law, rule, or other regulation to be under oath, may be subscribed to by a written declaration in such form as the Administrator may prescribe, and such declaration shall be in lieu of the oath otherwise required.

(2) Whenever a written declaration under paragraph (1) is used, the document containing the declaration shall state that willful false statements are punishable by fine or imprisonment, or both, pursuant to section 1001 of title 18, and may jeopardize the validity of the application or document or a registration resulting therefrom.

§ 1313. Examination of application and issue or refusal of registration

(a) Determination of Registrability of Design; Registration. Upon the filing of an application for registration in proper form under section 1310, and upon payment of the fee prescribed under section 1316, the Administrator shall determine whether or not the application relates to a design which on its face appears to be subject to protection under this chapter, and, if so, the Register shall register the design. Registration under this subsection shall be announced by publication. The date of registration shall be the date of publication.

(b) Refusal to Register; Reconsideration. If, in the judgment of the Administrator, the application for registration relates to a design which on its face is not subject to protection under this chapter, the Administrator shall send to the applicant a notice of refusal to register and the grounds for the refusal. Within 3 months after the date on which the notice of refusal is sent, the applicant may, by written request, seek reconsideration of the application. After consideration of such a request, the Administrator shall either register the design or send to the applicant a notice of final refusal to register.

(c) **Application to Cancel Registration.** Any person who believes he or she is or will be damaged by a registration under this chapter may, upon payment of the prescribed fee, apply to the Administrator at any time to cancel the registration on the ground that the design is not subject to protection under this chapter, stating the reasons for the request. Upon receipt of an application for cancellation, the Administrator shall send to the owner of the design, as shown in the records of the Office of the Administrator, a notice of the application, and the owner shall have a period of 3 months after the date on which such notice is mailed in which to present arguments to the Administrator for support of the validity of the registration. The Administrator shall also have the authority to establish, by regulation, conditions under which the opposing parties may appear and be heard in support of their arguments. If, after the periods provided for the presentation of arguments have expired, the Administrator determines that the applicant for cancellation has established that the design is not subject to protection under this chapter, the Administrator shall order the registration stricken from the record. Cancellation under this subsection shall be announced by publication, and notice of the Administrator's final determination with respect to any application for cancellation shall be sent to the applicant and to the owner of record. Costs of the cancellation procedure under this subsection shall be borne by the nonprevailing party or parties, and the Administrator shall have the authority to assess and collect such costs.

§ 1314. Certification of registration

Certificates of registration shall be issued in the name of the United States under the seal of the Office of the Administrator and shall be recorded in the official records of the Office. The certificate shall state the name of the useful article, the date of filing of the application, the date of registration, and the date the design was made public, if earlier than the date of filing of the application, and shall contain a reproduction of the drawing or other pictorial representation of the design. If a description of the salient features of the design appears in the application, the description shall also appear in the certificate. A certificate of registration shall be admitted in any court as prima facie evidence of the facts stated in the certificate.

§ 1315. Publication of announcements and indexes

(a) **Publications of the Administrator.** The Administrator shall publish lists and indexes of registered designs and cancellations of designs and may also publish the drawings or other pictorial representations of registered designs for sale or other distribution.

(b) **File of Representatives of Registered Designs.** The Administrator shall establish and maintain a file of the drawings or other pictorial representations of registered designs. The file shall be available for use by the public under such conditions as the Administrator may prescribe.

§ 1316. Fees

The Administrator shall by regulation set reasonable fees for the filing of applications to register designs under this chapter and for other services relating to the administration of this chapter, taking into consideration the cost of providing these services and the benefit of a public record.

§ 1317. Regulations

The Administrator may establish regulations for the administration of this chapter.

§ 1318. Copies of records

Upon payment of the prescribed fee, any person may obtain a certified copy of any official record of the Office of the Administrator that relates to this chapter. That copy shall be admissible in evidence with the same effect as the original.

§ 1319. Correction of errors in certificates

The Administrator may, by a certificate of correction under seal, correct any error in a registration incurred through the fault of the Office, or, upon payment of the required fee, any error of a clerical or typographical nature occurring in good faith but not through the fault of the Office. Such registration, together with the certificate, shall thereafter have the same effect as if it had been originally issued in such corrected form.

§ 1320. Ownership and transfer

(a) **Property Right in Design.** The property right in a design subject to protection under this chapter shall vest in the designer, the legal representatives of a deceased designer or of one under legal incapacity, the employer for whom the designer created the design in the case of a design made within the regular scope of the designer's employment, or a person to whom the rights of the designer or of such employer have been transferred. The person in whom the property right is vested shall be considered the owner of the design.

(b) **Transfer of Property Right.** The property right in a registered design, or a design for which an application for registration has been or may be filed, may be assigned, granted, conveyed, or mortgaged by an instrument in writing, signed by the owner, or may be bequeathed by will.

(c) **Oath or Acknowledgment of Transfer.** An oath or acknowledgment under section 1312 shall be prima facie evidence of the execution of an assignment, grant, conveyance, or mortgage under subsection (b).

(d) **Recordation of Transfer.** An assignment, grant, conveyance, or mortgage under subsection (b) shall be void as against any subsequent purchaser or mortgagee for a valuable consideration, unless it is recorded in the Office of the Administrator within 3 months after its date of execution or before the date of such subsequent purchase or mortgage.

§ 1321. Remedy for infringement

(a) In General. The owner of a design is entitled, after issuance of a certificate of registration of the design under this chapter, to institute an action for any infringement of the design.

(b) Review of Refusal to Register. (1) Subject to paragraph (2), the owner of a design may seek judicial review of a final refusal of the Administrator to register the design under this chapter by bringing a civil action, and may in the same action, if the court adjudges the design subject to protection under this chapter, enforce the rights in that design under this chapter.

(2) The owner of a design may seek judicial review under this section if—

(A) the owner has previously duly filed and prosecuted to final refusal an application in proper form for registration of the design;

(B) the owner causes a copy of the complaint in the action to be delivered to the Administrator within 10 days after the commencement of the action; and

(C) the defendant has committed acts in respect to the design which would constitute infringement with respect to a design protected under this chapter.

(c) Administrator as Party to Action. The Administrator may, at the Administrator's option, become a party to the action with respect to the issue of registrability of the design claim by entering an appearance within 60 days after being served with the complaint, but the failure of the Administrator to become a party shall not deprive the court of jurisdiction to determine that issue.

(d) Use of Arbitration to Resolve Dispute. The parties to an infringement dispute under this chapter, within such time as may be specified by the Administrator by regulation, may determine the dispute, or any aspect of the dispute, by arbitration. Arbitration shall be governed by title 9. The parties shall give notice of any arbitration award to the Administrator, and such award shall, as between the parties to the arbitration, be dispositive of the issues to which it relates. The arbitration award shall be unenforceable until such notice is given. Nothing in this subsection shall preclude the Administrator from determining whether a design is subject to registration in a cancellation proceeding under section 1313(c).

§ 1322. Injunctions

(a) In General. A court having jurisdiction over actions under this chapter may grant injunctions in accordance with the principles of equity to prevent infringement of a design under this chapter, including, in its discretion, prompt relief by temporary restraining orders and preliminary injunctions.

(b) Damages for Injunctive Relief Wrongfully Obtained. A seller or distributor who suffers damage by reason of injunctive relief wrongfully obtained under this section has a cause of action against the applicant for such injunctive relief and may recover such relief as may be appropriate, including damages for lost profits, cost of materials, loss of good will, and punitive damages in instances where the injunctive relief was sought in bad faith, and, unless the court finds extenuating circumstances, reasonable attorney's fees.

§ 1323. Recovery for infringement

(a) **Damages.** Upon a finding for the claimant in an action for infringement under this chapter, the court shall award the claimant damages adequate to compensate for the infringement. In addition, the court may increase the damages to such amount, not exceeding $50,000 or $1 per copy, whichever is greater, as the court determines to be just. The damages awarded shall constitute compensation and not a penalty. The court may receive expert testimony as an aid to the determination of damages.

(b) **Infringer's Profits.** As an alternative to the remedies provided in subsection (a), the court may award the claimant the infringer's profits resulting from the sale of the copies if the court finds that the infringer's sales are reasonably related to the use of the claimant's design. In such a case, the claimant shall be required to prove only the amount of the infringer's sales and the infringer shall be required to prove its expenses against such sales.

(c) **Statute of Limitations.** No recovery under subsection (a) or (b) shall be had for any infringement committed more than 3 years before the date on which the complaint is filed.

(d) **Attorney's Fees.** In an action for infringement under this chapter, the court may award reasonable attorney's fees to the prevailing party.

(e) **Disposition of Infringing and Other Articles.** The court may order that all infringing articles, and any plates, molds, patterns, models, or other means specifically adapted for making the articles, be delivered up for destruction or other disposition as the court may direct.

§ 1324. Power of court over registration

In any action involving the protection of a design under this chapter, the court, when appropriate, may order registration of a design under this chapter or the cancellation of such a registration. Any such order shall be certified by the court to the Administrator, who shall make an appropriate entry upon the record.

§ 1325. Liability for action on registration fraudulently obtained

Any person who brings an action for infringement knowing that registration of the design was obtained by a false or fraudulent representation materially affecting the rights under this chapter, shall be liable in the sum of $10,000, or such part of that amount as the court may determine. That amount shall be to compensate the defendant and shall be charged against the plaintiff and paid to the defendant, in addition to such costs and attorney's fees of the defendant as may be assessed by the court.

§ 1326. Penalty for false marking

(a) In General. Whoever, for the purpose of deceiving the public, marks upon, applies to, or uses in advertising in connection with an article made, used, distributed, or sold, a design which is not protected under this chapter, a design notice specified in section 1306, or any other words or symbols importing that the design is protected under this chapter, knowing that the design is not so protected, shall pay a civil fine of not more than $500 for each such offense.

(b) Suit by Private Persons. Any person may sue for the penalty established by subsection (a), in which event one-half of the penalty shall be awarded to the person suing and the remainder shall be awarded to the United States.

§ 1327. Penalty for false representation

Whoever knowingly makes a false representation materially affecting the rights obtainable under this chapter for the purpose of obtaining registration of a design under this chapter shall pay a penalty of not less than $500 and not more than $1,000, and any rights or privileges that individual may have in the design under this chapter shall be forfeited.

§ 1328. Enforcement by Treasury and Postal Service

(a) Regulations. The Secretary of the Treasury and the United States Postal Service shall separately or jointly issue regulations for the enforcement of the rights set forth in section 1308 with respect to importation. Such regulations may require, as a condition for the exclusion of articles from the United States, that the person seeking exclusion take any one or more of the following actions:

(1) Obtain a court order enjoining, or an order of the International Trade Commission under section 337 of the Tariff Act of 1930 excluding, importation of the articles.

(2) Furnish proof that the design involved is protected under this chapter and that the importation of the articles would infringe the rights in the design under this chapter.

(3) Post a surety bond for any injury that may result if the detention or exclusion of the articles proves to be unjustified.

(b) Seizure and Forfeiture. Articles imported in violation of the rights set forth in section 1308 are subject to seizure and forfeiture in the same manner as property imported in violation of the customs laws. Any such forfeited articles shall be destroyed as directed by the Secretary of the Treasury or the court, as the case may be, except that the articles may be returned to the country of export whenever it is shown to the satisfaction of the Secretary of the Treasury that the importer had no reasonable grounds for believing that his or her acts constituted a violation of the law.

§ 1329. Relation to design patent law

The issuance of a design patent under title 35, United States Code, for an original design for an article of manufacture shall terminate any protection of the original design under this chapter.

§ 1330. Common law and other rights unaffected

Nothing in this chapter shall annul or limit—

(1) common law or other rights or remedies, if any, available to or held by any person with respect to a design which has not been registered under this chapter; or

(2) any right under the trademark laws or any right protected against unfair competition.

§ 1331. Administrator; Office of the Administrator

In this chapter, the "Administrator" is the Register of Copyrights, and the "Office of the Administrator" and the "Office" refer to the Copyright Office of the Library of Congress.

§ 1332. No retroactive effect

Protection under this chapter shall not be available for any design that has been made public under section 1310(b) before the effective date of this chapter.

*

THE 1909 COPYRIGHT ACT (EXCERPTS)

CHAPTER 1—REGISTRATION OF COPYRIGHTS

§ 1. **Exclusive Rights as to Copyrighted Works.** – Any person entitled thereto, upon complying with the provisions of this title, shall have the exclusive right:

(a) To print, reprint, publish, copy, and vend the copyrighted work;

(b) To translate the copyrighted work into other languages or dialects, or make any other version thereof, if it be a literary work; to dramatize it if it be a nondramatic work; to convert it into a novel or other nondramatic work if it be a drama; to arrange or adapt it if it be a musical work; to complete, execute, and finish it if it be a model or design for a work of art;

(c) To deliver, authorize the delivery of, read, or present the copyrighted work in public for profit if it be a lecture, sermon, address or similar production, or other nondramatic literary work; to make or procure the making of any transcription or record thereof by or from which, in whole or in part, it may in any manner or by any method be exhibited, delivered, presented, produced, or reproduced; and to play or perform it in public for profit, and to exhibit, represent, produce, or reproduce it in any manner or by any method whatsoever. The damages for the infringement by broadcast of any work referred to in this subsection shall not exceed the sum of $100 where the infringing broadcaster shows that he was not aware that he was infringing and that such infringement could not have been reasonably foreseen; and

(d) To perform or represent the copyrighted work publicly if it be a drama or, if it be a dramatic work and not reproduced in copies for sale, to vend any manuscript or any record whatsoever thereof; to make or to procure the making of any transcription or record thereof by or from which, in whole or in part, it may in any manner or by any method be exhibited, performed, represented, produced, or reproduced; and to exhibit, perform, represent, produce, or reproduce it in any manner or by any method whatsoever; and

(e) To perform the copyrighted work publicly for profit if it be a musical composition; and for the purpose of public performance for profit, and for the purposes set forth in subsection (a) hereof, to make any arrangement or setting of it or of the melody of it in any system of notation or any form of record in which the thought of an author may be recorded and from which it may be read or reproduced: *Provided,* That the provisions of this title, so far as they secure copyright controlling the parts of instruments serving to reproduce mechanically the musical work, shall include only compositions published and copyrighted after July 1, 1909, and shall not include the works of a foreign author or composer unless the foreign state or nation of which such author or composer is a citizen or subject grants, either by treaty, convention, agreement, or law, to citizens of the United States similar rights. And as a condition of extending the copyrighted control to such mechanical reproductions, that whenever the owner of a musical copyright has used or permitted or knowingly acquiesced in the use of the copyrighted work upon the parts of instruments serving to reproduce mechanically the musical work, any other person may make similar use of the copyrighted work upon the payment to the copyright proprietor of a royalty of 2 cents on each such part manufactured, to be paid by the manufacturer thereof; and the copyright proprietor may require, and if so the manufacturer shall furnish, a report under oath on the 20th day of each month on the number of parts of instruments manufactured during the previous month serving to reproduce mechanically said musical work, and royalties shall be due on the parts manufactured during any month upon the 20th of the next succeeding month. The payment of the royalty provided for by this section shall free the articles or devices for which such royalty has been paid from further contribution to the copyright except in case of public performance for profit. It shall be the duty of the copyright owner, if he uses the musical composition himself for the manufacture of parts of instruments serving to reproduce mechanically the musical work, or licenses others to do so, to file notice thereof, accompanied by a recording fee, in the copyright office, and any failure to file such notice shall be a complete defense to any suit, action, or proceeding for any infringement of such copyright.

In case of failure of such manufacturer to pay to the copyright proprietor within thirty days after demand in writing the full sum of royalties due at said rate at the date of such demand, the court may award taxable costs to the plaintiff and a reasonable counsel fee, and the court may, in its discretion, enter judgment therein for any sum in addition over the amount found to be due as royalty in accordance with the terms of this title, not exceeding three times such amount.

The reproduction or rendition of a musical composition by or upon coin-operated machines shall not be deemed a public performance for profit unless a fee is charged for admission to the place where such reproduction or rendition occurs.

(f) To reproduce and distribute to the public by sale or other transfer of ownership, or by rental, lease, or lending, reproductions of the copyrighted work if it be a sound recording: *Provided,* That the exclusive right of the owner of a copyright in a sound recording to reproduce it is limited to the right to duplicate the sound recording in a tangible form that directly or indirectly recaptures the actual sounds fixed in the recording: *Provided further,* That this right does not extend to the making or duplication of another sound recording that is an independent fixation of other sounds, even though such sounds imitate or simulate those in the copyrighted sound recording; or to reproductions made by transmitting organizations exclusively for their own use.

§ 2. **Rights of Author or Proprietor of Unpublished Work.** – Nothing in this title shall be construed to annul or limit the right of the author or proprietor of an unpublished work, at common law or in equity, to prevent the copying, publication, or use of such unpublished work without his consent, and to obtain damages therefor.

§ 3. **Protection of Component Parts of Work Copyrighted; Composite Works or Periodicals.** – The copyright provided by this title shall protect all the copyrightable component parts of the work copyrighted, and all matter therein in which copyright is already subsisting, but without extending the duration or scope of such copyright. The copyright upon composite works or periodicals shall give to the proprietor thereof all the rights in respect thereto which he would have if each part were individually copyrighted under this title.

§ 4. **All Writings of Author Included.** – The works for which copyright may be secured under this title shall include all the writings of an author.

§ 5. Classification of Works for Registration. – The application for registration shall specify to which of the following classes the work in which copyright is claimed belongs:

(a) Books, including composite and cyclopedic works, directories, gazetteers, and other compilations.

(b) Periodicals, including newspapers.

(c) Lectures, sermons, addresses (prepared for oral delivery).

(d) Dramatic or dramatico-musical compositions.

(e) Musical compositions.

(f) Maps.

(g) Works of art; models or designs for works of art.

(h) Reproductions of a work of art.

(i) Drawings or plastic works of a scientific or technical character.

(j) Photographs.

(k) Prints and pictorial illustrations including prints or labels used for articles of merchandise.

(*l*) Motion-picture photoplays.

(m) Motion pictures other than photoplays.

(n) Sound recordings.

The above specifications shall not be held to limit the subject matter of copyright as defined in section 4 of this title, nor shall any error in classification invalidate or impair the copyright protection secured under this title.

* * * *

§ 7. Copyright on Compilations of Works in Public Domain or of Copyrighted Works; Subsisting Copyrights Not Affected. – Compilations or abridgements, adaptations, arrangements, dramatizations, translations, or other versions of works in the public domain or of copyrighted works when produced with the consent of the proprietor of the copyright in such works, or works republished with new matter, shall be regarded as new works subject to copyright under the provisions of this title; but the publication of any such new works shall not affect the force or validity of any subsisting copyright upon the matter employed or any part thereof, or be construed to imply an exclusive right to such use of the original works, or to secure or extend copyright in such original works.

* * * *

§ 9. Authors or Proprietors, Entitled; Aliens. – The author or proprietor of any work made the subject of copyright by this title, or his executors, administrators, or assigns, shall have copyright for such work under the conditions and for the terms specified in this title: *Provided, however,* That the copyright secured by this title shall extend to the work of an author or proprietor who is a citizen or subject of a foreign state or nation only under the conditions described in subsections (a), (b), or (c) below:

(a) When an alien author or proprietor shall be domiciled within the United States at the time of the first publication of his work; or

(b) When the foreign state or nation of which such author or proprietor is a citizen or subject grants, either by treaty, convention, agreement, or law, to citizens of the United States the benefit of copyright on substantially the same basis as to its own citizens, or copyright protection, substantially equal to the protection secured to such foreign author under this title or by treaty; or when such foreign state or nation is a party to an international agreement which provides for reciprocity in the granting of copyright, by the terms of which agreement the United States may, at its pleasure, become a party thereto.

The existence of the reciprocal conditions aforesaid shall be determined by the President of the United States, by proclamation made from time to time, as the purposes of this title may require: *Provided,* That whenever the President shall find that the authors, copyright owners, or proprietors of works first produced or published abroad and subject to copyright or to renewal of copyright under the laws of the United States, including works subject to ad interim copyright, are or may have been temporarily unable to comply with the conditions and formalities prescribed with respect to such works by the copyright laws of the United States, because of the disruption or suspension of facilities essential for such compliance, he may by proclamation grant such extension of time as he may deem appropriate for the fulfillment of such conditions or formalities by authors, copyright owners, or proprietors who are citizens of the United States or who are nationals of countries which accord substantially equal treatment in this respect to authors, copyright owners, or proprietors who are citizens of the United States: *Provided further,* That no liability shall attach under this title for lawful uses made or acts done prior to the effective date of such proclamation in connection with such works, or in respect to the continuance for one year subsequent to such date of any business undertaking or enterprise lawfully undertaken prior to such date involving expenditure or contractual obligation in connection with the exploitation, production, reproduction, circulation, or performance of any such work.

The President may at any time terminate any proclamation authorized herein or any part thereof or suspend or extend its operation for such period or periods of time as in his judgment the interests of the United States may require.

(c) When the Universal Copyright Convention, signed at Geneva on September 6, 1952, shall be in force between the United States of America and the foreign state or nation of which such author is a citizen or subject, or in which the work was first published. Any work to which copyright is extended pursuant to this subsection shall be exempt from the following provisions of this title: (1) The requirement in section 1(e) that a foreign state or nation must grant to United States citizens mechanical reproduction rights similar to those specified therein; (2) the obligatory deposit requirements of the first sentence of section 13; (3) the provisions of sections 14, 16, 17, and 18; (4) the import prohibitions of section 107, to the extent that they are related to the manufacturing requirements of section 16; and (5) the requirements of sections 19 and 20: *Provided, however,* That such exemptions shall apply only if from the time of first publication all the copies of the work published with the authority of the author or other copyright proprietor shall bear the symbol © accompanied by the name of the copyright proprietor and the year of first publication placed in such manner and location as to give reasonable notice of claim of copyright.

Upon the coming into force of the Universal Copyright Convention in a foreign state or nation as hereinbefore provided, every book or periodical of a citizen or subject thereof in which ad interim copyright was subsisting on the effective date of said coming into force shall have copyright for twenty-eight years from the date of first publication abroad without the necessity of complying with the further formalities specified in section 23 of this title.

The provisions of this subsection shall not be extended to works of an author who is a citizen of, or domiciled in the United States of America regardless of place of first publication, or to works first published in the United States.

§ 10. Publication of Work With Notice. – Any person entitled thereto by this title may secure copyright for his work by publication thereof with the notice of copyright required by this title; and such notice shall be affixed to each copy thereof published or offered for sale in the United States by authority of the copyright proprietor, except in the case of books seeking ad interim protection under section 22 of this title.

§ 11. Registration of Claim and Issuance of Certificate. – Such person may obtain registration of his claim to copyright by complying with the provisions of this title, including the deposit of copies, and upon such compliance the Register of Copyrights shall issue to him the certificates provided for in section 209 of this title.

§ 12. Works Not Reproduced for Sale. – Copyright may also be had of the works of an author, of which copies are not reproduced for sale, by the deposit, with claim of copyright, of one complete copy of such work if it be a lecture or similar production or a dramatic, musical, or dramatico-musical composition; of a title and description, with one print taken from each scene or act, if the work be a motion-picture photoplay; of a photographic print if the work be a photograph; of a title and description, with not less than two prints taken from different sections of a complete motion picture, if the work be a motion picture other than a photoplay; or of a photograph or other identifying reproduction thereof, if it be a work of art or a plastic work or drawing. But the privilege of registration of copyright secured hereunder shall not exempt the copyright proprietor from the deposit of copies, under sections 13 and 14 of this title, where the work is later reproduced in copies for sale.

§ 13. Deposit of Copies After Publication; Action or Proceeding for Infringement. – After copyright has been secured by publication of the work with the notice of copyright as provided in section 10 of this title, there shall be promptly deposited in the Copyright Office or in the mail addressed to the Register of Copyrights, Washington, District of Columbia, two complete copies of the best edition thereof then published, or if the work is by an author who is a citizen or subject of a foreign state or nation and has been published in a foreign country, one complete copy of the best edition then published in such foreign country, which copies or copy, if the work be a book or periodical, shall have been produced in accordance with the manufacturing provisions specified in section 16 of this title; or if such work be a contribution to a periodical, for which contribution special registration is requested, one copy of the issue or issues containing such contribution; or if the work belongs to a class specified in subsections (g), (h), (i) or (k) of section 5 of this title, and if the Register of Copyrights determines that it is impracticable to deposit copies because of their size, weight, fragility, or monetary value he may permit the deposit of photographs or other identifying reproductions in lieu of copies of the work as published under such rules and regulations as he may prescribe with the approval of the Librarian of Congress; or if the work is not reproduced in copies for sale there shall be deposited the copy, print, photograph, or other identifying reproduction provided by section 12 of this title, such copies or copy, print, photograph, or other reproduction to be accompanied in each case by a claim of copyright. No action or proceeding shall be maintained for infringement of copyright in any work until the provisions of this title with respect to the deposit of copies and registration of such work shall have been complied with.

§ 14. Same; Failure to Deposit; Demand; Penalty. – Should the copies called for by section 13 of this title not be promptly deposited as provided in this title, the Register of Copyrights may at any time after the publication of the work, upon actual notice, require the proprietor of the copyright to deposit them, and after the said demand shall have been made, in default of the deposit of copies of the work within three months from any part of the United States, except an outlying territorial possession of the United States, or within six months from any outlying territorial possession of the United States, or from any foreign country, the proprietor of the copyright shall be liable to a fine of $100 and to pay to the Library of Congress twice the amount of the retail price of the best edition of the work, and the copyright shall become void.

* * * *

§ 19. Notice; Form. – The notice of copyright required by section 10 of this title shall consist either of the word "Copyright", the abbreviation "Copr.", or the symbol ©, accompanied by the name of the copyright proprietor, and if the work be a printed literary, musical, or dramatic work, the notice shall include also the year in which the copyright was secured by publication. In the case, however, of copies of works specified in subsections (f) to (k), inclusive, of section 5 of this title, the notice may consist of the letter C enclosed within a circle, thus ©, accompanied by the initials, monogram, mark, or symbol of the copyright proprietor: *Provided,* That on some accessible portion of such copies or of the margin, back, permanent base, or pedestal, or of the substance on which such copies shall be mounted, his name shall appear. But in the case of works in which copyright was subsisting on July 1, 1909, the notice of copyright may be either in one of the forms prescribed herein or may consist of the following words: "Entered according to Act of Congress, in the year ___, by A.B., and in the office of the Librarian of Congress, at Washington, D.C.," or, at his option the word "Copyright", together with the year the copyright was entered and the name of the party by whom it was taken out; thus, "Copyright, 19__, by A.B."

In the case of reproductions of works specified in subsection (n) of section 5 of this title, the notice shall consist of the symbol P (the letter P in a circle), the year of first publication of the sound recording, and the name of the owner of copyright in the sound recording, or an abbreviation by which the name can be recognized, or a generally known alternative designation of the owner: *Provided,* That if the producer of the sound recording is named on the labels or containers of the reproduction, and if no other name appears in conjunction with the notice, his name shall be considered a part of the notice.

§ 20. Same; Place of Application of; One Notice in Each Volume or Number of Newspaper or Periodical. – The notice of copyright shall be applied, in the case of a book or other printed publication, upon its title page or the page immediately following, or if a periodical either upon the title page or upon the first page of text of each separate number or under the title heading, or if a musical work either upon its title page or the first page of music, or if a sound recording on the surface of reproductions thereof or on the label or container in such manner and location as to give reasonable notice of the claim of copyright. One notice of copyright in each volume or in each number of a newspaper or periodical published shall suffice.

§ 21. Same; Effect of Accidental Omission From Copy or Copies. – Where the copyright proprietor has sought to comply with the provisions of this title with respect to notice, the omission by accident or mistake of the prescribed notice from a particular copy or copies shall not invalidate the copyright or prevent recovery for infringement against any person who, after actual notice of the copyright, begins an undertaking to infringe it, but shall prevent the recovery of damages against an innocent infringer who has been misled by the omission of the notice; and in a suit for infringement no permanent injunction shall be had unless the copyright proprietor shall reimburse to the innocent infringer his reasonable outlay innocently incurred if the court, in its discretion, shall so direct.

* * * *

§ 24. Duration, Renewal and Extension. – The copyright secured by this title shall endure for twenty-eight years from the date of first publication, whether the copyrighted work bears the author's true name or is published anonymously or under an assumed name: *Provided,* That in the case of any posthumous work or of any periodical, cyclopedic, or other composite work upon which the copyright was originally secured by the proprietor thereof, or of any work copyrighted by a corporate body (otherwise than as assignee or licensee of the individual author) or by an employer for whom such work is made for hire, the proprietor of such copyright shall be entitled to a renewal and extension of the copyright in such work for the further term of twenty-eight years when application for such renewal and extension shall have been made to the copyright office and duly registered therein within one year prior to the expiration of the original term of copyright: *And provided further,* That in the case of any other copyrighted work, including a contribution by an individual author to a periodical or to a cyclopedic or other composite work, the author of such work, if still living, or the widow, widower, or children of the author, if the author be not living, or if such author, widow, widower or children be not living, then the author's executors, or in the absence of a will, his next of kin shall be entitled to a renewal and extension of the copyright in such work for a further term of twenty-eight years when application for such renewal and extension shall have been made to the copyright office and duly registered therein within one year prior to the expiration of the original term of copyright: *And provided further,* That in default of the registration of such application for renewal and extension, the copyright in any work shall determine at the expiration of twenty-eight years from first publication.

* * * *

§ 26. Terms Defined. – In the interpretation and construction of this title "the date of publication" shall in the case of a work of which copies are reproduced for sale or distribution be held to be the earliest date when copies of the first authorized edition were placed on sale, sold, or publicly distributed by the proprietor of the copyright or under his authority, and the word "author" shall include an employer in the case of works made for hire.

For the purposes of this section and sections 10, 11, 13, 14, 21, 101, 106, 109, 209, 215, but not for any other purpose, a reproduction of a work described in subsection 5(n) shall be considered to be a copy thereof. "Sound recordings" are works that result from the fixation of a series of musical, spoken, or other sounds, but not including the sounds accompanying a motion picture. "Reproductions of sound recordings" are material objects in which sounds other than those accompanying a motion picture are fixed by any method now known or later developed, and from which the sounds can be perceived, reproduced, or otherwise communicated, either directly or with the aid of a machine or device, and include the "parts of instruments serving to reproduce mechanically the musical work", "mechanical reproductions", and "interchangeable parts, such as discs or tapes for use in mechanical music-producing machines" referred to in sections 1(e) and 101(e) of this title.

§ 27. Copyright Distinct From Property in Object Copyrighted; Effect of Sale of Object, and of Assignment of Copyright.

– The copyright is distinct from the property in the material object copyrighted, and the sale or conveyance, by gift or otherwise, of the material object shall not of itself constitute a transfer of the copyright, nor shall the assignment of the copyright constitute a transfer of the title to the material object; but nothing in this title shall be deemed to forbid, prevent, or restrict the transfer of any copy of a copyrighted work the possession of which has been lawfully obtained.

§ 28. Assignments and Bequests.

– Copyright secured under this title or previous copyright laws of the United States may be assigned, granted, or mortgaged by an instrument in writing signed by the proprietor of the copyright, or may be bequeathed by will.

* * * *

§ 30. Same; Record.

– Every assignment of copyright shall be recorded in the copyright office within three calendar months after its execution in the United States or within six calendar months after its execution without the limits of the United States, in default of which it shall be void as against any subsequent purchaser or mortgagee for a valuable consideration, without notice, whose assignment has been duly recorded.

§ 31. Same; Certificate of Record.

– The Register of Copyrights shall, upon payment of the prescribed fee, record such assignment, and shall return it to the sender with a certificate of record attached under seal of the copyright office, and upon the payment of the fee prescribed by this title he shall furnish to any person requesting the same a certified copy thereof under the said seal.

§ 32. Same; Use of Name of Assignee in Notice.

– When an assignment of the copyright in a specified book or other work has been recorded the assignee may substitute his name for that of the assignor in the statutory notice of copyright prescribed by this title.

CHAPTER 2—INFRINGEMENT PROCEEDINGS

Sec.
§ 101. Infringement.
 (a) Injunction.
 (b) Damages and profits; amount; other remedies.
§ 104. Willful infringement for profit.

§ 101. Infringement.

– If any person shall infringe the copyright in any work protected under the copyright laws of the United States such person shall be liable:

(a) Injunction. – To an injunction restraining such infringement;

(b) Damages and Profits; Amount; Other Remedies. – To pay to the copyright proprietor such damages as the copyright proprietor may have suffered due to the infringement, as well as all the profits which the infringer shall have made from such infringement, and in proving profits the plaintiff shall be required to prove sales only, and the defendant shall be required to prove every element of cost which he claims, or in lieu of actual damages and profits, such damages as to the court shall appear to be just, and in assessing such damages the court may, in its discretion, allow the amounts as hereinafter stated, but in case of a newspaper reproduction of a copyrighted photograph, such damages shall not exceed the sum of $200 nor be less than the sum of $50, and in the case of the infringement of an undramatized or nondramatic work by means of motion pictures, where the infringer shall show that he was not aware that he was infringing, and that such infringement could not have been reasonably foreseen, such damages shall not exceed the sum of $100; and in the case of an infringement of a copyrighted dramatic or dramatico-musical work by a maker of motion pictures and his agencies for distribution thereof to exhibitors, where such infringer shows that he was not aware that he was infringing a copyrighted work, and that such infringements could not reasonably have been foreseen, the entire sum of such damages recoverable by the copyright proprietor from such infringing maker and his agencies for the distribution to exhibitors of such infringing motion picture shall not exceed the sum of $5,000 nor be less than $250, and such damages shall in no other case exceed the sum of $5,000 nor be less than the sum of $250, and shall not be regarded as a penalty. But the foregoing exceptions shall not deprive the copyright proprietor of any other remedy given him under this law, nor shall the limitation as to the amount of recovery apply to infringements occurring after the actual notice to a defendant, either by service of process in a suit or other written notice served upon him. . . .

* * * *

§ 104. **Willful Infringement for Profit.** – (a) Except as provided in subsection (b), any person who willfully and for profit shall infringe any copyright secured by this title, or who shall knowingly and willfully aid or abet such infringement, shall be deemed guilty of a misdemeanor, and upon conviction thereof shall be punished by imprisonment for not exceeding one year or by a fine of not less than $100 nor more than $1,000, or both, in the discretion of the court: *Provided, however,* That nothing in this title shall be so construed as to prevent the performance of religious or secular works such as oratorios, cantatas, masses, or octavo choruses by public schools, church choirs, or vocal societies, rented, borrowed, or obtained from some public library, public school, church choir, school choir, or vocal society, provided the performance is given for charitable or educational purposes and not for profit.

(b) Any person who willfully and for profit shall infringe any copyright provided by section 1(f) of this title, or who should knowingly and willfully aid or abet such infringement, shall be fined not more than $25,000 or imprisoned not more than one year, or both, for the first offense and shall be fined not more than $50,000 or imprisoned not more than two years, or both for any subsequent offense.

* * * *

APPENDIX C

REGULATIONS OF THE U.S. COPYRIGHT OFFICE (EXCERPTS)

37 Code of Federal Regulations

PART 201—GENERAL PROVISIONS

§ 201.3 Fees for registration, recordation, and related services, special services, and services performed by the Licensing Division.

(a) *General*. This section prescribes the fees for registration, recordation, and related services, special services, and services performed by the Licensing Division.

(b) *Definitions*. For purposes of this section, the following definitions apply:

(1) Registration, recordation, and related service fee. This is the fee for a registration or recordation service that the Office is required to perform under 17 U.S.C., or a directly related service. It includes those services described in section 708(a)(1)-(9) and authorized by Pub. L. 105–80.

(2) Special service fee. This is a fee for a special service not specified in title 17, which the Register of Copyrights may fix at any time on the basis of the cost of providing the service, as provided by 17 U.S.C. 708(a)(10).

(3) Licensing Division service fee. This is a fee for a service performed by the Licensing Division.

(c) *Registration, recordation and related service fees*. The Copyright Office has established the following fees for these services:

Registration, recordation and related services	Fees
(1) Basic registrations: Form TX, Form VA, Form PA, Form SE, (including Short Forms), and Form SR	$ 30
(2) Registration of a claim in a group of contribution to periodicals (GR/CP)	30
(3) Registration of a renewal claim (Form RE):	
Claim without Addendum	45
Addendum	15
Registration of a claim in a Mask Work	75
(5) Registration of a claim in a group of serials (Form SE/Group) $30 minimum	10^1

445

Registration, recordation and related services	Fees
(6) Registration of a claim in a group of daily newspapers, and qualified newsletters (Form G/DN)	55
(7) Registration of a restored copyright (Form GATT)	30
(8) Registration of a claim in a group of restored works (Form GATT Group) $30 minimum	10^2
(9) Registration of a correction or amplification to a claim (Form CA)	65
(10) Providing an additional certificate of registration	25
(11) Any other certification, per hour	65
(12) Search—report prepared from official records, per hour	65
(13) Search—locating Copyright Office records, per hour	65
(14) Recordation of documents (single title)	50
Additional titles (per group of 10 titles)	15
(15) Recordation of a notice of intention (NIE) to enforce a restored copyright containing no more than one title	30
Additional NIE titles (each)	1
(16) Recordation of Notice of Intention to Make and Distribute Phonorecords	12
(17) Issuance of a receipt for a deposit	4

[1] Per issues.
[2] Per claim.

(d) *Special service fees.* The Copyright Office has established the following fees for special services:

Special services	Fees
(1) Service charge for deposit account overdraft	$ 70
(2) Service charge for dishonored deposit account replenishment check	35
(3) Service charge for insufficient fee	[1]
(4) Appeals:	
(i) First appeal	200
Additional claim in related group	20
(ii) Second appeal	500
Additional claim in related group	20
(5) Secure test processing charge, per hour	60
(6) Copying charge, 15 pages or fewer	15
Each additional page over 15	50
(7) Inspection charge	65
(8) Special handling fee for a claim	500
Each additional claim using the same deposit	50
(9) Special handling fee for recordation of a document	330
(10) Full-term storage of deposits	365
(11) Surcharge for expedited Certifications and Documents Section services:	
(i) Additional certificates, per hour	75
(ii) In-process searches, per hour	75
(iii) Copy of assignment or other document, per hour	75
(iv) Certification, per hour	75

Special services		Fees
(v)	Copy of registered deposit:	
	First hour	95
	Each additional hour	75
(vi)	Copy of correspondence file:	
	First hour	95
	Each additional hour	75
(12)	Surcharge for expedited Reference & Bibliography Section searches:	
	First hour	125
	Each additional hour	95

¹Reserved.

(e) *Licensing Division service fees.* The Copyright Office has established the following fees for certain services performed by the Licensing Division:

Licensing Division services		Fees
(1)	Recordation of a Notice of Intention to Make and Distribute Phonorecords (17 U.S.C. 115)	$ 12
(2)	Certificate of Filing a Notice of Intention (17 U.S.C. 115)..	8
(3)	Filing Fee for Recordation of License Agreements under 17 U.S.C. 118	50
(4)	Recordation of Certain Contracts by Cable Television Systems Located Outside the Forty–Eight Contiguous States	50
(5)	Initial Notice of Digital Transmission of Sound Recording (17 U.S.C. 114)	20
	Amendment of 17 U.S.C. 114 Notice	20
(6)	Statement of Account Amendment (Cable Television Systems and Satellite Carriers, 17 U.S.C. 111 and 119)..	15
(7)	Statement of Account Amendment (Digital Audio Recording Devices or Media, 17 U.S.C. 1003)......	20
(8)	Using Public Photocopier, per page	25
	Photocopies Made by Licensing Staff, per page	40
(9)	Search, per hour	65
(10)	Certification of Search Report	65

§ 201.13. Notices of objection to certain noncommercial performances of nondramatic literary or musical works.

(a) *Definitions.* (1) A "Notice of Objection" is a notice, as required by section 110(4) of Title 17 of the United States Code as amended by Pub. L. 94–553, to be served as a condition of preventing the noncommercial performance of a nondramatic literary or musical work under certain circumstances.

(2) For purposes of this section, the "copyright owner" of a nondramatic literary or musical work is the author of the work (including, in the case of a work made for hire, the employer or other person for whom the work was prepared), or a person or organization

that has obtained ownership of the exclusive right, initially owned by the author of performance of the type referred to in 17 U.S.C. 110(4). If the other requirements of this section are met, a Notice of Objection may cover the works of more than one copyright owner.

(b) *Form.* The Copyright Office does not provide printed forms for the use of persons serving Notices of Objection.

(c) *Contents.* (1) A Notice of Objection must clearly state that the copyright owner objects to the performance, and must include all of the following:

(i) Reference to the statutory authority on which the Notice of Objection is based, either by citation of 17 U.S.C. 110(4) or by a more general characterization or description of that statutory provision;

(ii) The date and place of the performance to which an objection is being made; however, if the exact date or place of a particular performance, or both, are not known to the copyright owner, it is sufficient if the Notice describes whatever information the copyright owner has about the date and place of a particular performance, and the source of that information unless the source was considered private or confidential;

(iii) Clear identification, by title and at least one author, of the particular nondramatic literary or musical work or works, to the performance of which the copyright owner thereof is lodging objection; a Notice may cover any number of separately identified copyrighted works owned by the copyright owner or owners serving the objection. Alternatively, a blanket notice, with or without separate identification of certain copyrighted works, and purporting to cover one or more groups of copyrighted works not separately identified by title and author, shall have effect if the conditions specified in paragraph (c)(2) of this section are met; and

(iv) A concise statement of the reasons for the objection.

(2) A blanket notice purporting to cover one or more groups of copyrighted works not separately identified by title and author shall be valid only if all of the following conditions are met:

(i) The Notice shall identify each group of works covered by the blanket notice by a description of any common characteristics distinguishing them from other copyrighted works, such as common author, common copyright owner, common publisher, or common licensing agent;

(ii) The Notice shall identify a particular individual whom the person responsible for the performance can contact for more detailed information about the works covered by the blanket notice and to determine whether a particular work planned for performance is in fact covered by the Notice. Such identification shall include the full name and business and residence addresses of the individual, telephone numbers at which the individual can be reached throughout the period between service of the notice and the performance, and name, addresses, and telephone numbers of another individual to contact during that period in case the first cannot be reached.

(iii) If the copyright owner or owners of all works covered by the blanket notice is not identified in the Notice, the Notice shall include an offer to identify, by name and last known address, the owner or owners of any and all such works, upon request made to the individual referred to in paragraph (c)(2)(ii) of this section.

(3) A Notice of Objection must also include clear and prominent statements explaining that:

(i) A failure to exclude the works identified in the Notice from the performance in question may subject the person responsible for the performance to liability for copyright infringement; and

(ii) The objection is without legal effect if there is no direct or indirect admission charge for the performance, and if the other conditions of 17 U.S.C. 110(4) are met. . . .

§ 201.14. Warnings of copyright for use by certain libraries and archives.

(a) *Definitions.* (1) A "Display Warning of Copyright" is a notice under paragraphs (d)(2) and (e)(2) of section 108 of Title 17 of the United States Code as amended by Pub. L. 94–553. As required by those sections the "Display Warning of Copyright" is to be displayed at the place where orders for copies or phonorecords are accepted by certain libraries and archives.

(2) An "Order Warning of Copyright" is a notice under paragraphs (d)(2) and (e)(2) of section 108 of Title 17 of the United States Code as amended by Pub. L. 94–553. As required by those sections the "Order Warning of Copyright" is to be included on printed forms supplied by certain libraries and archives and used by their patrons for ordering copies or phonorecords.

(b) *Contents.* A Display Warning of Copyright and an Order Warning of Copyright shall consist of a verbatim reproduction of the following notice, printed in such size and form and displayed in such manner as to comply with paragraph (c) of this section:

NOTICE WARNING CONCERNING COPYRIGHT RESTRICTIONS

The copyright law of the United States (Title 17, United States Code) governs the making of photocopies or other reproductions of copyrighted material. Under certain conditions specified in the law, libraries and archives are authorized to furnish a photocopy or other reproduction. One of these specific conditions is that the photocopy or reproduction is not to be "used for any purpose other than private study, scholarship, or research." If a user makes a request for, or later uses, a photocopy or reproduction for purposes in excess of "fair use," that user may be liable for copyright infringement.

This institution reserves the right to refuse to accept a copying order if, in its judgment, fulfillment of the order would involve violation of copyright law.

(c) *Form and manner of use.* (1) A Display Warning of Copyright shall be printed on heavy paper or other durable material in type at least 18 points in size, and shall be displayed prominently, in such manner and location as to be clearly visible, legible, and comprehensible to a casual observer within the immediate vicinity of the place where orders are accepted.

(2) An Order Warning of Copyright shall be printed within a box located prominently on the order form itself, either on the front side of the form or immediately adjacent to the space calling for the name or signature of the person using the form. The notice shall be printed in type size no smaller than that used predominantly throughout the form, and in no case shall the type size be smaller than 8 points. The notice shall be printed in such manner as to be clearly legible, comprehensible, and readily apparent to a casual reader of the form.

§ 201.24. Warning of copyright for software lending by nonprofit libraries.

(a) *Definition.* A Warning of Copyright for Software Rental is a notice under paragraph (b)(2)(A) of section 109 of the Copyright Act, title 17 of the United States Code, as amended by the Computer Software Rental Amendments Act of 1990, Pub. L. 101–650. As required by that paragraph, the "Warning of Copyright for Software Rental" shall be affixed to the packaging that contains the computer program which is lent by a nonprofit library for nonprofit purposes.

(b) *Contents.* A Warning of Copyright for Software Rental shall consist of a verbatim reproduction of the following notice, printed in such size and form and affixed in such manner as to comply with paragraph (c) of this section.

NOTICE: WARNING OF COPYRIGHT RESTRICTIONS

The copyright law of the United States (Title 17, United States Code) governs the reproduction, distribution, adaptation, public performance, and public display of copyrighted material.

Under certain conditions specified in law, nonprofit libraries are authorized to lend, lease, or rent copies of computer programs to patrons on a nonprofit basis and for nonprofit purposes. Any person who makes an unauthorized copy or adaptation of the computer program, except as permitted by title 17 of the United States Code, may be liable for copyright infringement.

This institution reserves the right to refuse to fulfill a loan request if, in its judgement, fulfillment of the request would lead to violation of the copyright law.

(c) *Form and manner of use.* A Warning of Copyright for Software Rental shall be affixed to the packaging that contains the copy of the computer program, which is the subject of a library loan to patrons, by means of a label cemented, gummed, or otherwise durably attached to the copies or to a box, reel, cartridge, cassette, or other container used as a permanent receptacle for the copy of the computer program. The notice shall be printed in such a manner as to be clearly legible, comprehensible, and readily apparent to a casual user of the computer program.

PART 202—REGISTRATION OF CLAIMS TO COPYRIGHT

§ 202.1.   **Material not subject to copyright.**

The following are examples of works not subject to copyright and applications for registration of such works cannot be entertained:

(a) Words and short phrases such as names, titles, and slogans; familiar symbols or designs; mere variations of typographic ornamentation, lettering or coloring; mere listing of ingredients or contents;

(b) Ideas, plans, methods, systems, or devices, as distinguished from the particular manner in which they are expressed or described in a writing;

(c) Blank forms, such as time cards, graph paper, account books, diaries, bank checks, scorecards, address books, report forms, order forms and the like, which are designed for recording information and do not in themselves convey information;

(d) Works consisting entirely of information that is common property containing no original authorship, such as, for example: Standard calendars, height and weight charts, tape measures and rulers, schedules of sporting events, and lists or tables taken from public documents or other common sources.

(e) Typeface as typeface.

§ 202.10.   **Pictorial, graphic, and sculptural works.**

(a) In order to be acceptable as a pictorial, graphic, or sculptural work, the work must embody some creative authorship in its delineation or form. The registrability of such a work is not affected by the intention of the author as to the use of the work or the number of copies reproduced. The availability of protection or grant of protection under the law for a utility or design patent will not affect the registrability of a claim in an original work of pictorial, graphic, or sculptural authorship.

(b) A claim to copyright cannot be registered in a print or label consisting solely of trademark subject matter and lacking copyrightable matter. While the Copyright Office will not investigate whether the matter has been or can be registered at the Patent and Trademark Office, it will register a properly filed copyright claim in a print or label that contains the requisite qualifications for copyright even though there is a trademark on it. However, registration of a claim to copyright does not give the claimant rights available by trademark registrations at the Patent and Trademark Office.

§ 202.11. Architectural works.

(a) *General.* This section prescribes rules pertaining to the registration of architectural works, as provided for in the amendment of title 17 of the United States Code by the Judicial Improvements Act of 1990, Pub. L. 101–650.

(b) *Definitions.*

(1) For the purposes of this section, the term *architectural work* has the same meaning as set forth in section 101 of title 17, as amended.

(2) The term *building* means humanly habitable structures that are intended to be both permanent and stationary, such as houses and office buildings, and other permanent and stationary structures designed for human occupancy, including but not limited to churches, museums, gazebos, and garden pavilions.

(c) *Registration—*

(1) *Original design.* In general, an original design of a building embodied in any tangible medium of expression, including a building, architectural plans, or drawings, may be registered as an architectural work. . . .

(5) *Publication.* Publication of an architectural work occurs when underlying plans or drawings of the building or other copies of the building design are distributed or made available to the general public by sale or other transfer of ownership, or by rental, lease, or lending. Construction of a building does not itself constitute publication for purposes of registration, unless multiple copies are constructed.

(d) *Works excluded.* The following structures, features, or works cannot be registered:

(1) *Structures other than buildings.* Structures other than buildings, such as bridges, cloverleafs, dams, walkways, tents, recreational vehicles, mobile homes, and boats.

(2) *Standard features.* Standard configurations of spaces, and individual standard features, such as windows, doors, and other staple building components.

(3) *Pre-December 1, 1990 building designs.* The designs of buildings where the plans or drawings of the building were published before

December 1, 1990, or the buildings were constructed or otherwise published before December 1, 1990.

§ 202.20. Deposit of copies and phonorecords for copyright registration.

(a) *General.* This section prescribes rules pertaining to the deposit of copies and phonorecords of published and unpublished works for the purpose of copyright registration under section 408 of title 17 of the United States Code, as amended by Pub. L. 94–553. The provisions of this section are not applicable to the deposit of copies and phonorecords for the Library of Congress under section 407 of title 17, except as expressly adopted in § 202.19 of these regulations.

(b) *Definitions.* For the purposes of this section:

(1) The "best edition" of a work has the meaning set forth in § 202.19(b)(1) of these regulations.

(2) A "complete" copy or phonorecord means the following:

(i) *Unpublished works.* Subject to the requirements of paragraph (b)(2)(vi) of this section, a "complete" copy or phonorecord of an unpublished work is a copy or phonorecord representing the entire copyrightable content of the work for which registration is sought;

(ii) *Published works.* Subject to the requirements of paragraphs (b)(2)(iii) through (vi) of this section, a "complete" copy or phonorecord of a published work includes all elements comprising the applicable unit of publication of the work, including elements that, if considered separately, would not be copyrightable subject matter. . . .

(iii) *Contributions to collective works.* In the case of a published contribution to a collective work, a "complete" copy is one complete copy of the best edition of the entire collective work, the complete section containing the contribution if published in a newspaper, the contribution cut from the paper in which it appeared, or a photocopy of the contribution itself as it was published in the collective work;

(iv) *Sound recordings.* In the case of published sound recordings, a "complete" phonorecord has the meaning set forth in § 202.19(b)(2) of these regulations;

(v) *Musical scores.* In the case of a musical composition published in copies only, or in both copies and phonorecords;

(A) If the only publication of copies took place by the rental, lease, or lending of a full score and parts, a full score is a "complete" copy; and

(B) If the only publication of copies took place by the rental, lease, or lending of a conductor's score and parts, a conductor's score is a "complete" copy;

(vi) *Motion pictures.* In the case of a published or unpublished motion picture, a copy is "complete" if the reproduction of all of the visual and aural elements comprising the copyrightable subject matter in the work is clean, undamaged, undeteriorated, and free of splices, and if the copy itself and its physical housing are free of any defects that would interfere with the performance of the work or that would cause mechanical, visual, or audible defects or distortions.

(3) The terms *architectural works, copy, collective work, device, fixed, literary work, machine, motion picture, phonorecord, publication, sound recording, transmission program,* and *useful article,* and their variant forms, have the meanings given to them in 17 U.S.C. 101.

(4) A "secure test" is a nonmarketed test administered under supervision at specified centers on specific dates, all copies of which are accounted for and either destroyed or returned to restricted locked storage following each administration. For these purposes a test is not marketed if copies are not sold but it is distributed and used in such a manner that ownership and control of copies remain with the test sponsor or publisher.

(5) "Title 17" means title 17 of the United States Code, as amended by Pub. L. 94–553.

(6) For the purposes of determining the applicable deposit requirements under this § 202.20 only, the following shall be considered as unpublished motion pictures: motion pictures that consist of television transmission programs and that have been published, if at all, only by reason of a license or other grant to a nonprofit institution of the right to make a fixation of such programs directly from a transmission to the public, with or without the right to make further uses of such fixations.

(c) *Nature of required deposit.*

(1) Subject to the provisions of paragraph (c)(2) of this section, the deposit required to accompany an application for registration of claim to copyright under section 408 of title 17 shall consist of:

(i) In the case of unpublished works, the complete copy or phonorecord.

(ii) In the case of works first published in the United States before January 1, 1978, two complete copies or phonorecords of the work as first published.

(iii) In the case of works first published in the United States on or after January 1, 1978, two complete copies or phonorecords of the best edition.

(iv) In the case of works first published outside of the United States, one complete copy or phonorecord of the work either as first published or of the best edition. For purposes of this section, any works simultaneously first published within and outside of the

United States shall be considered to be first published in the United States.

(2) In the case of certain works, the special provisions set forth in this clause shall apply. In any case where this clause specifies that one copy or phonorecord may be submitted, that copy or phonorecord shall represent the best edition, or the work as first published, as set forth in paragraph (c)(1) of this section.

(i) *General.* In the following cases the deposit of one complete copy or phonorecord will suffice in lieu of two copies or phonorecords:

(A) Published three-dimensional cartographic representations of area, such as globes and relief models;

(B) Published diagrams illustrating scientific or technical works or formulating scientific or technical information in linear or other two-dimensional form, such as an architectural or engineering blueprint, or a mechanical drawing;

(C) Published greeting cards, picture postcards, and stationery;

(D) Lectures, sermons, speeches, and addresses published individually and not as a collection of the works of one or more authors;

(E) Musical compositions published in copies only, or in both copies and phonorecords, if the only publication of copies took place by rental, lease, or lending;

(F) Published multimedia kits or any part thereof;

(G) Works exempted from the requirement of depositing identifying material under paragraph (c)(2)(xi)(B)(5) of this section;

(H) Literary, dramatic, and musical works published only as embodied in phonorecords, although this category does not exempt the owner of copyright in a sound recording;

(I) Choreographic works, pantomimes, literary, dramatic, and musical works published only as embodied in motion pictures;

(J) Published works in the form of two-dimensional games, decals, fabric patches or emblems, calendars, instructions for needle work, needle work and craft kits; and

(K) Works reproduced on three-dimensional containers such as boxes, cases, and cartons.

(ii) *Motion pictures.* In the case of published or unpublished motion pictures, the deposit of one complete copy will suffice. The deposit of a copy or copies for any published or unpublished motion picture must be accompanied by a separate description of its contents, such as a continuity, pressbook, or synopsis. . . .

(iv) *Certain pictorial and graphic works.* In the case of any unpublished pictorial or graphic work, deposit of identifying material in compliance with § 202.21 of these regulations may be made and will suffice in lieu of deposit of an actual copy. In the case of a published pictorial or graphic work, deposit on one complete copy, or of identifying material in compliance with § 202.21 of these regulations, may be made and will suffice in lieu of deposit of two actual copies where an individual author is the owner of copyright, and either:

(A) Less than five copies of the work have been published; or

(B) The work has been published and sold or offered for sale in a limited edition consisting of no more than 300 numbered copies.

(v) *Commercial prints and labels.* In the case of prints, labels, and other advertising matter, including catalogs, published in connection with the rental, lease, lending, licensing, or sale of articles of merchandise, works of authorship, or services, the deposit of one complete copy will suffice in lieu of two copies. . . .

(vi) *Tests.* In the case of tests, and answer material for tests, published separately from other literary works, the deposit of one complete copy will suffice in lieu of two copies. In the case of any secure test the Copyright Office will return the deposit to the applicant promptly after examination: Provided, That sufficient portions, description, or the like are retained so as to constitute a sufficient archival record of the deposit.

(vii) *Computer programs and databases embodied in machine-readable copies other than CD–ROM format.* In cases where a computer program, database, compilation, statistical compendium, or the like, if unpublished is fixed, or if published is published only in the form of machine-readable copies (such as magnetic tape or disks, punched cards, semiconductor chip products, or the like) other than a CD–ROM format, from which the work cannot ordinarily be perceived except with the aid of a machine or device, the deposit shall consist of:

(A) For published or unpublished computer programs, one copy of identifying portions of the program, reproduced in a form visually perceptible without the aid of a machine or device, either on paper or in microform. For these purposes, "identifying portions" shall mean one of the following:

(1) The first and last 25 pages or equivalent units of the source code if reproduced on paper, or at least the first and last 25 pages or equivalent units of the source code if reproduced in microform, together with the page or equivalent unit containing the copyright notice, if any.

If the program is 50 pages or less, the required deposit will be the entire source code....; [O]r

(2) Where the program contains trade secret material, the page or equivalent unit containing the copyright notice, if any, plus one of the following: the first and last 25 pages or equivalent units of source code with portions of the source code containing trade secrets blocked-out, provided that the blocked-out portions are proportionately less than the material remaining, and the deposit reveals an appreciable amount of original computer code; or the first and last 10 pages or equivalent units of source code alone with no blocked-out portions . . .

(B) Where registration of a program containing trade secrets is made on the basis of an object code deposit the Copyright Office will make registration under its rule of doubt and warn that no determination has been made concerning the existence of copyrightable authorship.

(C) Where the application to claim copyright in a computer program includes a specific claim in related computer screen displays, the deposit, in addition to the identifying portions specified in paragraph (c)(2)(vii)(A) of this section, shall consist of:

(1) Visual reproductions of the copyrightable expression in the form of printouts, photographs, or drawings no smaller than 3x3 inches and no larger than 9x12 inches; or

(2) If the authorship in the work is predominantly audiovisual, a one-half inch VHS format videotape reproducing the copyrightable expression, except that printouts, photographs, or drawings no smaller than 3x3 inches and no larger than 9x12 inches must be deposited in lieu of videotape where the computer screen material simply constitutes a demonstration of the functioning of the computer program.

(D) For published and unpublished automated databases, compilations, statistical compendia, and the like, so fixed or published, one copy of identifying portions of the work, reproduced in a form visually perceptible without the aid of a machine or device, either on paper or in microform....

(viii) *Machine-readable copies of works other than computer programs, databases, and works fixed in a CD–ROM format.* Where a literary, musical, pictorial, graphic, or audiovisual work, or a sound recording, except for works fixed in a CD–ROM format and literary works which are computer programs, databases, compilations, statistical compendia or the like, if unpublished has been fixed or, if published, has been published only in machine-readable form, the deposit must consist of identifying material.

(A) For pictorial or graphic works, the deposit shall consist of identifying material in compliance with § 202.21 of these regulations;

(B) For audiovisual works, the deposit shall consist of either a videotape of the work depicting representative portions of the copyrightable content, or a series of photographs or drawings, depicting representative portions of the work, plus in all cases a separate synopsis of the work;

(C) For musical compositions, the deposit shall consist of a transcription of the entire work such as a score, or a reproduction of the entire work on an audiocassette or other phonorecord;

(D) For sound recordings, the deposit shall consist of a reproduction of the entire work on an audiocassette or other phonorecord;

(E) For literary works, the deposit shall consist of a transcription of representative portions of the work including the first and last 25 pages or equivalent units, and five or more pages indicative of the remainder.

(ix) *Copies containing both visually-perceptible and machine-readable material other than a CD–ROM format.* Where a published literary work is embodied in copies containing both visually-perceptible and machine-readable material, except in the case of a CD–ROM format, the deposit shall consist of the visually-perceptible material and identifying portions of the machine-readable material.

(x) *Works reproduced in or on sheetlike materials.* In the case of any unpublished work that is fixed, or any published work that is published, only in the form of a two-dimensional reproduction on sheetlike materials such as textiles and other fabrics, wallpaper and similar commercial wall coverings, carpeting, floor tile, and similar commercial floor coverings, and wrapping paper and similar packaging material, the deposit shall consist of one copy in the form of an actual swatch or piece of such material sufficient to show all elements of the work in which copyright is claimed and the copyright notice appearing on the work, if any. If the work consists of a repeated pictorial or graphic design, the complete design and at least part of one repetition must be shown.

(xi) *Works reproduced in or on three-dimensional objects.*

(A) In the following cases the deposit must consist of identifying material complying with § 201.21 of these regulations instead of a copy or copies:

(1) Any three-dimensional sculptural work, including any illustration or formulation of artistic expression or information in three-dimensional form. Examples of such works include statues, carvings, ceramics, moldings, constructions, models, and maquettes; and

(2) Any two-dimensional or three-dimensional work that, if unpublished, has been fixed, or, if published, has been published only in or on jewelry, dolls, toys, games, except as provided in paragraph

(c)(2)(xi)(B)(3) of this section, or any three-dimensional useful article. . . .

(xviii) *Architectural works.*

(A) For designs of unconstructed buildings, the deposit must consist of one complete copy of an architectural drawing or blueprint in visually perceptible form showing the overall form of the building and any interior arrangements of spaces and/or design elements in which copyright is claimed. For archival purposes, the Copyright Office prefers that the drawing submissions consist of the following in descending order of preference:

(1) Original format, or best quality form of reproduction, including offset or silk screen printing;

(2) Xerographic or photographic copies on good quality paper;

(3) Positive photostat or photodirect positive;

(4) Blue line copies (diazo or ozalid process).

The Copyright Office prefers that the deposit disclose the name(s) of the architect(s) and draftsperson(s) and the building site, if known.

(B) For designs of constructed buildings, the deposit must consist of one complete copy of an architectural drawing or blueprint in visually perceptible form showing the overall form of the building and any interior arrangement of spaces and/or design elements in which copyright is claimed. In addition, the deposit must also include identifying material in the form of photographs complying with § 202.21 of these regulations, which clearly discloses the architectural works being registered. For archival purposes, the Copyright Office prefers that the drawing submissions constitute the most finished form of presentation drawings and consist of the following in descending order of preference:

(1) Original format, or best quality form of reproduction, including offset or silk screen printing;

(2) Xerographic or photographic copies on good quality paper;

(3) Positive photostat or photodirect positive;

(4) Blue line copies (diazo or ozalid process).

With respect to the accompanying photographs, the Copyright Office prefers 8 X 10 inches, good quality photographs, which clearly show several exterior and interior views. The Copyright Office prefers that the deposit disclose the name(s) of the architect(s) and draftsperson(s) and the building site.

    (xix) *Works fixed in a CD–ROM format.*

      (A) Where a work is fixed in a CD?ROM format, the deposit must consist of one complete copy of the entire CD–ROM package, including a complete copy of any accompanying operating software and instructional manual, and a printed version of the work embodied in the CD–ROM, if the work is fixed in print as well as a CD–ROM. A complete copy of a published CD–ROM package includes all of the elements comprising the applicable unit of publication, including elements that if considered separately would not be copyrightable subject matter or could be the subject of a separate registration.

(d) *Special relief.*

(1) In any case the Register of Copyrights may, after consultation with other appropriate officials of the Library of Congress and upon such conditions as the Register may determine after such consultation:

    (i) Permit the deposit of one copy or phonorecord, or alternative identifying material, in lieu of the one or two copies or phonorecords otherwise required by paragraph (c)(1) of this section;

    (ii) Permit the deposit of incomplete copies or phonorecords, or copies or phonorecords other than those normally comprising the best edition; or

    (iii) Permit the deposit of an actual copy or copies, in lieu of the identifying material otherwise required by this section; or

    (iv) Permit the deposit of identifying material which does not comply with § 202.21 of these regulations.

(2) Any decision as to whether to grant such special relief, and the conditions under which special relief is to be granted, shall be made by the Register of Copyrights after consultation with other appropriate officials of the Library of Congress, and shall be based upon the acquisition policies of the Library of Congress then in force and the archival and examining requirements of the Copyright Office. . . .

PART 253—USE OF CERTAIN COPYRIGHTED WORKS IN CONNECTION WITH NONCOMMERCIAL EDUCATIONAL BROADCASTING

§ 253.4. Performance of musical compositions by PBS, NPR and other public broadcasting entities engaged in the activities set forth in 17 U.S.C. 118(d).

The following schedule of rates and terms shall apply to the performance by PBS, NPR and other public broadcasting entities engaged in activities set forth in 17 U.S.C. 118(d) of copyrighted published nondramatic musical compositions, except for public broadcasting entities covered by §§ 253.5 and 253.6, and except for compositions which are the subject of voluntary license agreements.

(a) *Determination of royalty rates.*

			2003–2007
(1)	For the performance of such a work in a feature presentation of PBS:		$224.22
(2)	For the performance of such a work as background or theme music in a PBS program:		$ 56.81
(3)	For the performance of such a work in a feature presentation of a station of PBS:		$ 19.16
(4)	For the performance of such a work as background or theme music in a program of a station of PBS:		$ 4.04
(5)	For the performance of such a work in a feature presentation of NPR:		$ 22.73
(6)	For the performance of such a work as background or theme music in an NPR program:		$ 5.51
(7)	For the performance of such a work in a feature presentation of a station of NPR:		$ 1.61
(8)	For the performance of such work as background or theme music in a program of a station of NPR:		$ .57

(9) For the purposes of this schedule the rate for the performance of theme music in an entire series shall be double the single program theme rate.

(10) In the event that the work is first performed in a program of a station of PBS or NPR, and such program is subsequently distributed by PBS or NPR, an additional royalty payment shall be made equal to the difference between the rate specified in this section for a program of a station of PBS or NPR, respectively, and the rate specified in this section for a PBS or NPR program, respectively.

(b) *Payment of royalty rate.* The required royalty rate shall be paid to each known copyright owner not later than July 31 of each calendar year for uses during the first six months of that calendar year, and not later than January 31 for uses during the last six months of the preceding calendar year.

(c) *Records of use.* PBS and NPR shall, upon the request of a copyright owner of a published musical work who believes a musical composition of such owner has been performed under the terms of this schedule, permit such copyright owner a reasonable opportunity to examine their standard cue sheets listing the nondramatic performances of musical compositions on PBS and NPR programs. Any local PBS and NPR station that shall be required by the provisions of any voluntary license agreement with ASCAP or BMI covering the license period January 1, 2003, to December 31, 2007, to prepare a music use report shall, upon request of a copyright owner who believes a musical composition of such owner has been performed under the terms of this schedule, permit such copyright owner to examine the report.

(d) *Terms of use.* The fees provided in this schedule for the performance of a musical work in a program shall cover performances of such work in such program for a period of four years following the first performance.

§ 253.5. Performance of musical compositions by public broadcasting entities licensed to colleges or universities.

(a) *Scope.* This section applies to the performance of copyrighted published nondramatic musical compositions by noncommercial radio stations which are licensed to colleges, universities, or other nonprofit educational institutions and which are not affiliated with National Public Radio.

(b) *Voluntary license agreements.* Notwithstanding the schedule of rates and terms established in this section, the rates and terms of any license agreements entered into by copyright owners and colleges, universities, and other nonprofit educational institutions concerning the performance of copyrighted musical compositions, including performances by noncommercial radio stations, shall apply in lieu of the rates and terms of this section.

(c) *Royalty rate.* A public broadcasting entity within the scope of this section may perform published nondramatic musical compositions subject to the following schedule of royalty rates:

(1) For all such compositions in the repertory of ASCAP, $239 annually.

(2) For all such compositions in the repertory of BMI, $239 annually.

(3) For all such compositions in the repertory of SESAC, $80 annually.

(4) For the performance of any other such compositions: $1.

(d) *Payment of royalty rate.* The public broadcasting entity shall pay the required royalty rate to ASCAP, BMI and SESAC not later than January 31 of each year.

(e) *Records of use.* A public broadcasting entity subject to this section shall furnish to ASCAP, BMI and SESAC, upon request, a music-use report during one week of each calendar year. ASCAP, BMI and SESAC shall not in any one calendar year request more than 10 stations to furnish such reports.

§ 253.8. Terms and rates of royalty payments for the use of published pictorial, graphic, and sculptural works.

(a) *Scope.* This section establishes rates and terms for the use of published pictorial, graphic, and sculptural works by public broadcasting entities for the activities described in 17 U.S.C. 118. The rates and terms established in this schedule include the making of the reproductions described in 17 U.S.C. 118(d)(3).

(b) *Royalty rate.*

(1) The following schedule of rates shall apply to the use of works within the scope of this section:

(i)		*For such uses in a PBS-distributed program:*	2003–2007
	(A)	For a featured display of a work	$ 64.78
	(B)	For background and montage display	$ 31.59
	(C)	For use of a work for program identification or for thematic use	$127.71
	(D)	For the display of an art reproduction copyrighted separately from the work of fine art from which the work was reproduced, irrespective of whether the reproduced work of fine art is copyrighted so as to be subject also to payment of a display fee under the terms of the schedule	$ 41.95
(ii)		For such uses in other than PBS-distributed programs:	2003–2007
	(A)	For featured display of a work	$ 41.95
	(B)	For background and montage display	$ 21.51
	(C)	For use of a work for program identification or for thematic use	$ 85.76
	(D)	For the display of an art reproduction copyrighted separately from the work of fine art from which the work was reproduced, irrespective of whether the reproduced work of fine art is copyrighted so as to be subject also to payment of a display fee under the terms of this schedule	$ 21.51

For the purposes of this schedule the rate for the thematic use of a work in an entire series shall be double the single program theme rate. In the event the work is first used other than in a PBS-distributed program, and such program is subsequently distributed by PBS, an additional royalty payment shall be made equal to the difference between the rate specified in this section for other than a PBS-distributed program and the rate specified in this section for a PBS-distributed program.

(2) "Featured display" for purposes of this schedule means a full-screen or substantially full-screen display appearing on the screen for more than three seconds. Any display less than full-screen or substantially full-screen, or full-screen for three seconds or less, is deemed to be a "background or montage display".

(3) "Thematic use" is the utilization of the works of one or more artists where the works constitute the central theme of the program or convey a story line.

(4) "Display of an art reproduction copyrighted separately from the work of fine art from which the work was reproduced" means a transparency or other reproduction of an underlying work of fine art.

(c) *Payment of royalty rate.* PBS or other public broadcasting entity shall pay the required royalty fees to each copyright owner not later than July 31 of each calendar year for uses during the first six months of that calendar year, and not later than January 31 for uses during the last six months of the preceding calendar year.

(d) *Records of use.*

(1) PBS and its stations or other public broadcasting entity shall maintain and furnish either to copyright owners, or to the offices of generally recognized organizations representing the copyright owners of pictorial, graphic and sculptural works, copies of their standard lists containing the pictorial, graphic, and sculptural works displayed on their programs. Such notice shall include the name of the copyright owner, if known, the specific source from which the work was taken, a description of the work used, the title of the program on which the work was used, and the date of the original broadcast of the program.

(2) Such listings shall be furnished not later than July 31 of each calendar year for displays during the first six months of the calendar year, and not later than January 31 of each calendar year for displays during the second six months of the preceding calendar year. . . .

§ 253.10.   Cost of living adjustment.

(a) On December 1, 1998, the Librarian of Congress shall publish in the Federal Register a notice of the change in the cost of living as determined by the Consumer Price Index (all consumers, all items) during the period from the most recent Index published prior to December 1, 1997, to the most recent Index published prior to December 1, 1998. On each December 1 thereafter the Librarian of Congress shall publish a notice of the change in the cost of living during the period from the most recent index published prior to the previous notice, to the most recent Index published prior to December 1, of that year.

(b) On the same date of the notices published pursuant to paragraph (a) of this section, the Librarian of Congress shall publish in the *Federal Register* a revised schedule of rates for § 253.5 which shall adjust those royalty amounts established in dollar amounts according to the change in the cost of living determined as provided in paragraph (a) of this section. Such royalty rates shall be fixed at the nearest dollar.

(c) The adjusted schedule of rates for § 253.5 shall become effective thirty days after publication in the *Federal Register.*

PART 255—ADJUSTMENT OF ROYALTY PAYABLE UNDER COMPULSORY LICENSE FOR MAKING AND DISTRIBUTING PHONORECORDS

§ 255.1. General.

This part 255 adjusts the rates of royalties payable under the compulsory license for making and distributing phonorecords, including digital phonorecord deliveries, embodying nondramatic musical works, under 17 U.S.C. 115.

§ 255.2. Royalty payable under compulsory license.

With respect to each work embodied in the phonorecord, the royalty payable shall be either four cents, or three-quarters of one cent per minute of playing time or fraction thereof, whichever amount is larger, for every phonorecord made and distributed on or after July 1, 1981, subject to adjustment pursuant to § 255.3.

§ 255.3. Adjustment of royalty rate.

(a) For every phonorecord made and distributed on or after January 1, 1983, the royalty rate payable with respect to each work embodied in the phonorecord shall be either 4.25 cents, or 0.8 cent per minute of playing time or fraction thereof, whichever amount is larger, subject to further adjustment pursuant to paragraphs (b) through (m) of this section....

(k) For every phonorecord made and distributed on or after January 1, 2002, the royalty rate payable with respect to each work embodied in the phonorecord shall be either 8.0 cents, or 1.55 cents per minute of playing time or fraction thereof, whichever amount is larger, subject to further adjustment pursuant to paragraphs (l) through (m) of this section.

(l) For every phonorecord made and distributed on or after January 1, 2004, the royalty rate payable with respect to each work embodied in the phonorecord shall be either 8.5 cents, or 1.65 cents per minute of playing time or fraction thereof, whichever amount is larger, subject to further adjustment pursuant to paragraph (m) of this section.

(m) For every phonorecord made and distributed on or after January 1, 2006, the royalty rate payable with respect to each work embodied in the phonorecord shall be either 9.1 cents, or 1.75 cents per minute of playing time or fraction thereof, whichever amount is larger.

PART 256—ADJUSTMENT OF ROYALTY FEE FOR CABLE COMPULSORY LICENSE

§ 256.1. General.

This part establishes adjusted terms and rates for royalty payments in accordance with the provisions of 17 U.S.C. 111 and 801(b)(2)(A), (B), (C), and (D). Upon compliance with 17 U.S.C. 111 and the terms and rates of this part, a cable system entity may engage in the activities set forth in 17 U.S.C. 111.

§ 256.2. Royalty fee for compulsory license for secondary transmission by cable systems.

(a) Commencing with the first semi-annual accounting period of 1985 and for each semi-annual accounting period thereafter, the royalty rates established by 17 U.S.C. 111(d)(1)(B) shall be as follows:

(1) .893 of 1 per centum of such gross receipts for the privilege of further transmitting any non-network programming of a primary transmitter in whole or in part beyond the local service area of such primary transmitter, such amount to be applied against the fees, if any, payable pursuant to paragraphs (a)(2) through (4) and (c);

(2) .893 of 1 per centum of such gross receipts for the first distant signal equivalent;

(3) .563 of 1 per centum of such gross receipts for each of the second, third and fourth distant signal equivalents; and

(4) .265 of 1 per centum of such gross receipts for the fifth distant signal equivalent and each additional distant signal equivalent thereafter.

(b) Commencing with the first semi-annual accounting period of 1985 and for each semi-annual accounting period thereafter, the gross receipts limitations established by 17 U.S.C. 111(d)(1)(C) and (D) shall be adjusted as follows:

(1) If the actual gross receipts paid by subscribers to a cable system for the period covered by the statement for the basic service of providing secondary transmission of primary broadcast transmitters total $146,000 or less, gross receipts of the cable system for the purpose of this paragraph shall be computed by subtracting from such actual gross receipts the amount by which $146,000 exceeds such actual gross receipts, except that in no case shall a cable system's gross receipts be reduced to less than $5,600. The royalty fee payable under this paragraph shall be 0.5 of 1 per centum regardless of the number of distant signal equivalents, if any; and

(2) If the actual gross receipts paid by the subscribers to a cable system for the period covered by the statement, for the basic service of providing secondary transmissions of primary broadcast transmitters, are more than $146,000 but less than $292,000, the royalty fee payable under this paragraph shall be: (i) 0.5 of 1 per centum of any gross receipts up to $146,000 and (ii) 1 per centum of $146,000 but less than $292,000, regardless of the number of distant signal equivalents, if any.

(c) Notwithstanding paragraphs (a) and (d) of this section, commencing with the first accounting period of 1983 and for each semi-annual accounting period thereafter, for each distant signal equivalent or fraction thereof not represented by the carriage of:

(1) Any signal which was permitted (or, in the case of cable systems commencing operations after June 24, 1981, which would have been permitted) under the rules and regulations of the Federal Communications Commission in effect on June 24, 1981, or

(2) A signal of the same type (that is, independent, network, or non-commercial educational) substituted for such permitted signal, or

(3) A signal which was carried pursuant to an individual waiver of the rules and regulations of the Federal Communications Commission, as such rules were in effect on June 24, 1981; the royalty rate shall be, in lieu of the royalty rates specified in paragraphs (a)(2) through (4) and (d) of this section, 3.75 per centum of the gross receipts of the cable systems for each distant signal equivalent; any fraction of a distant signal equivalent shall be computed at its fractional value.

(d) Commencing with the first semi-annual accounting period of 1990 and for each semi-annual accounting period thereafter, in the case of a cable system located outside the 35–mile specified zone of a commercial VHF station that places a predicted Grade B contour, in whole or in part, over the cable system, and that is not significantly viewed or otherwise exempt from the FCC's syndicated exclusivity rules in effect on June 24, 1981, for each distant signal equivalent or fraction thereof represented by the carriage of such commercial VHF station, the royalty rate shall be, in addition to the amount specified in paragraph (a) of this section,

(1) For cable systems located wholly or in part within a top 50 television market,

    (i) .599 per centum of such gross receipts for the first distant signal equivalent;

    (ii) .377 per centum of such gross receipts for each of the second, third, and fourth distant signal equivalents; and

    (iii) .178 per centum of such gross receipts for the fifth distant signal equivalent and each additional distant signal equivalent thereafter;

(2) For cable systems located wholly or in part within a second 50 television market;

    (i) .300 per centum of such gross receipts for the first distant signal equivalent;

    (ii) .189 per centum of such gross receipts for each of the second, third, and fourth distant signal equivalents; and

    (iii) .089 per centum of such gross receipts for the fifth distant signal equivalent and each additional distant signal equivalent thereafter;

(3) For purposes of this section "top 50 television markets" and "second 50 television markets" shall be defined as the comparable terms are defined or interpreted in accordance with 47 CFR 76.51, as effective June 24, 1981.

*

BERNE CONVENTION FOR THE PROTECTION OF LITERARY AND ARTISTIC WORKS

(Paris Text 1971, Excerpts)

The countries of the Union, being equally animated by the desire to protect, in as effective and uniform a manner as possible, the rights of authors in their literary and artistic works,

Recognising the importance of the work of the Revision Conference held at Stockholm in 1967,

Having resolved to revise the Act adopted by the Stockholm Conference, while maintaining without change Article 1 to 20 and 22 to 26 of that Act.

Consequently, the undersigned Plenipotentiaries, having presented their full powers, recognised as in good and due form, have agreed as follows:

Article 1

The countries to which this Convention applies constitute a Union for the protection of the rights of authors in their literary and artistic works.

Article 2

(1) The expression "literary and artistic works" shall include every production in the literary, scientific and artistic domain, whatever may be the mode or form of its expression, such as books, pamphlets and other writings; lectures, addresses, sermons and other works of the same nature; dramatic or dramatico-musical works; choreographic works and entertainments in dumb show; musical compositions with or without words; cinematographic works to which are assimilated works expressed by a process analogous to cinematography; works of drawing, painting, architecture, sculpture, engraving and lithography; photographic works to which are assimilated works expressed by a process analogous to photography; works of applied art; illustrations, maps, plans, sketches and three-dimensional works relative to geography, topography, architecture or science.

(2) It shall, however, be a matter for legislation in the countries of the Union to prescribe that works in general or any specified categories of

works shall not be protected unless they have been fixed in some material form.

(3) Translations, adaptations, arrangements of music and other alterations of a literary or artistic work shall be protected as original works without prejudice to the copyright in the original work.

(4) It shall be a matter for legislation in the countries of the Union to determine the protection to be granted to official texts of a legislative, administrative and legal nature, and to official translations of such texts.

(5) Collections of literary or artistic works such as encyclopaedias and anthologies which, by reason of the selection and arrangement of their contents, constitute intellectual creations shall be protected as such, without prejudice to the copyright in each of the works forming part of such collections.

(6) The works mentioned in this Article shall enjoy protection in all countries of the Union. This protection shall operate for the benefit of the author and his successors in title.

(7) Subject to the provisions of Article 7(4) of this Convention, it shall be a matter for legislation in the countries of the Union to determine the extent of the application of their laws to works of applied art and industrial designs and models, as well as the conditions under which such works, designs and models shall be protected. Works protected in the country of origin solely as designs and models shall be entitled in another country of the Union only to such special protection as is granted in that country to designs and models; however, if no such special protection is granted in that country, such works shall be protected as artistic works.

(8) The protection of this Convention shall not apply to news of the day or to miscellaneous facts having the character of mere items of press information.

Article 2bis

(1) It shall be a matter for legislation in the countries of the Union to exclude, wholly or in part, from the protection provided by the preceding Article political speeches and speeches delivered in the course of legal proceedings.

(2) It shall also be a matter for legislation in the countries of the Union to determine the conditions under which lectures, addresses and other works of the same nature which are delivered in public may be reproduced by the press, broadcast, communicated to the public by wire and made the subject of public communication as envisaged in Article 11bis (1) of this Convention, when such use is justified by the informatory purpose.

(3) Nevertheless, the author shall enjoy the exclusive right of making a collection of his works mentioned in the preceding paragraphs.

Article 3

(1) The protection of this Convention shall apply to:

(a) authors who are nationals of one of the countries of the Union, for their works, whether published or not;

(b) authors who are not nationals of one of the countries of the Union, for their works first published in one of those countries, or simultaneously in a country outside the Union and in a country of the Union.

(2) Authors who are not nationals of one of the countries of the Union but who have their habitual residence in one of them shall, for the purposes of this Convention, be assimilated to nationals of that country.

(3) The expression "published works" means works published with the consent of their authors, whatever may be the means of manufacture of the copies, provided that the availability of such copies has been such as to satisfy the reasonable requirements of the public, having regard to the nature of the work. The performance of a dramatic, dramatico-musical, cinematographic or musical work, the public recitation of a literary work, the communication by wire or the broadcasting of literary or artistic works, the exhibition of a work of art and the construction of a work of architecture shall not constitute publication.

(4) A work shall be considered as having been published simultaneously in several countries if it has been published in two or more countries within thirty days of its first publication.

Article 4

The protection of this Convention shall apply, even if the conditions of Article 3 are not fulfilled, to:

(a) authors of cinematographic works the maker of which has his headquarters or habitual residence in one of the countries of the Union;

(b) authors of works of architecture erected in a country of the Union or of other artistic works incorporated in a building or other structure located in a country of the Union.

Article 5

(1) Authors shall enjoy, in respect of works for which they are protected under this Convention, in countries of the Union other than the country of origin, the rights which their respective laws do now or may hereafter grant to their nationals, as well as the rights specially granted by this Convention.

(2) The enjoyment and the exercise of these rights shall not be subject to any formality; such enjoyment and such exercise shall be independent of the existence of protection in the country of origin of the work. Consequently, apart from the provisions of this Convention, the extent of protection, as well as the means of redress afforded to the author to protect his rights, shall be governed exclusively by the laws of the country where protection is claimed.

(3) Protection in the country of origin is governed by domestic law. However, when the author is not a national of the country of origin of the work for which he is protected under this Convention, he shall enjoy in that country the same rights as national authors.

(4) The country of origin shall be considered to be:

(a) in the case of works first published in a country of the Union, that country; in the case of works published simultaneously in several countries of the Union which grant different terms of protection, the country whose legislation grants the shortest term of protection;

(b) in the case of works published simultaneously in a country outside the Union and in a country of the Union, the latter country;

(c) in the case of unpublished works or of works first published in a country outside the Union, without simultaneous publication in a country of the Union, the country of the Union of which the author is a national, provided that:

(i) when these are cinematographic works the maker of which has his headquarters or his habitual residence in a country of the Union, the country of origin shall be that country, and

(ii) when these are works of architecture erected in a country of the Union or other artistic works incorporated in a building or other structure located in a country of the Union, the country of origin shall be that country.

Article 6

(1) Where any country outside the Union fails to protect in an adequate manner the works of authors who are nationals of one of the countries of the Union, the latter country may restrict the protection given to the works of authors who are, at the date of the first publication thereof, nationals of the other country and are not habitually resident in one of the countries of the Union. If the country of first publication avails itself of this right, the other countries of the Union shall not be required to grant to works thus subjected to special treatment a wider protection than that granted to them in the country of first publication.

(2) No restrictions introduced by virtue of the preceding paragraph shall affect the rights which an author may have acquired in respect of a work published in a country of the Union before such restrictions were put into force.

(3) The countries of the Union which restrict the grant of copyright in accordance with this Article shall give notice thereof to the Director General of the World Intellectual Property Organisation (hereinafter designated as "the Director General") by a written declaration specifying the countries in regard to which protection is restricted, and the restrictions to which rights of authors who are nationals of those countries are subjected. The Director General shall immediately communicate this declaration to all the countries of the Union.

Article 6bis

(1) Independently of the author's economic rights, and even after the transfer of the said rights, the author shall have the right to claim authorship of the work and to object to any distortion, mutilation or other modification of, or other derogatory action in relation to, the said work, which would be prejudicial to his honour or reputation.

(2) The rights granted to the author in accordance with the preceding paragraph shall, after his death, be maintained, at least until the expiry of the economic rights, and shall be exercisable by the persons or institutions authorized by the legislation of the country where protection is claimed. However, those countries whose legislation, at the moment of their ratification of or accession to this Act, does not provide for the protection after the death of the author of all the rights set out in the preceding paragraph may provide that some of these rights may, after his death, cease to be maintained.

(3) The means of redress for safeguarding the rights granted by this Article shall be governed by the legislation of the country where protection is claimed.

Article 7

(1) The term of protection granted by this Convention shall be the life of the author and fifty years after his death.

(2) However, in the case of cinematographic works, the countries of the Union may provide that the term of protection shall expire fifty years after the work has been made available to the public with the consent of the author, or, failing such an event within fifty years from the making of such a work, fifty years after the making.

(3) In the case of anonymous or pseudonymous works, the terms of protection granted by this Convention shall expire fifty years after the work has been lawfully made available to the public. However, when the pseudonym adopted by the author leaves no doubt as to his identity, the term of protection shall be that provided in paragraph (1). If the author of an anonymous or pseudonymous work discloses his identity during the above-mentioned period, the term of protection applicable shall be that provided in paragraph (1). The countries of the Union shall not be required to protect anonymous or pseudonymous works in respect of which it is reasonable to presume that their author has been dead for fifty years.

(4) It shall be a matter for legislation in the countries of the Union to determine the term of protection of photographic works and that of works of applied art in so far as they are protected as artistic works; however, this term shall last at least until the end of a period of twenty-five years from the making of such a work.

(5) The term of protection subsequent to the death of the author and the terms provided by paragraphs (2), (3) and (4) shall run from the date of death or of the event referred to in those paragraphs, but such terms shall

always be deemed to begin on the first of January of the year following the death or such event.

(6) The countries of the Union may grant a term of protection in excess of those provided by the preceding paragraphs.

(7) Those countries of the Union bound by the Rome Act of this Convention which grant, in their national legislation in force at the time of signature of the present Act, shorter terms of protection than those provided for in the preceding paragraphs shall have the right to maintain such terms when ratifying or acceding to the present Act.

(8) In any case, the term shall be governed by the legislation of the country where protection is claimed; however, unless the legislation of that country otherwise provides, the term shall not exceed the term fixed in the country of origin of the work.

Article 7bis

The provisions of the preceding Article shall also apply in the case of a work of joint authorship, provided that the terms measured from the death of the author shall be calculated from the death of the last surviving author.

Article 8

Authors of literary and artistic works protected by this Convention shall enjoy the exclusive right of making and of authorising the translation of their works throughout the term of protection of their rights in the original works.

Article 9

(1) Authors of literary and artistic works protected by this Convention shall have the exclusive right of authorising the reproduction of these works, in any manner or form.

(2) It shall be a matter for legislation in the countries of the Union to permit the reproduction of such works in certain special cases, provided that such reproduction does not conflict with a normal exploitation of the work and does not unreasonably prejudice the legitimate interests of the author.

(3) Any sound or visual recording shall be considered as a reproduction for the purposes of this Convention.

Article 10

(1) It shall be permissible to make quotations from a work which has already been lawfully made available to the public, provided that their making is compatible with fair practice, and their extent does not exceed that justified by the purpose, including quotations from newspaper articles and periodicals in the form of press summaries.

(2) It shall be a matter for legislation in the countries of the Union, and for special agreements existing or to be concluded between them, to

permit the utilisation, to the extent justified by the purpose, of literary or artistic works by way of illustration in publications, broadcasts or sound or visual recordings for teaching, provided such utilisation is compatible with fair practice.

(3) Where use is made of works in accordance with the preceding paragraphs of this Article, mention shall be made of the source, and of the name of the author if it appears thereon.

Article 10bis

(1) It shall be a matter for legislation in the countries of the Union to permit the reproduction by the press, the broadcasting or the communication to the public by wire of articles published in newspapers or periodicals on current economic, political or religious topics, and of broadcast works of the same character, in cases in which the reproduction, broadcasting or such communication thereof is not expressly reserved. Nevertheless, the source must always be clearly indicated; the legal consequences of a breach of this obligation shall be determined by the legislation of the country where protection is claimed.

(2) It shall also be a matter for legislation in the countries of the Union to determine the conditions under which, for the purpose of reporting current events by means of photography, cinematography, broadcasting or communication to the public by wire, literary or artistic works seen or heard in the course of the event may, to the extent justified by the informatory purpose, be reproduced and made available to the public.

Article 11

(1) Authors of dramatic, dramatico-musical and musical works shall enjoy the exclusive right of authorising:

(i) the public performance of their works, including such public performance by any means or process;

(ii) any communication to the public of the performance of their works.

(2) Authors of dramatic or dramatico-musical works shall enjoy, during the full term of their rights in the original works, the same rights with respect to translations thereof.

Article 11bis

(1) Authors of literary and artistic works shall enjoy the exclusive right of authorising:

(i) the broadcasting of their works or the communication thereof to the public by any other means of wireless diffusion of signs, sounds or images;

(ii) any communication to the public by wire or by rebroadcasting of the broadcast of the work, when this communication is made by an organisation other than the original one;

(iii) the public communication by loudspeaker or any other analogous instrument transmitting, by signs, sounds or images, the broadcast of the work.

(2) It shall be a matter for legislation in the countries of the Union to determine the conditions under which the rights mentioned in the preceding paragraph may be exercised, but these conditions shall apply only in the countries where they have been prescribed. They shall not in any circumstances be prejudicial to the moral rights of the author, nor to his right to obtain equitable remuneration which, in the absence of agreement, shall be fixed by competent authority.

(3) In the absence of any contrary stipulation, permission granted in accordance with paragraph (1) of this Article shall not imply permission to record, by means of instruments recording sounds or images, the work broadcast. It shall, however, be a matter for legislation in the countries of the Union to determine the regulations for ephemeral recordings made by a broadcasting organisation by means of its own facilities and used for its own broadcasts. The preservation of these recordings in official archives may, on the ground of their exceptional documentary character, be authorised by such legislation.

Article 11ter

(1) Authors of literary works shall enjoy the exclusive right of authorising:

(i) the public recitation of their words, including such public recitation by any means or process;

(ii) any communication to the public of the recitation of their works.

(2) Authors of literary works shall enjoy, during the full term of their rights in the original works, the same rights with respect to translations thereof.

Article 12

Authors of literary or artistic works shall enjoy the exclusive right of authorising adaptations, arrangements and other alterations of their works.

Article 13

(1) Each country of the Union may impose for itself reservations and conditions on the exclusive right granted to the author of a musical work and to the author of any words, the recording of which together with the musical work has already been authorised by the latter, to authorise the sound recording of that musical work, together with such words, if any; but all such reservations and conditions shall apply only in the countries which have imposed them and shall not, in any circumstances, be prejudicial to the rights of these authors to obtain equitable remuneration which, in the absence of agreement, shall be fixed by competent authority.

(2) Recordings of musical works made in a country of the Union in accordance with Article 13(3) of the Conventions signed at Rome on 2 June

1928, and at Brussels on 26 June 1948, may be reproduced in that country without the permission of the author of the musical work until a date two years after that country becomes bound by this Act.

(3) Recordings made in accordance with paragraphs (1) and (2) of this Article and imported without permission from the parties concerned into a country where they are treated as infringing recordings shall be liable to seizure.

Article 14

(1) Authors of literary or artistic works shall have the exclusive right of authorising:

(i) the cinematographic adaptation and reproduction of these works, and the distribution of the works thus adapted or reproduced;

(ii) the public performance and communication to the public by wire of the works thus adapted or reproduced.

(2) The adaptation into any other artistic form of a cinematographic production derived from literary or artistic works shall, without prejudice to the authorisation of the author of the cinematographic production, remain subject to the authorisation of the authors of the original works.

(3) The provisions of Article 13(1) shall not apply.

Article 14bis

(1) Without prejudice to the copyright in any work which may have been adapted or reproduced, a cinematographic work shall be protected as an original work. The owner of copyright in a cinematographic work shall enjoy the same rights as the author of an original work, including the rights referred to in the preceding Article.

(2)(a) Ownership of copyright in a cinematographic work shall be a matter for legislation in a country where protection is claimed.

(b) However, in the countries of the Union which, by legislation, include among the owners of copyright in a cinematographic work authors who have brought contributions to the making of the work, such authors, if they have undertaken to bring such contributions, may not, in the absence of any contrary or special stipulation, object to the reproduction, distribution, public performance, communication to the public by wire, broadcasting or any other communication to the public, or to the subtitling or dubbing of texts, of the work.

(c) The question whether or not the form of the undertaking referred to above should, for the application of the preceding subparagraph (b), be in a written agreement or a written act of the same effect shall be a matter for the legislation of the country where the maker of the cinematographic work has his headquarters or habitual residence. However, it shall be a matter for the legislation of the country of the Union where protection is claimed to provide that the said undertaking shall be in a written agreement or a written act of the same effect. The countries whose legislation so provides shall notify the Director General by means of a written declaration, which will be immediately communicated by him to all the other countries of the Union.

(d) By "contrary or special stipulation" is meant any restrictive condition which is relevant to the aforesaid undertaking.

(3) Unless the national legislation provides to the contrary, the provisions of paragraph (2)(b) above shall not be applicable to authors of scenarios, dialogues and musical works created for the making of the cinematographic work, or to the principal director thereof. However, those countries of the Union whose legislation does not contain rules providing for the application of the said paragraph (2)(b) to such director shall notify the Director General by means of a written declaration, which will be immediately communicated by him to all the other countries of the Union.

Article 14ter

(1) The author, or after his death the persons or institutions authorised by national legislation, shall, with respect to original works of art and original manuscripts of writers and composers, enjoy the inalienable right to an interest in any sale of the work subsequent to the first transfer by the author of the work.

(2) The protection provided by the preceding paragraph may be claimed in a country of the Union only if legislation in the country to which the author belongs so permits, and to the extent permitted by the country where this protection is claimed.

(3) The procedure for collection and the amounts shall be matters for determination by national legislation.

Article 15

(1) In order that the author of a literary or artistic work protected by this Convention shall, in the absence of proof to the contrary, be regarded as such, and consequently be entitled to institute infringement proceedings in the countries of the Union, it shall be sufficient for his name to appear on the work in the usual manner. This paragraph shall be applicable even if this name is a pseudonym, where the pseudonym adopted by the author leaves no doubt as to his identity.

(2) The person or body corporate whose name appears on a cinematographic work in the usual manner shall, in the absence of proof to the contrary, be presumed to be the maker of the said work.

(3) In the case of anonymous and pseudonymous works, other than those referred to in paragraph (1) above, the publisher whose name appears on the work shall, in the absence of proof to the contrary, be deemed to represent the author, and in this capacity he shall be entitled to protect and enforce the author's rights. The provisions of this paragraph shall cease to apply when the author reveals his identity and establishes his claim to authorship of the work.

(4)(a) In the case of unpublished works where the identity of the author is unknown, but where there is every ground to presume that he is a national of a country of the Union, it shall be a matter for legislation in that country to designate the competent authority which shall represent the author and shall be entitled to protect and enforce his rights in the countries of the Union.

(b) Countries of the Union which makes such designation under the terms of this provision shall notify the Director General by means of a written declaration giving full information concerning the authority thus designated. The Director General shall at once communicate this declaration to all other countries of the Union.

Article 16

(1) Infringing copies of a work shall be liable to seizure in any country of the Union where the work enjoys legal protection.

(2) The provisions of the preceding paragraph shall also apply to reproductions coming from a country where the work is not protected, or has ceased to be protected.

(3) The seizure shall take place in accordance with the legislation of each country.

Article 17

The provisions of this Convention cannot in any way affect the right of the Government of each country of the Union to permit, to control, or to prohibit, by legislation or regulation, the circulation, presentation, or exhibition of any work or production in regard to which the competent authority may find it necessary to exercise that right.

Article 18

(1) This Convention shall apply to all works which, at the moment of its coming into force, have not yet fallen into the public domain in the country of origin through the expiry of the term of protection.

(2) If, however, through the expiry of the term of protection which was previously granted, a work has fallen into the public domain of the country where protection is claimed, that work shall not be protected anew.

(3) The application of this principle shall be subject to any provisions contained in special conventions to that effect existing or to be concluded between countries of the Union. In the absence of such provisions, the respective countries shall determine, each in so far as it is concerned, the conditions of application of this principle.

(4) The preceding provisions shall also apply in the case of new accessions to the Union and to cases in which protection is extended by the application of Article 7 or by the abandonment of reservations.

479

Article 19

The provisions of this Convention shall not preclude the making of a claim to the benefit of any greater protection which may be granted by legislation in a country of the Union.

Article 20

The Governments of the countries of the Union reserve the right to enter into special agreements among themselves, in so far as such agreements grant to authors more extensive rights than those granted by the Convention, or contain other provisions not contrary to this Convention. The provisions of existing agreements which satisfy these conditions shall remain applicable.

* * * *

Article 33

(1) Any dispute between two or more countries of the Union concerning the interpretation or application of this Convention, not settled by negotiation, may, by any one of the countries concerned, be brought before the International Court of Justice by application in conformity with the Statute of the Court, unless the countries concerned agree on some other method of settlement. The country bringing the dispute before the Court shall inform the International Bureau; the International Bureau shall bring the matter to the attention of the other countries of the Union.

(2) Each country may, at the time it signs this Act or deposits its instrument of ratification or accession, declare that it does not consider itself bound by the provisions of paragraph (1). With regard to any dispute between such country and any other country of the Union, the provisions of paragraph (1) shall not apply.

(3) Any country having made a declaration in accordance with the provisions of paragraph (2) may, at any time, withdraw its declaration by notification addressed to the Director General.

* * * *

Article 36

(1) Any country party to this Convention undertakes to adopt, in accordance with its constitution, the measures necessary to ensure the application of this Convention.

(2) It is understood that, at the time a country becomes bound by this Convention, it will be in a position under its domestic law to give effect to the provisions of this Convention.

* * * *

UNIVERSAL COPYRIGHT CONVENTION, AS REVISED AT PARIS, 1971 (EXCERPTS)

The Contracting States,

Moved by the desire to ensure in all countries copyright protection of literary, scientific and artistic works,

Convinced that a system of copyright protection appropriate to all nations of the world and expressed in a universal convention, additional to, and without impairing international systems already in force, will ensure respect for the rights of the individual and encourage the development of literature, the sciences and the arts,

Persuaded that such a universal copyright system will facilitate a wider dissemination of works of the human mind and increase international understanding,

Have resolved to revise the Universal Copyright Convention as signed at Geneva on 6 September 1952 (hereinafter called "the 1952 Convention"), and consequently,

Have agreed as follows:

Article I

Each Contracting State undertakes to provide for the adequate and effective protection of the rights of authors and other copyright proprietors in literary, scientific and artistic works, including writings, musical, dramatic and cinematographic works, and paintings, engravings and sculpture.

Article II

1. Published works of nationals of any Contracting State and works first published in that State shall enjoy in each other Contracting State the same protection as that other State accords to works of its nationals first published in its own territory, as well as the protection specially granted by this Convention.

2. Unpublished works of nationals of each Contracting State shall enjoy in each other Contracting State the same protection as that other State accords to unpublished works of its own nationals, as well as the protection specially granted by this Convention.

3. For the purpose of this Convention any Contracting State may, by domestic legislation, assimilate to its own nationals any person domiciled in that State.

Article III

1. Any Contracting State which, under its domestic law, requires as a condition of copyright, compliance with formalities such as deposit, registration, notice, notarial certificates, payment of fees or manufacture or publication in that Contracting State, shall regard these requirements as satisfied with respect to all works protected in accordance with this Convention and first published outside its territory and the author of which is not one of its nationals, if from the time of the first publication all the copies of the work published with the authority of the author or other copyright proprietor bear the symbol © accompanied by the name of the copyright proprietor and the year of first publication placed in such manner and location as to give reasonable notice of claim of copyright.

2. The provisions of paragraph 1 shall not preclude any Contracting State from requiring formalities or other conditions for the acquisition and enjoyment of copyright in respect of works first published in its territory or works of its nationals wherever published.

3. The provisions of paragraph 1 shall not preclude any Contracting State from providing that a person seeking judicial relief must, in bringing the action, comply with procedural requirements, such as that the complainant must appear through domestic counsel or that the complainant must deposit with the court or an administrative office, or both, a copy of the work involved in the litigation; provided that failure to comply with such requirements shall not affect the validity of the copyright, nor shall any such requirement be imposed upon a national of another Contracting State if such requirement is not imposed on nationals of the State in which protection is claimed.

4. In each Contracting State there shall be legal means of protecting without formalities the unpublished works of nationals of other Contracting States.

5. If a Contracting State grants protection for more than one term of copyright and the first term is for a period longer than one of the minimum periods prescribed in Article IV, such State shall not be required to comply with the provisions of paragraph 1 of this Article in respect of the second or any subsequent term of copyright.

Article IV

1. The duration of protection of a work shall be governed, in accordance with the provisions of Article II and this Article, by the law of the Contracting State in which protection is claimed.

2. (a) The term of protection for works protected under this Convention shall not be less than the life of the author and twenty-five years after his death. However, any Contracting State which, on the effective

date of this Convention in that State, has limited this term for certain classes of works to a period computed from the first publication of the work, shall be entitled to maintain these exceptions and to extend them to other classes of works. For all these classes the term of protection shall not be less than twenty-five years from the date of first publication.

(b) Any Contracting State which, upon the effective date of this Convention in that State, does not compute the term of protection upon the basis of the life of the author, shall be entitled to compute the term of protection from the date of the first publication of the work or from its registration prior to publication, as the case may be, provided the term of protection shall not be less than twenty-five years from the date of first publication or from its registration prior to publication, as the case may be.

(c) If the legislation of a Contracting State grants two or more successive terms of protection, the duration of the first term shall not be less than one of the minimum periods specified in sub-paragraphs (a) and (b).

3. The provisions of paragraph 2 shall not apply to photographic works or to works of applied art; provided, however, that the term of protection in those Contracting States which protect photographic works, or works of applied art in so far as they are protected as artistic works, shall not be less than ten years for each of said classes of works.

4. (a) No Contracting State shall be obliged to grant protection to a work for a period longer than that fixed for the class of works to which the work in question belongs, in the case of unpublished works by the law of the Contracting State of which the author is a national, and in the case of published works by the law of the Contracting State in which the work has been first published.

(b) For the purposes of the application of sub-paragraph (a), if the law of any Contracting State grants two or more successive terms of protection, the period of protection of that State shall be considered to be the aggregate of those terms. However, if a specified work is not protected by such State during the second or any subsequent term for any reason, the other Contracting States shall not be obliged to protect it during the second or any subsequent term.

5. For the purposes of the application of paragraph 4, the work of a national of a Contracting State, first published in a non-Contracting State, shall be treated as though first published in the Contracting State of which the author is a national.

6. For the purposes of the application of paragraph 4, in case of simultaneous publication in two or more Contracting States, the work shall be treated as though first published in the State which affords the shortest term; any work published in two or more Contracting States within thirty days of its first publication shall be considered as having been published simultaneously in said Contracting States.

Article IVbis

1.   The rights referred to in Article I shall include the basic rights ensuring the author's economic interests, including the exclusive right to authorize reproduction by any means, public performance and broadcasting. The provisions of this Article shall extend to works protected under this Convention either in their original form or in any form recognizably derived from the original.

2.   However, any Contracting State may, by its domestic legislation, make exceptions that do not conflict with the spirit and provisions of this Convention, to the rights mentioned in paragraph 1 of this Article. Any State whose legislation so provides, shall nevertheless accord a reasonable degree of effective protection to each of the rights to which exception has been made.

Article V

1.   The rights referred to in Article I shall include the exclusive right of the author to make, publish and authorize the making and publication of translations of works protected under this Convention.

2.   However, any Contracting State may, by its domestic legislation, restrict the right of translation of writings, but only subject to the following provisions:

(a) If, after the expiration of a period of seven years from the date of the first publication of a writing, a translation of such writing has not been published in a language in general use in the Contracting State, by the owner of the right of translation or with his authorization, any national of such Contracting State may obtain a non-exclusive licence from the competent authority thereof to translate the work into that language and publish the work so translated.

(b) Such national shall in accordance with the procedure of the State concerned, establish either that he has requested, and been denied, authorization by the proprietor of the right to make and publish the translation, or that, after due diligence on his part, he was unable to find the owner of the right. A licence may also be granted on the same conditions if all previous editions of a translation in a language in general use in the Contracting State are out of print.

(c) If the owner of the right of translation cannot be found, then the applicant for a licence shall send copies of his application to the publisher whose name appears on the work and, if the nationality of the owner of the right of translation is known, to the diplomatic or consular representative of the State of which such owner is a national, or to the organization which may have been designated by the government of that State. The licence shall not be granted before the expiration of a period of two months from the date of the dispatch of the copies of the application.

(d) Due provision shall be made by domestic legislation to ensure to the owner of the right of translation a compensation which is just and conforms to international standards, to ensure payment and transmittal of such compensation, and to ensure a correct translation of the work.

(e) The original title and the name of the author of the work shall be printed on all copies of the published translation. The licence shall be valid only for publication of the translation in the territory of the Contracting State where it has been applied for. Copies so published may be imported and sold in another Contracting State if a language in general use in such other State is the same language as that into which the work has been so translated, and if the domestic law in such other State makes provision for such licences and does not prohibit such importation and sale. Where the foregoing conditions do not exist, the importation and sale of such copies in a Contracting State shall be governed by its domestic law and its agreements. The licence shall not be transferred by the licencee.

(f) The licence shall not be granted when the author has withdrawn from circulation all copies of the work.

* * * *

Article VI

"Publication", as used in this Convention, means the reproduction in tangible form and the general distribution to the public of copies of a work from which it can be read or otherwise visually perceived.

Article VII

This Convention shall not apply to works or rights in works which, at the effective date of this Convention in a Contracting State where protection is claimed, are permanently in the public domain in the said Contracting State.

* * * *

Article X

1. Each Contracting State undertakes to adopt, in accordance with its Constitution, such measures as are necessary to ensure the application of this Convention.

2. It is understood that at the date this Convention comes into force in respect of any State, that State must be in a position under its domestic law to give effect to the terms of this Convention.

* * * *

Article XVII

1. This Convention shall not in any way affect the provisions of the Berne Convention for the Protection of Literary and Artistic Works or membership in the Union created by that Convention.

2. In application of the foregoing paragraph, a declaration has been annexed to the present Article. This declaration is an integral part of this Convention for the States bound by the Berne Convention on 1 January 1951, or which have or may become bound to it at a later date. The signature of this Convention by such States shall also constitute signature of the said declaration, and ratification, acceptance or accession by such States shall include the declaration, as well as this Convention.

Article XVIII

This Convention shall not abrogate multilateral or bilateral copyright conventions or arrangements that are or may be in effect exclusively between two or more American Republics. In the event of any difference either between the provisions of such existing conventions or arrangements and the provisions of this Convention, or between the provisions of this Convention and those of any new convention or arrangement which may be formulated between two or more American Republics after this Convention comes into force, the convention or arrangement most recently formulated shall prevail between the parties thereto. Rights in works acquired in any Contracting State under existing conventions or arrangements before the date this Convention comes into force in such State shall not be affected.

Article XIX

This Convention shall not abrogate multilateral or bilateral conventions or arrangements in effect between two or more Contracting States. In the event of any difference between the provisions of such existing conventions or arrangements and the provisions of this Convention, the provisions of this Convention shall prevail. Rights in works acquired in any Contracting State under existing conventions or arrangements before the date on which this Convention comes into force in such State shall not be affected. Nothing in this Article shall affect the provisions of Articles XVII and XVIII.

Article XX

Reservations to this Convention shall not be permitted.

Appendix Declaration Relating to Article XVII

The States which are members of the International Union for the Protection of Literary and Artistic Works (hereinafter called "the Berne Union") and which are signatories to this Convention,

Desiring to reinforce their mutual relations on the basis of the said Union and to avoid any conflict which might result from the co-existence of the Berne Convention and the Universal Copyright Convention,

Recognizing the temporary need of some States to adjust their level of copyright protection in accordance with their stage of cultural, social and economic development,

Have, by common agreement, accepted the terms of the following declaration:

(a) Except as provided by paragraph (b), works which, according to the Berne Convention, have as their country of origin a country which has withdrawn from the Berne Union after 1 January 1951, shall not be protected by the Universal Copyright Convention in the countries of the Berne Union;

(b) Where a Contracting State is regarded as a developing country in conformity with the established practice of the General Assembly of the United Nations, and has deposited with the Director–General of the United Nations Educational, Scientific and Cultural Organization, at the time of its withdrawal from the Berne Union, a notification to the effect that it regards itself as a developing country, the provisions of paragraph (a) shall not be applicable as long as such State may avail itself of the exceptions provided for by this Convention in accordance with Article V^{bis};

(c) The Universal Copyright Convention shall not be applicable to the relationships among countries of the Berne Union in so far as it relates to the protection of works having as their country of origin, within the meaning of the Berne Convention, a country of the Berne Union.

*

Agreement on Trade–Related Aspects of Intellectual Property Rights (Excerpts)

MTN/FA II–A1C

Members,

Desiring to reduce distortions and impediments to international trade, and taking into account the need to promote effective and adequate protection of intellectual property rights, and to ensure that measures and procedures to enforce intellectual property rights do not themselves become barriers to legitimate trade;

Recognizing, to this end, the need for new rules and disciplines concerning:

(a) the applicability of the basic principles of the GATT 1994 and of relevant international intellectual property agreements or conventions;

(b) the provision of adequate standards and principles concerning the availability, scope and use of trade-related intellectual property rights;

(c) the provision of effective and appropriate means for the enforcement of trade-related intellectual property rights, taking into account differences in national legal systems;

(d) the provision of effective and expeditious procedures for the multilateral prevention and settlement of disputes between governments; and

(e) transitional arrangements aiming at the fullest participation in the results of the negotiations;

Recognizing the need for a multilateral framework of principles, rules and disciplines dealing with international trade in counterfeit goods;

Recognizing that intellectual property rights are private rights;

Recognizing the underlying public policy objectives of national systems for the protection of intellectual property, including development and technological objectives;

Recognizing also the special needs of the least-developed country Members in respect of maximum flexibility in the domestic implementation of laws and regulations in order to enable them to create a sound and viable technological base;

Emphasizing the importance of reducing tensions by reaching strengthened commitments to resolve disputes on trade-related intellectual property issues through multilateral procedures;

Desiring to establish a mutually supportive relationship between the WTO and the World Intellectual Property Organization (WIPO) as well as other relevant international organizations;

Hereby agree as follows:

PART I—GENERAL PROVISIONS AND BASIC PRINCIPLES

Article 1

Nature and Scope of Obligations

1. Members shall give effect to the provisions of this Agreement. Members may, but shall not be obliged to, implement in their domestic law more extensive protection than is required by this Agreement, provided that such protection does not contravene the provisions of this Agreement. Members shall be free to determine the appropriate method of implementing the provisions of this Agreement within their own legal system and practice.

2. For the purposes of this Agreement, the term "intellectual property" refers to all categories of intellectual property that are the subject of Sections 1 to 7 of Part II.

3. Members shall accord the treatment provided for in this Agreement to the nationals of other Members.[1] In respect for the relevant intellectual property right, the nationals of other Members shall be understood as those natural or legal persons that would meet the criteria for eligibility for protection provided for in the Paris Convention (1967), the Berne Convention (1971), the Rome Convention and the Treaty on Intellectual Property in Respect of Integrated Circuits, were all Members of the WTO members of those conventions.[2] Any Member availing itself of the possibilities provided in paragraph 3 of Article 5 or paragraph 2 of Article 6

---

1. When "nationals" are referred to in this Agreement, they shall be deemed, in the case of a separate customs territory Member of the WTO, to mean persons, natural or legal, who are domiciled or who have a real and effective industrial or commercial establishment in that customs territory.

2. In this Agreement, "Paris Convention" refers to the Paris Convention for the Protection of Industrial Property; "Paris Convention (1967)" refers to the Stockholm Act of this Convention of 14 July 1967. "Berne Convention" refers to the Berne Convention for the Protection of Literary and Artistic Works; "Berne Convention (1971)" refers to the Paris Act of this Convention of 24 July 1971. "Rome Convention" refers to the International Convention for the Protection of Performers, Producers of Phonograms and Broadcasting Organizations, adopted at Rome on 26 October 1961. "Treaty on Intellectual Property in Respect of Integrated Circuits" (IPIC Treaty) refers to the Treaty on Intellectual Property in Respect of Integrated Circuits, adopted at Washington on 26 May 1989.

of the Rome Convention shall make a notification as foreseen in those provisions to the Council for Trade–Related Aspects of Intellectual Property Rights.

Article 2

Intellectual Property Conventions

* * * *

2. Nothing in Parts I to IV of this Agreement shall derogate from existing obligations that Members may have to each other under the Paris Convention, the Berne Convention, the Rome Convention and the Treaty on Intellectual Property in Respect of Integrated Circuits.

Article 3

National Treatment

1. Each Member shall accord to the nationals of other Members treatment no less favourable than that it accords to its own nationals with regard to the protection[3] of intellectual property, subject to the exceptions already provided in, respectively, the Paris Convention (1967), the Berne Convention (1971), the Rome Convention and the Treaty on Intellectual Property in Respect of Integrated Circuits. In respect of performers, producers of phonograms and broadcasting organizations, this obligation only applies in respect of the rights provided under this Agreement. Any Member availing itself of the possibilities provided in Article 6 of the Berne Convention and paragraph 1(b) of Article 16 of the Rome Convention shall make a notification as foreseen in those provisions to the Council for Trade–Related Aspects of Intellectual Property Rights.

2. Members may avail themselves of the exceptions permitted under paragraph 1 above in relation to judicial and administrative procedures, including the designation of an address for service or the appointment of an agent within the jurisdiction of a Member, only where such exceptions are necessary to secure compliance with laws and regulations which are not inconsistent with the provisions of this Agreement and where such practices are not applied in a manner which would constitute a disguised restriction on trade.

Article 4

Most–Favoured–Nation Treatment

With regard to the protection of intellectual property, any advantage, favour, privilege or immunity granted by a Member to the nationals of any other country shall be accorded immediately and unconditionally to the nationals of all other Members. Exempted from this obligation are any advantage, favour, privilege or immunity accorded by a Member:

3. For the purposes of Articles 3 and 4 of this Agreement, "protection" shall include matters affecting the availability, acquisition, scope, maintenance and enforcement of intellectual property rights as well as those matters affecting the use of intellectual property rights specifically addressed in this Agreement.

(a) deriving from international agreements on judicial assistance and law enforcement of a general nature and not particularly confined to the protection of intellectual property;

(b) granted in accordance with the provisions of the Berne Convention (1971) or the Rome Convention authorizing that the treatment accorded be a function not of national treatment but of the treatment accorded in another country;

(c) in respect of the rights of performers, producers of phonograms and broadcasting organizations not provided under this Agreement;

(d) deriving from international agreements related to the protection of intellectual property which entered into force prior to the entry into force of the Agreement Establishing the WTO, provided that such agreements are notified to the Council for Trade–Related Aspects of Intellectual Property Rights and do not constitute an arbitrary or unjustifiable discrimination against nationals of other Members.

Article 5

Multilateral Agreements on Acquisition or Maintenance of Protection

The obligations under Articles 3 and 4 above do not apply to procedures provided in multilateral agreements concluded under the auspices of the World Intellectual Property Organization relating to the acquisition or maintenance of intellectual property rights.

Article 6

Exhaustion

For the purposes of dispute settlement under this Agreement, subject to the provisions of Articles 3 and 4 above nothing in this Agreement shall be used to address the issue of the exhaustion of intellectual property rights.

Article 7

Objectives

The protection and enforcement of intellectual property rights should contribute to the promotion of technological innovation and to the transfer and dissemination of technology, to the mutual advantage of producers and users of technological knowledge and in a manner conducive to social and economic welfare, and to a balance of rights and obligations.

Article 8

Principles

1.   Members may, in formulating or amending their national laws and regulations, adopt measures necessary to protect public health and nutrition, and to promote the public interest in sectors of vital importance to their socio-economic and technological development, provided that such measures are consistent with the provisions of this Agreement.

2. Appropriate measures, provided that they are consistent with the provisions of this Agreement, may be used to prevent the abuse of intellectual property rights by right holders or the resort to practices which unreasonably restrain trade or adversely affect the international transfer of technology.

PART II—STANDARDS CONCERNING THE AVAILABILITY, SCOPE AND USE OF INTELLECTUAL PROPERTY RIGHTS

Section 1:

Copyright and Related Rights

Article 9

Relation to Berne Convention

1. Members shall comply with Articles 1–21 and the Appendix of the Berne Convention (1971). However, Members shall not have rights or obligations under this Agreement in respect of the rights conferred under Article 6*bis* of that Convention or of the rights derived therefrom.

2. Copyright protection shall extend to expressions and not to ideas, procedures, methods of operation or mathematical concepts as such.

Article 10

Computer Programs and Compilations of Data

1. Computer programs, whether in source or object code, shall be protected as literary works under the Berne Convention (1971).

2. Compilations of data or other material, whether in machine readable or other form, which by reason of the selection or arrangement of their contents constitute intellectual creations shall be protected as such. Such protection, which shall not extend to the data or material itself, shall be without prejudice to any copyright subsisting in the data or material itself.

Article 11

Rental Rights

In respect of at least computer programs and cinematographic works, a Member shall provide authors and their successors in title the right to authorize or to prohibit the commercial rental to the public of originals or copies of their copyright works. A Member shall be excepted from this obligation in respect of cinematographic works unless such rental has led to widespread copying of such works which is materially impairing the exclusive right of reproduction conferred in that Member on authors and their successors in title. In respect of computer programs, this obligation does not apply to rentals where the program itself is not the essential object of the rental.

Article 12

Term of Protection

Whenever the term of protection of a work, other than a photographic work or a work of applied art, is calculated on a basis other than the life of a natural person, such term shall be no less than fifty years from the end of the calendar year of authorized publication, or, failing such authorized publication within fifty years from the making of the work, fifty years from the end of the calendar year of making.

Article 13

Limitations and Exceptions

Members shall confine limitations or exceptions to exclusive rights to certain special cases which do not conflict with a normal exploitation of the work and do not unreasonably prejudice the legitimate interests of the right holder.

Article 14

Protection of Performers, Producers of Phonograms (Sound Recordings) and Broadcasting Organizations

1. In respect of a fixation of their performance on a phonogram, performers shall have the possibility of preventing the following acts when undertaken without their authorization: the fixation of their unfixed performance and the reproduction of such fixation. Performers shall also have the possibility of preventing the following acts when undertaken without their authorization: the broadcasting by wireless means and the communication to the public of their live performance.

2. Producers of phonograms shall enjoy the right to authorize or prohibit the direct or indirect reproduction of their phonograms.

3. Broadcasting organizations shall have the right to prohibit the following acts when undertaken without their authorization: the fixation, the reproduction of fixations, and the rebroadcasting by wireless means of broadcasts, as well as the communication to the public of television broadcasts of the same. Where Members do not grant such rights to broadcasting organizations, they shall provide owners of copyright in the subject matter of broadcasts with the possibility of preventing the above acts, subject to the provisions of the Berne Convention (1971).

4. The provisions of Article 11 in respect of computer programs shall apply *mutatis mutandis* to producers of phonograms and any other right holders in phonograms as determined in domestic law. If, on the date of the Ministerial Meeting concluding the Uruguay Round of Multilateral Trade Negotiations, a Member has in force a system of equitable remuneration of right holders in respect of the rental of phonograms, it may maintain such system provided that the commercial rental of phonograms is not giving rise to the material impairment of the exclusive rights of reproduction of right holders.

5. The term of the protection available under this Agreement to performers and producers of phonograms shall last at least until the end of a period of fifty years computed from the end of the calendar year in which the fixation was made or the performance took place. The term of protection granted pursuant to paragraph 3 above shall last for at least twenty years from the end of the calendar year in which the broadcast took place.

6. Any Member may, in relation to the rights conferred under paragraphs 1–3 above, provide for conditions, limitations, exceptions and reservations to the extent permitted by the Rome Convention. However, the provisions of Article 18 of the Berne Convention (1971) shall also apply, *mutatis mutandis,* to the rights of performers and producers of phonograms in phonograms.

*

WORLD INTELLECTUAL PROPERTY ORGANIZATION COPYRIGHT TREATY (EXCERPTS)

(Geneva 1996)

CRNR/DC/94

Preamble

The Contracting Parties,

Desiring to develop and maintain the protection of the rights of authors in their literary and artistic works in a manner as effective and uniform as possible,

Recognizing the need to introduce new international rules and clarify the interpretation of certain existing rules in order to provide adequate solutions to the questions raised by new economic, social, cultural and technological developments,

Recognizing the profound impact of the development and convergence of information and communication technologies on the creation and use of literary and artistic works,

Emphasizing the outstanding significance of copyright protection as an incentive for literary and artistic creation,

Recognizing the need to maintain a balance between the rights of authors and the larger public interest, particularly education, research and access to information, as reflected in the Berne Convention,

Have agreed as follows:

Article 1

Relation to the Berne Convention

(1) This Treaty is a special agreement within the meaning of Article 20 of the Berne Convention for the Protection of Literary and Artistic Works, as regards Contracting Parties that are countries of the Union established by that Convention. This Treaty shall not have any connection with treaties other than the Berne Convention, nor shall it prejudice any rights and obligations under any other treaties.

(2) Nothing in this Treaty shall derogate from existing obligations that Contracting Parties have to each other under the Berne Convention for the Protection of Literary and Artistic Works.

(3) Hereinafter, "Berne Convention" shall refer to the Paris Act of July 24, 1971 of the Berne Convention for the Protection of Literary and Artistic Works.

(4) Contracting Parties shall comply with Articles 1 to 21 and the Appendix of the Berne Convention.[1]

Article 2

Scope of Copyright Protection

Copyright protection extends to expressions and not to ideas, procedures, methods of operation or mathematical concepts as such.

Article 3

Application of Articles 2 to 6 of the Berne Convention

Contracting Parties shall apply *mutatis mutandis* the provisions of Articles 2 to 6 of the Berne Convention in respect of the protection provided for in this Treaty.[2]

Article 4

Computer Programs

Computer programs are protected as literary works within the meaning of Article 2 of the Berne Convention. Such protection applies to computer programs, whatever may be the mode or form of their expression.[3]

1. **Agreed statement concerning Article 1(4):** The reproduction right, as set out in Article 9 of the Berne Convention, and the exceptions permitted thereunder, fully apply in the digital environment, in particular to the use of works in digital form. It is understood that the storage of a protected work in digital form in an electronic medium constitutes a reproduction within the meaning of Article 9 of the Berne Convention.

2. **Agreed statement concerning Article 3:** It is understood that in applying Article 3 of this Treaty, the expression "country of the Union" in Articles 2 to 6 of the Berne Convention will be read as if it were a reference to a Contracting Party to this Treaty, in the application of those Berne Articles in respect of protection provided for in this Treaty. It is also understood that the expression "country outside the Union" in those Articles in the Berne Convention will, in the same circumstances, be read as if it were a reference to a country that is not a Contracting Party to this Treaty, and that "this Convention" in Articles 2(8), 2*bis*(2), 3, 4 and 5 of the Berne Convention will be read as if it were a reference to the Berne Convention and this Treaty. Finally, it is understood that a reference in Articles 3 to 6 of the Berne Convention to a "national of one of the countries of the Union" will, when these Articles are applied to this Treaty, mean, in regard to an intergovernmental organization that is a Contracting Party to this Treaty, a national of one of the countries that is member of that organization.

3. **Agreed statement concerning Article 4:** The scope of protection for computer programs under Article 4 of this Treaty, read with Article 2, is consistent with Article 2 of the Berne Convention and on a par with the relevant provisions of the TRIPS Agreement.

Article 5

Compilations of Data (Databases)

Compilations of data or other material, in any form, which by reason of the selection or arrangement of their contents constitute intellectual creations, are protected as such. This protection does not extend to the data or the material itself and is without prejudice to any copyright subsisting in the data or material contained in the compilation.[4]

Article 6

Right of Distribution

(1) Authors of literary and artistic works shall enjoy the exclusive right of authorizing the making available to the public of the original and copies of their works through sale or other transfer of ownership.

(2) Nothing in this Treaty shall affect the freedom of Contracting Parties to determine the conditions, if any, under which the exhaustion of the right in paragraph (1) applies after the first sale or other transfer of ownership of the original or a copy of the work with the authorization of the author.[5]

Article 7

Right of Rental

(1) Authors of

(i) computer programs;

(ii) cinematographic works; and

(iii) works embodied in phonograms, as determined in the national law of Contracting Parties, shall enjoy the exclusive right of authorizing commercial rental to the public of the originals or copies of their works.

(2) Paragraph (1) shall not apply

(i) in the case of computer programs, where the program itself is not the essential object of the rental; and

(ii) in the case of cinematographic works, unless such commercial rental has led to widespread copying of such works materially impairing the exclusive right of reproduction.

(3) Notwithstanding the provisions of paragraph (1), a Contracting Party that, on April 15, 1994, had and continues to have in force a system

4. Agreed statement concerning Article 5: The scope of protection for compilations of data (databases) under Article 5 of this Treaty, read with Article 2, is consistent with Article 2 of the Berne Convention and on a par with the relevant provisions of the TRIPS Agreement.

5. Agreed statement concerning Articles 6 and 7: As used in these Articles, the expressions "copies" and "original and copies," being subject to the right of distribution and the right of rental under the said Articles, refer exclusively to fixed copies that can be put into circulation as tangible objects.

of equitable remuneration of authors for the rental of copies of their works embodied in phonograms may maintain that system provided that the commercial rental of works embodied in phonograms is not giving rise to the material impairment of the exclusive right of reproduction of authors.[6] [7]

Article 8

Right of Communication to the Public

Without prejudice to the provisions of Articles 11(1)(ii), 11bis(1)(i) and (ii), 11ter(1)(ii), 14(1)(ii) and 14bis(1) of the Berne Convention, authors of literary and artistic works shall enjoy the exclusive right of authorizing any communication to the public of their works, by wire or wireless means, including the making available to the public of their works in such a way that members of the public may access these works from a place and at a time individually chosen by them.[8]

Article 9

Duration of the Protection of Photographic Works

In respect of photographic works, the Contracting Parties shall not apply the provisions of Article 7(4) of the Berne Convention.

Article 10

Limitations and Exceptions

(1) Contracting Parties may, in their national legislation, provide for limitations of or exceptions to the rights granted to authors of literary and artistic works under this Treaty in certain special cases that do not conflict with a normal exploitation of the work and do not unreasonably prejudice the legitimate interests of the author.

(2) Contracting Parties shall, when applying the Berne Convention, confine any limitations of or exceptions to rights provided for therein to certain special cases that do not conflict with a normal exploitation of the work and do not unreasonably prejudice the legitimate interests of the author.[9]

6. Agreed statement concerning Articles 6 and 7: As used in these Articles, the expressions "copies" and "original and copies," being subject to the right of distribution and the right of rental under the said Articles, refer exclusively to fixed copies that can be put into circulation as tangible objects.

7. Agreed statement concerning Article 7: It is understood that the obligation under Article 7(1) does not require a Contracting Party to provide an exclusive right of commercial rental to authors who, under that Contracting Party's law, are not granted rights in respect of phonograms. It is understood that this obligation is consistent with Article 14(4) of the TRIPS Agreement.

8. Agreed statement concerning Article 8: It is understood that the mere provision of physical facilities for enabling or making a communication does not in itself amount to communication within the meaning of this Treaty or the Berne Convention. It is further understood that nothing in Article 8 precludes a Contracting Party from applying Article 11bis(2).

9. Agreed statement concerning Article 10: It is understood that the provisions of Article 10 permit Contracting Parties

Article 11

Obligations concerning Technological Measures

Contracting Parties shall provide adequate legal protection and effective legal remedies against the circumvention of effective technological measures that are used by authors in connection with the exercise of their rights under this Treaty or the Berne Convention and that restrict acts, in respect of their works, which are not authorized by the authors concerned or permitted by law.

Article 12

Obligations concerning Rights Management Information

(1) Contracting Parties shall provide adequate and effective legal remedies against any person knowingly performing any of the following acts knowing, or with respect to civil remedies having reasonable grounds to know, that it will induce, enable, facilitate or conceal an infringement of any right covered by this Treaty or the Berne Convention:

(i) to remove or alter any electronic rights management information without authority;

(ii) to distribute, import for distribution, broadcast or communicate to the public, without authority, works or copies of works knowing that electronic rights management information has been removed or altered without authority.

(2) As used in this Article, "rights management information" means information which identifies the work, the author of the work, the owner of any right in the work, or information about the terms and conditions of use of the work, and any numbers or codes that represent such information, when any of these items of information is attached to a copy of a work or appears in connection with the communication of a work to the public.[10]

Article 13

Application in Time

Contracting Parties shall apply the provisions of Article 18 of the Berne Convention to all protection provided for in this Treaty.

---

to carry forward and appropriately extend into the digital environment limitations and exceptions in their national laws which have been considered acceptable under the Berne Convention. Similarly, these provisions should be understood to permit Contracting Parties to devise new exceptions and limitations that are appropriate in the digital network environment.

It is also understood that Article 10(2) neither reduces nor extends the scope of applicability of the limitations and exceptions permitted by the Berne Convention.

10. Agreed statement concerning Article 12: It is understood that the reference to "infringement of any right covered by this Treaty or the Berne Convention" includes both exclusive rights and rights of remuneration.

It is further understood that Contracting Parties will not rely on this Article to devise or implement rights management systems that would have the effect of imposing formalities which are not permitted under the Berne Convention or this Treaty, prohibiting the free movement of goods or impeding the enjoyment of rights under this Treaty.

501

Article 14

Provisions on Enforcement of Rights

(1) Contracting Parties undertake to adopt, in accordance with their legal systems, the measures necessary to ensure the application of this Treaty.

(2) Contracting Parties shall ensure that enforcement procedures are available under their law so as to permit effective action against any act of infringement of rights covered by this Treaty, including expeditious remedies to prevent infringements and remedies which constitute a deterrent to further infringements.

* * * *

Article 22

No Reservations to the Treaty

No reservation to this Treaty shall be admitted.

* * * *

WORLD INTELLECTUAL PROPERTY ORGANIZATION PERFORMANCES AND PHONOGRAMS TREATY (EXCERPTS)

(Geneva 1996)

CRNR/DC/95

Preamble

The Contracting Parties,

Desiring to develop and maintain the protection of the rights of performers and producers of phonograms in a manner as effective and uniform as possible,

Recognizing the need to introduce new international rules in order to provide adequate solutions to the questions raised by economic, social, cultural and technological developments,

Recognizing the profound impact of the development and convergence of information and communication technologies on the production and use of performances and phonograms,

Recognizing the need to maintain a balance between the rights of performers and producers of phonograms and the larger public interest, particularly education, research and access to information,

Have agreed as follows:

CHAPTER I—GENERAL PROVISIONS

Article 1

Relation to Other Conventions

(1) Nothing in this Treaty shall derogate from existing obligations that Contracting Parties have to each other under the International Convention for the Protection of Performers, Producers of Phonograms and Broadcasting Organizations done in Rome, October 26, 1961 (hereinafter the "Rome Convention").

(2) Protection granted under this Treaty shall leave intact and shall in no way affect the protection of copyright in literary and artistic works.

Consequently, no provision of this Treaty may be interpreted as prejudicing such protection.[1]

(3) This Treaty shall not have any connection with, nor shall it prejudice any rights and obligations under, any other treaties.

Article 2

Definitions

For the purposes of this Treaty:

(a) "performers" are actors, singers, musicians, dancers, and other persons who act, sing, deliver, declaim, play in, interpret, or otherwise perform literary or artistic works or expressions of folklore;

(b) "phonogram" means the fixation of the sounds of a performance or of other sounds, or of a representation of sounds, other than in the form of a fixation incorporated in a cinematographic or other audiovisual work;[2]

(c) "fixation" means the embodiment of sounds, or of the representations thereof, from which they can be perceived, reproduced or communicated through a device;

(d) "producer of a phonogram" means the person, or the legal entity, who or which takes the initiative and has the responsibility for the first fixation of the sounds of a performance or other sounds, or the representations of sounds;

(e) "publication" of a fixed performance or a phonogram means the offering of copies of the fixed performance or the phonogram to the public, with the consent of the rightholder, and provided that copies are offered to the public in reasonable quantity;[3]

(f) "broadcasting" means the transmission by wireless means for public reception of sounds or of images and sounds or of the representations thereof; such transmission by satellite is also "broadcasting"; transmission

---

1. **Agreed statement concerning Article 1(2):** It is understood that Article 1(2) clarifies the relationship between rights in phonograms under this Treaty and copyright in works embodied in the phonograms. In cases where authorization is needed from both the author of a work embodied in the phonogram and a performer or producer owning rights in the phonogram, the need for the authorization of the author does not cease to exist because the authorization of the performer or producer is also required, and vice versa.

It is further understood that nothing in Article 1(2) precludes a Contracting Party from providing exclusive rights to a performer or producer of phonograms beyond those required to be provided under this Treaty.

2. **Agreed statement concerning Article 2(b):** It is understood that the definition of phonogram provided in Article 2(b) does not suggest that rights in the phonogram are in any way affected through their incorporation into a cinematographic or other audiovisual work.

3. **Agreed statement concerning Articles 2(e), 8, 9, 12 and 13:** As used in these Articles, the expressions "copies" and "original and copies," being subject to the right of distribution and the right of rental under the said Articles, refer exclusively to fixed copies that can be put into circulation as tangible objects.

of encrypted signals is "broadcasting" where the means for decrypting are provided to the public by the broadcasting organization or with its consent;

(g) "communication to the public" of a performance or a phonogram means the transmission to the public by any medium, otherwise than by broadcasting, of sounds of a performance or the sounds or the representations of sounds fixed in a phonogram. For the purposes of Article 15, "communication to the public" includes making the sounds or representations of sounds fixed in a phonogram audible to the public.

Article 3

Beneficiaries of Protection under this Treaty

(1) Contracting Parties shall accord the protection provided under this Treaty to the performers and producers of phonograms who are nationals of other Contracting Parties.

(2) The nationals of other Contracting Parties shall be understood to be those performers or producers of phonograms who would meet the criteria for eligibility for protection provided under the Rome Convention, were all the Contracting Parties to this Treaty Contracting States of that Convention. In respect of these criteria of eligibility, Contracting Parties shall apply the relevant definitions in Article 2 of this Treaty.[4]

(3) Any Contracting Party availing itself of the possibilities provided in Article 5(3) of the Rome Convention or, for the purposes of Article 5 of the same Convention, Article 17 thereof shall make a notification as foreseen in those provisions to the Director General of the World Intellectual Property Organization (WIPO).[5]

Article 4

National Treatment

(1) Each Contracting Party shall accord to nationals of other Contracting Parties, as defined in Article 3(2), the treatment it accords to its own nationals with regard to the exclusive rights specifically granted in this Treaty, and to the right to equitable remuneration provided for in Article 15 of this Treaty.

(2) The obligation provided for in paragraph (1) does not apply to the extent that another Contracting Party makes use of the reservations permitted by Article 15(3) of this Treaty.

4. Agreed statement concerning Article 3(2): For the application of Article 3(2), it is understood that fixation means the finalization of the master tape ("bande-mère").

5. Agreed statement concerning Article 3: It is understood that the reference in Articles 5(a) and 16(a)(iv) of the Rome Convention to "national of another Contracting State" will, when applied to this Treaty, mean, in regard to an intergovernmental organization that is a Contracting Party to this Treaty, a national of one of the countries that is a member of that organization.

505

CHAPTER II—RIGHTS OF PERFORMERS

Article 5

Moral Rights of Performers

(1) Independently of a performer's economic rights, and even after the transfer of those rights, the performer shall, as regards his live aural performances or performances fixed in phonograms, have the right to claim to be identified as the performer of his performances, except where omission is dictated by the manner of the use of the performance, and to object to any distortion, mutilation or other modification of his performances that would be prejudicial to his reputation.

(2) The rights granted to a performer in accordance with paragraph (1) shall, after his death, be maintained, at least until the expiry of the economic rights, and shall be exercisable by the persons or institutions authorized by the legislation of the Contracting Party where protection is claimed. However, those Contracting Parties whose legislation, at the moment of their ratification of or accession to this Treaty, does not provide for protection after the death of the performer of all rights set out in the preceding paragraph may provide that some of these rights will, after his death, cease to be maintained.

(3) The means of redress for safeguarding the rights granted under this Article shall be governed by the legislation of the Contracting Party where protection is claimed.

Article 6

Economic Rights of Performers in their Unfixed Performances

Performers shall enjoy the exclusive right of authorizing, as regards their performances:

(i) the broadcasting and communication to the public of their unfixed performances except where the performance is already a broadcast performance; and

(ii) the fixation of their unfixed performances.

Article 7

Right of Reproduction

Performers shall enjoy the exclusive right of authorizing the direct or indirect reproduction of their performances fixed in phonograms, in any manner or form.[6]

6. Agreed statement concerning Articles 7, 11 and 16: The reproduction right, as set out in Articles 7 and 11, and the exceptions permitted thereunder through Article 16, fully apply in the digital environment, in particular to the use of performances and phonograms in digital form. It is understood that the storage of a protected performance or phonogram in digital form in an electronic medium constitutes a reproduction within the meaning of these Articles.

Article 8

Right of Distribution

(1) Performers shall enjoy the exclusive right of authorizing the making available to the public of the original and copies of their performances fixed in phonograms through sale or other transfer of ownership.

(2) Nothing in this Treaty shall affect the freedom of Contracting Parties to determine the conditions, if any, under which the exhaustion of the right in paragraph (1) applies after the first sale or other transfer of ownership of the original or a copy of the fixed performance with the authorization of the performer.[7]

Article 9

Right of Rental

(1) Performers shall enjoy the exclusive right of authorizing the commercial rental to the public of the original and copies of their performances fixed in phonograms as determined in the national law of Contracting Parties, even after distribution of them by, or pursuant to, authorization by the performer.

(2) Notwithstanding the provisions of paragraph (1), a Contracting Party that, on April 15, 1994, had and continues to have in force a system of equitable remuneration of performers for the rental of copies of their performances fixed in phonograms, may maintain that system provided that the commercial rental of phonograms is not giving rise to the material impairment of the exclusive right of reproduction of performers.[8]

Article 10

Right of Making Available of Fixed Performances

Performers shall enjoy the exclusive right of authorizing the making available to the public of their performances fixed in phonograms, by wire or wireless means, in such a way that members of the public may access them from a place and at a time individually chosen by them.

7. Agreed statement concerning Articles 2(e), 8, 9, 12 and 13: As used in these Articles, the expressions "copies" and "original and copies," being subject to the right of distribution and the right of rental under the said Articles, refer exclusively to fixed copies that can be put into circulation as tangible objects.

8. Agreed statement concerning Articles 2(e), 8, 9, 12 and 13: As used in these Articles, the expressions "copies" and "original and copies," being subject to the right of distribution and the right of rental under the said Articles, refer exclusively to fixed copies that can be put into circulation as tangible objects.

CHAPTER III—RIGHTS OF PRODUCERS OF PHONOGRAMS

Article 11

Right of Reproduction

Producers of phonograms shall enjoy the exclusive right of authorizing the direct or indirect reproduction of their phonograms, in any manner or form.[9]

Article 12

Right of Distribution

(1) Producers of phonograms shall enjoy the exclusive right of authorizing the making available to the public of the original and copies of their phonograms through sale or other transfer of ownership.

(2) Nothing in this Treaty shall affect the freedom of Contracting Parties to determine the conditions, if any, under which the exhaustion of the right in paragraph (1) applies after the first sale or other transfer of ownership of the original or a copy of the phonogram with the authorization of the producer of the phonogram.[10]

Article 13

Right of Rental

(1) Producers of phonograms shall enjoy the exclusive right of authorizing the commercial rental to the public of the original and copies of their phonograms, even after distribution of them by or pursuant to authorization by the producer.

(2) Notwithstanding the provisions of paragraph (1), a Contracting Party that, on April 15, 1994, had and continues to have in force a system of equitable remuneration of producers of phonograms for the rental of copies of their phonograms, may maintain that system provided that the commercial rental of phonograms is not giving rise to the material impairment of the exclusive rights of reproduction of producers of phonograms.[11]

9. Agreed statement concerning Articles 7, 11 and 16: The reproduction right, as set out in Articles 7 and 11, and the exceptions permitted thereunder through Article 16, fully apply in the digital environment, in particular to the use of performances and phonograms in digital form. It is understood that the storage of a protected performance or phonogram in digital form in an electronic medium constitutes a reproduction within the meaning of these Articles.

10. Agreed statement concerning Articles 2(e), 8, 9, 12 and 13: As used in these Articles, the expressions "copies" and "original and copies," being subject to the right of distribution and the right of rental under the said Articles, refer exclusively to fixed copies that can be put into circulation as tangible objects.

11. Agreed statement concerning Articles 2(e), 8, 9, 12 and 13: As used in these Articles, the expressions "copies" and "original and copies," being subject to the right of distribution and the right of rental under the said Articles, refer exclusively to fixed copies that can be put into circulation as tangible objects.

Article 14

Right of Making Available of Phonograms

Producers of phonograms shall enjoy the exclusive right of authorizing the making available to the public of their phonograms, by wire or wireless means, in such a way that members of the public may access them from a place and at a time individually chosen by them.

CHAPTER IV—COMMON PROVISIONS

Article 15

*Right to Remuneration for Broadcasting
and Communication to the Public*

(1) Performers and producers of phonograms shall enjoy the right to a single equitable remuneration for the direct or indirect use of phonograms published for commercial purposes for broadcasting or for any communication to the public.

(2) Contracting Parties may establish in their national legislation that the single equitable remuneration shall be claimed from the user by the performer or by the producer of a phonogram or by both. Contracting Parties may enact national legislation that, in the absence of an agreement between the performer and the producer of a phonogram, sets the terms according to which performers and producers of phonograms shall share the single equitable remuneration.

(3) Any Contracting Party may in a notification deposited with the Director General of WIPO, declare that it will apply the provisions of paragraph (1) only in respect of certain uses, or that it will limit their application in some other way, or that it will not apply these provisions at all.

(4) For the purposes of this Article, phonograms made available to the public by wire or wireless means in such a way that members of the public may access them from a place and at a time individually chosen by them shall be considered as if they had been published for commercial purposes.[12] [13]

---

12. Agreed statement concerning Article 15: It is understood that Article 15 does not represent a complete resolution of the level of rights of broadcasting and communication to the public that should be enjoyed by performers and phonogram producers in the digital age. Delegations were unable to achieve consensus on differing proposals for aspects of exclusivity to be provided in certain circumstances or for rights to be provided without the possibility of reservations, and have therefore left the issue to future resolution.

13. Agreed statement concerning Article 15: It is understood that Article 15 does not prevent the granting of the right conferred by this Article to performers of folklore and producers of phonograms recording folklore where such phonograms have not been published for commercial gain.

Article 16

Limitations and Exceptions

(1) Contracting Parties may, in their national legislation, provide for the same kinds of limitations or exceptions with regard to the protection of performers and producers of phonograms as they provide for, in their national legislation, in connection with the protection of copyright in literary and artistic works.

(2) Contracting Parties shall confine any limitations of or exceptions to rights provided for in this Treaty to certain special cases which do not conflict with a normal exploitation of the performance or phonogram and do not unreasonably prejudice the legitimate interests of the performer or of the producer of the phonogram.[14][15]

Article 17

Term of Protection

(1) The term of protection to be granted to performers under this Treaty shall last, at least, until the end of a period of 50 years computed from the end of the year in which the performance was fixed in a phonogram.

(2) The term of protection to be granted to producers of phonograms under this Treaty shall last, at least, until the end of a period of 50 years computed from the end of the year in which the phonogram was published, or failing such publication within 50 years from fixation of the phonogram, 50 years from the end of the year in which the fixation was made.

Article 18

Obligations concerning Technological Measures

Contracting Parties shall provide adequate legal protection and effective legal remedies against the circumvention of effective technological

14. Agreed statement concerning Articles 7, 11 and 16: The reproduction right, as set out in Articles 7 and 11, and the exceptions permitted thereunder through Article 16, fully apply in the digital environment, in particular to the use of performances and phonograms in digital form. It is understood that the storage of a protected performance or phonogram in digital form in an electronic medium constitutes a reproduction within the meaning of these Articles.

15. Agreed statement concerning Article 16: The agreed statement concerning Article 10 (on Limitations and Exceptions) of the WIPO Copyright Treaty is applicable *mutatis mutandis* also to Article 16 (on Limitations and Exceptions) of the WIPO Performances and Phonograms Treaty. [The text of the agreed statement concerning Article 10 of the WCT reads as follows:

It is understood that the provisions of Article 10 permit Contracting Parties to carry forward and appropriately extend into the digital environment limitations and exceptions in their national laws which have been considered acceptable under the Berne Convention. Similarly, these provisions should be understood to permit Contracting Parties to devise new exceptions and limitations that are appropriate in the digital network environment.

It is also understood that Article 10(2) neither reduces nor extends the scope of applicability of the limitations and exceptions permitted by the Berne Convention.]

measures that are used by performers or producers of phonograms in connection with the exercise of their rights under this Treaty and that restrict acts, in respect of their performances or phonograms, which are not authorized by the performers or the producers of phonograms concerned or permitted by law.

Article 19

Obligations concerning Rights Management Information

(1) Contracting Parties shall provide adequate and effective legal remedies against any person knowingly performing any of the following acts knowing, or with respect to civil remedies having reasonable grounds to know, that it will induce, enable, facilitate or conceal an infringement of any right covered by this Treaty:

(i) to remove or alter any electronic rights management information without authority;

(ii) to distribute, import for distribution, broadcast, communicate or make available to the public, without authority, performances, copies of fixed performances or phonograms knowing that electronic rights management information has been removed or altered without authority.

(2) As used in this Article, "rights management information" means information which identifies the performer, the performance of the performer, the producer of the phonogram, the phonogram, the owner of any right in the performance or phonogram, or information about the terms and conditions of use of the performance or phonogram, and any numbers or codes that represent such information, when any of these items of information is attached to a copy of a fixed performance or a phonogram or appears in connection with the communication or making available of a fixed performance or a phonogram to the public.[16]

Article 20

Formalities

The enjoyment and exercise of the rights provided for in this Treaty shall not be subject to any formality.

16. Agreed statement concerning Article 19: The agreed statement concerning Article 12 (on Obligations concerning Rights Management Information) of the WIPO Copyright Treaty is applicable *mutatis mutandis* also to Article 19 (on Obligations concerning Rights Management Information) of the WIPO Performances and Phonograms Treaty.

[The agreed statement concerning Article 12 of the WIPO Copyright Treaty reads as follows:

It is understood that the reference to "infringement of any right covered by this Treaty or the Berne Convention" includes both exclusive rights and rights of remuneration.

It is further understood that Contracting Parties will not rely on this Article to devise or implement rights management systems that would have the effect of imposing formalities which are not permitted under the Berne Convention or this Treaty, prohibiting the free movement of goods or impeding the enjoyment of rights under this Treaty.]

Article 21

Reservations

Subject to the provisions of Article 15(3), no reservations to this Treaty shall be permitted.

Article 22

Application in Time

(1) Contracting Parties shall apply the provisions of Article 18 of the Berne Convention, *mutatis mutandis*, to the rights of performers and producers of phonograms provided for in this Treaty.

(2) Notwithstanding paragraph (1), a Contracting Party may limit the application of Article 5 of this Treaty to performances which occurred after the entry into force of this Treaty for that Party.

Article 23

Provisions on Enforcement of Rights

(1) Contracting Parties undertake to adopt, in accordance with their legal systems, the measures necessary to ensure the application of this Treaty.

(2) Contracting Parties shall ensure that enforcement procedures are available under their law so as to permit effective action against any act of infringement of rights covered by this Treaty, including expeditious remedies to prevent infringements and remedies which constitute a deterrent to further infringements.

* * * *

†